SWINDON'S WAR RECORD

prepared for the
SWINDON TOWN COUNCIL

by

W. D. BAVIN

LOCo1
2018

First published in 1922.
Facsimile edition first published in the United Kingdom in 2017;
second facsimile edition 2018

Published for Local Studies (Swindon Libraries)
Central Library, Regent Circus, Swindon SN1 1QG
www.swindon.gov.uk/localstudies

by The Hobnob Press, Unit 30C, Deverill Road Trading Estate, Sutton Veny, Warminster
BA12 7BZ

LOC01

British Library Cataloguing in Publication Data
A catalogue record for this book is available from the British Library

ISBN 978-1-906978-51-8

Additional material typesetting and origination by John Chandler

Printed by Lightning Source

Also available

LOC02 *Roll of Honour 1939–1945, Swindon & District* compiled by Katherine Cole,
2017.

Swindon's War Record.

PRINTED AND PUBLISHED BY

JOHN DREW (PRINTERS) LTD.,

51, BRIDGE STREET,

SWINDON.

Swindon's War Record

Prepared for the Swindon Town Council

BY

W. D. BAVIN.

Illustrated.

JOHN DREW (PRINTERS) LTD.,
51 BRIDGE STREET, SWINDON.

1922.

Preface.

To the Mayor, Aldermen and Councillors of the Borough of Swindon :

GENTLEMEN,

The war had lasted three and a half years when I was asked to undertake the compilation of this record. No one had contemplated the preparation of such a work, and consequently accurate memoranda of much that was of great interest had been kept by no one. I had, therefore, to rely upon what I could learn from persons interested in the work, from reports in the local journals, and from whatever records had been preserved. Even then the information I could gather was far from complete, and not always accurate, and I have had to reject much that might perhaps have found a place in the record, if it could have been coherently and truly stated. I wish, however, to acknowledge the uniform courtesy and the ready assistance I have met in my search for material, from nearly every one of those—far too many to enumerate—whom I approached ; not a letter of mine remained unanswered, no tradesman refused me information from his private ledgers, no one declined me any audience, and many went out of their way to obtain the information they themselves could not give.

It may possibly strike some that much of the substance of this work is trivial— " the rustic cackle of our bourg,"—without interest beyond the limits of Swindon. Well, it is true that the borough was spared the horrors of the East Coast Towns ; and as that country has been called happy that has no history, so may Swindon be reckoned fortunate in having nothing more stirring to record than lies within the pages of this book. But the sketch of the civil life of a large community during such a momentous period as that through which we have passed is not trivial, and if such an account could be found for some town of England during one of the great wars of the Plantagenets every detail would be prized by the historian. It was doubtless with an eye to the future value of all such records that the Government asked that these local histories should be prepared whilst the facts were fresh in men's minds. If any part of this imperfect account has value for the future student it will probably be the fairly full record of the increase in the prices of commodities in Swindon as the war went on, the story of the patriotic co-operation of all classes of the community in philanthropic work, and the detailed account of the labours of the more important committees ; these, it is hoped, will be found to be adequately set out.

As far as possible the order of the first part of the work—the civil record—is chronological, but in the case of two committees it was not possible to distribute the narrative amongst the successive years without seriously disfiguring the story, and these committees have been given separate chapters at suitable points in the chronological series. As regards the second part—the military record—it would have been presumptuous on my part to have pretended to give anything but a mere sketch of the service of the several military units that have a claim on Swindon's interest. It was felt, however, that it would have been unpardonable to have omitted the relation, even though it should be little more than a résumé, of the trials and heroism of Swindon's sons. In the preparation of the chapters dealing with the different units every care has been used in checking the details, but it would be surprising if no errors could be found, and omissions will certainly be apparent to many. The stories have, nevertheless, a special interest in being the narratives of Swindon men of what they themselves saw and experienced; but they are not " old soldiers' tales "; the facts have been checked from other sources, and in all cases none but men of high character and intelligence have been consulted. A very striking feature was the modesty of the narrators and the reluctance to allow the personal element to obtrude itself, and the work has left me proud to have met these men; my estimate of the quality of Swindon's manhood has been raised by the privilege—for such it has been—of conversing with " men that have hazarded their lives " for the sake of their fellows, and who speak of their gallant service " as men averse from war." They are too numerous to thank by name, and indeed they would not wish it, for many would only speak on condition their names were not mentioned.

In conclusion, Gentlemen, I must ask you to judge the work with leniency, remembering that it has had to be done in " the intervals of business," during a time of stress and transition in my professional duties under your Education Committee. I am conscious of many defects that more leisure and adequate assistance would have prevented, but I am content to leave the work to your generous judgment and to sign myself,

Your obedient servant,

W. D. BAVIN.

Swindon, 1921.

Contents.

Illustrations.

August, 1914.

―――――

" What ails the world, with sin and crime accursed ?
   O God | What bloody rule is this begun ?
   Why do Earth's teeming children pant and run,
Maddened with War's abhorred, consuming thirst ?
What rancorous bosom hath the Fury nursed,
   And dared to breathe it forth beneath the sun ?
   Thou slave of Hell | This evil hast thou done |
The pagan scourge hath from his dungeon burst.
O Europe | who hast long, for Freedom's sake,
   The swelling tyrant's insolence withstood,
   And strove in vain his frenzy to assuage,
From thy proud limbs the galling fetters shake |
   Scatter the arch-contriver's brutish brood,
   And hurl him down, the Traitor of the age."

*(The first of Mr. Alfred Williams' war-sonnets in the ' Swindon
Advertiser,' 21st August, 1914).*

In Memoriam – 1914-18. Swindon.

PART I.

LOCAL AFFAIRS DURING THE WAR.

SWINDON'S WAR RECORD

CHAPTER I

1914 : First Effects of the War.

A Peaceful On Saturday, August 1st, 1914, the Wilts Battery and Ammunition
homecoming. Column of the 3rd Wessex Brigade of Royal Field Artillery returned
The R.F.A. to Swindon from Larkhill Camp, having finished its annual training
under canvas. The men returned in excellent spirits from their
enjoyable and invigorating fortnight on the breezy expanse of "the Plain,"
and the Swindon Battery was elated by its triumph in having won Colonel
Bedford-Pim's cup for general efficiency ; Brigadier General Fanshawe had paid
them the high compliment of stating that their drill was the best he had ever
witnessed in Territorial troops.

These men returned to the peaceful avocations of the factory or the office,
but in less than a week they were leaving Swindon in response to a royal proclamation summoning the Territorials and the Reserves to the colours.

The call The order to mobilise was given on Tuesday, August 4th, at 7.49 p.m.,
to Arms. by the pre-arranged signal of ten blasts on the "hooter" at the
Great Western Railway Works, and within a few minutes excited
crowds were streaming towards the Park in New Town or the Old Town Drill Hall,
where the men were promptly reporting themselves. All day on Wednesday the
men of the R.F.A. were busily engaged in transporting to the Old Town Station
their guns, baggage, and ammunition, and towards 6 p.m. they were met at the
station by Ald. C. Hill, the Mayor of Swindon, and the members of the Town
Council, with the Chief officials of the Corporation, supported by a dense crowd that
had assembled to give the men a good send-off. The Mayor, speaking
Send-off of for the town, expressed the admiration and good wishes that all
the R.F.A. felt, and his words were seconded by a great volume of cheers from
the crowd ; he said, " You are leaving home and friends at the call of
duty, and you can depend upon us to see that those homes and friends, where
necessary, are cared for in your absence. We will see they do not want. Our good
wishes go with you, believing that you will, as worthy sons, uphold the best
traditions of our fore-fathers................What we say to you, we say to your
comrades who have gone on in advance, to those who are to follow you, and also
to those who have gone to active service straight from camp, without the opportunity of coming back to Swindon and saying good-bye to their friends. Be of good
cheer. Good-bye, Good luck, and God bless you all !" Colonel Bedford-Pim
r. plied with much feeling, and a few minutes after six o'clock, amid many pathetic
farewells, the train steamed out of th · station en route to Portsmouth.

The contingent consisted of eighty officers and men, and was under the command
of Col. Bedford-Pim, and Major the Earl of Suffolk, who was accompanied to the
train by the Countess of Suffolk (Lord Suffolk's mother), Lady Suffolk, and the

little Lord Andover with his two brothers. It was not then known what the ulti-
mate destination of these young men would be,—young men representative of the
finest physique and intelligence of the Wiltshire railway town,—and most people
thought it would not be long before they were using their guns in Flanders and
France ; but early in the new year they were in distant India, and many novel
experiences and terrible fights were to be gone through before those who were
fortunate enough to " pull through " would resume their wonted toil at the desk
or bench in Swindon. [1]

Call of the Yeomanry. The public excitement was augmented when the " hooter " again
sounded ten blasts on Thursday, August 6th, at 8.50 p.m., calling
the Swindon Squadron of the Royal Wilts Yeomanry to the Drill
Hall. At 10.45 the police cleared the M. and S.W.J. Rly. station for the troops,
and the men marched up and were speedily got away amidst the cheers of a large
crowd. They returned in the morning, having been engaged on special guard duty
upon the railway all night. This was the Yeomanry's first piece of service in the
Great War, and hardly foreshadowed the rigorous nights some of them were to
spend near Peronne early in 1917, or the thrilling charge at Houdecourt, or the
terrible stand some were to make at Morchies in 1918, when, as members of the
6th Wilts, some were to fall into the hands of the Germans and others were to find
a grave far from the quiet Wiltshire Town that was now buzzing with excitement
over their call to service. The story of " D " Squadron's gallant and loyal share
in the war will be treated, though but briefly and inadequately, in a later section,
and it is a story of patient waiting and preparation, ready response to the call of
duty, hard service, and willing sacrifice. [2]

The Reserves called. The departure of the Territorials and the Yeomanry was not lacking
in spectacular glamour and the enthusiasm of numbers, but a large
number of men were leaving daily with no other God-speed than the
tears and forced smiles of wives and parents,—men who had already given their
country long and good service, who had doffed their uniform for civilian clothes,
had exchanged the rifle for the mechanic's tools, and had settled down in middle
life with wife and children in a little home in Swindon. On Sunday, Aug. 2nd,
the Naval Reserves had been called up, and on Tuesday the order was issued summoning the Army Reservists and Territorials to the colours ; large numbers departed
at once, ten leaving the Swindon Post Office alone. It is sad to think of these men
parted from their families and sent in all directions, some never to return ; but
they formed an invaluable element in the great armies Britain was called upon to
form,—steady and experienced men-at-arms.

The Army Reserve. The Army Reserve consisted of service men of two classes ; section "B"
formed the " 1st class Army Reserve," and comprised all men who
had joined the Army between the ages of 18 and 25, who had completed
their period with the colours, but not the period necessary to make up
the full period of enlistment, which was 12 years, or thirteen if required. Thus if a man
had enlisted for three years, he would have nine in the Reserve ; if for seven years,
he would have five in the Reserve ; and so on. These men used to have reserve pay
of 6d. a day. Section " D," the " 2nd class Army Reserve," comprised men who had
completed the full term of twelve years and had then re-enlisted in the Reserve for
four more years, their reserve pay being 4d. a day. Thus when the Government called

(1) See Part II., ch. ii.   (2) See Part II., ch. iii.

up these men, it was but calling upon them to fulfil the contract of their enlistment; only, as the nation was now at war, however near a man was to the completion of his service he could not hope for release.

Swindon Battalion of the Wilts National Reserve. These reservists must not be confused with the " National Reserve " of whom there were 1,300 in Swindon at the beginning of August, 1914, ex-service men who had not necessarily been in the regular army. The Swindon Battalion of the Wilts National Reserve was under the command of Major F. P. Goddard, in the absence of Col T. C. P. Calley, who, being on a visit to Germany at the time, was thought to be a prisoner of war there. At a parade held in the Great Western Railway Company's park, on August 12th, 600 men responded to the summons and were addressed by Major Goddard upon the courses open to the men and the arrangements contemplated ; men of Class I. under 42 years of age could volunteer to rejoin their old corps, but not the Territorial Army. Instructions were shortly afterwards received from Trowbridge as to the provision of local guards to be formed of men of fifty years of age or more, who were unsuitable for service in the field ; these men were attested for one year or for the duration of the war.

The Reserve was organized into twelve companies, and the men were given the opportunity of joining the 4th Wilts Battalion for home defence, all men of Class II. being eligible ; there was a splendid response to the appeal and the first batch of men left for Trowbridge on Saturday, September 12th. The more honour is due to these men in that they were mainly elderly men with homes and families dependent upon them, and in volunteering they made great sacrifices ; the spirit of the men was shown at a parade held on Wednesday, October 14th, when the men of the Swindon No. 1 Company were invited to volunteer for service as railway-guards; 120 were required and 79 names were given in at the parade, showing that more than were required would readily be found.

Guarding the Railway. These guards were for a long time a familiar sight at important spots on the line—at bridges, tunnels, etc. ; the work had its dangers, and on December 11th, Lance Corporal W. J. Nurden was buried at the Swindon Cemetery with military honours after a service at the Parish Church, having lost his life in crossing the line at Newton Toney when he was going to relieve a sick comrade of his duty.

By November, the Swindon National Reserve had been depleted of nearly 400 men who had gone to all parts of the country, and of whom some were already in the firing line.

Swindonians in Germany. The war came upon England so suddenly and unexpectedly that large numbers of British subjects were enjoying a holiday in Germany at the very time war was secretly determined upon by the German Government ; amongst these were well-known local residents.

Colonel Calley's Escape. Most interest was felt in the fate of Col. T. C. P. Calley, of Burderop Park, commanding officer of the Swindon Battalion of the Wilts National Reserve : he had gone to Homburg on account of his health, and when no news of him had been obtainable for a fortnight, it was feared that he had been made a prisoner of war. It turned out that he had tried to leave Homburg on Saturday, August 1st, but was prevented by the dislocation of traffic occasioned by the mobilization of the German forces, so that he was still present in Homburg when war was declared on Monday. On the Wednesday a proclamation was issued ordering visitors of enemy nationality to leave Homburg by 6 p.m., on Thursday ; Col. Calley therefore left the town and reached Frankfort, only, however, to be sent back to Homburg and detained there till August 15th. On the 16th he was again allowed to start, but by a roundabout route to Cologne, taking seventeen hours to make a journey that usually takes four.   The next day the company got as far as Goch, near Cleves, and although they were not molested they were made very uncomfortable by the manifestations of strong animosity against the British ; they had much difficulty in getting away from Goch, and three young men of the party were marched away and sent to a concentration camp in Westphalia.   At the frontier a German official gave orders that no British were to cross, but the train was manned by Dutch railway-men, and whilst the passengers, already seated, were arguing with the German, the Dutch driver suddenly started off and left him furiously gesticulating and shouting on the platform.

The Colonel now could make for home via Flushing, and on August 20th he arrived in Swindon to the delight of many who recognised and cheered him as he passed through the streets. The next day he received at the Drill Hall an enthusiastic reception from the Swindon Company of National Reserves, and was at the close of the parade carried shoulder-high amid tumultuous cheering to the Goddard Arms, from the balcony of which he thanked his friends for their welcome home.

Holiday Makers Threatened.   Mr. C. G. Macdonald, son of Mr. Colin Macdonald of Kent Road, was spending a holiday with his family and some friends at a sanatorium at Godesberg, near Bonn.   War was a question of a few hours, and the party had some difficulty in getting away. On their way to Bonn their car was stopped by soldiers, with rifles levelled at the passengers, and they refused to recognise their pass-ports until a certificate from the doctor of the sanatorium was produced.   At Bonn they were surrounded by a terrible mob, and feared the car would be pushed over the embankment into the river, but they succeeded in getting to the station and had a trying journey to Goch, where they changed for Flushing. A dramatic episode occurred near Crefeld ; as the train passed over a bridge the patrol guarding the bridge fired shots at the last car, and as the train drew into the station a Frenchman jumped out and was immediately shot dead : he had tried to bomb the bridge.

Corporation Official's Experience.   Mr. J. Boulton, Foreman of the Swindon Corporation Staff, was on holiday in Switzerland. On August 1st he realised the situation, and decided to return at once ; he was booked to return through Alsace-Lorraine on Bank-Holiday, but at Basle he was asked for his passport, which he had not obtained, and on showing his ticket a German soldier spat on it and threw it on the ground.   Mr. Boulton sought the aid of the British Consul at Basle, who turned out to be a German and refused any aid.

Acting on the advice of an acquaintance he went to Delle on the French border, and with a crowd of other tourists set out on a tedious and uncomfortable journey, with hardly any food.   At one point they found the Germans had pulled up the line, and they had to return and wait for another train, travelling via Dijon to Paris, which was reached thirty-six hours after leaving Basle.   There Mr. Boulton had to wait ten hours in a gigantic queue to obtain a pass-port ; delays occurred at Paris, Dieppe, and Newhaven, and when Mr. Boulton arrived in Swindon it had taken him 5½ days to get from Lucerne,—days of great hardship, anxiety and privation.

Others, however, were not so fortunate as these ; for instance, Mr. W. Winterson, formerly on the M. and S.W.J. Rly, and at this time a driver on the Soudan railway, was on his way from Khartoum, and, being taken into Hamburg on August 2nd, before war was declared, was detained and then interned as a civilian prisoner of war.

Off to India, the R.F.A.

The Mayor of Swindon's Farewell to the R.F.A.'s. M. & S.W.J. Rly. Station.

The Red Cross. The Red Cross Society in Swindon was organised with remarkable alacrity. Mrs. T. C. P. Calley, the President, and Mrs. Waugh, of the Vicarage, Chiseldon, the Honorary Secretary, summoned a public meeting in the Swindon Town Hall, for Aug. 10th. The room was filled to overflowing and Mr. Hankey, the County Director, explained to the meeting the object for which it was convened. He pointed out that there was no Voluntary Aid Detachment in Swindon, and said that two or three members of the County detachments were prepared to come and work there if assistance was needed ; volunteers were invited for the work, an appeal was made for funds, and ladies were invited to enrol themselves in classes that would be formed for instruction in nursing and first aid. The spirit of the gathering may be judged from the fact that a committee was appointed forthwith, and about £322 was collected or promised on the spot.

By the end of the week two detachments had been formed in Swindon in addition to a Rest Station party; when the intimation was sent to the County Director he was so surprised by the expedition shown that he thought a mistake had been made and asked for complete lists ; these were sent him and comprised a Commandant, Lady Superintendent, and Quarter-Master, and seventeen nurses to each detachment, with the same officers and six nurses for the Rest Station party. By September 24th, another sum of £303 had been collected in Swindon and the surrounding district.

The President, Honorary Secretary, and Mr. W. G. Little speedily arranged with the Education Committee for special classes to be held at the Technical School for the training of nurses. The lecturer was Dr. S. Rattray, and training in practical work was given by Miss E. B. Walker, Matron of the Victoria Hospital, and Mrs. Dismorr, of Wroughton ; the first course was concluded by an examination held on October 14th, when one second-course certificate and twenty-eight first-course certificates were awarded.

The Hospital at the Baths. The Rev. C. A. Mayall, Vicar of Swindon, had at the out-set generously placed the Vicarage in Bath Road at the disposal of the local 'Red Cross Society, for use as a hospital or convalescent home ; but on October 2nd Col. Geddes, R.A.M.C., had an interview with Mrs. Waugh and said that, in view of the large camp which was growing up at Draycott, the War Office urgently needed a hospital for a hundred beds in Swindon, and he asked the Red Cross Society to provide one with the necessary staff and equipment. The Society therefore rented from the G.W.R. Medical Fund the large Baths in Faringdon Street, at a rent of £12 per week, paid by the War Office. Miss C. Deacon, the Commandant, and an enthusiastic staff took charge of the building on October 8th ; generous assistance was given by the G.W.R. Company in the equipment, for they lent a great variety of necessaries, such as springs for mattresses, blankets, pillows, and a large number of sundry articles. The services of the doctors were given gratuitously and Major R. Swinhoe, the Chief of the G.W.R. Medical Staff, gave invaluable assistance in organising the hospital. By the middle of October ninety-five patients were under treatment or had been discharged, presents of fruit, vegetables, flowers, papers, books, tobacco, etc., were steadily flowing in, and the hospital well merited the praise bestowed upon it by Col. Fletcher, the County Director of the Br. R. C. S., and Col. Melville, R. A. M. C., of Tidworth Camp, when they came down to inspect it. In October and November it was overflowing with patients, as many as one hundred and forty-seven being present on one night.

B

Garments, The ladies of Swindon set to work with much zeal to make the garments
etc. so badly needed by the Society ; in six weeks the division sent to the
central depôt at Salisbury 198 pairs of socks, 112 night-shirts, 140 day-
shirts, 56 vests, 59 pairs of bed-socks, as well as Bracknel shirts, pyjamas, nightingales,
bed-jackets, cholera-belts, pillows, draw-sheets, bandages, mittens, and scarves,
along with the inevitable pipes and tobacco.   Mothers' meetings and working parties
were formed, not only in Swindon but in the out-lying villages, to carry on this
work, and the school children, who always freely respond to generous impulses,
knitted a large quantity of the simpler articles.   It must not be overlooked that
the neighbouring villages co-operated readily in this work, and special credit should
be given to Wootton Bassett, Highworth and Cricklade, where also classes in Nursing
and First Aid were held.

The In the report on the work of the society up to December 31st, 1914,
Director's Mr. Basil Hankey, the County Director, stated that Swindon division
Report. had collected 2,491 garments, had sent £125 to the funds, and had
contributed £15 towards a motor ambulance : the invaluable help given
to the Army by the hospital is proved by the fact that in the twelve
weeks that had elapsed since its opening 588 patients has been admitted, whose
treatment made 7,063 "patient-nights" ; besides these there had been 1,600
out-patients.   The cases came from Draycott Camp, Tidworth, the lines of
communication and from units stationed in Swindon. [1]

The G.W.R. Reference having been made to the help given by the Great Western
Ambulance Railway Company to the Red Cross Society, it may be mentioned here
Trains. that on August 24th and 26th, 1914, the first two of a series of magnificent Ambulance Trains left the Swindon Works.   Each train was
made up of nine coaches ; two coaches were for doctors, nurses and orderlies ;
there were five ward-coaches, a dining-car, and a pharmacy-car with dispensary and
operating-room ; and the total bed-accommodation was for 98 patients and 12 of
the staff.   The interior was painted white, and the trains were lighted by gas and had
ample water-storage and steam-heating apparatus : a gang-way wide enough for
the passage of a patient on a stretcher gave communication with the operating room
from any part of the train.   Each side and the roof of every coach bore a large
red cross painted on a white ground.

Visiting the On the afternoon of the Sunday previous to their despatch, the public
Trains. was admitted to the Great Western Railway Works to view the trains
on payment of 6d. each ; the money was to go to the Red Cross Society,
and so great was the interest of the townsfolk that although they were
admitted in a queue four deep at the main entrance, the stream of visitors was
continuous from 2 p.m. to 6 p.m.   The local Red Cross Nurses were in attendance,
giving the necessary touch of life to the trains and acting as guides to the visitors
passing through them.

The Young Steps were taken without delay for establishing organizations for
Citizens' recruiting, though few realized the arduous struggle that lay before
League. the nation and the strain it was going to put upon its man-power.
The schemes at first devised were purely voluntary in character,
and compulsory national service was as yet undreamt of.   On August 8th, at a
meeting held at the Town Hall under Mr. T. Kimber's chairmanship, a " Young

(1) Continued, p. 53.

Citizens' League " was formed ; it was in reality a development of the " Junior
Imperial League," an organization of about 350 young men in which Mr. Kimber
had taken great interest.   The object of the new league was the enrolment of young
men from seventeen to twenty-four years of age, who were anxious to play a part
in helping the nation in this emergency ; they would be ready at a moment's notice
to serve in any capacity required by the Government or the local authorities, and
it was hoped that a good proportion of those who joined the League would offer
themselves to some branch of the Army or Navy ; it was, however, contemplated
that many who felt they could not do this would find in the League avenues of
service suited to their circumstances.   The League was inaugurated at a large
meeting of young men presided over by the Mayor, Ald. C. Hill, and addressed also
by Major F. P. Goddard and Mr. T. Kimber ; practically all the young men present
enrolled themselves as members of the League.

The Junior Imperial League was dissolved upon the formation of the Young
Citizens' League, and its members were appealed to by the officers to join the new
organization.   They proved worthy of the confidence placed in them, for of the 350
all but about half a dozen were accounted for, and the members of the League were
amongst the readiest to enlist in the armed forces of the Crown.   Hence the Young
Citizens' League soon ceased to have any further existence in the town, all its
members finding a place in some branch of the national services.   It served its
purpose as one of the first recruiting agencies in the Borough, and those who were
responsible for its origin were satisfied that it had well fulfilled its function.

Swindon   Meanwhile, recruiting in the armed forces had been going on vigor-
Volunteer   ously ; a public notice was issued by the Mayor on August 11th,
(Temporary) establishing the " Swindon Volunteer (Temporary) Force," and
Force.   inviting men from seventeen to thirty years of age to enroll at the
Drill Hall in Prospect ; instruction in drill was to be given on four
evenings a week and on Saturday afternoons.   The intention was that this body should
be auxiliary to the Territorial Force, but later, when the territorial ranks were
closed, the men were given the option of joining the regular army.   Major F. P.
Goddard was associated with the Mayor as a president, and training began at once
under Sergeants Archer, Morse, Trimmer, and Woolford ; within a month, of 200
men who had enrolled, 60 joined " Kitchener's army " and 100 joined the Wilts
Yeomanry and the R.F.A.

This body must not be confused with the Volunteer Training Corps that was
established in 1915, and became a marked feature of the town's life.   The earlier
of the two bodies was but a transient organization, useful only as a feeder for the
national military forces.

Recruiting.   Recruiting for " Kitchener's Army " had been going on vigorously
"Kitchener's in Swindon, as elsewhere, almost from the outbreak of war ; on August
Army."   26th a great meeting in support of Lord Kitchener's appeal for 100,000
men was held at the Mechanics' Institution, when the Mayor was
supported by Col. T. C. P. Calley, Major F. P. Goddard, General Jefferys, and many
of the leading citizens ; nearly a hundred young men were enrolled at the meeting.

By October there were 2,634 Swindon men in various branches of the
2,000 by   forces, of whom 2,000 had joined since the outbreak of war.   Before
October.   the war there were 496 Swindon men in the Army and 167 in the Navy
—663 in all ; since the war began the additions up to October were :
Army Reserve, 312 ; Special Reserve, 75 ; Territorials (foot), 627 ; Yeomanry, 251 ;

Naval Reserve, 45; "Kitchener's Army," 661; thus the total additions to the forces were 1971, of whom two-thirds went to the Territorial regiment and "Kitchener's Army."

The Wiltshire Regiment naturally engaged local interest more particularly, and on October 29th another large meeting was held at the Mechanics' Institute in order to foster this interest. The Mayor again presided, and his chief supporters were Field Marshal Lord Methuen, Lieut. Col. Steward (in command of the Wilts Depôt), and Mr. R. C. Lambert, the Member of Parliament for the division. Lord Methuen stated that up to the end of September, 3190 Wiltshiremen had enrolled, and he paid a tribute to the sobriety of the men, saying that the way in which they had resisted the temptations of drink was an honour to Wiltshire.

Billetting in Swindon. But what brought the war most vividly before the town was the enormous influx of troops almost immediately after the declaration of war, and the dislocation of the ordinary life which it entailed. In the second week of August large numbers of troops began to be billetted in Swindon, as many as five or six soldiers sometimes being lodged in one house; in nearly every case the men were warmly received and entertained with more hospitality than the War Office notices demanded.

The Schools requisitioned. Somewhat hastily and ill advisedly certain schools were requisitioned as mess-rooms, hospitals, or sleeping quarters, but better counsels prevailed and they were soon restored to their proper use; the Technical School in Victoria Road was fitted up as a hospital for the 3rd South Midland Field Ambulance (R.A.M.C. Territorials), and the men were billetted in the vicinity; Sanford Street School, too, was converted into a hospital; Clarence Street School was for a short time used as a barracks, and on the morning when work should have been re-commenced after the Summer Vacation the lady-teachers devoted themselves to repairing damaged uniforms for the soldiers in occupation of the building. Other schools similarly commandeered were Westcott School and Ferndale Road School. It was a most fortunate thing for the welfare of Swindon that this policy was speedily abandoned, for the moral and intellectual damage sustained by those towns where the children were sacrificed to the exigences of the troops in this way is incalculable.

Entertaining the Troops. The entertainment of the troops was not left entirely to private good-will; with commendable promptitude marquees were erected adjacent to the Church Hall in Devizes Road to serve as recreation-rooms for the soldiers; there facilities for reading and writing were provided, and concerts were arranged under the management of the Rev. R. W. Philipson. Many of the Free Churches, too, converted schools and class-rooms into recreation-rooms, notably Faringdon Street Wesleyan Church and the Presbyterian Church, whose pastor, the Rev. J. H. Gavin, threw himself ardently into the work of ministering to the welfare of the troops—in the town, at Chiseldon Camp, and later on the battlefront in France where he served for two years as a chaplain.

Boy-Scouts as Guides. The duty of guiding the men to their billets upon their first arrival devolved upon the police, but the Boy Scouts speedily recognized a fine opening for service in this direction; the Town Council placed a room in the Town Hall at their disposal, where, under the direction of Mr. W. Arnold-Forster, they were on duty for emergency work day and night. As the trains arrived they were met by a number of scouts, and the celerity with which the lads got the men to their lodgings quite out-did the police methods. This was but a part of the invaluable help given by the boys, whose zeal and energy seemed inexhaustible, and whose services were in constant demand for several weeks.

The month of August, 1914, was one of tropical heat and exceedingly trying to the new troops, of whom many thousands were suddenly billetted in Swindon ; the men, fresh from offices, colleges, schools, factories and farms, stood it well upon the whole, though minor mishaps were common, especially when certain officers injudiciously took their men on long route-marches in the trying heat, burdened with full kit ; then it was no uncommon sight to see exhausted lads brought in by country carts or straggling in long after the main body had reached home. The people of Swindon, and especially the youth, were intensely interested in all the military movements, and its quiet streets were transformed by the frequent passage of long columns of troops and sometimes of gun-columns or long trains of motor-lorries and ambulances. It would be difficult to reproduce the gaiety and eager excitement of those early days when nearly everyone was saying, " It will be all over by Christmas " : no one then dreamt of rationing, and food-queues, and zeppelin-warnings, and universal service for men up to fifty years of age. All were conscious of the righteousness of Britain's cause, and did not yet realize the gigantic forces arrayed against the Allies.

Appreciation of Swindon's Hospitality. Between August 15th and 17th this first great contingent of friendly invaders left Swindon, chiefly on the Sunday, when 45 trains left the Great Western Railway Station ; the officers in command, address-ing the men, spoke warmly of the way in which the town had entertained them, whilst the officers of the 6th Battalion of the Gloucester Regiment and Lieut. Col. T. F. Ash, commanding the 7th Battalion of the Royal Warwicks, wrote letters to the Mayor thanking the people of Swindon for their " overwhelming hospitality " and " the willing help and good wishes of all ranks." The Mayor of Rugby, too, sent a letter of thanks to the Mayor for the town's welcome to the 1st Howitzer Battery (Warwicks) of the 4th South Midland Brigade, a local battery in which Rugby took great interest ; the letter remarked specially that those with whom the men had been billetted had refused the money payment for their accommodation. Similarly the 3rd South Midland Field Ambulance left with cordial expressions of appreciation for the hospitality they had received ; one of their number, writing to the local press, said, ' At the last, on parting, it appeared to be quite a strain for the men to leave, and also for the people to allow them to leave. In fact, there was one case of a couple of small children going to the Colonel's billet and saying to him " Please, sir, daddy sent us to ask couldn't Private................ stay for a few more days ? " When the Colonel answered in the negative, the poor little mites broke into tears.'

The welcome given these soldier lads was indeed warm ; they were of the pick of England's youth, full of enthusiasm and gaiety, and many a mother and wife looking on them said in her heart, as more than one said aloud, " I have a son—or husband—in the army, and I know how I should feel if some woman gave him a decent home for a day or two." It was a pleasure to meet the long columns of lads singing some catchy air as they marched ; singing, in fact, seemed their chief delight, and in the evening about an hour before the roll-call crowds of soldiers would assemble at the appointed spot and sing popular airs and hymns indiscrimi-nately, to the genuine enjoyment of the onlookers. As the Mayor said at the Council Meeting on September 1st, "How the inhabitants of the Borough stood the strain of having over 17,000 men billetted on them, and how well the men were

received and treated, was one of the most pleasant things to be remembered."
But equally pleasant was the memory these Territorials left by their chivalry,
decorum, and cheerfulness.

Glimpses of Swindon men were present at the retreat from Mons, the battles of
the War.   the Aisne and Marne, the siege of Antwerp, and in the naval fights,
          and vivid letters describing their experiences appeared in the " *Swindon
Advertiser* " and the " *North Wilts Herald.*" The casualty lists and honours lists,
and then the list of prisoners of war began to contain names familiar in the Borough;
thus, the local press reported on October 23rd that Captain T. E. Estcourt, (Scots
Greys), son of Canon Estcourt, the late Vicar of Swindon, was a prisoner of war,
and the same issue announced the mention, in Sir John French's despatches, of
the Rev. T. S. Goudge, son of Mr. Jno. Goudge, of Bath Road; he was one of eight
chaplains mentioned by the General and was attached to the 13th Field Ambulance,
5th Division, and had been present at the Mons battle, where the 1st Wiltshire
Regiment was engaged.
      The casualty lists now assumed a painful interest for many in Swindon, serving
to " bring the war home " to the townsfolk more acutely than anything else.   It
was about the first week in September that the names of men known in Swindon
began to find a place in these terrible lists, when the 3rd casualty list contained the
Wilts regimental losses.   One of the first Swindon men notified as having lost his
life in his country's cause was William George Sheldon, son of Mr. Sheldon of Dean
Street ; he was an engine-room artificer on H.M.S. " Pathfinder " which was blown
up by a mine on September 5th ; the ill-fated vessel was cruising about twenty
miles from the East Coast when it struck one of the diabolical floating mines that
had been strewn broadcast by the Germans upon the North Sea, and was literally
blown to fragments, all traces of the vessel disappearing in about four minutes.
Another name of mournful interest that appeared in these earliest lists was that of
Capt. Gerald Ponsonby, son of the late respected Vicar of St. Mark's Church, Swindon ;
he was the Canon's eldest son, and his death from wounds received in battle aroused
wide-spread sympathy for his parents, who had moved from Swindon to Wantage.
These are but amongst the fore-runners of the great number whose names figure in
the Swindon roll of honour.

Delusion still Yet a curious commentary upon the total misapprehension of the
cherished.   state of affairs, involving the expectation of a speedy return to normal
          conditions, is afforded by an advertisement that appeared in the
" *Swindon Advertiser* " for November 11th.   It ran—

DRESDEN ROYAL CONSERVATOIRE
FOR MUSIC AND DRAMA.
(59th Year).
Full or Special Courses.
Entry at any time.   Principal courses commence 1st April and 1st September.
Prospectus from the Directorium.

      This astonishing notice could have met with little response in Swindon at the
best of times.

Prevention of Distress. It was the universal belief that the outbreak of war would be immediately followed by serious economic disturbance resulting in wide-spread distress, and those upon whom lay the responsibility of ameliorating such hardship began promptly to take measures to combat it. One class, indeed, was in urgent need of immediate attention,—the families of the soldiers and sailors,—but the idea that there would soon be a large section of the community unemployed turned out to be an entire miscalculation. The army allowance to the wives and dependents of service men was, however, quite inadequate, not having been designed for circumstances such as those in which the nation now found itself. The Great Western Railway Company was quick in taking steps to ameliorate the situation by arranging to supplement service-pay and separation-allowances of married men in their employ according to the circumstances of their families, and at the same time guaranteed them their posts upon the conclusion of the war ; by September over 4,000 reservists and territorials had been released from the Company's service, and of course a large number were Swindon men. The Town Council adopted the same generous course with their employees ; thus, employees of the Corporation would continue to receive half their wages or salary, whilst the Education Committee decided that teachers joining the Army were to receive full pay less their army allowance, and service with the colours was to count as service under the Committee.

The Prince of Wales' Fund. It was anticipated, however, that there would be a serious slackening of business and industrial enterprise with a consequent increase of unemployment, especially in the ensuing winter. The Prince of Wales inaugurated a National Fund for the relief of the distress that was thought inevitable, and on receipt of letters from His Royal Highness and from Queen Mary, who warmly supported her son's enterprise, the Mayor convened a large meeting of representative citizens at the Town Hall on August 7th to deal with the matter. An executive committee was formed to organize the work of various sub-committees, a subscription list was opened, and steps were taken to obtain information as to Reservists and Naval men called away and as to the position of their families. The fund was to be essentially national ; subscriptions were therefore to be sent in full to the central fund, and then what was needed locally would be drawn thence ; a fortnight later His Worship was able to announce that £675 : 10 : 9 had already been subscribed. The town was divided into 84 districts, a visitor being appointed to each to enquire personally into every case where a man had joined the forces ; urgent cases of need were to be reported immediately and to receive direct attention.

Growth of the Fund. By the end of August the local subscriptions to the fund reached nearly £1,000, and by the end of September over £2,000. At a meeting of the General Committee held on Oct. 9th, it was reported that there were 1,882 cases on the register of whom 1,701 were those of men in the Great Western Railway Company's service ; 147 homes had received relief, all but 10 being homes where a man had gone away on military service. By mid-November the subscriptions reached £2,800, the registered cases were 1,983, and the number receiving weekly assistance was 216, of whom 15 were civilian cases. The increase in the separation allowance about this time caused a considerable reduction in the numbers needing relief, and they fell to 57 military and naval and 13 civilian cases. The last public statement of the year 1914 gave a total contribution to the Prince of Wales' Fund from Swindon of £3,345 : 9 : 11½. [1]

[1] Continued on page 48.

The Camp   The activities of Swindon could not be restricted to the bounds of
at Chiseldon. the Borough, with a big camp springing up at Draycott for the men
               of which Swindon was the great attraction during leisure hours.   In
August it was known that a scheme was afoot for purchasing large tracts of land in
the vicinity of Chiseldon for military purposes, and early in September it was
announced that Messrs. Chivers and Sons, of Devizes, had secured a contract for
building barracks on land that had been bought at Draycott, and that the estimate
was between fifteen and sixteen thousand pounds ; the buildings were to be constructed on wooden frames, with asbestos linings and corrugated iron coverings.   At
the beginning of October four regiments, numbering about five thousand men,
were already quartered there, consisting of Cheshires, Royal Welsh Fusiliers, South
Wales Borderers, and the Welsh Regiment ; the barracks were then growing rapidly,
and the Midland and South Western Junction Railway Company had constructed
a siding at the camp.

               Acting with the promptitude that distinguished its splendid work during
The Y.M.C.A. the war, the Young Men's Christian Association opened three large
               marquees at the camp almost as soon as the men arrived; there they pro-
vided refreshments, facilities for reading and writing, amusements, and a good series
of entertainments under the management of Mr. H. M. Gould, the Camp-leader.
About a fortnight later the Association formally opened the premises of the old
Conservative Club in Fleet Street, Swindon, for the accommodation of soldiers
coming into the town ; Field Marshal Lord Methuen, supported by the Mayor
(Ald. C. Hill), Mr. R. C. Lambert (M.P. for the division), the Rev. A. G. Gordon Ross,
and many others, officiated at the opening ceremony, and a company of the Royal
North Lancashires with their band acted as a guard of honour to the distinguished
general.

               It was not long before the Y.M.C.A. replaced its marquees by a large "Hut"
within the Camp and erected another in Chiseldon, and throughout the war the
Y.M.C.A. "Hut" was the centre of the social amenities of the Camp.

Combating   An ugly feature of the general perturbation caused by the outbreak
Food Panic. of war was the selfish haste of some people to lay in a large stock of
               provisions, and the equally selfish action of some wholesalers and trades-
men in raising the price of commodities at once.   The questions of maintaining
an adequate supply of necessities, of regulating prices, and of stimulating economy
were to form the most difficult problems for both national and local administrators,
involving enormous labour and anxiety.

               On August 6th, in consequence of the panic-purchase of food by many folk,
the Mayor issued a public notice urging upon householders the patriotic duty of not
making purchases beyond their usual requirements; he also appealed to all
provision dealers to decline to supply any customers with more than their usual
supply of provisions, and called attention to the assurances of the Chancellor of
the Exchequer (Mr. Lloyd George) and Mr. Austen Chamberlain that there were
ample supplies of food available and that there was no need for any great increase
in prices.

               Several tradesmen and the local co-operative societies patriotically refrained
from raising prices, but naturally they had also to restrict their sales to their regular
customers and to limit the amounts in the way the Mayor suggested.   Flour had
risen, however, 5/- a sack in the first week of August, entailing an increase of 1d. on
the quartern loaf ; wheat, maize, and barley also rose considerably in price, whilst

other necessities were rising. In consequence of this and of the Mayor's appeal a large number of retail provision dealers held a conference at the Town Hall on August 6th, Mr. A. W. Burson, the principal of " Freeth & Co." presiding ; the meeting decided to point out to the public that the exorbitant increases in wholesale prices justified the rise in retail prices ; furthermore, as the wholesale dealers in many instances were refusing to accept payment in any form but gold, the public was urged to pay cash for their purchases. After a long discussion, however, the meeting could not agree on the impotant matter of a table of prices for retail sales.

Swindon Corn-Market. At the Swindon Corn-Market on August 10th, there was little old wheat for sale, the supply now having nearly run out, and the price asked was 45 /- per qr., an advance of 8 /- to 10 /- in a fortnight. The new wheat began to come in the following week, 155 qrs. being sold in Swindon market at an average price of 37 /3; an examination of the prices in successive weeks shows a steady increase, 40 /- being reached by the end of August, when the price became steady for some weeks ; 40 /- to 42 /- was asked on Nov. 2nd, 44 /- the next week (as against 32 /- for the corresponding date in 1913) and on Dec. 21st, 46 /-. The rates for barley in the same period varied between 26 /3 per qr. and 31 /-, and oats between 23 /7 and 27 /9.

Bread. The effect upon the price of bread was that the quartern loaf, which cost 4½d., before the war, rose to 5½d. in August and 6d. in September ; it was, however, pure and not adulterated with the unpalatable ingredients with which the public became familiar in 1917.

Maximum Prices. The Board of Trade began very early to regulate in some measure the prices of the chief necessities, announcing lists of maximum prices every few days at first ; thus, from Aug. 14th to Aug. 18th, the maximum retail rates permitted were,

Sugar, granulated,	3¾d.	per lb.
Sugar, lump,	4d.	,,
Butter, imported,	1 /6	,,
Cheese, colonial,	9½d.	,,
Lard, American,	8d.	,,
Margarine,	10d.	,,
Bacon (by the side) foreign,	1 /1	,,
Bacon, British,	1 /2	,,

At the time even these prices seemed heavy to the small housekeeper, but before the end of 1920 they would have seemed ridiculously low, when English butter was 5 /- a pound and the best cuts of bacon were about 3 /6 a pound.

Sugar Fixed. In October sugar prices were fixed by Royal Commission at 3½d. per lb., and 4d. per lb., for granulated sugar and cubes respectively, but the time had not yet come when the public was put on rations.

The Borough Market. The commodities sold in the Borough Market, chiefly vegetables, fruit, and fish, continued plentiful and cheap ; right through the autumn tomatoes were sold at 2d. to 4d. the lb., apples at 1d. and 2d.; potatoes were 8d. a peck ; plums sold at 13 to 6 lbs a shilling according to quality, and damsons were 1d. a lb ; oranges were sold at 16 to 24 a shilling. Eggs, which were 11 a shilling in August, began to rise in price very early owing to the growing demand for them in the military hospitals ; they rose in price to 8 a shilling in

September and 6 a shilling in October, but even then no one contemplated seeing eggs at 5d. each by July, 1918. Similarly, fish was cheap ; bloaters were obtainable at 8 and 12 a shilling, and in September as many as 16 were bought for a shilling ; plaice, which was 4d. and 5d. a lb, in August, was being sold at from 4d. to 6d., in October.

Christmas Fat Stock Market. Meat was plentiful at the customary rates, but the Christmas Fat Stock Show was abandoned, the chief reason being the anticipated difficulty of obtaining sufficient subscriptions to the Prize Fund, owing to the many calls made for the War Funds. There was, however, an exceptionally good entry of fat stock at the Christmas Market, held on Dec. 14th, at which Mr. J. A. Y. Matthews gave prizes in place of the usual trophies ; there were sold by auction 72 head of cattle, 125 calves, 60 fat sheep, and 229 heavy fat sows, baconers, and porkers. Fat sows fetched £6 : 12 : 6 to £11 : 15 : 0, baconers £4 to £9 : 2 : 0, and porkers £2 : 1 : 0 to £2 : 11 : 6. The best fat cows realised from £28 : 5 : 0 to £37, and the best fat bulls from £24 : 10 : 0 to £42, whilst the best five fat sheep (Brig. Gen. Calley's) went for 64 /- each, and the second five (also Brig. Gen. Calley's) for 64 /6 each.

Meat. At Christmas some increase in the retail price of meat was also observable ; English beef, which in June was sold at from 4d. to 1 /2 per lb., according to cut, was now selling at from 4d. to 1 /6 ; foreign beef, 3d. to 10d. per lb. in June, was now sold at 4d. to 1 /- ; English Mutton, 6d. to 1 /1 in June, now cost 6d. to 1 /4, and foreign mutton had gone up from prices between 2½d. and 8d. a pound to rates between 2½d. and 10d. ; suet had risen from 9d. to 1 /- per lb ; veal, which sold at prices from 6d. to 1 /- per lb. in June, now cost from 8d. to 1 /4, and pork had gone up 2d. since June when its price was 6d. to 1 /-. Thus there was an all-round increase of 2d. to 4d. per lb on meat,—nothing very remarkable, but the beginning of an upward progress that was to bring good cuts of beef and mutton to 2 /6 per lb.

Leather and Boots. Before the war one could buy in Swindon a good pair of men's boots, well-finished and neat in appearance, for anything from 12 /6 upwards, and good women's boots for about 15 /- or shoes from 7 /6 upwards. Four years later these prices were tripled and the quality had deteriorated. This was due to several causes, amongst which were the cessation of imports of hides and the requisition of leather for military use. As early as October 19th, a meeting of the Swindon and District Boot and Leather Trades Association discussed the price of leather and the increase in it already caused by the war ; the military demands were shown to have interfered very seriously with the ordinary trade, and as the advance in price entailed an increase in the cost of repairs a schedule of new rates was adopted by the members of the Association.

Restriction of Drink. The proximity of a large camp and the presence of the large works caused Swindon to be one of the first localities where restrictions were placed upon the sale of intoxicating liquors. At a meeting of the Borough Licensing Justices held on Oct. 8th, it was decided to make a Closing Order under the act recently passed, affecting all licensed houses, clubs, and grocers' licenses ; it prohibited the sale of any intoxicating drink after 9 o'clock in the evening, and the order was to hold good till Jan. 28th., 1915 : the Licensed Victualler's Association described this as a vindictive attack upon the trade, and appealed to the General in command of the camp, at whose instance the order was made, to reconsider the question ; he firmly refused to interfere with the Justices' Order, and declared that since it was made there had been a very marked decrease of trouble at the camp in consequence of it. On Nov. 14th, the order was supplemented by one issued by the Superintendent of Police ; this order placed all premises where intoxicating drink was sold out of bounds for soldiers, between 6 a.m., and mid-day ; furthermore, it prohibited the sale of bottles of spirits or other intoxicating liquors to soldiers, directly or indirectly, at all times.

Industrial Life. Beyond the changes made in the character of the work in certain shops in the Great Western Factory, the industry of the town was but slightly affected during 1914. There was a foolish catch-word chanted from one end of the country to the other by the " gramophone press " and unthinking speakers ; it was, " Business as usual,"—as though anything could go on " as usual " whilst the most momentous war of History was being waged at the very doors of England ; it sprang from the persistent delusion that modern warfare could not possibly last more than a few months owing to the tremendous waste of life and wealth. But the phrase very well described the life of the country as a whole when the first shock was past, until it began to be realized that the nation was engaged in a life and death struggle with an immensely powerful foe.

A War Office Order. The only notable industrial event in Swindon, perhaps, outside the factory, was the giving of an enormous order to Messrs. McIlroy & Co. by the War Office ; the firm received an order for 45,000 beds and as many pillow-cases, of which 15,000 were to be made in Swindon ; 250 new hands were taken on in the town, two large workshops were organized out of rooms in the Regent Street establishment, 40 new machines were immediately installed, and the buzz of the workrooms could be heard throughout the premises.

The M. & S.W.J. Railway. The establishment of huge camps upon Salisbury Plain, at Chiseldon, and elsewhere in Wiltshire entailed an enormous increase in traffic upon the Midland and South Western Junction Railway. This erstwhile quiet little line, which had for long been a favourite theme for jests amongst Swindon folk who compared it with good-humoured superiority with their own famous line, was transformed into a bustling, crowded, and important line of communication, necessitating the enlargement of stations and the increase of staff. From August 5th to Dec. 31st, 1914, the railway ran 566 special troop-trains, conveying 154,671 men and 2,137 officers, 22,291 horses, 74 guns, 1102 wagons, 1,170 tons of luggage and 1,323 bicycles ; besides these there were 53 ambulance trains, and also vast quantities of stores despatched to Tidworth, Ludgershall, and Chiseldon. Swindon formed an important centre, and it was a common sight to see long columns of soldiers crossing the town from one station to the other, and the bridge in Devizes Road was a favourite point of view for the interested observer until the spy-mania or some other military notion caused the parapet to be raised some feet by an unsightly fence.

A Foolish Order. When a nation goes to war it must be prepared to put up as cheerfully as it can with the orders of the class to whom it entrusts the conduct of the war ; military necessity then comes first. The men into whose hands the power falls have neither any special qualifications for conducting any but purely military affairs nor any special interest in concerning themselves with civilian needs or sentiments ; consequently civilians find themselves frequently tried by what seems to them inept and unnecessary orders, though they can generally do nothing but submit in silence. One such military order, however, raised a storm of protest throughout the country ; it was issued through the Home Office, where one would have expected a little appreciation of public sentiment, and it made it part of the duty of the police to watch over the conduct of the wives of soldiers and sailors who were absent on service. Good as were the intentions behind the order, it only needs to be stated to see the tactlessness of it and the insult it conveys to the women of the country. The Swindon Trades and Labour Council, in common with public bodies throughout the land, was up in arms and passed a resolution, "That this Council strongly protests against the Home Office order imposing upon the Police the duty of supervising the conduct of the wives of the soldiers and sailors, and demands the withdrawal of this odious order." Needless to say, such an order could not be justified and was heard of no more. Of course there were instances of unworthy women betraying their trust, and they would have been bad wives had their husbands been at home, but the women of Swindon rose splendidly to their responsibilities, and a proof of it lies in the comparatively small increase—for there was some increase as time went on,—in juvenile crime.

Reduction in Vagrancy. A very marked effect of the changed conditions of the country, and one to which reference will have to be made again, was apparent in the returns of the Boards of Guardians. After the war had begun nearly all the Wiltshire Unions began to record a diminution in the number of vagrants relieved, as compared with the numbers for the corresponding periods of the previous year. The Wilts Vagrancy Committee, meeting at Trowbridge on October 29th, found that during the quarter just ended the number of vagrants relieved had fallen by 1,147 in comparison with the same quarter of 1913. No doubt a certain number of able-bodied vagrants had found their way into the army, but there was also more work to be obtained. There was a good deal of loose talk about the many "fine, strapping fellows" on the road, but investigation did not substantiate the assertions ; thus, a question was asked at a meeting of the Swindon and Highworth Board of Guardians early in December, by a Guardian who said "he had seen men walking in the direction of the Workhouse who should not be allowed to live on the ratepayers" ; but the Master said he had only had one man of military age, who, when spoken to, produced a certificate showing that he suffered from heart disease.

The November Elections. The November municipal elections excited hardly any interest, and there were contests only in two wards,—in the North Ward, where only 488 burgesses out of 2,726 troubled to vote, and in the King's Ward, where 951 out of 1,936 electors voted ; Mr. W. E. Morse was one of the candidates returned in the King's Ward, and he succeeded Alderman Chas. Hill in the Mayoral chair.

The Retiring Mayor. At the last Council meeting, on October 27, high and well-earned praise was bestowed upon the work of the retiring Mayor, who had served during the most strenuous year in the history of the municipality hitherto,—one that, apart from the many duties entailed by the war, had seen the initiation of matters of great importance for the Borough,—notably the acquisition by the town of the Canal as far as was contained within the borough boundaries, the billetting of about 20,000 troops in Swindon in the early days of the war, the help given by the authorities of the town in recruiting, the work done for the Prince of Wales' Fund which at this time had been augmented by about £2,600 collected in Swindon, the supervision of the relief granted to the dependents of soldiers and sailors, and the provision of hospitality to Belgian refugees; all these had immensely added to the Mayor's duties and he had spared neither time nor labour in attending to them. The late Mr. J. J. Shawyer voiced the general feeling when he said, " Mr. Hill leaves the chair not only with the respect of the Council, but with the respect of all the inhabitants of Swindon."

The New Mayor. The new Mayor, Mr. Wm. Ewart Morse, was the son of a former Mayor of Swindon, the late Mr. Levi Lapper Morse, founder of the large furnishing firm associated with the name. He was the youngest member of the Council, of which he has been a member for six years, and had occupied the positions of Chairman of the Health Committee and Vice-Chairman of the Watch and Pleasure Grounds Committee. Mr. Morse was also one of the King's Ward's representatives on the County Council, president of the Swindon Chamber of Commerce, and secretary of the North Wilts Liberal and Radical Association. Mr. Morse entered upon his year of office with universal good-will and confidence in his power to uphold the dignity of the chair and to sustain the heavy and important duties attached to it at this momentous time. It was hoped that as his father had had the privilege of announcing the declaration of peace after the South African War, so the son might be able to read the King's proclamation of peace before his year of office closed. But before that happy event came Mr. Morse was to be Swindon's Mayor for two years, and to serve as an officer in His Majesty's forces ; so little did men appreciate the true nature of the struggle that had begun.

A Graceful Act. One of the new Mayor's early notices was as follows :—
" The children of the United States of America have sent a large number of Christmas gifts for the children of Soldiers and Sailors of British or Belgian nationality, whose Fathers or Guardians are, or have been, on active service abroad, and a number of these gifts is being sent for distribution amongst such children residing in Swindon.

Parents or other relatives of children of soldiers and sailors serving abroad may obtain forms of application for such gifts on applying at the Town Hall, or at the Mechanics' Institute."

On Christmas Eve over 500 expectant children assembled at the Mechanics' Institute, where a table reaching from one side of the room to the other was laden with toys, some of which had crossed the Atlantic Ocean in America's Christmas Ship, " Jason." A large body of ladies and gentlemen was present to support the Mayor and Mayoress in the performance of perhaps the pleasantest duty of their official life. The Mayor spoke briefly to the children, explaining that Swindon's share of America's gift was only 150 gifts, but not a single boy or girl was to be disappointed if they could help it ; he explained to them that children in Russia, France, and Belgium had also received gifts from their American cousins, and asked them to show their gratitude by a hearty cheer. Then the Mayor gave out the gifts for the girls, 273 in number, and the Mayoress distributed those for the 263 boys, and the 35 Belgian children,—16 girls and 19 boys. A choir of Belgian children, dressed in the uniform of the " combattants de 1830," delighted the audience by singing the Belgian and Flemish national anthems, and boys of Clarence Street School responded with several English and American songs.

American policy caused many heart-burnings in Britain before she came into the war with such splendid help as she sent three years later, but such an incident as this served to show where the real heart of America lay, and the memory of it is worthy of being treasured.

The Belgian   Mention has just been made of the presence of thirty-five Belgian
Refugees.   children at this distribution of gifts.   The invasion of Belgium by the
                   Germans and their ruthless treatment of the civil population from the
very moment of their entrance caused wide-spread panic in the unhappy land.
Great numbers fled to England and offers of hospitality poured in from all parts
of the country, Swindon being one of the first to invite some of the refugees to come
and settle amongst its townsfolk.   It has been found impracticable to deal with
the work of the Belgian Relief Committee in yearly sections, as is also the case with
the work of the Committee for the provision of Comforts for the Wiltshire Regiment
and Prisoners of War.[1]   Each of these subjects has been treated separately, as
a whole, and this seems a convenient place for dealing with the Belgian Relief
Committee.   The interest centres in the early days of the war, since as time went on
the work became more automatic, many of the refugees became self-supporting, and
the numbers fell off as some moved to other parts or hopelessly returned to live
under German rule.   The next chapter, therefore, traces the subject of Belgian
relief throughout the whole course of the war, even though this somewhat disturbs
the chronological order of the book.

(1) Chapter V, p. 89.

CHAPTER II.

The Belgians in Swindon.

One of the earliest philanthropic movements to enlist public sympathy was that for the relief of the Belgian Refugees. Nothing stirred so deeply the national heart in the early days of the war as the plight of Belgium ; the indignation excited by the unspeakable brutalities inflicted by the Germans upon the helpless population was equalled by the pity aroused for the thousands who had fled to England, in many cases utterly destitute.

Inception of the Belgian R. Com. Early in September, 1914, the "Liberal Women" of Swindon collected and sent to London for the refugees six large hampers of garments—526 in all,—and the offers of housing that were made led the Mayor, Alderman C. Hill, to convene a public meeting for the purpose of forming a committee to deal with the matter. Mrs. Arnold-Forster was elected President and Miss E. Blake was made Secretary, and with the assistance of a large number of willing workers they organized the work with enthusiasm and business-like skill. The Committee at once devoted itself whole-heartedly to the cause, its efforts never flagging throughout the four and a half years that the work lasted ; Mrs. Arnold-Forster remained President during the whole period.

Miss Blake relinquished the Secretaryship in December, 1914, and the office was filled by Miss Arnold-Forster until September, 1916, by Mrs. Tanner from then, till October, 1917, and then by Miss Kathleen Withy until the repatriation of the refugees. A debt of gratitude is due to these ladies, for the work called for great sacrifices of time and energy, and demanded exceptional powers of organization, especially in the first two years. The office of Treasurer was occupied first by Mrs. W. H. Williams, then by Miss Kathleen Withy, and, upon her becoming Secretary, by Mr. S. H. Webber. Mr. Ainsworth, until he left Swindon on special service in 1917, and Mr. W. Johnson acted as Auditors.

Method. In Swindon and several of the neighbouring villages local sub-committees were formed, who raised funds and took houses in their own localities for use as Belgian "homes" ; they solicited the loan of furniture and gifts of money, clothes, and food, and in this way personal interest was created in each district and there was excited a spirit of hospitality and friendliness that did much to ensure success ; in many cases houses were lent free of rent, and large quantities of furniture were readily found in response to the appeals of Mrs Tindle, Secretary of the Furnishing Committee, and her many helpers. In this way the Committee furnished about thirty homes in Swindon, including—

Swindon "Homes."

"Belmont," Devizes Road	60, Curtis Street
144, Goddard Avenue	36, Hythe Road
36, Ashford Road	12a, Hythe Road
South Street	58, York Road
23, Swindon Road	97, Redcliffe Street
"Deben House," Victoria Road	127, Redcliffe Street

297, Cricklade Road	56, Dixon Street
63, Cheltenham Street	17, Drew Street
" Downside," Westlecot Road	15, John Street
8, William Street	8, Commercial Road
2, Regent Close	6, Park Lane
73, Gooch Street	92, Clifton Street
47, Kingshill Road	49, Dryden Street
9, John Street	10, Haydon Street
23, King William Street	

Of course these were not all furnished at once, but they are all separate furnished homes, and no account is taken in this list of removals of homes to other addresses.

The Hostel. Until the system of separate homes could be fully carried out, the Vicar of Swindon generously placed his large house in Bath Road at the Committee's disposal for use as a Hostel, and it became the head-quarters of the work. The little meeting-room in the front garden was used as a store-house and was soon filled to overflowing with parcels of clothing and other necessaries. The hostel was later on moved to 53, Bath Road, and then to 88, Bath Road.

The First Guests. Mrs. Arnold-Forster had been up to the Alexandra Palace where many refugees were sheltered ; she found the poorest class, mainly Flemish refugees, quite without home comforts, and she brought back on September 26th, 1914, the first company of Belgians to come to Swindon ; this included a peasant family from Malines, consisting of a husband and wife with their five children, whose home had been burned down, and they were taken to Stratton by Mrs. Arkell. Another family was passed on to Purton and another to Wroughton ; M. and Mme. Georday and their four children were installed in Devizes Road, the family of M. Boelpaepe, from Brussels, in Goddard Avenue, and M. Barbe with his aged mother, from Charleroi, at the Vicarage, where a large circle of refugees was soon formed ; Dr. Bivar, a Portuguese royalist who had escaped from Lisbon three years previously, was at Liège when the German invasion rolled over Belgium, and escaped with his five-year-old son; he was entertained by Dr. Lavery. These were amongst the first comers, and they were soon followed by others, amongst whom were M. Hollebeke, the accomplished 'cellist of the Royal Flemish Conservatoire at Antwerp, and Mme. Hollebeke, and also a large group of ladies and girls, the family of Professor Cajot of Liège, who were settled at Deben House, Victoria Road. M. Van Gelder, who became the recognised spokesman for his compatriots, was one of the earliest comers, and M. Adrianssens, too, was soon a leading member of the Belgian community in Swindon.

Villages that helped. It will have been noticed that from the outset neighbouring villages played a part in the scheme for entertaining the refugees ; amongst those that received and supported families, besides Purton, Stratton, and Wroughton mentioned above, were Cricklade, Highworth, Shrivenham, Wootton Bassett, Hannington, Liddington, and Bassett Down. In most instances there were local committees, as in Swindon, who took and furnished homes and raised funds for the support of the visitors.

Effect of the presence of Belgians. The presence of the refugees created a more vivid realization of the horrors of the war than any newspaper report could have done. Here was a peasant family from near Malines, who related how they had been aroused from their beds at dawn, had been driven at the point of the bayonet along the highway—grandparents, husband, wife and four little ones, clothed merely in the garments they could hastily snatch before their house was set ablaze ; they told how the children cried with hunger and cold and how the poor old grandfather fell exhausted by the roadside, never to be heard of again. One lady related how for eight days her family and friends had found in a cellar refuge from the horrors of bombardment. Here, again, was a little girl of five years of age, whose tiny arm bore the cruel gash of a German sabre. Two lonely girls from a convent, passing through Swindon to a home at Hindon, near Salisbury, described their horrible passage from Antwerp in a vessel crowded to overflowing and the target for Zeppelin bombs as it crept down the Scheldt. Certainly, had a politic government wished to devise a plan for stimulating the national zeal, they could hardly have found one more to their purpose than that which the Germans themselves provided in driving by their cruelty this host of refugees to England.

Numbers. Within a few months upwards of three hundred Belgians had received hospitality in Swindon and the district, and altogether 350 were entertained ; a considerable number of those who came during these early months remained till the end of the war; for others, suitable openings were found in other parts of England, but 117 were still in the Committee's care when arrangements for repatriation were made early in 1919.

Return of some. A reduction in the numbers occurred in the early part of 1915, when the Germans had confirmed for the time being their grip on Belgium ; they recalled the refugees on pain of confiscation of their property and posts in Belgium, and some of the refugees in Swindon, as elsewhere, were induced to return. One gentleman, M. François Boelpaepe, who had made many friends in Swindon, was amongst these, and managed to keep up a correspondence with some of his acquaintances in Swindon ; in one letter he expresses his regret at having been induced to take the step :—

" Here in Brussels freedom has been but a name, and many and many a time have we regretted bitterly that we ever left the hospitable shores of England. When we returned to Belgium in May, 1915, life in Brussels had undergone practically no change, and except for the disagreeable sight of Boche uniforms you would not have thought that war was raging. This state of things, however, did not last long ; and when, owing to the blockade, stocks in Germany began to run low, our existence, bearable so far, quickly grew more and more intolerable, until it resolved itself finally into a state of abject wretchedness and want. The Germans ruthlessly seized upon all stocks of goods found in Belgium and erected central depôts or " centrales," for their reception. These " centrales " had at their disposal a whole army of officials who methodically set to work to sack the country."

Then, after giving the prices of several articles—for instance, eggs 2/- each ; sugar 6/6 per lb ; coal 22/- per cwt ; men's shoes £10 per pr ; and so on, he says :

" Then again, certain articles of food were only procurable by stealth. For instance, I used to spend my Sundays and holidays in tramping the countryside to try to get a pound or two of butter or a few potatoes at some farmhouse or other. In this way you paid about 20 to 30 per cent less than what you had to give for the same things in town. But matters did not always end here. There was the problem of getting back to Brussels in safety, for Hun gendarmes were everywhere on the look-out to arrest all Belgians obtaining food indirectly from the farmer or gardener."

Subscriptions. The appeal made for funds upon the formation of the Belgian Relief Committee met with a ready response ; by October 15th, 1914, the public subscription list reached beyond £350, and many people had promised monthly subscriptions ; by November 14th, £524 : 19 : 10 had been contributed and the total receipts for 1914, covering only just over three months, were £786 : 13 : 0.

c

Children's help. To these sums must be added valuable gifts in kind, and it is pleasing to remember how heartily the children entered into schemes for obtaining supplies ; hampers and sacks placed in the schools were speedily filled with potatoes and other vegetables, and some really splendid consignments were thus obtained and sent up to the Hostel. Some of the Boy-scouts became a sort of " A.S.C." company in the service of the Belgian Relief Committee, collecting and distributing the supplies, and it is pleasant to note in the subscription lists such items as " Three scouts (sweeping snow) 3 /6."

Balance Sheet. The receipts and expenditure by the Committee during the course of the war amounted to over £5,000, and the following table shows the amounts contributed annually ; it will be seen that from September 7th, 1917, the local subscriptions failed to meet the expenses, and the Committee had to accept assistance from the War Refugee Committee in London ; but let it be recorded that the Swindon Committee was one of the last in the Country to seek outside help.

Amounts raised by the Swindon and District Committee.		£	s.	d.	Expenditure by the Committee.	£	s.	d.
1914 (3mths)	....	786	13	0		5106	12	5
1915	....	1469	10	1				
1916	....	1073	4	7				
1917	....	740	5	11				
1918	....	94	17	8				
1919 (4 mths)	....	86	19	6				
Total contributions	....	4251	10	9				
Amount received from the War Refugee Committee.					Balance returned to the War Refugee Committee:—	37	16	8
1917 (from Sept 7)	....	142	10	0				
1918	....	503	0	0				
1919	....	247	8	4				
Total Aid.	....	892	18	4				
Total Receipts	....	5144	9	1	Total	5144	9	1

This amount, £4,251 : 10 : 9, raised in the district for the central local fund, does not represent the total amount raised in Swindon even for local needs, to say nothing of contributions sent elsewhere, for the district sub-committees raised and expended large sums for the work of their own districts : thus,

The District Committee for		Secretary			Raised £	s.	d.
60, Curtis Street	....	Mrs. Sawyer	....	....	174	13	4½
58, York Road	....	Mrs. Seaton & Mrs. Kinneir	....		*195	2	9
144, Goddard Avenue	....	Mrs. Tindle	....	....	305	5	0
47, Kingshill	....	Miss Colborne,					
56, Dixon Street	....	(for Mme. Dockray's			300	0	0
49, Dryden Street	....	Ladies' Choir)					
23, Swindon Road	....	Mrs. Sargent and					
36, Hythe Road	....	Mrs. Norris	....	....	350	0	0
Gorse Hill	....	Mrs. Turk	....	....	200	0	0
		Total from Sub-Committees		....	£1525	1	1½

* Includes £85 subscribed by the Municipal Officers' Guild.

Adding this amount to the £4,251 : 10 : 9, a grand total of £5,776 : 11 : 10½ is obtained. Some of it was due to great personal effort on the part of individual ladies, Mrs. G. Brooks alone collecting £250 for the central fund.

Besides the sub-committees mentioned, there were also others for 73 Gooch Street, (Secy. Mrs. Lavery) and for "Downside" (Secy. Mrs. C. A. Plaister, succeeded by Mrs. Marillier).

Fêtes, etc. A good deal of money was raised by public entertainments in which the Belgian guests took a prominent part. The first was the Fête in the Town Gardens on August 28th, 1915, a Belgian "Flag-Day," the fête being preceded by a procession through the town. It was certainly the best procession the town had seen for many years, and some very beautiful tableaux were presented.

A crowded concert in aid of the funds on March 6th, 1916, showed there was no waning of sympathy, and on September 2nd a delightful carnival was held in the Great Western Park ; the day was "Belgian Flag-Day," and the Mayor, Mr. W. E. Morse, presided at the opening of the carnival, Mrs. Currie, of Upper Upham, performing the ceremony; what with music, gymnastic displays, songs, games and dancing, the scene was one to be remembered and had an unwonted touch of gaiety that was undoubtedly due to the influence of the Belgian guests.

In 1917 an afternoon concert and gymnastic display, held in the Town Gardens on May 30th, was followed by an evening concert at the Mechanics' Institute, and they were as successful as the previous concert given at the Institute.

But more enjoyable than these, to those who were privileged to attend, were the private parties given to the refugees. The first was given on the Saturday before Christmas, 1914, when the Workers' Educational Association entertained the Belgian guests at the Higher Elementary School ; Mrs. Arnold-Forster welcomed them in a beautiful speech in French, and then handed to each child present a Christmas Gift. The programme that followed the tea included 'cello solos' by Professor Hollebeke, songs by both Belgian and English singers, and a song composed by Mr. Alfred Williams with a rendering into French by Dr. Bivar.

Similar parties were held at the Mechanics' Institute,—a tea, with Christmas Tree and distribution of presents on December 30th, 1914, a New Year's Party on January 6th, 1916, a Christmas Party in December, 1916, and a Farewell Party on January 6th, 1919.

The Belgian National Day, July 21st, was signalised in 1916 by a picnic in Mr. Balch's fields at Westlecott, and in 1918 Mrs. Tindle and Miss Withy entertained the women and children at " Westlecott."

These were by no means the only occasions upon which hospitality was extended to Swindon's guests, and private hospitality to special families was very general, resulting in the formation of many lasting friendships.

There were also occasions upon which the Belgians organized public gatherings ; on December 18th, 1914, for example, they arranged a very beautiful Belgian Fancy Fair at the Town Hall, for the benefit of their wounded compatriots. The Fair was opened by the Mayor, Mr. W. E. Morse, and in their speeches in reply both the president, M. Adrianssens, and the director of the bazaar, M. Van Gelder, alluded in glowing language to the hospitality they had received and the friendships they had formed in Swindon.

Mrs. Arnold- At these friendly gatherings Mrs. Arnold-Forster was a frequent visitor,
Forster.   and by her kindness and charm she won the deepest affection of the
                 refugees,—a feeling that found expression in the beautiful album of
names presented to her, which was the work of the talented young artist, M. Emile
Boelpaepe. The Committee, too, felt the greatest admiration for Mrs. Arnold-
Forster's gifts of organization and leadership, and at the close of their labours they
expressed their " great appreciation of her splendid work for the Belgians thoughout
the war," saying that " without her able leadership and powers of organization
the work of the Committe : could not have continued so successfully to the end."

Miss Arnold- The work owed a good deal of its success, too, during the most strenuous
Forster.   period, to Miss Iris Arnold-Forster, and it was felt that her departure
                 to take up war-work elsewhere was a severe loss ; she had been
Secretary for nearly two years when she left Swindon, in the latter part of 1916,
and her labours had been incessant and heavy. The Committee showed their
regard for her by the presentation of a silver tea-service, and the Belgians of the
district presented her with a silver toilet-set, which, with a bouquet, was gracefully
handed to her by three little Belgian children, accompanied by a happy speech
from M. Adrianssens.

The   Mention should be made, also, of the great help derived from the
Language   services of Mrs. Neville who acted as Interpreter to the Committee,—
Difficulty. a very necessary service in the earlier period when most of the refugees
                knew no language but French or Flemish. As time went on and it
became apparent that the war would last a long time, steps were taken to teach
English to the exiled ; a class was formed for adult refugees, and the Education
Committee established a special class at the Secondary School for Belgian children,
drafting them to the Elementary Schools as they attained to some degree of proficiency in English ; many of the English pupils made excellent progress in French
through their association with their Belgian fellow-pupils at the Secondary School,
but, on the other hand, the younger Belgian children became so proficient in English
that they forgot their mother-tongue in time and were indistinguishable from
English children.

Work.   It was not the Committee's intention, when once it was realized that
                the Belgians' stay might be a long one, that they should live in the
town in a state of dependence if means of self-support could be found ; work was
therefore found for those able to undertake it, and some were engaged in the Railway
Works, some at the Munitions Works, some at the Chiseldon Camp, and several
in private businesses.

                In 1915 a Belgian Workshop was opened in a building at the corner
The   of Eastcott Road and Bath Road, lent by Mr. Webb for the purpose ;
Workshop.   Mrs. Norris gave two workman's benches for the workshop and Mr.
                Jinks a magnificent chest of tools. The men engaged at this workshop
were employed first in making furniture which was to be the property of the
Belgian Government, and was to be kept for furnishing Belgian houses ; later on the
place became a small toy-factory and sent out some beautiful specimens of
handicraft. A good deal of furniture was sent to France, and Messrs. McIlroy
bought a large quantity of toys for their Christmas Bazaar. M. Emile Geys, the
foreman, spoke gratefully of the many ways in which Mr. Webb helped on the

work, and at the time when arrangements were being made for repatriation M. Geys was prepared to take on eight or ten more unemployed Belgians,—so successfully was the scheme working. The Great Western Company also helped materially in allowing the workshop to have what waste wood it needed for the toys, and at a time when timber was almost unobtainable this was no slight gift. As an example of the workshop's success it may be noted that between September, 1916, and January, 1917, £60 was realized from the toy manufacture of which £30 was paid in wages.

Help from Aldwych. Reference has been made to the fact that in September, 1917, the Committee was driven to accept aid from the Central War Refugee Fund. At that time the income was only about £6 per week whilst the expenses were about £12 weekly ; an appeal had been issued in July stating these facts, and pointing out that from £250 to £300 over the normal subscriptions would be required to carry the work through the winter, and to allow the means of providing supplementary allowances to the wives of Belgian soldiers, of maintaining the elderly and infirm, and of supplementing the incomes of those earning low wages. The appeal did not, however, attract sufficient to obviate the necessity of drawing upon the Central Committee in Aldwych ; but this must not be construed as a reflection upon local philanthropic feeling, for there were now many other pressing appeals, commodities were exceedingly dear, multitudes of people had no " bonus " coming in or had a bonus that by no means brought up their incomes in proportion to their expenditure, and there was a very general feeling of anxiety and apprehension. Swindon had indeed done well, and hitherto had met all the expense unaided, and this had been £26 per week in 1915

£23 and £24 ,, 1916
£20 ,, ,, the first 3 months of 1917.

Honours. Swindon was one of the very few towns to keep its Committee to the end, and honour was reflected upon the whole band of workers when King Albert conferred upon Mrs. Arnold-Forster, Mrs. Tanner, and Mrs. Tindle the " Medaille de la Reine Elizabeth," in recognition of their unflagging services to Belgian refugees and soldiers.

Acts of kindness. It has been impossible to refer to all the many acts of kindness and assistance—multitudes of instances are unknown—or to name all who deserve gratitude. A glance down the subscription lists reveals many, and the Committee from time to time passed resolutions of thanks, such as, " The Belgian Committee owes a debt of gratitude to Mr. Toomer, who, since the beginning of the war, has given £13 worth of coal amongst the Belgian homes " (May, 1915), or again, " Mrs. Parker has collected £13 : 6 : 7 in the year " (Dec, 1915 : Mrs. Parker personally collected altogether £28 : 9 : 4 for the central fund). But no subscription list records such acts as that of a kindly housewife, pinched for money herself, who ordered her dairyman to leave a quart of butter-milk regularly at a poor home where an old peasant woman was pining for a taste of her national " butter-milk soup," ignorant of the means of getting its ingredients.

Thanks, too, are due to Dr. Beatty for the time and trouble he freely gave to the sick amongst the refugees,—work in which Dr. Lavery gave generous assistance.

Besides the ladies who have been mentioned in the course of the narrative, gratitude is due to the many other ladies of the Committee whose support was given through so long a period,—to Mrs. Ainsworth, Mrs. Ashford, Mrs. Currie,

Mrs. English, Mrs. Gilbert, Mrs. Harvey, Mrs. Horton, Mrs. H. C. King, Mrs. Kirby, Mrs. S. Morris, Mrs. Perry, Mrs. Pollard, Mrs. Rattray, Mrs. Reeson, Mrs. Sandling, Mrs. Skurray, Mrs. Whitworth, and others.

Farewell.   One hundred and seventeen Belgians still remained under the Committee's care when steps towards their repatriation began to be taken in January, 1919.   A pleasant store of memories was crowned by a delightful social gathering held at the Town Hall, when the Committee and other friends bade the company of refugees farewell.   The Mayor and Mayoress (Mr. and Mrs. C. A. Plaister), Mrs. Arnold-Forster, Mr. & Mrs. Ashford (of Burderop), Miss Withy (Secretary), Dr. Beatty, and many members of the Committee were present and gave the Belgians a hearty welcome ; music, song, and dance passed a merry hour or two, and during an interval in the mirth, M. Mommens, replying to a felicitous speech by the Mayor, expressed the gratitude of the Belgians for Swindon's hospitality.

One face was missing that all would gladly have seen there, for M.
A Sorrow.   Vanderheyden had not lived to see his country's release from German tyranny, and Madame and little Georgette had to return to Brussels in sorrow instead of joy.

When the last party set off from Swindon in April the Mayor and
Departure.   many of the Committee and friends wished them good-bye on the Great Western Station.   This party numbered 63,—12 men, 24 women, and a crowd of children.   One family of three had to remain till the end of the month at their "home" in Wroughton; they came from Ypres, and the devastated state of that part of Belgium delayed their return till accommodation was ensured for them.

A happy thought on the part of the Red Cross Hospital Committee
The Red   was to distribute amongst the returning refugees the blankets left
Cross Gift,   on their hands, and 50 were sent to the Belgian Relief Committee for the purpose,—a comforting provision for the voyage.

As a further illustration of the good relations existing between different
and the B.R.   Committees working in the Borough, the Belgian Relief Committee
Committee's   handed to the Victoria Hospital Committee the balance of £42 : 17 : 9,
Gift to the   that remained in its hands,—the net balance of the sale of furniture
hospital.   left after people had reclaimed what they had lent the Committee in 1914 and 1915.

Letters.   Many grateful letters and postcards were received from Belgium, of which one or two examples will be of interest.   Mrs. Neville received the following from Antwerp. :

(Translation by Mrs. Neville).

Antwerp, February 9th, 1919.
    Dear Madam—Just a few words to let you know that my wife and child arrived here on Wednesday, February 5th.   They had a splendid sea vogage, and they are both in excellent health.   I wish to take this opportunity to express to you my deep and heartfelt thanks for all you have done for them, both as interpreter and in visiting them from time to time, to make their life as happy as possible during their long exile in a strange land ; also for the happy time they spent at your home with you and your husband a few days before leaving Swindon.
    We shall often think of you for the great services you have rendered to the Belgian Refugees, not only as interpreter, but for all your other good works.
    My parents, who had the great pleasure of meeting their daughter and grand-daughter again after their long exile wish me to express their gratitude to you for your great kindness to them. Once more, dear Madam, accept our heartfelt thanks.
    My wife and little daughter say they hope to see you again in Belgium should you be spared to come here again.   They also wish to be remembered to your husband.

We should feel very grateful if you would express our thanks to the Committee, also to the people of Swindon and district for all they have done on behalf of the Belgians during their long exile in England.

Accept, dear Madam, our sincere friendship and salutations, also a big kiss from my little daughter,
                                                                Yours sincerely,
                                                                J. VANDYCK.

Here is one from a family whose home was for many months visible from the British trenches near Dixmude :—

(Extract from the Swindon Advertiser, May 26th, 1919).

BELGIANS' THANKS—Mrs. H. E. Norris, of 45, Kent Road, Swindon, has received the following letter expressing the thanks of Belgians who made many friends during their stay in Swindon :—" We have the honour to express our best thanks to the ladies of the Committee, Dr. Beatty, and all friends for the kind attentions shown to us during our stay in Swindon, at 36, Hythe Road. We sincerely apologise for not visiting personally and thanking our friends before our departure, but the short notice prevented us doing so. Accept once more our best thanks. The family, Inghelbrecht."

Others say—

" If you could hear all the good we say of the English people I am sure you would be quite proud of being English."

" We were so happy in England ! We were in Paradise compared with those who stayed in Belgium. We don't know how to thank all those who have been so good to the Belgians."

" I can never forget the good English folk, and all they did to relieve and encourage us in our exile."

" How hospitable Swindon has been ! And what great sympathy we received everywhere ! "

These are but a few extracts from the large pile of letters and postcards in Miss Withy's possession.

Conduct of the Visitors. On the other hand it should be stated that the demeanour and conduct of Swindon's guests throughout their long stay in the town and district were most gratifying, and gave no grounds for the complaints made in some towns. Most of the refugees came from the peasant and lower middle class, but, as regards the latter section, it is doubtful whether an equal number of English representatives of the class, chosen haphazard, would have displayed so much good-breeding and cultivation, and they have left behind them some very pleasant memories of their sojourn in the town.

The Prime Minister's Letter. In conclusion one cannot do better than quote the letter of thanks received by the Committee from the Prime Minister, the Rt. Hon. David Lloyd George :—

                                                        10, DOWNING STREET,
                                                        LONDON, S.W.1.
                                                        May, 1919.

Now that the repatriation of the Belgian Refugees is drawing to a close, I desire on behalf of His Majesty's Government to express to all who have taken a part in helping these unfortunate victims of the War our warm appreciation both of the services rendered and of the generous and kindly spirit which has throughout inspired them. When the first refugees from Belgium reached these shores, few could have guessed what their final numbers would be or how long their sojourn here would last. At that time the War Refugees Committee in London and the Local Committees throughout the Country, which so rapidly came into being, took upon themselves the task of organising the great national sentiment of hospitality, and in the result the mass of refugees were received into the country, homes were found for them, and their necessities relieved with singular speed and efficiency.

Since then many changes have taken place, many problems have had to be solved, and many developments in the organisation have been evolved, and the last act in the drama has been the repatriation of the refugees.

The Belgian Government have expressed themselves deeply sensible of the hospitality and friendliness which have been shown to their compatriots in their exile, and of the thoughtful care with which the arrangements for their repatriation have been made.

It will, I am sure, be a lasting pleasure to all who have been engaged in this great act of humanity to feel that at a time when so much of the energies of mankind has been devoted to destruction, it has been their privilege to take a part both in alleviating distress and in creating a new bond of fellowship between nations which will continue long after the tragic circumstances that brought it into being have passed into history.

D. LLOYD GEORGE.

CHAPTER III.

1915. – Settling down to War Conditions.

The year 1915 finally opened the eyes of most people to the true nature of the struggle in which England was involved, especially when the hopes of decisive victories in the summer were found to be deceptive ; it was realized that folk at home must settle down to a long period of " war conditions," and that in the making of plans to deal with these conditions longer views would have to be taken than were taken in many of the hastily devised schemes of 1914. In Swindon the year was marked by a considerable extension of philanthropic work and by great industrial prosperity ; but, as elsewhere, the public mind was much perturbed by the rapidly growing cost of living, which persistently outran the hesitating efforts first made to deal with it by small increases of wages ; these increases took the form of bonuses granted on the understanding that when normal conditions returned they would cease to be given,—which shows not only a very curious view of human nature, but also a very surprising estimate of the consequences of so vast an upheaval as Europe was experiencing.

Swindon Corn Market. The steady increase in the price of corn remarked in the last half of the year 1914 continued throughout 1915. The last sales at Swindon Corn-market in 1914 were—147 qrs. of wheat at an average price of 46/7, 89 qrs. of barley at 28/9, and 41 qrs. of oats at 27/3. It is to be noted that these are average rates, and were exceeded for the best varieties of grain ; the prices quoted below are also average figures unless otherwise specified. Although a very slight reduction might occur in an odd week now and then, the rise in price went on steadily until, in April, record rates were reached, not only locally, but throughout the country, for the price of wheat was higher than it had been for fifty years. On April 26th, 688 qrs. of wheat were sold in Swindon Corn-market, but even this was not the highest figure reached, for on May 17th, 65/- was demanded and given. The effect of this upward tendency was of course evident in the prices of flour and bread ; at the beginning of 1915 **Flour and Bread.** flour was 40/- the sack of 280 lbs ; in March the Swindon and Highworth Board of Guardians had to pay 48/- the sack, and in April, in consequence of the record rates of wheat just noted, the London millers advanced the price of flour to 53/- for town-households and 56/- and 57/- for top grades. Bread was raised in Swindon from 6½d. the quartern loaf to 7d. on January 4th ; on March 19th, the Board of Guardians contracted for bread at 7¼d. the qtn. loaf ; in June the Kingshill Co-operative Society had to charge 4d. for the 2 lb. loaf as against 2¾d. in June, 1914, whilst throughout the town the general price was 7½d. the qtn. loaf. Barley and Oats showed the same steady rise, though in a less degree, for barley advanced from the 28/9 quoted above to 33/11, at which price 44 qrs. were sold in Swindon on April 19th; and oats advanced to 34/1, 61 qrs. averaging that price in the local market on May 3rd.

The high figure just quoted for wheat could not be long maintained ; on June 7th, buyers in the market demanded a reduction of 4/- to 5/- on the previous week's price of wheat (60 /-) and as the farmers persisted in their refusal to come down, no business was done, but the next week saw a drop of 6 /- or 7 /- ; it was not, however, till the new wheat came in in September that there was any substantial fall in the rate ; the lowest average for the year was reached on September 20th, when 284 qrs. at 41 /4 was the quantity sold ; oats, too, fell to 25 /10, but barley had continued to rise, reaching 42 /- at the end of August, and now only fell to 36 /4.   The September contracts of the Board of Guardians also showed a slight amelioration, for they accepted flour at 1 /1 per 7 lbs., (being at the rate of 43 /4 the sack), and bread at 6½d., the qtn.

Closing Prices.   Henceforth there was a gradual rise to the end of the year, and in December wheat was fetching 53 /6 a quarter, 57 /- being paid for the best red ; 284 qrs. of barley were sold at 49 /2 on December 6th, but the highest figure for the year was reached on November 15th, when 218 qrs. were sold at 50 /3; the last sales of oats were at 31 /6, 32 /11 being the price on November 22nd. Flour went up rapidly in the middle of October, advancing 4 /- the sack in a fortnight, and bread was now 8d. the quartern in Swindon, although 9d. was charged in many towns.

Meat.   It was not till towards the end of 1915 that the increase in the price of meat was accentuated, and in March the Board of Guardians was able to obtain meat at the moderate rates of—beef 6d. a lb., mutton 7d., joints 9½d., shin of beef 3½d., and suet 4d., but in September they had to give 8½d. for beef, 9d. for mutton, 11d. for joints, 7d. for shin of beef, and 6d. for suet. By the end of May the wholesale price of meat had gone up 75% on pre-war rates, and in November beef was 30 to 35% dearer than in November, 1914, and mutton only a little less. A few quotations from the Swindon Cattle-Market illustrate the way in which prices were rising ; at the end of July prices were reckoned

Swindon Cattle Market.   high and fat bulls were sold from £29 : 10 : 0 downwards. At the beginning of October. when trade was slow, fat steers ran from £25 downwards, fat heifers from £24 : 5 : 0, fat sows from £11 : 2 : 6 to £6 : 10 : 0, fat pigs from £7 : 2 : 0 and porkers from 70 /- downwards. On November 15th calves were sold from £3 : 15 : 0 down, fat pigs from £7 : 4 : 0 to £4 : 17 : 6, and porkers from 88 /- down. A week later the prices paid were heifers and calves £28 : 10 : 0, £26, and £25 downwards, fat beasts £22, and fat sows £11 : 2 : 6. At the Christmas market—when, at Smithfield, wholesale prices as compared with those of Christmas, 1913, showed increases of 1d.

Christmas Sale.   to 2½d. a lb., and 3d. on British pork,—in Swindon there was a short supply of mutton but a plentiful supply of beef and pork ; prices were high, fat beasts fetching from £36 : 10 : 0 downwards, fat bulls from £39 : 10 : 0, and cows and heifers from £27 : 10 : 0 ; fat sows sold from £16 : 5 : 0 to £11, and one even fetched £20 : 5 : 0, whilst fat pigs ruled from £7 and porkers from 74 /- downwards. Veal was unobtainable as the Board of Agriculture had now imposed stringent restrictions upon the slaughtering of calves. It will be noticed that some of these figures are a substantial increase upon those of the 1914 Christmas market.

Naturally there was a corresponding increase in the cost of birds at the **Christmas Poultry Sale,** at which 11,000 were offered for sale, though 1 /- to 1 /7 a lb. for fat turkeys and 8d. to 1 /- for geese could perhaps not be regarded as excessive considering the conditions and the season; but chickens at 8 /6 to 10 /- a couple and ducks at 8 /- to 10 /- a couple seemed high after what people had been accustomed to pay.

Milk. About the middle of 1915 milk began the upward career that raised it to 11d. a quart by January, 1920. In August a meeting of farmers was held in Swindon with the aim of securing concerted action in demanding higher prices at the next contracts, and when the Board of Guardians made their September contract the price was raised to 1/2 per gallon, although the Swindon Victoria Hospital secured milk at 1/1 per gallon. At another farmers' meeting held at Swindon in September it was agreed to demand 1/2 per gallon for Winter milk and 10d. a gallon for Summer supplies, the farmers alleging that there was a great shortage of hay—of which the Army absorbed large quantities—and that feeding stuffs had doubled in price. In October, when the Guardians invited tenders for the supply of milk to Olive House, they had to give 1/2½ per gallon, and the Michaelmas contracts gave to the farmers an average rate of 1/1¼ per gallon for Winter supply and 10d. a gallon for Summer milk. Meanwhile the retail price in Swindon was 1/2 per gall. from Oct. 1st 1914, to Sept. 30th, 1915, having been 1/- a gallon in the summer of 1914 ; for the rest of the year 1915 and to June 30th, 1916, milk was 1/4 per gallon.

Fodder. The increased cost of fodder alluded to above was well illustrated by the contracts made for the supply of the **Swindon Corporation** in September, when the Town Council purchased 400 qrs. of English oats at 35/6 and 36/- per qr., 10 tons of broad bran at £8 a ton, 80 tons of meadow hay at £5:5:0, and £5:15:0 a ton, and 30 tons of sanfoin hay at £5:10:0 and £5:15:0 a ton. The circumstances operating in this respect to the disadvantage of the Corporation had, however, tended to their advantage earlier in the year, for at the letting of the **meadow grass at Broome Sewage Farm** in April, they had secured very favourable offers ; the conditions of letting were that the lands should be mown once only and the aftermath fed with cattle or sheep up to December 1st.; altogether the Town Council had about 112 acres to let and, excluding one acre near the filter beds let at £1 the acre, the bids ranged from £4:13:6 to £3:4:0 an acre, the whole letting at an average of about £3:18:0 per acre.

Increases in cost. More general interest attaches to the increases in the cost of **household food-stuffs** ; in July, 1915, prices had advanced, as compared with the cost in July, 1914, by the following amounts :—

British butter	........22/- per cwt.	Canadian cheese	....20/- per 120 lb.
Imported butter	........31/- ,,	Irish & Canadian bacon	22/6 per cwt.
British eggs	...............3/5 per 120	Danish bacon	...............25/- ,,
Irish eggs	...............4/- ,,	American bacon	.... 4/- ,,
Danish eggs	............4/11 ,,	English hams	.... 8/- ,,
Cheddar cheese	........24/6 per 120 lb.	Canadian hams	.... 3/- ,,
Cheshire cheese	........22/6 ,,	American hams	........fell 1/6 ,,

During this month the rise in prices had become accentuated, for the increases over the June prices were 8/-, 3/6 and 9/- per cwt. for British, Irish and Danish butter respectively, and British eggs had gone up 1½d. per dozen.

Protest Meetings. The public were much exercised by this question, and earlier in the year—in February—meetings of protest had been held by the Swindon Branch of the Amalgamated Society of Engineers, the Trades and Labour Council, and the New Swindon Co-operative Society, at which resolutions were passed expressing apprehension at " the uncalled-for rise in prices of food and fuel," and urging the Government to take " steps to remove that burden from the worker." At a conference of delegates of the National Union of Railwaymen held in the Mechanics' Institute on March 28th, for the purpose of demanding an increased war-bonus, the grounds for the demand were that by the end of January commodities had risen in price 23% above pre-war rates, and were 41% higher than in 1900, and 50% higher than in 1896.

Provisions. The Board of Guardians—who, buying in quantity and by contract, obtain more favourable rates than the public,—had to pay in September the following prices (bread and flour have been spoken of previously)—

Cheese ....62/- per cwt.	Lemons ....9d. per doz.	Sultanas ....7d. per lb.
Bacon ....96/- ,,	Onions ....11/- per cwt.	Tea ....1/9 ,,
Fresh butter 1/6½ per lb.	Split peas 25/- ,,	Rice ....15/- per cwt
Margarine ....1/- ,,	Loaf sugar 4d. per lb.	Currants ....4½d. per lb.
Apples ....16/- per cwt.	Gran. sugar 30/- per cwt.	Yellow soap 24/- per cwt
Marmalade ....4d. per lb.	Sago ....2½d. per lb.	

By November the cost of food was 41% higher than in July, 1914, and 26% higher than at the corresponding date of that year ; compared with prices at that time (November 1914) tea and fish were 50% dearer, butter 25%, eggs, bacon, milk and cheese 20%, potatoes 14% and sugar 13%; at that very time potatoes were being sold in the **Borough market** at 90/- to 105/- the ton ; and finally, at the Christmas Provision Market the following prices ruled.—

Sprats ....1½d. per lb.	Lard ....6½d. & 7d. lb.	Sp. Nuts ....6d. per lb.
Bloaters ....1½d. each.	Butter 1/5 to 1/8 per lb.	Braz. Nuts ....9d. ,,
Oysters ....6d. per doz.	Cheese ....10d. ,,	Walnuts ....6d. ,,
Rabbits ....1/2 to 1/5.	Eggs ....4 a 1/-.	Chestnuts ....2d. & 3d.
Bacon (best white) 1/3 lb.	Apples ....1½d. to 4d. lb.	
,, (smoked) 1/4 ,,	Tomatoes 3d. per lb.	
Hams ....1/1 ,,	Oranges ....24 & 30 a 1/-	

There was a plentiful supply of vegetables and fruit, but fish was scarce.

Coal, Gas, etc. There was as yet no pronounced shortage of coal, but the price was going up, and whereas the Board of Guardians could, in June 1914, obtain house coal at 19/- per ton and steam coal at 15/8 per ton, in June, 1915, the contracts were 26/2 per ton for house coal and 26/11 for steam coal. The men in the Great Western Railway Works, who have always been favoured by the Company in this particular, were allowed coal at 17/6 per ton before the war ; during 1915 the price was raised, twice,—to 20/- per ton on March 8th, and to 22/6 on August 30th. The prices charged by the coal-merchants of the town rose from 28/- for superior kinds and 26/- for common house coal in the middle of 1914, to 35/- per ton for the better quality and 32/- for ordinary house coal in 1915.

Similarly 1915 saw a substantial addition to the price of gas in Swindon, for on July 1st the Swindon United Gas Company increased its pre-war rate of 3/6 per 1,000 cub.feet to 3/10 per thousand, with monthly rents of 4d. and 2d. for meter and stove respectively. The Town Council, too, raised the electricity rate from 4d. per unit to 4½d. per unit on October 1st, and increased the charges for power by 12½%, public lighting by 10%, and the tramway system by 10%, the cost of coal being of course the deciding factor.

Tobacco. A young man who commenced to smoke, say, at Christmas 1918, paying 9½d. or 10½d. an ounce for his tobacco, would probably have been astonished to learn that in the days of his innocence " before the war," tobacco of excellent quality was purchasable at 4½d. and 5d. an ounce. But the price of tobacco is very largely dependent upon taxation, and the Chancellor of the Exchequer worked this lucrative vein to the fullest extent during the war.   The first pronounced increase in retail prices came in September, 1915, when advances were made of 1½d. per ounce on tobaccoes up to 4½d. an ounce, and 2d. on those over 4½d. ; cigarettes rose from 25% to 50% the packet, and cigars that were sold at prices varying from 1d. to 6d. each bore increases ranging from 2 /6 to 7 /6 per hundred, while the humble " Woodbine " was sold at four a penny instead of five a penny, as formerly.

Wool.   It would be impracticable to enumerate all the familiar commodities, and it is true to say that all showed the same tendency to advance in cost ; but it may be remarked that the gigantic demand for clothing and especially for wool in the Army and Navy materially affected the situation as regards clothing.   Some light is cast upon the question by a comparison of the figures relating to the **Swindon Wool Sale** of 1915 with those of the sale of 1914, which transaction took place annually and was usually held at the V.W.H. Repository in High Street.   In July, 1915, only 8,000 fleeces were sold as against 15,000 in 1914 ; washed Hampshires, which fetched 1 /2 to 1 /2½ in 1914, sold for 1 /10¼ per lb, in 1915 ; cross-breed fleeces ranged from 9¾d. to 1 /1½ in 1914, but in 1915 cross-bred fleeces went for 1 /9 and unwashed fleeces for 1 /4¾ ; thus there was a substantial increase in price along with a great diminution in supply.

Licensed   It has been noticed that the Closing Order made by the Borough
Houses.   Justices on October 8th, 1914, was to operate until January 28th, 1915.   When that date arrived the Justices extended the order indefinitely, being unmoved by the many protests from interested parties who had voiced their dissatisfaction in the columns of the local papers.   A police report made early in February, when it was too soon to judge of the effect of the order, showed that during 1914 convictions for drunkenness were about the same as for 1913 in the case of residents, but that there was an increase of 35 in the case of non-residents. Of 81 charges, 34 were against residents and 47 against non-residents, of whom 30 were soldiers.   Considering the vast number of soldiers who frequented the Borough it would be unjust not to pay a high tribute to the sobriety, orderliness, and good humour that distinguished the overwhelming majority ; on one or two occasions certain regiments who happened to be at the Camp, and who shall be nameless, left unsavoury memories behind them, but their stay was brief, and most of the troops who poured into the town in interminable streams on Saturday afternoon proved themselves worthy of His Majesty's uniform.

Swindon   Evidence that the limitations and difficulties under which tradesmen
County   laboured were no bar to business prosperity may be found in the
Court.   record of County Court cases in Swindon, where a striking reduction is observable.   In 1914 there were 2,762 cases before the Court as against 3,784 in 1913,—a fall of 1,022.   The same thing is seen in the returns for 1915, when the number of plaints fell to 1,675,—a reduction upon those for 1914 of 1,087,—and the amount concerned was only £3,808 as against £5,122 for 1914. This effect of the war was general, and in the country as a whole the number of plaints had not been so low since the year 1864.

The Tobacco What was expected to be a valuable addition to Swindon's industrial
Factory.   organization was destined to serve very different ends before it had really taken firm root in the town ; the Imperial Tobacco Company

had for some time been erecting a very fine factory in the east end of the Borough, and the premises were ready for work in the later part of 1915 : all who saw them were loud in their praise of the conditions of labour and the attention paid to the convenience of the employees, and there was keen competition amongst girls to obtain a post in the new factory. A large number was engaged at good wages, and the work was light and congenial ; it was hoped that the town might see an extension of this field for girl-labour, but not many months elapsed before the Ministry of Munitions, in the middle of 1916, laid hands upon the factory and for three years it became a cog in the great military machine.

The Munitions Works. Late in the year the War Office acquired an extensive tract of land in the same neighbourhood—between Gorse Hill and Stratton—for the purpose of erecting buildings for Munitions Works, and the clearance of the ground was immediately begun ; and about the same time a new industry, though small in comparison with the tobacco factory's addition to Swindon's industrial life, was introduced into the town by Messrs. J. Gundry and Co., of Bridport; they opened a small factory in Newcastle Street where employment was given to about fifty girls in rope and net manufacture.

The Net and Rope Factory.

The Munitions Tribunal. As is well known, Labour submitted during the war to certain conditions that were alien to the spirit of Trade Union policy and that were confessedly only temporary expedients to meet exceptional circumstances. One of the temporary measures put into practice in 1915 for the purpose of securing regular production of munitions was the Munitions Act ; its effect was to restrict the liberty of the employees of munition firms in the interests of the State, for if an employee left the service of his employer without consent it was unlawful for him to enter the service of another firm within six weeks, and anyone employing him would be liable to penalty ; the object was of course to prevent the disturbance of work by men leaving to secure higher wages elsewhere, a very great temptation at this time, when in many places wages unparalleled in English History were being paid. If the employer consented to the employee's leaving, or if he dismissed the man, then he must give him a leaving certificate,— which was not a testimonial, but only a statement that the man left by consent, without which no other employer dare engage him.

For the purpose of administering the Act, tribunals were established in those places where munitions were being made, and these tribunals were composed of representatives of both employers and men. Most of the cases that came before them were concerned with disputes as to leaving certificates, matters of wages, or charges of slackness. In many parts men were prosecuted for losing time or for shirking, and as the men were represented on the tribunal itself, and every opportunity for stating the case was given, the system gave very general satisfaction.

Swindon's First Case. The first case heard in Swindon did not arise till November, and this speaks well for the tone of the Borough. It was one in which a member of the Amalgamated Society of Engineers complained that the Great Western Railway Company was unreasonably withholding from him a leaving certificate. The tribunal consisted of Mr. E. H. C. Wethered (Chairman), Mr. E. Ireland, representing the employers, and Mr. F. V. Harper representing the employees. The Amalgamated Society presented the case for the complainant through Mr. G. W. Davis, and Mr. C. B. Collett defended on behalf of the Great Western Company, pleading that it was the interference of the man's

Union that caused him to leave. After a patient hearing the Tribunal upheld the Company. It is pleasant to note that few tribunals had so little work to do as the Swindon Tribunal.

Earlier Closing. What discussion and agitation amongst shop-assistants and trades-people had for long failed to secure, the pressure of war-conditions very soon effected,—the shortening of business hours. Two or three considerations combined in attaining the result ; the lack of assistants made the arrangement of proper meal-times very difficult, especially in the smaller shops, and towards the close of 1915 it had become common for shops to close from 1 to 2 p.m., so as to give an hour for luncheon; but when the question first came up for discussion at the local Chamber of Commerce there was much opposition to the general adoption of this policy, as well as to the suggestion of making 7.30 the closing-time in the evening. But it was not till 1916 that the darkening of the streets, the compulsory shading of shop lights, and the need of economising light made it futile to try to keep open till 8 o'clock. " D.O.R.A." then stepped in with an order compelling tradesmen to close at 8 p.m. on all nights except Saturday, when 9 o'clock was fixed ; but Swindon traders " went one better," and adopted 7 o'clock closing-time, many even making it 6 o'clock.

Decrease in Vagrancy. Both the shortage of labour and the prosperity of trade at home are evidenced by the Vagrancy returns for 1915. The periodical reports of the Swindon and Highworth Union and of the Cricklade and Wootton Bassett Union—and indeed of all Wiltshire Unions—regularly showed reduced figures ; for instance, Swindon and Highworth Guardians relieved 22 fewer casuals in one fortnight than in the corresponding period of 1914, 17 in another, 64 in another, and so on ; in similar periods for the other union mentioned the figures are even more striking, showing decreases such as 91 and 104. At the second quarterly meeting of the Wilts Vagrancy Committee in 1915 (July), it was reported that the number of vagrants relieved by the police during the quarter was 7,584— a reduction of 659 on the figures for the second quarter of 1914,—and the total number of night's relief granted by all the unions in the county was 10,311, or 2,347 less than in 1914 during the same period. An increase was remarked in the number of casuals in lodging-houses, and this was attributed to the attraction of the camps where a good deal of casual employment was to be obtained.

Similarly, in the quarter ending December 22nd, the Master of Stratton Work-house reported a decrease of 231 vagrants relieved as compared with the same quarter of 1914, ascribing the fall to the absorption of much casual labour by Government works ; the number relieved by the police, however, under the mid-day relief system, had increased by 118, and this was said to be due to men passing to and from various Government works.

Finally, the annual vagrancy returns for Wiltshire showed a decrease of 3,740 upon the 1914 returns,—a striking evidence of good facilities for labour. Never-theless, complaint was made at a meeting of the Cricklade and Wootton Bassett Board in April that there were a great many able-bodied tramps upon the roads, whilst on the other hand at a meeting at Stratton in September it was stated that many casuals had joined the forces and there were now very few tramps of military age. The Master said that out of a hundred examined there were only 5 of military age and 3 of these were defective.

Stratton Workhouse. In the Stratton Workhouse itself there was also a reduction in the number of inmates. In May these were 192 in all, consisting of 91 men, 76 women, and 25 children and infants ; if to these are added the children in the scattered homes and thirty people maintained by the Guardians in other institutions, the total number of indoor poor was 267, 50 less than a year before. Those in receipt of out-door relief were 1,048, 77 less than a year before. In October the indoor poor had decreased in number still further, the total then being 246, as against 313 a year previously.

Prosperity of 1915. Thus, as regards business and employment the year 1915 was one of prosperity for the Borough ; there was plenty of work and none too many hands for it. There was a big demand for boys in the Works, and girls too were being engaged in considerable numbers in the Great Western Offices, it being understood that the majority of the posts were temporary and would have to be relinquished when the young men returned from the Army. This was the beginning of a period of unheard-of financial prosperity for boys and girls, a not entirely unmixed blessing.

The Prince of Wales' Fund. The Prince of Wales' Fund maintained its hold upon the public sympathies, and a very satisfactory report of over a year's progress was given at a public meeting in October, when the Mayor, Mr. W. E. Morse, presided, and the Honorary Secretary (Mr. R. Hilton) and the Honorary Treasurer (Mr. A. E. Dean) reviewed the work of the Committee and of the Committees for providing Vegetables for the Navy and for sending Comforts to the Wiltshire Regiment.

Subscriptions. Up to the date of the report, £5,587 : 0 : 0 had been sent up to the Central Committee, of which £3,545 : 14 : 8 had been subscribed by men in the Great Western Railway Works, and £2,042 : 2 : 4 by other subscribers. For the sixty weeks covered this gives the creditable average of £93 : 2 : 8 per week.

Local Relief. For the purposes of local relief the Central Committee had remitted to Swindon £1,094 : 18 : 5 and the local Committee had distributed of this sum £830 : 18 : 11 to the wives and dependents of soldiers and sailors, and £263 : 19 : 6 in civilian cases of necessity. The total number of cases relieved from the Fund was 490, viz :—

262 naval and military, involving 262 wives		and 596 children
178 ,, ,, ,, 178 dependents		,, 154 ,,
50 civilian cases, ,, 50 ,,		,, 40 ,,
490 cases in all, ,, 490 ,,		,, 790 ,,

But in addition to these cases there were others relieved from the Royal Patriotic Fund, which had sent to Swindon the sum of £319 for the dependents of deceased soldiers and sailors, and this sum was employed in assisting—

33 cases involving 33 widows		and 64 children
30 ,, 30 dependents		
63 cases in all ,, 63 ,,		,, 64 ,,

Furthermore, the Soldiers' and Sailors' Help Society, of which Mr. Geo. Brooks was the Honorary Secretary, had assisted 15 discharged soldiers with 30 dependents to the extent of £32 : 14 : 6.

Thus from these three sources a total of £1,446 : 12 : 11 had been employed in assisting 568 cases, involving 1,452 persons. Swindon, therefore, having sent £5,587 : 17 : 0 to the Central Committee of the Prince of Wales' Fund, had hitherto more than fulfilled the promise made to the departing soldiers on her behalf by Ald. C. Hill in 1914. There were those who regretted that this large sum was not kept in Swindon for local use, but upon reflection no right-minded person would wish that Swindon should cut herself off from the great national movement, helping her own and giving no thought to others, especially as Swindon was one of the places to which the war brought increased work and money.

The assistance given by the Prince of Wales' Fund Committee was not limited to money ; 152 free medical books and 10 maternity vouchers had been granted during the period, and many wives and mothers of wounded men had been given facilities for visiting their husbands and sons at the hospitals where they were being treated. The work was carried out by eight visitors, each with an assigned district, and these visitors went to the homes weekly, distributing the sums granted and often giving valuable help in getting the allowances from the military authorities, whose remissness was often a source of much anxiety and suffering. [1]

A Gift from Overseas. In August Swindon received a pleasing mark of the sympathy of Britain's kinsfolk across the seas ; the Queensland Government gave, for distribution to families in Swindon that were in need on account of the war, 25 quarters of beef and 25 carcases of mutton. The offer was most gratefully accepted, and the meat was put down in cold storage, the Swindon Cold Storage and Ice Company generously accepting it on reduced terms, and the Butchers' Association undertaking to see to the cutting up and distribution of the joints. The first distribution was made on October 1st, when 71 families received 185 lbs. of meat in portions of from 1½ to 5 lbs ; the sub-committee who had charge of the distribution arranged for weekly or bi-weekly allotments from this date.

Comforts for the Wilts. The Committee for the Provision of Comforts for the Wiltshire Regiment had a splendid record of work done, but the nature, extent, and importance of its duties demand treatment in a separate section, [2] when the story can be told as a whole ; but it may be noted here that it was in January, 1915, that the more important part of the work—the care for the Prisoners of War—was begun, and henceforth it absorbed by far the greater part of the Committee's energy.

Vegetables for the Navy. Although an inland town, Swindon is not without personal links with the Navy and the Mercantile Marine ; it is true that she sends very few sailors to the fleet or the merchant service, but she sends not a few skilled mechanics as engine-room artificers and engineers, and the war has taken its toll of these. At this critical period of the nation's history the eyes of all Britain were turned upon the fleet, first with confidence not unmixed with apprehension, at times with impatience to know what was taking place amidst the dark waters of the Orkneys and in the great ocean routes, and finally with a quiet trust that was abundantly justified on that great day when the German dreadnoughts

(1) Continued on Page 79.   (2)—See Chapter V.

D

and cruisers tamely crept into the Firth of Forth.   Any appeal for the Navy, therefore, was certain to meet with a ready response, and when it was known that fresh vegetables and fruit were a necessity badly wanted and not easily obtained by the fleet, Swindon was one of the first places to organize a system of collection of these articles and one of the most regular and persistent in forwarding supplies.

Genesis of the Movement. On October 30th, 1914, a group of market-gardeners met at the Town Hall under the presidency of the Mayor, Ald. C. Hill, to consider a letter that had been received from the National Vegetable Production Committee, of which Admiral Sir Chas. Beresford was the president ; the letter asked the farmers and market gardeners of the district to assist in the very important work of maintaining the health of the men of the Navy. The Admiralty, "for satisfactory reasons," does not include fresh vegetables in the ships' rations, having found it impracticable to execute any plan to provide them ; hence the need of the voluntary organization that had undertaken the task. A scheme of co-operation was inaugurated by the new Mayor, Mr. W. E. Morse, at a second meeting held on November 9th, when a committee was formed to collect and despatch fruit and vegetables weekly to a salvage depôt at Paddington, Mr. W. H. Trowbridge being elected chairman, and Mr. F. W. Trineman secretary.

First Despatches. The Market Hall in Cromwell Street was opened as a local depôt, and nearly a ton of vegetables and fruit was received during the first three days, whilst within four weeks three and a half tons were despatched to the Navy, the first consignment being sent off on December 2nd.   Most appreciative letters were received by the committee from Rear-Admiral Bayley, H.M.S. Marlborough, and from H.M.S. Illustrious.   The same hearty response was made to a special appeal for Christmas fruit, for two tons of fruit and vegetables came in within a week, and as the weekly consignments had become so large the central body in London asked the Swindon Committee to send its contributions henceforth direct to the Naval Base at Lowestoft.

Whence Obtained. Messrs. Trowbridge and Trineman and their colleagues laboured persistently at this work, and succeeded in placing Swindon in 'the very fore-front of local contributory bodies, maintaining to the close of the war the same zeal as was shown at the outset.   The sympathies of local farmers were enlisted over an area stretching from Tockenham to Coleshill and Sevenhampton, and from Latton to Draycott ; many of them sent in large packages ready for despatch ; some put aside the produce of an acre of cabbages or roots for the committee, either gathering the crop themselves or letting the committee crop it at their convenience; others put aside the produce of certain fruit-trees, and some acted as collecting agents in their locality, bringing in the load at their own expense.   It would be invidious to try to name all the generous donors, but the Committee, at their first annual meeting, in December, 1915, publicly recorded their gratitude to some, whose contributions serve to exemplify the generosity of many ; thus, Mr. Haine, of Sevenhampton, had given the produce of one acre of cabbages and one of turnips; the Hon. Mrs. Agar, besides sending a package weekly, had devoted the crops of eight apple-trees and five walnut-trees to the Committee's work : Mr. Hussey, of Draycott, had given one acre of cabbages and an acre and a half of swedes, which the Committee cropped ; Mr. Butt, of Coleshill, had sent a truck-load of turnips ; General Calley had forwarded large quantities of roots, vegetables and fruit ; Sir Frederick Banbury had lent wagons and teams ; whilst others, too numerous to mention, had made the delivery of packages of vegetables a regular part of their weekly visit to Swindon.

The borough also contributed its share, though in its case the quota was made up by the accumulation of small donations; a large receptacle was placed in the market-hall, so that the housewife who made her Friday purchase there might drop into it a potato or two, a few carrots, or an odd cabbage or swede. The schools had special "potato-days" or "vegetable days," when each child brought a small contribution from the father's allotment or the family larder; and the results were incredible, a large cart being sometimes required to remove the collection of a single school. When the Harvest Festivals were held, the produce displayed would sometimes be given to the Navy, and the exhibits at vegetable shows were devoted to the same end.

Appreciation. Nearly eighty tons of fruit and vegetables were sent in the first four months of the Committee's activities, to Lowestoft, Harwich, Parkeston Quay, Immingham, and Aberdeen, and the General Secretary wrote from London, " If the work of our various branches were measured by tonnage, I think that our Swindon Branch would be in the top rank." The general committee evidently did not meet the same zeal in all its branches, for in April, 1915, they sent out a circular to the local committees deploring the great falling-off in the contributions, and appealing to the public to try to realize the sacrifices made by the men of the fleet, and the dangers and horrors to which they were daily exposed; at this time the number of branches was 170, and they were sending an average of 12,000 lbs. a day to the ships. The General Secretary wrote again in June, that, " besides being one of the oldest, the Swindon Committee are also the best and most regular contributors," and it is to be noted that the committee was at that time the only one in Wiltshire.

First Year's Results. When the first annual meeting was held early in December, 1915, the chair being occupied by Ald. C. Hill, the summary of the year's work proved most encouraging. Out of 500 branches then in existence Swindon was only excelled by four, and these were the Irish Branch, the West of Scotland Branch, and those of Liverpool and Bradford. During the year 250 donors had sent in 552 packages of fruit, vegetables, nuts, honey, and jam, and besides these 11 trucks of cabbages and 40 tons of turnips had been given; altogether, about 100 tons of food had been forwarded to the Navy from Swindon. A remarkable feature was the economical working of the committee; money donations had not been large, but had been sufficient, for although the donations only amounted to £17 : 11 : 0, the expenses only came to £17 : 5 : 0½, much of which was used in directly purchasing goods, as, for instance, when three crates of onions were purchased in July on account of a falling-off in the contributions; whilst the hire of labour for cropping and horse-hire accounted for the rest.

It was a splendid record of a year's voluntary work, and the Admiralty recognized it in a special—and, indeed, an unusual—form, for they bestowed a beautifully embellished badge inscribed, " With the thanks of the Navy," not only upon the Secretary, Mr. Trineman, but also upon eight other members of the Committee, viz: Messrs. Trowbridge (Chairman), R. Hilton (the Town Clerk), A. Currey, F. W. Drew, H. Haine, A. Austin, W. Groves, and G. Gibbs. [1].

The Soldiers' Rest at the Town Hall. The vast number of soldiers encamped at Draycott could find relief from the monotony of camp-life only in Swindon, and an obligation lay upon the town to do what it could to exercise hospitality towards the swarms of men who sought recreation in Swindon on the Saturday

(1). continued on page 81.

and Sunday. Victoria Street often presented an astonishing sight on Saturday afternoons, with its apparently endless stream of men pouring down the hill, all in the highest of spirits and bent upon enjoyment.

Other Soldiers' Rests. From the first the duty of providing accommodation was recognized, and the Young Men's Christian Association and several churches did what they could in affording it ; thus the Y.M.C.A. rooms in Fleet Street were opened in October, 1914 ; Mrs. Streeten and an influential Ladies' Committee were doing splendid work at their "Soldiers' Rest" in Newport Street, and on Sunday afternoons and evenings the Presbyterian Church provided shelter and light refreshments for visiting soldiers. The extent of the field may be judged from the work done at one of these centres alone, —the one in Newport Street ; there, Mrs. Streeten and her colleagues had furnished a tea-room, reading and writing room, lavatory, etc., had provided means of amusement such as whist-tables, and gave a good tea to all who wished it ; at first the cost was defrayed entirely from money subscribed and from what the visitors chose to put into a box that was placed in the rooms. In the last week-end—Saturday and Sunday—of May, 1915, three thousand men availed themselves of the hospitality offered, and a fortnight previously two thousand had done so. The cost was now becoming greater than the income from subscriptions, and the Committee had to begin to make a regular charge of 3d. per head. It is with deep regret that one remembers how, just at this time, Mrs. Streeten was so deeply struck by the tragic death of her husband, Dr. E. Streeten, the Medical Officer of Health for Swindon, that she had to relinquish her kindly work at Newport Street and speedily sank beneath the blow.

Formation of the Committee. It was obvious that if so small an institution as the Newport Street rooms could so do much, there was need for provision on a far larger scale, and in May, 1915, during the first mayoralty of Mr. W. E. Morse, the Mayoress convened a meeting of ladies at the Town Hall, and the Mayor and the Town Clerk met them with promises of support for whatever scheme they should formulate.

The Committee selected to carry out the work comprised the Mayoress (Mrs. W. E. Morse, followed in subsequent years by her successors, Mrs. A. J. Gilbert, Mrs. A. W. Haynes, and Mrs. C. Plaister in turn), acting as President, Mrs. G. Merricks as Vice-President, Miss E. Deacon as Treasurer, and Mrs. H. Perry as Secretary ; with them were associated Mrs. G. Brooks, Mrs. N. Butler, Mrs. L. Harris, Misses F. & D. Hayward, Mrs. Jones, Mrs. S. Norris, Mrs. H. Reynolds, Mrs. Sargent, Mrs. Sawtell, Mrs. Seaborne, Mrs. Sloan, and Mrs. B. Tyler.

Opening of the Town Hall Rest. On May 15th the large hall of the Town Hall was opened as a soldiers' rest, and soon became the recognized hostelry of the majority of the soldiers visiting Swindon on Saturday or Sunday. The weekly conversion of this large room into a tea-room and concert-hall undoubtedly caused enormous inconvenience and extra work to the Town Hall Staff, but anyone who looked in between the hours of 4 and 7 p.m., for instance, would say the premises had never been put to better use. Long tables ran down the full length of the hall, so close as to leave only just room to pass, and not only would every seat often be occupied but a throng would be waiting at the door for vacancies ; an ample and appetising meal was provided, and a large staff of young ladies saw that the men were served promptly ; and for a large part of the time a concert was being given from the platform. It was a scene of brightness, comfort, and cheerfulness that must have been a welcome change to multitudes of young fellows wearied by the coarse and rough life of the camp.

First Visitors. The first visitors were men who have left many pleasant memories behind them,—the gallant Scottish Division, who afterwards covered themselves with honour at Loos ; and when they left, their place at the camp was taken by a body of men whose name became a household word,—the famous " Bantams,"—men below the regulation height who were formed into a special unit ; many will never forget the ludicrous sight that might be seen in Swindon on a Saturday evening at that time ; one would meet a picket of "Bantams" averaging something like five feet in height, strutting slowly in file alongside the pavement, whilst a tall, thin sergeant of six feet in height ambled along the pavement vainly trying to find a step that would harmonize with that of his picket, and painfully conscious of his unseemly stature. Whilst the " Bantams " were here, in November, 1915, Swindon was placed " out of bounds " to troops, owing to the severe epidemic of scarlet-fever with which the town was afflicted ; consequently the Rest was closed from then until the embargo was raised in March, 1916, by which time there had been great changes in the establishment at the camp.

The work of the Soldiers' Rest Committee will receive further notice in later sections of this work, when details as to the management and expenses of the " Rest " at the Town Hall will find a place in the narrative. [1]

Flag-Days. This year witnessed the inauguration of a form of raising funds which in the next four years became a very common institution. Tiny flags of various nationalities and design, according to the objects for which the collections were made, were sold in the streets by women and girls, and the days were therefore known as " Flag Days." There were four special Flag-Days in 1915, viz—

DATE.	FUND.	AMOUNT RAISED.
		£ s. d.
July 14th	French Flag Day.	150 0 0
,, 24th	Serbian Flag Day	219 11 4
Aug. 28th	Belgian Flag Day	141 1 5
Sept. 11th	Russian Flag Day	325 11 11
	TOTAL	£836 4 8

At first the idea " caught on " with the public, as can be seen from the substantial amounts realized, and as the occasions were generally fine Saturdays in the Summer, the girls came out in their gayest attire and proved very efficient collectors ; it is pretty certain that an equal number of staid middle-aged " Benedicts " would not have attracted so much money, and obvious considerations caused some restrictions to be made later on as to the age of the girls engaged as collectors.

The Red Cross Society. The Red Cross Hospital at the Baths continued to attract public sympathy so long as its existence lasted, and the Christmas of 1914 was the occasion for a fine list of presents from friends amongst the public, especially presents of plum-puddings, fruit, and cigarettes. Before the end of February, 1915, 815 patients had been admitted to the hospital, of whom 752 had been discharged, 3 had died, and 60 were still under treatment ; the number of out-patients up to that time was nearly 2,000.

(1). continued on page 83.

In June, 1915, a hospital was established within Draycott Camp
Closing the itself, and this substantially reduced the work that came to the Swindon
Hospital. Red Cross Hospital. The building in Faringdon Street, too, designed
with a glass roof admirably suited for its real purpose, was now un-
comfortably hot, and application was made to the War Office for leave to close for
the Summer at least; permission was granted, and on July 5th, when the building
was closed, there were only six patients in the hospital, and these were transferred to the hospital at the Camp.

During the time the hospital had been in existence from three to
Total of four thousand out-patients had been treated, 1070 patients had been
Patients. admitted, and although there had been a large number of serious cases
the number of deaths was only three. The public had not ceased
to contribute generous supplies of fruit, flowers, vegetables, eggs, tobacco, and
luxuries of all kinds, being keenly interested in an institution which they regarded
as a trust handed over to Swindon. Surgeon-General Bedford, R.A.M.C., the head
of the Southern Command Medical Service, wrote upon the occasion of the closing
of the hospital, "I do not know what we should have done without it, and I am most
deeply indebted to you and all the organization for the immense help which you
have been." The fine staff who had worked so devotedly with the Commandant,
Miss C. Deacon, richly merited these words of praise, and thanks were no less due to
Dr. W. Boxer Mayne and Dr. H. Evans for the services they had given quite freely.
Miss Deacon had worked unremittingly, and it was regretted that she was now obliged
to give up the commandantship, being succeeded by Mrs. Colledge.

The funds for the Red Cross Hospital came from the Government,
Finance. and altogether £2,309 : 6 : 9 had been received from that source ;
the principal expenses were £1917 : 15 : 6 for the maintenance of
patients, £312 for rent, £34 : 12 : 3 for sheets, £16 : 13 : 9 for nurses' expenses, and
£20 for the improvement of the ventilation of the building.

The Balance Sheet of the Swindon branch of the Red Cross Society, presented
at a meeting held at the Town Hall on September 9th, showed the year's receipts
and expenses as follows :—

INCOME.	£	s.	d.		EXPENDITURE	£	s.	d.
Donations	362	3	9		Flannel	155	6	10
Village Balances	 79	8	5		Wool	 51	12	8
From Entertainments	 24	13	7½		County Emergency Fund	100	0	0
From Sundry Sales	 4	10	11½		Serbian Relief Fund	50	0	0
					Wilts Pris. of War Fund	25	0	0
					Motor Ambulance	15	0	0
					Other expenses	55	9	9½
						452	9	3½
					Balance in bank	18	7	5½
	£470	16	9			£470	16	9

Working The working parties had been steadily and persistently working
Parties. throughout the year, and had made an enormous quantity of garments;
for in addition to what they had forwarded to the British Red Cross
Depôt, at Salisbury, they had sent 326 pairs of socks, 140 shirts, 74 mufflers, 12 wool

helmets, and 12 pairs of mittens to the Navy, the men on the trawlers, and Belgian, Indian, and Wiltshire soldiers. An epidemic of knitting had come upon the whole country, and Swindon caught the fever as soon as any place ; no sooner was it known that a certain article was badly needed than a host of women and girls were busily knitting ; at one time it was knee-caps that were wanted, and before the army of knitters had fairly settled to work word was sent that the supply was now ample; all who could handle the needles could knit the long, broad mufflers of khaki wool ; socks could not be too abundant, and the appeal for these was most insistent; the more ambitious crafts-women aspired to sleeping-helmets, which also formed ideal protection for motor cyclists and airmen. In those first two winters of trench warfare, when the men faced novel conditions for which the military authorities were quite unprepared, innumerable soldiers blessed the unknown fingers that had woven the warm wrap or socks that reached them, often with a few words of cheer pinned to the gift. It is impossible to estimate the number of these articles made by the women and girls of Swindon, for they were despatched through a variety of channels, some going to the committee for Comforts for the Wiltshire Regiment, some to central agencies in London, and some being sent direct to soldiers in whom the donors had an interest.

The members of the Red Cross Society were not at all content to see their hospital closed without any attempt to re-establish it elsewhere. In October, therefore, Mrs. Waugh sent out an appeal for helpers in forming another Red Cross
Red Cross Depôt. Hospital in Swindon. The realization of the plan belongs, however, to 1917, when the hospital at Stratton was established. In the meantime a War-work Depôt was established at 43, Regent Street, to provide wounded soldiers with the necessary garments upon their admission to hospital. The Committee consisted of the Mayoress, Mrs. Waugh, and Miss Rose, Miss Calley and Mrs. R. W. Goddard being joint Secretaries and Treasurers. A subscription list was opened for funds for the purchase of material, and workers were invited to assist in making it up. The depôt was opened on November 29th, and met with instant success, as will be seen from figures given in February, 1917, which cover the work done up to December 31st, 1916 [1].

Farmers and the Red Cross. Some reference should be made to the work done for the Red Cross Society by the Farmers of Wiltshire. The Wiltshire branch of the Farmers' Union was very regular in its contributions to the Society. By April, 1915, the British Farmers' Red Cross Fund had reached £17,788 : 16 : 11, and was already preparing its second hospital in Serbia ; of the sum named the Wiltshire Farmers had subscribed £362 : 18 : 0, of which £170 : 6 : 0 was from the North Wilts section. By the 30th of July, the national fund reached £39,804 : 11 : 0, the North Wilts Farmers contributing £736 : 14 : 2 out of £920 : 17 : 8 for the County. By the end of October Wiltshire's contribution to the British Farmers' Red Cross Fund was £4,727 : 16 : 2, out of a total of £94,399 : 5 : 8, the fund advancing by leaps and bounds. [2]

The Volunteer Training Corps. On February 3rd, 1915, at a meeting of the Swindon Town Miniature Rifle Club a proposal was made to form a local Volunteer Training Corps such as was being raised in many towns, and in which ablebodied men ineligible for the army might be trained in arms with a view towards forming a body of men available for home-defence.

(1) Continued on page 77.   (2) Continued on page 77.

The idea of a German invasion of the country, which would have been laughed to scorn a few months before, was beginning to be seen as a very real possibility, and the Germans were loudly boasting of their intention to invade England and of the " frightfulness " they would wreak upon its inhabitants.   The necessity for guarding the country against such an event tied up a large number of soldiers at home, and such a force as was contemplated by the organizers of the Volunteer Training Corps might release a part of these for foreign service.

Initiation.   The members of the Rifle Club invited the Mayor to call a public meeting to discuss the matter, and this was held on March 9th, under the chairmanship of Councillor T. Kimber, with the result that the proposal was approved and a committee was formed to put it into effect. A few days later the Committee met and elected as its officers, Mr. T. Kimber, Chairman; Mr. W. J. Ainsworth, Vice-Chairman ; Mr. W. P. McAllister, Secretary; Mr. J. Belcher, Correspondence Secretary; Mr. W. H. Kinneir, Treasurer; and the lately retired Deputy Chief Constable, Mr. T. J. Robinson, Commandant.

Work Begun.   Squad drills were begun forthwith at the Drill Halls in Park Lane and Prospect Place, the officers being F. G. Comley, Sergt. Maj.; W. P. McAllister, Orderly-room Sergt. ; A. W. Phillips, Sergt-instructor of musketry ; A. Potbury, Platoon-sergt. ; H. Barnes, C. H. Ockwell and O. M. Gee, Platoon-sergeants; and C. Johnson, Sergeant.   Musketry instruction also began at once at the rifle range on Canal Side.   By the middle of April the corps numbered 225 members, not counting 5 who had in the meantime enlisted in the army, and they were made up of 19 under 19 years of age, 51 between 19 and 38 years of age, and 155 over 38 years of age.   Of these 81 were cyclists, 12 were motorists, and several had horses.   Brassards were obtained for the members of the corps—red armlets bearing the letters " V.T.C."—and a uniform, estimated to cost 30/-, was adopted but was not a compulsory item in the equipment.   The Town Council showed its readiness to assist the movement by constructing an out-door rifle-range on the spare ground adjacent to the Town Gardens, and the Education Committee granted the use of the Gorse Hill School playground for drills.   Thus, within a few weeks a considerable number of recruits had joined the Corps, and it had fairly got to work, having regular drills, route-marches, church-parades, etc., in quite the regular manner.

It will have been noticed that some of the members were of military age, and evidently this was the case elsewhere, for the War Office issued in June a general order, saying, " Any man below the age of 40 who joins the V.T.C., on and after June 1st, 1915, will be required to sign an undertaking that he will enlist into the Army if specially called upon to do so ; " so that instead of the Corps' forming a refuge for young men unwilling to enlist it was to be a potential reservoir for recruits for the regular forces.

Growth by July.   In July the Town Council gave the Corps permission to use the Pleasure Grounds and the County Ground once a week for drills.   By this time the membership had risen to 426, of whom 103 (58 married and 45 single men) were of military age.   The first musketry tests had been held, and 40 candidates had passed, viz: 25 as marksmen, 12 in the first class, and 3 in the efficiency class.   Special classes were now being held for officers and non-commissioned officers, and the Corps stood well financially, having a balance of £80 in hand.

The Commandant. The excellent progress made reflected great credit upon the Commandant, and the Corps recognized his devotion to the work by presenting to him a sword at a smoking-concert held at the Goddard Arms on September 8th ; and, indeed, he expected the same earnest attention to duty from the men, issuing a notice that the completion of 40 drills did not cancel the obligation to attend drill, and that any member who did not make at least four attendances a month might be struck off the roll. A summary of the Commandant's " orders " for the week ending September 18th well illustrates Mr. Robinson's thoroughness :—

Monday evening :	two " A " Company drills ;
	two " B " Company drills ;
	Platoon drill for Gorse Hill section ;
	Signalling instruction at Prospect ;
	Musketry instruction for two sections of " B " Company.
Tuesday evening :	Bugle practice.
Wednesday evening:	General Meeting of members.
Thursday evening :	Bugle practice ;
	Platoon drill, Gorse Hill section.
Friday evening :	Signalling class ;
	Musketry instruction for two sections of " A " company.
Saturday 5 p.m. :	Route March, " A " Coy.
	Route march, " B " Coy.

The Sunday previous had seen a Church Parade at Bath Road Wesleyan Church, about 100 members turning out.

Colonel Steward's Inspection ; growth and successes. Lieut. Col. Steward, of the Wilts Regiment, held a review of the Corps in the Great Western Park, on Sunday, October 3rd, when 332 members appeared on parade. He expressed satisfaction with the results of the training and complimented the Corps on its careful preparation. The membership had by this time reached 626, made up of 98 married and 45 single men of military age, 339 married and 16 single men above military age, 80 under age, 34 who had enlisted, and a small number who had been transferred to other battalions ; six had resigned. Already 95 members had obtained their efficiency badges for musketry, of whom more than half were marksmen, and five had their names inscribed on the roll of marksmen of England, whilst five were enrolled as skilled shots and six as riflemen of the N.R.A. Members of the Corps also formed a team which held the principal Wiltshire trophies for rifle-shooting—the Lansdowne Shield, the Kynoch Shield, the County Cup, and the Astor Cup—and a large number held medals for shooting, including three with the Donegal Medal. An ambulance section had recently been formed, one member holding the First Aid Certificate, one a Nursing Certificate, and five held labels or medallions. A signalling section had also been formed, a full engineering section was in course of formation, and the Corps had a bugle band.

The Corps had already been called upon to perform certain duties outside its regular training ; it had provided orderlies for the Red Cross Hospital, guards at Draycott Camp, and volunteers for the Swindon Fire Brigade.

These facts were stated by the Commandant at Lieut. Col. Steward's inspection, and shortly afterwards the Secretary of the Military Committee of the V.T.C. Central Association wrote to the Adjutant saying :—

Reported "Efficient." "I am instructed to inform you that the report of Colonel Steward relative to his inspection of the Swindon and District Corps has been received. The Inspecting Officer states, ' This is a strong, efficient, and well-drilled Corps. Extended order drill requires more practice; general intelligence is good ; a very serviceable corps for any defence purposes or for guarding duties.' It is stated that all men of military age have signed the acceptance of the terms of the War Office letter of Nov. 19th, 1914, and in these circumstances the Military Committee have given directions that the Corps be now affiliated to this Association."

The staff of officers had of course been largely increased, and at this review there were present,—the Commandant, Mr. T. J. Robinson : the Sub-Commandant, Mr. W. H. Kinneir ; Captains Comley, Kimber, Ockwell, Ainsworth and Arkell ; Platoon Commanders Kirby, Harvey, C. A. Plaister, G. R. Plaister, Johns, Jones, Wellicombe, Stamper, Watts, Horsell, Maundrell, Blackwell, Hatt and Elwell ; the Adjutant, Mr. W. P. McAllister ; Quartermaster Bottomley ; and Sergt.-Major Potbury.

Service at Didcot. When the year closed many members of the Corps were giving very valuable service on Sundays in assisting the Army Ordnance Corps to pack, load, and unload material at the vast depôt that was established at Didcot, as many as 60 or 70 men going from Swindon and putting in a strenuous day's work.

It will be seen that the growth and training of the V.T.C. in the nine months of its existence hitherto, was a triumph of energy and organization on the part of its forceful and able Commandant and his staff of officers, such as few towns of Swindon's size could excel. The finances of the Corps were in good order, thanks to the special efforts that had been made throughout the year, these having brought in the substantial sum of £74 : 6 : 1, made up as follows :—

			£	s.	d.
Mr. A. Manners' Concert	....	....	34	13	6
Mr. S. A. Morley's Concert	....	....	17	2	0
Madame Dockray's Concert	....	....	9	16	9
The Cricket Match	....	....	6	5	0
The Whist Drive	....	....	3	10	7
Messrs. Studts'	....	....	2	18	3
	TOTAL		£74	6	1

Balance Sheet. The Balance Sheet (to Dec. 31st, 1915) [1] is here given :—

RECEIPTS.		£	s.	d.	EXPENDITURE.		£	s.	d.
Donations	....	67	1	6	Orderly room Equipment		9	9	2
Concerts, etc. (as above)	....	74	6	1	Stationery, books, etc.	....	13	2	1
Uniforms, badges, etc.	....	28	7	2	Printing and postage	....	8	4	3
Contributions from—					Corps' equipment	....	101	9	1
Wootton Bassett Platoon		10	15	2	Drill Hall Expenses	....	6	15	0
Stratton Platoon	....	22	0	6	Lighting	....		8	8
Unaccounted	....	....			5	Hire of cars	....	6	2	4
					Instructors' Expenses	....	1	19	0½
					Camp Expenses	....	6	11	7½
					Sundry Expenses	....	4	4	6
					Balance in hand	....	44	5	1
TOTAL	....	£202	10	10	TOTAL	....	£202	10	10

(1) Narrative Continued on page 75.

The Derby Scheme. The last quarter of 1915 witnessed the final effort of the Government to stave off compulsory service in the army by means of the expedient of the "Derby Scheme," so named after its author, Lord Derby, who made his explanatory statement in Parliament on October 19th. Under this recruiting scheme men were invited to " attest," *i.e.*, they were enlisted as recruits but were to continue at their ordinary employment until they were summoned along with all others of the same grade to join the colours. For the purpose of grading, 46 "groups" were formed and these groups would be called up in order : a man's group depended upon his age, and whether he was married or single ; thus, at the beginning of the scale, " Group 1 " was formed of single men eighteen years of age, " Groups 2 to 5 " of single men from nineteen to twenty-two years old, and so on ; the last four " groups," 42 to 46, consisted of the oldest married men—those from 36 to 40 years of age.

The men were to be summoned by proclamations in the press and on the hoardings, and any attested men thus summoned who had reasons for doing so could send in claims for postponement within ten days. In any case a man who had attested was now an enlisted soldier and subject to being called up when the military authorities decided that the time for his group had come ; and herein lay the weakness of the scheme, for it involved compulsory service on those who had attested, whilst it did not touch a large section of eligible men. It did not endure six months, as will be seen later. But in that short time the response in Swindon was excellent ; anyone who knew Sergt. Fry, the local recruiting officer, must have pitied him during the " rush " for attestation ; with no extra assistance, and overwhelmed with the huge amount of forms that had to be filled in, he was frequently at work from 3.15 a.m., to 9 p.m., and if the attestation and registration of the men of the Great Western Railway Works had not been carried out inside the Works he would have needed a large extra staff ; there, nearly 5,000 men were attested in the space of a month.

Prior to the " Derby Scheme," that is, up to October 30th, 1915, Sergt. Fry had enlisted 1,418 men during the war. [1]

Changes on the Council. In the course of the year two by-elections were necessary, resulting in the return of Mr. Reuben George for the West Ward and Mr. H. J. Vaisey for the same ward later in the year, when a vacancy was caused by the death of Mr. J. J. Shawyer in May ; Mr. Shawyer was one of Swindon's earliest Mayors, and his decease removed from the Council one of its ablest business men and one whose unquestioned integrity had won universal respect; he will be remembered by many on account of his capable handling of Swindon's affairs at the time of the sad tramway accident that cost the town £30,000 in indemnities. A passing reference should also be made to Mr. R. George, for his untiring labours throughout many years in organizing weekly outings did more than can be calculated to bring health and brightness into many lives ; although these were nominally part of the Summer programme of the Workers' Educational Association, they were open to all, and they were so arranged that the expense was negligible ; right through the years of the war he continued these innocent and delightful excursions into the country, usually attended by some speaker or writer, who gave an appropriate address on some vicarage lawn or in the recesses of a wood or park.

And Staff. The Corporation staff suffered a sudden loss in June, when the Medical Officer of Health, Dr. Streeten, died. His post was not filled till December, Dr. W. F. Whitley then being appointed. Dr. Streeten

[1] Derby Scheme continued p. 73.

had also fulfilled the duties of School Medical Officer, and in this part of the work Dr. S. J. Moore was for some time engaged.

The Elections Dropped. In 1915 the usual Municipal Elections were abandoned, both on account of the absence of so many voters and because of the disturbance of life and business they would entail at a time when the nation was preoccupied by weighty national concerns. The small amount of public interest in such matters is seen in the poll in the West Ward, when Mr. Vaisey was returned, only 473 voting on a register of 2021. As the same reasons weighed even more heavily as the war dragged on, there were no Municipal Elections after those of 1914 until 1919, when there were members of the Council who had been continuously upon it for seven years.

Mr. Morse's Second Mayoralty. There was also no change this year in the Mayoralty, Mr. W. E. Morse being elected by 27 votes to 5 to a second year of office. The past year had made many calls upon the Mayor, and much attention had been demanded by the Prince of Wales' Fund, the provision of Comforts for the Wiltshire Regiment, Flag-days, and other matters extraneous to the usual municipal duties, and Mr. Morse's re-election was a tribute to the manner in which he had executed the many duties of his office ; he was the first Mayor of Swindon honoured by a second call to the chair.

Draycott Camp's Water and Drainage. The provision of a water supply for Chiseldon Camp was undertaken by the Swindon Town Council, and was a rather serious undertaking in view of the Borough's own limited facilities for obtaining water, and the extension of the town. At the first council meeting of the year a letter from the Military Authorities was read saying that more than 60,000 gallons of water were needed daily. The Military Authorities wished the Council to enter into an agreement with them to supply the Camp, and to let them have water at a lower rate than was being charged under the temporary arrangement ; but the Council declined, and preferred to continue the temporary arrangement with its charge of 1 /- per thousand gallons. Up to within a few weeks of the end of the municipal year 1915 the Council carried out the whole of the sanitation of the Camp and supplied it regularly with water.

Trams and Electricity. The presence of so many soldiers in the town, especially on Saturdays, led to a large increase in the tramway receipts ; thus, to take an example at random, in a certain five-week period 22,447 more passengers used the trams than in the same period of the previous year, giving an increase of £94 : 18 : 4 in the takings. The enlistment of so many tramway-men led to the decision to engage youths from 16 to 17 years of age as temporary conductors at the rate of 3d. per hour. A considerable extension, too, in the electric-main system was made by the laying of mains to the Imperial Tobacco Company's new factory in Colbourne Street. In September, however, the Council was compelled to raise its charges for lighting and power by 12½% and public lighting and trams by 10% from October 1st.

Lighting and the Raids. In January 1915 the public of Swindon was notified that a warning of six blasts of "the hooter" would be given upon the approach of hostile aircraft. The Germans had threatened terrible things and had every confidence in their "Zeppelins'" power to penetrate into the interior of England,—a confidence that later events amply justified. Upon hearing this warning householders were to extinguish all lights and the corporation officials were to cut off the electric light at the power station. Happily Swindon experienced no raid, but on several occasions the warning was given, news having been received that Zeppelins were attacking places not too far away to make precautions needless in Swindon. These warnings were a source of great disturbance to many ; and the state of nervous tension may be judged from the fact that many upon the first occasion or two declared they distinctly heard bombs fall and even saw the airships.

In the winter of 1915-16 Swindon streets were a gloomy picture by night ; considerations of economy as well as precautions against raiders led the Council to reduce the number of street lamps to about one-third their normal number, and also to extinguish them at 10 o'clock instead of 11. Householders were responsible for obscuring the lights in their homes, but as yet the lighting restrictions were not the stringent regulations they became in 1916 ; complaints, however, were frequent concerning the darkness of the streets in the winter nights, and the wise ones stayed indoors unless business compelled them to go out, for it was indeed dangerous in bad weather and on moonless nights to try to get about in the darkness.

Wages and Salaries under the Council. In common with all other folk the employees of the Council began to find the expenses of living too high for their income. The system of " War-bonuses " had been adopted in the Great Western Works, and seemed a suitable expedient for meeting what everyone hoped was merely a brief phase of the economic situation. The Council therefore resolved to adopt the general policy, and in March, 1915, it took what was to be the first of several steps in this direction, by granting a war-bonus of 2 /- per week to all married men over eighteen years of age, whose wages with the bonus would not exceed £2 a week ; single men over eighteen were to have a bonus of 1 /- a week provided it did not bring their wages to more than 30 /- a week. The bonus also went to married men with the colours. In December the Council decided that the salaries of all members of the clerical staff who had joined the forces or attested by December 14th, should rise according to the scale in their absence.

Market Tolls. The scarcity of supplies and the drainage of manpower soon made an appreciable difference to the business done in the Borough Market, and as early as January, 1915, the Council felt bound to accede to applications for reduction in the rent of certain stalls, whilst the year showed a growing deficiency in the market stallages ; thus, for the year ending March 31st, the receipts were £45 : 12 : 7 less than in the previous year ; in June 1915 alone, the figures were £15 : 13 : 4 down, and several more rents had to be reduced; and for the half-year, April 1st to October 16th, the fall in the stallages was £74 : 1 : 11.

Roads. One branch of the Council's work that was very difficult to keep up to its usual level of efficiency was the upkeep of the roads. The extra-ordinary military traffic, especially by means of heavy motor-lorries, made great havoc with the roads ; much of the road-material was expensive and difficult to obtain, and labour was scarce ; hence the roads and streets often fell into a deplorable state before they could be dealt with. Hearing that a Pioneer Battalion was to be billetted in Swindon, the Council hoped that the men might be allowed to give assistance in laying the roads, but those expectations were disappointed when the War Office wrote saying that they could not undertake the work, and the pioneers would not be sent to Swindon. The Corporation sent in a claim to the War Office for £1,666 as compensation for damage done to the roads by the military, but on the recommendation of the Road Department the War Office offered £676, which the Council had perforce to accept.

Health.   The latter part of 1915 saw the Borough visited by a severe epidemic of scarlet fever ; on August 31st, there were no fewer than 64 cases of fever in the hospital besides 3 diphtheria patients and 4 suspected cases.   On October 12th the number of fever patients had risen to 73 ; between October 14th and November 17th, 81 fresh cases were notified and 10 cases of diphtheria, and on December 14th, there were 111 fever patients in the hospital and 8 cases of diphtheria.   Alongside this epidemic was also an epidemic of measles, and it was not till January, 1916, that any abatement began to be observed.

The Education Committee.   Reference will be made elsewhere [1] to the valuable work done by the Education Committee in instructing the public in the principles of " war-time cookery " and in the use of substitutes for foods that were growing scarce, as well as in the need and principles of economy in food.   Their assistance to the Red Cross Society by the establishment of Ambulance classes has also been noted. [2]   Late in 1915 the Committee, in view of the increasing demand for women in the place of men called to the colours, formed classes at the Technical School for women who wished to take temporary posts as clerks.   The course was to be an intensive one lasting about three months, and was intended for women of no regular occupation who had already had a good general education ; three or four weeks were to be devoted to Arithmetic and Office Routine, followed by eight or ten weeks given to Type-writing and Shorthand.   Thus, the students would be fitted to enter banks, offices, and business houses.

In the winter, with the object of economising in light and fuel, the Committee reduced the hours of attendance at the Elementary Schools from two to one and three-quarter hours for Infant Schools and from two and a quarter to two hours for Upper Schools.   The accommodation in Elementary Schools was becoming a serious problem for the Committee, and this year they secured the approval of the Board of Education for a new school in Ferndale Road and for plans for one in Broad Street ; the war, however, delayed the execution of these projects for some years, although the need was very pressing.

The Swindon Education Committee, whilst suffering inconvenience like all other committees from the enlistment of so many teachers, never experienced an actual shortage of teachers.   It had been its policy for many years to train a good number of young teachers, most of whom were desirous of coming back to the town after their college training ; in course of time many of the women had married and were settled in the town, and occasionally gave a few weeks' service in the schools as " Supply Teachers " ; these now formed a large source from which the Committee could draw, and they came back into the schools to replace the young men who had joined the colours.   Some of these ladies were in continuous service for four years or more, and the efficiency and industry of some of them were beyond praise. In October the Committee reported that already the number of those of its employees who had joined the forces included 24 teachers in the primary schools, 3 of the office staff, 22 teachers in the Secondary School or part-time instructors in the technical departments, and 4 other employees of the secondary school governors,—a total of 53.   Some of these were of course irreplacable and certain work had to be dropped ; a serious loss to many clever young engineer-apprentices resulted from the suspension of the Great Western Railway day-studentships and from the inordinate amount of over-time demanded of youths who would otherwise have attended engineering classes.

(1) See page 113.   (2) See page 17.

Teachers and Enlistment. At its first meeting in 1916 the Education Committee received a complete return of its male teaching-staff in relation to military service ; the statistics were :—

	Elem. Schools	Secondary School
No. serving with the colours.	31	6
Attested under Lord Derby's scheme	10	1
Physically unfit	16	2
Of military age, unattested or not enlisted	0	1
Over military age	32	4
TOTALS	89	14

In examining these figures it must be borne in mind that the military age had not yet been raised beyond 45 ; this took place in 1918.

The National Register. One of the outstanding events in 1915 amongst home affairs was the compilation of the National Register, a duty which brought a great deal of heavy work upon local authorities ; it absorbed most of their attention and energy during the whole of August and September. The Borough of Swindon was divided into 119 enumeration districts, and the work of preparing, distributing, collecting, and tabulating the forms was done entirely by voluntary workers, the teaching staff being largely engaged in the task. The forms were delivered at the homes in the week August 9th to 14th, and had to be ready for collection by Sunday, the 15th. For every member of the household between the ages of 15 and 65 the following particulars had to be given :—

The Form.
Name.   Address.   Nationality.
Single, married, widow or widower.
How many children dependent, (a) under 15 years.
*   (b) over 15 years.*
How many other people dependent (a) wholly,
*   (b) partially.*
Occupation : kind of work fully stated, and material worked in.
Name, Business, and Address of Employer.
If employed by a Government department.
If skilled in any other work.
If able and willing to do such work.

The purpose of the register was to obtain complete information as to the available resources of the nation in man-power in the different industries of vital importance at this time of national stress. It was denied that it had anything to do with conscription, but its importance in the event of the nation's being driven to this expedient was obvious to anyone.

In Swindon the forms were all collected by Wednesday, August 25th, when the work was handed over to a fresh body of voluntary workers who were engaged at the Town Hall in the evenings upon the compilation of the register ; besides the general register a special register was compiled, consisting of the names of all men between 18 and 45 years old,—the military age ; these were the men who had the famous " pink form " and this register had to be completed within two or three weeks. The work was so expeditiously executed in Swindon that many people had their certificates delivered to them by September 3rd ; the certificate was as follows :—

The Certificate.

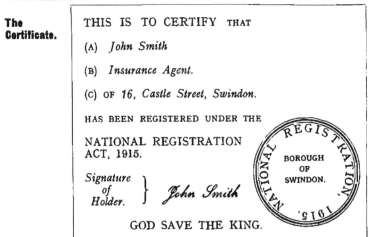

THIS IS TO CERTIFY THAT

(A) *John Smith*

(B) *Insurance Agent.*

(C) OF *16, Castle Street, Swindon.*

HAS BEEN REGISTERED UNDER THE

NATIONAL REGISTRATION ACT, 1915.

Signature of Holder. } *John Smith*

GOD SAVE THE KING.

BOROUGH OF SWINDON.

The holder of the certificate was bound to preserve the certificate and to produce it when called upon to do so by any authorised official—in fact, it was advisable to carry it about with one, especially when travelling,—and the holder had to notify any change of address other than temporary at a Post Office or the Council Offices within twenty-eight days.

The expenses of the registration in Swindon only came to about £10, and the Council recorded in its minutes an expression of high appreciation for the way in which the work was performed, and of its thanks to those who had so freely given their time and labour.

No 1915 "Trip." The serious state of public affairs caused the Great Western Railway Company to abandon the annual " Trip " in July, though at the time hopes were held out that the general holiday might be given in September. The factory had so much government contract work on hand in July that a general stoppage of work for a week was impracticable, and, furthermore, the great demands of the military authorities upon the traffic department made it impossible to arrange for the customary excursions. The situation was no better in September, but the Company tried to compensate its employees by the liberal issue of passes and by granting individual holidays.

Football. The enlistment of many of the professional football-players, and the strong feeling engendered by the spectacle of some of the most athletic men in the country indulging in sport during the nation's life and death struggle, caused the Swindon Town Football Company to open the season of 1915-16 with a purely amateur team. Its first match, played on the 4th of September, was with Portsmouth, resulting in the victory of Portsmouth by five goals to two.

CONTINENTAL AMBULANCE TRAIN
Built at G.W.R. Works Swindon 1916.

For France, 1916.   Ambulance Train built in Swindon Works.

**The
" Fair."**
Similarly, the September hiring fair reflected the seriousness of the position ; there was a large number of farm-hands present for hiring and much was done at advanced rates of pay, but the usual " pleasure fair " was entirely absent.

**A Quiet
Christmas.**
Christmas-tide was a season of very boisterous weather, but the exuberant spirit of the elements was in striking contrast with the depression that marked the national festival in the home ; gaiety and conviviality were entirely lacking, for people's thoughts were full of the privations and dangers of husbands and brothers, and at many gatherings an empty chair checked the spirit of mirth. The absent ones were not, however, suffered to go without tokens of remembrance, and there was a very heavy despatch of parcels from Swindon to the troops overseas, necessitating the temporary engagement of many women at the Post-Office. The inmates of the Workhouse, too, were not allowed to lose their usual treat, and enjoyed their Christmas dinner, the Christmas-tree, and a concert at the " Arcadia " picture-house as in other years. The Christmas football-matches with Reading were also played ; the one on Christmas Day gave the Reading team a win by four goals to three, but on Boxing Day a farcical game in a hurricane resulted in Swindon's winning by four goals to two.

**" Life in a
Railway
Factory."**
Before the close of the year much local interest was aroused by the publication, in November, of a remarkable prose volume by Mr. Alfred Williams—" Life in a Railway Factory," the factory being, of course, the Great Western Factory at Swindon. The work, besides exhibiting the writer's perfect mastery of a fine prose style, was full of intimate touches and picturesque description that delighted readers both from within and without the Works, and even when Mr. Williams ventured into the realm of criticism those who disputed his judgments could not withhold their admiration for his literary power. This book is undoubtedly the chief work, from a literary point of view, dealing exclusively with Swindon, that has hitherto been published, and it was unfortunate that it had to be launched at so unpropitious a time. Shortly afterwards, in February, 1916, a further volume of poetry was published by Mr. Williams, entitled " War Songs and Sonnets," consisting of poems that had appeared at intervals in the " Swindon Advertiser " and the " Wilts and Gloucester Standard." This formed the fifth volume of poetry put forth by Mr. Williams, whose next poems were to appear in a far different quarter—the " Times of India,"—when he was serving in the R.F.A. in the " Land of the Moguls."

Little reference has been made in this survey of 1915 to the terrific struggle taking place across the waters, but many a Swindon family was grieving for the loss of a dear one. In May, the whole town was moved by the news that a German submarine had torpedoed the magnificent Cunard liner, the " Lusitania," sending to their deaths nearly 1,200 innocent men, women and children. Amongst the hapless victims was a Swindon lady, Mrs. F. Chirgwin, with her baby, on her way home from Cuba for a holiday ; she was the second daughter of the late Councillor Cox, and all hearts went out in sympathy to the afflicted relatives, bereaved in so cruel and tragic a manner. Daily, the war was taking toll of England's best, and it was under a cloud of anxiety and sorrow that people went about their daily work, looking forward to the Spring campaign of 1916 with mingled hopes and forebodings.

E

CHAPTER IV.

1916. In the full Tide of War-Work.

The year 1916 opened with an innovation in business circles, inasmuch as New Year's Day was constituted a " Bank Holiday,"—not, however, to give employees in banks and business-houses a respite from work, but to enable the banks, working on depleted staffs, to get out their annual balance sheet. The following

A Day of Intercession.
day, Sunday, was observed as a day of Public Intercession, when the Mayor (Mr. W. E. Morse), the Town Council, and representatives of all public bodies and various societies, along with a large number of the citizens, walked in procession from the Town Hall to the Parish Church ; there a united service was held, the Vicar of Swindon, the Rev. C. A. Mayall, M.A., being assisted by the Mayor's Chaplain, the Rev. S. A. Barron, minister of the Primitive Methodist Church, and by the Rev. J. E. Simon, B.A., the minister of Sanford Street Congregational Church, and president of the Free Church Council.

Swindon Corn Market.
The year saw a continuance of the rising tendency in prices of all kinds of commodities, but without reaching the stage of compulsory limitation. Corn, of course, is the article of prime interest ; the price of wheat in Swindon Market remained fairly steady until September, when an alarming increase began; in January wheat was sold at about 60/- per qr. ; a slight fall set in in March, and prices ranged between 60/- and 50/- until the middle of June, when there was a sudden drop to 45/- ; recovery began at once and 60/- and 62/- were being asked on August 18th ; there was considerable shortage of grain, and the arrival of supplies of new English wheat in September was unable to check the rise which had set in ; October saw the rate for wheat advance to 63/-, 65/-, 66/- and 69/-, and the first November market witnessed a sensational increase to 75/-, some lots even fetching 78/-, the highest price since the Crimean War. Still the advance continued, and in December 80/- per qr. was obtained,—the record price hitherto for Swindon market, though even that was to be exceeded in 1917. Other cereals showed the same tendency, for barley began the year at 42/2 per qr., and finished at between 70/- and 80/- the qr., whilst oats began the year at 32/3 and finished at 51/-.

Bread.
In January bread remained at 1/4 the gallon (8d. a quartern) in Swindon, whilst 1/5 was being charged in other Wiltshire towns, and even 1/6 in London, but the price rose to 1/5 in Swindon in the middle of February ; the Swindon and Highworth Board of Guardians, however, secured tenders in March for bread at 7½d. the 4 lb. loaf and flour at £2 : 8 : 6 the sack. The 4 lb. loaf dropped from 8½d. to 8d. in June and to 7½d. at the Co-operative Society's Stores, only to rise again to 8½d. on the 1st of September ; in November it rose to 9d., and in December to 9½d. December 31st was the last day upon which fine wheaten bread could be anywhere obtained, for with the New Year " War Bread " only could be made ; at first many had welcomed the appearance of a bread made from flour in which a higher percentage of the grain was present, but the praise grew fainter as more and more foreign ingredients—maize, barley,

rice, peas, beans, potatoes, etc.—found a place in the bread, until in 1917 the contrast between the unpalatable and unwholesome-looking war-bread and the crisp white loaf of "pre-war days" silenced even the warmest advocates of the substitute.

Groceries.   In March, 1916 the Grocer's bill ran as follows : English bacon 1 /10 per lb ; foreign bacon 1 /- to 1 /4 ; hams, 1 /- the lb in the Borough Market, where butter was also obtainable at 1 /6 to 1 /8 ; cheese was 11d. and 1 /- a lb ; lard 7d., and 8d. ; granulated sugar was 4½d. and cubes 5d. a lb ; margarine was 10d. ; currants were 7d. a lb and sultanas 10d., but were becoming scarce, and when in March the Guardians sought tenders for the ensuing half-year, they were asked and refused to give 1/4 a lb ; rice was 4d. and 6d., tea of average quality 2 /6, and coffee of ordinary quality 1 /8 a lb.

By the end of the year some of these prices were considerably higher : English bacon was 2 /- a lb by Christmas, and lard 1 /- ; butter was 1 /11 by September, cheese 1 /2 by October, and similar increases had taken place in most articles. Eggs, which began the year at 6 a shilling, were cheapest in April when 8 or 9 could be got for a shilling ; in September they were 5, and by Christmas they were 4 for 1 /-.

Meat.   Retail meat prices in 1916 began to be a source of anxiety to the housekeeper ; the following table will show at a glance the rate of increase, and the figures given in each column show the rates for the cheapest and dearest qualities and cuts at the period indicated at the head of the column ; they are taken from the books of a leading Swindon Butcher.

	Christmas, 1915.	March, 1916.	Christmas, 1916.
English Beef	....5d. to 1s. 10d.	6d. to 2s. 0d.	6d. to 2s. 2d.
English Mutton	....7d. ,, 1s. 9d.	9d. ,, 2s. 0d.	9d. ,, 2s. 4d.
Foreign Beef	....7d. ,, 1s. 9d.	6d. ,, 2s. 0d.	7d. ,, 2s. 2d.
Foreign Mutton	....5d. ,, 1s. 2d.	6d. ,, 1s. 4d.	7d. ,, 1s. 6d.
Suet	.... 1 /2	1 /2	1 /4
Pork	....8d. to 1s. 4d.	9d. to 1s. 6d.	9d. to 1s. 10d.
Veal	....9d. ,, 1s. 6d.	9d. ,, 1s. 8d.	9d. ,, 2s. 0d.

The Swindon and Highworth Board of Guardians obtained tenders for meat in the Spring at the rates of 7½d. per lb for beef, 9½d. for mutton, 5d. for shin, and 6d. for suet. In the autumn contract the figures rose to 9½d. per lb. for beef, 10½d. for mutton, 6½d. for shin, 7d. for suet, and 1 /1 per lb. for officers' joints.

Swindon Cattle Market.   In Swindon Cattle Market, on May 8th, unprecedented prices were realized, at the same time as records were being made at Smithfield ; fat bulls ranged up to £43 and fat beasts up to £37 : 15 : 0 ; "barreners" sold at an average of £22, some bringing in over £25,—higher prices than had been obtained for 30 years ; cows with calves made up to £32, in-calf heifers up to £30 : 15 : 0, and calves up to £6 ; and two-year old steers made £24. Fat pigs fetched £15. These high prices continued through the year, and early in the following January we find fat beasts sold at prices from £49 down to £24 : 10 : 0, lambs from 79 /6 downwards, tegs from 105 /- downwards, ewes 81 /-, and rams 93 /- down.

The Guardians' Pigs.   The Board of Guardians, too, obtained prices for the pigs they reared and sold that were records hitherto ; in February they sold 9 pigs at 16 /6 per score, 9 more in March at 16 /9 per score (16 /3 for animals under 9 score in weight), and in June or July 10 pigs at 17 /6 a score.

Milk.

Milk, which had gone up to 1/4 a gallon in October, 1915, remained at that figure till June 30th, 1916, when it rose to 1/6, a further increase to 1/8 (5d. a quart) taking place in October. The farmers had held a meeting in Swindon on September 11th, at which they were urged not to make contracts for less than 1/5 per gallon for the winter; when, a fortnight later, the buyers from the large dairy-companies appeared at the Market, the farmers generally declined their offers, standing out for the price they had fixed; in one case 1/6 a gallon was obtained, and another dealer obtained 1/6 and 1/5 for the two halves respectively of the winter term. The Board of Guardians, too, was compelled to accept a tender of 1/6 per gallon. When the public realized how the farmers were uniting to keep up milk prices there was wide-spread resentment, and this, coupled with the alarm excited by the enhancement of the cost of nearly all other commodities, expressed itself in resolutions of protest and appeals to the Government to intervene.

Protests.

On September 6th the Town Council had unanimously passed a resolution, "that this Council views with alarm the continued high prices of commodities, and calls upon the Government to introduce at once measures whereby this may be prevented and a decrease in prices be brought about, and that a copy of the resolution be sent to the Prime Minister, the War Secretary, and the Member for the Division." The Board of Guardians now followed suit and resolved, "that this Board views with alarm the high prices now appertaining to the people's food and fuel, and appeals to His Majesty's Government to take urgent steps to control, supply, and restrict prices of the same on behalf of the masses." Similar resolutions of protest were passed by the Swindon Trades and Labour Council, the Swindon Women's Society, and other bodies.

The Borough Market.

Fortunately, vegetables, fruit and fish were in good supply and remained at comparatively moderate rates throughout the year, and the following are some of the prices asked in the Borough market:—Old potatoes gradually rose from 10d. to 1/6 a peck till the new potatoes came in, and these were soon selling at 1¼d. a pound; onions fell from 3½d. a pound (in April) to 1½d.; the cheaper sorts of apples were obtainable at 1½d. and 2d. a pound for the greater part of the year, and better kinds at from 3d. to 5d.; foreign tomatoes varied from 3d. to 5d. a pound, and the English fruit came in at 9d. and soon fell to 7d. and 5d.; cabbages, broccoli, and cauliflowers were cheap, and in June broad beans were selling for 1/4 a peck and peas for 1/6, whilst French beans were 2½d. a lb. at the end of August. In their proper season cucumbers fetched from 3d. to 5d. each, and marrows from 2½d. to 5d.; strawberries sold at 8d. to 6d. a pound, gooseberries at 2d., cherries at 7d., plums at 1½d. to 4d., greengages at 6d., and pears at 3d.

As regards fish, hake was usually about 1/- a pound, and in October haddock was the same price, but herrings and bloaters were almost uniformly 1½d. and 2d. each,—dealers had not yet learned to sell these at so-much per lb; kippers ranged from 3d. to 5d. a pair, and mackerel were 3d. and 4d. each; cod rose from 6d. a pound, in the earlier part of the year, to 10d., and soles varied from 9d. to 1/- a pound.

Rates of Increase.

The Board of Trade returns issued in May, 1916, showed that the general level of prices had risen 23% since the previous May, and that in the same period meat and fish had gone up by 30%, sugar and potatoes by 50%, bacon, milk, and tea by 20 to 25%, butter, cheese and eggs by

17 or 18%, bread by 7%, and flour by 4%. Since the war started the increase in the cost of food for a working-man's household was 55%, and some of the items showed a startling advance, such as : British meat 50%, foreign meat 70 to 80%, bread, tea and cheese 50%, fish 99%, sugar 152%, flour 60%, potatoes 47%, bacon 37% and butter 34%. After September these rates increased greatly in many cases.

Liquor Traffic. The drink trade was subjected to further restrictions early in the year ; a new Licensing Order issued in February limited the hours for the sale of intoxicating liquors to the times between noon and 2.30 p.m., and between 6 p.m. and 9 p.m., on weekdays, and to the same periods on Sundays except that 12.30 was substituted for noon. Orders for spirits to be consumed off the premises could only be taken on five days of the week—Monday to Friday— and then only for quantities of not less than a reputed quart. "Treating" was prohibited, but although prosecutions for the violation of this order occasionally took place it was in reality impracticable, and when it is considered that a man who paid for a glass of beer for his wife at the same time as he paid for one for himself was guilty of a breach of the order, many will be disposed to doubt the expediency of the clause. The new order embraced clubs as well as licensed houses, and strong protests came from both sources, but when the Farmers' Union was asked to support the protest of the licensed victuallers they declined to do so.

Drink, however, had not been a serious cause of disorder in Swindon, and Superintendent Millard was able to give a very satisfactory report on the year's cases (1915) to the Justices in February ; there had been only one prosecution against a licensee in Swindon and that had been dismissed ; prosecutions for drunkenness numbered eleven—an increase of seven, and eight convictions were recorded ; during the year not one soldier had been convicted for drunkenness or for any other offence.

In February 1916 the price of beer was 3½d. and 4d. a pint ; spirits rose by 1d. the quartern, so that Scotch and Irish Whiskey were 11d. a quartern, gin was 10d., brandy 1/4, and proprietary whiskies 1/2. In June bottled beers were raised from 3½d. to 4d. per bottle (½pt) and beer on draught was 6d. a quart for mild and 8d. for bitter beer.

Fuel. It will have been noticed that the Guardians' resolution of protest referred to the cost of fuel as well as of food ; coal of which the retail prices in Swindon had been £1 : 8 : 0 (superior coal) and £1 : 6 : 0 (ordinary house coal) per ton in the latter half of 1914, and £1 : 15 : 0 and £1 : 12 : 0 in 1915, advanced to £1 : 16 : 0 and £1 : 14 : 0 respectively in 1916, In March the Gas Company asserted that they were paying about 6/- per ton more for their coal than a year before, and the Great Western Railway Company had to raise the price of coal supplied to their employees to 25/- in March and again to 27/6 per ton in June, 1916.

The Gas Company made another advance in the price of gas towards the close of the year, charging now 4/- per thousand cubic feet. The price charged by the Corporation for electricity for lighting purposes remained at 4½d. per unit for three quarters of the year, and was then raised to 5d.

Fodder, etc. Whilst the Town Council had to give £2 : 18 : 6 a ton on the year's contract for straw in March and £6 : 10 : 0 per ton on its contract for meadow hay in September, it obtained prices that were a record hitherto when it let the grass land at Broome Sewage Farm in April; the rates

obtained created a sensation amongst the farmers, for the six lots made respectively
£6 : 3 : 0 per acre, £5 : 9 : 0, £5 : 7 : 0, £5 : 2 : 0, £5 : 15 : 0, and £5 : 1 : 0 ; the
total received was £665 as against £340 obtained a year before.

Wool. Although it is not intended to trace out here the rise in the cost of
the many other necessities that enter into ordinary life and business,
it must be remembered that clothing showed the same tendency as
food ; the shortage of wool for civilian needs was made more acute by the action
of the Government about the middle of the year, when, in order to meet the military
requirements, it prohibited anyone from buying, selling or dealing in raw wool
produced in Great Britain or Ireland during 1916 ; at the beginning of 1917 a further
order required all farmers to sell to the Government all wool still in their possession.
These are two examples of the famous " Dora " regulations which hedged in the
helpless civilian during the war.

Decline
of the
Market. The food shortage was emphasised by the continued fall in the
Market Stallages in 1916 ; thus, to take one example only, in the
five weeks ending January 15th, the receipts were only £40 : 7 : 10,
as against £47 : 11 : 0 for the corresponding period a year before.

Horse-
Flesh. A more remarkable evidence lay in the granting of a license in September, 1916, to Mr. S. Cooper for a slaughter-house on Stratton Road,
for the slaughter of horses only for human consumption. The meat
was readily purchased by Swindon's Belgian visitors, but national prejudice was too
strong to allow it to become a popular food though many did rise superior to
prejudice.

Shortage
of Male
Labour. In June the Imperial Tobacco Company's premises were taken by the
Government for the Ministry of Munitions ; the Company gave the
girls who had to leave a promise of first consideration after the war,
and many of them were engaged by the Ministry of Munitions. Girls
and women, in fact, were entering upon a fortunate period as regards employment,
for the shortage of male labour was becoming daily more acute. In March the
postal deliveries were reduced to two a day owing to the loss of so many men ; the
number of girl clerks in the Great Western Railway Works was growing rapidly ;
and the Education Committee, acting through the Governors of the Secondary
School, had established early in the year classes where an intensive course of training
was given to women in order to fit them to replace men on active service ; these
classes were intended for women who had already received a good general education,
and provided training in type-writing, shorthand, business methods and allied subjects.

Decrease of
Vagrancy. The vagrancy returns, too, testified to the shortage of men and the
demand for labour. Thus, a report in March showed 80 vagrants
in a fortnight in the Cricklade and Wootton Bassett Union as compared
with 148 for the same period in 1915. The quarterly return of the Swindon and
Highworth Board of Guardians in April gave the substantial decrease of 540 as
compared with the parallel quarter a year previously, the figures being 698 as
against 1,238. On the night of May 16th, there was not a single male vagrant in
Stratton workhouse, a circumstance of which there was no record in thirty years ;
even this remarkable record was broken on June 10th, when not a single casual
applied for admission,—a fact the more surprising seeing that the day was a Saturday.
The number of inmates also showed a reduction, and at the beginning of 1916 was
only 185, being 39 less than in the previous January.

The Lighting Order. The outstanding feature of local interest in 1916 was probably the lighting question. In the interests of economy public lighting had already been reduced to a point that gave occasion for much complaint, but the danger from aerial raids now led to a stringent enforcement of the orders enjoining the public to obscure all lights from an hour and a half after sunset till nearly sunrise. From April to September nearly every sitting of the magistrates saw several cases of prosecution for neglect of the Lighting **Fines.** Order; for instance, on May 15th seven citizens were fined, three having to pay 40/-; three days later eight were fined, nearly all to the extent of 25/-; on August 31st, eleven delinquents paid the penalty of carelessness, the fines varying from 10/- to £2. It cannot be denied that the fines levied in Swindon were more severe than in many places more exposed to danger, and in September a comparison of the fines levied in Swindon with those levied in Bath showed those in Swindon to be on the average 14/6 heavier than those in the latter place. Possibly the presence of two munition works and the great railway factory influenced the magistrates, and certainly the Swindon public was slow to learn the lesson. An analysis of 102 fines levied at 16 petty sessions during this period gives 3 of 5/-, 7 of 10/-, 19 of 15/-, 19 of £1, 20 of 25/-, 14 of 30/-, 17 of £2, and one each of £2 : 5 : 0, £3, and £3 : 10 : 0.

Cases. The nature of the offences this penalised may be illustrated by one or two newspaper reports: thus—

" ...., of...................., Swindon, was summoned for contravening the Lighting Order on ....at 9.15 p.m. P.C....................stated the facts. Defendant did not appear, but was represented by his sister, who stated that she had pulled the blind up ready for morning, but had omitted to put out the light; her brother accepted responsibility."

" ...., of...................., Swindon, was summoned for contravening the Lighting Order at 10.45 p.m., on .... Defendant pleaded guilty, and he made the excuse that the blind had fallen down and he had been too busy to put it up."

" ...., of...................., was likewise summoned. P.C................ said that he saw a bright electric light shining from defendant's shop window. It threw a reflection across the roadway. When his attention was called to it defendant said he did not know the light was showing; had it not been for a few customers coming in just then the shop would have been closed : defendant, who said it was a side window where the blind was not drawn, was fined 30/-."

Church Lights and Bells. One effect of the Lighting Order was to lead the churches to fix an earlier time for the evening services, which were often very melancholy offices held in semi-darkness. In November, also, the bells of the Parish Church ceased to be rung for evening service, lest their notes should be a guide to some prowling foe in the air.

"Daylight Saving." The lighting question was to some extent one of fuel-economy as well as of precautions against attack, and the adoption of the "Daylight Saving" device resulted in great economy of fuel and light. It would have gladdened the heart of Mr. Willett, who had for years advocated the measure in the face of much opposition and ridicule, if he could have lived to see his idea embodied in an Act of Parliament and accepted with almost universal approbation. On Sunday, May 21st, at 2 a.m., the act came into operation, but of course the public put the clocks forward an hour before going to bed on Saturday evening. The long summer evenings that enabled one to do without artificial light till nearly bedtime were a boon to the gardener, and to the youth of the town who had been confined to the factory or shop all day; but the effect was not altogether good in the case of young children who either had to be put to bed in full sunshine or had to be deprived of the rest their health demanded. But there was an actual shortage of fuel and need to economise, accounting to some extent for the raising of the price of electricity in Swindon from 4½d. to 5d., a unit in September. The Lighting restrictions had hit the Electricity Department severely, for at the annual presentation of the municipal budget in March, it was stated that there was a decrease of £700 in the electricity account, and the adoption of "Daylight Saving" would accentuate the fall in consumption.

The Electricity Dept.

War Savings. Early in this year the Local Central Committee for War Savings was formed ; it was elected at a public meeting convened by the Mayor, Mr. W. E. Morse, on March 30th, and Mr. H. A. Stanier was appointed Honorary Secretary. It did good educative work during the year, but it was not till 1917 that the movement seized the public imagination to any great extent. In the latter part of 1916, however, a "War Savings Campaign" was organized by the Committee, lasting through the week, November 13th to 18th. Open-air meetings were held during the dinner-hour outside the main entrances of the Great Western Railway Factory and elsewhere, and on the Thursday evening a mass-meeting was held in the large hall of the Swimming-baths under the presidency of the new Mayor, Mr. A. J. Gilbert ; there was a very strong platform of supporters, and speeches were delivered by the Mayor, Mr. R. Toothill (Labour Member of Parliament for Bolton), Mr. W. Brace, M.P., (Labour : then Under Secretary for Home Affairs), and Mr. R. Lambert, M.P. for the locality. The meeting pledged itself to support the Government financially in the following resolution :—

"This mass-meeting of the citizens of Swindon cordially supports the Government in its strenuous endeavour to achieve a great victory over Germany ; and pledges itself to form a joint War Savings Association, and to practise economy in all departments of life, and will do this until a great and glorious victory is achieved."

War Savings Certificates. War Savings Certificates, issued at 15/6 and worth £1 at the end of five years, were now being offered to the public and were certainly the best investment ever offered the small depositor ; to invest 15/6 and to get £1 at the end of five years was to obtain just over 5.8% on the investment. There was also the additional advantage that the investor could present his certificate at any Post Office and realize it at any time according to a printed table of values. During the first year its value remained at 15/6, but thereafter it increased at the rate of 1d. a month, being worth 19/8 at the end of 4 years 11 months, and at the end of the next month 4d. was added to the value. It was very popular in the schools, where the children saved their money by affixing sixpenny stamps upon a special card bearing thirty-one spaces. "War Savings Associations" had sprung up in considerable numbers all over the country, and Swindon had twenty-five already ; in these, the money saved was pooled and a quantity of certificates was purchased immediately ; these were inscribed in the names of members chosen by some form of ballot or by rotation, and were held by the association until the member had completed the amount ; by this means, a certificate began to bear interest before the 15/6 subscribed by the member whose name it bore had been

War-Savings Associations.

deposited. Several of the schools became "War Savings Associations," but it is a curious fact that the Post Office Savings Bank, which only paid 2½%, was obstinately preferred by very many children—under the influence, or course, of their parents,—either from an illogical idea that the Post Office was safer, or from mere lethargy, or, as some affirmed, because "father did not believe in the war."

Working of the Derby Scheme. In December, 1915, the first proclamation calling up men attested under the "Derby Scheme" appeared on the hoardings, when Groups 2 to 5 —single men from nineteen to twenty-two years of age—were summoned on December 12th, to present themselves for service with the colours on January 1st. This caused no surprise, but what did cause surprise—and was due to the inadequate number of attestations,—was the rapidity with which the proclamations calling up the other groups followed this one. The dates are as follows :—

No. of Group.	Date of Proclamation.	Called up for.
Group 1	Feb. 25th, 1916	March 28th, 1916
Groups 2—5	Dec. 12th, 1915	Jan. 20th, 1916
„ 6—9	Jan. 8th, 1916	Feb. 8th, 1916
„ 10—13	Jan. 30th, 1916	Feb. 29th, 1916
„ 14—24	Feb. 16th, 1916	Mar. 18th, 1916
Group 24	May 13th, 1916	June 13th, 1916
Groups 25—32	March 7th, 1916	April 4th, 1916
„ 33—41	April 27th, 1916	May 29th, 1916
„ 42—46	May 13th, 1916	June 13th, 1916

Thus within about seven months of the adoption of the "Derby Scheme" its resources were exhausted, though it is to be remembered that great numbers who attested had escaped being called up through being engaged on munition-work or other important labour.

The New Military Service Act. It had been repeatedly stated in the early part of the war that the Government had no intention of applying conscription to the nation, and that the nation would never endure it ; these prophecies were based upon an utter miscalculation of Germany's resources, and 1916 saw Great Britain adopt the principle of conscription. The "Derby Scheme," under which men voluntarily attested and were called up by age-groups, was pronounced by the military authorities to be inadequate, and, moreover, it was obviously unfair and often unwise in its effects, since a married man or one engaged in valuable work might be called up whilst a young, single man, engaged in unimportant work, was left behind because he had not attested. In January, 1916, therefore, a new Military Service Act was passed, whereby every man between the ages of 18 and 40 was made liable to military service ; certain occupations of national importance were exempted, and Tribunals were set up with power to exempt cases of special hardship.

The Borough Tribunal. On February 9th, the last day allowed for the purpose by the provisions of the new Act, a special meeting of the Town Council was held to appoint a Tribunal for Swindon ; it consisted of the tribunal appointed some months before in connection with Lord Derby's scheme, with the addition of five new members,—eleven in all, viz :—

Mr. A. W. Deacon, J.P.
,, A. E. Harding
,, T. Butler, J.P.
,, J. Clark, J.P.
,, J. Crewe Wood
,, S. Walters

Mr. W. R. Robins
,, C. E. Taylor, J.P.
,, H. Watkins, J.P.
,, R. M. Forder
Mrs. E. Whitworth

First Session. The new tribunal held its first session on February 21st, when the Town Clerk was present as clerk to the tribunal and Mr. A. E. Withy as the military representative; there were twenty-two applications to be dealt with. Mr. Withy ceased to attend very shortly, having been appointed on the County Appeal Tribunal, and the military representative was henceforth Mr. T. Kimber or Mr. J. Crewe Wood; on Mr. Crewe Wood's acceptance of this office he resigned from the Tribunal and his place was taken by Mr. W. H. Kinneir. Mr. A. W. Deacon was elected chairman.

Other Tribunals. On the same day upon which the tribunal held its first sitting another tribunal also sat for the first time in Swindon; this was the one for the Highworth Rural District, of which Mr. J. K. Coleing was the chairman; whilst on March 31st, yet another held its sitting in the Borough, when the Military Appeal Tribunal sat at the Town Hall, under the presidency of Lord Bath, to hear appeals from the local tribunals of Swindon, Highworth, Calne, and Ramsbury. This Tribunal eventually settled down at Trowbridge.

Typical Cases. The mere newspaper reports, bald as they are, are full of illuminating glimpses as to the serious nature of the Tribunal's labours and the need for both courage and sympathy. For example :—

The Widow's Son. " ...., of...................., a bricklayer, claimed total exemption 'If I can get it.' He was 38 years of age, and said he was the sole support of his widowed mother, who was 73 years of age and in a bad state of health. Applicant had no brothers, but he had one sister married and living in ....shire. Replying to Mr. Kimber, applicant said his mother could not go and live with his sister, as she had two children and her husband was expecting to be called up in the Army. Temporary exemption for two months was granted."

Another. " ...., aged 39, of ...., a labourer, appeared accompanied by his widowed mother, who made an appeal on behalf of her son. Applicant said he supported his mother. He had one sister, who was single, and a brother who was married. ' I would thank you gentlemen to extend his time for a few months, pleaded the widowed mother, ' Oh, don't you take him from me, gentlemen. I shall be left all alone.' The tribunal granted 14 days' exemption, but he will have a further two months as he has not been attested, and un-attested men get two months' exemption beyond the period granted by the Tribunal."

A one-man Business. " ...., 26, grocer, applied for exemption. He said he came home from abroad four years ago and had invested all his savings in the business. His only brother had been serving in the Army since the outbreak of war. Applicant was married and had a child 14 months of age.

Mr. Wood : Could not your wife manage the business ?
Applicant : She helps a little, but could not carry on the business herself.
The Chairman : You may come back again soon.

Applicant : Well, we don't know how long the war will last.

The Chairman : The nation badly needs young men like you.

Temporary exemption was granted for six months."

"Total exemption was granted to ....26, a G.W.R. porter,
The Pink Card. who produced a ' pink card ' issued by his employers, and which denotes that his services are indispensable."

"A month's exemption was granted................, a carriage fitter, and
A Widower. widower with three children. He said that he cooked the meals and made the beds."

Conscientious " ....applied for exemption on conscientious grounds. He
Objection. said he was a firm believer in the teachings of Count Leo Tolstoi. He could not take the military oath to kill anyone. He belonged to no religious sect. He firmly believed that to take part in fighting of any kind was contrary to his religious belief. He held that force was no remedy. He objected to military service of any kind. He was quite willing to help in saving life in his private capacity, but he could not undertake any duties in a military capacity. He had held his present views for some years, since July, 1912. Applicant asked that other points he had to put forward should be heard in camera. After considerable discussion and argument on important points, the applicant was granted conditional exemption."

Such cases might be multiplied a hundred-fold and they illustrate the painful nature of the duty which lay on the Tribunal and the variety of the problems they had to solve. The names of the members of the Swindon Tribunal themselves would vouch for the humane spirit in which they performed their task, and it could never be said that this Tribunal was either unduly harsh or that it shrank from its duty ; it certainly compared well in both respects with other tribunals that could be named, and it had a real cause for complaint at times in the way in which its decisions, upon the appeal of the military representative, were altered at Trowbridge, feeling rightly that they, on the spot and familiar with the circumstances, were better able to judge rightly than were the county gentlemen in the west of the County.

Not many cases of "Conscientious Objectors" came before the
Conscientious Tribunal,—a thing for which it might well be thankful ; but occasionally
Objectors. these perplexing cases did arise, and at one petty sessions the police brought two objectors before the Bench, who fined them each £2 and handed them over to the military as absentees. These men had had their appeals rejected both by the Local and the Appeal Tribunals. Such cases were often solved by granting exemption upon the appellants' undertaking some particular work of national importance, such as farm work.

A substitution scheme was formulated by the Army Council and explained to the Tribunal by Mr. Kimber in October. He said the Military Authorities recognised the hardships of employers and would try to find substitutes for any further men taken for the Army. [1]

Volunteer The Volunteer Training Corps was, as has been seen, firmly established
Training and efficiently working at the close of 1915, and the new year saw
Corps. all branches actively engaged, for the weekly orders included section drill, rifle practice, instruction classes for N.C.O.'s, signalling instruction, engineering instruction, and ambulance instruction. The orders were now signed by Mr. G. R. Plaister, appointed Adjutant upon Mr. McAllister's resignation.

(1) Continued, p. 188.

Another office that had changed hands was the treasurership, Mr. C. E. M. Harvey having accepted that post after Mr. Kinneir's resignation in the summer of 1915.

Change in Status. Early in 1916 the Government accorded to the Volunteer Training Corps the military rank and status of the old Volunteer Force, under the command of the Lord Lieutenant of the County, and the Swindon and District branch therefore became the Swindon Detachment of the Wilts Volunteer Regiment ; later in the year Col. T. C. P. Calley, C.B., M.V.O., was gazetted County Commandant of the Wiltshire Volunteers.

Decline and its causes. The miniature rifle-range near the Town Gardens was opened on July 8th, and this was a boon to the members of the Corps, who had little enough encouragement from head-quarters. A general order had been issued at the close of last year giving the Volunteer Training Corps permission to use the military ranges, but they had no rifles. The comparative lack of recognition by the War Office was undoubtedly responsible for some of the heavy decline in numbers which occurred in 1916, though other causes contributed to the falling-off ; but the lack of equipment and the absence of rifles were a very discouraging feature of the movement, for it was extremely difficult to make men take an interest in their work when they were without the means to make themselves efficient. True, they were equally without these in 1915, but the Corps had then plenty of elementary work to do ; it had not reached a stage when it was pulled up for lack of means of going further. But there were other reasons for a good many of the losses ; numbers of men were absorbed in the manufacture of munitions and several others had gone into the regular army.

Lord French's Inspection. The reduction in the size of the Swindon detachment was apparent when Lord French held an inspection of the Swindon, Trowbridge and Marlborough detachments of the Wilts Volunteers on the County Ground on October 8th. The number present was 231, and another 73 were absent on patrol duty, whereas a year before Swindon and District alone had presented 332 for Col. Steward's inspection. Viscount French was accompanied by a distinguished staff of officers and conducted a very thorough inspection. Captain Usher, of Trowbridge, was in command of the volunteers and was supported by Capt. T. J. Robinson and Lieuts. W. J. Ainsworth, G. R. Plaister, and Comley of the Swindon detachment, and Lieut. W. S. Butler of Marlborough. Lord French made to the men a very encouraging speech, and evidently he was aware of the feeling caused by the Government's neglect, for he said that it was very necessary before they were armed and equipped, and before the Government spent vast sums of money upon them, that the Government should have some guarantee from the Volunteers that they would continue the kind of service they were doing until the end of the war. If they made sacrifices the Government was ready at once to go a considerable way towards providing them with the necessary arms and equipment.

The Corporation's Help. The Swindon Town Council, indeed, gave the volunteers more substantial encouragement than the Government had done hitherto, for it made them a grant of £50 towards their expenses. There was this much to be said for the reluctance of the War Office to go to any great expense on behalf of the Volunteers, that under their existing conditions of service any man could withdraw from the Corps by giving fourteen days' notice of his intention to do so ; and although every member would repel with indignation the idea that he would do so if circumstances seemed to be leading him to danger and sacrifice, the Government could not undertake the tremendous expense of furnishing great numbers of men on the chance of their remaining in service. That their services were valuable was admitted by Lord French, alluding to those who were engaged in defending the railway and other vulnerable points, and it is not to be assumed that the Government had no desire to see the Volunteers a strong and well-trained body.[1].

The Red Cross. No longer having a hospital to look after, the energies of the Swindon Branch of the Red Cross Society in 1916 were devoted mainly to the Depôt in Regent Street, opened at the close of November, 1915. The workers had a busy year, for up to the close of 1916 they made and sent away from the Depôt 2,333 articles ; amongst them were included

Work of the Depôt.

351 bed-jackets.	57 pairs of socks.
69 helpless-case shirts.	133 pairs of bed-socks.
93 day-shirts.	212 pairs of operation-stockings.
252 knitted washing-squares.	84 night shirts.
54 pyjamas.	173 knitted caps.
99 hot water bottle covers.	41 pillows.

The purely voluntary nature of all this work is apparent from the balance-sheet for 1916, in which the working expenses stand at the nominal sum of 16 /-.

INCOME	£	s.	d.	EXPENDITURE	£	s.	d.
Grant from Swindon Branch of Red Cross Society	100	0	0	Material bought	241	19	4
Subscriptions and Donations	101	0	7	Expenses of Depôt		16	0
Envelope Collection (less expenses of collection)	41	14	9				
	£242	15	4		£242	15	4

The " Envelope Collection " alluded to in the statement of income was made early in February and Mrs. Calley and Mrs. Swinhoe, thanking the collectors, gave the total proceeds as £43 : 5 : 9.

In April Mrs. Calley (The President) resigned the office of Commandant of the Swindon Red Cross Society, owing to the pressure of other duties, and she was succeeded by Mrs. Colledge, of Mannington Farm.[2].

The Farmers. The Wiltshire branch of the Farmers' Union had by the end of February contributed £4,921 : 8 : 8 to the total of £232,679 : 10 : 11, reached by the British Farmers' Red Cross Fund, and three beds had been allocated to Wiltshire in the Farmers' Exterior Hospital at Calais and had the name of the County inscribed above them. But it was felt by the farmers of Swindon district that a special effort should be made in this locality, and the success of such enterprises in other districts spurred them to make their effort conspicuously fruitful in results. It took the form of a " Jumble Sale " held at the Monday market at Swindon, on May 22nd, when Mrs. Calley opened the sale by putting up to auction the first lot,—a fine white bullock given by the Swindon Master Butchers' Association,—which fetched £61. The total proceeds of the sale reached the excellent figure of £2,020 net profit, a result due largely to the enthusiasm inspired by the indefatigable Secretary,Mr. J. S. Protheroe. A similar sale held at Savernake brought in £1,005, so that the North Wilts Farmers added to the funds £3,025 by the two sales.[3].

(1) Continued on page 134.   (2) Continued on page 136.   (3) Continued on page 138.

Flag Days.

The " Flag Days " arranged for 1916 were :—

April 29th	English Flag Day (B.R.C.S.)	146	2	3
Sept. 23rd	Mayor's War Fund	95	10	8½
Oct. 7th	Sailors' Day	105	5	10½
Oct. 21st	Lord Kitchener's Memorial Fund	100	4	3½
Nov. 4th	Red Cross Fund	144	12	6
	Total	£501	15	7½

But to these must be added certain other " Flag Days," privately arranged viz :

June 3rd	For Blinded Soldiers and Sailors	162	6	6
June 24th	" Rose Day " (Victoria Hospital)	162	15	0¼
Sept. 3rd	Belgian Flag Day	154	0	1½
Sept. 15th	R.S.P.C.A. (Wounded horses)	137	6	6
	Total	£616	8	1¾

Thus the Grand Total is over £1,200 for the nine collections.

The Budget.

The Corporation's Annual Budget was presented by Councillor T. Kimber, and reflected much credit upon those who had managed the Corporation business during a trying and anxious period. The total expenditure on all accounts for the past year resulted in a saving of £966 upon the estimate put forward in March, 1915, and the income was £5,439 in excess of the estimate. Actually, the expenditure was £143,957 and the income was £143,052. As a matter of fact the economies effected on the rate-fund accounts amounted to approximately £5,000 ; but owing to the epidemic of infectious disease the Corporation had to pay the Hospital Board £1,078 more than had been estimated, and a sum of £1,600 had been expended in the purchase of property for street improvements not provided for in the previous estimates ; the trading accounts, too, exceeded the estimate by £1,308, and thus the net saving was reduced to £966. The increase of £5,439 in the income was accounted for, in round numbers, as follows :

Increase in Education Grants	£2500
Increase in Tramway Receipts	£ 900
Increase in Waterworks Revenue received mainly from the Military Camp at Draycott	£1900
Amount due to Corporation on settlement of outstanding Income Tax Claims	£1000
	£6300

Deduct—

Decreased income on Electricity A /c.	£700	
Decreased income on District and Borough Rate, due chiefly to the reduction in the County Main Roads Grant	£200	
		900
Net Increase		£5400

The rates levied during the past year had been 8/4 in the pound as against 8/5 in the estimate, and for the ensuing year the estimate was 8/- in the pound.

The Trams. The increase in the Tramway receipts will be observed in the statement just given, and a further report made to the Town Council at the beginning of May said the trams had just had the best year on record; the receipts for the year ending March 31st were £10,175, exceeding those for the year before by £945, and the previous best year by £429.

Wages and Bonuses. At this meeting the Council raised the wages of tramway conductors over twenty-one years of age from 5d. to 5½d. per hour. This was, of course, apart from bonuses already granted in 1915, these being presumably a temporary expedient to meet the greater cost of living. But the cost of living was still going up, and before the end of the year the Council had to reconsider the subject of salaries and bonuses; in November a bonus of 5/- per week was granted to members of the clerical staff receiving less than £100 a year, and 3/- to those receiving between £100 and £160 a year; an additional bonus of 2/- a week was given to the workmen provided that it did not bring their wages to more than 45/- a week. This settlement endured but for a short time, for the matter had to be re-opened in the following March, and the year 1917 saw it a frequent subject of discussion.

Special Constables. It has often been felt that a town of the size and importance of Swindon should have the control of its own police, and the state of affairs had not infrequently given rise to a little friction between the local and the county authorities; but there was no justification for the direct snub administered to the Town Council by the Standing Joint Committee of the County Council in response to a letter sent by the Town Council in April. All over the country the depletion of the police force had led to the enrolment of bodies of Special Constables, and the sight of the civilian constable wearing his armlet was common. The police staff in Swindon had never been a large one, and now, when many police had been called to the colours, it was felt by many that it was inadequate; the town was often thronged with soldiers from the camp, there had been an influx of munition workers into the town, the darkening of the streets was a source of danger, and the administration of the numerous "Orders" made in the name of "Dora" cast additional burdens upon the police. The Town Council therefore wrote to the County authority suggesting that special constables should be appointed in Swindon, particularly as plenty of citizens were prepared to volunteer. Their representations were only met by the statement that special constables were not needed in Swindon and a reminder that the Town Council was not reponsible for the police-force.

The Prince of Wales' Fund. When 1916 opened Swindon had contributed to the Central Committee of the Prince of Wales' Fund just about £6,000. The National Fund itself had reached imposing dimensions, and in March, 1916, the total subscriptions came to £5,827,874 of which £3,073,000 had been expended in relief.

Towards the end of July, 1916, a meeting of the local Committee was called to receive a report upon the work done up to that time, and the report was necessitated by the fact that the formation of the War Pensions Committee relieved the Prince of Wales' Fund of a great part of its responsibilities. As is mentioned elsewhere, [1] the new committee was to administer the new Naval and Military Pensions Act and began its duties on July 1st, and the work hitherto done by the Executive Committee

(1) Page 84.

of the Prince of Wales' Fund was transferred to the Pensions Committee. Although the relief of civil cases was not affected by the act, the new Committee agreed to take these over, only 26 being on the books at the time.

Work done. Since the outbreak of war the subscriptions to the Prince of Wales' Fund collected in Swindon amounted to £6,384 : 9 : 8, of which the collections in the works provided £4,310 : 11 : 3, and other subscriptions £2,073 : 18 : 5. This gives an average of £64 : 9 : 9 for the 99 weeks. The Central Committee had returned £1,733 : 14 : 0 for the purpose of local relief, £1,196 : 6 : 0 going to naval and military cases and £537 : 8 : 0 to civil cases. The sum of £1,196 : 6 : 0 was eventually repaid to the Prince of Wales' Fund by the Government, for, as from the 1st July, 1916, the Government accepted the responsibility for all payments made to dependents of soldiers and sailors, and the amount already advanced from the National Relief Fund for these cases was refunded by the Government. Hence it should be noticed that in future reports this sum of £1,196 : 6 : 0 will not be included in the statement of the amount disbursed in relief. The cases relieved were—

344 naval and military, involving	344 wives	and	799 children
217 ,,	,,	217 dependents	,, 195 ,,
68 civilian	,,	68 ,,	,, 52 ,,
629 cases in all,	,,	629 ,,	,, 1046 ,,

Additional grants from the Royal Patriotic Fund Corporation for the dependents of deceased soldiers amounted to £498, being distributed to

45 cases involving 45 widows and 101 children
48 cases, involving 48 dependents

93 cases involving 93 dependents and 101 children.

The Soldiers' and Sailors' Help Society had used £381 : 8 : 8 in assisting 79 discharged soldiers with 132 dependents. Thus a total sum of £2,613 : 2 : 8 had been expended in relieving 801 cases involving 2,080 people.

Other assistance had been given in the form of 260 free medical books and 11 maternity vouchers, whilst in 208 cases loans amounting to £350 : 17 : 4 had been granted to tide over the time before allotment and separation allowances began to be received. It is gratifying to find that at the time of the report £296 : 3 : 10 had already been repaid. [1]

Mayor's Local War Fund. A fund similar in character to the Prince of Wales' Fund was established late in 1916 to meet local requirements that could not be dealt with adequately by existing funds. It was known as the Mayor's Local War Fund, and its chief object was to assist disabled men or their families. The Great Western Works collectors decided to continue for this fund the collections hitherto made for the Prince of Wales' Fund, and also to hand over to it a balance of £350 which they had in hand. Canon Ross sent a cheque for £150 and Mr. T. Arkell sent one for £50, whilst several local gentlemen sent £25. Thus the fund started with contributions and promises amounting to about £800, and by the end of the year it reached £1,056 : 11 : 11½. The fund was administered by a committee of ten, including the Mayor. [2]

(1) Continued on page 128.   (2) Continued on page 128.

Vegetables for the Navy. The year 1916 saw the work of the Vegetable Products Committee carried on with unflagging zeal, in spite of the difficulties presented by a bad season and the serious shortage of labour caused by the growing demands of the army for men. The fruit harvest was especially poor, and it was a great cause of regret to the Committee that they were able to send to the fleet hardly any apples.

General Facts. The figures transmitted to the Committee by the General Secretary in the Spring show the extensive nature of the work in which the Committee was participating, for they showed that on March 1st, Swindon was one of 670 centres engaged, which had already sent 10,000,000 lbs., inclusive of 80,000 lbs of Christmas puddings, to the sailors ; 670 cases had been forwarded to the Eastern Mediterranean Squadron. The work was also assisted by parts of the empire beyond the seas, for 2000 cases and barrels of fruit and vegetables had been sent, chiefly by the Dominion of Canada, Singapore, the West Indies, and Mauritius.

Unweary in Well-doing. Contributions continued to be received from the surrounding villages with a regularity that is a proof not only of the generosity of the donors, but also of the persistence of the Committee in keeping the cause prominently before the public ; thus, not only did Mr. H. Haine himself make lavish contributions, but he enlisted the sympathy and help of many others in the neighbourhood of Sevenhampton. Mr. Hiscock, of Highworth, presented a truck of cabbages ; valuable lots were sent by Mr. Eddols, of Sevenhampton, Mr. Butt, of Coleshill and Mr. Hickman, of Bishopstone ; Mr. Willis, of Overtown, brought in many consignments, including welcome gifts of Christmas puddings, and excellent lots were frequently sent in by Mr. Ashford, of Burderop, Mr. Drew, of Purton, Mr. Chandler, of Aldbourne, and Mr. Taylor, of Idstone. Amongst the local tradesmen, Messrs. Trowbridge, Berry and Clements proved staunch friends, and other tradesmen helped greatly by giving empty cases and barrels for the packing of the goods. Mr. Currey, of Wroughton, Mr. Austin, of Highworth, and others far too numerous to mention, rendered valuable assistance, and the churches and schools of the district sent in many large assortments collected from small contributors.

Floss. A picturesque recruit was found in Mr. Trineman's collie-dog " Floss," who on market-days used to frequent the Borough Market wearing a kind of saddle bearing a union-jack and a collecting box ; as the balance sheet shows, she proved a very efficient collector, and was borrowed to carry on her work at Highworth and other markets.

Cash Assistance. The poor season and the increased cost of everything made it more necessary to obtain contributions in cash, and in the course of the year £38 : 10 : 0 was obtained, of which the greater part was used in the purchase of onions, apples, marrows and other food. The Committee expressed much gratitude for the handsome monetary assistance given by the girls and women at Messrs. Compton's factory, who sent the largest donations from any one source.

At the end of the year the balance-sheet stood thus :—

F

	£	s.	d.
Balance in hand at beginning		5	10½
Employees of Messrs. Comptons	11	1	11
National Farmers' Union	5	2	3
Miss Manners' Xmas Pudding fund	2	2	0
Mr. Murphy's Draycott Concerts	1	15	0
Collected by Mr. Austin	2	0	6½
„ Mr. Gibbs		13	0
„ " Floss "	15	5	5
Small Sums		4	0

	£	s.	d.
Expenditure	27	11	3
Balance to carry forward	10	18	9

£38 10 0   38 10 0

Sailors' The best evidence of the beneficent character of the work came
Tributes. from the gallant fellows whose life was brightened by it ; letters
were always coming, bearing the thanks of the men, and these un-
solicited tokens of appreciation frequently came from the hand of some
Swindonian aboard the ship receiving packages from Swindon ; sailors on short
leave, too, called upon the Chairman, Mr. Trowbridge, or upon the Secretary, Mr.
Trineman, to express the gratitude of themselves and their mates, one of them
saying that the day the crates arrived was a real holiday for them. The packages
were not confined to one or two ships, but letters came from many sources,—the
Thunderer, the Barham, the Superb, the Blanche, the Daphne, the Cyclops, the
Neptune, etc.,—although H.M.S. Marlborough seems to have been considered as
more especially a protegee of Swindon.

2nd Year's At the close of the year it was found that 616 packages had been sent
Results. off, as compared with 552 in the previous year, in addition to four
truck loads of cabbages, turnips, and swedes, and already the Committee had the promise of three more trucks of cabbages and turnips
for the following season. At the final meeting the Mayor, Mr. A. J. Gilbert, spoke
with just pride in congratulating the Committee upon an excellent year's work,
a result due to the enthusiasm and perseverance of the members, and the excellent
organization they had created ; a well-merited compliment was paid to Mrs. Trineman
who had carried out most of the clerical duties, when, upon the Mayor's proposition
the meeting decided to send her a special letter of thanks for her able assistance [1].

Prisoners It will be seen in the chapter [2] devoted to the Committee for providing
of War Comforts for the Wilts Regiment that this committee had a strenuous
Committee. time throughout 1916, sending off a hundred parcels per week to
individual prisoners of war in the early summer, and a total of 3,758
such parcels in the months July to November inclusive. Before the close of the
year drastic changes were made in the system of relieving prisoners of war, the
work being placed under the Red Cross Society ; it was then that the Museum in
Regent's Circus became the Committee's depôt and headquarters.

Club for Although the subject will be dealt with more fully in a following
Wives and section (1917) it is proper to mention here the Social Club for the
Mothers. Wives and Mothers of Soldiers and Sailors, which for over three years
brought a great deal of happiness into the lives of many Swindon

(1) Continued on page 129.   (2) Chapter V.

women and was maintained by the persevering attention of a large group of ladies. One must imagine the forlorn lot of many a housewife whose husband was in France or Mesopotamia ; she had her separation allowance and children's allowance, but she was left without assistance in the management of her family and the family affairs, and her life was likely to be very drab and monotonous ; the design of those who promoted the Club was to give these women a thorough change once a week, to bring them together to chat and listen to music whilst they enjoyed a tea they had not had to prepare, and so to help to keep up their spirits and courage.

The Club was founded on November 4th, 1915, and was really an offshoot of the Swindon Welfare Association, and 331 members were enrolled forthwith. A nominal annual subscription of a half-penny was charged, and meetings were held every Wednesday afternoon in the large hall of the Town Hall regularly throughout 1916, except in the month of July. The character of the meetings will be described later, but one may note that everything was done to make the Club accessible to the most straightened purse, for the charges were : tea, ½d. per cup, bread and butter, ½d. per slice, and cakes, ½d. each.

The Committee, and officers and helpers, consisted of :—

The *President*—Mrs. H. C. King.

The *Secretary and Treasurer*—Miss M. Rattray (Mrs. Saddler).

The *Registrars*—Mrs. T. Tindle and Miss Webb.

Committee—Mrs. Whitworth, Mrs. Rattray, Mrs. Chamberlain, Mrs. Horton, Miss Deacon.

Helpers—Mrs. G. Brooks, Mrs. Stewart, Mrs. Tindle, Mrs. Dimmack, Mrs. H. Thomas, Mrs. Hornby, Miss Sumner, Miss Eacot, Miss Beswick, Miss King, Miss Timms.

War Savings Secretary—Mrs. R. Goddard : and

Treasurer—Mrs. P. Webb.

The first general report covered 1916 and 1917, and is referred to in describing the events of the latter year. [1]

The Soldiers' Rest. The re-opening of the Soldiers' Rest at the Town Hall, after the interval occasioned by the outbreak of scarlet fever, took place on the 25th of March, 1916. By that time the little men with the big hearts had gone, and their places were occupied by the Cyclists' Corps, amongst whom were some Colonial Troops.

Catering. When the Rest was first opened the Committee was able to give each visitor as much food and tea as he wished at the very low charge of threepence ; no restrictions had yet been imposed and prices had not risen unduly. When, however, the hall was re-opened in March, 1916, conditions had changed, and it was found necessary to raise the charge to fourpence. The food provided included tea, coffee, and cocoa, white and brown bread and butter, three kinds of cakes, buns, and pastries. In October, 1916, the prices of provisions had mounted to such an extent that a further increase in the charge had to be made, but, whilst raising it to sixpence, the Committee added fish and ham sandwiches to the generous menu detailed above. The work of catering was undertaken by Miss Deacon, and in its report of December, 1917, the Committee pays a warm tribute to her and her helpers :—

"Everyone will understand, the helpers most of all, how much we owe to Miss Deacon, upon whom falls the responsibility and work of catering. By hook or

[1]   See page 132.

by crook she has invariably managed to procure provisions, a task which those who have to purchase for their homes will very fully realize. No words can adequately do justice to the enormous amount of work the catering entails, and the thanks of everyone are due to Miss Deacon for the splendidly successful way in which she sees after the men's material comfort."

Mrs. Perry, in the admirable report she presented in December, 1917, from which the above extract is taken, gives some surprising details as to the numbers of men using the Rest, and some interesting facts as to the method of conducting it ; these will be mentioned in the narrative of that year's events, and further details will complete the account when those of 1918 are considered. [1].

The Pensions Committee. The most notable addition to the public bodies of the Borough in 1916, was the Local Committee set up for the administration of the new Naval and Military War Pensions Act. A memorandum prepared by the Town Clerk, Mr. R. Hilton, states :—The Act received the Royal Assent on the 10th of November, 1915, and its general object is to make certain provisions relating to pensions and grants and allowances in respect of the present war to officers and men in the Naval and Military Service of the Crown, and their wives, widows, children, and other dependents, and the care of officers and men disabled in consequence of the war. For this purpose, the Act directs that a Statutory Committee of the Royal Patriotic Fund Corporation shall be constituted for the whole country, to be known as the Statutory Committee. This Committee has been formed, and H.R.H. the Prince of Wales has undertaken to act as Chairman of the Committee. The functions of this Statutory Committee are set out in the Act," and the memorandum goes on to give them in detail. Continuing, the statement says, "Section 2 of the Act provides as follows : For the purpose of assisting the Statutory Committee in the execution of their duties a Local Committee shall be established for every County and County Borough, and for every Borough and Urban District having a population of not less than 50,000, the Council of which so desires, and for any other Borough or Urban District for which the Statutory Committee, on the application of the Council thereof, consideres it expedient that, having regard to the special circumstances of the case, a separate Local Committee should be established."

The Swindon Town Council, therefore, set up a Committee of twenty-six members appointed for three years. It held its first meeting on June 22nd, when the Deputy Mayor, Mr. C. Hill, was elected Chairman, and it entered upon its **End of the Prince of Wales' Fund Committee.** duties on July 1st. With the establishment of this Pensions Committee the Prince of Wales' Fund passes from public notice, for the duties hitherto carried out by the Executive Committee of this Fund were transferred to the New Committee. It became one of the most hard-working and important of local public bodies, and, from the nature of its duties, its work was bound to extend to a time long after the war's termination. In reading the account of this Committee's labours, one cannot help being struck by the wisdom that handed over to a body of sympathetic fellow-citizens of the noble fellows who fought and died for their country, the settlement of many painful and pitiful cases, rather than to a distant and slowly moving bureau. The dilatoriness of the military authorities in dealing with pensions and allowances was often a public scandal, but in the Local Committee the claimants found a prompt, just, and sympathetic source of assistance.

(1) Continued on page 130.

The Finance and Grants Sub-Committee. The Pensions Commitee's work was carried on by two sub-committees, the Finance, Grants, and Allowances Sub-Committee and the Disablement Sub-Committee. The Chairman and Vice-chairman (Messrs. C. Hill and W. Parry) of the Pensions Committee acted in those capacities on the Finance Sub-Committee, which dealt with all matters relating to supplementary pensions, grants, and allowances, and was authorised to make grants in certain cases not covered by the Prince of Wales' Fund or other funds; for instance, it could deal with separation allowances to relatives of soldiers who had left motherless children in their care; it could grant supplementary separation allowances to childless wives who were physically unfit for work; dependents who were ineligible for the State separation allowance could be helped by the Committee, and it could grant separation allowances in respect of soldier or sailor sons who used to contribute towards the support of the home. Thus the Committee's scope was wide, and embraced exceptional circumstances not covered by the military pension scheme; the Committee was, however, guided by definite principles laid down for its operations, as, for instance, the instruction that it must not consider increased cost of living as an "exceptional circumstance." As an example of its work, the facts reported in its first monthly report may be quoted:—

Meetings held, —4.

Grants in the 5 weeks ending July 29th :—

122 cases under War Pensions Act	£114	17 9
17 cases under Royal Patriotic Fund	23	2 5
28 civil cases	33	5 0
167 cases	....£171	5 2

Several cases were referred to the Central Statutory Committee with a view to increase of pension.

The Disablement Sub-Committee. The other sub-committee was the Disablement Sub-Committee, of which Ald. A. Haynes was chairman, and Mr. R. M. Forder vice-chairman. It was concerned with provision for disabled officers and men after their discharge from the forces, whether in regard to health or training and employment. The first report stated, "The Disablement Sub-Committee have held six meetings, and interviewed a considerable number of men, with the gratifying result that in nearly every case suitable employment has been found. These men have, where necessary, been granted financial assistance until they have secured work or received the Government temporary allowance or pension." The question of training men became an important subject of consideration, as will be seen when the work of the Committee is more fully treated in the sections dealing with the years 1917 and 1918.

Personnel of the Committee. The Pensions Committee consisted of a large and representative number of members : in October, 1916, they were—

The Mayor (Mr. Morse)	Mr. C. Hill	Mr. A. E. Harding
Mr. A. Haynes	,, W. Parry	,, G. Brooks
,, T. Kimber	,, J. Powell	,, T. Butler
,, G. J. Churchward	,, F. King	,, C. B. Collett
,, R. M. Forder	,, W. S. White	,, W. E. Reeves
,, T. E. Morgan	,, E. C. Ayres	,, W. R. Robins
,, J. S. Protheroe	,, E. Jones	,, L. J. Newman
Mrs. A. E. Jenner	Mrs. L. Baxter	Mrs. E. Whitworth
Miss L. M. Govier	Mrs. E. A. Sandling	

Honorary Secretary—Mr. R. Hilton (Town Clerk).

Treasurer—Mr. A. E. Dean, (Borough Treasurer).

Councillor C. Hill resigned the chair at the close of the year and was succeeded by the new Mayor, Mr. A. J. Gilbert.

Visitation. In order that proper attention might be given to every case the Committee divided the Borough into eight districts, and prepared a rota of visitors to visit periodically all discharged soldiers and sailors in each district. The work thus done by the members of the Committee was most valuable and formed no light portion of their duties. The visitors acted as distributors of the allowances made, and had therefore to go on their rounds weekly ; as the work increased the number of districts had to be doubled, and their work was often the means of bringing to the notice of the Committee special cases of distress arising from the death or serious illness of the wives or dependents of men on service. This system of regular visitation and the payment of all grants at the homes of the recipients illustrate the sympathetic spirit and the thoroughness with which the Pensions Committee carried out its duties. [1].

Protection of Tenants. Although it was no part of the Council's duties to administer the various new orders and acts that were frequently coming into operation, or even to advise the public of their existence, they acted in a very proper manner in deciding in October to notify the public of its rights under the recent Act of Parliament which made it illegal on the part of a landlord to raise the rents of houses let at less than £26 a year. In spite of the Act many landlords were raising rents ; the Trades and Labour Council of Swindon stated that they had found as a result of enquiries that 300 householders had had their rents illegally increased, and the mere fact that enquiries were being made resulted in the refunding of the excess in some instances. It was frequently argued, with some justice, that, whilst others were getting more return for their labour or commodities and the purchasing power of money was falling, the landlord was unfairly treated in being compelled to let his houses at the pre-war rate. In view, however, of the growing inadequacy of housing in such centres as Swindon, it is certain that house-rents would soon have soared to extortionate figures but for this provision, and the equally necessary one which prevented landlords from giving notice to tenants who paid their rent. The act might have been fraught with hardship for a few, but it was a protection to multitudes, and it was the only measure that totally prevented " profiteering " in the object it dealt with. Other acts merely prevented prices going up indefinitely ; this prevented their going up at all.

The New Mayor. Mr. W. E. Morse was succeeded as Mayor by Mr. A. J. Gilbert,[2] who had long been one of the most active members of the Council and one of the most sagacious of Swindon's business men. At the time he accepted office his only son, Mr. Clifford Gilbert, was fighting with the 5th Wiltshires in Mesopotamia, and few citizens had during the last two years done so much as Mr. Gilbert to maintain the patriotic spirit of the Borough.

(1) Continued on page 125.

(2) As this volume goes to press the melancholy news is received that Mr. Gilbert has passed away after a painful illness.

The Mayor's Survey of the year. The retiring Mayor closed his year of office by an admirable survey of the year's work and the financial situation of the Borough, alluding to the energetic way in which the various committees set up for special war-work had carried out their duties,—the Prisoners of War Committee, that for providing Vegetables for the Navy, that for managing the Soldiers' Rest, the one for entertaining the Soldiers' and Sailors' Wives, the Committee for providing entertainments at the Camp, the War Savings Committee, the now defunct Prince of Wales' Fund Committee, and its successor, the Pensions Committee,—and referring to the fresh committees that had had to be formed,—the Recruiting Committee, the Tribunals, the Advisory Committee, the War Charities Committee, and others of lesser degree. The mere recital of the names of these bodies—all working with almost feverish zeal—is strong evidence of the spirit of sacrifice and determination that inspired the people of Swindon at a time when men were anxiously asking, " When will this terrible struggle end ?

The Town's well-being. Can we really overcome a foe like this ? " Mr. Morse also spoke of the general well-being of the Borough, " In Swindon we have every reason to congratulate ourselves on this point. The town is a healthy borough possessing a vigorous community. On three occasions it has had the lowest weekly death-rate in the country. There is no unemployment, there is no distress, there is very little crime, and we have no slums."

The Maternity Centre. This led the Mayor to pay a tribute to the Health Committee's work in regard to child-welfare ; the Maternity Centre which they had established over twelve months before had already proved its need and its worth ; in January, 197 attendances had been registered, while in July the number had risen to 867,—an evidence of the public confidence which had been won. It would be difficult to over-estimate the value of this work in producing the healthy atmosphere needed for the proper upbringing of the children of the town.

The new Mayor entered upon his duties with zest, inaugurating his work with a vigorous " War Savings "campaign that lasted a week. On the last Sunday of the year Mr. Gilbert joined, as his predecessor had done on the first Sunday of the year, in a united Intercession Service at the Parish Church, when the Vicar was again assisted by the Rev. J. E. Simon, of Sanford Street Congregational Church, and also by the Wesleyan Superintendent minister, the Rev. J. Hall.

The Mayor's Christmas. It may not be without interest to notice the Mayor's " Christmas Diary," which will in any case illustrate the demands Swindon makes of its chief magistrate :—

Christmas Eve :—

4.0 p.m.—Soldiers' Rest.

7.30 p.m.—Concert at the Theatre for Xmas gifts to the Forces.

Christmas Day—

9.30 a.m.—Xmas breakfast to old folk at Sanford Street Congregational School.

12 noon—Workhouse.

1.0 p.m.—Children's Homes at Stratton.

1.30 p.m.—Victoria Hospital.

4.0 p.m.—G.W.R. Hospital.

5.0 p.m.—Olive House Children's Home,

and then—Soldiers' Rest, Newport Street.

A Generous
Bequest.

Before leaving 1916, one may remark a very pleasing—and, as far as Swindon is concerned, unusual act of civic benevolence ; for Mr. C. L. Brooke, formerly secretary of the Midland and South Western Joint Railway, left the Borough by his will £800 to apprentice necessitous and deserving boys.

The Committee for the provision of comforts for the Wilts Regiment and its offshoot, the Prisoners of War Committee, having now become involved in the full tide of their work, a suitable point is reached for narrating the history of their labours throughout the war,—a subject well worthy of a separate chapter.

CHAPTER V.

The Care of the Prisoners of War.

Where many committees were working in various directions with unremitting zeal it is hard to select one for special praise, and yet if one had to be singled out few would begrudge the honour if it were awarded to the Prisoners of War Committee. As an offshoot of the Committee formed for the provision of Comforts for the Wiltshire Regiment, it must be dealt with at the same time, but its work became by far the more important branch and came to have the greater claim upon local sympathy.

Inception of the Committee for Comforts for the Wilts. In the beginning of the Autumn of 1914 the Mayor of Swindon, Ald. C. Hill, received an appeal from Lady Heytesbury for gifts for the Wiltshire Regiment, and on October 15th the Swindon Committee for the provision of " Comforts for the Wilts Regiment " was formed. It was composed of the ladies of the Prince of Wales' Committee, and others co-opted by them; the work, therefore, was entirely managed by ladies with the exception, to be noted later, that two or three gentlemen came in to do some of the heavy work connected with the packing.

Officers. The Committee elected as its Chairman Miss Slade, and she retained the position to the close of the Committee's labours; Miss F. K. Coleman was associated with Miss Slade as Hon. Secretary until ill-health compelled her to resign the office in March, 1915, and sincere regret was felt at her untimely death soon afterwards. Miss Coleman was succeeded as Secretary by Miss K. Handley, and it is impossible to speak too highly of the devotion, energy, and skill with which Miss Handley fulfilled the office for four years,—work that gradually grew heavier and more complex, and that needed the most scrupulous care in its details.

The Committee. The Committee for providing " Comforts for the Wilts Regiment " consisted, as has been indicated, of all ladies upon the Prince of Wales' Relief Fund Committee, but not all could find time to devote themselves to this additional work; many others were co-opted both at first and as time went on, so that the working committee gradually settled down to a number of ladies who made this work their special care, along with the small group of gentlemen engaged on the heavier work. The names of these workers will be recorded when mention is made of the more rigid organization required when, in December, 1916, the Red Cross Society was made responsible for what had by then become the more important branch of the work,—the provision of necessities for the Prisoners of War. Moreover, the nature of the work demanded concentration in the hands of those who could attend constantly; division of labour within a limited field was the only way to success.

First Labours. The work for the first three months consisted entirely of making or buying woollen goods and despatching them to the men of the Wilts Regiment at the front. The response to the letter of appeal sent out by the Mayor was immediate, and within three weeks there were forwarded to the regimental depôt at Devizes 90 prs. of mittens, 75 prs. of socks, 100 body-belts, 24 scarves, besides jerseys, helmets, and other articles, and £93 : 3 : 0 in cash had been received. A fortnight later the quantities had increased to 214 prs. of mittens, 224 prs. of socks, 193 body-belts, 122 scarves, 77 cardigans, 134 helmets, 10 vests, 150 handkerchiefs, besides lint, boric powder, vaseline and cigarettes; £100 had been subscribed and was spent mainly on cardigans and wool for the workers.

The Need. It was found that there was pressing need for the articles, for the weather conditions were most trying, not only in Flanders, but also in many of the hastily improvised camps where the mud was an appalling trial and the rain a source of great danger to youths hitherto accustomed to domestic comforts. Undoubtedly these garments were a great boon to the men and many grateful letters from officers of the various companies testify to the appreciation with which they were received.

Kindly Messages. In many instances children sent little notes with the goods they had knitted, and these often called forth delightful responses such as,— "Writing a few lines to thank you for your kind gift, and I must say your father and mother are quite proud of you, and I am quite proud of you too. If God spares me to come home I shall come and see you. I will send you a letter later on. Hoping this letter will find you in the best of health."

Every Thursday evening a great heap of parcels was lying at the Town Hall, waiting for the workers' attention ; many were specially designated,—"To a brave soldier," "To one who has no home," "To one who has received no Christmas present," and so on,—testifying to the tide of sympathy and gratitude that then swept over all classes, whilst the memory of the marvellous deliverance from what had seemed irresistible forces was still fresh in all memories, and before the first enthusiasm was dulled by hope deferred, high prices, scarcity, familiarity with suffering and war-weariness.

Total Comforts from Swindon to the men on Service. It will be convenient to state here the extent of this work—the provision of Comforts for the Wilts Regiment—during the 4¼ years of the Committee's existence. Swindon sent to the depôt at Devizes for despatch to the front—

4463 prs. of socks,	2373 scarves,
1408 prs. of mittens,	758 helmets,
901 knee-caps,	238 belts,

besides a great quantity of miscellaneous comforts and medicaments. But this does not represent all, for Swindon forwarded direct to various local companies that had a claim upon her special interest—

766 pairs of socks,	100 scarves,
44 pairs of mittens,	122 helmets,

32 footballs, and many games. Tobacco and cigarettes were also sent to the fighting units in large quantities. The packing of the goods involved much labour, and in this respect the greatest thanks are due to the army of knitters, to Mrs. Slade for acting as collector and distributor, and to Mrs. Williams for making up the packages.

Inauguration of Work for Prisoners. Until January, 1915, it was not realized that there was any need to send food or clothing to the prisoners of war ; it was assumed that the German Government would fulfil its obligations under international law ; but when letters began to arrive from the men themselves begging for bread, it was soon realized that they were in dire need, and in imminent risk of dying from starvation, exposure, and disease,—an end which the German treatment seemed purposely designed to attain. Many of the articles the Committee was handling were therefore sent to the Prisoners of War, and thus was originated the scheme which undoubtedly saved the lives of many Wiltshiremen, who had the ill-fortune to fall into the hands of a brutal and callous enemy. But at first there was no strict division between the two branches of the work—provision of comforts for the fighting men and the assistance of the prisoners.

Early efforts and Difficulties. At the outset the Committee decided to spend £2 a week on groceries to be sent to Göttingen and other camps where the large number of Wiltshiremen was interned after their capture during the fall of 1914. The Committee had but little cash in hand, and they made appeals to the public for more money and for gifts of bread and groceries. Funds came in but slowly at first, for the general public feared they would be feeding the Germans and that the men would not receive what was sent ; but the publication of the men's responses and the Committee's perseverance in making appeals prevailed, and funds began to come in, whilst the institution of a monthly collection in the Great Western Railway Factory afforded invaluable help. It was only gradually, however, that public confidence was established, and the Committee acted wisely in publishing the men's acknowledgments. Thus the public could read such confirmatory letters as the following :—

Letters of Thanks. " On behalf of myself and the N.C.O.'s and men of the regiment I wish to thank you and all concerned for the parcels which were received by us from you. Needless to say, the contents came in very handy. The men, and myself, will never forget the kindness shown to us by you and the people of Swindon, also by Mrs. Steward, the Barracks, Devizes. I must say we have been treated far better than any other regiment here, and we are proud to think we have such good people looking after us." (*Sergt. C. MacLeod, 1st Wilts, writing to the Town Clerk, Mr. R. Hilton*).

" How well the people of Swindon are responding to the call for money to buy groceries for us ! We get a fine parcel out here every week. We take it in turns to have it, as there is so many here." (*To Miss Slade*).

" Many thanks from the N.C.O.'s and men for bread received in excellent condition. Please would you kindly write to Mrs. Steward and thank her very much for tobacco and cigarettes. In fact anything sent is most thankfully received by the men. They tell me they shower their thanks on the people of Wiltshire for their kindness shown. All are in good health and content under the circumstances." (*The Mayor of Swindon, Mr. W. E. Morse, from Sergt. G. Mills*).

When the system of the transmission of parcels was fully established, most acknowledgments were restricted to an official postcard, such as the following, in which the italics show the part filled in by the prisoner :—

RECEIPT FOR PARCEL.
GÖTTINGEN.

Dear Miss Handley,

I have received your parcel posted *on June 30th,* for which I thank you.

(Signature) *A. Sellwood, Sergt.*

P.S.—It is forbidden to enclose letters in parcels.

These cards varied in form at the different camps; in the one above the front gave the address to which it was sent and on the left of that the details as to the sender,—number, rank, name, regiment, and name of the prison camp. The next differs somewhat from this :—

CAMP OF PRISONERS OF WAR, CASSEL (Germany).
Sender (Name) *Cpl. H. A. Green, 5167, Wilts Regt.*
Company No. *10.* Section No. *116.*

Cassell, *Dec, 4th,* 1916.

Receipt Card.

Dear *Miss Handley,*

Many thanks for parcel of *Oct. 28th,* received *Nov. 28th,* in good condition.

Believe me,
Pte. J. Holland,
Wilts Regt.

It must be observed that nothing was to be learnt of the prisoners' mode of life from the sacksful of letters and postcards—all carefully preserved and docketted by Miss Handley—until the N.C.O.'s were interned in Holland and could write freely.

Numbers. Early in December, just before Mrs. Steward wrote to the Mayor of Swindon, there were 500 men of the 2nd Wiltshires alone imprisoned in Germany, so there was a big field of labour awaiting it when the Committee began its work for the prisoners. By October, 1915, the Committee was sending parcels to 660 men, distributed in various camps as follows :—

Göttingen	332	Münster	152
Wahn	74	Sennelager	25
Doeberitz	40	Hameln	8
Cellelager	8	Suderzollhaus	1
Friedrichsfeld	13	Wittenberg	6
Merseburg	1	Minden	1
Flensburg	1	Ohrdruf	2
Querlinburg	2	Osnabrück	2
Glissen	1	Angora (Turkey)	1

Method. The depôt for collecting and packing the goods was at first located in the Town Hall; bread was the article in greatest demand and an appeal was early made to the bakers and private citizens for gifts of bread : there was a good response; many bakers contributed so many loaves weekly, many private persons gave their bakers orders to send a weekly loaf in their names, and in the schools weekly collections of bread were made, Sanford Street School giving generous help. Every Thursday evening and every Saturday morning the packers met to deal with the goods. The bread was packed in small wooden boxes—three loaves in each box—which were made by Messrs. Mattingly, Nethercot, and Martin from wood supplied on special terms by the Great Western Railway Company ; now and then the demand for the boxes outran the supply and the boys of the Higher Elementary School devoted a lesson or two to making them, or a kindly gift of a few boxes helped to keep up the supply. Many men in the G.W.R. Works also made boxes for the Committee, Mr. Filtness, of Lansdowne Road, making over a thousand ; this help was most timely and was greatly appreciated by the Committee. Members of the Town Hall Staff wrote out the despatch notes, and tradesmen helped with gifts of paper, string and packing.

Parcels for Distribution. In October, 1915, the Committee was sending to prisoners £6 worth of food weekly ; this was insufficient to send a parcel of food to each camp weekly, so parcels were sent every week to the two largest camps in the list already given, and one every seven weeks to the rest ; these parcels alone preserved the men from starving. Up to the end of March, 1915, the Committee had despatched big parcels—40 to Göttingen and 11 to Doeberitz—for distribution by the non-commissioned officers ; by the end of October, 1915, the numbers of big parcels sent for distribution were—

to Göttingen 471 of groceries, 504 of bread ;
„ Doeberitz 25 of groceries, 21 of bread ;
parcels of bread and groceries,—

to Münster	90	to Friedrichsfeld	11
„ Hameln	40	„ Limburg	12
„ Sennelager	47	„ Cellelager	11
„ Wahn	115	„ Wittenberg	2

and to scattered prisoners 23.

Individual Parcels. This system was continued until the end of June, 1916, by which time there had been sent to the prisoners, 1,365 parcels of groceries, 1,419 of bread comprising 4,741 loaves, 38 of clothing, and 15 of books.

By that time it was found that the arrangements were not quite satisfactory to the men away from camp in working parties ; many men had been moved to farms, mines, roads, workshops, and gardens, and were not always easy to communicate with ; the Committee therefore adopted the plan of sending parcels addressed personally to the men, taking them in order ; in the early summer of 1916 a hundred individual parcels per week were being sent off, any one man receiving a parcel about once in seven weeks in addition to what relatives sent him ; each parcel contained five shillings' worth of food. In this way 3,758 individual parcels were despatched in the five months to the end of November, 1916, when the whole system of sending goods to prisoners was re-organized and placed under the control of the Red Cross Society.

The Depôt at the Museum. Before this time the work had grown to such dimensions that a special building was required for the stores and the packing. It must be remembered, also, that the sending of comforts to the regiment was going on regularly at the same time. The depôt was therefore transferred to the Museum in Regent's Circus in December, 1916 ; this building, formerly the Roman Catholic Church, was then being arranged as a museum by Mr. Gore, and the work was proceeding apace, but all his cherished cases were carefully boarded up and hidden by stacks of groceries, tins of meat, boxes, and other goods, and the hall became a ware-house and packing-shed.

Funds. It is obvious, too, that subscriptions must have increased to allow such an expansion of the work, but as no distinction was made between the monies devoted to the comforts for the fighting units and those devoted to the prisoners until 1917, only combined figures can be given, thus—

	RECEIPTS			EXPENDITURE		
	£	s.	d.	£	s.	d.
To June 30th, 1915	 321	9	6	244	19	0
July 1, 1915—June 30, 1916	 778	14	8	781	10	1¼
July 1, 1916—Sept. 30, 1916	213	16	7	213	18	6
Oct. 1, 1916—Dec. 31, 1916	 657	10	5	450	3	9½
	£1971	11	2	£1690	11	4¾

To these monetary contributions must be added the great quantity of gifts in kind ; of the 12,257 loaves sent up to November 30th, 1916, most were given. Until this date parcels were despatched to prisoners by relatives or "adopters"
Adopters. themselves. The Committee had induced many families to "adopt" a prisoner, to whom they sent regular parcels of goods, and similarly certain schools "adopted" one or more prisoners. After November 30th, 1916, under the Red Cross Scheme all these parcels had to be packed and despatched by the Committee itself. In 1915 and 1916 hundreds of people subscribed either by gifts or money for the benefit of men—soldiers or prisoners—in whom they were interested, through the Devizes Committee ; many had "adopted" one, two or more men, paying money to Mrs. Steward for their particular benefit. She sent the names of the men and of the "adopters" to the Swindon Committee, with a statement of the amount paid, but the money does not appear in the Swindon accounts. If relatives and friends brought money to the Swindon Committee direct those sums do enter into the accounts.

The Red Cross Scheme. From December 1st, 1916, the entire organization for sending parcels to prisoners of war was placed by the War Office under the control of the Red Cross Society ; there was need for a change, for whilst some men got plenty, others received but little ; the relatives of some men supplied them generously, others had no friends to send them parcels ; in some parts there was overlapping of organizations ; and it was asserted that there was not sufficient stringency in regard to illicit communications. Now the whole charge of the prisoners was vested in a central committee composed of representatives of the British Red Cross Society, and of the Order of St. John of Jerusalem ; they were to co-ordinate all voluntary efforts and thus prevent overlapping, and were responsible for the prevention of the transmission of any prohibited goods or communications. This central committee authorised an association in any given locality, and no parcel could go except through that association ; it took charge of a certain number of prisoners, and had to send to every prisoner three parcels per fortnight—that is, about 30 lbs. of goods altogether. Elaborate precautions against violations of the rules were taken ; each helper must be a British born subject, vouched for by the Association and given a certificate enabling him to help ; the premises used had to be closed to all others ; and the books and premises were open to government inspection at any time.

The Wiltshire Association. In November, 1916, a meeting of representatives from each district in Wiltshire was held at Devizes to consider the formation of a committee to undertake the care of the Wiltshire prisoners. The number of prisoners was at that time 700, the third largest of any regiment, and the cost for a year's food, estimated at 6/- per parcel, was £17,000. It was decided that each district should be asked to provide a sum proportionate to its rateable value, and the amount allotted to Swindon was £2,855. The Mayor of Swindon for the time being (then Mr. A. J. Gilbert), Miss Slade and Miss K. Handley were elected as representatives on the county committee from Swindon, and Mrs. Steward, reviewing the work already done in the county, spoke most highly of the work done by the Swindon Committee and hoped they would continue their labours as a branch of the County body.

The Swindon Committee. The Swindon Committee at once accepted the responsibility laid upon it, and asked for permission to send parcels to 87 Swindon men of the regiment; they received permission, and on December 12th despatched the first batch of parcels. The new conditions now demanded a definite body of certificated workers, and thus a specific " packing Committee " had to be formed. The members were at first:—

Mrs. Bull	Miss J. E. Handley	Miss Slade
,, Mattingly	,, K. Handley	,, G. E. Smith
,, F. Morris	,, M. Hill	,, Tallyn
,, S. Nethercot	,, Hilton	,, E. White
,, S. J. Thomas	,, Kent	,, C. H. Williams
,, Perrin	,, V. Kinneir	Mr. Mattingly
,, Tute	,, Pickett	,, S. Nethercot
Miss Gover	,, Rowe	,, Perrin.

Certificates had also to be given to the curator of the museum, Mr. Gore, to enable him to go in and out, to Mr. Haynes, the caretaker, and to the cleaner, Mrs. Fry.

Later on there were added to the Packing Committee—

Miss Crofts	Miss E. Stevens	Mr. W. R. Jones
,, E. Gee	,, E. Strean	,, F. Smith
,, Harding	Mr. J. Adams	,, Jos. Williams.
,, M. Hartley		

Method. The goods for transmission to prisoners of war were allowed to be purchased free of duty, and the accounts had to be kept separate from those relating to comforts for the Wiltshire Regiment. In purchasing goods the Committee had at first worked on a rota of shopkeepers (including the Co-operative Society), dividing the orders as evenly as possible throughout the town; but at length the inequality of the prices charged at different establishments and the growing stringency of the food situation compelled the Committee to resort to wholesale buying. Furthermore, the Central Prisoners of War Committee received special privileges from Government, and was thus enabled to supply the branches at shippers' rates with goods already packed suitably for despatch. The goods were obtained to a large extent through the Central Prisoners of War Committee in West Kensington and the British Red Cross Society's branch at Bristol, and the most minute accuracy was demanded in the accounts, every half-ounce of tobacco, sugar, tea, cocoa, jam, syrup, etc., having to be accounted for. The depôt was now a bonded store, and special accounts of all dutiable goods had to be kept, as weekly and quarterly inspections were made by government officials. Mr. Mattingly kept the ordinary stock accounts till he was called up on military service, and then Mr. Nethercot undertook the duty. Precise instructions as to packing and labelling had to be followed, and only the official label could be used; the label is here reproduced in fac-simile:

Donor'sName and Address Name und Wohnort des Gebers.	Kriegsgefangenensendung.
	Packed and despatched by **The Wiltshire Regiment Prisoners of War (Swindon Branch),** under authority granted by the Central Prisoners of War Committee of the British Red Cross Society and the Order of St. John of Jerusalem in England. *Verpackt und versendet mit der Autorisierung des Central Komite fur Kriegsgefangene des Britischen Roten Kreuzes und der Vereinigung St. Johannes von Jerusalem in England.*

CONTENTS.　INHALT.	Parcel No. and Date of Despatch.........................
	BRITISCHER KRIEGSGEFANGENER. **WILTSHIRE REGIMENT.** **GERMANY.**

Inside the parcel were placed two postcards, already addressed, one to the Secretary of the Swindon Committee and one to the prisoner's " adopter " ; these were for the prisoner's acknowledgment of the receipt of the parcel, and in order that both he and the Committee might know whether he was receiving his parcels regularly the cards were stamped with the date and the number of the parcel ; here is one of the returned cards :—

No. 127.　　　　　ACKNOWLEDGMENT.
25-7-18.　　　　　　　　　　　　Oct. 6th, 1918.
　　　　Sirs,
　　　　　I beg to thank you very much for parcel No. 127,
which I received with the following things.
1lb. of Biscuits　　　　1 tin of Salmon
¼ lb. of Tea　　　　　1 tin of Pudding
1 tin of Jam　　　　　½lb. of Rice
1 tin of Dripping
1 tin of Milk　　　　　　　Yours sincerely,
1 tin of Army Ration　　　　Pte. H. R. Brooks.

Then, beside the Red Cross label already described, the parcel bore an English (Swindon) label and another was placed inside the parcel ; thus every care was taken to ensure its reaching the proper quarter.

Raising the Money. The responsibility of raising £2,855 for the year was great and called for special effort. The Mayor, Mr. A. J. Gilbert, issued through the press an appeal for subscriptions, and addressed a meeting of the collectors in the Great Western Railway Works, when they decided to give their fortnightly collections to the Prisoners of War Fund ; he also approached the Chamber of Commerce and employers of labour, asking for regular collections to be made in works and business houses. The Committee also organized a weekly house-to-house collection, 130 ladies being enrolled for this duty,—one not always pleasant, and calling for much patience and self-denial. A Treasurer was now needed, and Miss M. Withy acted in this capacity for a short time, being followed by Miss Gover, than whom a more competent and devoted officer could not have been found ; the treasurer attended at the Town Hall twice weekly to receive the contributions. The result exceeded the promise. When Miss Handley presented her report in December, 1917, she was able to announce a total of £3,075 : 8 : 8 for the Prisoners of War Fund and £359 : 5 : 5 for the comforts for the fighting men. Of this large sum £932 : 12 : 11¼ came from the collections in the Great Western Railway Works, £626 : 13 : 6¼ from the house-to-house collections, and £386 : 11 : 5 from the Chamber of Commerce. Many special efforts had added considerably to the amount collected ; to mention a few only,—there were the Mayor's Flag Day, Mr. A. Manners' concerts and matinee at the theatre, the Wags' concert, Mr. Kenneth Ellis's concert, the football match between

Total Raised Under the Red Cross Scheme. the Tidworth and Chiseldon teams, the sports of the Worcester Regiment, and the collections made in the schools. Until the close of the Committee's work the same steady effort had to be made, and the results were as given below.

Period	General Fund divided into		(a) Comforts Fund		(b) Pris. of War Fund.	
	Receipts	Expenditure	Receipts	Expenditure	Receipts	Expenditure
Jan. 1, 1917 Mar. 31, 1917	£ s. d. 1078 2 4	£ s. d. 929 10 5	£ s. d. 100 0 0	£ s. d. 74 19 4	£ s. d. 355 0 0	£ s. d. 414 13 7
April 1—June 30, 1917	1591 7 6	1768 16 6	100 0 0	33 5 9	1832 19 11	1437 2 5½
July 1—Nov. 30, 1917	1197 18 4½	1004 10 8	125 0 0	150 16 0	1599 1 0½	1239 4 4½
Dec. 1, 1917— Feb. 28, 1918.	734 3 11	808 4 11½	100 0 0	24 8 11	901 7 6	950 9 3
Mar. 1—May 31, 1918	847 0 2½	499 4 10	....	41 2 6	1090 19 1	873 13 9
Jun. 1—Aug. 31, 1918	859 16 6	920 10 0	....	62 0 3	1570 5 4	1406 14 1
Sept. 1—end.	1022 4 10	1368 16 2	50 0 0	50 0 0	1377 14 7	2865 13 4

Total During the 4½ years of the Committee's work Swindon raised the
Raised splendid sum of £10,967 : 3 : 0 for the fund. Of this amount the
During Great Western Railway Works raised £3,252 : 6 : 4, first by monthly
the War. collections, then by fortnightly collections in response to the Mayor's
    appeal, and then by weekly collections when in 1918 Mr. A. W. Haynes,
who succeeded Mr. A. J. Gilbert as Mayor, asked for further support in consequence
of increased prices and the larger number of prisoners.   Then the house-to-house
collections inaugurated in February, 1917, brought in £1612 : 9 : 6, 105 ladies continuing to call regularly for subscriptions and handing their cards to Miss
Gover every Thursday or Saturday evening.   The Chamber of Commerce contributed
£786 : 9 : 4 from the business houses of the town and the money raised by its Waste
Paper Scheme. Mr. A. Manners was instrumental in adding £767 : 8 : 2 by
collections at the Empire Theatre; the Flag Days for the fund brought in £263 : 1 : 3 ;
the clothing and munition factories made splendid contributions, while the children
of the schools must not be omitted, for in some cases they were the most regular
of all subscribers.

    In the disposal of this huge sum the Committee spent £1,091 : 9 : 6½
How on comforts for the regiment, and was left in December, 1918, with a
Allotted. balance of £58 : 13 : 5. The expenditure on Prisoners of War came
    to £9,444 : 9 : 5¾ of which £1,372 : 10 : 0 had been received in grants
from the County Committee at Devizes, making Swindon's contribution to the
expenditure £8,072 : 3 : 5¾; this branch, however, was left with a huge stock in hand,
and the proceeds nearly paid off the advances from Devizes, so that Swindon can
claim to have defrayed practically the whole of the nine thousand odd pounds spent.

    These figures illustrate the growth of the work ; from £2 weekly spent in
February, 1915, the weekly expenditure had risen to £210 in October, 1918, and
this alone speaks volumes for the persistence, devotion, and self-sacrifice of those
who carried on the work. The work was all purely voluntary and freely given,
but the reward of the workers is the certain knowledge that the lives of many of
their fellows were saved by their efforts ; over 90% of the parcels reached their
owners in good condition, and the men say that but for them they could never
have returned to England.

Nos. of The prisoners handed over to Swindon's care under the Red Cross
Swindonian Scheme in December 1916 were, as has been said, just under 90 in
Prisoners. number, and they kept in the neighbourhood of that figure till the
    German offensive of March 1918, when a rapid increase began ; in
    October the Committee was packing 274 fifteen-pound parcels weekly.
Total No. Altogether, under the Red Cross Scheme, they packed and sent off
of Parcels 16,914 parcels weighing 79 tons 9 cwt ; to these must be added the
sent. 6,580 parcels of 11 lbs. and over sent during 1915 and 1916,
    and then one can get some idea of the magnitude of the effort
made and of the patience and constancy of those ladies and gentlemen whose
perseverance never faltered through those long years.

    The Red Cross Scheme was efficient ; it attained its end ; but the
Reassuring relatives of the unfortunate men felt it hard that they could not do
Relatives. for their men what they would have liked to do ; they could not
    appreciate the need of all this " red tape " and they feared that their
loved ones were not being well and regularly fed. To allay their apprehensions the
Committee sent out the subjoined invitation :

TOWN HALL,
SWINDON,
16th Aug., 1917.

Wiltshire Regiment Care Committee.

SWINDON BRANCH.

DEAR SIR OR MADAM,

His Worship the Mayor (Mr. A. JOHN GILBERT) and the above Committee have decided to invite the Wives and Children of the Swindon Prisoners of War, and two of the Nearest Relatives of the Unmarried Prisoners, to a SOCIAL GATHERING at the Town Hall, on Wednesday, 29th August, at 6.30 p.m., to 9.0 o'clock.

Yours faithfully,
MARY E. SLADE, *Chairman.*
K. M. HANDLEY, *Hon. Sec.*

A very interested and grateful audience listened to an account of the Committee's methods and inspected the stores and arrangements for packing, and thus a good deal of misapprehension was removed. Furthermore, measures were taken to allow them to do a little personally for their men's comfort by means of a "personal parcel" sent occasionally through the Committee. The

Quarterly "Personal Parcels." circular sent from head-quarters governing the special parcel is very definite as to its character ; it runs as follows—

Wiltshire Regimental Care Committee.

DEVIZES,
November, 1917.

The War Office has now sanctioned the sending of a "Personal Parcel" to prisoners by the relatives under the following conditions :—

1. Any of the articles noted below may be included.

Pipe	Handkerchiefs (one a	Clothes Brushes
Sponge	quarter)	Buttons
Pencils	Shaving Soap (one	Chess
Tooth Powder	stick a quarter)	Draughts
Pomade	Insecticide Powder	Dominoes
Cap Badge and	Braces and Belts (pro-	Dubbin
Badges of Rank	vided they are made	Hobnails
Shaving Brush	of webbing and in-	Sweets
Safety Razor	clude no rubber or	Medal Ribbons
Bootlaces (Mohair)	leather)	Brass Polish
Pipe Lights	Combs	Mittens and Mufflers
Housewife	Hair Brushes	(one pair each every
Health Salts	Tooth Brushes	quarter)

2. The "Personal Parcel" may be sent once a quarter only. The maximum weight is 11 lbs. It is advised that such parcels should not weigh less than 3 lbs. so as to minimize the risk of loss in the post.

3. It may not be packed and despatched by any authorised Association and must not bear the Red Cross label. It must be packed and despatched through the Post Office by the friend or relative of the prisoner who receives the coupon to be mentioned below, and the coupon must be affixed to the parcel.

4. A supply of coupons has been issued by the Central Prisoners of War Committee to this Committee, and one of these coupons will be furnished by us in the case of each prisoner once a quarter on application.

5. The next-of-kin of the Prisoner has the right to the coupon or to designate the person to whom it is to be given.

6. The scheme will come into force on the 1st December, 1917.

7. Applicants should note that the inclusion in the parcel of any article not mentioned in the above list may entail the confiscation of the parcel.

The County As the Swindon Committee was, under the Red Cross Scheme, a
Committee's branch of the County Association, a few words are needed as to the
Success. way in which the County Scheme had worked. It was seen that
in the first year the new plan entailed the raising of £17,000, allotted
to the various districts according to their rateable value. Practically every Urban
and Rural District responded splendidly, and at the close of the year (1917) the
income was nearly double what had been asked for, made up as follows :—

	£	s.	d.
Balance handed over by Mrs. Steward	854	7	7
Contributions from the Districts	19,839	13	10
From " adopters " and others outside the Co., ...	12,455	1	8
Bank Interest	145	14	4
	£33,294	17	5

Nearly 58,000 parcels had been despatched to prisoners during the year, and
£25,962 : 15 : 10 had been expended, leaving a satisfactory balance to start the
new year's work. The average number of prisoners provided for was about 690,
but towards the end of the year the number was substantially reduced by the
transfer of men to Holland, and at the year's close stood at about 600. Having looked
into the prospective needs for the next year, the Committee again asked for the
raising of £17,000.

The Heavy The events of the Spring of 1918 completely overthrew the Com-
increase of mittee's plans, and at a meeting held at Trowbridge in June, under
1918. the presidency of Lord Roundway, a serious increase in the number
of prisoners was revealed,—no less than 1,100 odd, making the total
to be provided for about 1,700 officers and men. The Committee
therefore had to make a special appeal for £55,000.

Support The sum seemed a large one to aim at, but Mr. A. J. Gilbert,
from representing Swindon, along with Miss Slade and Miss Handley,
Swindon. supported the issue of the appeal and was confident that Swindon
would do its share. When the representatives from Swindon had
reported the state of affairs at home, the Mayor issued the following
weighty appeal to the Borough :

WILTSHIRE REGIMENT.
Prisoners of War in Germany.

In March last I made an earnest appeal to all sections of the Community on behalf
of the 700 or 800 men of the Wiltshire Regiment who are prisoners of war in Germany, in
which I stated that the sum desired to be raised by Swindon would not be less than £3,000.

Since then about 1,500 additional men of the Wiltshire Regiment have been made
Prisoners of War. As a consequence the calls on the Fund for sending parcels to the men
have been more than doubled. The regulations require that three parcels of food per
fortnight should be sent to every man, and the cost of each parcel is now at least 9s. It
is estimated, therefore, that the cost for the year 1918 will be not less than £58,000. Towards
this there is a surplus of about £4,000 brought forward from last year (which has been
temporarily invested by the County Committee), and the sum of about £15,000 which is
expected to be received from adopters and others outside Wiltshire, leaving £39,000 to
be raised throughout the County. Swindon is, therefore, asked to increase its contribution
from £3,000 to £6,000. It is hoped that some relief may eventually be obtained from the
arrangements which are now under consideration for the exchange of Prisoners of War ;
but, under the circumstances, it will be a considerable time before any relief is obtained in
consequence of the return of Prisoners from Germany.

It is my unfortunate duty, therefore, to make an urgent appeal to the inhabitants of Swindon to increase their already very generous contributions to this Fund.

Recent reports shew the deplorable conditions under which many of these men are living, and the necessity for sending them food in order to keep them alive.

Under the circumstances I feel sure, great as the burden is, Swindon will not be behind the rest of the County in providing the funds to enable the necessary succour to be sent to our brave men who are suffering so much on our behalf.

In making this further appeal I should like once again to thank all sections of the community for their generous support of the fund in the past.

A. W. HAYNES, Mayor.

Town Hall, Swindon,
9th August, 1918.

The Balance after the Armistice. Fortunately, events falsified the anticipation that "it would be a considerable time before any relief would be obtained in consequence of the return of prisoners from Germany,"and the County Committee was not only able to carry on its work until the Armistice, but when all was cleared up—a process that took a very long time—the Committee found itself with a balance of £11,000 in hand. Of this sum £3,400 was money sent by "adopters," and it was decided that this sum should go to the Prisoners of War Care Committee at Devizes for them to dispose of. They determined to devote the money to the Wilts Regiment Old Comrades' Association Fund,—a fund that existed for the purpose of helping the men of the regiment, as, for instance, when they needed a little assistance upon their discharge to enable them to set up in business, and so forth. Colonel Steward was the Chairman of the Old Comrades' Association and Devizes was its headquarters.

This left a sum of £7,600 to be disposed of,—money that had been subscribed from all parts of the County; it was only fair that the places that had subscribed should be consulted as to the disposal of this sum; letters were therefore sent out asking whether the money should be returned to the associations, pro rata, so that they could use it as seemed best in their own localities, or whether it should be managed by a joint committee, or given to the Old Comrades' Association. Ten branches chose the "pro rata" scheme, two supported the idea of a joint committee, and two favoured giving the money to the Old Comrades' Association,

The Last Meeting. whilst five branches sent up other suggestions. And now a curious situation arose; a meeting of delegates was called at Trowbridge on December 19th, 1919, attended on behalf of Swindon by the Mayor (Mr. S. Walters), Miss Slade and Mr. A. J. Gilbert, and the question was put to the vote; only delegates present were allowed to vote, the written replies being ignored; the more distant branches had not sent delegates in many instances, and thus a different electorate was now voting upon the subject, with the result that by fifteen votes to six it was decided to form a joint committee.

The Joint Committee. The Joint Committee was formed of six representatives of the Wiltshire Prisoners of War Fund and six of the Old Comrades' Association. The six representatives of the Wilts Prisoners of War Fund were,—the Mayors of Salisbury and Swindon for the time being, the Rev. H. Sanders, of Trowbridge, Mrs. Steward, Mrs. Hogan, of Warminster, and Mr. Howard Bell (of Seend).

The money, capital and interest, was to be expended for the benefit of men of the Wiltshire Regiment, so that the practical outcome was that this £7,600 was expended in the same way as the £3,400, only differing in the fact that in the case of the larger sum persons outside the Old Comrades' Association had a voice in the disposal of the money.

The result did not meet the desires of the Swindon Branch, for it was felt that the money which would have been returned to Swindon could have been most advantageously employed for the benefit of the many Swindon men who had been in the Wilts Regiment, and whose needs would be best known by the Swindon Committee.

Release of the N.C.O's. Early in 1918 an arrangement was made whereby non-commissioned officers were interned in Holland, and then more detailed letters began to arrive, of which the three following will serve as examples—

Scheveningen, Holland.
18/3/18.

Dear Miss Handley,—No doubt you will be surprised and pleased to hear that I have arrived in Holland after being in Germany 3½ years. I wish to thank you and the committee for the great kindness you all have shown to me during the time I have been in Germany. If it was not for the parcels you sent to me I would have had a very hungry time indeed, in fact I think I would have been starved to death, if I had to live only on German rations, and I am sure you cannot realise how thankful I am to you all. We cannot realise our good fortune in being here, after so long a time in Germany, where we were being continually punished because we were Englishmen, because the Germans hate us more than any other nation. Well, I must not bore you with my misfortunes, so I will close. Again thanking you all for your great kindness to me,

I remain,
Yours sincerely,
E. J. TALBOT,
Lance-Corporal.

Scheveningen,
14/3/18.

Dear Miss Handley,—It is with great pleasure that I write these few lines to let you know we are at last out of Germany, also to thank you for the comforts and all those kind gifts received from the Swindon Branch of the Wiltshire Care Committee, and for the excellent way in which they have looked after us with reference to food. I can say without fear of contradiction that since the New Scheme was started your parcels have at least been as good as any I have seen. We have here two men who were receiving the same kind of parcels as myself; they are both Swindon lads—namely, Sergts. Sellwood and Matthews, who agree with me in my opinion of your parcels, without which we should all have been poor specimens of humanity by now. Not wishing to waste your valuable time, I will close this brief note, again thanking you for all you have done for us during our long stay in captivity.

I remain,
Yours sincerely,
J. COOMBS, Lance-Sergt.

Scheveningen, Holland,
March 17th, 1918.

Dear Miss Slade—Will you please convey and accept my very best sincere thanks to the ladies and friends who asisted you in sending the parcels I was always very grateful to receive. I am very pleased to say they were second to none that came into the country, and I am sure that a lot of thought must have been taken in considering the contents. I must apologise for what may have appeared very abrupt remarks on the acknowledgment cards, but a few words will easily explain. In different camps the regulation as regards correspondence varies, and in many cases we were only supposed to write three words on them, and so of course I had to curtail them accordingly. I left Hameln for Aachen on the 8th inst., from which place the exchange took place on the 11th inst. At Colin, which is the first station, we were met by many ladies who had sandwiches and coffee for us. Unfortunately we were not allowed to cheer entering the station, as there had been previous demonstrations by the parties who had come before us when they were getting rid of the German Hun. I need not mention we made up for it when we were leaving it. We arrived here about 10.30 p.m. The streets to the hotel were lined with our comrades. After a terrible amount of handshaking we eventually arrived at the hotel. There we were met by the General in Command and various other officials, the General reading their Majesties the King and Queen's speech, and after various other speeches we eventually sat down to dinner. A great deal of care must have been taken in arranging for our coming. I must ask you to excuse this scrawl, as it is nearly four years since I had the privilege of handling a pen, so again thanking you for your kindness, I will close with very best wishes.

Yours sincerely,

WALTER G BULL, Sergeant.

Such letters as these are precious mementos both of sufferings bravely endured by Swindon men, and unflinching devotion to a sacred task by Swindon women and men.

Return of the Prisoners. Their treatment in Germany. When the Armistice was signed and the men began to get back home from imprisonment, their stories confirmed the meagre hints that had been gathered from other sources as to the ill-treatment of many and the dire need of all during their imprisonment. Mr. T. Saddler said, "had it not been for the parcels received out there from Great Britain we should have been starved," all they had given them was one slice of brown bread for breakfast and one for tea—and nothing on it; " we had a bowl of soup for dinner, which I can honestly say would not have been eaten by a dog or a pig. That was all we had served out to us in **" Luxurious "** camp by the Germans. When we received the parcels from England **Parcels.** they contained nothing but what was a luxury to us. If I told you what these parcels contained it would really surprise you, and it would do you good to see how the boys enjoyed it."

Sergt. Jerram, of the 6th Wiltshires, said the ration at his camp was a quarter of a loaf per day, and "a drop of what they call coffee, which is really made of burnt barley ground up, without milk or sugar." This had to last till 6.30 p.m., except that at midday they had a soup made of dried vegetables and water, with a bit of horse-flesh thrown in occasionally. One morning, at 6.30, when **The Brutal** the men were ordered to go to the workshop they refused to go unless **Guard.** given more bread. The guard was turned out with fixed bayonets, but meanwhile the men had gone to the workshop. The guard, however, turned them out, bayoneting one man through the arm the full length of the bayonet, and knocking others down with the butts of their rifles. This was followed by rigorous punishment consisting of nine hours marching per day, prohibition of smoking or conversation, and stoppage of all packages from home, till the non-commissioned officers—exempt by international law from forced labour—were driven to give in.

A Wanton Sword-cut. Lance Sergt. Sellwood (2nd Wilts) describes how a German Field Marshal wantonly slashed a prisoner, whom he named, with his sword whilst the men were marching along in a perfectly orderly manner. He also was forced to work at turning virgin soil on the moors, having been sent with a large number of other non-commissioned officers to a punishment camp in order that they might be compelled to work.

Such experiences might be multiplied many times from the narratives of the returned men, and in the relations of each the only bright spot is usually the reception of the parcels from home. No excuses can palliate the brutal treatment meted out to the poor fellows ; they found it on the railway and on the road as well as in the camps ; they were deprived of the veriest necessities, forced in many instances to live in the most debasing conditions, and subjected often to revolting **An Album** brutality. There was shown round Swindon at one time an album **of Views.** of views in one camp, showing a clean, jovial, and well cared-for set of prisoners in nice surroundings. When the young man who had sent it was questioned on his return, he said, " You see, ours was a ' show-camp ' ; things were really awful at first and I could tell you of dreadful things ; then when the Americans came to have a look round we were spruced up a great deal for the purpose of impressing them ; then when the Germans were getting short of men we were formed into a self-governing camp, and things went on very nicely, except that we couldn't get food, and it was the parcels from home that kept us going." But all the men were not in " show-camps," and many will carry to their dying day the marks of their cruel imprisonment in bodily or mental injury.

The Mayor's Welcome. Great was the relief when the prisoners were released, and it gave additional pleasure to the people of Swindon to have then back for Christmas. The Mayor, Alderman C. A. Plaister, addressed to each a letter of welcome and an invitation to meet him at the Museum to receive a Christmas parcel which had been packed ready for despatch to Germany before the Armistice was signed :

Town Hall, Swindon,
19th December, 1918.

Dear Sir,

I understand that you have just returned to Swindon on furlough after being a Prisoner of War in Germany for some considerable time. On behalf of the inhabitants of Swindon I desire to give you a hearty welcome home and to assure you that we have not been unmindful of your sufferings while in Germany.

We have all read with horror of the brutalities practised by the Germans on our Prisoners of War, many of whom have died, and whose bodies are now resting in foreign soil.

I think we can rest assured that when the peace terms are finally settled one of the conditions will be the exacting of adequate punishment of all those who so cruelly illtreated our men while prisoners of war in their hands.

I trust that with the comforts of home you will soon be restored to your usual health and strength.

In due course, I hope it will be my privilege and pleasure on behalf of the town to welcome at an official gathering all the men of Swindon who have been prisoners of war in Germany, when the town generally will be able to show its appreciation of your services, and its sympathy with your sufferings on behalf of your country,

Accompanying this letter is a small gift from the Wilts Regiment Prisoners of War Committee, which is similar to some of the parcels sent to our men while in Germany. I trust you will find this acceptable.

With every good wish, believe me,
Yours faithfully,
C. A. PLAISTER, Mayor.

On Monday afternoon, December 23rd, the men responded to the Mayor's invitation by meeting at the Packing Depôt at the Museum, which was gay with flags and bunting. They were delighted to meet again old comrades and to compare notes ; two had returned only that day from Lagensalza, and many had been more than four years in captivity in various camps in Germany. The men much appreciated the Christmas parcels and the Mayor's letter of welcome, and Sergt. A. Sellwood gave expression to their feeling in a short speech, ending with the remark that, " without the parcels the majority of them would never have returned to England."

Official Reception and Dinner. The official welcome of the repatriated men took place on Tuesday evening, January 21st, 1919, when about 400 returned prisoners and their friends' were entertained at dinner in the Large Swimming Baths. Rarely has the building presented so gay an aspect. Mr. A. J. Gilbert had lent flags and Mr. and Mrs. Nethercot had designed and executed a large number of very beautiful emblems, recalling places where the heroism of the Wiltshire Regiment had won renown in the great war ; amidst flags drooping from the balcony were the names of these battlefields in great white letters,—unforgettable names: Mons, Ypres, Cambrai, the Aisne, the Somme, Gallipoli, Salonika, Mesopotamia, Palestine, the Piave, and East Africa. The roof was hung with a shower of pendent decorations, a string band was playing from the platform encircled with plants and emblems, and thirteen huge tables were decked with flowers and other decorations.

All ex-prisoners of war were invited to the dinner, and many heart-burnings were soothed by the opportunity afforded for clearing away mis-understandings. There were Swindon men who felt aggrieved that no parcels had been sent to them, until they learned that the Committee was absolutely prevented from sending to any but men of the Wiltshire Regiment. Others thought the Government should have sent to them and should not have left the work to a voluntary body, and it had to be made clear that under the arrangements that existed the Government was prohibited from packing and the work had to be voluntary.

Representatives of the Hosts. The Mayor, Ald. C. A. Plaister, presided at the first table, supported on his right by Major F. P. Goddard and having the Mayoress on his left, next to whom sat Brig. Gen. Calley, C.B., M.V.O.; a large number of supporters of the cause sat with them—the " War Mayors," Mr. C. Hill, Lieut. W. E. Morse, Mr. A. J. Gilbert, and Ald. A. W. Haynes, with the Ex-mayoresses; Sir. Fredk. Young, M.P.; the Vicar of Swindon, the Rev. C. A. Mayall; the Town Clerk, Mr. R. Hilton; the Rev. J. H. Gavin, whose strenuous work for the soldiers in Swindon and in France had endeared him to many; Mr. A. E. Withy; Mr. T. Butler; Lieut. Col. Stewart; Mr. A. J. L. White; Mr. T. H. Chandler; Lieut. Chandler; Mr. Young; Police Supt. Moore; Lieut. A. J. Jones; Mr. F. Ayres; the Rev. Father Cashman; Mr. W. Johnson; Capt. Arkell; Mr. Arkell; Mr. R. M. Forder; Mr. Hemmins; Lieut. Hemmins; Mr. F. Reeves; Mrs. Stewart; Mrs. F. P. Goddard; Mrs. Calley; Mrs. Gavin; Mrs. A. Hart; Miss Withy; Mrs. Johnson; Mrs. Reeves; and representatives of the press.

The tables were served by the members of the Prisoners of War Committee and their friends, and the dinner was one worthy of the occasion; then followed appropriate toasts and speeches, the Mayor taking occasion to address a hearty welcome home to the men, and Sir. F. Young pronouncing a warm eulogy upon the Wiltshire Regiment. But probably no speech went more to the hearts of the men than Major Goddard's tribute of gratitude to the ladies who for over four years had worked so arduously on their behalf, and the toast to them, coupled with the names of Miss Slade and Miss K. Handley, was drunk with generous applause.

Honour to a Zeebrugge Hero, His Worship then rose to do honour to a native of Swindon who shared in the glorious action that blocked up Zeebrugge harbour on April 23rd, 1918, when the *Vindictive* covered herself with glory. Mr. Plaister's predecessor in the mayoral office had presented gold watches to three Swindonians who had shared in the enterprise, and now he handed to a fourth, Pte. F. J. Gee, a similar token of admiration on behalf of the Borough.

and to Workers for the Soldiers. Another pleasing presentation followed, the Mayoress handing Queen Victoria Red Cross Certificates to Miss Slade, Miss Handley, and Miss Gover, officers of the Committee, and Mrs. Bull, Mrs. Thomas, Mrs. A. Hart, Mrs. F. Morris, Mrs. Perrin, Mr. Mattingly, Mrs. Tute, Miss J. Handley, Miss Rowe, Miss C. Williams, Miss White, Miss Pickett, Miss Kent, Miss Smith, Miss Challen, Miss Hill, Miss Kinneir, Mr. S. Nethercot, Mr. Perrin, and Mr. Jones. The Certificate ran as follows :—

THE BRITISH RED CROSS SOCIETY.

To ....

It is a sincere pleasure to me to learn that at a Meeting of the Council of the British Red Cross Society, held at St. James's Palace, your name has been inscribed upon the Roll of Honourable Service.

I cordially congratulate you upon your good work, and gratefully thank you for your services in connection with the Cause which I have so much at heart.

ALEXANDRA

SEAL   *Date*.............................19................

This certificate is the only material reward that was received by any of the workers, but it will be treasured highly by a band of workers whose sole motive was love and pity for their brethren, regardless of any reward.

The gathering was enlivened by a delightful concert given by several of Swindon's most talented singers, and the guests departed declaring they had never passed a happier evening.

It may be mentioned at this point that a few months later (on July 25th, 1919) the King and Queen entertained at Buckingham Palace representatives of war-work associations throughout the country, when Miss Slade and Miss Handley represented the Swindon Prisoners of War Committee. The King and Queen spent nearly three hours with their guests, and other members of the Royal Family were present ; everything was done to make the visitors feel quite at ease ; their Majesties conversed with many, two military bands were in attendance, and refreshments were served in marquees erected in the grounds. It was interesting to note that quite two-thirds of the guests were women.

Clearing Up. This dinner practically brought to a close the Committee's labours, though there was a great deal to be done in the way of " clearing-up." As has been said, the Committee was left with a great stock of goods on hand, and these had to be disposed of ; sales were held at the Town Hall, the Museum, and the Market, until quite £900 worth of the stores had been sold locally, and then the central Committee took over the rest for £1,073 : 13 : 5½. Some idea of the fare sent out to the prisoners may be gained from the list of articles advertised for sale :

Tinned sausages and onions....	....	....	....	18 /6 per doz.
Libby's corned beef	....	....	....	16 /6 ,,
Harris's Camp pies (bacon)	....	....	....	15 /9 ,,
Harris's " Sunset " sausages	....	....	....	16 /3 ,,
Morton's Oxford sausages	....	....	....	13 /8 ,,
Libby's loaf goods (medium size)	....	....	....	16 /6 ,,
Preserved beef	....	....	....	14 /- ,,
Beef stew (1lb. net)	....	....	....	12 /- ,,
Morton's Army rations	....	....	....	12 /9 ,,
Chivers' Army rations	....	....	....	16 /9 ,,
Meat and potato puddings	....	....	....	11 /10½,,
Sausage and potato puddings	....	....	....	10 /4½ ,,

Maconochie's fresh herrings	....	....	....	13/6 per doz.
Blanchflower's fresh herrings	....	....	....	13/1 ,,
Pilchards and tomato (1lb.)	....	....	....	16/9 ,,
Butter beans	....	....	....	....	8/- ,,
Baked beans	....	....	....	....	6/4½ ,,
Rhubarb puddings	....	....	....	10/10½,,

In addition to these there were numerous other articles, including a large stock of tobacco and 70,000 cigarettes ; as these last were obtained duty free they could not be sold and were amongst the things returned to the Central Committee. After paying off all outstanding accounts, the Committee had a balance of over £1,000 to return to Devizes in repayment of the advances they had received, which, it has already been seen, amounted to £1,372 : 10 : 0.

Conclusion. Few places can show a nobler record in this connection than Swindon and Wiltshire. The Wiltshires were one of the most heavily smitten territorial regiments of the army ; if the County had refused to care for its own prisoners—and it might have argued that it ought not to be expected to do more than other counties,—they would not have been neglected ; but the men would have missed the note of personal interest that was present in what was done for them, and it was an additional joy to feel, whenever a parcel came, that it came from home ; and so those at home accepted as a privilege and honour the duty of providing for the men of the Wiltshire Regiment, and it is a source of pride that they did this without growing weary of the work or passing on the expense to strangers.

List of the Prisoners. By the courtesy of Miss Handley it has been possible to give at full the list of Swindon men who were Prisoners of War, so far as the Wiltshire Regiment was concerned. The first ninety-two are those for whom the Committee was packing in January 1918, and the rest are those who were captured during the severe struggles of the following Spring.

WILTSHIRE REGIMENT.

SWINDON PRISONERS OF WAR.

In January, 1918.

(1)	8323	Pte. E. A. Beaumont	(19)	5113	Pte. G. Eatwell
(2)	8609	Pte. R. S. Blunsden	(20)	8202	Pte. E. Ellison
(3)	8265	Pte. B. Bolter	(21)	9255	Pte. G. W. Evans
(4)	8239	Pte. C. A. H. Brooks	(22)	4222	Pte. J. Forest
(5)	8814	Cpl. C. A. Brown	(23)	7275	Pte. T. Fowler
(6)	5826	Sgt. W. G. Bull	(24)	10518	Pte. H. E. Foyle
(7)	5408	Pte. T. Butcher	(25)	8639	Pte. J. Gale
(8)	8015	Pte. W. H. Castle	(26)	8388	Pte. P. J. Gallichan
(9)	8645	Pte. J. Clarke	(27)	8057	Pte. C. C. Gee
(10)	8638	Cpl. L. Colborne	(28)	8067	Pte. W. Godwin
(11)	7931	Pte. G. Compton	(29)	8380	Pte. C. E. Haggard
(12)	4844	Pte. H. Cook	(30)	5445	Pte. W. F. Hall
(13)	8168	L-Sgt. A. J. Coombs	(31)	8062	Pte. W. H. Hall
(14)	8904	Pte. P. Coombes	(32)	7392	Pte. S. D. Hillier
(15)	8664	Pte. W. Cox	(33)	7538	Pte. J. Holland
(16)	8736	Pte. A. N. Dash	(34)	8329	L-Cpl. G. Hooper
(17)	6157	Pte. T. H. Davis	(35)	9883	Pte. J. W. Hunt
(18)	9152	Pte. R. P. B. Dixon	(36)	8720	Pte. C. Hutt

(37)	7674	Pte. H. C. Iles
(38)	9433	Pte. W. H. Iles
(39)	8802	Pte. A. R. Gibbs
(40)	7569	Pte. F. Kent
(41)	8984	L-Cpl. R. F. Kent
(42)	8696	Pte. L. Kirby
(43)	6164	Pte. B. Law
(44)	8526	Pte. E. Lawrence
(45)	7192	L-Cpl. W. Lester
(46)	8147	Pte. T. J. Love
(47)	7883	Cpl. McLoughlin
(48)	9607	Pte. C. Malin
(49)	8233	Sgt. P. Matthews
(50)	6303	Sgt. G. Mills
(51)	9320	Cpl. A. Nash
(52)	8690	Pte. C. Norris
(53)	7950	Pte. H. Page
(54)	7833	Pte. E. Painter
(55)	8316	Pte. E. G. Painter
(56)	10230	Pte. E. H. Pickett
(57)	7837	Pte. H. W. Pickett
(58)	8593	Pte. P. Pinniger
(59)	8687	Pte. C. Mead
(60)	8041	Pte. E. Purdue
(61)	8423	Pte. G. E. Razey
(62)	8237	L-Sgt. A. Sellwood
(63)	6232	Pte. G. F. Smith
(64)	7515	Pte. T. F. Smith
(65)	9435	Pte. F. Smith
(66)	7324	Pte. G. Spackman
(67)	8729	Pte. H. Spackman
(68)	7579	Pte. A. E. Ashton
(69)	8724	Pte. B. Stokes
(70)	9054	Pte. E. F. Stuart
(71)	9002	Pte. W. Sylvester
(72)	8562	L-Cpl. E. J. Talbot
(73)	7115	Pte. H. E. Tarrant
(74)	6935	Pte. W. E. Titcombe
(75)	8167	Pte. F. C. Turton
(76)	60	Pte. W. Underwood
(77)	8406	Pte. E. Walklate
(78)	8794	Pte. C. Wareham
(79)	9102	Pte. W. B. Weston
(80)	7770	Pte. C. J. Wheeler
(81)	8511	Pte. F. J. Williams
(82)	6126	Pte. A. Witts
(83)	7432	Cpl. F. Woof
(84)	7030	Pte. W. T. Woolford
(84)	7797	Pte. C. Young
(86)	8236	Pte. W. Mullis
(87)	8731	Cpl. F. Hopkins
(88)	8642	Cpl. E. S. Smith
(89)	7961	Pte. W. Titcombe
(90)	7244	L-Cpl. A. E. Windslow
(91)	9289	Pte. T. Drew
(92)	1688	Pte. J. Titcomb

Additions in 1918.

(93)	8828	Pte. W. J. Johnson
(94)	8560	Pte. E. S. Ponting
(95)	1681	Pte. E. Stacey
(96)	11615	Pte. A. Cox
(97)	8203	Pte. E. Stratton
(98)	20020	Pte. A. Burden
(99)	18125	Pte. H. V. Blake
(100)	22417	L-Cpl. G. H. Camille
(101)	21102	Pte. W. Eamer
(102)	22356	Pte. A. J. Embling
(103)	203058	Pte. F. J. Enstone
(104)	27272	Cpl. A. R. Franklin
(105)	22319	Pte. F. Fry
(106)	3/291	Sgt. A. Grace
(107)	32991	Pte. R. Habgood
(108)	32637	Pte. V. W. King
(109)	33538	Pte. W. A. Lamport
(110)	33918	Pte. J. Liddon
(111)	6716	Sgt. F. Porter
(112)	33218	Pte. E. Skinner
(113)	21282	Pte. F. H. Skuse
(114)	18474	Pte. W. A. Tyler
(115)	18431	Cpl. C. E. Tuck
(116)	18563	Pte. A. W. Llewellyn
(117)	31780	Pte. A. E. Wild
(118)	14101	Pte. W. G. Wheeler
(119)	13786	Pte. A. Hamley
(120)	27074	Pte. A. Tyler
(121)	10580	Cpl. B. J. Solomon
(122)	10233	Pioneer E. A. Sturgess
(123)	10033	Pte. S. Puffett
(124)	27392	Pte. W. O. Lavington
(125)	18538	Pte. H. Richens
(126)	24577	Pte. W. F. E. Gill
(127)	22761	Pte. A. Hazell
(128)	18523	Pte. F. Cook
(129)	11270	Pte. D. H. Lucas
(130)	25905	Pte. J. Morse
(131)	11575	Pte. J. Matthews
(132)	25540	L-Cpl. H. Ballard
(133)	35300	Pte. A. Beck
(134)	27231	Pte. R. J. Bedington
(135)	26776	Pte. W. G. Bennett
(136)	35543	Pte. C. Boulter
(137)	204395	Pte. G. W. Brine
(138)	3/194	Pte. J. T. Bromley
(139)	9288	Pte. R. Rolls
(140)	25531	Pte. H. Brooks
(141)	21777	Pte. J. Burr
(142)	11453	Pte. C. Bye
(143)	24523	Pte. E. Carter
(144)	11082	Pte. A. N. Clarke
(145)	27108	Pte. F. Cooper
(146)	203044	Sgt. J. W. Clapp
(147)	6122	Sgt. J. W. Cook
(148)	8092	Pte. G. Dobson
(149)	26965	Pte. T. Dowson
(150)	9380	Pte. H. Edwards
(151)	22928	Pte. W. J. England
(152)	19719	Pte. W. E. Elismore
(153)	10296	Pte. E. J. Gregory
(154)	26866	Pte. W. Goodwin
(155)	35503	Pte. W. H. Green
(156)	220004	L-Cpl. J. C. W. Guy

(157)	25804	Pte. J. House
(158)	21551	Pte. C. P. Hamlin
(159)	203110	Pte. W. Handcock
(160)	26973	Pte. S. Hirschman
(161)	229489	Pte. L. Hitchcock
(162)	220006	Sgt. D. C. Hutton
(163)	20783	Pte. H. B. Herbert
(164)	35536	Pte .W. E. Knight
(165)	26753	Pte. F. S. King
(166)	204071	Pte. F. A. J. Lovelock
(167)	26982	Pte. A. McCall
(168)	204076	Sgt. T. S. Mortimore
(169)	11916	Cpl. P. R. Ockenden
(170)	203079	Pte. T. H. Phillips
(171)	220051	Pte. W. Pitts
(172)	203014	Pte. M. W. Perry
(173)	29619	L-Cpl. S. G. Pipkin
(174)	21565	Pte. E. L. Roberts
(175)	29737	Pte. G. Sladden
(176)	20931	Pte. R. Sainsbury
(177)	203337	Pte. G. S. Phillips
(178)	18866	L-Cpl. G. Swaine
(179)	26887	Pte. C. W. Smedley
(180)	20864	Pte. W. H. Sprules
(181)	18440	Pte. C. Viveash
(182)	203308	Pte. E. Legg
(183)	12765	Pte. A. L. Wright
(184)	19951	L-Cpl. A. H. Williams
(185)	25602	Pte. A. Coombes
(186)	11283	L-Cpl. C. Cavalo
(187)	7082	Pte. C. Bridges
(188)	21921	Pte. C. W. J. Gibbs
(189)	24147	Pte. J. Driscoll
(190)	204272	Pte. A. Golding
(191)	9661	Pte. A. W. Harris
(192)	19145	Pte. H. C. Holley
(193)	18671	Pte. W. Lawrence
(194)	204176	Pte. H. Kilminster
(195)	7189	Sgt. W. J. Sharpe
(196)	29919	Pte. E. Warren
(197)	10970	Pte. J. T. Lang
(198)	204221	Pte. A. Withers
(199)	24588	Pte. S. W. Sutton
(200)	203174	Sgt. H. Godwin
(201)	806	Pte. G. H. Harman
(202)	37511	Pte. F. Hill
(203)	37498	Pte. A. Morse
(204)	24578	Pte. J. Munro
(205)	18111	Pte. J. Chivers
(206)	9338	Pte. W. Shilton
(207)	8931	Cpl. S. W. Westall
(208)	13937	L-Cpl. Beale
(209)	1022	Pte. H. Bromage
(210)	9851	Pte. E. G. Dash
(211)	10614	Pte. F. French
(212)	8148	L-Cpl. G. Wright
(213)	34817	Pte. R. C. Strange
(214)	9202	Pte. F. Ayers
(215)	10386	Pte. C. Cowley
(216)	203295	Pte. F. J. Hinton
(217)	3/9709	L-Cpl. W. T. Curtis
(218)	203192	Cpl. A. Haynes
(219)	6416	Sgt. F. Cook, D.C.M.
(220)	26944	Pte. C. Wiggins
(221)	26154	Pte. C. Furze
(222)	203358	Pte. F. Smart
(223)	32208	Pte. F. Couzens
(224)	25895	L-Cpl. F. Neate
(225)	20737	Pte. H. Goodenough
(226)	18458	Pte. V. C. Angell
(227)	203258	Pte. W. J. Cowlard
(228)	203352	Pte. A. F. Rouse
(229)	23770	Pte. V. Lansdowne
(230)	26343	Pte. A. H. Robins
(231)	320022	Sgt. A. Jerram
(232)	22486	L-Cpl. F. E. Hayward
(233)	9271	Cpl. F. Hiet
(234)	202815	Pte. H. G. Mills
(235)	5461	Sgt. B. Dobson
(236)	10031	Pte. B. Beasley
(237)	36887	Pte. E. G. Johnson
(238)	24557	Pte. H. Trueman
(239)	204160	Pte. E. Egglestone
(240)	19434	Pte. T. R. Button
(241)	18115	Pte. C. E. Webb
(242)	9935	Cpl. A. Kitching
(243)	10213	Cpl. S. A. Leonard
(244)	6685	Pte. A. Chandler
(245)	202100	Pte. W. Boswell
(246)	24580	Pte. M. Middleton
(247)	25773	Pte. W. C. Eveleigh
(248)	18526	Cpl. F. Miles
(249)	11289	Cpl. J. T. H. Hinchcliffe
(250)	27876	Pte. M. E. Postlethwaite
(251)	6843	Sgt. W. H. G. Walker
(252)	22596	Pte. P. A. Bowly
(253)	10460	Pte. J. Pile
(254)	22079	Pte. J. Holliday
(255)	22382	Pte. F. J. Bourton
(256)	29839	L-Cpl. W. W. Addison
(257)	27430	Pte. C. Alexander
(258)	34804	L-Cpl. J. G. Apsey
(259)	36525	Pte. H. Avery
(260)	27437	Pte. W. E. Bacon
(261)	27436	L-Cpl. H. Back
(262)	11887	Pte. W. Baker
(263)	21505	Pte. H. V. Baker
(264)	10502	Pte. E. Bancroft
(265)	33111	Cpl. H. J. Barker
(266)	31850	Pte. A. Beard
(267)	20925	L-Cpl. G. S. Beasant
(268)	27440	Pte. L. Bellamy
(269)	203597	Pte. J. Best
(270)	27324	Pte. A. W. Bird
(271)	26339	Pte. C. Blackford
(271)	21776	Pte. W. D. Blake
(273)	27045	Pte. C. Bourdon
(274)	204306	Pte. F. G. Bowden
(275)	39624	Pte. V. Bown
(276)	7341	L-Cpl. L. Bray
(277)	8716	L-Cpl. F. G. Britten
(278)	27961	Pte. J. Brooks
(279)	10596	Pte. A. Burgin
(280)	35649	Pte. H. Carter
(281)	33938	Pte. G. E. Chard
(282)	37273	Pte. T. G. Churcher

(283)	27749	Pte. E. G. Clarke		(294)	6th Wilts	Pte. W. E. Kent
(284)	20623	Pte. G. A. Cocks		(295)	8949	Pte. F. Merritt
(285)	13919	Pte. T. Cook		(296)	35750	Pte. E. T. Perrett
(286)	21654	Pte. H. Cottingham		(297)	204109	Pte. E. V. Purdue
(287)	203262	Pte. W. Crook		(298)	204201	Pte. C. Rust
(288)	35709	Pte. H. W. Fallen		(299)	14566	Pte. S. Telling
(289)	9650	L-Cpl. E. G. Ferris		(300)	203383	Pte. S. G. White
(290)	26959	Pte. E. J. Field		(301)	10888	Pte. E. Webb
(291)	204235	Pte. J. H. Fletcher		(302)	9536	Pte. G. J. Yeates
(292)	26321	Pte. V. W. Gould		(303)	27868	Pte. T. Nurden
(293)	26462	Pte. A. P. Hobbs				

Deaths. Not all these men lived to see their home again, and the brief record here made will be sufficient to call forth the pity of every citizen of Swindon who reads it :

Sergt. H. Godwin, died of tuberculosis induced by exposure and starvation.

Pte. M. E. Postlethwaite, died in hospital in Germany, November, 1918.

Pte. Eveleigh, died of starvation on the way home from Germany after the armistice was signed.

Pte. C. E. Haggard lived to see his home again, but died suddenly in the street in Swindon three weeks later.

To these must be added :—

Pte. A. H. Cox, 5th Wilts,   died in Turkey,

Pte. E. Stacey, 1/4th Wilts   „   „

Pte. E. Ponting, 1/4th Wilts   „   „

Of all Swindon men of the Wiltshire Regiment who were prisoners in Turkey only Pte. J. Titcombe, of the 1/4 Wilts, returned.

Inscribed in an autograph album amongst the Committee's records are the signatures of 217 returned Prisoners of War, mostly written when the men came to the depôt at the Mayor's invitation to receive their Christmas parcels. These include many who were not in the Wiltshire Regiment and who were therefore not on the list of prisoners cared for by the Swindon Committee. The album is a pathetic memento of the War and the mere record of dates sometimes tells a story of deep suffering. Here is an entry of six successive names taken at random from the top of one of the pages :

Name	Reg.	Date of Capture.	Last Camp	Returned Swindon	Address
B. Davis	M.G.C.	28/4/18	Gustrow	1/12/18	13, Dowling St.
W. J. Kethero	M.G.C.	11/4/18	Gardelegen	5/12/18	33, Eastcott Hill.
A. H. Chandler	2, Wilts.	25/5/18	Maintz	5/12/18	" Silbury," Bath Road.
E. Blount	R.E.	25/4/18	Limburg	5/12/18	78, Manchester Rd.
T. Saddler	R.I. Fus.	23/10/18	Dülmen	2/12/18	Bath Road.
A. J. Coombs	2, Wilts.	24/10/14	Saltau, Z, 3036	22/11/18	170, Beatrice St.

This album, the many scrupulously kept account-books of the Committee, collections of letters and postcards, lantern-slides of photographs of many postcards used at the Swindon Cinema-houses, specimens of labels and forms, lists, and other records, have been carefully packed and deposited in the Town Hall, where some future historian of Swindon may perhaps find the material for a striking chapter upon the civic spirit of the Borough in the early part of the Twentieth century.

CHAPTER VI.

1917. Growing Restrictions and Unflagging Work.

The year 1917 saw the principle of Food-Control gradually forced upon the nation by the increasing shortage of provisions due to the withdrawal of so many men from production, the falling-off of imports—which was much more pronounced than in 1916 on account of the havoc worked upon our shipping by the German submarines,—and the vast needs of the Army. It was with great reluctance that the Government adopted the rationing policy, and they deferred it almost to the danger-point.

Voluntary Food-Control. At first it was hoped to secure the desired end by voluntary means, and voluntary food-control committees were formed all over the country in order to stimulate and direct public opinion. The Town Council and the Local War Savings Committee were asked by the Food Controller to organise the campaign in Swindon, and an overflowing meeting of delegates from the trade societies, churches, friendly societies, and practically every notable organisation, was held in the Town Hall on April 16th, in order to give effect to the Food Controller's demand. This meeting elected an Executive of about fifty members, and left to it the election of an Advisory Committee which was to consist of experts upon the various matters that were bound to arise. The meeting was full of nervous tension and it required all the ability of the Mayor (Mr. A. J. Gilbert), to guide the business successfully,—a task which he fulfilled with rare tact. His Worship had taken this question to heart and throughout the months in which the voluntary food-control campaign was carried on he devoted himself unsparingly to what he conceived as a duty laid upon him. The Executive speedily got to work; it appointed an Advisory Committee consisting of representatives of the various traders' societies, labour societies, domestic teachers, allotment holders, clergy, etc., with Mr. W. K. Procter as Hon. Treasurer, and Mr. H. Stanier as full-time Secretary; a Publicity Committee was elected for propagandist work; and the Swindon Education Committee, supplemented by suitable other persons, was entrusted with the educative work. This last committee was to make arrangements for instructing housewives in the preparation of food-substitutes, and to prepare a comprehensive scheme of demonstrations, lectures, and exhibitions conducted by qualified advisers.

Sugar and Bread. The two most pressing questions at the time were those of the supply of sugar and bread. Steps had been taken to obtain an adequate supply of sugar for the town on the basis of ¾lb. per head, but the great influx of billeted soldiers and newcomers had reduced the average weekly allowance to ½lb. per head; this, therefore, was the "voluntary ration" which good citizens were in honour bound not to exceed; cases of disloyalty of course came to light,—as for instance that of a woman who, by sending out her children in turn, obtained three or four times her share,—but in the main consumers and tradesmen co-operated in loyally carrying out the scheme. The "voluntary ration" of bread was 4lbs. per head weekly, including flour, and at the time the campaign started it was found that consumption was going on at the rate of 6lbs. per head ; the public was notified that unless it reduced consumption to the 4lb. standard within six weeks " bread tickets " were inevitable ; they were urged to banish bread from the dinner-table, to use more oatmeal, beans, peas, and rice, and to learn how to prepare maize for the table.   The difficulty, however, was great, for bread still remained the cheapest form of food, and thrifty housewives found that as soon as they began to turn to these substitutes they quickly rose in price. The subject of " profiteering " was therefore one that continually arose at the Food-Control Committee's meetings, and a resolution was sent to the Food-Controller pointing out the difficulty, and urging him to check profiteering by limiting the prices of substitutes as he had just done in the case of new arrivals of peas and beans. At the same time the Bakers' Association was called into counsel, particularly as complaints were rife as to the quality of the bread ; 25% of other substances were now present in wheat and flour, and the bakers asserted by their secretary

War-Bread. that these could not be regarded as food ; it was said that people found the " war-bread " less satisfying and ate more of it ; it was said also that it was difficult of digestion since many of the foreign ingredients were but half cooked, and the Committee arranged a conference between the Bakers and Dr. Whitley and Mr. Burkhardt, to discuss methods of preparing the flour.   A great difficulty, however, lay in the fact that these other substances were added by the miller and hence the baker was precluded from suitably preparing them.   A severe epidemic of sores upon all parts of the body, especially amongst children, was generally believed to be due to the bread, and doctors advised people to eat less bread and as much fresh vegetable food as they could.   Upon the Bakers' advice a leaflet was drawn up for public distribution embodying a statement of the reasons that necessitated a reduction in consumption, an explanation of the hardships that would ensue from compulsory rationing, and a request to house-holders to limit their custom to one baker ; the committee refused to adopt a clause suggested by the Bakers, which formed a pledge to take a certain (reduced) quantity weekly ; it was felt that this might lead sometimes to hardship and sometimes to waste.

Food Orders. The voluntary nature of this Committee explains its lack of power either to enforce its ideas, however admirable, or to take legal proceedings against violators of existing regulations ; it could give information against offenders just as it was open to any private individuals to lodge complaints with the police, who had full powers to act upon information as to breaches of the Controller's regulations.   There were many such now in operation ; for instance, Tuesdays in London and Wednesdays elsewhere were " meatless days" when it was forbidden to serve meat in restaurants ; on other days the amount that could be served at a meal was limited; potatoes, the scarcity of which will be dealt with later,[1] could only be served on meatless days and Fridays ; tradesmen must not "impose any condition" upon the sale of any article,—for example, a grocer might not refuse to sell sugar unless the buyer purchased other goods ; "hoarding" was illegal—purchasers must not obtain more than enough for their current needs; waste of food-stuffs was a punishable offence ; no chocolates were to be sold at over 3d. per oz., or other sweets 2d ; tea had to be packed net-weight ; milk-sellers were not to charge on any date more than 2d. per quart above the price on the corresponding date of 1914.   These are examples of the regulations that were now being

[1] See pages 116, 117.

In G.W.R. Factory. 6in. Guns on Travelling Carriages.

issued every few days under the authority of " D.O.R.A." but which lay outside the scope of the Voluntary Committee, except in so far as they chose to inform the police of any infringements.

Education of the Public. The work done by the Food Control Committee through the Education authority was of the greatest value, for in many homes the food question was really critical ; people were asked to find substitutes for food they had never been without before, and to use dietary articles which they did not know how to prepare, and thus there was a danger to health as well as much inconvenience.   The Education Committee decided to suspend for a week the ordinary instruction at its different domestic centres, in order to allow continuous lectures and demonstrations in "war-time cookery" to be given by the Domestic Teachers ; through the schools and by advertisement housewives were invited to attend at any time, and they were encouraged to inspect, discuss, and test various food preparations which were quite new to most of them.   The visitors were given lists of foods, facts as to their health value, and printed sheets of recipes; in the first week over a thousand housewives came for instruction, and at two of the centres the attendance was so good as to lead the Committee to continue the work for a second week, so that this education of the house-wives was going on from May 3rd to the 17th.

The instruction at the centres was supplemented by similar work done at four Exhibitions or Shops opened in Regent Street, Victoria Road, the Gorse Hill Girls' Club, and in Rodbourne Lane.   These, being located in such public spots, attracted large numbers of shoppers and passers-by, who could watch cookery going on, obtain samples, leaflets, and recipes, or sit down and partake of food prepared on the spot ; at times the shops would be crowded, and the interest of the women was shown by the way in which they questioned those in charge and the attention with which they followed the short lectures given from time to time.

No effort was spared to reach the women of the town and to accustom them to the use of new articles of diet, and it must be acknowledged that the people as a whole cheerfully strove to overcome prejudices and the suspicion of novel articles of diet ; and although maize failed to seize the popular fancy, it is certain that the breakfast plate of oatmeal dates in many families from the pinch that began to be acute in 1917.

The large meeting of soldiers' wives and other women held at the Town Hall every Wednesday afternoon was another field for propaganda, and several lectures were given there by ladies and gentlemen who understood the food question ; further efforts were made to reach every home by sending leaflets out by the school-children, who themselves received instruction at school, especially in regard to the waste of food ; inspection of the playgrounds after the lunch interval showed almost an entire absence of waste, and in many instances children ceased to bring to school the customary packet of "lunch."   At the Food Control meetings some allegations of waste were made, supported by specific examples, but there was very little throughout the town, and an inspection of the ash-boxes enabled the Borough Surveyor to report that there was no waste whatever of bread-stuffs in the Borough.

Sugar. The sugar shortage continued to give the Committee much anxiety, for large " queues " began to be an ugly feature of the streets ; these were caused by the unpatriotic action of those who went from shop to shop for sugar and thereby prevented others from getting their fair share, so that a sort
G

of panic drove promiscuous crowds of buyers to certain stores as soon as, or before they were opened, and these shops sold out their day's supply in an hour or two. In order to remedy this evil, the Food Control Committee called into conference the Grocers' Association and representatives of the Co-operative Society and the multiple stores ; after one or two meetings the Grocers' Association surprised the Committee by reporting against a local "sugar-ticket system " as unworkable, although one of the chief multiple shops had adopted a ticket-system that allowed 2lb. of sugar to its regular customers. The real difficulty lay in the fact that Swindon was receiving 50% of its 1915 supplies, but tradesmen's customers had fluctuated greatly ; thus, one grocer might have the same number of customers as in 1915, and he could give them half the 1915 allowance ; but another might have double the number of customers, and he would have to give them one-quarter of the 1915 allowance. A resolution was sent to the Food Controller indicating the unsatisfactory nature of the method of distribution, but nothing came of it,— probably because the use of sugar-tickets for the whole nation was plainly now but a matter of time.

As the Food Controller had released a certain amount of sugar for private growers of fruit, and many had applied for it for the purpose of making jam, the Committee arranged lectures and demonstrations in bottling and preserving fruit and vegetables without sugar, so that those who grew no fruit themselves could still lay in a stock of bought fruit. At the Committee's request the Board of Agriculture sent down one of its expert demonstrators, Mrs. Parsons, of Crewkerne, who showed how vegetables and fruit could be dried or bottled, and the work was continued after her departure by the mistresses of the Domestic Centres. To assist householders the Committee ordered 300 dozen bottles for preserving, retailing them at cost price.

Close of the Voluntary Food-Control Committee's Work. The labours of the Voluntary Food-Control Committee came to a close in August, when, by order of the Government, Statutory Food Control Committees were set up all over the country to administer the compulsory rationing scheme that was shortly to come into force. The Executive Committee had met weekly, and although the difficulties were great, in view of the lack of any powers but those of persuasion and advice, its work had been very valuable ; it had caused people to think seriously upon a subject that had been regarded all too lightly ; it had excited a patriotic feeling of sacrifice and a readiness to bear inconveniences cheerfully ; it had educated the public in new principles of economy and diet ; and it had prepared the public for the compulsory rationing that was anticipated at first with the greatest repugnance. Amongst material results the Committee could claim to have reduced the consumption of bread by about 10%, and the attention and experiment devoted to the subject had given Swindon a bread superior to what was obtainable in many places. It had not done all it would have liked ; for instance, it had wished to see communal piggeries established at Broome Sewage Farm, where the waste products of allotments and households could be profitably used ; the Sewage Farm Committee, however, could not see its way to take up the matter, although it offered to allow the Food Control Committee to do so ; but this body, having no funds at its disposal beyond a trifling sum allowed for its organizing expenses, was not in a position to attempt the work. Another question—that of Communal Kitchens—was repeatedly examined, but finally it was not thought that at the time there was any local need of them.

Mr. A. J. Gilbert, in his farewell speech to the Committee over which he had, as Mayor of the Borough, invariably presided, rightly spoke of the desire shown by all to do everything possible to meet the crisis reached in the struggle to avert the privation by which the enemy hoped to break the British spirit.   There had been sharp differences of opinion in the meetings, but a most amicable feeling had been preserved, and it would be hard to say how greatly its work had contributed to mould local opinion.

The Corn To turn to the subject of prices in 1917.   It has been shown that the
Market. price of wheat reached a record in Swindon market at the end of 1916 ; even that was surpassed before the Government fixed prices, for by the end of March wheat was selling at 86/- and 87/- a quarter, and oats at 61/- and 62/-, whilst barley reached 80 /- in April.   It is also noteworthy that the markets were uniformly very poor, the attendance being small and supplies short,—in fact sometimes there was no grain on offer at all.   In April the Food Controller fixed the maximum prices of cereals ; wheat was not to be sold at more than 78 /- per qr. of 480 lbs., barley at 65 /- per qr. of 400 lbs., and oats at 55 /- per qr. of 312 lbs.; these were " maximum prices," but the public soon discovered that the maximum price of an article at once became its current price.

The price of bread continued to rise, and the Cricklade and Wootton
Bread Bassett Guardians could not get tenders in June for less than 10½d.
Control. the four-pound loaf, and had to pay 45 /- a sack for barley-meal ; in the same month the Co-operative Society's report stated that flour had gone up 110% and bread 90% since the beginning of the war.   In September the price of the quartern loaf was fixed by the Controller at 9d., and it remained about that price throughout the rest of the war.   Various regulations issued by the Controller during the year point to the anxiety felt concerning the bread-supply ; restaurants, tea-shops, and other places of refreshment were bound to limit the amount of flour served in any form ; between 3 and 6 p.m. not more than 2 oz. of bread and cakes could be served to anyone taking a meal,—and yet, as illustrating the difficulties and anomalies that attended much of the system of control, there was nothing to prevent the customer from leaving his seat, going to the shop counter and purchasing as much cake and pastry as he liked, and bringing it to his table to be eaten at once. Confectioners were not allowed to make light fancy-pastry, crumpets, or muffins, and other cakes or pastry-goods had to conform to a set standard ; the sale of new bread, currant, sultana, and milk bread was forbidden ; the shape of the loaf was defined, and the use of sugar in bread was prohibited.   The limits between which other materials could be added to wheaten flour were raised, and whilst these ingredients could form 25% of the whole, they were not to form less than 10%. Horses, too, were rationed, the Controller's order limiting them to 16lbs. of oats per day ; this order formed the subject of criticism in a Town Council meeting, when it was said that the Corporation horses—particularly fine and well-kept animals—had never had more than 10½ lbs. per day.

As grain was now so dear it was only to be expected that the
Milk and Town Council would have to pay dearly for its straw, and in February
Fodder. its contract was 11 /6 per ton higher than the last, forty tons being tendered at £3 : 10 : 0 a ton.

Milk, which had risen to 5d. a quart in October, 1916, was sold at 6d. a quart by most retailers in Swindon for the first three quarters of 1917 ; in April the contract price to the farmer was 1 /5 per gallon, and, contrary to public expectation, there was no fall in the retail price to " summer prices," and in June it was announced in the press that there would probably be great scarcity of milk in the ensuing winter. In October the retail price was raised to 7d. a quart, and the best terms the Board of Guardians could obtain were 2/- per gallon for October, 2/1 for November, and 2/2 from December to March, with delivery at " Olive House " Home at 6d. a quart in October and at 7d. afterwards.   The increase in milk prices, a great hardship where there were young children, created great concern and excited much feeling, but the farmers pointed to the greater expense of keeping cattle, and the large increase in the cost of beasts ; for instance, the Town Council had in April to pay £7 : 5 : 0 a ton in its contract for hay, being an increase of 15/- per ton since September ; as a set-off they again received remarkably high prices for the grass-land they had to let at Broome Farm, making £567 : 15 : 6 for just over 89 acres,—an average of about £6 : 7 : 0 per acre.   Again, cattle-cake was very expensive, so much so that the Food Controller had to fix a miximum price of £19 per ton in November, when the market rates were £22 and £23 per ton.   The number of cattle in the district had fallen to a serious extent, and this naturally affected the milk question; in March, 1917, it was stated at a meeting of the Farmers' Union held in Swindon that the number of cattle in the Swindon and North Wiltshire district was 800 less than in 1913,—a point to bear in mind also when considering the situation in regard to meat.

Provisions.   As illustrating the growth in domestic expenditure upon groceries a few figures may be quoted for March 1917. Both English and Foreign bacon were 2/4 a lb., and from this month the price remained steady at that figure, for the Food Controller had taken the matter in hand and henceforth the prices of bacon, ham, butter, and lard were controlled. Both English and Foreign butter sold at 2/6 a lb. retail, though 2/2 was usually asked about this time in the Borough Market. Cheese was very scarce at 2/6 per lb., and did not fall until controlled ; lard was 1/8 per lb. Other prices in March were :—granulated sugar 7d. and loaf sugar 7½d. a pound ; margarine 1/-, rice 4d. and 6d., tea 3/-, coffee 1/6 and 2/4, and currants 1/2 a pound ; sultanas were unobtainable and currants nearly so, and by the end of the year were quite absent from the shops. Later on tea fell to the controlled price of 2/8 per lb., and there were times during the year when people found a little difficulty in getting as much tea as they would have wished, but no real hardship was experienced.

The wholesale price of eggs was 5 a shilling in January, 7 and 8 in March, 6 in June, 5 again in October, 4 by the beginning of December, and 3/6 a dozen by Christmas ; retail prices were usually at the rate of one egg less per shilling or thereabouts, so that eggs were 4½d. and 5d. each at Christmas-time,—a price that excluded them from the average family's table.

Vegetables and fruit were dearer than in 1916 to some extent, but in the market one could still buy in October apples at 1d. to 2½d a pound, pears at prices up to 4d., plums at 2d. and 3d., tomatoes at 6d. and 7d. and onions at 3d.   Potatoes,

Potato Shortage.   however, had been a subject of concern for the greater part of the year ; in January they were sold in Swindon at 10/- to 12/- per cwt., and in March there was an unprecedented scarcity. It is to be remembered that the effort to economize in bread, as well as the unpalatable nature of the bread, made people turn to potatoes in place of it, and the winter's store was depleted before the new potatoes were ready ; thus, multitudes of people went for many weeks without potatoes, seeking to replace them by swedes and parsnips ; the hitherto cheap and neglected swede—esteemed by many till then as fit only for cattle and sheep—suddenly acquired a position of great importance, and its price went up at an incredible rate, so much so that the Food Controller had to intervene ; in a month the price had rushed up from £4 a ton to £12, when the Controller stepped in and fixed the retail price at 1½d. per lb., which gave undreamt of profits to those who had large stocks of swedes. As to parsnips, these were nearly all gone in March when the Controller checked the rise in the price of swedes.

This experience led the Government to take steps to increase the quantity of potatoes grown by a promise to farmers that they should have a fixed price of £6 per ton after September 15th, for all stocks of sound potatoes that would not pass through the 1⅝inch sieve. The promise was made in May, giving time enough to get in the seed, and indeed, the matter was urgent, seeing that the German "U-Boats" were inflicting more and more damage upon our shipping ; there was the double loss of cargoes and vessels, and in spite of the optimism of the general public the authorities had serious grounds for anxiety in face of an enemy who avowed his intention to hesitate at no means of starving his opponent into submission.

The Swindon Town Council applied for 120 tons of seed-potatoes in furtherance of its efforts—shortly to be noticed,—to assist in increasing the amount of food produced by allotment-holders, and these potatoes were sold to the holders at 15/- per cwt., at a time when the catalogue price was 26/- per cwt. The season, however, was doomed to be one of great disappointment, for in the first week of June one of the most disastrous outbreaks of potato-disease ever experienced swept over a large part of the country, and especially the southern portion. It was the disease known as "Black-leg," and it was favoured by the heavy rains and close weather that prevailed in the early summer. Spraying had been practised perhaps more than ever before, but it failed to do good because the potato haulms were too tall by the time the danger was realized and had fallen all about the rows. Wherever there were potato patches in or around the town they soon presented a pitiable spectacle, as though fire had swept over them, and when the roots came to be stored they rapidly deteriorated.

From September, then, it was illegal for the grower to sell his potatoes at less than £6 a ton, forward on rail, and the highest price he could charge was £6 : 10 : 0 ; the retailer was not to exceed 1¼d. per lb., and the usual price was a penny a pound. Special arrangements were made for bakers—for at the end of the year it was permissible to use potatoes in bread to the extent of one pound to seven of flour ; bakers were allowed potatoes at £3 : 10 : 0 per ton through the Food Control Committee who made up to the grower the full price of £6 : 0 : 0 per ton.

Fish, etc.   Fish remained at pretty much the same prices as in 1916 ; thus, in October and November kippers were sold in the Borough Market at 4d. a pair, herrings at 1½d. to 3d. each, and cod, plaice, and hake at 1/- a lb. At the same time rabbits were 1/9 each.

The Liquor Trade. There is little to note concerning the liquor trade, for every one had accepted as inevitable the restrictions imposed in 1916 ; when prices were re-adjusted in March, ale was 4d. a pint, and the best beer and stout 6d ; the "long pull" was abolished and the gravity of the beer was still further diminished. The retail prices of spirits were—4d. for a "small whisky," gin, or rum, 5d. for a "Johnny Walker," and 6d. for "specials" in whisky and brandy. By the quartern, "Johnny Walker" was 2/- and special whiskies and brandies 2/6.

Rates of increase. A few general figures as to the increase in the cost of living may be instructive. On February 1st, 1917, a comparison with July, 1914, showed that the cost of living in towns over 50,000 in population had risen 93%, and 89% for the country as a whole. The increase since February 1st, 1916, was 30%. Again, in June it was officially announced that in the large towns prices had risen since July, 1914, to the following extent : fresh butter 70% or 10¼d. a lb., salt butter 67% or 9½d. a lb ; milk 63% or 2¼d. a quart ; cheese 121% or 10½d. a lb ; fresh eggs 83% or 1/- a dozen ; and potatoes 162% or 7¼d. per 7 lbs. The Board of Trade returns in June showed that food prices were 102% above those of July, 1914, 28% above those of a year ago, and 2% over those current only a month ago. Finally, in November it was found that they had further risen to 106% above the rates for July, 1914.

In all directions the same state of affairs existed ; clothes were proportionally dearer and fabrics were also much poorer in quality, for wool was all commandeered by the Government—at a price 50% above the 1915 price—and only released for civilian clothing in very limited quantities. A similar condition existed in the case of boots and leather, and boot-repairers raised their prices also. And, to take an instance outside domestic expenditure, the Swindon Education Committee found the cost of stationery becoming a very heavy item, and in the last quarter of 1916 it had had to pay increases of 87½% on paper goods and 20% to 25% on others.

Swindon Cattle Market. A table of meat prices for 1916 has been given earlier in this work [1] and if reference is made to it the reader will see that good joints had reached a point of cost that was prohibitive to the average household ; the limit was not yet reached, for in 1917 English beef ranged from 6d. a pound for the poorest cuts to 2/4 for good joints, English mutton ranged from 9d. to 2/6, whilst Foreign beef and mutton were sold at the same rates as English ; suet was 1/6 a pound.

When the figures for cattle and other animals, as sold in the Swindon market, are examined, no surprise will be felt at these high prices for meat. On May 1st, a fat bull from Brig. Gen. Calley's farm at Burderop was sold for £63, and other beasts were sold at various prices from £47 : 15 : 0 downwards ; heifers and calves fetched prices as high as £41 : 10 : 0, stirks were £18 : 2 : 6 each, and calves varied from £4 : 8 : 0 to £5 : 4 : 0 ; pigs were sold for £17 : 7 : 0 each. On June 4th an astonishing figure was obtained for a prime maiden heifer, which was sold for £52, and a week later a remarkable sale gave the following high prices : four of Brig. Gen. Calley's steers sold for £209 : 15 : 0, an average of £52 : 8 : 9 each, the best one going for £53 : 10 : 0 ; Sir Frederick Banbury sent in six maiden heifers whose prices varied from £38 : 15 : 0 to £49 : 0 : 0 ; two in-calf heifers fetched £50 : 5 : 0 and £45 respectively ; and calves were sold at rates from £7 : 17 : 6 downwards. At the same market a fat sow obtained £34 : 5 : 0 and bacon pigs were twelve guineas each. Still the price of stock rose, and in July record prices for

A record Market. Swindon were reached when on the third Monday of that month a pair of in-calf heifers were sold for £117 : 10 : 0, and two others sold for £57 and £50 respectively ; twenty-six heifers averaged £40 : 13 : 0 a head. What would have happened is hard to imagine if the Food Controller had not taken the meat question in hand. It is possible that money may not be again of so high a purchasing power as in the early part of 1914, when these prices would have seemed incredible ; but the reader must imagine what they seemed to

(1). See page 67.

folk who had been accustomed to such figures as £30 per pair for heifers, £22 per pair for stirks, £6 : 15 : 0 for fat sows,—noted as "excellent" prices in June, 1914.

It may here be remarked that the same issue of the local papers that announced the terms of the arrangements for controlling the retail price of meat, reported the sale of six pigs by the Swindon and Highworth Board of Guardians at 25/- per score ; only about eighteen months previous they had congratulated themselves on getting "record prices," when they sold nine at 16/6 per score.

The action of the Food Controller in fixing prices at pretty much the current high rate was criticised adversely by many who were in no position to form a judgment upon the matter, and it is no part of the function of this work to enter into an explanation of the case, involving, as it would, reference to the dwindling national stock of animals, the great demands of the armed forces, the growing losses of shipping and the inability to build fresh vessels fast enough, the interruption of communication with foreign fields of production, the obligation to see that Britain's allies had a fair supply, and many other considerations. Suffice to say that the Food Controller's action stabilized the situation. Before going into this, however, it is necessary to speak of the new Food Control Committee.

The official The official Food Control Committee came into being in August, **Food-Control** 1917, and was a much smaller body than the voluntary committee **Committee.** that had paved the way. It was composed of the Mayor (Mr. A. J. Gilbert), Aldermen A. E. Harding, C. A. Plaister, and A. W. Haynes, Councillors T. Butler, H. J. Vaisey, and A. Bull, with the Secretary of the Amalgamated Society of Engineers (Mr. G. W. Davies), the Secretary of the Grocers' Association (Mr. E. Mackleden), the Manager of the New Swindon Co-operative Society (Mr. J. Lowes), the Secretary of the "Court Violet" of the Ancient Order of Foresters (Mrs. E. L. Lowe), and Mrs. A. J. Colborne, with the Town Clerk as the Hon. Executive Officer ; the Mayor was Chairman and Mr. T. Butler Vice-Chairman of the Committee's Meetings.

Sugar The first business was to deal with the sugar question, and retailers **Registration.** were ordered to register by September 15th ; after October 1st, none but registered tradesmen would be allowed to deal in sugar. At the same time special arrangements were made to supply the needs of caterers, manufacturers, keepers of boarding establishments, and similar special cases ; by December 30th the distribution of sugar throughout the entire trade would be completely regulated. The registration of consumers for the purpose of rationing everyone for sugar went on parallel with the registration of dealers ; the sugar-registration cards were issued to all householders between September the 15th and the 29th ; October 6th was the latest date for applying for "sugar cards," and the 26th the last day of issue ; the consumer had to hand these in to his retail tradesman by November the 5th. On November 28th, however, the Committee ordered that a fresh declaration of the number composing the household should be handed in, as so many changes had necessarily taken place since the registration of 1915.

Meat The regulation of meat prices was another of the first matters to **Regulation.** be attended to. On September 3rd the Food Controller fixed the wholesale prices of fresh meat and limited butchers' profits, leaving the local committee to adjust the prices of the various joints. The maximum retail prices were not to exceed an addition of 2½d. per lb. to the price paid by the butcher, or 20% profit, whichever was the less, and these were reckoned not on any specified cut but upon the total sales for each fortnight. Butchers had to display a list of their prices in their shops and to send a copy of it to the Town Clerk, and they were bound to keep accurate records of all the business done. The public, too, was notified that it must not pay prices above the maximum and that it should see that lists were displayed in the shops ; the customer who paid more than the maximum was equally liable with the tradesman to a heavy penalty, and Police-Superintendent Moore was appointed officer under the Orders at a small salary ; it was decided also to appoint a Food Inspector, and in December Mr. J. Belcher was given this office. The retail prices of the various joints were settled at a conference of the Committee with representatives of the Butchers' Association, and, irksome as was a great deal of the Committee's work, every effort was made to meet the just wishes of all bodies of traders with whom its regulations were concerned.

Penalties. Various articles were now being fixed in price by the Food Controller, and it was part of the Committee's duty to take action when any of these orders were contravened ; the first case to attract public notice was one in which a young assistant sold some dried peas at 8d. a pound, whereas the fixed price was 6d.; the manageress of the shop was prosecuted as a matter of course, but the public was somewhat taken aback when the magistrates imposed a penalty of £20, especially as the act was inadvertent, and not one of wilful " profiteering." Shortly afterwards, tradesmen were prosecuted for contravening the Milk Order, when fines ranging from 10 /- to £7 : 10 : 0 were imposed ; a dealer was fined 25 /- for failing to display a price list ; the manageress of a café was fined £5 for contravening the Meals Order; a grocer was penalised for contravening the Tea Order, and a brewery company was mulcted in £50 for exceeding the barrellage it was entitled to brew.

Fixing of Prices. In November prices were fixed for beans at from 5½d. to 8d. per lb., for jam at 9d. to 1 /- per lb., for bread at 9½d. the four pound loaf, for flour at 8½d. the quartern, and butter and cheese could not be retailed at a price that gave the tradesman more than 2½d per lb. over what he had paid ; oatmeal was 5d., blue and green peas 9d., and yellow peas 6d. per lb. maximum price ; whilst tea was not to exceed 4 /- per lb., and varied from 2 /4 to that figure. The public was urgently asked to assist in economising transport by carrying away purchases instead of expecting them to be delivered by the shopkeepers, and, in fact, very soon many shopkeepers refused to deliver goods and when paper became short insisted on customers' bringing their own wrappings.

Coal. In the same month a schedule of coal-prices was issued after consultation with the merchants, fixing sales of over half a ton at 39 /- per ton for " Controlled " coal and 42 /- per ton for Forest of Dean coal ; sales of less than half a ton by hawkers were at a slightly higher rate, and sales at depôts, sidings, or wharves, where customers carried away their own coal, were a trifle lower in price.

Another order fixed the retail price of milk for November at 2 /2 per gallon, 2d. less being charged for it if sold over the counter.

These prices, though by no means low, gave on the whole general satisfaction, for the public now knew where it stood in regard to many commodities, and was no longer in the position of wondering from day to day what it would have to pay for them. Sometimes the fixed price was higher than one had to pay a short time before,—for instance, coal could be purchased at lower rates only a day or two before the prices quoted were fixed,—but there was no guarantee that in a short time the price would not have been much in excess of that fixed. At the same time the dealers had been consulted, and could not say their point of view had been ignored.

Further Regulations. December saw the list of regulations still further extended ; retailers of imported bacon, hams, and lard were to register themselves, so had makers of potted meats, etc., and caterers who dealt with wholesale firms in these foods ; the retailer was not to make more than 3d. a pound on bacon or ham, or 2d. on lard, and was to display his price list and keep correct records. Dairymen were to give priority of supply to young children and sick patients, and were to sell fresh cream only for invalids and children under five years of age, and then only upon receipt of a written statement of the case ; all other cream was to be reserved for butter-making. The maximum price of coffee was put at 1 /4 for raw coffee and 1 /6 for roasted or ground coffee, with the provision that superior kinds might be sold at prices up to 2 /6 per lb., if a notice was displayed in the shop to the effect that the grocer also had supplies of coffee at 1 /6 the pound.

Margarine Queues. Towards Christmas margarine assumed an importance it had never before had in Swindon ; butter was so scarce as to be practically unobtainable and the public had to fall back upon margarine, of which the maximum price was fixed at 1 /- per lb., excepting the brand known as " oleo " which, sold in its proper wrapper, was 1 /4 per lb. The main supply of margarine reached the town chiefly through certain multiple firms, and more especially through the " Maypole Company," and so eager was the public to obtain the article that big crowds formed outside the shops long before they opened in the morning, until the police had to undertake the arrangement of the crowds in " queues ; " in the depth of winter people had to stand in some cases for hours in the cold and wet to obtain a pound of margarine, and the queues became so alarming a feature of the streets that the police complained to the Food Control Committee. To make matters worse the supply ran out, and large numbers of people had the prospect of a " fatless " Christmas, for lard was as scarce as butter. The Town Clerk telegraphed to the Divisional Commissioner and the Ministry of Food, whereupon an extra 2½ tons of margarine were sent down to the Maypole Stores ; the distribution was undertaken by the Food Control Committee who asked the services of the Teachers and a few others ; tickets were obtained at the Town Hall, and at one time a queue, four deep, reached round the Town Hall until the end was close to the beginning of the queue ; the margarine was then sold to ticket-holders at certain schools, and thus on Monday, December 24th, over 2,500 persons were supplied with one-pound packets of margarine by one o'clock. There were obvious objections to the system and there were undoubtedly people who selfishly acquired unfair amounts, but a scheme had to be devised hastily to meet a sudden crisis, and it saved the situation, for not only did every family have a supply of the precious fat for Christmas, but a little was left over.

Meat Rations. By order of the Food Controller the supply of cattle and meat for sale was restricted in December to one half of the quantity sold in October ; the Committee and the butchers did all they could to supply the allowance of 12 oz. for an adult and six ounces for a child, consumers being supplied with coupons. The first week of the new scheme it was found that the demand for fresh meat was greater than in any other week since October, the explanation being that many households which had been content with small joints now demanded the full quota allowed by their coupons ; many persons, therefore, were unable to get meat at all, and the Food Control Committee decided that for the time being no family should be supplied with more than 5 lbs. of fresh meat per week. Seeing that sausages, cooked and preserved meats, bacon, and ham were not yet rationed, this was no great hardship. People were asked to go to the same butcher regularly, registering themselves with a butcher for beef and mutton, but not with any particular butcher for pork. This scheme, however, was but preliminary to a more rigid rationing scheme that came into operation in February, 1918. [1]

Food Production. It has already been noticed that the Swindon Town Council assisted local efforts for increasing the food-supply early in 1917, by enabling allotment holders to purchase seed-potatoes upon advantageous terms. Early in the year a sub-committee of the Town Council had been formed to put into operation the "Cultivation of Lands Order" of 1916. This committee decided to break up for allotments $32\frac{1}{8}$ acres of land at Broome Sewage Works, $5\frac{1}{8}$ acres at Rodbourne Sewage Works, a strip east of County Road with another south of the County Ground making over $2\frac{1}{4}$ acres, 5 acres of the Rodbourne Recreation Ground, and 3 acres adjoining the Town Gardens. Public notices were issued inviting applications for allotments, and they were immediately taken up.

As many of the allotment-holders were novices in gardening, Mr. T. Sharpe, F.R.H.S., the Horticultural Instructor to the County Council, was asked to give a course of lectures at the Technical Institution upon cottage-gardening ; these were well attended and were not the last delivered in Swindon by Mr. Sharpe.

Allotments. Some striking facts concerning the stimulus which allotment-holding had received were given at a large meeting of allotment-holders in March, the Mayor, Mr. A. J. Gilbert, presiding. It was reported that the Town Council had supplied 700 cultivators with seed potatoes, that it had 155 acres of land in 2,139 plots, and that it had already 1,775 tenants. These figures, however, were almost immediately improved, for there were 740 fresh applicants, and the Corporation took a further 48 acres of land for plots—as already detailed above ; even then 100 applicants were waiting for six acres that still remained to be obtained. In addition to the Corporation land, 90 acres were let by Major F. P. Goddard in 1,250 plots, and 20 acres by other owners in 300 plots. Thus about 318 acres of garden land were being cultivated by 4,115 tenants—a truly astonishing number. Women, too, were encouraged to interest themselves in the subject, a meeting of women being convened under the Mayoress at which they were asked to send in their names and to apply for advice and help in the work ; consequently, it was no uncommon sight to see women at work on their husbands' plots, and in many cases women held allotments of their own. So earnest was everyone in this matter that some of the ministers of the town preached from their pulpits upon the subjects of food-economy and food production.

The Committee's Work. When the "Cultivation of Lands" sub-committee reported to the Town Council in October, the chairman, Councillor T. Kimber, stated that up to the date of the report thirty meetings had been held ; the committee had taken over 62 acres $16\frac{1}{2}$ perches of land altogether, of which $16\frac{1}{2}$ acres had had to be obtained by the exercise of its compulsory powers ; besides the lands already enumerated a large slice of the Radnor Street Cemetery had been brought under cultivation, and although the Committee

(1) See page 149.

had not been able to satisfy the large number of new applicants, numbering 1,084, they had provided 870 with allotments ; the land was mostly let at 6d. per perch rental, but where the land was rough a reduction of 50% was made in some instances, and in others the first year's rent was remitted.   The Committee had engaged the services of Mr. A. Currey, of Wroughton, as Horticultural Instructor for the Borough from April 9th to July 31st, and besides publicly lecturing to gardeners Mr. Currey had visited the various plots, helping and advising the men at their work.   The quantity of seed-potatoes purchased by the Town Council in the Spring was 130 tons altogether, costing £1,800 ; the sale of these to allotment holders brought in £2011 : 12 : 8, leaving a good balance which was devoted to the purchase of five spraying-machines and spraying-mixtures, as well as artificial manures for sale to the tenants of the allotments.   The spraying-machines were let out to the tenants at a very small fee.

As fresh applications continued to come in it was decided to take up 3¾ acres of fresh land on Drove Road for the following season, and before the year was out the Council was advertising for applications for seed-potatoes again and was making arrangements to supply all applicants.   The close of the year was marked, too, by a second course of lectures by Mr. T. Sharpe, whose work was highly appreciated by the many who came to hear him and who found they could learn much from his simple and practical lessons, and found him always ready with counsel when they brought him their horticultural problems.

An experiment carried out by the Council at the Whitworth Road Cemetery had not been so successful as the work already described.   In March it was decided to plough up six acres of the ground there and to plant the ground with potatoes. Considering the lateness of the date, which did not allow the upturned soil to come under the action of frost or the buried turf to have time to decay, it was a risky experiment ; but, as has been said, the food-question was pressing and risks had to be taken.   The crop was not a success, for it was found that the soil was not deep enough, and was infested by wire-worms, and the old roots stifled the plants. Mr. Sharpe was called in to advise as to what should be done next season ; more land was taken in, and under his direction the whole was treated with manures and insecticides and prepared for mangolds, wheat and potatoes.

The Allotment-Holders' Association. The Allotment Holders' Association, inaugurated with about 80 members early in the year, had a very successful season ; its first president was Mr. Alderman S. E. Walters, with Mr. J. Day as Chairman of Committees, Mr. J. K. Partington as Secretary, and Mr. W. H. Major as Assistant Secretary.   By the end of September 400 members were enrolled ; they worked on co-operative lines, purchasing at wholesale prices seed, fertilisers, and other necessaries, and buying sprayers for the common use.   During the year they did not hold a show, but on September 29th exhibits of their products were sent to the Town Hall and afterwards despatched as a free gift to the forces.   Out of an income of £69 : 3 : 6 for the season the Association was left with a balance of £16 : 7 : 0 and had every prospect of a flourishing career.

Pig-keeping. A further effort to encourage food-production was made in January, 1917, when the Town Council made some relaxation in the bye-laws relating to the keeping of pigs ; the distance of sixty feet between a pig-sty and a dwelling-house, that was hitherto insisted upon, was reduced to thirty feet, provided that application was made to the Medical Officer of Health and sanction for the erection of the sty was granted.

War   The effort made in November 1916, to stimulate saving and investment
Savings   in the war-loan was repeated in February, 1917. Monday, February
Campaign.   5th, was a special day, for Sir. R. Ashton Lister and the Rt. Hon W.
F. Massey, the Prime Minister of New Zealand, came down and
addressed a Farmers' meeting in the Goddard Arms Assembly Room, and in the
evening they spoke at a large meeting at the Mechanics' Institute presided over by
the Mayor.

Prior to this day Swindon had invested £103,134, of which £97,163 had gone
through the Post Offices and Banks, and £714 was to be credited to the children in
the schools. But the present campaign gave a remarkable stimulus to the movement; at the farmers' meeting one farmer invested £5,000 in war loan and two
brothers invested another £5,000. The progress of the campaign can be seen from
the daily payments into the Banks and Post Offices during the last week, as
proclaimed from the Town Hall by " Swindon's Daily Barometer "—a huge clock-
face indicator—which showed the gradually mounting total :—

		£
Up to Monday, Feb. 5th		103,134
Feb. 6th to 9th	....	65,869
„ 10th	....	7,784
„ 12th	....	26,110
„ 13th	....	18,006
„ 14th	....	46,436
„ 15th	....	47,086
„ 16th	....	48,667
		363,092
G.W.R. Swindon Employees		6,555
TOTAL		£369,647

Of this sum the Town Council took up £25,000 new stock and £2,500 converted stock.

No pains were spared to ensure the success of the campaign; advertisements
were sent to the local press, great posters were displayed, the Boy-Scouts distributed
circulars from house to house, special slides were shown at the Theatre and Picture-
houses accompanied by short addresses, and special sermons were preached at
Christ Church by the Vicar.

By the end of March Swindon had 61 " War-Savings Associations "
The War-   with a membership of 4,186 contributors, and these associations
Savings   had obtained certificates to the value of £50,065 by February 17th,
Associations. which sum they increased to £62,328 by March 24th.

From February 17th to December 1st Swindon invested £62,606 in
war-savings certificates through the local banks and post-offices, and £33,496 in
National War Bonds taken out through the same channels, giving a total of £96,102
in about 9 months. The school-children of the Borough invested £1,594 : 1 : 9
in certificates during the eleven months ending December 1st; and by that time,
also, the number of " Associations " had risen to sixty-four, working in connection
with various workshops, church-guilds, clubs, and other bodies. The year had
witnessed a steadily growing spirit of thrift and of patriotic lending in Swindon,
and the result was owing to the persistent way in which the subject was now kept
before the public by the War Savings Committee and its Secretary, Mr. H. A.

Stanier ; much of the credit belonged to the Mayor, whose feelings were strongly aroused by the Government's appeals for thrift and food-economy.

National Service. A campaign that met with far less success than that in favour of economy was the "National Service Campaign" which caused the whole town, and, as far as one could judge, the whole country, to be placarded with flamboyant appeals to everyone to register for "national service." It was hoped that everyone between the ages of 18 and 61 and not in military service would enrol, and, in particular, all engaged in "non-essential industries" were expected to do so, the idea being that they thereby placed themselves at the service of the Government to do the work for which they were best fitted. Public meetings were held, and a special campaign was inaugurated at the end of March, when addresses were delivered at the Cinema houses, the Theatre and elsewhere, describing Mr. Neville Chamberlain's scheme and urging men to enrol by the 31st of the month. Nevertheless, in spite of the Mayor's assiduity the scheme came to little in Swindon, as was the case elsewhere, doubtless because of the general suspicion that the scheme was a device for bringing all under military jurisdiction, and because none considered his own work "non-essential."

War Pensions Committee. One or two changes in the personnel of the Pensions Committee took place during 1917. Mr. A. J. Gilbert acted as chairman during his mayoralty and was succeeded in November by Mr. A. W. Haynes upon his election to the mayoral office. Mr. F. Coles replaced Mr. L. J. Newman upon the Committee after Mr. Newman's call to military service, and in October Mr. C. Heavens replaced Mr. W. Parry who left Swindon for Newport where he was at once co-opted upon the Pensions Committee there. Mr. Parry's position as a representative upon the Western Counties' Joint Committee was taken by Mr. E. C. Ayris. In November Mr. W. E. Baylis was co-opted on the Finance Sub-Committee, of which Mr. F. King became chairman and Mr. E. C. Ayris vice-chairman. Two ladies, Mrs. A. Arman and Mrs. Hill, were early in the year appointed on the Visiting Committee.

Growth of the Work. An interesting glimpse of the growth of the work since July, 1916, and during 1917 may be obtained by comparing the figures given in the reports of the January and December meetings. In January the report upon the previous month's work gave—

	£	s.	d.
Cases under the War Pensions Act	201	19	1
Grants from the Royal Patriotic Fund, etc.	27	15	10
Cases of civilian distress	41	5	6
	£271	0	5

The December report gave—

	£	s.	d.
Cases under the W.P.A.	308	10	9
Special fund cases	13	14	3
Civilian cases	21	19	6
	£344	4	6

By the time that the Pensions Committee delivered to the Town Council its first Annual Report (for the year ending June 30th, 1917) it had granted assistance in 486 military and naval cases, 26 civilian cases, and 53 cases assisted from various special funds,—a total of 565 cases.

Sources of the Funds. The fact that the Committee was, at the request of the Local Representative Committee of the Prince of Wales' National Relief Fund, dealing with civilian cases, created an impression in some minds that the funds of the Committee came from charitable sources. This was not so ; the money expended by them in naval and military cases came entirely from funds provided by the Government. Small amounts, to meet special cases outside the scope of the War Pensions Act, were occasionally advanced from special funds ; thus, the January report acknowledges £6 from the Mayor's Local War Fund, £5 and £4 from a special fund for the dependents of wounded soldiers and sailors, and £6 and £5 from one for the dependents of deceased sailors ; in June receipts of £5 and £13 from the Navy League are acknowledged, and there is a pleasing reference to a sum of £5 : 6 : 8 subscribed by officers and men in India to assist in the Committee's work ; then in July we read of £2 from the "Queen Mary" Benevolent Fund, sent for the mother of a lad killed in the Jutland Fight. Nevertheless, the fact remains that the great bulk of the sums expended came from money provided by Government, and that the sums obtained from the Royal Patriotic Fund and other special funds were trifling beside this.

The Distributors. The work of distribution and visitation entailed much sacrifice on the part of those members who undertook it, and the first annual report (already alluded to) states that the average number of visits paid by each of the eight visitors was thirty per week ; the names of the visitors are given as—

Mr. F. King	Mr. A. W. Haynes	Mrs. L. Baxter
„ J. S. Protheroe	„ A. E. Harding	„ A. E. Jenner.
„ W. Parry	Miss L. Govier	

New Regulations. The Committee's duties were not made any the easier by the frequency with which new regulations were notified to them by the Statutory Committee, but happily these were nearly always imbued with the spirit of humanity and common sense; for instance, in March the Committee was authorized to make an increase of 4/- in the grant to a childless wife unable to work, and to give in special cases supplementary separation allowances $33\frac{1}{3}\%$ in excess of the assessment. In May a new Royal Warrant made eligible for pensions the parents of soldiers who had been killed or had died of wounds, provided they had been wholly or partially dependent upon their lost son ; another concession permitted grants not exceeding £3 to the widows of soldiers and sailors notified of their husband's deaths after April 4th. Later in the year widows who were being trained under a new scheme that embraced training in nursing, midwifery, massage, French polishing, etc., were granted a weekly allowance up to 12/6, and in December the Committee availed itself of the power granted by a new circular to make advances to widows of members of the Forces who had died after their discharge, by making payments of 30/- per week in one such case. Thus it will be seen that the tendency of these many regulations was to assist and not to hamper the Committee in their humane endeavours.

Training Discharged Men. The duty of rendering discharged and disabled men capable of entering industrial life properly equipped, fell to the Disablement Sub-committee ; it was not an easy task, for in some directions they encountered reasonable objections on the part of Trade Unions, in others the men themselves were not always easy to satisfy, and there had to be in any case a prospect that employment could afterwards be found.

The Committee arranged for one or two men to be trained at the " Lord Roberts' Memorial Workshops," but they found a general disinclination on the part of the men to leave the town; they therefore turned to local avenues of training, and, as a result of a conference with the Governors of the Secondary School, arrangements were made for training men in a variety of pursuits at the Technical Institution in Victoria Road; in September the Committee reported that three men were being trained in metal-plate work, one in light woodwork and polishing, two in poultry-keeping and gardening, and one in mechanical drawing and tracing; Mr. E. C. Skurray, too, had agreed to train men, and was instructing five in motor-driving, repairs, tractor ploughing, and agricultural engineering. Besides these, one man was being trained as a cinematograph operator and one as a switch-board attendant. Before the close of the year the Committee had further arranged for other men to be trained at the Technical Institute,—two in light woodwork, five in mechanical drawing, one in painting and decorating, four in metal-work, and one in poultry keeping. The Corporation had two in training at the switch-board at the Electricity Works and two others under training as plumbers, whilst Mr. Haskins was training two and Messrs. Greenaway and Sons one in boot-repairing; Mr. Skurray, too, had taken on another man in his motor-works.

Union Difficulties.   As has already been remarked, the training of these men brought the Committee face to face with some Trade Union difficulties. A trades-unionist, discussing the case of the metal-workers with an official—a trained engineer—asked, "Do you, as an engineer, think any man, after a few months' training, can be made an engineer ? " " Of course not," he replied, " it takes years to make an engineer." " Then what can these men do ? " " They could take charge of a simple machine, and undertake other simple duties." " But would you feel you could trust them with the hundred and one jobs any trained fitter will tackle at a moment's notice ? " " Certainly not." " Then," answered the fitter, " I want to know where we stand ; I have every sympathy with these men and would not stand in their light ; but if they are, after three months' training, to enter the labour-market as engineers and to take the place of a man who has learnt the trade, I am not having it." It was this attitude that led to the suspension about May of the training in metal-work until an arrangement had been made with the Trades Union ; a conference was held at which it was agreed, in view of the imminent appointment of Advisory Committees for each national industry, that a local panel of employers and trades-unionists should be set up to fix fair rates of pay in each case.

It may be noted, in passing, that the Corporation granted the men in training free passes on the trams to and from the Technical Institution. The absorption into industry of the trained men formed the subject of a conference between employers and the Committee in the Spring.

Visitors.   Besides the distributors already named a visitor was appointed to each of the eight districts, whose duty was to call periodically on all disabled men and to give advice and help in regard to medical treatment, pensions, industrial training, and employment ; the visitors named in the September report were Messrs. R. M. Forder, W. S. White, J. Powell, W. E. Reeves, E. C. Ayris, Edwin Jones, T. C. Morgan, L. J. Newman and W. R. Robins.

Medical Treatment.   Up to the date just referred to eleven discharged soldiers had been sent for medical treatment to various hospitals, sanatoria, and convalescent homes and, in addition, three motherless children of a soldier had been sent to a Boys' Home ; in October nine more men were reported as sent to various hospitals, and in November special treatment was arranged for five other cases. The Committee found many cases of tuberculosis amongst discharged men, and pressed the Wilts Insurance Committee to provide hospital accommodation for advanced cases, renewing their efforts in December by an appeal to the Ministry of Pensions to cause this to be done.

The Committee had kept in touch with other local pensions **Co-ordination** committees, and nearly every meeting considered letters upon **of the work.** all manner of principles and details from all parts of the country.

But now the work was co-ordinated over wider areas by the division of the whole country into districts, and Swindon formed a unit in the district under the Western Counties Joint Committee, which comprised Wiltshire, Dorset, Somerset, Gloucester, Devon and Cornwall. Each local War Pensions Committee had two representatives upon the Joint Committee—except Bristol, which had four, and Plymouth with three,—and there were also three representatives for employers, six for labour, three for the medical profession, and four for technical training ; Swindon's representatives were Messrs. A. W. Haynes and W. S. White, with Mr. W. Parry as the nominee of the Swindon Trades and Labour Council and Mr. G. Burkhardt as one of the representatives for technical training. [1]

The Mayor's The Mayor's Local War Fund, which has been mentioned once or
Local twice, and which was noticed as one of the subsidiary sources upon
War Fund. which the Pensions Committee had drawn occasionally for cases
that could not be dealt with under the War Pensions Act, received in subscriptions during the municipal year ending in November the sum of £351. [2]

Prince of It was seen that the subscriptions to the Prince of Wales' Fund in
Wales' Fund. Swindon ceased with the establishment of the Pensions Committee
(July 1st, 1916) ; the total amount sent up to the Central Committee was £6,384 : 9 : 8, and a balance of £350 in hand was given by the G.W.R. collectors as a nucleus for the new Mayor's Local War Fund. There was, therefore, not a great deal to report concerning the Prince of Wales' Fund at the close of 1917, when Mr. A. E. Dean, the Borough Treasurer, gave his account of the year's working of the fund. But although subscriptions had ceased, Swindon was still drawing from the central fund; during 1917 an average of 24 persons per week drew assistance amounting to an average of £5 : 4 : 6 per week, and the total amount for the year was £271 : 11 : 0. This brought the full amount drawn from the fund since its inauguration to £2,156 : 6 : 0, from which must be deducted £1,196 : 6 : 0 repaid to the Fund by the Government (as already related), leaving a net draft upon the Fund of £960.

In addition to these grants there had been various contributions from the general fund in the form of grants to widows of deceased soldiers, and in other ways. The issue of free medical books to soldiers' wives, enabling them to obtain drugs from chemists at cost price, was discontinued when the government-grant to wives was increased, but the Committee gave help in special cases.

Prisoners of As regards the Committee for providing Comforts for the Wilts
War Regiment—or, to use the term now most commonly employed, the
Committee. Prisoners of War Committee,—the account given elsewhere [3] of its
work shows that under the new Red Cross Scheme the Borough was committed to the raising of a sum of nearly £3,000, the quota for which Swindon was

(1) Continued on p. 171.   (2) See page 219 ; the figure quoted here   (3) Chapter V.
overlaps to some extent that on p. 80.

assessed by the County Association. The exact amount was £2,855 and the town exceeded the expectations of the Committee by raising over £3,075 for the Prisoners of War Fund besides nearly £360 for comforts for the fighting men. The work done by the packing committee at its depôt in Regent's Circus was heavy and continuous ; right through the year the Committee was sending three parcels per fortnight to each of about 90 prisoners, working under a very rigid system that demanded the utmost care and precision.

Vegetables for the Navy. A difficult Year. The year 1917 did not open auspiciously for the Vegetable Products Committee, for the winter of 1916-17 was one of much severity, and vegetables of all kinds were scarce ; the high standard which the committee had set themselves in the duty of providing vegetables for the Navy could not, therefore, be maintained. Another obstacle to their work was the ever-growing shortage of agricultural labour, illustrated by the position of Mr. Currey himself, who, at the final meeting of 1917, said that whereas he was accustomed to employ nine men on his land at Wroughton, he had now to manage with only two,—one an old man of seventy-five and the other a man fifty-eight years old.   The Committee, however, relaxed none of its efforts ; and indeed, it had earned so good a reputation that there could be no drawing back even if there had been any cooling of enthusiasm, for expectant eyes were now turned towards them. Thus, in January a letter came

A Swindonian's Appeal. from H.M.S. Inflexible, signed by an old Swindonian, Lieut. A. E. Hall, asking if the Committee could send some vegetables to that ship ; immediately they decided to send a truck-load, but found to their chagrin that they could not raise so much. Mr. H. Haine, of Sevenhampton, who had more than once helped them in a difficulty, generously provided a truck-load of swedes, turnips, and cabbages, and these were sent to the Inflexible. A letter of thanks was sent by Lieut. Hall, saying that 57 sacks and casks were received and remarking : " Officers and men very greatly appreciate your valuable gift, and desire me to convey to you their sincerest thanks. A surplus over and above our immediate needs was presented to H.M.S. Tiger. It has been most kind and generous of you, and we wish you all good luck and a very prosperous year."

In February the General Secretary, praising the work of the Swindon branch, said that their total consignments now amounted to over 180 tons. Amongst the ships sending messages of thanks were the Marlborough, the Constance, the Tiger, the Orion, the Bellerophon, the Bellona, the Benbow, the Iron Duke, etc ; from the Cyclops came the following letter from two artificers :—

Thanks from the Cyclops, " I am just writing you a few lines conveying the most sincere gratitude of the engine-room artificers for the splendid support and encouragement received from you, in assisting us in the gardening enterprise. We have the greatest hopes of success, and look forward eagerly to the gathering-in time and the fruits of our labours. May I assure you of the deepest gratitude and appreciation we feel for your kindly help." This letter was an acknowledgment of a gift of 200 cabbage plants sent for the garden which the men of the " Cyclops " were trying to cultivate.

and from the Lion and the Ramilies. A man from H.M.S. Lion called upon the secretary to thank the Committee verbally, and he stated that there were seven Swindon men on board his vessel ; and a Highworth lad wrote from H.M.S. Ramilies :—" We have been receiving fruit and vegetables for a considerable time now, and I have often wondered from whom they originated.   Reading the local papers which I have sent me, I saw what the Swindon and District Vegetables Committee are doing in supplying us with vegetables.   I have instructions to thank all concerned in this grand work.   I can assure you that the boys always greatly appreciate the gifts.   Nothing is wasted.   We are all deeply grateful to you for what you are doing for us.''

Sources of Supply.   In spite of the scarcity of fruit and vegetables, the list of donors for the year was a very long one and included many fresh contributors both from Swindon and the villages ; the area drawn from stretched from Dauntsey to Ashbury, and from Cricklade to Aldbourne, generous gifts being received from some friend or other in nearly every village.   In Swindon, besides the produce sent by private persons, churches, and schools, a considerable amount was forwarded by the Allotment Holders' Association, and on the Gorse Hill Allotments several boxes had been set up for the collection of gifts, however small.   A surprising quantity was obtained by such simple devices as the one just mentioned, and the good consignments so regularly sent in by Mr. Drew from Purton School were got together in this way, a large basket always standing open by his desk.   Amongst monetary gifts those sent by the girls of Messrs. Compton's factory were the chief, for they contributed during the year £21 : 1 : 7, raising their total subscriptions to £32 : 4 : 0 ;   it is to be remembered, too, that this was not the only cause supported by them.

Total for the 3rd year.   During the year purchases had to be made to keep up an adequate supply, in view of the difficulty of obtaining vegetables, and £25 : 1 : 0 was spent in buying 40 dozen cabbages, 31 bushels of carrots, about a thousand onions, 50 bushels of apples, twelve hundred head of lettuce, six dozen marrows, two bushels of parsnips, two bushels of swedes, and the same quantity of beetroot.   The total amount despatched to the Fleet consisted of 279 packages—as against 616 in 1916—and a truck-load of turnips presented by Mr. Haine.

For the last four months of the year the Committee was deprived of the services of the secretary, Mr. F. W. Trineman, who had been called away on work of national importance, and Mrs. Trineman had efficiently discharged the duties of secretary and treasurer.   At the concluding meeting of the year she was appointed to the joint offices, and the Town Clerk was asked to send a letter of thanks to Mr. Trineman for his faithful services ever since the inauguration of the work.   The Mayor, Ald. A. W. Haynes, and Councillor C. Hill (during whose mayoralty the Committee was formed) both paid a high tribute to the work of the Committee, and heartily supported the proposal to leave the work in their hands for the following year.[1]

The Soldiers' Rest.   The year 1917 was one of great activity for the ladies in charge of the Soldiers' Rest at the Town Hall, and their self-imposed duties were made doubly arduous by the situation as regards food.   The difficulty of catering, already great, was vastly increased when compulsory rationing came into effect, and in the spring of 1917 an intimation was received from the Southern Command that the provision made must be on rationing principles ; but the Committee succeeded in framing a satisfactory scheme which was put into operation on April 28th, whereby the men were supplied with tea, coffee, or cocoa, two sandwiches, two pieces of bread and butter, and one piece of cake for fourpence.

(1)   Continued on page 163.

By this time the Cyclists had left Draycott, and they were succeeded by regiments of the Training Reserve, who in their turn made way for the London Division.

Numbers. The numbers making use of the Rest are a proof of the need that called it into being and of its utility. When the Secretary, Mrs. Perry, presented her report in December, 1917, she was able to state that up to that time 66,805 men had had tea at the Rest in the fifteen months— allowing for the period when it was closed,—during which it had been open. The numbers varied week by week, and the record for any one week-end **The function of the Rest.** was hitherto 970, but it must be borne in mind that many others used the Rest ; it was more than a tea-room, and many came to write letters, to read, and to rest and enjoy the music. Every Saturday and Sunday, from 4.30 to 6 o'clock, a musical programme was arranged, and no small part of the men's enjoyment was due to the excellent singing and instrumental music they could always be sure of hearing ; the Committee met with a ready response to their appeals for help in this direction, and these concerts were frequently made more attractive by the voluntary contributions of some of the men, amongst whom there were often to be found gifted amateur musicians or professional instrumentalists. Altogether, up to December, 1917, 220 of these concerts had been given, whilst the piano was always available for any who desired to play.

The year 1917 was fittingly brought to a close by a delightful Christmas party held on Boxing Day, when 650 men were entertained and spent what they said was the finest time they had had since joining the forces.

Expenses. The total expenditure up to this date amounted to £1,147 : 2 : 8, a small enough figure for the huge number of soldiers entertained, working out at just about 4d. per head. Such a result was only possible through the assiduous and self-sacrificing efforts of so many voluntary workers. The work, continuing for some hours at a time, was strenuous and exacting, and all thanks are due to the many ladies who gave up their week-ends, sacrificing their own comfort and leisure, solely to brighten the lives of the men and lads whom the German madness had compelled to leave their homes and families. No man who accepted the hospitality offered will forget the breezy good humour, courtesy, and frank kindness with which he was treated by these daughters of Swindon. Their efforts were to be continued yet another year before demobilization released them from their humane undertaking.[1]

The Camp Concerts Committee. The camp at Chiseldon, with its thousands of youths fresh from comfortable homes, made a strong appeal to the sympathies of Swindon, and amongst other forms in which these sympathies took practical shape the formation of the Mayor's Camp Concerts Committee was not the least valuable ; the object of those who formed this committee was to try to relieve a little of the monotony inseparable from camp-life and to bring a little brightness to those in hospital there. From November 4th, 1916, to November 27th, 1917, the Committee succeeded in providing no less than 161 concerts for the troops at Chiseldon,—51 on Tuesday evenings in the Y.M.C.A. Hut, 56 on Saturday evenings mostly in the same building, and 54 at the Camp Hospital. Various members of the Committee were responsible for the programme, and the concerts were distributed amongst them as follows :—

(1) Continued on page 186.

Madame Dockray	 51	Mr. W. J. Young	 8
Mr. J. Gale (elocutionist)	 24	Miss F. Owens	 6
Mr. W. Richardson (the 'Wags')	8	Mr. A. E. Ford	 6
Mr. C. K. Warner (Sec.)	15	Mrs. McHardy	 2
Mr. F. Barnett	 6	Mrs. E. Hughes	 4
Miss A. Haines	 8	Miss Brown	 4
Mr. C. Daniels	 8	Miss Thomas (the ' Cheerios ')	2
Mr. J. L. Williams	 8	Miss Gilbert	 1

The Chairman and Secretary of the Committee, which consisted of working members, was Mr. C. K. Warner, who, previous to the establishment of the Committee, had endeavoured to bring some enjoyment into the Camp by forming a choir amongst the soldiers themselves,—work for which he was peculiarly fitted by his long experience as leader of the G.W.R. Temperance Choir in Swindon ; he had succeeded in building up an excellent choir from men of the Gloucesters, Warwicks, Hampshires, and Cyclists Corps, and after regular practices had given one concert, when the middle of the next week saw the men in France.

The concerts were thoroughly enjoyed by the men, and not only would the Hut often be full to overflowing, but the doorways and windows would be thronged by men unable to get inside ; and certainly everything was done to give a high tone to programmes upon which the best talent of Swindon was represented. It should be remarked, too, that no fee was ever paid to any performer, but naturally the companies could not be taken to and from Swindon without some expense and a sum of £28 : 15 : 6 was drawn from the Mayor's Fund for the hire of cars, though very often the artistes went at their own expense. Against this comparatively small expenditure must be placed a return of nearly £8 to the Mayor's Fund from a concert organised by Mr. W. J. Young, a member of the Committee, on January 25th, 1917, when scholars of the Secondary School trained by Mr. Young gave a capital programme at the Town Hall. In respect of conveyance the Committee was much indebted to Sergt. Hancock (late 11th Hussars) without whose valuable services with the car the expense would have been much greater. The Mayor, Mr. A. J. Gilbert, went with the party and presided at the concert on two occasions, and took a very special interest in the progress of the Committee's work. His successor, Ald. A. W. Haynes, also showed his appreciation of their efforts by attending with the Town Clerk at some of the Committee's meetings, and, as will be seen later, by utilizing the Committee's talents in other directions during his mayoralty.[1].

The Club for Wives and Mothers. Reference has already been made to the formation of the Social Club for the Wives and Mothers of members of the forces, and the Committee responsible for this beneficent work has been described. The average attendance at the weekly meetings through 1916 and 1917 was 160, not including the children whom the mothers brought with them. But by December, 1917, the membership had risen to 511, and the average attendance at the meetings was 240. From the opening of the club to the time of the general report of the work issued in December, 1917, the number of Wednesday afternoon meetings at the Town Hall was 94 ; in 1917, July and August were vacation months. The meetings were much more than "tea-meetings,"

Character of the Meetings. for every one was enlivened by music and song, and at many short addresses were given. All the available local musical talent was requisitioned upon occasion, and freely responded to the call ;

(1). Continued on page 185.

members of the theatrical profession engaged at the Empire Theatre generously accepted Mr. Stone's invitation to appear at the Town Hall, and parties of soldiers from the Chiseldon Camp or the Drill Hall also gave their services. The addresses were of an educational character as a rule, dealing with such subjects as the care of children, women's work in the war, war-savings, food-economy, and cottage-gardening. In connection with the last-named subject the Committee distributed to members of the Club eighteen sacks of seed-potatoes to meet the needs of those who were growing potatoes.

Cost. Owing to the voluntary nature of the labour and the generosity of various outside bodies the cost up to December, 1917, was defrayed entirely out of the nominal subscription and the small charges for refreshments, and the Committee was left with a balance in hand of about £4. The Committee expressed its gratitude in particular to the G.W.R. Temperance Union for the loan of china, to the Amalgamated Society of Engineers for table-cloths, and to the Presbyterian Church for urns, cloths, and tables. Apart from the cost of tea and food the only serious items of expenditure the Committee had to meet were for printing and piano-hire.

Entertainments. The weekly meetings were supplemented by some exceedingly enjoyable entertainments provided by generous patrons of the club, amongst whom Councillor J. Powell was one of the most constant in supporting it ; in the period covered by the report he entertained the members to tea in the Town Gardens on 14 occasions ; he also engaged the Central Cinema for the exclusive enjoyment of the members, and on another occasion engaged the Theatre, inviting all wives and mothers of men serving in any branch of the forces, whether they were members of the Club or not. The Mayors of the Borough for the two years, Messrs. W. E. Morse and A. J. Gilbert, both showed their kindly interest in the Club by inviting the members to a garden-party in the Town Gardens during the Summer, and Mr. and Mrs. H. Heard entertained 52 mothers and 141 children—though not as members of the Club,—at the Mechanics' Institute in December, 1916, when, after the tea, the Mayor addressed the guests, and the party was entertained by the " Wags " and by a cinema display; the children each received a bag of sweets and fruit given by the Rifle Club.

Support for the Pris. of War Fund. Many wives and mothers were by now mourning the loss of a loved one or were consumed with anxiety for one in a German prison, and the Club felt a touching interest in the Prisoners of War. In March, 1916, they raised £24 : 4 : 1 for the Prisoners of War Fund by a Sale of Work, the exhibits being either made or collected by the members, and every week they collected amongst themselves about £1 for the fund.

Savings. The members were encouraged to participate in the Government's War-Savings scheme, and up to the end of 1917 the sum of £203 : 18 : 6 had been invested by 122 contributors.

It will be realized that Mrs. H. C. King's committee of ladies had no light task in providing a tea and entertainment week after week, especially in view of the growing difficulty of catering. The mere labour of arranging tea on such a scale was great, and Mrs. Saddler and her colleagues must have felt much anxiety as they saw their sources of supply endangered by the rising cost of the goods, but they were yet to present another report upon what continued to be a very flourishing and admirable institution. [1]

(1). Continued on page 187.

The
Volunteer
Training
Corps.

Numbers.

Early in 1917 a determined attempt was made to check the decline in the numbers of the Volunteers which was a feature of 1916. A public meeting was called for February 20th, when the Mayor presided and was supported by Lord Roundway, Mayor. F. P. Goddard, the officers of the Swindon Detachment of the V.T.C., and others. Lieut. W. J. Ainsworth reported upon the condition of the detachment, and it appeared that the total membership stood at 233 of whom 38 were in "A" section, 42 in "B" section, and 153 in the Supernumerary section. "A" section consisted of men over military age and "B" section contained those of military age ; under the new regulations now in force both these sections were bound to pass a moderate examination on the basis of "C 1" of the army categories ; they were also bound to attain moderate proficiency in drill, and when they had fulfilled these two conditions the Government paid £2 per head for equipment ; all members of these sections who undertook to serve for the period of the war were equipped and armed free of expense.

Lieut. Ainsworth was able to state that 20 rifles were already on the way, and that instructors were to be provided from permanent camps, whilst certain Volunteer Officers and N.C.O.'s were to be permitted to go to instruction-camps in order to qualify as instructors ; the Swindon detachment was also allowed to use Chiseldon Camp and its equipment upon making proper application.

An interesting detail revealed by the report was the fact that from 100 to 150 men had passed from the corps into the Army, where they would find that the training they had received as volunteers would be of the greatest value to them.

Trench
Training.

The result of the encouragement now given by the Government was seen in the interest and zest with which the detachment entered into its training rather than in any great access of numbers. For instance, in the summer the Volunteers spent some weeks upon the construction of two sets of trenches in a field off Redcliffe Street ; the work was fairly complete and up-to-date, comprising fire and control trenches connected by communication trenches, with crump-holes and shell-slits, and part of the system was effectively reveted, part built up with sand-bags, and part protected by wire-entanglement. On August 5th, the work was inspected by Gen. Sclater, Col. Lord Roundway, Col. Fletcher and other officers. A trench attack was carried out in presence of these officers in thoroughly orthodox style, the men being divided up into rifle-men, bombers, lewis-gunners, rifle-bombers, and "moppers-up," and the attack being delivered in two waves. The inspecting party expressed their approbation of the display and complimented the Volunteers upon their smartness and careful preparation.

In Camp.

Almost directly after this inspection the Volunteers went into camp near Liddington ; owing to the nature of their business few of the men could devote a full ten-days to the camp, so a permanent party of twenty-five was settled there and other units came and went as opportunities permitted them. The programme for one day will show how thoroughly the men entered into the training under canvas ; it is the routine for Monday :—Reveille, 6.30 ; parade at 7.0 for an hour's physical training ; breakfast at 8.0 ; parade for drill at 9.30 ; parade for bayonet practice at 11.0 ; dinner at 1.0 ; parade for bombing at 2.30 ; tea at 4.30 ; parade for drill at 7.30 ; tattoo at 10.0. Interesting lectures on such subjects as bombing and musketry varied the routine on certain days, and the first Sunday morning was devoted to an instructive scheme of open attack upon an objective bristling with obstacles and a stoutly defended "strong-point."

Sergt. Major T. Trimmer (Royal Sussex) was responsible for the development of this very interesting scheme, which was executed to the satisfaction of the officers conducting and witnessing it.   The instruction in the different branches of training was carried out by instructors who had undergone regular courses at Lyndhurst and Tidworth,—Sergt, Maj. Potbury, Corp. J. E. Greenhalgh, Corp. W. M. Greenaway, Pte. H. Atkins and Pte. G. Dockray,—and the camp was well equipped with material ; the men themselves were full of zest and everything went off in the best style, whilst the commissariat under the supervision of Acting Q.M.S. H. W. Thomas won commendation from everyone.   Towards the close of the ten days, ending on Sunday,

A Trophy.   August 19th, as many as 70 men were in camp ; on Saturday afternoon a team marched into Swindon to compete at the miniature rifle-range for Capt. R. A. Gill's Silver Cup, which they won by a substantial margin, the scores being—

Swindon Coy., 1st Wilts Volunteers	....	2341 points
15th (T.W.) Worcesters	....	2307 ,,
Military Foot Police	....	2288 ,,

Three matches of eight a side were arranged and the highest score of all was made by a Swindon shot, Sergt. Moran, who took part in all three matches and scored 299 out of a possible 300.

On the last Sunday more serious tests were carried out in Camp, for the new rifles were to be used with live ammunition upon the ranges at Liddington. 91 men, of whom 43 were efficients and 48 recruits, assembled to undergo their class-firing tests, and more than half had never fired a rifle with live cartridges before.   The result was gratifying in the extreme and no one was more satisfied then Sergt. Major Potbury who had been indefatigable in his efforts to train the men for the tests; the figures were—

Success at   Efficient Class   ....   36 passed 7 failed
the Ranges.   Recruits Class   ....   42 passed 6 failed.

After a hard day spent in packing, marching, shooting, striking camp, and marching home,—14 hours activity,—the detachment reached home just in time for eight of their members, who formed part of the Fire-Brigade, to join in the effort to extinguish a conflagration at the Southern Laundry.

The high degree of efficiency of the Swindon Company was again demonstrated in October, when it presented the first batch of recruits in the Wilts Battalion to become " efficients."   They were examined by Adjut. Capt. Lawrence in squad drill, extended order, bayonet fighting, bombing, and musketry, including range firing.   Thirty of the candidates passed the examination, thus becoming entitled to their uniform and equipment ; several of these were youths between 17 and 18 years of age, and a capital course of instruction for the ensuing winter was in course of preparation in the hope that a considerable number of lads of that age would join the Company.

Keenness   Thus the year 1917 was marked, as regards the Volunteers, by a devotion to the work of training that secured great success and the
in 1917.   commendation of the authorities, and this was due to the zeal of the officers, the encouragement and facilities now provided by the Government, and the consequent interest that the men felt in their training.   The practice in open field and trench warfare, studied under Coy. Sergt. Major T. Trimmer, was entered upon with the enthusiasm of schoolboys, and equal keenness was shown in the musketry course under the instruction of Sergt. Major Potbury and Sergt. Dainty of the 22nd Training Reserve Battalion.

In November, Brig. Gen. T. C. P. Calley, the Commandant of the Wiltshire Volunteers, was gazetted a Staff Officer for the Volunteer Service.   He took the greatest interest in the Swindon Company, and on more than one occasion expressed his regret that a town of Swindon's size should not support quite two companies of Volunteers, each 250 strong.   This deficiency in numbers was, in fact, the only point at which the movement in Swindon was open to criticism. [1]

Red Cross   In March, 1917, Mr. Basil Hankey, the Director of the Wiltshire
Society :   Branch of the Red Cross Society, wrote to the Swindon Town Council
a new   stating that if Swindon could offer a suitable building for a hospital
Hospital.   for wounded men, providing 50 or more beds, he would undertake
that the offer should be accepted by the War Office at once.   The Wesleyan Institute in Faringdon Street was suggested as a very suitable building, capable of accommodating over 120 beds, and was reported upon favourably by Col. A. R. Hall, R.A.M.C.   It was available at a rent of £450, and the Council resolved that if the Institute were accepted by the War Office they would, subject to the Local Government Board's sanction, pay the rent.

The Council was much chagrined to receive a week or two later a
Council's   letter from an official of the Army Council declining the offer, saying
Offer refused.   that another scheme involving the use of the Infirmary at Stratton
Workhouse had been favourably considered.   Mrs. Calley and Mrs. Waugh had inspected the Stratton accommodation and they found that the wards were practically ready and equipped for a hospital, whereas some structural alterations would be required at the Institute.   At the Council Meeting held on April 17th, very strong feeling was excited by what was considered a " snub " to the Council by the War Office, and warm protests were made against the idea of associating soldiers, wounded in the service of their country, in any way whatever with a pauper institution.   The Mayor, Deputy-Mayor, and Town Clerk were instructed to take what immediate steps they deemed necessary to secure the end desired by the Council.

The officials of the War Office, however, decided that the Stratton scheme was the preferable one for their purpose, and an agreement was made whereby the Red Cross Society took over a portion of the Infirmary, the Guardians waiving any claim for rates upon the occupied portion.   One regrettable result of the disagreement concerning the choice of a building for the hospital was that several of the members of the local branch of the Red Cross Society sent in their resignations, in token of their disapproval of the course that had been pursued.

Apart from objections connected with the character of the institution,
The Stratton   the Infirmary was undoubtedly the better place ; there the inmates
Hospital.   could have quietude and fresh country air, and they had plenty of
open ground for exercise and recreation—an important detail quite lacking in Swindon unless one considered the G.W.R. Park as supplying the need. The hospital formed an auxiliary to the military hospital at Reading, and about the middle of June was ready for the reception of eighty patients, Mrs. Calley (The President), and Mrs. Waugh (The Secretary), being present to receive the first batch, along with an excellent staff of from thirty to forty trained nurses and V.A.D. workers. The charge of the hospital was entrusted to Mrs. Muir, assisted by Miss Whistler, and the medical officers were Drs. Muir, Beatty and Powell ; Mrs. Yule had charge of the clothing department, Miss Scott of the kitchens, and Mrs.

(1) Continued on page 188.

Fuller and Mrs. Cholmeley acted as general quarter-masters.   Shortly afterwards Miss K. Rose was made Secretary to the Hospital Committee.

One result of the locating of the Hospital at Stratton was that it was removed to a large extent out of Swindon's immediate sphere of interest, and although fine lists of gifts and donations were acknowledged weekly, Swindon did not at first figure largely in them ; but as the weekly acknowledgments and the sight of the "hospital blue " uniform familiarised the public with the idea that the hospital was just " at their elbow," interest was awakened ; frequent parties went over to Stratton to entertain the men with music in the wards, Mr. A. Manners fetched men over to performances at the theatre, and right through the Summer the men had invitations to garden-parties both in and about the town.

A visit to the hospital with one of the orchestras that went periodically from Swindon was a delightful, if somewhat saddening experience ; the well-lighted, clean, and airy wards were a picture of comfort; chairs were brought into one ward and these and the beds were crowded with convalescent men whose reception of their entertainers was full of welcome and of courtesy, who followed the programme with far more intelligence and attention than the average concert audience, and who never failed to put up one of their number to voice their thanks at the close.   During the evening a jovial interval occurred when patients, nurses, and guests took light refreshments together, and chatted with one another, and throughout the evening a happy, free-and-easy atmosphere prevailed, with plenty of cigarettes and sweets for all who wished for them.   Attendance was of course quite voluntary, but few whose condition or duties allowed them to be present chose to remain outside, and members of the companies who went over used to say that they never sang or played better than in the appreciative atmosphere of the hospital ward.

Visitors were admitted to the hospital from 5 to 7 p.m. on Wednesdays and from 2 to 4 p.m. on Sundays.   Only occasionally were inmates natives of Swindon or the locality, but many friendships were formed between the men and people of the neighbourhood and many visitors came out of pure interest, bringing small gifts of luxuries with them.

At a concert held on November 1st, Mrs. Muir, the Matron in charge of the Hospital, and Sister Whistler were presented with the Royal Red Cross in recognition of their services.   Shortly afterwards an exhibition and sale **Sale of** of work was held at the Hospital, the articles being the work of **Work.** wounded soldiers,—chains, chip-carving, golliwogs, jig-saw puzzles, basket work, model aeroplanes, etc. ; the object was to raise special funds for giving the men a good Christmas, and the result was extremely gratifying for £91 : 9 : 5 was left after paying expenses.   In the same paragraph that notified this result, Mrs. Calley acknowledged the receipt of a cheque for £18 : 17 : 3 from Mr. A. E. Harding on behalf of the Swindon Horticultural Society and two other cheques for £5 each as well as a very large number of gifts of every description. The number of patients in the hospital at the close of 1917 was 97.

Depôt, etc.   The Depôt in Regent Street continued its activities throughout the year ; it was open on Mondays from 11.30 a.m. to 12.30 p.m. and on Thursday from 3 to 4 p.m., for the distribution of materials and the receipt of finished articles.   An envelope collection for funds for buying material was made in April and produced £70 : 19 : 10.   About the same time a new course of lectures in First Aid was begun at the Technical Institution by Dr. T. P. Berry.

The Balance-sheet for 1917 for the war-work Depôt was as follows :—[1]

(1) Narrative continued on page 168.

Balance Sheet

INCOME		£	s.	d.	EXPENDITURE		£	s.	d.
Balance from 1916	....	11	15	0	Materials	....	138	6	8
Subscr. & Donations	....	32	9	6	Grant to Bourton Depôt		5	0	0
Whist Drives	....	27	15	0	Printing, Advertising, etc.		4	5	3
Chapel Collection	....	1	0	6	Expenses of Room	....	1	3	8
Envelope Collection	....	71	1	4	Balance in hand	....	2	7	1
Grant from Swindon					Balance at Bank	....	11	9	11
Branch, B.R.C.S.	....	10	0	0					
V.A.D. Uniforms	....	8	11	3					
		£162	12	7			£162	12	7

North Wilts Farmers. The Wiltshire Branch of the British Farmers' Red Cross Society repeated its special effort to raise funds by a " Jumble Sale " at Swindon Market on Monday, May 21st, and succeeded in raising a net return of £1,649 : 13 : 7. The first "lot" was the King's Proclamation (read by the Mayor, Mr. A. J. Gilbert) urging economy in the use of food ; it was put up to auction and finally knocked down to the Mayor for £5 on behalf of his son, Lieut. J. C. Gilbert, then in Mesopotamia. Mrs. Calley now opened the sale of the various lots presented to the Red Cross Society, the first being a pedigree bull give by General Calley which realized by successive sales nearly £110. The proceeds of the sale were thus allocated :—

				£	s.	d.
Relief of the Allies Fund	....	....	....	750	0	0
British Farmers' Red Cross Fund	....	....		750	0	0
Swindon Prisoners of War Fund	....	....		100	0	0
Mayor's Ambulance Fund	....	....		20	0	0
Swindon Red Cross Hospital	....	....		10	0	0
Marlborough Red Cross Hospital	....	....		10	0	0
Bourton Supply Depôt	....	....	....	9	13	7
				£1649	13	7

As the 1915 sale at Swindon brought in £181 : 0 : 6 and those at Swindon and Savernake in 1916 realized £3,025, and the present sale nearly £1,650, the total receipts from " Jumble Sales " already organised by the Swindon Branch of the National Farmers' Union came to nearly £4,900 up to date,—a fine contribution to the funds of the Red Cross Society.

The Wages Question. Throughout 1917 the high cost of living caused the greatest unsettlement amongst all but the richest classes ; it was recognized that the public was almost powerless to cope with the question of prices, and therefore the wage-earners turned their attention to increases of wages in order to meet the increase in prices ; this was a course where no finality could be reached so long as prices continued rising, and thus new claims for consideration were made with startling frequency. It would be impracticable to enter upon a general survey of wages in the G.W.R. Factory and elsewhere, and the **Bonuses under the Council.** remarks will be confined to the Town Council's workers. It has been seen that in March, 1915, the workmen received a bonus of 2/- per week, an increment of ½d. an hour in March, 1916, and a bonus of 2/- per week in Nov. 1916 ; now, in March, 1917, another ½d. per hour was granted, and the result was that the men's wages were 29 /- and 27 /- per week in Summer and Winter respectively, with the addition of the total bonus of 4 /- ; —the entire increase hitherto being 8 /4 per week.

A month later a 2 /- bonus was granted to the tramway-men, with the proviso that it was not to raise any wages over 45 /- a week, and it was agreed that the full bonus of no employee was to exceed 4 /-.

But in the Summer the Council was approached by the Workers' Union, and in response to their representations an additional bonus of 4 /- per week was conceded in July to married men provided that it did not raise their weekly wages beyond 60 /-, and to single men provided their weekly wages were not raised above 34 /-. A similar concession was made to the tramway-men in September, the bonus dating back from July.

In October bonuses were granted to the Town Hall Staff ; the members under 18 years of age received 4 /- ; those between the ages of 18 and 26 received 7 /- if they were married and 6 /- if they were single ; married men over 26, whose salary was under £140 a year, received 8 /- and single men of that class 7 /- ; and those whose salaries were between £140 and £160 had 5 /-.

Again, in November an additional bonus of 2 /- per week was given to the Council's employees who were under 18 years of age.

Female Labour under the Council. The ever-increasing scarcity of male labour caused the Council, like other employers, to have recourse to female-labour ; in March it was decided to appoint women tram-conductors, and very soon they were a familiar sight upon the cars. Many people criticised, but it is unjust and absurd to generalize concerning the way they fulfilled their duties; there were women who were all that could be wished as regards alertness and courtesy, and there were others who were disobliging and perfunctory ; but the same could be said of any class of men-conductors, and certainly the women carried on the work successfully till the men came back.

In September, too, girl-clerks were introduced into the Town Hall ; by this time the presence of girls in the railway-works' offices and elsewhere was so common that there was no novelty in seeing them in the public offices.

Teachers' Salaries. The Education Committee, too, had in March felt constrained to consider the position of the Teaching Staff, upon whom, in the absence of any war-bonus or extraordinary increments of salary, the situation was pressing very severely ; the Council passed its scheme, which gave a bonus to every married assistant master, consisting of £7 : 10 : 0 per annum with an additional allowance of £2 : 10 : 0 for each child under 14 years of age up to three in number, providing that his salary did not thereby exceed £180 a year. To all other assistant teachers was given a bonus of £7 : 10 : 0, so long as the salary was not raised above £180 for men and £130 for women. Uncertificated mistresses such as sewing-mistresses, were to receive a bonus of £5 providing that it did not bring the salary above £70 per annum. These arrangements proved to be but transitory, for the salary scale itself was admittedly inadequate, and it was not long before the Committee set about a radical revision of the scale.

Juvenile Crime. In most parts of the country much apprehension was felt concerning the increase in juvenile crime and the unhealthy degree of liberty enjoyed by young people who were receiving inordinate wages. The absence of so many fathers and teachers was bound to have the effect of relaxing the strings of discipline, and in some places a very grave state of affairs was brought about. Happily there was less cause for anxiety in Swindon than in many towns, but indications of the danger were not absent ; thus, at one session of the Juvenile Court in March, 1917, there were three cases of theft by children before the Court, and about the same time reference was made in the Chamber of Commerce to the increase in juvenile crime, and tradesmen were urged to lessen the **Huge** temptation presented by lavish displays in shop-fronts. The **Wages of** excessive wages paid to mere children were also illustrated at the **Young folk.** same court, when a boy of fifteen, summoned for riding a bicycle without lights after dark, admitted receiving wages of 35 /- per week at the Munitions factory. The consequence of this premature command of large sums of money by mere boys and girls was the production of an offensive type of young person—loud, swaggering, and spendthrift,—that frequently made the streets unpleasant for quiet folk ; they were quite above restraint at home as their high wages made them independent, and they would not infrequently leave their homes and go into lodgings. To see this type in its full flower, however, one had to go to certain other munition centres, but it was not unrepresented in Swindon.

It was therefore a timely step which was taken in October, when **Juvenile** a local committee was set up to co-ordinate the efforts of the several **Organization.** organisations in the town that were concerned in the welfare of children. This Committee was a large and varied body formed of representatives of all these organisations and it met to consider first how boys and girls might be attracted into clubs or brigades, how the difficulty of obtaining workers might be overcome, how the weaker units might be strengthened, how overlapping might be prevented, and how the development of the work might be furthered. At a subsequent meeting in November, an Executive Committee was elected and officers were appointed, viz:—Chairman, the Mayor (Ald. A. W. Haynes) ; Vice-Chairman, Mr. A. J. Gilbert ; Joint Secretaries, Miss E. A. Gough, Mr. W. J. Young, and Mr. W. Bullock ; Treasurer, Mr. A. E. Dean. Amongst the suggestions discussed at this meeting and referred to the Executive's consideration were the formation of a Boys' Club Union, the preparation of a handbook descriptive of all existing organisations and classes, the association of Sunday Schools in the work especially as a means of obtaining suitable workers, the provision of gymnasia, and the possibility of obtaining the use of premises belonging to religious and other bodies for use as welfare centres.

Births and Some concern was expressed at a meeting of the Council in July at the **Deaths.** figures for Births and Deaths in Swindon, for the Medical Officer's report stated that the average monthly death-rate for the five months commencing January 1st, 1917, exceeded the average monthly birth-rate, the figures being 17.6 per 1,000 and 14.8 per 1,000 respectively. In September, however, a more reassuring report was received giving the average monthly death-rate for the seven months commencing January 1st as 13.82 per 1,000 and the birth-rate for the same period at 16.4 per 1,000. The effect of the war upon the birth-rate was clearly seen by a statement issued about this time comparing the birth-rate in Swindon for the year 1916 with that for 1915, by which it was shown that it had fallen from 21.16 per 1,000 in 1915 to 18.9 per 1,000 in 1916 ; thus the 16.4 quoted for the first seven months of 1917 was seriously low.

Increase in At a special meeting of the Town Council held on March 20th to **the Rates.** consider the annual budget a somewhat heavy increase in the rates was found to be necessary, the total amount being 1 /2 in the £, made up of 8d. on the District Rate, 5d. on the Education rate, and 1d. for the Tramways ; the reasons are interesting as showing the activities of the Council at the time and the difficulties that beset its work. Increased wages, rates, and taxes account for some of the increase ; £400 was required for the new Maternity Hospital ; the lighting restrictions accounted for a deficiency of £1,910 in the electric light account ; then there was excess expenditure on the Rodbourne sewage-farm, roads, etc. ; the hospital board made an unexpected precept upon the Council ; the cost of school materials, fuel, etc., had gone up enormously and there was also a sensible reduction in the education grant due to a fall in the attendance caused by infectious disease and severe weather ; increased expenditure was needed on the tram track ; and, along with these heavier calls on the rates, must be noted the disability under which the Council lay by the Treasury's prohibition against the raising of loans.

Reduction of the Debt. A satisfactory feature of the statement made by the Chairman of the Finance Committee (Mr. T. Kimber) was the reduction in the Borough's loan debt which on March 31st, 1909, stood at £451,518, and had now been reduced to £367,000, whilst by the end of another year it would be approximately £350,000,—a reduction of £100,000 in nine years.

Electricity Extension. The Electricity Department, hard hit by the lighting restrictions, was called upon in 1917 to make an important extension of the system, for the Ministry of Munitions required a supply of current for the new munition factory in Gipsy Lane, Stratton, and was prepared to pay part of the cost of installation. The proposal was laid before the Council in February, and on July 4th the current was switched on to the new factory by Mr. Bull, the chairman of the Electricity and Tramways Committee, under the guidance of the Electrical Engineer, Mr. Dimmack. This was the first occasion in Swindon for the use of the high-tension alternating-current three-phase system and caused the erection of some very fine new plant at the electricity works.

Trams. The deficiency in the Tramways account reported in the Budget statement was practically entirely accounted for by increased expenditure on the maintenance of the permanent way ; it demanded from the rates 2½d. in the £, as compared with 1½d. for the past year. The receipts, however, continued to go up, and in June an increase of £570 on the year's working was reported, the largest on record.

The Lighting Restrictions. The restriction of the public lighting was, in the opinion of many of the Council and the public, carried to an unnecessary and dangerous degree, and at the September meeting of the Council there were many protests made ; it was said, very truly, that the streets were dangerous during the moonless nights and that the state of things was detrimental to public morality and decency. In response to representations made to the authorities—for the Council was not free in the matter—a letter was received from the Home Office allowing some relaxation of the lighting order if suitable precautions were taken. Those who lived in Swindon and had to go out in those wintry evenings of 1916-1918 will not forget the pitchy darkness of the streets, intensified by a glimmer here and there coming from some lamp that had the greater part of the glass blackened ; now and then the wayfarer was dazzled by the sudden flash of an electric torch borne by another wary pedestrian and sometimes one would meet someone carrying a subdued light in a lantern or bicycle-lamp. Collisions and falls were not infrequent, and the neglected state of many of the roads allowed numerous traps to lie about in the form of large pools of water or slush. Some efforts to ameliorate the perilous state of the roads was made by painting tree trunks, curbs, and posts with white paint ; but this was of no use unless there was a little light that could be reflected, when of course the paint was hardly necessary. Another concession that might be remarked here was the allowing of the Town Hall clock to strike again (in March) after a long silence.

Placards and Newspapers. It will be impossible for people of a later generation, should they be blessed with the inexperience of a great war, to imagine the many unexpected points at which civilian life felt the influence of the war.

For instance, the October Council report baldly states that it was agreed to reduce the rent of certain hoardings in Swindon from £10 to £8,—another consequence of the war ; paper was becoming dear, much wood-pulp was used in making munitions, and the Government had prohibited the use of newspaper placards and the posting of placards over a certain size ; moreover, advertisers were becoming fewer and there were fewer commodities and public functions to advertise ; consequently the hoardings often presented a barren surface to the public eye. The paper question also affected the price of newspapers, as well as their size ; so on August 3rd, the price of the weekly edition of the " *North Wilts Herald* " was raised from 1d. to 1½d., although its contemporary, " *The Swindon Advertiser*," maintained the old price for the present.

The Waste-Paper Scheme. Whilst the subject of paper is before the reader allusion should be made to the scheme so successfully carried out by the Chamber of Commerce, whereby assistance was given to the paper manufacturers and at the same time considerable sums were obtained for local funds. The scheme was initiated at the Chamber's last meeting in 1916 and was put into operation immediately. The aim was to collect the great amount of waste-paper that most people accumulate, including such things as old ledgers and account-books lying in tradesmen's cellars. The aid of the Boy Scouts and Girl Guides was enlisted for the collection, patrols going round on Saturdays and fine evenings and conveying the paper given them to depôts where it was stored until there was sufficient to be sent to a central depôt for baling. The central depôt was at the Repository, kindly lent by Mr. Chappell, and Mr. Prowse lent a coach-house in Newport Street for a store as well as a shed near his house ; the New Swindon depôt was a store in Merton Street lent by Mr. Heard. The work was organized by two Committees, one formed by Mr. Horder for Old Town and one by Mr. Tranter for New Town.

The Mayoress, Mrs. A. J. Gilbert, formed a small Committee to collect enough to defray the initial expenses, the chief of which was £7 : 10 : 0 for a baling-machine, and Messrs. Heard, Mason, Raven and Coleman gave 220 sacks. By the middle of February the baling-machine was at work, and a contract had been entered into with Messrs. Bradford & Co., of Bath, whereby the Chamber was to receive £3 a ton for scrap-paper, £5 a ton for magazines, and £9 a ton for ledgers without covers. A good impetus was given to the collection by the gift of a large quantity of ledgers and other paper from the Town Hall cellars, and many promises of similar gifts were readily given.

When the military authorities took over the Repository for motor-transport workshops, the Chamber rented a store in Eastcott Road, and then Mr. Maundrell kindly provided excellent accommodation free of charge in Cricklade Street. The Scouts and Girl Guides worked splendidly, and as a result of their efforts 500 bales, 253 sacks of waste paper were collected and disposed of, the total tonnage of which was 42 tons, by the time the annual meeting of the Chamber of Commerce was held in November.

This large quantity of waste-paper had enabled the Chamber to send £30 to the Victoria Hospital, £20 to the Wiltshire Prisoners of War Fund, £10 to the Red Cross Society, and £2 to the Boy Scouts and £1 for the Girl Guides in recognition of their labours. The work was going on as briskly as ever, and the results already attained were but an earnest of what was ultimately accomplished [1].

Flag-days. Whilst the subject of these minor contributions to local philanthropic bodies is being spoken of, one may note the list of " Flag-Days " for 1917,—a long list that speaks well for the generosity of the people of Swindon; they were—

		£	s.	d.
21st April	Wilts Prisoners of War	143	17	5
5th May	Russian Flag Day	129	15	4
12th May	National Egg Collection for the Wounded	156	13	4
26th May	Motor Ambulance	236	5	5
9th June	Mesopotamia Day	131	13	6
30th June	Wounded Horses' Flag Day (R.S.P.C.A.)	93	19	11
14th July	France's Day	118	18	6
28th July	Blinded Soldiers' and Sailors' Hostel	97	5	11
25th Aug.	Sailors' Day (R.N. Lifeboat, Minesweepers, and Jutland Funds)	92	16	2
8th Sept.	Womens' Day	164	18	11
22nd Sept.	Recreation Huts, Chiseldon	80	12	1
6th Oct.	Lord Roberts' Memorial Fund	56	10	7
13th Oct.	" Our Day " (British Red Cross)	155	17	4
	TOTAL	£1,659	4	5

Even this long list does not exhaust the record of street collections, for it does not include the Annual " Rose Day " (June 22nd) in aid of the Victoria Hospital, when £136 : 19 : 1½ was collected in Swindon and £77 : 5 : 3 in the district around, making a total of £214 : 4 : 4½, and leaving a balance of £125 : 3 : 7½ for the Hospital after expenses were deducted. Then there was " Scarlet Pimpernel Day," arranged by the Ancient Order of Buffaloes, whereby £102 : 3 : 2½ was raised towards the cost of a Red Cross Motor-Ambulance which was presented to the War Office through Major F. G. Wright, at a meeting in the G.W.Rly. Park on August 18th, in the presence of the Mayor and Town Council, the Bishop of Bristol, and a numerous company of citizens.

A Novel Tax. The Government had perforce to look in new directions for money to carry on the war, and the public was not always aware of the sums it was paying in taxation ; but one novel tax was levied in 1917 which the taxpayer could not overlook. A tax on amusements had often been advocated, and this year saw its first imposition. It was levied by means of stamps of graduated value attached to the ticket of admission, the cost being added to the cost of the ticket. As first imposed in July the tax began at 1d. on tickets up to 4d. in cost and rose to 6d. on tickets costing from 7 /6 to 15 /- ; but this scale was replaced in October by one that was more nicely graduated and rose to a much higher figure ; it began at ½d. on tickets up to 2d. in price, and rose gradually until 6d. was charged on tickets costing from 2 /1 to 3 /-, then 9d. on those up to 5 /-, 1 /- on those up to 7 /6, and so on until tickets costing 15 /- or more carried a tax of 2 /6 and additional half-crowns for every 5 /- above 15 /- in price.

(1) Continued on page 181.

The 3rd Anniversary of the War. Saturday, August 4th, was the third anniversary of the declaration of war, and in common with most parts of the Empire, Swindon made it the occasion for demonstrating its conviction that the war was a righteous war, the sword having been forced into the nation's hand by an unscrupulous and ambitious aggressor, and for re-affirming the determination not to draw back from the struggle till victory was won. A great meeting of citizens was held in the open space by the Town Hall on Sunday evening, when the Mayor, supported by members of the Council and Magistracy and Ministers of the various Churches, proposed a resolution :—

"That, on this third anniversary of the declaration of a righteous war, this meeting of the Citizens of Swindon records its inflexible determination to continue to a victorious end the struggle in maintenance of those ideals of liberty and justice which are the common and sacred cause of the Allies."

It was the same resolution as had been passed by multitudes of people in all parts of the British Empire on the anniversaries in 1915 and 1916, and on this occasion it received a loud and unanimous endorsement from the great body of Swindon's citizens assembled at the Town Hall. The Mayor proposed it in a speech of great fervour, and was followed with equal warmth by the Rev. John Hall, the Wesleyan superintendent minister, Major F. G. Wright, Mr. C. Hill and Mr. T. Butler. Then the enthusiasm of the meeting was raised to the highest pitch by the appearance of Sergt. William Gosling, V.C. on the platform ; he was introduced by the Mayor and delivered an address full of encouragement and hope, and one that paid a high tribute to the way in which the Territorials, "whom you used to call feather-bed soldiers," had stood the test of battle.

A Local V.C. Sergt. Gosling was a Wroughton man and had just returned from France ; two days before this meeting his Wroughton friends had given him a great reception in the Oddfellows Hall at Wroughton, when Brig. Gen. T. C. P. Calley had presented him with a purse and an illuminated address subscribed for by the people of Wroughton. General Calley congratulated Sergt. Gosling upon the honour bestowed upon him by the King for an act that had saved the lives of a great many of his comrades ; for, when a high explosive shell dropped just in front of his trench, Sergeant Gosling rushed towards it, and in less time than it takes to read of the act, unscrewed the fuse-cap and tossed it away. On the day following the presentation at Wroughton Sergt. Gosling was invited to the Empire Theatre in Swindon, and was the recipient of a handsome antique silver tobacco-box at the hands of the Mayor, supported by Aldermen W. H. Williams and C. A. Plaister, and other members of the Council.

A Resolution of Protest. United as the nation might be in its determination to win the war, similar unanimity did not prevail in its views concerning the conduct of the war ; in fact, a storm of indignation swept the country when the incompetence which nearly ruined the Mesopotamian campaign was revealed. Wiltshire was peculiarly interested in this campaign, as the 5th Wiltshires had been transferred there after their withdrawal from the Dardanelles. In July the Swindon and District Trades and Labour Council passed a resolution typical of many :—

"That this Council, noting the terrible exposure (and by no means the first exposure) of the criminal incompetence of high officials and the governing classes generally, as disclosed by the report of the tragic campaign in Mesopotamia, expresses its utter abhorrence of such dastardly conduct, and demands that the severest punishment be visited upon the parties responsible for this sorry record of humiliating failures and disasters ; and we recognize that no scheme of re-organization can be of real effective service unless direct representatives of soldiers and workmen sit upon all War Office administrative bodies."

Though there will be much diversity of opinion as to the efficacy of the remedy suggested in the concluding sentence,—a " non-sequitur " even if the statement be true,—the feeling expressed was universal ; but, as people had learned to expect, the " severest punishment " failed to be meted out to " the parties responsible."

The Mayor's busy year. At the last Council Meeting of Mr. A. J. Gilbert's mayoralty high tribute was paid to the energy and determination that had characterized his work during his year of office ; it had been a strenuous year for him, and he had been unsparing of his time and strength.   He had represented Swindon on the County Finance Committee of the Prisoners of War Fund ; he had been Chairman of both the War Savings Committee and of the War Loan Campaign Committee, and as Chairman of the Pensions Committee had visited Roehampton Hospital for Disabled Soldiers, St. Dunstan's Hospital for blinded men of the forces, and Lord Roberts' Memorial Workshops.   Then, as chairman first of the Voluntary Food Control Committee and afterwards of the Food Control and Coal Committees, he had been unremitting in his efforts to arouse the public to a serious view of the situation as regards supplies and to foster an unselfish and patriotic spirit.   With the Mayoress he had taken a kindly interest in the meetings for Soldiers' Wives and Mothers, held every Wednesday at the Town Hall, and hardly a religious, philanthropic, or social organization in the town had lacked the encouragement of his presence and support.

The New Mayor. The New Mayor was Mr. A. W. Haynes, for many years chairman of the G.W.R. Sick Fund Society, a leading Trade Unionist on the Council, and one of the Borough Justices.   In the past year he had, as chairman of the Disablement Sub-Committee of the Pensions Committee, done splendid service ; as one of his colleagues said, " He had shown a fine brotherly spirit, and had been most sympathetic and wise in his advice to the poor fellows who had come before that body."   Alderman Haynes also represented the Swindon Local Committee on the Joint Committee for the Western Counties, being elected at its first meeting on July 11th.

Enough has been said to show that the year 1917 was one full of anxiety, privation, and work, calling forth the best qualities of the citizens,—patience, endurance, cheerfulness, and unselfishness,—and it can faithfully be said that the inhabitants of Swindon stood the test well.   The town was prosperous as regards **Vagrancy.** employment, and there was no need for any able-bodied person to be out of work.   The decline of vagrancy observed in the previous years of the war, due to the great demand for labour on Government and other work and to the calling up of men for the Army, continued during 1917, and the local figures relating to the opening and close of the year will sufficiently show this.   In January the Swindon and Highworth Board of Guardians received the report for the quarter ending December 22nd, 1916, showing that during the quarter there had been 275 admissions to the casual ward,—a decrease of 210 upon the corresponding quarter of the previous year ; the mid-day meals provided, 150 in number, were less by 77. The returns made to the Board in October, 1917, told a similar tale, for 401 had been admitted to the casual-ward during the quarter just ended, and this was 65 fewer than in the same period in 1916.

H

CHAPTER VII

1918. The Year of Rationing.

Rationing. The outstanding feature of the Food question in 1918 was the adoption of a general system of rationing for the principal articles of diet and fuel. It had indeed become plain in the last months of 1917 that such a policy was inevitable and was at hand. The sight of the long queues in the streets in the depth of winter not merely reconciled people to the idea of universal rationing but caused them to welcome it and to complain that it was delayed so long; strong letters of protest appeared in the local press, but the Town Council was not so idle as the writers appeared to think, and was formulating a temporary scheme to carry the borough through the crisis until a national scheme was inaugurated.

Margarine. Margarine and meat were the articles needing most urgent attention. For the first two or three weeks of the year margarine continued to be issued at the schools upon the production of tickets, the Town Council having taken over the distribution of the Maypole Company's weekly consignment, which was by far the most important supply coming into the town. The Mayor, Mr. Alderman A. W. Haynes, published an appeal in the following terms: "There is a great scarcity at present of butter and margarine . . . Notwithstanding this scarcity many persons have been obtaining more than their fair share . . . The ration is 4 oz. of butter or margarine, or 4 oz. made up partly of butter and margarine, for each person per week, and I wish to appeal to the inhabitants of Swindon and District on their personal honour, to limit themselves to these quantities." This scale could not be strictly adhered to, and on January 25th, the Town Clerk had to publish the following notice: "The Public is respectfully informed that the supply of margarine available only admits of a ration of 3 oz. per head." A week later he announced: "If supplies arrive in time, the ration this week of margarine or of margarine and butter combined will be 4 oz. per head." Still the unscrupulous could readily obtain more than their share, and the Food Control Committee prepared a scheme of rationing which was approved by the Food Controller; this scheme embraced tea, butter and margarine. A large staff of voluntary workers, consisting mainly of Teachers and Trades Union Workers, placed their services at the disposal of the Committee. Application forms were distributed to every householder at his home; the distributors called for these a few days later, examined them to see if they were correctly filled up, and handed in exchange for them ration cards for each person named on the form. The householder had to deposit the cards at the shops where he wished to obtain his supplies, but he might hand in the tea portion of the card at one shop and the butter and margarine portion at another; henceforth he could get only his legitimate share at the shop he had chosen and none elsewhere. The card was provided with blank coupons intended to be used later for other foods that might be rationed. The price of the margarine was fixed at one shilling per lb.

Tea, Butter and Margarine; local Scheme.

The First Food-Card. It will be of interest to future readers to see what these first "food-cards" were like; the front was as shown below :—

FOOD CARD——D.3. SWINDON.
BOROUGH OF SWINDON.

Holder's Name ....
Address ....

A.
H.N.

BUTTER AND MARGARINE.

1	2	3	4	5	6	7	8	9	10
11	12	13	14	15	16	17	18	19	20

B.....
H.N.

TEA.

1	2	3	4	5	6	7	8	9	10
11	12	13	14	15	16	17	18	19	20

C.
H.N.

1	2	3	4	5	6	7	8	9	10
11	12	13	14	15	16	17	18	19	20

D.
H.N.

1	2	3	4	5	6	7	8	9	10
11	12	13	14	15	16	17	18	19	20

Issued under the Swindon Tea, Butter and Margarine Scheme, 1918

CUSTOMER'S PART.

D. ....
Shopkeeper's Name :
....
Address : ....

C. ....
Shopkeeper's Name ;
....
Address : ....

B. TEA.   **Give this part to your Shopkeeper.**
Shopkeeper's Name :
....
Address : ....

Give this part to your Shopkeeper for—
A. BUTTER AND MARGARINE.
Shopkeeper's Name :
....
Address : ....

Here is shown the back of the card :—

FOOD CARD.——D. 3. SWINDON.

A. Butter and Margarine, Shopkeeper's Name : Address :	**B. TEA.** Shopkeeper's Name : Address :
C .... Shopkeeper's Name : Address :	**D** .... Shopkeeper's Name : Address :

INSTRUCTIONS.

1. Fill in your Name and Address clearly opposite (**E**) and (**F**) and register this Card **at once** with your Shopkeepers by giving them those parts of the Card. They will fill up the spaces marked **A** and **B**.
2. Do nothing with the rest of the Card unless public notice is given that the Card is to be used for buying other goods besides Butter, Margarine and Tea.
3. This part must be produced every time you want to buy Butter, Margarine or Tea.
4. It is only available at the shops where you have registered.
5. It is not transferable.

Name :   (H.N............)
(**H**) ....
Full Address :
....

Name :   (H.N............)
(**G**) ....
Full Address :
....

Name :   **TEA.**   (H.N............)
(**F**) ....
Full Address :
....

BUTTER AND MARGARINE.

Name :   (H.N............)
(**E**) ....
Full Address :
....

Meatless Sunday. The first Sunday in January, 1918, was a meatless day for many households in Swindon; on Saturday the butchers were sold out early in the day and closed their shops before evening; regular customers who had ordered beforehand fared fairly well, but the majority of the working-classes generally shop with ready money and are not regular customers at one particular shop; their chances of securing a Sunday joint were very remote. On the following Monday there was not a single head of cattle, sheep, or pigs in Swindon Market, and only a small number of calves. On January 15th, the Mayor issued an appeal to all consumers to reduce their meat-consumption by one half, and urging sedentary workers to go even beyond this so as to allow as much as possible for manual workers. At a meeting of Farmers in Swindon on January 28th the serious position was fully discussed and a proposal was carried to the effect that a weekly cattle-market should be held instead of the usual fortnightly market. Mr. J. N. Read, a prominent local butcher, was present and explained the situation to the meeting; after reminding his audience that Swindon was only allowed 50% of the supplies the Town consumed in October, he said that the butchers now required 25 bullocks and 125 sheep weekly for the Borough, and an additional number of 15 bullocks and 50 sheep for the immediate environs; in the previous week the whole supply available was only 17 bullocks and 70 sheep, and very little could be obtained at the Cold Storage. His plea convinced the meeting that a weekly supply of cattle ought to be sent in, and received the sympathetic treatment recorded above.

Meat; local Scheme. The Food Control Committee saw the need of formulating a temporary meat-rationing scheme on the lines of the scheme already detailed; voluntary workers distributed ration-cards and explanatory circulars at every house on January 31st, and the system came into operation at once. The public was asked to leave the first week's coupons with their butchers before mid-day on Friday, and the available supply of beef and mutton was allocated to the butchers in proportion to the number of coupons held by them. The ration was 12 oz. for adults and 6 oz. for children under 14 years of age, and the householder might take out a weekly ration entirely in pork, or entirely in beef or mutton, but he could not divide his ration between a pork-butcher and another butcher. Having deposited his first week's coupon with a certain butcher the house-holder was thereby registered with that butcher and had to continue dealing there except for pork, which he could obtain from any pork-butcher by handing him the coupon not later than Thursday morning. This scheme was elaborated by the Committee after conferring with the Butchers' Association and Trade Union representatives, and worked very satisfactorily, for every one was sure of receiving a supply, even though small.

The following is a fac-simile of the first Meat-ration-card ;

FOOD CONTROL COMMITTEE.

RATION CARD FOR BEEF, MUTTON AND PORK.

1. Customer's Name ....

2. Address ....

3. Number of Persons in the Household, as per Sugar Tickets : ....

    Adults................................ Children ....

NOTE—The Coupon for the appropriate week must be detached and handed to the Retailer when the week's Ration is obtained.

SEE INSTRUCTIONS ON BACK.

23rd February.	2nd March.	9th March.
Adults	Adults	Adults ....
Children	Children	Children ....
Address	Address	Address ....
....	....	....
....	....	....
2nd February.	**9th February.**	**16th February.**
Adults	Adults	Adults ....
Children	Children	Children ....
Address	Address	Address ....
....	....	....
....	....	....

On the other side the following " Instructions " were printed :—

1. This card is not transferable.
2. In the event of the holder leaving the district this Card, together with the unused Coupons, must be surrendered immediately to the Local Food Office.
3. Each Coupon is available only during the week of issue, and unless presented during that week is useless.
4. No Supplies are guaranteed by the Committee.
   This ticket must be carefully preserved, as under no circumstance will a duplicate be issued.

Name of Butcher with
whom Ration Ticket deposited..

Address of Butcher ....

Along with the cards there was sent to each household the circular given below :—

BOROUGH OF SWINDON.

FOOD CONTROL COMMITTEE.

RATIONING SCHEME FOR BEEF, MUTTON AND PORK.

1.—In order to avoid queues, and to secure an equitable distribution of the meat supplies, the Food Control Committee have decided to bring a Rationing Scheme into operation at once.

2.—Herewith is a Ration Card for your household.

3.—You are to state on this card the number of persons living in your house, including lodgers, or boarders, giving those over 14 years of age, and those of 14 years of age and under separately.

4.—A household may take out its weekly ration entirely in pork or entirely in beef and mutton, or partly in beef and partly in mutton (if the butcher having regard to his supplies can make it convenient to supply it in this way), but a person who desires pork must take the whole week's ration in pork.

5.—This week you should take the coupon dated the 2nd February to your butcher on Friday. If he can supply you on that day he will. If not, you should be able to obtain your supplies on Saturday.

6.—In subsequent weeks you should take your coupon to your butcher at the time you make your purchase.

7.—The ration is 12 ozs. for adults and 6 ozs. for children of 14 years of age and under.

8.—Having deposited your first coupon with your butcher, you must continue to obtain your weekly supplies from him, unless your coupon is transferred to another butcher by the Committee. You cannot change your butcher yourself, but when you desire to take your week's ration in pork you should take your coupon not later than the Thursday morning, to a butcher who deals in pork.

9.—The Committee may at any time transfer your Ration Card from one butcher to another.

10.—The ration may be varied from time to time by the Committee, according to the supplies of meat available.

Town Hall, Swindon.

29th January, 1918.

Fixed Prices. Meanwhile the number of foods of which the price was fixed by the Food Controller was growing. Onions, which had been sold at as much as 8d. per pound, were given a maximum price of 3d. ; rabbits had a maximum price of 2/- unskinned or 1/9 skinned, and if part of a rabbit was sold it was to be at the maximum rate of 10d. per lb., skinned and cleaned. The purchase of " a portion " of a rabbit would have seemed ludicrous not long before, but was now a serious reality. Under the somewhat offensive term of " offals " edible portions of meat-carcases, such as liver, kidneys, hearts, tripe, chitlings, sweet-breads, etc., were regulated in price, and shop-keepers were required to exhibit lists of the maxima as fixed from time to time. Some shops began to exhibit an unwonted display of " offal " and one would see huge slabs of liver, or astonishing arrays of hearts or kidneys, that made one wonder where the carcases were from which they were derived ; they were, of course, imported offal and owing to the shortage of meat found a ready sale. Lists of maximum prices for fish were also prepared and revised from time to time, and it was now that one began to buy herrings at so much per lb.—an unwelcome novelty to housewives who could recollect buying herrings at two a penny. The maximum retail price of rice and its derivatives was put at 4d. per lb., but certain varieties could be sold at prices up to 6d. if the retailer displayed a conspicuous notice stating that he had also rice on sale at 4d. a lb.

Milk. The high cost of milk in 1918 was one of the special grievances of the public and was also a very serious matter in families where young children were being reared. In January at a meeting of the local branch of the National Farmers' Union held in Swindon the Secretary put forward recommendations from the executive of the N.F.U., which the meeting unanimously adopted ; they were to the effect that April should be reckoned a winter month ; that prices should run as follows,—May and June 1/2 a gallon forward on rail, July 1/4, August and September 1/6 ; that the farmer should have 5d. a gallon if he acted as distributor ; and that the buyer should pay the railway rates. These demands foreshadowed high prices for the consumer, but retail rates were even higher than the farmers' demands suggested. In February all retail milk-sellers had to register themselves under the local Food Control Committee, and henceforth the public was notified periodically of changes in the retail price of milk, which depended upon the wholesale rate fixed by the Food Controller. It has been noted that the price in Swindon from October 1917 was 2/4 per gallon (7d. per quart) ; now, for May 1918 it was fixed at 1/8 ; in June, July and August 2/- ; in September 2/4 ; in October and November 2/8 ; and from December 1st to April 30th, 1919, the price was raised to 3/- per gallon or 9d. per quart.

As has been remarked, the local Food Control Committee was bound in its action by the Food Controller's policy in fixing wholesale prices, and they themselves felt that the prices were too high ; they gave expression to their view in a resolution of protest sent to the Food Controller, stating that they were unanimously of opinion that the producers' price (2/3 per gal. for October) was much too high.

National Rationing. The local rationing scheme tided Swindon over until the national scheme was ready; it was intended that this should come into operation early in March and the Committee made use of the services of a large body of voluntary workers at the Town Hall in preparation for the inauguration of the scheme. March 4th was the eventful day, but there was some delay in making the arrangements for the new meat scheme, and tea, butter and margarine were the first articles dealt with in the national scheme;

Tea. under this the tea-ration was 1½oz. per head weekly—an allowance which effectively disposed of the " early morning cup of tea," to say

Butter and Margarine. nothing of the after-dinner cup,—and the ration of butter and margarine combined was 4 ozs. per head, raised to 5 ozs. in May; the method of supply was similar to that under the local scheme which this replaced, but consumers had perfect freedom in registering with fresh retailers if they wished to change, and could go to one shop for tea and another for butter and margarine; in fact, as the rationing was extended there were people who were registered at four or five different shops.

Meat. The meat-rationing scheme had to be deferred for a fortnight or so, the local scheme being continued for the interval. Under the new scheme were included all meats, cooked, tinned, or uncooked; each consumer had four coupons for the week, and each coupon would purchase five-pennyworth of butchers' meat but only three coupons could be so used; the fourth was to be used for the purchase of other kinds of meat or of a meat meal at some restaurant. It will be noted that the ration is not stated as so many ounces, but as fivepennyworth per coupon; the amount varied with the joint, but even with the cheapest joints this was very small—so small that a scheme of supplementary rations for heavy workers had to be immediately devised, not, however, including butcher's meat or pork. It was by no means easy for the butchers to satisfy their customers and they had to exercise much ingenuity in cutting the meat into the small portions permitted by the rationing scheme; householders with large families had the advantage here, for they could at any rate get a respectable joint by putting all their coupons together, but a couple with no children were hard put to in devising how best to employ their coupons for the week. Another result was that the shops were closed from Saturday night till Thursday morning; the coupons were available from Thursday to Thursday, but the supply of meat was so limited and people were so eager to make sure of their allowance that the coupons were presented at once on Thursday and the meat was soon all gone.

Sugar and Jam. In view of the fact that a great many people grow small quantities of fruit and that much of it would be wasted unless sugar for preserving it could be obtained, applications for sugar for this purpose were invited in the Spring, on the basis of not more than 10lbs. per head for the household. Forms had to be filled up stating the amount of sugar required, the kind of fruit grown, the number of members of the household, etc., and the forms were passed to the Food Control Committee through the grocers. The allotment was made in two parts, that for soft fruit being delivered in June and that for stone fruit and marrows in September. As a rule people received only a portion of the amount they had applied for, with the result that the conscientious applicant received less than he needed whilst others who had viewed their needs too generously received all they needed and perhaps more, for there was little possibility of checking the figures quoted.

This relaxation of the sugar restriction was the more welcome as jam was very scarce indeed in Swindon, and in April the Committee made representations to the Divisional Authority and secured a special consignment of seven tons, which, however, was only about ½lb. per head for the Borough. The jam shortage continued, and it was really a great relief to many when jam was rationed in November and they could make sure of a little.

Education in Cookery and Preserving. The desirability of preserving as much of the fruit crop as possible led the Food Control Committee—through the Education Committee— to continue the educational work of the previous year. In the Spring a course of six lectures was given at the Technical Institution in " War-time Cookery," and this was followed in June by a series of lectures and demonstrations at different centres in the town, on bottling and pulping fruit, bottling vegetables, drying fruit and vegetables, and jam-making. Then in September Mrs. Candy, of the Fruit-Production Department in London, delivered two lectures at the Technical Institution on the canning of fruit. All these were free lectures to the public and were well attended.

Beer Famine. There was a " shortage " of most commodities all through 1918, but at Easter-tide an unwonted experience befell the town ; on Easter Sunday and Monday nearly all the public-houses in the locality were closed, and most of them remained closed till the following Thursday ; on the doors were to be seen notices saying : " Closed : no beer," or, " Closed : sold out," and one inn-keeper's flamboyant—if not ambiguous—announcement ran, " Closed, no beer : God Save the King." Through the summer such notices as these were frequently to be seen, and stout, in particular, was unprocurable for long periods.

More Coupons. New ration books were issued in July and they covered sugar, butter and margarine, meat, bacon, and lard, and had also spare leaves for new articles that might have to be rationed. Consumers had had **Bacon.** to register with the retailers for bacon and ham in April and were rationed in May ; but by the end of July it was found possible to free bacon from coupons, and people could now use all the four meat-coupons, available for any one week, in purchasing fresh or other meats to the extent of five-pennyworth per coupon ; along with this concession, however, the " supplementary ration" for heavy workers was cancelled. Retailers of bacon could still supply only customers who were registered with them, and they were required to supply their customers with not less than 8 oz. of bacon or 12 oz. of ham if it were demanded. The price of bacon was fixed at 2 /4 a pound. In August the Ministry of Food announced that it was releasing a large quantity of bacon " suitable for boiling " at 1 /8 a pound ; there was a dubious air about the announcement, which emphasised the direction that the bacon should be well-soaked before boiling, or that it should be boiled in two changes of water. About this time the Food Control Committee received numerous complaints that bad bacon was being sold, and their inspector ascertained that a good deal of unwholesome bacon had been delivered in the town and proceedings were instituted in some cases ; the joint committee of the National Union of Railwaymen also sent to the Food Control Committee a strong protest concerning the matter.

Fruit. Fruit was neither plentiful not cheap in the summer; the spring had given promise of an abundant crop, but a prolonged spell of dry east wind and some night frosts had occurred just as the fruit was setting; prices were prohibitive for the average household, and in Swindon the difficulty of getting fruit at a reasonable rate was enhanced by the proximity of the camp, which took up a good deal of the supply. An effort was made to give the public an opportunity to taste—it was little more—the strawberry crop, for at the end of June the price was fixed at a maximum of 9d. per lb. for small sales, but as the bulk of the crop was "commandeered" for jam-making the fruit made but a brief appearance in Swindon. What the price would have been if not controlled may be judged from the fact that logan-berries did not fall below 2/- per lb., apples were sold in Swindon market at 1/- per lb. in August and were much dearer in the shops, greengages were 2/- per lb., and so with most other fruit.

Rabbits. In fact, nearly everything was so scarce and in such demand, that unless the price was "controlled" it tended to soar to exorbitant heights. It was the fixing of the price that saved the consumer in spite of the fact that people were loud in their complaints that the Food Controller favoured the dealer; sometimes he intervened to reduce prices already fixed; thus, it was seen above that when the price of rabbits was fixed the maximum was 1/9 for a skinned rabbit and 10d. per lb. for a portion; in August a new order fixed the prices at 6d. per lb. for the producer, 8d. for the middleman—collector and distributor,—and 8½d per lb. for the retailer. Rabbits were nevertheless very scarce in the Borough, and complaints were made that most of them were sent up to London, but it must be remembered that the farmers and dealers were so short-handed that there was not anything like the customary extent of shooting and trapping.

Protests and Threats. The public, however, was much exercised upon the question of prices and could not be convinced that the Food Controller could not fix lower rates. On Saturday, September 28th, a meeting of the Great Western Railway workmen was held at noon and passed a resolution that, " This meeting of organized workmen calls upon the officials of our Unions to take immediately such steps as are necessary to warn the local Food Control Committee that no further increases in the price of essential commodities will be tolerated. Further, this meeting pledges itself to take whatever action is necessary, no matter how drastic, to combat the ever-growing evil of profiteering out of the people's food."

On the following Tuesday, at 4 o'clock, the tradesmen of all grades in the Works laid down their tools and marched in procession, led by two brass bands, to the Town Hall, where a meeting of many thousands—some put it as high as 10,000— was held to protest against the high prices. It was a most orderly meeting, but the short addresses given by the different speakers were received with frequent outbursts of cheers, or cries of " Shame ! " as reference was made to specific instances of unfair prices. Mr. W. M. Noble, J.P., of the Amalgamated Society of Engineers, presided, and he acknowledged the endeavours of the local Food Control Committee to act justly in their delicate duties, instancing the fact that only the previous day they had fixed the price of milk in opposition to the retailers, who had asked for a higher rate.

It was decided to send a deputation to the Committee to lay the facts before them, and to ask attention to be given to several points, including a demand for better bread, for the municipalization of the milk supply, for powers for the Education Committee to supply children with boots at cost price during the coming winter, for a reduction in farmers' prices for milk, and for an increase in Old Age Pensions. Obviously, as many of these matters were beyond the powers of the Food Control Committee, it was intended that representations should be made by the Committee to higher authorities.

The day before this meeting the Committee had met and had received from Mr. Noble a letter embodying the resolution passed at the Saturday's meeting; another was received from Mr. A. Creber, Secretary of the Amalgamated Society of Carpenters and Joiners, expressing the same views and suggesting that, "unless reasonable action is taken we shall feel justified in taking such action as commends itself to us, in conjunction with other organizations." A third letter, from Mr. J. Wilson, Secretary of the Swindon 2nd Branch of the A.S.E., protested against the price of milk, and yet a fourth from Mr. F. H. Beavis, Secretary of the Swindon Branch of the N.U.R., protested against the bad bacon coming into the town. The Committee considered all these communications and instructed the Town Clerk to forward them to the Divisional Commissioner with a request that he would lay them before the Food Controller, and a meeting was arranged for representatives of the societies to confer with the Committee.

It must not be thought that these were merely academic discussions ending where they began; the leaders were in earnest and the Divisional Commissioner recognised the fact by sending to the Food Control Committee a long and carefully reasoned statement in reply to a letter from Mr. W. M. Noble, which the committee had sent him. The situation in Swindon was paralleled by that in many towns, and the authorities had real cause for anxiety, and it was distinctly fortunate that the Armistice came on November 11th., diverting the public mind and holding out hopes of speedy relief. Many retailers were naturally anxious to allay the suspicions —doubtless often unfounded—that shopkeepers as a class were responsible for the inflated prices that prevailed, and at a meeting of the Chamber of Commerce held in December it was asserted that traders were doing their best to keep prices down and even often sold goods in stock below the market price; but owing to the continual advances made by wholesalers, through increased cost of materials and labour, new stock was bound to show a considerable advance on previous prices.

New Ration Books. Fresh ration books were issued for November covering sugar, fats, meat, lard, and jam or syrup, and containing a supplementary leaf for extra jam for persons between six and eighteen years of age. A curious detail in regard to jam was an injunction to those people who had received earlier in the year more than six pounds of sugar for jam-making, requiring them to cancel one jam coupon for every quarter-pound of sugar received in excess of six pounds, with a maximum of sixteen coupons cancelled; this order was probably hardly observed at all, for people were often registered for jam at a different shop from that where they had obtained the sugar, and there was no real check. It had seemed probable that a little more butter and margarine might be granted under the new rations; the price of butter had been raised from 2/4 to 2/6 in September, but the ration was raised from October 1st to 6oz. per head— two of butter and four of margarine; the lack of transport, greatly drawn upon in October for shipping American troops to France, compelled the Food Controller to reduce the allowance to 1 oz. of butter and 4 oz. of margarine again on October

20th. Margarine, which had for some time been 1/2 a lb., was in November temporarily reduced to 1/-. New meat prices had already reduced the quantity for which the coupons were available, for in September prices were raised 2d. per lb., and pork was similarly increased in price in October.

A deficiency that caused much hardship was that of cheese, which, had it been plentiful, would have gone far to make up for the shortage of meat, now being imported in greatly reduced quantities. But cheese was very scarce in Swindon throughout the year, although visitors from other towns could often bring a good piece with them and were pressed to do so. In October the Committee appealed to the Divisional Commissioner for extra supplies and he responded with an extra thousand pounds,—a welcome but very slight alleviation of the hardship.

There was also in the Autumn a temporary scarcity of soap and soda in the Borough, and the Committee appealed to the Commissioner for supplies ; there was, however, no general scarcity and the deficiency was soon remedied. The adequacy of the supply of soap right through the war was indeed remarkable, for a great scarcity was generally feared ; by this time soap was three and four times its pre-war price and was decidedly inferior in quality, but it could always be obtained.

National Kitchens. Ever since any kind of food-control had been exercised in Swindon there had been a section who pressed for the establishment of National Kitchens, but both the Voluntary and the Official Food Control Committees, after devoting much time and discussion to the subject, had failed to be convinced of the need for them in Swindon. The Trades and Labour Council, however, invited in November the Director of National Kitchens for the South Midland Area to come and address a public meeting upon the subject, and asked the Food Control Committee to associate themselves with the promoters of the meeting ; the Committee complied and arranged for the meeting to be held in the Town Hall under the presidency of Mr. C. J. Heavens ; the result was a resolution in favour of opening National Kitchens in Swindon, and a demand for a town's meeting to create interest in the project and thus secure its success. This town's meeting was held in January, the Mayor, Ald. C. A. Plaister, presiding ; but the attendance was very poor and led the opponents of the scheme to deny the existence of any public demand. A resolution in favour was passed, but there the matter ended for the time being.

Christmas Cheer. Meantime the Food Control Committee had been busy with many matters, and in common with everyone else they were anxious that the " Armistice Christmas " should be marked by some relaxation of the stringency as regards food. Swindon was to have a good supply of oranges at 10d. per lb.—an unheard-of price, averaging 3d. each, but after so great a scarcity of fruit this formed a grateful addition to a fare that had afforded little variety. The Food Controller had arranged for double meat rations at Christmas, and this was secured by raising the value of the coupon to 8d., prices remaining at the fixed rates. Game, poultry and similar food were to be coupon-free, also at the fixed prices. A good supply of currants and raisins would have been especially welcome, but there was great scarcity of all classes of dried fruits, and in November no sultanas at all could be had ; it was stated that there was sufficient in the country to allow everyone a share consisting of 4½ozs. of currants and 1½ozs. of raisins ; but dried fruits were not rationed, and when a supply was delivered in the Borough the Committee had no power to control and distribute the fruit ; they did what they could in informing the public that the fair share per head was 6ozs., and in asking grocers to supply customers with no more than that amount. An extra ¼lb. of sugar per head was allowed for Christmas, and the Committee granted permission to bodies like the Great Western Railway Mechanics' Institution and the Gorse Hill Adult School to procure extra sugar for Christmas Teas to old folk and children. It may be noted here that the sugar ration was raised from 8 ozs. to 12ozs. on January 27th, 1919, with no reduction in the price of sevenpence. A little more cheese came into the town in December, and tinned meats were freed from coupons, as also was lard, though in its case customers had still to be registered with some retailer.

Alcohol for Invalids.   The Food Control Committee received several complaints towards the end of the year about the difficulty of purchasing whiskey and brandy for medical use ; there was considerable demand for these spirits due to the severe influenza epidemic that prevailed in the autumn. The wine and spirit merchants refused to supply any but regular customers except upon production of a medical certificate, asserting that their supplies were insufficient. Enquiries were made as to the facts by a canvass of the Medical Faculty of the Town, and two doctors affirmed that there was a shortage of spirits and seven said they had not found any scarcity.   This was hardly conclusive as it was the persons who had to fetch the spirits who experienced the difficulty, and not the doctors who ordered the stimulant. Application was made to the Divisional Commissioner, who replied that nothing could be done in the matter, when the very next day the Ministry of Food announced that arrangements had been made to provide at once extra supplies for medicinal purposes without contravening the regulations of the Liquor Control Board for limiting consumption.

Matches,   Before leaving the subject of the shortage of commodities one may allude to the great dearth of matches that had now been experienced for some time ; a penny a box was the usual price, and tobacconists refused as a rule to supply any but their own customers; it was illegal to " impose a condition " upon the sale of any article, and, theoretically, if a retailer had an article in stock he should sell it on demand unless it was one for which customers had to be registered. The trader very naturally wished to keep his regular customers supplied, and therefore he often ceased to display his stock, and when a chance customer asked, for instance, for matches, he would be told that there was " none in stock,"—a phrase whose technical meaning was very often, " under the counter." Towards December the supply of matches began to improve.

and Tobacco.   Tobacco, too, was very scarce about this time, especially in the form of cigarettes ; the stock in the country was greater than in the earlier part of the year, but manufacture and distribution were much impeded by the influenza epidemic and by the scarcity of labour and machinery ; Swindon was particularly short of tobacco and the shops were for some time quite devoid of cigarettes. The usual price of loose Gold Flake and similar tobaccoes was 9½d. an ounce, and the ordinary packet tobaccoes were 10½d. an ounce.

Cereals and Bread.   There is little to say about wheat and other cereals in 1918. The farmers had been guaranteed their 78/- a quarter for wheat, and there was no reason why they should bring samples into Swindon and try to effect sales when all their store was known to the authorities, and was collected by a Government agent as it was wanted. The farmer could no longer declare that he could do as he liked with his own; his corn was not his own, and in January an order under the Defence of the Realm Act made it illegal to use grain or beans for feeding horses other than certain classes provided for in the order, and these were rationed. It was followed by another order containing a strong warning against using wheat, barley, rye, or rice for any other purpose than for human food; only damaged grain could be used for feeding poultry and animals. There was much complaint amongst the farmers, for, as one said, whilst they could not use their cereal " tailings " for feeding their pigs, they were compelled to buy pig-meal —which, he said with pardonable redundancy, was nothing but "dirty muck,"—at £24 per ton. It was at times pitiable to see the emaciated condition of some of the horses in the streets and the fields, but the truth was—and it was hard to convince the nation,—that there was not enough corn for man, to say nothing of the beasts.

Bread and Flour. The " War-bread," supplied only after it was twelve hours old, varied in quality according to the cargoes that came into Bristol, and other supplies that found their way into Swindon; at times one would get bread little different, apparently, from " pre-war " bread and then it might be followed by bread tasting strongly of beans, rank in odour, and dark in colour. The flour, when kneaded into dough and put into the oven, would sometimes give off an almost unendurable smell, and it would be rash for a layman to try to name the constituents; but even as it was the Food Controller was not satisfied that the bakers were doing all they could to dilute the wheaten flour, and in October he issued an order to enforce the use of potatoes in bread. The bakers had had for some months a free hand in adopting a percentage of potatoes in flour, but the optional scheme had not produced results that satisfied the Controller; a compulsory order would have been made in 1916 but for the difficulties of transport, and now that they had been overcome the order was made. The potato-flour was really an improvement upon some ingredients, and the bread was whiter and more palatable than some that had been made.

Potatoes in Bread.

Hopes of Improvement. In December, during the Armistice, it was stated that the white loaf was likely to be on sale everywhere very soon, and that the Twelve Hours Order might soon be abandoned. The order was suspended for Christmas, but was put into operation again afterwards and time went on without any sign that the Controller intended to withdraw it, and proceedings were instituted against any who infringed the regulation. The matter was complicated by the movement to do away with night-labour in bakeries, and the agitation to restore the customary white bread took no account of the fact that there were gigantic stocks of " war-flour " in the country that had to be used, and that there was a world-shortage of wheat necessitating sacrifices for the sake of the continental nations. Nevertheless, a decided improvement in the quality of the bread began about this time, and people ceased to complain.

Hay and Straw. The 1918 crop of hay and straw was strictly controlled by the Government by an Army Council Order of the 30th of July, applying to all consumers other than producers. These had all to be registered with some dealer, to whom they had to state the number of animals for which forage was wanted, details as to the animals and forage, and the place where the forage was required; increases or decreases in the number of the animals had to be notified immediately. Similarly, all producer-distributors, dealers, wholesale-traders, and lifters desiring to sell hay or straw had to obtain a licence from the Wilts County Distributing (Forage) Committee if they traded in Wiltshire. Current prices may be judged from the tenders accepted by the Swindon Town Council in September, when they paid 107/6 a ton for oat-straw, and for meadow-hay a fluctuating price of about £10 a ton.

The   Most Swindon folk at some time have watched on the Downs Brig.-
Burderop   Gen. Calley's oxen ploughing, and strangers have stood in amazement
Draught-   to see on English soil a picture that recalled such scenes as that in
Oxen.   which Elijah " found Elisha the son of Shaphat who was plowing with
                 twelve yoke of oxen before him, and he with the twelfth." The
Burderop oxen had long been preserved and employed on the Chiseldon hills, and were a source of pride to Swindon's esteemed neighbour ; but the needs and limitations of the time now compelled the gallant general to adopt the more expeditious plan of ploughing with motor-tractors. It was therefore not without regret that the famous teams were sold at Swindon Market in July of this year ; one team of four oxen realized £240, and went to Kintbury, Berkshire; and Mr. Rich, of Wootton Bassett, paid £180 for another team of three oxen. Within recent years one might have seen oxen ploughing elsewhere in the locality—for instance, at Liddington and Cirencester,—but few of the rising generation will probably ever have the experience.

Light   Few things caused the householder so much anxiety in 1918 as the
and Fuel.   consumption of coal, gas, and electricity. The price alone was a
                 sufficient source of worry for gas was 4/- per thousand cubic feet and
coal was well over £2 per ton, but now a further cause for anxiety was added in the limitation of supplies. A hint of the coming control of fuel occurred in January, when the Town Clerk announced that, " The Coal Controller has informed the Council that there are large stocks of Coke on hand in Swindon, and urges that this Coke should be made use of in household consumption so as to economise coal"; but, unfortunately for the success of the endeavour to induce the public to buy
                 coke, this was as dear as coal   In April, however, all-powerful
"D.O.R.A."   " Dora " intervened with an order forbidding anyone to consume
                 more than five-sixths of the quantity of gas or electricity that was
consumed in the corresponding quarter of 1916 or 1917, whichever was the greater, and now the poor householder began to have dreams of fines and imprisonment ; to economise coal his wife used the gas-stove, for the range ate up coal by the scuttleful, and now she was to cut down the gas ; but the gas supplied was of an atrocious quality, both as an illuminant and as a heating-agent, for it was subject to processes that abstracted materials valuable for war-purposes, whose loss reduced its value for household purposes. The same order forbade cooking or the serving of hot meals in hotels and restaurants between 9.30 p.m. and 5 a.m., and no light beyond what was necessary for cleaning was to be used in the dining-room between 10 p.m. and 5 a.m.

                 In June the "Household Fuel and Lighting Order" was issued,
Fuel and   fixing the quantities of fuel and lighting for every household, and
Light   the rates, as set out in the leaflet sent out by the authorities,
Rations.   were as follows :—

Where the No. of occupied rooms is not more than	Fuel. The year's allowance shall not exceed	Lighting. The year's allowance shall not exceed	
	Tons	*either* Gas cubic feet	*or* Electricity B.T. Units
2	3	7500	120
3	3½	7500	120
4	4	11250	180
5	4½	11250	180
6	5	11250	180
7	6	15000	240
8	7	15000	240
9	8	15000	240
10	9	18750	300

The table continued up to 21 rooms, and provisions were made for special cases ; for example, in any house up to 12 rooms in size an extra ton of fuel was allowed if the occupants exceeded six in number; additional allowances could be procured where there were aged or infirm persons, invalids, or young children, where lodgers occupied separate rooms, where rooms were used for business purposes, where there was illness, and so forth.

Arrangements had to be made for households where both coal and gas or electricity were used for fuel, and where both gas and electricity were used for lighting, and these complications caused great trouble to the local administration as well as to the consumer. In the former case 15,000 c.ft. of gas or 800 B.T. Units of electricity counted as a ton of fuel, and 3 tons of coke counted as two of fuel ; for lighting 750 c.ft. of gas and 12 B.T. Units of electricity were reckoned as equivalent.

The Fuel Overseer. The carrying-out of this Order demanded the appointment of a local Fuel Overseer, and the duties of that office were performed by Mr. W. H. Lawson with a good temper and patience beyond praise,— for his work brought him into daily contact with numbers of people too unpractised to fill in properly the bewildering forms presented to them, or discontented with their allowance, or anxious to get further supplies on all manner of grounds. The distribution, collection, and examination of the forms was a difficult and tedious task that had, nevertheless, to be performed with expedition. The householder had to state on the form the name of his retailer and thereby became registered with him, and the coal-merchant, who also was registered or licensed, could supply him with the quantity for which the house was assessed and no more.

Coal Prices. This, speaking generally, was the scheme for coal-rationing, but there was a long list of provisory clauses that gave every consideration to particular cases but caused the order to appear a most formidable document in the eyes of the public, and it was due very largely to the considerate way in which the order was administered in Swindon that so little trouble was experienced. The order did not touch prices, which were still regulated by the Retail Coal Prices Committee of the borough. It will be remembered that towards the end of 1917 the prices fixed were 39/- per ton for " Controlled " coal and 42/- for Forest of Dean coal ; in July 1918 the Committee revised prices in view of the fact that the Controller of Coal Mines had granted an increase of 2/6 per ton at the pit mouth, other increased expenses also entering into the question ; in Swindon the new rates were 42/- per ton for " Controlled " coal and 45/- for

Forest of Dean. The coal-merchants had to take just what was sent them, and sometimes a splendid coal was got by the consumer for 42/-, and the next time he might get the veriest rubbish at the same price.

The price of gas-coke came under control in October, and was not to exceed in any district the price of the second list of house coal; a special discount of 10% was to be allowed to industrial establishments which used 50 tons or more monthly.

The Coal Shortage. The coal shortage, due to the needs of the Allies of Britain, was made more pronounced by the withdrawal of large numbers of men from the mines by the army and by frequent stoppages of work in various districts. The need of the allies was really very great, for France had lost the best part of her coal areas for the time being, and Italy had always had to rely upon imported coal, which Britain alone was now in a position to supply. In withdrawing men from the mines the authorities had shown much lack of foresight, and now they hastily tried to save the situation by sending miners back again, but their efforts were sadly hampered by the temper of the miners and transport-workers in certain districts, and although in Swindon there was no privation in the winter of 1918-19 there was real suffering for lack of fuel in London and many other places. Stocks were frequently very low in the Borough, but the dealers could usually let one have a bag to go on with till the trucks came in, and they used discretion in distributing the coal so that each had a little when it did arrive. But many a cheerless evening would have been spent but for neighbourly loans or gifts of a bucketful of coal. The saving of fuel was felt to be all-important, and extensions of the existing gas and electricity systems were discouraged ; the local Fuel Overseer published in August a notice that no new supplies of lighting or fuel could be given nor could any premises be furnished with fresh appliances for using gas or electricity for fuel, without the previous consent of the Fuel Overseer.

Price of Electricity. The Swindon Corporation was compelled to raise its charges for electricity again from April 1st, 1918 ; the rate for electricity for lighting purposes was increased from 5d. to 6d. a unit, and this time the power and fuel charges were increased too, that for power going up from 2¼d. to 3d. a unit, and that for heating or cooking from 1¼d. to 1½d. per unit.

Food Production. In the spring of the year Swindon received a visit from Mr. Rowe, of the Food Production Department of the Board of Agriculture ; his mission was to urge the Cultivation of Lands Committee, with whom he had a Conference, to use every effort to bring under cultivation every available plot of ground. Councillor T. Kimber, describing to the Town Council the gentleman's visit, said he was greatly impressed with what the Borough had already done, affirming that, with the exception of some small towns where the residents had more leisure, Swindon had done as well as any town in England ; but he also urged them to go further, saying that the difference between " inconvenience " and " privation " would depend upon a sufficient supply of vegetables. The Committee therefore appealed through the Council that every man who had any leisure should do something, however small, towards growing vegetables. The response was admirable ; men of all classes sought allotments, and the snobbery that forbade " respectable " people to be seen in their shirt-sleeves and carrying tools and vegetables through the streets received a blow from which it should never recover. Cherished lawns were dug up to make potato patches, and it was no uncommon sight to see cabbages growing in front gardens where geraniums had bloomed in previous years.

Appeal to the Public.

Allotments. At the Town Council Meeting already alluded to, held in March, Mr. Kimber said that the total area under cultivation in the town in 1917 was 460 acres, with 4,770 tenants ; then there had been 65 acres taken this year, with 1,040 tenants, and now a further 44 acres had been provided of which 28 acres were already let; these included nine acres at Gorse Hill, another four of the Rodbourne Recreation Ground and three let by Major Goddard at the bottom of the Drove Road.   The Town Council assisted as they had done the previous year, in providing seed-potatoes, buying wholesale **Seed** large quantities of British Queen, King Edward, Arran Chief, and **Potatoes.** Up-to-date seed, which were sold to growers at 5/- a bushel, or 1/3 a peck.   About the same time the potatoes grown by the Town Council in 1917 on the ground at the Whitworth Road Cemetery were unearthed from the storage pits; there were nearly 5½ tons, mostly of seed size, and it was decided that these should be sold at the Market along with the Scotch and Irish seed, but at a different price.

The last year's experience made everyone anxious to be prepared to combat any recurrence of the disastrous potato-disease, and the Committee brought down Mr. T. H. Middleton, of the Board of Agriculture's Food Production Department, to lecture at the Town Hall in March upon potato-growing, with special reference to the diseases of potatoes and how to treat them.

An It has been related how and why the first effort at potato-growing on **Unfortunate** the Whitworth Road ground was disappointing, and how, upon the **Experiment.** advice of Mr. T. Sharp, the County Council expert, it had been decided to treat the land for other crops.   Mr. Rowe's representations induced the Cultivation of Lands Committee to alter its plans although the land had already been prepared, and to try potatoes once more.   Again unforeseen circumstances brought disappointment ; along with the allotment holders, the Committee suffered severe loss from disease, for just when the time for lifting potatoes came there occurred a long spell of cold and very wet weather that spoiled the crops all over the country ; the disease had already made its appearance, and it was essential that the roots should be got up and dried at once, and this was rendered impossible.   When Councillor J. Clark, now Chairman of the Committee, made his statement in February, 1919, he had to put against an expenditure of £211 : 19 : 6 an income of only £113 : 2 : 0, involving a deficit of £98 : 17 : 6 ; £48 of the income sprang from bad potatoes used for pig-food.

In view of this second failure the Borough Surveyor, Mr. H. J. Hamp, was instructed in October to arrange for six acres to be sown for oats for the next season's crop, as recommended by Mr. Sharp, as the oats would be valuable as food for the Corporation's horses.

The Corporation made this year another effort in the direction of food-production by breeding pigs at their sewage farms, for sale to allotment-holders and others in the Borough and District.

Vegetables The Vegetable Products Committee for the year 1918 comprised one **for the** or two new members ; besides the chairman (Mr. W. H. Trowbridge) **Navy.** and the secretary (Mrs. F. W. Trineman), there were present at the meetings the Mayor (Mr. A. W. Haynes, followed by Ald. C. Plaister), the Town Clerk, Mr. A. J. Gilbert, Messrs. H. Haine, of Sevenhampton, G. Gibbs, of Wanborough, A. Currey, of Wroughton, and F. Austin, of Highworth ; Messrs. G. Davis and J. Bennett ; Mr. P. Crockford, representing the Allotment

Holders' Association; and Mr. C. J. Averay, elected to represent Messrs. Comptons', in recognition of the generous support given by the employees of that firm.

The two facts that faced the Committee at the outset were firstly, the greatly increased need of supplies owing to the growing strength of our vast fleet, and secondly, the difficulty of restoring falling contributions in a period **Rising** of scarcity and high prices. Nevertheless, they entered upon their **to the** work with determination, and the result was a veritable triumph. **Occasion.** Mr. T. S. Taylor, of Idstone, did the Committee great service and brought them much encouragement early in the year, for, besides adding to his many previous gifts a donation of six tons of swedes, he brought the claims of the Navy before the Farmers' Union and enlisted the sympathy of many new contributors; thus, four farmers of the Burbage district—Messrs. J. G. Blanchard, W. Gauntlett, J. May, and Mr. Arthurs, of Savernake,—sent up a truck of swedes; Mr. Hervey White of Wootton Bassett, and Mr. E. Pritchard of Clyffe Pypard, joined in sending a second truck of swedes; Mr. C. Whatley, of Wanborough Plain, sent half a ton of beet-root, and many other gifts came in about this time, the whole forming a splendid outcome of Mr. Taylor's efforts. The following month brought equally fine gifts from another district, Mr. J. Rickards and Mr. J. Horton, both of Cricklade, sending between them five and a quarter tons of swedes; and there were also handsome gifts from Mr. Haine, Mr. Gibbs, and Mr. Taylor, of swedes, parsnips and apples.

In February it was announced that 780 branches were now engaged **Swindon** in this work, and that twenty-six million pounds of food had been **Still to** sent to the Navy up to date; the number shortly reached close on **the Fore.** eight hundred branches, and Swindon still maintained her position of fifth on the list for efficiency. A pleasing mark of appreciation **Beatty's** was bestowed upon the Chairman and Secretary, in the form of beauti- **Thanks.** fully executed engravings sent from the Grand Fleet Fund at Edinburgh, bearing the autograph of Admiral David Beatty; the inscription ran, " Christmas, 1917, to Mr............................, of the Vegetable Products Committee for Naval Supply, from the officers and men of the Grand Fleet, in grateful recognition of your devoted and untiring labours for their comfort and welfare." Shortly afterwards copies were obtained for each member of the Committee,—a slight but gratifying memento of a long course of purely voluntary service.

This year the Committee spent nearly forty pounds in supplementing **Cash** the gifts of vegetables, and purchased eight truck-loads of roots and **Assistance.** greens. This indicates a substantial increase in the amount of cash handled, and donations of money reached £42 : 10 : 11½, consisting of—

	£	s.	d.
Messrs. Comptons' employees	17	10	0
Proceeds of Whist Drive at Stratton	8	8	0
Mr. F. Hinton (Wanborough)	2	2	0
Mrs. J. Hinton (Isle of Wight)	1	1	0
Part Collection, Intercessory Service	5	0	0
Mr. G. J. Averay		10	6
Per. Mr. Gibbs, rebate to purchasers of seed potatoes at Wanborough	2	11	1
Collected by Floss	5	8	4½
	£42	10	11½

The contribution from Messrs. Comptons' brought the total given by the employees up to within six shillings of fifty pounds.

Show at the Town Gardens. Very substantial results accrued from a joint effort of the Vegetable Products Committee and the Swindon Horticultural Society in September. Mr. A. E. Harding, the Secretary of the latter Society, co-operated with Mr. G. R. Davis and Mrs. Trineman in organizing a Fruit and Vegetable Show at the Town Gardens on September 7th ; flower-shows, owing to the strenuous times through which all were passing, had been in abeyance for a year or two, but this show had a double object suitable to the times ; firstly, it was intended to encourage allotment-holders and gardeners generally to swell the national food supply, and secondly, it was hoped to secure a good quantity of fruit and vegetables for the Fleet, since all entries became the property of the Navy. A silver cup and two silver salvers were presented for the show by the officers of the Navy.

The Children's Effort. Mr. Harding worked indefatigably to ensure the success of the Show, and by his efforts the Vegetable Products Committee benefited to the extent of fourteen tons of vegetables and fruit, which were despatched to the Fleet in 263 large packages. This splendid result was in a large measure due to the school-children of Swindon and a few villages near, whose sympathies Mr. Harding had enlisted through his Association with them as a member of the Swindon Education Committee. Long rows of sacks and hampers stretched along the lawn, showing the contribution from each school and attracting great attention, and especial interest was shown in the huge amount sent from the Higher Elementary School and from Gorse Hill School, where Mr. Webber's instruction in gardening had created many enthusiastic boy-gardeners. The total value of all the exhibits amounted to £225.

Great Results. The fourth annual report contained a fine list of donors—churches, societies and individuals, too many to reproduce here,—and stated that during the year 1,493 packages of fruit and vegetables, including twelve truck-loads, had been forwarded to the Navy ; remembering that in 1917 the total despatched was 279 packages and one truck-load, one may see how fully the Committee had carried out its determination to recover and even extend the ground lost in 1917. Since December, 1914, 4,500 packages of produce had gone from Swindon to the Fleet, a substantial proof of gratitude to the patient heroes who had protected our shores from invasion and had saved the nation from starvation. Letters of thanks were frequent and from many vessels,—the Valiant, the Resolution, the Royal Oak, the Queen Elizabeth, the Bellerophon, the Meynell, the Lewes, the Penelope, the Neptune, the Indomitable, the New Zealand, the King Orry, the Maid of Thule, the Birmingham, the Lion, etc.

The following is the balance sheet for 1918 :—

INCOME	£	s.	d.	EXPENDITURE.	£	s.	d.
Balance from 1917	9	16	11	Purchase of vegetables	38	19	9
Donations (as per list above)	42	10	11½	Timber for crates	2	6	10
				G.W.R. Company	1	15	8
				Postage	1	0	2½
				Printing, Stationery, etc.		4	4
				Balance in hand	8	1	1
	£52	7	10½		£52	7	10½

Thus the Committee closed the year with a balance of over £8 in cash besides a banking account with £127 in hand on the Vegetable Show account and an anticipated sum of about £23 returned Excise tax making £150 from the Show alone.

Thanks.   The report closes : "We should like to take this opportunity of thanking everyone who has helped us in any way during the past year, and we ask your kind assistance during the next few months, as the need of our Navy is just as great to-day as ever it has been and a good supply of fresh vegetables will go a long way towards keeping our sailors fit and well.

We are also very grateful to Mr. Trowbridge and Mr. Davis for collecting and despatching goods to the railway-stations, thereby saving expense. Our very best thanks are also due to the Market Inspector, Mr. R. Bathe, who very ably assists us in packing and booking-in gifts.

We desire to place on record again our high appreciation of the devoted services of our Chairman, Mr. W. H. Trowbridge and of our Hon. Secretary, Mrs. Trineman, to whose labour so much of our success is due." [1]

National War-Bonds.   Another War Loan Campaign was made in March, 1918, when the public was asked to invest either in War Bonds carrying 5% interest or in War Savings Certificates issued for 15/6 and worth £1 in five years' time. The Mayor published the telegram from Mr. Bonar Law, the Chancellor of the Exchequer, which ran—

"To the Mayor, Swindon.

I know that I can depend upon your doing your utmost. Every War Bond bought this week will show Germany to what extent we are in earnest.
                                    Bonar Law."

The Mayor's message accompanying the telegram said,

"Swindon is in competition with other towns of similar size, and is asked to invest £150,000 in War Bonds this week. I should like to make an urgent appeal to the loyalty and patriotism of the inhabitants to raise this sum, and as much more as possible.   A. W. Haynes, Mayor."

In view of the large sum invested by the town only a year previously—£367,000—and of the fact that something like £150,000 had already been issued in 15/6 certificates by the local Banks and Post Offices, the sum now asked for was a very big one. The Borough did not succeed in attaining it, but it achieved the creditable result of £85,073 ; £84,621 had, however, been issued in the town in National War Bonds previous to the campaign week, making a total of £169,694.

The "War Savings Associations" had been steadily investing small sums for nearly two years now ; one association, for instance, took out 1,500 certificates in twelve months ; another, started on March 8th, 1918, took out ninety certificates the next day.

"Tank Week."   A second special effort was made in May during "Tank Week," so called because the centre of the effort—as well as the centre of attraction—was H.M. Tank, No. 113, named "Julian," weighing about 30 tons ; the tank took up its station in the Market Square on Monday —"Farmers' Day"—attended by a band of pipers from the London Scottish Regiment ; speeches were delivered by the Mayor, and by Mr. J. B. Stevens, President of the local branch of the Farmers' Union, and the Vicar of Swindon, after which business began, the Mayor being the first depositor by the purchase of a £50 bond. In the evening huge crowds lined the streets to

(1) Continued on page 212.

watch " Julian's " progress to the Town Hall ; he came accompanied by the band of the Worcester Regiment and a large procession, and provided a few thrilling moments when he reached a barrier thrown across his path ; it was a huge pile of sandbags backed by a barbed wire entanglement ; " Julian " slowly mounted the barrier till he was almost on end, snapped the wire, slowly came into position, and lumbered to his new station before the Town Hall. Here the tank remained till Saturday, each day being marked by a fresh batch of speakers and enlivened by songs and music. It was a great attraction to the children, for they could buy a War Savings Certificate in the Town Hall, take it to the Tank to be stamped, and thereby get a peep into the mysterious interior. £115,000 was realized by this effort, including £20,000 contributed by the Great Western Railway Company, and £5,000 by the Swindon Corporation.

Yet a third special effort was made in 1918, when July 16th to 20th was celebrated as " War Weapons Week," the aim being to raise £100,000, which would purchase forty aeroplanes, one of them to be named " The Swindon." This, however, was too great a sum to expect after so much had been deposited by the town ; moreover, the concerts arranged for the evenings were spoilt by heavy rain, and the amount realized by the effort was not known locally.

It will be convenient here to summarise the work of the Swindon War Savings Committee since its inauguration in 1916, up to the cessation of hostilities ; the figures were provided by Mr. H. Stanier, Hon. Secy. of the Committee, and of course refer only to sums ascertainable by the Committee, for many people took up bonds through Insurance Societies or other channels outside the Committee's knowledge :—

War Savings Certificates :—

Year ended 12th February, 1917.	....	....	£50,065
Feb. 12th, 1917, to Oct. 31st, 1918.	....	....	226,262
TOTAL	....		£276,327
National War Bonds	....	....	 385,750
War Loan	....	....	 363,092
GRAND TOTAL	....		£1,025,169

The sum is indeed creditable, and it is interesting to notice that of this sum £2,828 was subscribed by the children of the day-schools.

Nut-shells. No appeal to the children was made in vain, as the many fine collections in the schools attest, whether the money was intended for the relief of the Belgian sufferers, the provision of comforts for the troops and prisoners of war, the children of Armenia, or for any other philanthropic purpose. But an appeal of a different kind was made in July, 1918, by means of a circular sent to the schools by Mr. W. Seaton, the Education Secretary ; it ran as follows :

" The Director of National Salvage announces that fruit-stones, including date-stones and hard nut-shells, are immediately required for an urgent war-purpose, and it is desired that these should all be carefully collected in Swindon and forwarded weekly."

They were required for conversion into charcoal to be used in the making of respirators used by the soldiers as a protection against poison gas. The Town Clerk, too, published a notice asking the public to assist, sending their collections to appointed depôts.

Flag-Days. The "Flag-Days" were a constant source of interest to the children, for not only did many take a part in the day's work, but it became a hobby with many to make a collection of the numerous emblems associated with the days. In 1918 the flag-days arranged and the amounts collected were:—

		£	s.	d.
4th May	Wilts Regt. Prisoners of War	120	12	8
11th May	The Belgian Soldiers' Fund, the Armenian Refugees Fund,			
	and the Italian Red Cross Fund.	69	16	10
25th May	France's Day and the French War Emergency Fund	90	17	5
8th June	British Red Cross Society, " Our Day "	94	1	0
22nd June	Lord Roberts' Memorial Workshops Fund, and the			
	National Institution for the Blind	82	3	8
13th July	England's Day and Serbian Day	67	3	9
20th July	King George's Fund for Sailors, and the British and			
	Foreign Sailors' Society	60	5	10
3rd Aug.	" Women's Day "	68	7	3
31st Aug.	Smokes for Wounded Soldiers and Sailors	73	0	7
	To these may be added the following Special "Days":—			
26th June	Y.M.C.A. " Hut Day "	63	17	7
21st Sept.	N.S.P.C.C.	108	0	6
30th Nov.	Federation of Discharged Soldiers.	79	6	7¾
	TOTAL FOR 12 COLLECTIONS.	£977	13	8¾

Federation of Discharged Soldiers. By the beginning of 1918 branches of a "National Federation of Discharged Sailors and Soldiers" had been formed in many towns, Swindon included. The objects were mainly concerned with the care of the interests of the dependents of deceased members of the forces, the securing of adequate maintenance for the disabled and work for the discharged men, to watch over the grant and administration of pensions, to protect pensioners from exploitation by employers, to secure representation on public bodies, and to oppose conscription for men once discharged.

An example of the Swindon Society's activity arose in February when they protested against the attitude of the Carpenters' and Joiners' Union in advising their members not to assist in instructing discharged soldiers in learning their trade. There was considerable suspicion amongst the trade-unions in regard to the efforts of the Pensions Committee to get disabled men trained in various trades, and in 1917 the work of training men in metal-work at the Technical Schools had to be suspended until an arrangement was made with the local Federation of Trades Unions.

Red Cross Society. In 1918 funds came into the Red Cross Society's account fairly freely from Swindon, especially as the result of one or two special efforts.

A concert and sale of work held at the Swimming Baths on April 10th resulted in the sum of £232 : 19 : 3, which was divided between the Hospital Equipment and Dilapidation funds ; many whist drives and concerts held in the Borough brought in valuable additions to the Society's income ; the collection organized by Mr. A. Manners in November reached £258 : 12 : 11¾ and included the proceeds of a matinée at the Theatre, collections at the Cinema Houses, the proceeds of flag-sales, and numerous subscriptions ; and a house-to-house collection organized by the Mayor in December raised £126 : 1 : 3, to be divided between the Red Cross Hospital and the recently formed fund for providing comforts for the men at the newly established hospital at Chiseldon Camp.

Hospital. On December 19th the hospital patients were sent home on furlough and it was quite expected that at the close of the ten days it would be re-opened ; Mr. Basil Hankey wrote: " I spoke to the A.D.M.S., Salisbury Plain, on the subject, and he anticipates that your good work at Stratton will probably be asked for a little time longer, as it is expected that more troops will be moved to Chiseldon at an early date as part of the demobilization scheme." On December 19th a supper and dance was arranged to give the men a good send-off. In the morning Lady Lansdowne had visited the Hospital, and as President of the Wilts Branch of the British Red Cross Society had inspected the wards and had expressed much pleasure at all she saw. At the evening party General and Mrs. Calley and Mrs. Waugh were present and assisted at a pleasing little ceremony when Quarter-master Mrs. Iles and the Cook, Mrs. Keylock, were the recipients of gifts from the rest of the staff. Each of the patients and all local men who had been patients during the year received a Christmas present, and the next morning patients and staff departed to their homes. The following letter from Chatham Barracks speaks for itself :

" To the Committee, B.R.C.S., Stratton, Wilts.

A Cheering Please accept my best thanks for your great kindness in thinking of me **Letter.** this Christmas by way of a gift. I'm very proud of it, and have shown it around to my chums here to let them see that a Tommy is not easily forgotten down Swindon way. When one remembers the good times we had at Stratton, I think it is we Tommies that should send out the presents. I expect you are all very busy getting ready for a merry time at the Hospital. I know the best time I had in the Army was at Stratton, and I honestly think it was worth while being wounded for. Trusting you have a right royal time this Christmas, and wishing each one all that you wish yourselves,

I beg to remain, Yours very sincerely,

2nd Corp. Jas. Brooks, R.E."

However, the Hospital was not re-opened, and Gen. Sir. H. C. Sclater, G.C.B., wrote to Mrs. Calley a very appreciative letter in which he said, " I assure you that your work and theirs [*i.e.*, the Staff's] has been very highly appreciated, and will be most gratefully remembered as a noble example of devotion and charity."

The War Office sent a letter of thanks, too, to the Board of Guardians, as also did the Committee of the Swindon Branch of the B.R.C.S., in recognition of their kindness in allowing so large a part of their premises to be used as a hospital for 18 months. The Guardians received from the Red Cross Society £200 for dilapidations in connection with the use of the premises during the period.

No of During the time the Hospital was open 514 in-patients had been received **Patients.** and some hundreds of out-patients had been treated, and there can be no question that the men had received the greatest attention and kindness there. When it was known that the place was to be closed down, one of the men wrote, saying, " We don't want to leave ; we feel that we are leaving home."

The abstract of the accounts for the Hospital during its existence is here given :—

RECEIPTS.	£	s.	d.
To Loan from Swindon	30	0	0
Branch, B.R.C.S.			
,, Advance on account			
of Army Allowance	227	0	0
,, Do. Equipment Fund	117	0	0
,, Army Allowances	4810	6	2
,, Subsc.,Donat.,Collectns.			
Entertns.,General Fund	678	7	10
,, Do. Care&Comforts Fund	91	19	8
,, Do. Special Donation for			
Russia	18	16	7
,, Sundry Sales, Perishables	76	15	0
,, Sundry Sales			
Equipment	174	17	0
,, Interest, War Loan	4	9	8
	£6259	11	11

PAYMENTS.	£	s.	d.
By Repayment of Loan	30	0	0
By Repaymt. of Advance,	227	0	0
Army Allowance,			
,, Do. Equipment Fund	117	0	0
,, Cost of Maintenance	5088	9	11½
,, Cost of Administration	226	18	6½
,, Cost of Equipment	345	16	3
,, Cost of Care & Comforts	59	14	0
Balance	164	13	2
	£6259	11	11

Disposal of the Balance. Of the balance £100 (a War-Loan Bond) was presented to the Swindon Victoria Hospital and the remainder was sent to the B.R.C.S., earmarked for Russia. Bedding, provisions, drugs, surgical dressings, etc., to the value of £45 : 10 : 0 were sent to the Victoria Hospital, the Milton Road Nursing Home, and other institutions.

The Staff had been entertained by the Commandant at an " At Home " in the Bradford Hall at the end of January, when presentations were made to Mrs. Muir, the Matron; Miss Rose, the Secretary; and Mr. W. H. Lawson, the Treasurer. At the gathering a letter was read from Mr. Basil Hankey, warmly praising the work of the V.A.D's., and Mrs. Calley expressed the hope that the Detachment would be kept together by means of meetings and classes—a matter to be considered later.

The War-Work Depôt. The Depôt for war-work was removed early in 1918 from Regent Street, to an office kindly lent by Mr. W. J. Masters in his premises at the foot of Eastcott Hill, and the work went on throughout the whole of the year. As the depôt was finally closed at the end of January, 1919, the following balance sheet has been drawn up by Miss J. M. Calley to cover the thirteen months, January 1st, 1918, to January 31st, 1919.

INCOME	£	s.	d.
Balance, Dec. 31st, 1917	13	17	0
Subscriptions & Donations	37	11	10
Envelope Collections	113	7	8
	£164	16	6

EXPENDITURE	£	s.	d.
Materials, Wool, etc.	119	0	4
Printing, advts., etc.	2	13	3
Grant to County Expenses	3	0	0
Sundries	2	5	8
Balance	37	17	3
	£164	16	6

The total number of articles made and sent away by the Depôt during the time it was open exceeded 5,800,—a highly creditable record. The balance of £37 : 17 : 3 with which the Committee was left was paid over to the Divisional Red Cross Account

War Pensions Committee. The work of the War Pensions Committee for 1918 and the latter part of 1917 was well summarised in a report published by the Committee after the close of 1918. Throughout the year Mr. A. W. Haynes acted as chairman and Mr. F. King as vice-chairman. Mr. King was also chairman of the Finance Sub-Committee, with Mr. R. Evans as vice-chairman in succession to Mr. E. C. Ayris, whilst Mr. Haynes was Chairman of the Disablement Sub-Committee and Mr. R. M. Forder vice-chairman.

Cases Dealt with. During the eighteen months covered by the report the Committee had granted assistance in 2,891 cases, of which 2,800 were Naval and Military cases, 36 Civil cases, and 55 Special cases assisted from various funds, such as the King's Fund and the Mayor's Fund, available for cases ineligible under the government regulations.

The Borough was now divided into sixteen districts for purposes of distribution, and the number of distributors was correspondingly increased, the Committee continuing the wise, if laborious practice of paying all allowances and grants at the homes of the recipients. The members who served as distributors paid an average number of 50 visits per week,—no slight sacrifice of their time ; they were now mostly ladies—Mrs. A. Arman, Mrs. Beasant, Mrs. Baxter, Mrs. Baylis, Mrs. Dean, Mrs. Hornby, Mrs. Haynes, Mrs. King, Mrs. Russell, Mrs. Rattray, Mrs. Rees, Mrs. Saddler, Miss Beswick, Miss Govier, as well as Mrs. Whitworth, who reported on all specially difficult cases ; to these names must be added that of Mr. J. Protheroe. Not only did the distributors deliver the allowances at the homes, but they kept the Committee informed as to special circumstances of distress and hardship from death or illness.

Growth of the Work. The growth of the work is well indicated by a table of statistics for given weeks three months apart :

Week taken in	No. receiving allowances.	Amount of weekly payments £ s. d.
June, 1917	302	45 15 9
Sept., 1917	350	64 11 10
Dec., 1917	448	167 7 8
March, 1918	500	201 15 1
June, 1918	671	202 1 9
Sept., 1918	783	229 4 7
Dec. 1918	956	582 8 11.

The enormous increase in the work can also be seen by comparing the summary of the work done in November, 1918, with similar summaries quoted in earlier sections :—

Grants made to—	£ s. d.
Cases under the W.P. Act.	....1773 17 9
Civil Cases	.... 22 9 7
Cases under special funds	.... 35 2 10.

Additional work was laid upon the Committee in October, when the Military Service Civil Liabilities Committee handed over to it the administration of all cases in which grants not exceeding 12/- per week had already been made.

Care of Widows. A feature that deserves special note is the care exercised by the Committee to secure provision for widows whenever the regulations gave then grounds for doing so ; the report says, " During the period covered by the report, Alternative Pensions have been granted to eight widows on the recommendation of the Local Committee. The Committee has also been successful in obtaining pensions for the widows of a number of disabled men who died after their discharge from the army ; these cases have presented a great deal of difficulty, especially in connection with the deaths which occurred as a result of the influenza epidemic. The Committee have, however, been satisfied from medical evidence which they have obtained, that in the majority of these cases the man's death has been accelerated by his military disability, and in some instances it has been clear that the death could be regarded as attributable to the man's military service. In one recent case where the deceased soldier's disability was adjudged to be ' non-attributable ' and he was consequently not awarded a pension, the Committee were able to satisfy the Authorities that the case was one for special consideration, and a pension of over £3 a week was eventually awarded to the widow, for herself and eight children."

Children's Homes. The Committee was very anxious to see a Children's Home established in North Wilts for the orphans of deceased members of the forces, but hitherto had been unable to see their wish accomplished ; in the meantime they had secured the admission of several children to Homes elsewhere, at Torquay, Taunton, Truro, and also to private homes in Swindon.

Care of the Disabled. Disabled men, too, received a great deal of the Committee's attention, and in the eighteen months ending December 31st, 1918, arrangements were made for 189 men to receive treatment in hospitals and sanatoria, whilst 209 had permission to receive treatment in Swindon. In 19 instances the Committee provided surgical boots or appliances, or arranged for repairs to those already in use, and was also arranging for the provision of dental treatment locally instead of leaving this to the " Ivory Cross Society " which had attended to this work hitherto. The Committee had made representations on several occasions to the Wilts County Council and to the Ministry of Pensions upon the urgent need for hospitals for advanced cases of tuberculosis, and some fruit was borne in the opening of such a hospital at Salisbury, though the Committee hoped to see another established in North Wilts before long.

Appeals. An " Appeals sub-committee " had been formed to deal with the cases of men dissatisfied with the Government Pension, and anyone who ever had anything to do with the correspondence with which the men were bewildered when they had to deal personally with the military pensions department, will appreciate the relief afforded these men by the provision of local assistance. In 51 cases the Committee, relying upon reports from their medical referee, approached the Ministry of Pensions to obtain an increase of pension ; seven discharged soldiers also lodged an appeal against a decision of the Ministry that the disability for which they were discharged was not due to their military service, and, after examination, the Committee supported four of the appeals.

Training the Disabled. The training of disabled men in industrial pursuits made considerable headway after the Committee had succeeded, in August, 1917, in coming to a satisfactory agreement with the local federation of Trade Unions as to the conditions upon which such men should enter the labour-field upon completion of their training. In the year-and-a-half under consideration 87 men were admitted to training, not, however, all Swindon men ; in fact, the majority were sent to the Borough for training from other Pensions Committees : the list is striking :—

No. of men	Trade.		Where Trained.
11	Metal Plate Work	....	Swindon Technical Institute
12	Light Wood-work	....	,, ,,
19	Gardening and Poultry-keeping		,, ,,
7	Mechanical Drawing	....	,, ,,
9	Sign Writing	....	,, ,,
3	Chemistry	....	,, ,,
8	Electrical Work and Switchboard		Swindon Electricity Works
1	Tram Driving	....	Swindon Tramways Dept.
3	Boot making	....	Messrs. Haskins
3	Boot Repairing	....	Messrs. Greenaway
1	,, ,,	....	Mr. Waldron's
1	,, ,,	....	Co-operative Society
4	Motor Tractor Driving and Motor Repairs	....	Messrs. Skurray's
1	Woodwork	....	Lord Roberts' Memorial
1	Bicycle Mechanic	....	Mr. Salvage's [Workshops
1	Dental Mechanic	....	Mr. Barlow's
1	Sanitary Inspector	....	Leeds
1	Tailor's Cutter	....	Mr. Collard's
87			

Visiting the Discharged. A register of all discharged men returning to Swindon was kept by the Committee, and by December 31st, 1918, it comprised 950 men. But, further than this, the Borough was divided into ten districts in each of which a member of the Disablement Sub-Committee acted as a Visitor, calling periodically on all discharged men in the district to give counsel and help concerning pensions, treatment, or training. The ten visitors were—

Mr. F. Coles   Mr. W. S. White   Mr. J. Powell
,, G. Dunn   ,, E. Jones   ,, C. J. Packer
,, W. E. Reeves   ,, A. H. Tucker   ,, E. J. Wallis
,, C. J. Horder

Besides these, Mrs. Baxter and Mr. C. J. Lavington were appointed Hospital Visitors, and rendered excellent service in attending at the Military Hospital and Camp at Chiseldon to give help to men about to receive their discharge from the Army. The reports so obtained were forwarded to the local Pensions Committee of the districts where the men lived, and ensured their receiving proper assistance upon their return home.

Ladies' Work. The number of ladies upon the Committee had been greatly augmented since its inauguration, for it was found that in many ways their services were indispensable; it has been seen that the work of distribution was almost entirely transferred to them, and ever since 1916 a Ladies' Committee had met monthly at the Town Hall in order to overlook the provision for the orphans of deceased soldiers and sailors. For their purposes the Borough was divided into eight districts, and a member of the Sub-committee visited regularly all widows and orphans in each district. In this respect the Committee recorded its thanks to Mrs. Whitworth, Mrs. Guthrie, Mrs. Gray,

Mrs. Hemmings, Mrs. Warren, Mrs. Turk and Mrs. Arman. On the Finance Sub-committee, too, ladies found a place, the Mayoress, Mrs. A. W. Haynes, and Miss Crisford being co-opted, and the name of the last-named lady was added to the list of distributors.

New Regulations. New regulations continued to enlarge the Pensions Committee's responsibilities and powers, and amongst them may be noted one which increased materially the grants of a very large proportion of the wives and dependents of Swindon men. From October 1st, 1918, the Committee was empowered, in calculating the disproportion between the income of the wife or dependent and the pre-enlistment income, to take into account the increased wages and the war-bonus which the man would have received if he had remained in civil life until January 1st, 1918,—a regulation that affected practically all employees of the Great Western Railway Company, since a bonus or war-wage of over 20/- a week would have accrued to these men.

Another regulation allowed the granting of supplementary separation allowances of 6/6 per week to all childless wives who were not in employment.

The enormous amount of work that now devolved upon the Committee may be best realized by a perusal of the balance-sheet for the period of eighteen months up to December 31st, 1918, and the different classes of payments made show the humane spirit that pervaded the Act and its administration, and the great amount of anxiety and suffering which was averted :—

Balance Sheet.

NAVAL AND MILITARY CASES.

RECEIPTS.	£ s. d.	PAYMENTS	£ s. d.
Advances from Ministry of Pensions	12860 0 0	Advances recoverable from persons assisted	739 9 0
Advances recovered	610 10 1	Supplementary Separation Allowances to Wives and Dependents	4462 4 0
		Special Separation Allowances where no State Separation Allowance granted, including Grants to Post War Dependents	954 2 0
		Temporary Allowances to Widows and Disabled Men, ineligible for State Pensions	64 6 7
		Emergency Grants, Illness Grants, Maternity Grants, Funeral Expenses, &c.	800 2 7
		Payments to Disabled Men :—	
		Treatment 3860 14 6	
		Training 1921 14 9	
		Pensions 313 12 2	5916 1 5
		Pensions to Widows whose Husbands have died after discharge	40 13 4
		Fees to Medical Men for Reports	100 0 6
		Artificial Appliances for Disabled Men	26 11 3

CIVIL CASES.

Grants from Prince of Wales' National Relief Fund	....	450 0 0		Grants made principally to Widows who were dependent upon Lodgers who have joined the Army	....	.... 423 19 6
Repayments	....	5 5 0				

SPECIAL CASES.

Grants from various Charitable Funds, &c.	674 5 10		Grants made to Discharged Soldiers and Sailors and to Dependents of deceased Soldiers and Sailors, &c.	659 12 8
Balance in hand at 30th Jun, 1917—			. Balance in hand at 31st Dec. 1918—	
Naval & Military Cases 40 2 2			Naval & Military	
Special Cases 20 16 4			Cases 407 1 7	
————			Civil Cases 31 1 6	
60 18 6			Special Cases 35 9 6	
Less overdrawn :—			————	473 12 7
(Civil Cases) 4 0				
————	60 14 6			
	£14660 15 5			£14660 15 5

ROBT. HILTON, Hon. Sec.

ALFRED E. DEAN,
Treasurer.

A. W. HAYNES, DEPUTY MAYOR,
Chairman.

FRED KING,
Vice-Chairman.

Duly Audited by Mr. F. BAILEY (Hon. Auditor).

The Local Advisory Committee. In 1917 it was decided by the Ministry of Labour that a very useful purpose would be served by the formation of Local Advisory Committees in certain areas, and Swindon was considered sufficiently important to form one of the centres. The Committee was therefore constituted and held its first sitting on January 9th, 1918. Before describing its work, however, one must say a few words about the Swindon Labour Exchange, which forms the centre of the Committee's work and which, at the date mentioned, had already been in existence for some years.

The Labour Exchange. The Labour Exchange, or, as it was subsequently named, Employment Exchange, was established under the Labour Exchange Act of 1910, and was opened on May 1st, 1911, in premises in Regent Circus close by the Post Office; the growth of the work necessitated larger premises after a few years, and the establishment was transferred to Regent Street in September, 1918, the new offices comprising the buildings that had been numbered 43, 44, and 45, Regent Street.

The area served by the Exchange is about 1,000 square miles, with an approximate population of 90,000 people, and there are seven branch offices governed by the Swindon Exchange,—Cricklade, Cirencester, Highworth, Faringdon, Malmesbury, Wootton Bassett, and Marlborough. The Swindon district forms part of the South Western Division, of which the Divisional Office is at Bristol.

Staff. The present Manager of the Swindon Employment Exchange, and the Secretary of the Local Employment Committee (as the Advisory Committee is now called), is Mr. W. G. N. Sadler who was transferred to Swindon from Bristol in succession to Mr. R. D. Monk, prior to the removal of the Exchange to the larger premises; the Deputy Manager, Mr. T. E. Weight, was transferred from the Claims and Record Office at Kew upon the upgrading of the Exchange. A number of Clerks is needed to carry on the work of the Exchange, which has grown in importance immensely during the last few years.

Unemploy-
ment
Insurance.
A large part of the Exchange's activities is in connection with the administration of the National Insurance Act (Part II of the Unemployment Act of 1911). The original Act provided for compulsory insurance against unemployment on the part of all workmen in several great branches of industry, and in 1916 the scope of the act was extended to embrace, as a temporary measure, other trades mainly concerned in the production of munitions. The Exchange undertakes in all cases the receipt of applications for unemployment insurance books and claims for benefit, but members of a union or association which is an " approved society," that is, which is recognized as having a satisfactory machinery for administering the insurance clauses of the Act, may claim through their Society, when the Ministry of Labour reimburses the society. All associations are, however, connected with an Exchange and are encouraged to lodge their vacant books at the Exchange; in Swindon nearly all the Trade Union Branches do so.

The Court
of Referees.
Claims for Unemployment Insurance benefit are decided at the Claims and Record Office of the Ministry of Labour at Kew, and any claimant dissatisfied with the decision has the right to appeal to the "Court of Referees," which was elected in 1912, by work-people insured under the Act of 1911. As then constituted the Swindon and District Panel was composed of fifteen employers' representatives and nineteen workpeople's representatives, and the chairman of the Court was Mr. E. H. C. Wethered, Barrister-at-Law. In October, 1919, the panel was greatly different and Swindon was much more heavily represented on it; the Employers' representatives included fifteen Swindon Members and the Workpeople's representatives included forty Swindon residents, three being women. From this panel is formed the Court to which a dissatisfied claimant can appeal, and even if its verdict is adverse to him he has in certain cases the right of further appeal. The Court of Referees came to play an important part as will be seen later in connection with the Out-of-work Donation.

Numbers.
The number of work-people passing through the exchange varies of course with the local conditions of labour. The average monthly new registrations at the Swindon Exchange is 500, whilst the average monthly placings during the eighteen months ending October, 1919, was about 350. On October 10th, 1919, the numbers on the register were 1,026 men, 578 women, 128 boys, and 246 girls, giving a total of 1,978.

Functions
of the
Advisory
Committee.
The foregoing remarks indicate briefly the machinery that was in existence when the Local Advisory Committees were called into being, with functions of a much more general nature than those of the Labour Exchanges. These functions embraced all matters arising out of the work of the Exchange, questions of substitution in the cases where the conscription of certain men would cripple employers, the employment of discharged service-men, and the preparation for the re-settlement of labour at the close of the war. Later on there came the administration of the Out-of-Work Donations, the re-settlement of disabled soldiers and sailors, and the estimation of the earning capacity of applicants for Alternative Pensions. Then there were questions relating to interrupted apprenticeships, licenses for opening retail businesses, Civil Liabilities grants, and demobilization procedure. In Swindon a feature of the Committee's work was an arrangement with the management of the Great Western Railway Works, whereby all labour for that factory is now recruited by a special scheme; a sub-committee—the G.W.R. Technical

Great Guns in Swindon Works Battery of 6in. Guns with Limbers.

Sub-committee—interviews all applicants and decides whether their qualifications warrant inclusion on a special G.W.R. Register.

Constitution of the L.A.C. The constitution of the Local Advisory Committee at the first meeting differed but little, at the time of its inauguration in January, 1918, from what it is at the moment of writing, in October, 1919. The Chairman, Mr. A. E. Withy, was nominated by the Minister of Labour, and the vice-chairman was Mr. W. Hobson. The members of the Employers' panel were nominated by the various employers' organizations, the members of the workpeople's panel by the several trade organizations, and all were subsequently appointed by the Minister of Labour ; other authorities were given representatives on the Committee, and a number of ladies was appointed from both employers and workpeople on the Women's sub-committee. The composition of the panel (October, 1919), was as follows :—

Chairman—Mr. A. Ernest Withy.
Vice-Chairman—Mr. W. Hobson.

Employers' Panel—

Mr. J. G. Churchward, J.P.	G.W.R. Company
Mr. C. B. Collett	G.W.R. Company
Mr. E. Mackelden	Chamber of Commerce
Mr. E. J. Horder	Chamber of Commerce
Mr. A. Snow	National Farmers' Union.
Mr. W. Husselbee	M. & S.W. Junction Railway
Mr. R. Saunders	Saunders & Sons, Builders, Cirencester
Mr. A. G. While	Swindon United Gas Company.

Workpeople's Panel—

Miss D. M. Smith	Workers' Union
Mr. A. Crane	Boiler Makers, Iron and Steel Shipbuilders.
Mr. E. J. Griffiths	Amalgamated Society of Carpenters and Joiners
Mr. W. Hobson	Amalgamated Society of Engineers
Mr. F. J. Reeves	United Machine Workers' Union
Mr. W. Robbins	Swindon Trade Labour Council
Mr. G. Smith	Swindon Trade Labour Council (Agricultural Workers)
Mr. H. Vaisey	Workers' Union
Mr. A. Wentworth	National Union of Railwaymen
Mr. C. C. Barnes	Workers' Union (Malmesbury Branch).

Other Members—

Mr. A. W. Haynes, J.P.	Swindon War Pensions Committee
Major Wright	War Office
Capt. G. Rice	Representative for Juvenile Work
Mr. A. W. Pepler	Comrades of the Great War.

Women's Sub-Committee—

Employers' Panel	Mrs. A. Lee
	Miss I. M. Austin
Workpeoples' Panel—	Mrs. J. Retter
	Mrs. Gullis
	Miss A. Hopkins
Additional Members—	Mrs. Williamson
	Mrs. Arnold-Forster
	Miss Parr.

There is also a representative of the National Federation of Discharged Sailors and Soldiers, Mr. W. J. Bullock, as an additional Member to the Discharged Sailors and Soldiers Sub-Committee.

Secretary—Mr. W. G. N. Sadler, Employment Exchange.

I

Sub-Committees. The work of the Local Advisory Committee, or, to give it its later title, the Local Employment Committee, was carried on by a number of sub-committees; these were :—

(a) The Women's sub-committee, meeting monthly;

(b) The Standing sub-committee, meeting weekly, and dealing with all questions needing attention during the intervals between the meetings of the main Committee, held at the Exchange on the third Thursday of each month;

(c) The discharged Sailors and Soldiers sub-committee;

(d) The Building-trades sub-committee, formed for the purpose of recommending releases from the Army, and now defunct;

(e) The One-Man-Business sub-committee, similar in purpose and also now defunct. These sub-Committees were formed in 1918, and to them there were added in 1919—

(f) The G.W.R. Technical sub-committee, already mentioned;

(g) The alternative Pensions sub-committee formed to advise concerning the earning capacity and amount of pension of disabled men;

(h) The Disabled Ex-Service Men Sub-committee.

A 1918 Agenda. Some idea of the large amount of work that had to be done by the Committee in 1918—an amount, however, that has since increased,— may be obtained by a glance at a typical agenda for one of the monthly meetings. After confirming the minutes of the last meeting and those of the several sub-committees, the Committee went on to deal with applications for representation by the Federation of Discharged Soldiers, and several Trade organizations, after which a draft poster regarding the constitution and work of the Committee was considered. Next, 33 notifications of discharges from the Forces on medical grounds were dealt with, and three cases of substitution were investigated. The Exchange statistics were then examined, and a scheme for securing greater publicity for Exchange vacancies was considered. After this the Committee examined and approved a draft letter which was to be sent to all employers in the area asking for their co-operation in plans for the re-settlement of discharged soldiers and sailors, and a discussion upon the functions of the Committee in relation to the re-settlement of industry followed. Then approval was sought and given for the action taken by the Secretary in 29 cases where men called up were given the opportunity to do work of national importance. Following this, the employment of discharged men in the public services was considered and the Committee formulated recommendations dealing with the question. Even these matters do not exhaust the agenda of this one meeting, but they serve to give a general idea of what the Committee was doing in 1918.

Demobilisation. During the latter part of 1918 and the early part of 1919 a great deal of new work fell upon the Committee in connection with the demobilization of the troops, and the subjoined statistics show how important was the Committee's work :—

(a) 4132 post-cards were received from employers stating that posts were available for men on their release from the colours;

(b) 13 applications for pivotal men in building trades were received and passed;

(c) 222 similar applications for the release of "one man business" men were received;

(d) 5800 declaration-forms were received from employers stating that work was available for men;

(*e*) 8831 demobilization notices were received ;

(*f*) 5198 dispersal certificates were received.

In all, the Committee dealt with about 10,000 cases of demobilization.

Out of Work Donation. The inauguration of the Out-of-work Donation scheme at the end of November, 1918, also brought an immense increase of work to the Committee and the Exchange. The scheme met with a great deal of criticism from many, who of course were not out of work and whose attention was directed to the many cases of abuse inevitably involved in such a scheme before it could be properly organized and safe-guarded. But here was a great mass of labour suddenly made idle by the Armistice, and incapable of being absorbed in the other industries all at once, and both humanity and public policy called for immediate action. The number of claimants for this donation was soon considerable ; in fact, up to the 10th October, 1919, 4,738 policies were issued in the area of which Swindon is the centre, and of these 3,715 belonged to the Borough, viz :—

H.M. Forces Policies	....	....	Men	663
			Women	15
Civil Policies	....	....	Men	757
			Women	1763
			Boys	131
			Girls	386
			Total	3715

This total, moreover, does not include the number of policies issued to members of the forces at the dispersal camps.

The Young People. Looking at these figures, one is struck by the large proportion of women and girls. This is explained by the discharges from the shell factory and the Government Munitions Works after the Armistice, and the gradual replacement of girl-clerks in the G.W.Rly. Works by returned soldiers. In regard to the young people under eighteen it was felt that it would be disastrous to allow them to spend their time in idleness, perhaps for several months, whilst in receipt of an income, and in most cases living at home. It was therefore made a condition of the payment of the donation that the young people should attend day-classes established at temporary premises by the Education Committee. The school for the girls was organized at the Princes Street Mission Hall, and formed a very interesting and useful experiment providing valuable experience in view of the imminent establishment of universal Day Continuation Schools. The school was staffed by teachers from the day schools, acting under the general supervision of Miss Summers, the Committee's organiser for Domestic Instruction, and the influence of the work of these ladies was soon very apparent ; for it must be remembered that the bulk of the girls had left school at the age of fourteen, had been withdrawn from all educational influences ever since, had been working long hours often in very rough conditions, and had been earning wages sufficient to make them independent. Many came to the school at first in a spirit of resentment, only to obtain the out-of-work donation, and their presence was ensured by making them " sign on " at the school instead of at the Exchange ; but in all but a very few this spirit soon gave place to one of real interest in a curriculum wisely designed to give practical help as well as pleasure to girls who speedily realized how deficient they were in womanly accomplishments.

**Amount
of the
Donation.**
As suggested before, every recipient had to sign daily at the Exchange a certificate that he was out of work and unable to obtain employment, and at the end of the week he received payment for the number of days upon which he had signed the form.   At first the donation was 24/- per week for men, 20/- for women, and half these rates for juveniles, with an allowance of 6/- a week for the first child and 3/- for each succeeding one in the family of any man or woman claiming relief ; but on December 12th, 1918, the amounts were raised to 29/- and 25/- for men and women, juveniles continuing to receive half the adult rate, and the children's allowance remaining as before.   On May 25th, 1919, the rates were reduced to £1 and 15/-.   A policy was valid for one quarter, but might be extended for another thirteen weeks in the case of civilians and twenty weeks in the case of ex-members of the forces suffering from physical or mental disability.

**Weeding out
the
undeserving.**
Out of such a large number it was inevitable that cases of imposition should occur, and, in addition to these, cases where the donation, though legally claimable, was unfair.   For instance, cases were known in which married women whose husbands were in full work claimed the donation, having been discharged from well-paid work on munitions.   There were young people who were receiving out-of-work pay from a society, which, with the donation, exceeded their wages when at work.   Again, it was a rule that if a recipient of the donation refused work offered him his donation should cease ; and some, furnished with the card provided by the Exchange, went after a post determined not to accept it but managing to throw the onus of refusal upon the employer.   It was cases like these that brought undeserved blame upon a very necessary and beneficent scheme, and which it was the duty of the Employment Committee to discover and eliminate as soon as possible ; the way

**Variation
in Numbers.**
in which the Committee carried out this duty may be judged from the fact that up to October, 1919, they reviewed 2,056 cases, of which 1,190 policies were allowed to stand and 866 were refused.   The effect is seen in a table showing the variation in numbers in receipt of the donation over a period of ten months :—

			Men	Women	Boys	Girls	Total
31st January	1919	....	 600	683	74	121	1429
28th February,	1919	....	 623	758	45	121	1547
28th March,	1919	....	 750	840	40	198	1828
25th April,	1919	....	 826	749	25	196	1806
30th May,	1919	....	 790	294	24	157	1265
27th June,	1919	....	 648	99	17	141	905
25th July,	1919	....	 656	100	10	133	899
29th August,	1919	....	 576	134	8	69	787
26th September,	1919	....	 518	135	3	50	706
31st October,	1919	....	 617	157	10	52	836.

Expenditure.
As regards the amount of money expended in the donation, the amount first paid in Swindon was approximately £30 per week, the first payment being made on December 4th, 1918, in respect of H.M.'s Forces policies, and on December 5th in respect of Civil policies.   This amount increased towards the middle of 1919 to about £2,300 per week, and then fell to approximately £1,000 per week in October, 1919.   It is estimated that up to October 10th, 1919, £58,371 was paid in Out-of-Work Donation at the Swindon Exchange, whilst for the whole area the sum reached £79,030.

The Prince of Wales' Fund. Contributions to the Prince of Wales' Fund, which, it has been seen, had reached the sum of £6,384 : 9 : 8, had been discontinued now for some time; but in the course of 1918 £318 : 6 : 6 was received from the central fund, and was devoted to the assistance of an average weekly number of 24 persons. This brought the total draft upon the central fund up to the date of the report to £1,391 : 5 : 0 [1].

The King's Fund. In October, 1918, a letter from the Mayor, Mr. A. W. Haynes, appeared in the local press, appealing for public support for a fund hitherto but little noticed in Swindon,—one which the Mayor's work on the Pensions Committee had brought into his notice and which the Minister of Pensions (the Rt. Hon. J. Hodge) now commended to his special attention. The trustees of the " King's Fund for Disabled Officers and Men " hoped to raise £3,000,000 for the purpose of making grants to disabled men, and the Mayor now commended it to the public, saying,

" There is no doubt about the immense good which the voluntary funds of the Ministry of Pensions have hitherto done . . .and this will be multiplied many times by the operations of the King's Fund, which will be administered on a more generous and wider scale, and free from the rigid regulations... which necessarily apply to any State scheme. As Chairman of the Local War Pensions Committee, I can testify to the benefit which several of our own local men have received from the existing voluntary funds. However, what has already been done is as nothing compared with the task which confronts us if this good work is to be continued on an adequate scale."

The appeal met with a meagre immediate response, and this is no reflection upon the liberality of the Swindon public which had generously supported the many funds brought to its notice ; but the appeal came at a time of very great anxiety and apprehension, the fund was not a local one appealing intimately to the sympathies of Swindon, the economic pressure was almost insupportable for many, and shortly after the issue of the Mayor's letter the public mind was pre-occupied by the Armistice and hopes of peace. After the lapse of a few months the appeal was re-issued with better results.

Swindon benefited, however, to the extent of £80 received from the King's Fund in 1918; the money was paid to three discharged soldiers to give them a start in business, and to one widow in order to apprentice a son to a motor-engineering firm.

Waste-Paper. The Chamber of Commerce did well with its waste-paper scheme in 1917, but in 1918 the results exceeded expectation. The Town Council's co-operation had been sought, and handbills had been distributed to householders impressing upon them the importance of saving all paper, and asking them not to put it in the dust-bin but to tie it in bags or bundles and give it to the Corporation's men when they called on their rounds. The sales of paper in 1918 realized £638 : 8 : 4, and the profits, amounting to £428, had been distributed as follows :—The Wiltshire Prisoners of War Fund, £220 ; the Victoria Hospital, £130 ; the Red Cross Society, £65 ; the Committee for providing Vegetables for the Navy, £10 ; the Boy Scouts, £3 ; with a balance in hand of £84.

The scheme was brought to a close early the next year, owing to the fall in price of scrap paper. At the March meeting of the Chamber, Mr. Forder, the president, gave the total results of the work done :—

(1) Continued on page 219.

Tons collected	....	....	....	140
Bales packed	....	....	....	1692
Receipts	....	....	....	£1076
Profits	....	....	....	£ 750
Allocated (to date)		....	....	£ 679

The Committee did not entirely abandon its labours, but asked that higher-grade paper should still be sent in by their members and others, in order to be dealt with as hitherto.

The Boy-Scouts. The help of the Boy Scouts and Girl Guides had been an important factor in the success of the waste-paper scheme, and the stress of war conditions had in many ways revealed unsuspected possibilities for the skill and energy of these young people, whose enthusiasm was well maintained by the encouragement of the District Commissioner, Mr. W. R. Bird. He had been able to provide since the outbreak of war squads of Swindon boys for coast-guard duties in Cornwall, and their friends were amazed by their robust health and stalwart physique when they returned to Swindon on leave. In December, 1918, one of these lads had a dangerous experience on the north Cornwall coast ; the newspaper report says, " Whilst Charles **A Narrow Escape.** Henry Rolls, of Swindon, and Leslie Clint, of Liverpool, both Sea-Scouts, were on the edge of the Cliff in North Cornwall, watching the heavy sea, Clint suddenly saw the ground give way, and Rolls went headlong over a 270 ft. precipice. Clint at once gave the alarm, and help was immediately forthcoming. P.O. Burt and Pte. Pat Kearn, with very great gallantry and risk to their lives, went over the cliff and brought Rolls up. Although he had fallen such a distance, he had had the presence of mind to scramble on to a rock out of reach of the heavy breakers. Every possible assistance was given at the cliff-top, and many men assisted in the work of rescue. Rolls was immediately conveyed to the Military Hospital at Bodmin, where he is doing as well as can be expected. The action of P.O. Burt and Pte. Kearn has been warmly commended."

Eggs for the Wounded. Another interesting item in the minor philanthropic efforts maintained throughout the war was the collection, in Swindon and the District, of eggs to be sent to the military hospitals. This was part of a national movement under the patronage of Her Majesty Queen Alexandra, and very soon after its inception a branch was established in the Swindon district, due mainly to the activity of Mrs. A. M. Sellers, of Stratton St. Margaret, and Mr. W. J. Moran, secretary of the Swindon Fur and Feather Association. Stratton was the headquarters of the branch and Mrs. Sellers was the Controller for the District, but until nearly the end of the war Swindon carried on its part of the work independently with Mr. Moran as Controller, ably assisted by Mr. D. Hoare and other friends.

Mrs. Sellers appointed a lady-collector in each village of the neighbourhood, and these collectors formed the local committee with the late Mrs. T. Arkell as President. The Stratton depôt soon became one of the most thriving depôts in the country, and Mrs. Sellers' enthusiasm spread to other parts, for the editor of the official magazine, " *Eggs Wanted,*" remarked in August, 1916, " Mrs. Sellers was responsible for the formation of the go-ahead collection at Wroughton now under the control of Mr. Amos Curry." Mr. Curry, reporting on the work of his sub-depôt in the issue for March 18th, 1916, had already said, " I owe a deep debt of gratitude to Mrs. A. M. Sellers for all the great help given," and he goes on to state the method of work ; " There has been a steady increase all through, chiefly kept up by weekly house-to-house collections, and from people in the street who are asked for something to buy eggs for our wounded soldiers and sailors . . . I make a point of collecting all the eggs I buy at least three times a week, thus ensuring their perfect freshness." The collectors accepted, of course, both eggs and money for the purchase of eggs, being more likely to obtain the former in the country and the latter in Swindon.

The first list of donations and eggs collected by the Swindon depôt appeared in the local press on January 15th, 1915, and gave as the total up to date £1 : 5 : 6 in cash and 101 eggs ; by the end of the year the totals were over £122 in cash and nearly 5,000 eggs, largely due to the zeal of Messrs. D. Hoare and J. Tarrant ; the Fur and Feather Association presented each of these gentlemen a silver medal in November, 1915, Mr. Hoare having then collected £55, besides £10 for the Victoria Hospital, and Mr. Tarrant £43. Everyone will recollect the interest excited in the streets of Swindon when Mr. Hoare appeared with his Shetland pony, " Kitty," who soon became quite proud of her collecting-box and the attentions lavished upon her, or when Mr. Tarrant turned out with his organ and monkey. The Swindon depôt was located at Mr. Leach's Shop in Fleet Street, and Mr. Leach acted as receiver and helped Mr. Moran to pack and despatch the eggs. Much valuable help was given by Mr. & Mrs. A. J. Gilbert, Mr. & Mrs. C. A. Plaister, Mrs. H. Kirby, Mrs. Drewett, the various Day and Sunday Schools, and many others.

The eggs, and cash collected but not spent in purchasing eggs, were sent to the central depôt in London, except a few of the eggs which were sent to the Red Cross hospital at the Swimming Baths and the hospital at Stratton. From London the eggs were sent to various hospitals at home and abroad, especially the base hospitals in France, and sometimes they were the means of giving delightful surprises to soldiers far from home ; thus, Kathleen Sawyer, a Swindon girl, received in September, 1917, the following letter from her uncle in France ;

" My dear Kathleen,

Don't have a shock when you find out the writer of this, but having come across an egg bearing your name, I thought you would like the shell returned as a souvenir. One of our officers drew my attention to the eggs sent from Swindon, and the first one I noticed bore your name, so you will note that at least some of the good things sent to France by the people in England get near the fight-ing-line. I trust the shell will not get broken on its return journey," etc.

The issue of " Eggs wanted" for November 3rd, 1917, bore a capital photograph upon the cover, showing Kathleen holding her uncle's egg-shell.

Hundreds of letters of appreciation were received by the donors and officials, one of the most noteworthy being received by a little girl of Kingsdown. Her egg went from an egg-service held at St. Philip's Church, Upper Stratton, to a hospital in France, and was given to a sick lad who had left Swindon ten years before, and who had been lost to his parents, all efforts to trace him having been vain. A letter received by Mrs. Sellers ran as follows :—

" Dear Madam,

In the battle of.................. I had the misfortune to be shot through the head; I was taken to hospital, and after being made comfortable in bed my first meal consisted of an egg bearing your address, and as I come from Wootton Bassett I thought I must write and thank you for it. I wish you could see the joy on the poor fellows' faces when they get the eggs ; it would fully repay you for all your trouble. Again thanking you, Yours truly, T. Tucker."

The total collections for the Stratton Branch (including Swindon) during the war reached the splendid figures of £355 : 9 : 7½ in cash and 161,651 eggs. When one considers the care needed to pack eggs for transport and the fact that these large totals are made up of innumerable small contributions, one sees how great has been the patience and labour of those responsible. The total of the eggs was made up thus—

Depôt	Collectors	Eggs.
Wroughton	.... Mr. & Mrs. Curry	 55140
Stratton	.... Mrs. Stratford ; Mrs. Bartlett	 38304
Rodbourne Cheney	Miss Edwards	 14961
South Marston	Mrs. Snook	 13954
Blunsdon	.... Mrs. Hyett	 7728
Gorse Hill	.... Mrs. Miles ; Mrs. Francombe	 7389
Wanborough	.... Mrs. Pooles	 6916
Swindon	.... Mrs. Drewett	 6393
Stanton Fitzwarren	Miss Jeeves	 5260
Liddington	.... Miss Pitt : Miss Broughton	 2850
Little Hinton	Rev. C. E. Perkins	 991
Shaw	.... Miss Crees	 740
Sundries	....	.... · 1027
		161651

This was the local contribution to approximately 41,000,000 eggs forming the national total. The collection was brought to a close on May 2nd, 1919, when the Chairman (Horace Holmes, Esq.), speaking at the Connaught Rooms in London, mentioned Stratton as one of five depôts that had done remarkably well ; out of 2,000 depôts it finished eleventh.

The Y.M.C.A. The Young Men's Christian Association made two special efforts in 1918 to raise funds for Y.M.C.A. " Huts." The first was made in January when an endeavour was made to raise the balance of £100 required to complete the £400 which the local branch was raising for the purpose of building a " Swindon Hut " in France. The Committee invited Gipsy Smith down and he addressed a meeting on January 16th, his appeal being supported by Brig. Gen. Calley ; the response was excellent, calling forth a hearty letter of congratulation from Sir. Arthur Yapp, the National Secretary, to Mr. G. Wellicome, the Swindon representative.

Since the early days of the war no voluntary organization had done more sterling work for the men of the fighting forces than had the Y.M.C.A. Notepaper bearing the red-triangle found its way into nearly every home in the land, bringing messages from the 2,000 centres established throughout the world in camps at home and battle-areas abroad. Up to this time the average daily expenditure had been over £2,000, and now £600 a day was needed for the maintenance of the established centres, not a penny of the money going to the Association's ordinary work in civil centres. It would be impossible to estimate the enormous contribution of the Y.M.C.A. to the comfort of the troops and its beneficent effects upon their morale. In June, Swindon was asked to show its appreciation of

Hut week. the Association's work by keeping the 23rd to the 29th of the month as " Y.M.C.A. Hut Week," and by contributing to the great expenses

incurred in the society's work. The Mayor commended the scheme in a letter to
the public, and a fine programme was mapped out for the week. On Monday there
was a splendid concert at the Mechanics' Institute; on Tuesday envelopes were
distributed throughout the town; Wednesday was a " Flag-Day," and in the
evening a meeting was held in the Town Hall, presided over by the Mayor, Mr. A.
W. Haynes, and addressed by Sir. Arthur Yapp ; at the same time the Swindon
Military Band played in the Town Gardens, and an account of the work of "the
Red Triangle " preceded a collection for the funds ; on Thursday the band of the
National Reserve and the drummers and buglers of the 16th Worcesters played
in the G.W.R. Park, and there was a meeting at Gorse Hill Wesleyan Chapel addressed
by Mr. W. M. Oatts, J.P., of Glasgow ; on Friday the envelopes were collected and
the National Reserve Band played at a meeting behind the Town Hall ; and on
Saturday a Gymnastic Display, accompanied by a band of music, took place at the
rear of the Town Hall. The results of this strenuous week gave a total of £580,
of which £63 : 17 : 7 was derived from the " Flag Day " and £146 : 10 : 8½ from the
9,000 envelopes sent out.

The Order of the Red Triangle. The opportunity of recognizing long service was taken by the National
Council on this occasion and the Order of the Red Triangle was
conferred on several Swindon workers—Mr. H. Kearns, Mr. H. C.
Toller, Mrs. F. Green, Mrs. E. Whitworth and Mr. Longman of the
Fleet Street Staff ; Mrs. Phillips and Miss Hamon of the Chiseldon
Camp Staff ; Miss Major and Miss Jackson of the Chiseldon Village Hut Staff;
Madame Dockray for her long service in the entertainment of the men of the camp
and Mr. C. K. Warner, the Secretary of the Camp Concert Committee.

The Camp-Concert Committee. The Mayor's Camp Concert Committee had continued to perform the
valuable work at the Camp already described under the year 1917,
but its work had been checked in July by the very serious epidemic
of influenza that then broke out in the Camp. From October 17th,
1917, to July 18th, 1918, the Committee arranged 104 concerts at the Y.M.C.A.
Hut and the Camp Hospital, and, as in the previous year, the majority of the
concerts were conducted by Madame Dockray, whose kindly and disinterested
zeal on behalf of the soldiers knew no intermission. The 104 concerts were apportioned thus :—

Madame Dockray	 34	Mr. J. L. Williams	....	4
Mr. C. K. Warner	 16	Mr. W. J. Young	....	4
Mr. Jno. Gale (Elocutionist)	 12	Miss J. Brown	....	4
Mr. F. Barnett	 6	Mr. W. Bullock	....	2
Mr. C. Daniels	 6	Madame K. Difford	....	2
Mr. A. E. Ford ("Thalian Entertns") 8		Miss A. Haines	....	2
Mr. W. Richardson (The ' Wags ')	4			

When the epidemic had passed, the military situation had changed to such an
extent and things were so unsettled at the Camp, that it was not feasible to continue
the work ; but when the Armistice was declared in November the concerts were
resumed in order to provide amusement for the large number of men detained at
the Camp, and a further series of 17 concerts was given.

As was the rule from the beginning, all the work was purely voluntary, and the
total expenses in 1918 only amounted to £19 : 4 : 6 for the hire of cars, which sum
came from the Mayor's Fund.

At the request of the Mayor, members of the Camp Concerts Committee participated in the entertainments presented at the rear of the Town Hall during " Tank Week," in May, when " Julian " paid Swindon a visit, and also during " War Weapons Week " in July, though upon these occasions the weather was none too kind.

Swindon had very little opportunity of watching the work of this Committee, seeing that its labours were carried out at a distance and for the benefit of men and youths who were strangers. For this reason all the more praise is due to the unselfishness, perseverance, and ardour of the men and women who freely gave their time and talents, and were ready to face the inclemency of winter evenings in getting to the camp on the bleak downs, for the sake of the lads from distant parts of the country and from over the seas. Many a mother who had never heard of Swindon has cause to bless the Swindon folk who helped her boy to keep up his spirits in the weary Camp, and perhaps helped to save him from temptation as well as depression. It is a fact that numbers of young men preferred to remain in Camp when the Concert party was going over, and the eulogies they frequently uttered were a testimony of their gratitude and their enjoyment alike. Many of them made firm friends amongst the Swindon visitors, and after leaving for distant places they would refer in their letters to the delightful evenings they had spent in the concert-room ; whilst those amongst them who were possessed of musical talent often repaid their entertainers by assisting them in Swindon as well as on the platform at Chiseldon.

The Soldiers' During 1918 the Soldiers' Rest had to be closed for two periods, for
Rest. the town was placed " out of bounds " again for five weeks in March
and April on account of a severe epidemic of measles in Swindon, and the camp was unoccupied from July 21st to November 16th. The Rest was therefore open for thirty-seven weeks only ; but in that time 17,282 teas were served at a cost of £286 : 1 : 8, being a trifle under 4d. per head ; this gives a weekly average of 480 teas at a cost of about £8. The numbers fluctuated, however, a good deal, and on two successive weeks in March exceeded a thousand, this being during the sojourn of the London Division at Draycott.

Total Thus the total number of teas provided at the Rest is 84,087, and
Figures. the total expenditure £1,433 : 4 : 4. At the time these figures were
compiled the Committee was taking steps to bring its labours to a close, as the camp had ceased to be used for residential purposes and was being used as a Demobilization centre. In her final report Mrs. Perry expressed the Committee's thanks to the various bodies who had assisted them to
Helping carry out their duties with such success ; the Men's Liberal Associa-
Institutions. tion had lent china, as also had the G.W.R. Temperance Union ;
the Women's Liberal Association had lent urns, jugs, teapots, spoons, etc., and the G.W.R. Mechanics' Institute had lent their large urns ; the tables and bread-cutters were provided by the Baptist Tabernacle ; and much help was given by the Boy Scouts whose regular attendance was arranged by Mr. W. R. Bird, the District Commissioner of the Boy Scouts' organization.

Farewell. Of the many organizations established by the Town Council to
meet the various demands of the period of stress through which the
town,—and the whole nation,—was passing, no single one can be selected as excelling the rest in zeal and efficiency, when all displayed the same spirit of patriotism and self-sacrifice. But the ladies of Swindon may well reflect

with pride upon the splendid work carried out by their representatives who maintained the Soldiers' Rest ; they themselves, in their last report, gratefully acknowledge the able and ready assistance given them by the Town Clerk, who, as
the Town Council's deputy, embodied the spirit of kindly solicitude that
animated their efforts. But is is hardly correct to use the terms " duty " and
" work " in describing the activities of these ladies, for they, in their parting words,
use very different language :   " One great consolation will ever remain to each
of us who has taken a share in the various branches of the work, and that is, that
we were afforded such a great privilege." That spirit explains one fact that is very
noticeable in the work of the different committees, namely, that after three or
four years of unremitting effort the workers are nearly all the same people that
inaugurated the work ; this is a marked feature in the Committee for the Soldiers'
Rest, and indicates the spirit of unity that permeated it, as well as the tact of the
Secretary, Mrs. H. Perry, and her fellow officers and their power of communicating
their own enthusiasm to a large body of assistants.

Soldiers'   The Committee for entertaining the Soldiers' wives and mothers
Wives and   continued its work very successfully during 1918, and the Secretary,
Mothers'   Mrs. Mary Saddler, had some interesting figures to give in her report
Club.   at the close of the year.   The membership was 472, and between 200
              and 300 usually attended the Wednesday afternoon social gatherings,
of which 39 had been held in the year ; very often the large hall at the Town Hall
was filled to overflowing.   Starting the year with a balance of about £4, the Committee closed with £3 : 5 : 6½ in hand, although in face of enhanced prices they only
charged ½d. per cup for tea, ½d. for a bun, and ½d. for bread and butter, and the
annual subscription was 1d. as against ½d. previously.   At every meeting a collection
was made for the Prisoners of War Fund, bringing in about £1 weekly.   On November
27th, a sale was held, whereby £19 : 3 : 6 was raised for the Disabled Sailors and
Soldiers Fund, the Armistice having rendered it unnecessary for the purpose for
which it was planned,—the aid of the Prisoners of War.

Mr. J. Powell, always a good friend to the club, entertained the women at the
Theatre one afternoon, at the Central Cinema on another, and on eight occasions
provided them with tea.   The weekly gatherings were alway enlivened by music
and singing, and some delightful concerts were given by some of the best talent
in the town, whilst addresses and cookery demonstrations gave a more serious turn
to many of the gatherings.   During these dark and anxious times the bright
afternoons arranged for the lonely women whose husbands were in danger and trial,
must have helped and cheered them more than even Mrs. H. C. King and her band
of helpers imagined ; there was no flagging in zeal, no weariness in well-doing, but
the same steady persistence that marked the efforts of all Swindon's war-committees.
The Wednesday afternoon " socials " had become an institution, and if the war had
lasted another four years one can well believe that with little change of personnel
the Committee would have gone on arranging teas and concerts every week.

Raising   The Military situation in France in the Spring of 1918 caused so much
The Military concern that the military age was raised to fifty, and men of all
Age.   classes began to be summoned to Trowbridge for medical examination.
             Although the standard of examination was greatly lowered, and men
were put in " Grade 1 " who would have been rejected at the beginning of the war,
a decided effort was made to show consideration to these older men, and the doctors

at Trowbridge were very considerate. But the experience was in any case revolting and humiliating to men of refined sensibilities and sometimes in a state of health that should have saved them from being called to Trowbridge at all. In one party, summoned on a certain day in June, there were—a man with a wooden leg, one who was stone-deaf, and an imbecile ; the facts could have been easily verified before-hand, but the men were fetched from their homes thirty or forty miles away by the same "red-tape" spirit that has been responsible for so many disasters and so much waste.

The Tribunals. This raising of the age-limit threw a great extra strain upon the Tribunals, for many of the cases that arose under the new conditions were such as called for the sympathies of every feeling man, and yet the tribunals were ever being told that more and more men were needed. Probably no body of men in Swindon laid down their task with so much thankfulness that it was over, than did the members of the Borough Tribunal when the Armistice put a stop to their labours ; for two years and nine months they had had to sit in judgment upon their fellow-citizens, compelled at times by the nation's need to turn a deaf ear to appeals they would gladly have granted, but at the same time often standing as a shield to one whom an inexorable military system would have taken, regardless of all considerations. No bodies of Englishmen ever had to fulfil more solemn duties than did these tribunals, and few serious men would voluntarily undertake the heavy responsibility laid upon them,—that of deciding that the nation needed this man on the battle-field and that man at home, of parting this man from his wife and family and leaving that one in their midst, of ordering this man to close down his business and allowing that one to remain at his work. Accustomed as he was to individual freedom, it was hard for the Englishman to grasp the new—and yet very old—idea that the State was paramount to every private interest ; but he found himself reduced to a mere number in a register, circumscribed as to his movements, limited as to his purchases or the prices he should charge, and liable to be sent overseas to fight whether he would or no. The tribunals embodied this idea of the pre-eminence of the State, and they had the most thankless task of all the many bodies called into being by the War—a task that called for the highest qualities of judgment, courage, and humanity.

The Last Sitting. The members present at the last sitting of the Swindon Borough Tribunal were Mr. A. W. Deacon (Chairman), Mrs. E. Whitworth, Mr. J. Clark, Mr. W. H. Kinneir, Mr. R. M. Forder, Mr. A. E. Harding and Mr. T. Butler ; Mr. W. Marshall was present as the National Service representative, as well as the clerk, Mr. R. Hilton. The same issue of the local weekly papers that reported their sitting contained the following announcement : " The Town Clerk of Swindon has received intimation from the Local Government Board that the Government has decided that recruiting under the Military Service Acts is to be suspended. All out-standing calling-up notices, whether for medical examination or for service, are cancelled, and all cases pending before Tribunals are to be suspended." (*North Wilts Herald, Nov. 15th, 1918*).

The Volunteer Training Corps. There is little to add to what has been said of the activities of the Volunteer Training Corps. During 1918 they continued to be a most efficient company with but the one deficiency—that of numbers proportionate to the size of the Borough. This was the only adverse criticism made by Brig. Gen. T. C. P. Calley after his inspection of the Swindon Company on Sunday, March 10th. The inspection was carried out on the Rodbourne Recreation Ground, and Gen. Calley was accompanied by Major M. Allfrey, Commanding Officer of the Wiltshire Battalion, and Capt. F. Whiting, Adjutant.

Inspection by Gen. Calley. Ninety and odd men appeared on parade, under Capt. T. J. Robinson with Lieut. G. R. Plaister, Second. Lieuts. F. G. Comley and J. H. C. Maundrell, Co. Sergt. Major. A. S. Potbury, and Quartermaster Sergt. H. J. Brittain ; Warrant Officer T. Trimmer, who had rendered much expert assistance in the training of the Company, was also in attendance.

After the ceremonial inspection, Capt. Whiting took the Company through its drill, followed by an open attack in artillery formation upon an enemy strong-point, for which operation the Company acted in platoons divided into sections of bombers, riflemen, rifle-grenadiers, and hotchkiss gunners. General Calley said he was pleased and gratified by the display, and that appreciable progress had been made during the past year, but he urged the men to recruit others who ought to be training with them.

According to a recent order every recruit was now supplied with uniform and full equipment within a few weeks of joining.

In Camp. In August the Swindon Company went under canvas at Roundway Park, being joined with the Chippenham contingent to form " A " Company; in camp with them there were also detachments from Devizes, Calne, and Marlborough, forming " B " Company, whilst " D " Company was from Salisbury. Captain Mills was in Command of " A " Company, and Lieut. Plaister, Coy. Sergt. Major Potbury, Q.M. Sergt. Brittain, and Q.M. Sergt. Mattingly were the warrant officers.

The Swindon detachment attracted much notice by their proficiency in guard-mounting, and were specially selected to undertake the duty when General Ashburner inspected the camp and again when Gen. Sir H. Sclater did so. The incessant rain deprived them of the musketry course with ball cartridges at the range, but they took part in all the other exercises of the camp. Amongst those who inspected the camp and the troops were, besides the two generals already named, Brig. Gen. Calley, Col. Fletcher, and Col. Lord Roundway, and they were unanimous in their praise of the keenness and steadiness of the men, their good discipline, and the cleanliness and order of the camp.

In the drill competition " A " Company was placed second, the first place going to " D " Company, but the Commanding Officer said that the general level was so high that it was only upon small points that any differentiation could be made. The Medical Officer at the Barracks spoke in high terms of the skill of Pte. Watts, of Swindon, whose ambulance work had attracted special notice.

The Armistice Suspends Enrolment. The Armistice was followed very quickly by a War Office order suspending the appointment of candidates to commissions and the enrolment of men in the Volunteer Force ; the provisions of the various drill and training agreements were relaxed, and further attendance at drill was to be purely voluntary. This involved the suspension, too, of all action for the enrolment of men exempted by the tribunals upon condition of their joining the Volunteer Force,—a form of exemption now very common, and enjoined by the Military Service Act (No. 2) of 1918.

Thus the Volunteer Training Corps, without ceasing to exist, came to a period in its existence, and its immediate interest in the present connection closes with the concert held by the Swindon detachment on December 18th ; Lieut. G.

R. Plaister presided in place of Capt. T. J. Robinson, whose illness was universally deplored, for no more capable and popular Commandant could have been found than the late Deputy Chief Constable of Wiltshire. Supporting the Chairman were Capt. Mills, Second Lieuts. Maundrell and Comley, Reg. Sergt. Maj. May, Reg. Q.M. Sergt. Ellwood, Sergt. Maj. Shaw and Coy. Sergt. Maj. Potbury, whilst the Mayor (Ald C. A. Plaister), Mr. T. Kimber, Warrant Officer Trimmer, Messrs. H. W. Thomas, E. C. M. Harvey, A. Manners, and a few others from outside were present to do honour to the occasion. Practically all the Swindon detachment was present, the whole company numbering about 120.

Numbers. In the course of his speech Lieut. Plaister said that since July, 1916, over 260 members had been enrolled in the Swindon branch ; about 80, mainly engaged in agricultural pursuits, could not see their way to sign the agreement to continue membership for the duration of the war and had therefore resigned ; 80 others joined the regular army and some had given their lives for their country. About 100, therefore, were left in the detachment ; these had more than fulfilled their obligations, for instead of completing the minimum number of 120 drills for efficiency, the majority of them had been present at more than double that number. As regards the training, it had been exactly the same as that of the regular soldiers.

Thanks. Referring to the assistance given to the funds, Mr. Plaister gratefully acknowledged the £50 given by the Swindon Corporation, £25 given by the Highworth Urban District Council, and large monetary gifts from Mr. Alfred Manners. He also thanked the G.W.R. Company for valuable loans of materials and the use of land, and acknowledged the great debt the Volunteers owed to Reg. Sergt. Maj. Trimmer for assistance and tuition, and to Dr. Whitley for his services as Medical Officer of the detachment.

Presentation. During this meeting the Volunteers made to Mr. G. R. Plaister a presentation in token of the respect and affection with which he was regarded by all the men. Lieut. Plaister had had to act as Commanding Officer in place of the Commandant for some time now, and had earned the confidence of the men by his helpful and kindly spirit, and the approbation of his superior officers in the Battalion by his energy and competent leadership.

Au Revoir. The announcement by Captain Mills, who was the officer commanding " A " Company, that the War Office had requested that the Volunteers should continue to be kept in a state of efficiency, was received with general approbation ; for besides wishing to be in readiness to serve their country if their services were needed, the comradeship in arms and the active life they had been leading had begotten in most of them a love of the service ; most of them, too, had discovered that they were better in health and physique than when they first entered it, and to throw up the service now would leave a gap in their lives which they were unwilling to experience.

CHAPTER VIII.

The Close of the War.

The Armistice. It was on Monday, November 11th, 1918, that the Armistice was signed, suspending the terrible slaughter which had been wringing the heart of humanity. There were those who bewailed the fact that the war ceased just when the allied armies under the direction of General Foch were on the point of carrying the struggle into the enemy's own country, and who thought Germany was not so entirely beaten as the safety of the world demanded. Subsequent experience showed that Germany's defeat was more overwhelming than even the most sanguine believed, and November 11th will remain one of the greatest days in the annals of civilization.

Probably Swindon never saw a more delighted crowd than that which quickly thronged the streets after the news became known. Official confirmation was not received sufficiently early to allow notice to be sent to the schools before 12 o'clock, and the children met at 2 o'clock only to be immediately dismissed, when they joined the merry crowds which filled all the principal streets. Although the afternoon was dull and marred by drizzling rain, nothing could damp the gaiety of the demonstrators or spectators ; nearly all were bedecked with ribbons and miniature flags ; impromptu processions, sometimes with bands of music, were to be met in all directions ; the streets were gay with myriads of flags and the poorer streets were not always the least brilliant. At night " Dora " slept, the Borough awoke in an unwonted blaze of light, and it was an unutterable relief to walk through streets which only the night before had been plunged in gross darkness.

In the afternoon the Works were closed, but not all the citizens gave themselves up to boisterous merrymaking ; in many churches and chapels thanksgiving services were held in the evening, short though the notice was, and the bells which had rung for gladness in the afternoon called people to praise and thanksgiving ere the day closed. The Parish Church was filled to the doors, and the New Mayor, Ald. C. A. Plaister, and the Mayoress attended the service, accompanied by the Deputy Mayor, Ald. A. W. Haynes, and Mrs. Haynes, and the Town Clerk. The Vicar's sermon, upon the text, " O clap your hands, all ye people, shout unto God with the voice of triumph " (Ps. 47, 1), was a fervent expression of thankfulness and a plea for the re-consecration of each life as the only fitting mark of gratitude for this signal deliverance from a ruthless and violent tyranny.

The Mayor's Sunday. The Armistice celebrations practically coincided with the opening of a new mayoralty, and as the following Sunday was "Mayor's Sunday" a very special character marked the customary attendance of the Mayor and Corporation at the Parish Church ; the procession that attended the New Mayor was the most imposing that had ever taken part in the civic ceremony, which had all the features of a public Thanksgiving for peace, and the church was packed to overflowing. The service opened with the singing of the National Anthem, followed by the hymn, " Now thank we all our God," many of the congregation doubtless reflecting for a moment upon the German origin of this noble hymn, which has been since the seventeenth century the German hymn of thanks-giving used in all German national festivals. In the course of the service all joined in the special Hymn of Praise and Thanksgiving to be used "after victory or deliverance from an enemy,"—" If the Lord had not been on our side, now may we say : if the Lord himself had not been on our side, when men rose up against us, they had swallowed us up quick " (*Prayer Book* ; *Forms of Prayer to be used at Sea*). Many were deeply moved, especially when the hymn, "For all the saints who from their labours rest," was sung, for the thoughts of not a few turned to some gallant lad sleeping in France or beneath the waves, whilst the prayers for the sick and wounded, for prisoners of war, and for absent friends were poignant reminders to others.

What was taking place in Swindon was taking place in every part of the land, and though the cynical and shallow may rail at these public and official expressions of faith, it was well that the occasion should be solemnized in this way, rather than that its memory should recall nothing but scenes of revelry and foolish "mafficking." None who participated in the stately and moving act of worship could fail to be profoundly affected by it, or to take a more elevated view of the tremendous experiences through which the nation had passed.

Tokens of Peace. After the Armistice the town settled down to its ordinary life again, patiently awaiting the long-deferred declaration of Peace, until it seemed as though the formal act were never coming. Reminders that the war was at an end occurred from time to time,—reminders that were very various in their nature,—a sale of demobilised war-horses, victory balls, the appearance of a German gun outside the Town Hall, and so forth. As regards the horses, 99 were sold at the cattle-market on December 16th, from prices ranging from 49 to 10 guineas, and other consignments were promised, as many thousands had to be cleared out of the remount depôts, to say nothing of the great numbers that would soon be repatriated from France.

Greetings to F.M. Haig. It was about this time that Field Marshal Sir Douglas Haig returned as a victor to England, and the Mayor of Swindon expressed the thanks of the Borough in a telegram sent to him at the Admiralty Pier Station at Dover ; it ran,—

"On your victorious return home I desire on behalf of the inhabitants of Swindon respectfully to tender you our warmest thanks for the magnificent services you have rendered to the Empire in defeating and destroying Prussian militarism and so saving the liberties of all freedom-loving peoples. We tender our like appreciation and thanks to all the officers and men under your command. We beg also to assure you of our most heartfelt and lasting gratitude. —Mayor of Swindon."

To this congratulatory message Sir Douglas Haig replied,—

"Mayor, Swindon,—All officers and men under my command join with me in sending their grateful thanks to you and the inhabitants of Swindon for your message of welcome and generous appreciation.—D. Haig."

Amongst the "Victory Balls" held by various organizations the Municipal Victory Ball, held on February 21st, 1919, was the chief, partaking of the nature of a civic celebration. The Mayor and Mayoress received the guests, and amongst those present were Sir. Frederick Young, M.P. for the Division, and Lady Young, Major & Mrs. F. P. Goddard, Brig. Gen. & Mrs. T. C. P. Calley, Mr. R. Hilton,

Capt. S. Hilton, M.C., and a large gathering of Councillors and Citizens. After the expenses were defrayed the balance of £16 : 10 : 0 was divided between the Victoria Hospital and the Milton Road Nursing Home.

Demobilisation. But the chief reminder that the war was in reality finished consisted in the troops of demobilized men that were continually passing through the town. Chiseldon Camp was a demobilization camp, and it was a frequent occurrence to meet batches of war-worn soldiers, loaded with their kit, often caked in mud, and carrying home their steel helmets as souvenirs ; they were in the highest spirits as they tramped from Old Town to New Town Station, and it was often an inspiring sight to see the loaded trains departing from the G.W.R. Station, when no discomforts or over-crowding could damp the spirits of the men bound for home.

Chiseldon was not a demobilization camp for the Wiltshires nor for regiments with distant territorial names like the Northumberland Fusiliers or the Shropshires; and as the Swindon men who were not in the Wiltshires were as likely to be in the Dublin Fusiliers or the Lancashires as in any other regiment, they were demobilised in many distant camps and reached home in driblets. But gradually their presence began to be apparent ; for instance, Coate Road has long been a favourite promenade for the youth of the town on a Sunday afternoon ; during the war it had become little more than a feminine parade, but now it began to resume its former status as the recognized meeting-place of the youth of both sexes arrayed in their best plumage.

Comrades of the Great War. There already existed in the Borough a " Post " of the " Comrades of the Great War," and the demobilization of so many men gave an impetus to the Association, resulting in the formation of a " Branch." The movement of which the Swindon association was a part was not only a national one, but branches overseas were being formed ; the purpose was to keep alive the feeling of comradeship that existed amongst those who had passed through the Great War, to foster the spirit of patriotism, and to give practical help to discharged soldiers seeking employment as well as to watch over the interests of the dependents of comrades who had fallen in the War. In February, 1919, when the Swindon " Post " was converted into a " Branch," the membership was 142, and before the end of July it reached 1,335 and was rapidly growing. At the meeting in February which marked the change in constitution, Brig. Gen. T. C. P. Calley was elected Commandant of the Branch and Mr. S. Ellis Vice-Commandant ; speeches from Brig. Gen. Calley, Major A. J. Richardson, and Major F. G. Wright gave an enthusiastic tone to the meeting which was the first of several hearty gatherings. At a concert in aid of the Branch, held on April 1st, the Mayor pinned the Distinguished Conduct Medal on the breast of Pte. Evans (Somerset Light Infantry), of Savernake Street, amidst a great round of applause. On May, 12th the Comrades, to the number of 515, marched in procession behind their own band to a special service in memory of the fallen, which was held in St. Mark's Church. By July the Comrades had secured premises for a club, having purchased number 25, Milton Road and number 1, Tennyson Street, where the headquarters of the Branch were suitably housed. As Brig. Gen. Calley said in a letter appealing for funds for the Branch : " The Association is absolutely unpolitical and unsectarian, and its sole object is to protect the interests of our returned Soldiers and Sailors, and to give them an opportunity of social intercourse."

Another association has already been alluded to—the Swindon Branch of the National Federation of Discharged and Demobilised Sailors and Soldiers, and both associations secured recognition upon various public bodies and in various public functions.

Peace   The treaty of Peace was signed by the German plenipotentiaries
Signed.   on Saturday, June 28th, 1919, and in anticipation of this much
                 discussion and thought had been expended upon the manner in
which Swindon should celebrate the great occasion.   The news of the signing of
the treaty was the signal for a spontaneous outburst of rejoicing and very soon
the Borough assumed the picturesque aspect it had worn on "Armistice Day."
Innumerable flags flew from houses and shops, and the main thoroughfares were
almost impassable with dense crowds bedecked with favours and tiny flags, whilst
in the evening noisy processions of young folks paraded the streets, singing and
cheering ; the riotous excitement of " Armistice Day " was, however, much less in
evidence, although youthful folly caused much alarm and risk here and there by
letting off squibs and crackers in the thronged streets.   On the Sunday again,
thanksgiving services were held in the churches and chapels, which in many cases
were attended by crowded congregations.

                 The 6th of July was set apart by Royal Proclamation as " Peace
Thanksgiving Sunday," or, more correctly, as " A day of General Thanksgiving."
Sunday.   The Mayor, accompanied by members of the Town Council and
                 representatives of all the important bodies of the Borough, officially
attended service at the Parish Church.   A detachment of the 16th Worcesters,
under the command of Lieut. Col. Stewart, formed part of the procession and
a large contingent of discharged and disabled soldiers accompanied it ; but the
fact that it was " Trip Week " considerably affected the attendance, although a
very large congregation participated in a very impressive service.

                 The " Peace Celebrations " were fixed for Saturday, July 19th, and
Peace   were to include a Dinner to Old Folks and the Widows of Soldiers
Celebrations. and Sailors, public Sports at the County Ground, a Competition in
                 Decorations and Illuminations, a great Procession in the evening,
a united Memorial Service on the Sunday Afternoon, and a Tea and Sports for the
children on the Monday.

Unfortunately, the Saturday turned out a thoroughly wet day, the rain be-
coming heavier as the day wore on.   The morning was not particularly wet, and
                 the town was gaily decorated and an atmosphere of light-heartedness
Meeting of   prevailed.   The Mayor had sent out an invitation to all demobilised
Discharged   soldiers and sailors to meet him at the Town Hall in the morning,
Soldiers.   and his invitation met with a hearty response, a large number not
                 being able to find room in the densely packed hall.   His Worship
was accompanied by the Mayoress, the Town Clerk, Ald. A. W. Haynes, Coun.
A. J. Gilbert, the Borough Treasurer, and other supporters, and everything was
done to establish a homely feeling ; with kindly forethought the Mayor had provided
cigars and cigarettes for the guests, for, as was explained at the outset by Mr. R.
Padget, the Chairman of the local branch of the Discharged and Demobilised
Soldiers' and Sailors' Federation, it was the Mayor's personal wish that the men
should meet him on this occasion to shake hands and to have a smoke and
a chat together.   It was a happy idea, for the members of the Federation and the
Comrades' Association had decided that they could not participate in the official

celebrations,—for reasons that it would be out of place to discuss here,—and it was felt that it would be a painful feature of the day if it passed without some recognition of the men who had made the celebrations possible. The Mayor, and Mr. Gilbert and Mr. Haynes addressed the men in the friendliest and most sympathetic manner, without entering upon the grievances that had kept the members of the association from taking part in the celebrations, and Mr. Padget and two of his supporters responded in the same friendly tone, the meeting breaking up in the best of spirits.

During this meeting the Mayor gave the men a hearty invitation to an enter-tainment he and Mr. Alfred Manners had provided for ex-service men and their friends at the Empire Theatre on the Saturday evening. A crowded audience accepted the invitation and enjoyed an excellent variety programme ; during an interval in the programme Mr. Plaister addressed a few words of welcome to the guests, thanking Mr. Manners for his generosity and paying him a warm tribute for the many services he had rendered to numerous agencies for the cheering of the troops throughout the war.

It has been necessary to emphasise the good feeling that animated the associa-tions of discharged men as a whole, because undeserved blame has been cast upon the associations in connection with regrettable events that will shortly have to be noted, and which one would gladly see expunged from the record of these days.

Sports at the County Ground. Notwithstanding the heavy rain that marred the afternoon, the entire programme of sports drawn up for the occasion was carried out at the County Ground, though the great crowd of spectators showed a decided tendency to fall off before the close. There had been excellent entries for all the events, and several novel items—such as the relay race for local football clubs, the "needle and thread" race, and the "boat-race,"—afforded great amusement. Four of the events were for girls and women, and there were races for "veterans" over sixty and for wounded soldiers.

Dinner for the Old Folk. The Dinner for the Old Folks and Widows of members of the forces was a great success ; at the Drill Hall, where Ald. A. W. Haynes presided, about 650 sat down to an excellent menu, and over 200 partook of a similar meal at the Corn Exchange where Mr. A. J. Gilbert presided. Many of the guests were over eighty years of age, and the oldest was ninety years old,—Mrs. Walker, of Florence Street. Pipes and tobacco were provided after the dinner, and fruit and tea for the ladies, and one or two brief speeches were made by the Chairman and members of the Council and other gentlemen who supported the Chairman ; the Mayor and Mayoress visited both parties, at each of which Mr. Plaister read the telegram he was sending to the King in the name of the Borough, which ran as follows :—

To His Most Gracious Majesty the King,
Buckingham Palace, London.

The inhabitants of the Borough of Swindon humbly tender their loyal duty and devotion to Your Majesty and Your Most Gracious Consort the Queen on this auspicious occasion of the celebration of peace.

We desire to rejoice with Your Majesties in the glorious victory achieved by the British Empire and her Allies in the cause of right and freedom.

We remember with pride and affection the self-sacrificing labours and inspiring example of Your Majesty, the Queen, His Royal Highness the Prince of Wales and all the members of your Royal Household throughout the War.

With deep humility and reverence we desire to give thanks to Almighty God for our great deliverance and pray that His continued blessing may rest on Your Majesty's Royal House, and all the peoples of your world-wide dominions.

Again we humbly tender our renewed assurances of devotion and loyalty to your Majesty's Throne and person.   MAYOR, Swindon.

To this message the King's Private Secretary replied :—

"I am commanded to thank you for your loyal greetings on behalf of the inhabitants of Swindon.—Private Secretary."

The Theatre and Cinemas. Morning and afternoon, the children, who were to have their special celebration on the Monday, were being entertained free of charge at the Empire Theatre and the Picture Houses, the tickets having been distributed in the schools the day before. At the Theatre 2,300 children were present in the morning and over 2,000 in the afternoon ; at each performance the children joined lustily in singing the National Anthem and listened with attention to a brief address in which Mr. Manners, in the morning, and the Mayor in the afternoon, impressed upon them the momentous nature of the events they were celebrating that day. Similar arrangements were made at the Cinemas, and the performances were amongst the happiest children's entertainments ever given in Swindon. At the same time delightful free concerts were going on in the Town Hall, where the Borough Military Band, Madame Dockray's Choir, Madame Kingdon-Difford's Choir, and a massed choir under Mr. C. K. Warner, were assisted by well-known local soloists.

A Memorial Tree. The ceremony of planting a memorial tree in the Town Gardens was carried out at 2.30, and in spite of the deluge of rain a fairly good company assembled. The Chairman of the Watch and Pleasure Grounds Committee, Councillor Haskins, presented to the Mayor, who performed the ceremonial part of the planting, a spade suitably inscribed to serve as a souvenir given by the Corporation. It was a very pleasing little affair, and the spectators were in no way depressed by the rain, but cheerfully applauded Mr. Plaister's remark that it was just the right sort of weather for the work. The tree stands near the Westlecot entrance of the gardens by the left-hand approach.

The Procession, fixed for the evening, had to be deferred till the Monday, although many of the participants had already assembled at the County Ground, prepared to face the rain.

Sunday's Memorial Service. On Sunday afternoon weather conditions were not unfavourable for the Memorial Service ; the sky was overcast and the day was very cold for July, but the rain kept off and the ground in the Park was in good condition. The procession that accompanied the Mayor from the Town Hall numbered some hundreds and at the G.W.R. Park between 10,000 and 12,000 people assembled to take part in a service that was both beautiful and touching. Canon Talbot, D.D., the newly appointed Archdeacon of Swindon, the Rev. C. A. Mayall, M.A. (the Vicar of Swindon), the Rev. F. W. Harper (Primitive Methodist), the Rev. J. E. Simon, B.A. (Congregational), and the Rev. J. H. Gavin, B.A., B.D. (Presbyterian), in his uniform as a chaplain of the forces, all took part in the service, which reached its most impressive moment when, at the exhortation, "Let us remember before God the brave and the true who have died the death of Honour, and have departed into the Resurrection of Eternal Life, especially those men who from this town have fallen in the War," the vast assembly stood for some moments in silence and with bared heads. The addresses delivered by the Venerable Archdeacon and the Rev. J. E. Simon were eloquent and inspiring appeals for the recognition of God's overruling providence in the signal deliverance of civilization from a terrible danger, and for lasting gratitude to those who were the saviours of their country : "They have been," said Dr. Talbot, "our potential human saviours. By their stripes we have been healed, and let us take care that they are the first charge—a charge that cannot be repudiated—upon the gratitude of their country."

Children's Day. Swindon has always loved to see its children assembled in festive array, and its motto in these cases is " The more, the merrier." The huge gatherings at the " Children's Fête," the Schools' Swimming Sports, Children's processions, and in fact anything connected with the pleasure and welfare of the children excite an interest that is peculiar to the town and rarely equalled elsewhere. And so on Monday, July 21st, great crowds assembled early in the afternoon to watch the children march in procession to the G.W.R.

Sports. Park. The day was one of bright sunshine; the morning had been spent in watching a splendid programme of Inter-School Sports on the County Ground, after which the Mayor and Mayoress distributed the prizes; and now, at about half-past two, the children assembled at the various schools in holiday garb and with a cup or mug for later use.

The Procession. The arrangements for getting about 11,000 children into their allotted places in the park without confusion on the one hand or tedious waiting on the other were a triumph of organization. Each school knew exactly what station it was to go to in the G.W.R. Park, when it was to arrive at a given entrance, and what course would be followed when it had reached its station; distinctive colours were worn, indicating the gate that the wearers were to use, and the schools selected their own routes to their appointed gate.

It is hard to picture the appearance of Swindon about three o'clock on that afternoon; all the main thoroughfares were lined with dense throngs of parents and other spectators, and from all quarters of the town gay processions of children were converging on the Park, halting now and then as another procession crossed or entered their route, or slipping round by some unforeseen byway in order to avoid a collision. Some of these processions were extremely pretty spectacles, with their numerous flags, the girls in dainty paper bonnets in their distinctive colour, the boys in caps or sashes, and the little ones in decorated wagons upon some of which very artistic tableaux were presented.

Tea in the Park. Almost to the appointed minute all were in the Park where a couple of bands were enlivening the proceedings, and the sight of this multitude of children, seated in sections upon heavy planks lent by the G.W.R. Company, was a delightful spectacle, beautiful in colour and arrangement. Mr. J. Stafford, the Head Master of Clarence Street Boy's School, took his stand upon a high platform, and conducted the singing of two verses of the National Anthem and then the Grace, sung to the tune of the "Old Hundredth." With admirable quickness each child was now given a bag of provisions—six ounces of fruit cake and a two-ounce buttered bun—and the cups and mugs were filled with tea from jugs that were replenished from great urns stationed all around. The Wilts National Reserve Band played throughout the meal, during which the Mayor and Mayoress walked down the aisles and greeted the juvenile guests, and then, after singing the " Grace after meat," the children were free to roam round and enjoy the different shows provided for their entertainment —Punch and Judy, acrobatic performances, trick cycling, etc.

The execution of the gigantic scheme for the children's enjoyment without hitch of any kind was due to the skilful arrangements made by a Committee of about ninety members, mostly members of the Teaching Staff, of which the general secretary was Mr. Walter Anderson, the Head Master of Lethbridge Road Mixed School; this body had been divided into three Committees,—Mr. S. W. Matthews, Mr. W. Bullock and Mr. E. Blount acting as secretaries,—each with a definite part of the programme in its charge. The success of the sports held at the County Ground in the morning was due to the Swindon Schools' Sports Association, of which Mr. C. R. Jeffery was the President, and Mr. E. Blount the Secretary, and they enlisted the services of several local gentlemen to act as starters, judges and stewards. In fact, the day's success was the result of long and careful preparation on the part of a host of willing workers, and will remain as a model of bold and efficient organization that was prepared for every contingency.

The Pageant. The pageant that had to be postponed because of Saturday's downpour formed a fitting close to the day's enjoyment, and served the purpose of drawing the children from the Park before they began to weary of the entertainments provided there. The procession started at the County Ground after the judges had inspected the various competitive classes for which prizes were offered,—the tableaux, tradesmen's turnouts, fancy costumes, and decorated cycles,—and it presented a medley of quaint, comic and pretty items. The column was swelled by groups from the Friendly Societies and Trade Unions and other organizations in their regalia, the Town Military Band and the Borough Military Band, Boy Scouts, the Boys' Brigade, Girl Guides, and the Fire Brigade, and amongst the tableaux were some notable wagons,—Mrs. Hack's "Victory, with Peace greeting Britannia," the Temperance Union's "Peace," and Nurse Lancaster's "A little child shall lead them." Mr. A. Tyler was the secretary of the committee that organised the pageant, and proved an excellent Chief Marshal, whilst Mr. Marillier, the chairman, and Mr. J. Protheroe, the general secretary of the Music, Procession and Decorations Committee, had spared no pains in ensuring that the pageant should be a worthy one.

Expenses. Some little time before the Peace Celebrations the Local Government Board issued an order sanctioning any reasonable expenditure incurred by local authorities for the purpose, urging them, however, to use the power to supplement rather than to supersede voluntary funds. The Town Clerk, Mr. R. Hilton, reporting late in August upon the expense incurred in the Borough, said that the amount would be found to lie between £700 and £750,—a very moderate sum for a town of Swindon's size and in view of what had been done ; it was only because there had been such a great deal of voluntary service that the celebrations had been carried out so well at this moderate cost.

The Board of Guardians, too, had seen that those committed to their charge had had a share in the general rejoicings, and their extra expense, including the cost of a special dinner to the inmates of the Workhouse and extra out-relief, was £46.

A Discordant Note. At this point one would gladly end, but that would be to leave a false impression upon the minds of future readers who may care to look into the doings of their predecessors. Truth demands that the whole story should be told, and in the present instance, moreover, there is nothing that reflects discredit upon the authorities of the town or upon the great body of its citizens.

The Flag-Staff. It had been thought desirable to have a flag-staff erected in the centre of the town in time for the Peace Celebrations, and a very fine one had been erected at the north-west corner of the pavement in front of the Town Hall, a striking position as regards the approach from New Town.

During the celebrations a fine " Peace Flag " floated from its summit, and although the position did not please everyone a great many admired the new flag-staff, of which the first use was to signalise a glorious and victorious peace. Some discussion was caused in the Council by the fact that no formal resolution had been made upon the subject and that the responsibility for the erection was somewhat indefinite, this giving rise to some general gossip outside ; but on the whole the public was rather pleased with its new staff. This slight misunderstanding seems to have given a cue to a small section that was not in sympathy with the Peace Celebrations, and early in the day, on Monday, it was rumoured that there would be trouble at night ; in the Park children were saying that " they "—whoever " they " might be,—were going to burn the new flagstaff down.

Disorder. About 9 o'clock it was found that the cords of the flag had been cut, and the police secured the flag ; but very soon a large crowd, containing a small hostile element and a large proportion of merely curious onlookers, assembled round the Town Hall. The Mayor (Mr. C. A. Plaister) and Mr. Alfred Manners addressed the crowd, but no remonstrances could affect the small band of hooligans who were bent on mischief, and the staff was set on fire, falling about midnight when what remained was carried down Regent Street and thrown across the tram-lines at the Centre.

The police behaved with the greatest restraint and patience, but about one o'clock a crowd assailed the police-station in the erroneous belief that one of the men had been arrested, and they could only be pacified by the Superintendent's permission to some of their members to inspect the cells, but meanwhile some of the windows were smashed by stones.

Tuesday's Riot. If anything were needed to prove that the affair was not a demonstration on the part of dissatisfied citizens, but that dissatisfaction on the part of a few was made an excuse for riot by the small hooligan section that is always present, but usually dormant in every large town, the proof would be found in the events of the next two days. On Tuesday at about 11 p.m., a crowd assembled around the Town Hall, and again the great majority were merely sight-seers ; but a number of youths attacked the windows of the Labour Exchange and several shops with stones, looting the windows of two shops. The vast concourse of people seriously hampered the police in their efforts and formed an effectual cloak for the rioters, and in the early hours of Wednesday morning the police were forced to use their batons in repelling an ugly rush made upon them in Bridge Street.

Wednesday's Recovery. By Wednesday the sober elements of the town were thoroughly aroused to the necessity of taking serious steps to check the outburst of lawlessness. His Worship the Mayor issued an appeal to all loyal citizens to be indoors by 9 p.m., so as not to afford cover for the ill-disposed. The Swindon Trades and Labour Council and the Swindon Railway Federation of Trades Unions repudiated any connection with the disturbances and appealed to all their members to support the Mayor, and formed a joint committee to investigate any and every grievance that could be presented by any ex-service men, whilst the Mayor addressed a meeting of ex-service men in the Princes Street Recreation Ground, expressing his belief that the Trades Unions and the Ex-service Men's Associations had nothing to do with the rioting—as had been suggested in some of the London papers.

The Mayor's frank and sympathetic speech was met by a hearty response, and the Ex-service men formed pickets that paraded the town till after midnight on

Wednesday, effectually overawing any who wished to renew the riots, for only one person attempted to violate the public order and he was speedily handed over to the police.

Feeling in the Borough. No one believes the riots to have been more than a sudden outburst of lawlessness on the part of a small number who are ready for any excuse to break out into rowdyism, and it must be remembered that the burning down of the Town Hall at Luton only a few days before stimulated this baser element to some such attempts in Swindon. It did not need the emphatic disclaimers of both the Federation of Discharged Soldiers and Sailors and the Comrades of the Great War to relieve them of responsibility for the riots, and it was their action that put an end to them. But the occurrences served to show how near the surface, even in a quiet and law-abiding town, the forces of disorder lie, and it is a matter for congratulation that the citizens themselves were able to put down the outbreak without help from the police or the military. The general feeling of the Borough was that the affair was a most base and undeserved return for the strenuous exertions His Worship the Mayor had made to give universal pleasure; but even these untoward happenings served to bring out the qualities of tact and charm that prevented anyone from suspecting the slightest feeling of hostility to the chief magistrate himself.

Entertaining the Demobilized Men. No celebrations would have been complete without some special and official recognition of the demobilized soldiers and sailors; to fix this function early would have been to exclude many who might have been present, for the men were coming home daily; but the recognition could not be indefinitely postponed, and at length the middle of November was fixed for the purpose, and the Town Council resolved that part of the expense should be borne by the public funds, and voted £180 out of the rates.

By public notices and the distribution of printed invitations efforts were made to get in touch with all the men, and nearly 3,000 accepted the invitation to be present at an entertainment at the Baths or the Drill Hall on Thursday or Friday evening, November 13th and 14th,—for the great number necessitated the use of both halls on the Thursday evening.

The general arrangements were in the hands of a small sub-committee, consisting of Mrs. S. J. Thomas, Mrs. F. A. Morris, Mrs. H. Perry, Mrs. A. Bull, Miss K. Handley, Miss M. E. Rowe, Mr. T. A. Jenks, Mr. C. K. Warner, Mr. J. Davies, Mr. R. M. Forder, Mr. P. Pocock, and Ald. C. A. Plaister, with Ald. A. W. Haynes as Chairman, and Miss Slade as Secretary; Mr. J. S. Protheroe undertook the big task of issuing the invitations and the tickets sent to those who accepted them.

Each evening the festivities began at 7 o'clock; on their arrival the men found tobacco and cigarettes awaiting them, and there was a plentiful supply of sandwiches, cakes, fruit, and ale. Miss Slade had been responsible for the catering and had received generous support from the tradesmen of the town and the Town Hall Staff; in this her success was complete, and her energy was a repetition of the force that had made her efforts for the Prisoners of War so successful.

Councillor A. J. Gilbert presided at the Drill Hall and Ald. A. W. Haynes at the Swimming Baths on the Thursday, and Ald. Haynes at the Drill Hall on the Friday; they were supported by a number of ladies and gentlemen who visited both halls on the Thursday,—the Mayor (Ald. S. E. Walters) and Mayoress, Mr. and Mrs. C. A. Plaister, Mrs. Haynes, Major. F. P. Goddard, Brig. Gen. T. C. P. Calley, and others,—and the programme consisted of musical items interspersed with speeches.

Mr. C. K. Warner had made the musical arrangements, and the guests were charmed by as fine a display of talent as could be wished by the most fastidious, for Mr. Ken Ellis, adding to the invaluable services he had rendered the troops during the war, in France and at home, had brought down a select party to his native town, and the well-known " Wags " shared the programme with them.

The speeches of the members of the Council were warmly responded to by Mr. R. T. Padget, President of the Discharged Soldiers' and Sailors' Federation, Ex-Reg. Sergt. Maj. Dudley S. Foy, and Gen. T. C. P. Calley, Commandant of the Comrades of the Great War, and the gatherings broke up after singing " God save the King " and " Auld lang syne."

During the course of the evening a solemn moment occurred when the Chairman asked the company to pay silent tribute to the 900 comrades sleeping in France and other parts of the world, and to bear in remembrance the men still in hospital or not yet returned home. An impressive silence followed and there were few who could recall no friend whose presence they missed ; and then the Chairman softly repeated the verse from Ecclesiasticus, " Their bodies are buried in peace : but their name liveth for evermore."

The Souvenir. It was intended to present at these meetings to each man an illuminated souvenir, but the large number, each requiring the inscription of the recipient's name, caused the presentation of the souvenirs to be deferred, though the Mayor was able to display a specimen of the beautiful certificate which had been prepared for the purpose. When the souvenirs began to be inscribed the difficulty of obtaining a perfectly accurate list caused further delay whilst the roll of honour was being revised, and it was not till the middle of 1920 that the souvenirs began to be sent out. They were worded thus,—

PRESENTED BY
THE CITIZENS OF SWINDON
TO

....

In warm appreciation of the Services rendered by him in the Great War 1914—1918.

They desire by this Token to express their Heartfelt Thanks and Gratitude for the Devotion and Self-Sacrifice which made possible this Great Victory.

The Town has cause to be proud of the Triumphant Part played by her Gallant Sons in the Great Struggle for Freedom, Honour and Justice, and in Safeguarding the Shores and Homes of our Native Land.

June 28th, 1919. C. A. PLAISTER, *Mayor.*

The War Memorial. Before closing this account of Swindon's peace celebrations, one may refer to the " War Memorial." It is well that some visible reminder should be left to the children of those who suffered for their sakes. It is for them that a reminder may be needed; but as regards the generation that suffered, those nine hundred graves in distant lands meant nine hundred empty places in Swindon homes, and many a mother's or wife's aching heart needed no memorial but its own bitterness so long as life endured. The new generation will cease to be shocked by the sight of maimed and blinded men in the streets, and the past is soon forgotten. It is well, therefore, that they should occasionally be led, whilst enjoying the peaceful fruits of the long agony of their fathers, to give a passing thought to those whose trial they can never realize and whose fortitude in the trial secured the peace their children enjoy.

For many months and at several meetings the form the Memorial should take was debated, and on two occasions the matter seemed settled, only to be raised afresh. Finally, it was decided to erect the Cenotaph which now stands at the north-western corner of the Town Hall, upon the spot formerly occupied by the Fountain, which was removed to its present site to make way for the Cenotaph. For several months a wooden model of a cenotaph stood where the Fountain now stands ; this temporary memorial was severe and somewhat gloomy in style, but not inartistic or trivial in its general effect. All the time it stood there flowers were always to be seen about the base, brought by mourning relatives of fallen men. There was much relief when it was known that this was not the model for the actual cenotaph, which was executed by Messrs. John Daymond and Son, of Vauxhall Bridge Road, London, at a cost of £1,125, the greater part of which was raised by shilling subscriptions.

The cenotaph was unveiled on Saturday, October 30th, 1920, by the Mayor, Ald. S. Walters, in the course of one of the most impressive ceremonies ever conducted in Swindon. The day was one of those serene and sunny days that often mark the close of October, and a vast crowd assembled in silence around the Town Hall to participate in the dedicatory service. Detachments of the local military units, with the Boy Scouts and the Girl Guides, were in attendance, and a massed choir supported by the band of the Comrades of the Great War led the singing. The Mayor was accompanied by the members of the Town Council, General T. C. P. Calley and several military officers, the Archdeacon of Swindon (the Ven. R. T. Talbot), and many of the clergy and ministers of the town and neighbourhood.

After the singing of Dr. Watts' beautiful hymn, " How bright these glorious spirits shine," the Mayor paid an eloquent and moving tribute to the memory of Swindon's fallen sons, and uttered a plea that the Cenotaph should be a silent appeal to all who passed it for their efforts in the cause of peace. He then unveiled the monument and laid a wreath at its foot, and after the bugles had sounded "The Last Post" the great audience sang the hymn, "Nearer, my God, to Thee." The Archdeacon then offered the dedicatory prayer, and this was followed by intercessory prayers offered by the Rev. J. H. Gavin (Presbyterian) and the Rev. W. A. Prunell (Wesleyan), both of whom had served as Chaplains with the Forces. The service closed with the hymn, " For all the saints who from their labours rest," and then many relatives of the gallant dead came and laid their wreaths around the Cenotaph whilst the National Anthem gave the signal to disperse.

The silence and reverence that prevailed during this half-hour's service, during which all shops were closed and business was suspended, as well as the vast size of the assembly which densely packed all the approaches to the Town Hall, made the occasion one of the most memorable in the history of the Borough. The Cenotaph is Swindon's first public monument ; the day may come when, in an enlarged and embellished Swindon, many memorials may adorn her streets, but none will be founded so deeply in the sorrows and veneration of her citizens.

The following is the list of Swindon men who laid down their lives in the greatest struggle the world has ever seen. The exact number can never be ascertained, but about a thousand were killed or died on active service ; their names are recorded upon the Tablet in the Large Hall of the Town Hall.

Swindon's Roll of Honour.

"They sleep as well, and, roused from their wild grave,
Wearing their wounds like stars, shall rise again,
Joint heirs with Christ, because they bled to save
His weak ones, not in vain."

Alder, A. E.
Alder, W. G.
Allard, W. F.
Allaway, A. H. J.
Allen, J.
Amor, G.
Ansty, F. C.
Axford, A. J.
Baden, F.
Bailey, C.
Bailey, F. S.
Bailey, F. T.
Bailey, H.
Bailey, T. W.
Baker, E. F.
Baker, E. J.
Balch, F. A.
Baldry, A. E.
Ball, F.
Ball, G. G.
Ball, G
Ballard, J. H.
Barber, H. H.
Barker, A. J.
Barnes, A. A. S.
Barnes, W. H. F.
Barnes, W. H.
Barnett, R. T. F.
Barrett, J.
Barrett, J. F.
Barrett, W. F.
Bartlett, F.
Bartlett, T. E.
Barton, F.
Bathe, G.
Beales, E. N.
Beames, C. P.
Beard, F.
Beasant, F. A.
Beckett, H.
Bedwell, R.

Belcher, C.
Belcher, W. H.
Berry, W. W.
Berwick, R. T.
Bevan, E. W. R.
Bevan, G.
Bezzant, A. F.
Bick, C. A.
Biggs, L.
Biggs, E. L.
Bignall, S.
Birks, A. O.
Birks, G. A.
Bishop, L. W.
Bizeley, A.
Bizley, R. C.
Blackford, J. B.
Blake, F. B.
Blunsdon, F. A.
Bond, W.
Boulton, E. R.
Boulton, R. C.
Bourne, S. B.
Bowen, E.
Bowering, J. E.
Bown, P.
Bowron, F.
Boyles, T. H.
Bradley, H. W.
Brain, T. T.
Bramble, W.
Brewer, S. G.
Bridgeman, C. O.
Bridgeman, H.
Bright, J. C. G.
Brittain, H. B.
Broadhurst, B.
Brookham, F.
Brotheridge, W. J.
Brown, J. W.
Brown, T. N. T.

Brown, W. A. J.
Bryant, A. E.
Bryant, E. G.
Bryant, G. E.
Bryant, R. W.
Buckland, J.
Buckland, R. H.
Burchill, J. T.
Burchill, W. E.
Burness, W. J.
Burnes, S.
Burt, C. S.
Butler, F. C.
Butler, J.
Butler, R. H.
Butcher, A. S.
Butcher, A. E.
Butcher, G. E.
Butt, W. F. H.
Cann, R. G. F.
Cannings, E.
Cannons, S.
Canter, T.
Carpenter, W. H. E
Carter, B.
Carter, H. J.
Carter, P.
Carvey, J.
Cavill, W.
Chaplin, C. L.
Chapman, J. G.
Chapman, J.
Chapman, W. J.
Chambers, S. W. T.
Chandler, C. E.
Chanter, S. H.
Chequer, H. G.
Chesterman, P. T.
Child, A. R.
Clapham, F.
Clarke, A. H.

Clarke, C.
Clarke, C. J.
Clarke, J.
Clarke, W.
Clements, A. J.
Clifford, A. G.
Clifford, G. W.
Clifford, R.
Cole, J.
Cole, W. T.
Coleman, F.
Coles, C.
Collett, E. G.
Collett, J.
Collins, G.
Comley, J. G.
Comley, P. H.
Compton, G.
Cook, A. E.
Cook, H.
Cook, H. J.
Cook, W. C.
Cook, W. H.
Cook, W. J.
Cooksey, C. F.
Cooper, A.
Cooper, E.
Cooper, H.
Corbett, E.
Cornish, A.
Cornish, A. A.
Corser, H.
Corser, R.
Cotton, R.
Couldrey, H. A.
Cove, E.
Cove, H.
Cowley, F. J.
Cowley J. F.
Cox, A. H.

Cox, A. J.
Cox, H.
Cox, J.
Cox, J.
Cox, W. P.
Craddock, C. W.
Creber, S. W.
Crewe, P.
Crocker, G. A.
Crocket, R. H.
Crook, H.
Cullingford, F. E.
Cullip, G. W.
Cumner, V. G.
Curtis, S. H.
Curtis, W. G.
Cuss, C. H. V.
Dadge, G. G.
Darling, A. L.
Dash, J.
Dash, P.
Day, A. H.
Day, M.
Davenport, H.
Davenport, L. B.
Davis, H. V.
Davis, L. D.
Davis, S. J.
Davis, W. J.
Deacon, C. G. M.
Deacon, W. T.
Dean, G. F.
Deave, A. G.
Dennis, H. V.
Dent, B. R.
Denton, W. W.
Dewe, E. E.
Dewe, F. H. J.
Difford, W. M.
Dixon, E. A.
Dixon, N. R. W.
Dixon, W. J.
Dobson, A. J.
Dowers, F. J.
Drew, C. T.
Drewett, S. G.
Driver, W. G.
Duck, F. E.
Dulin, W. W. M.
Dunn, H. W.
Dunsdon, P. C.
Drury, H. P.
Drury, P. C.
Durrant, G.
Dyer, F. E.
Dyer, P. W.
Dyke, A.
Eaton, G. H.
Edge, C.
Edmonds, J.
Edwards, J. H.
Eggleton, E. T. E.
Eley, H. G.

Eley, W.
Ellis, A. C.
Elliott, L.
Elliott, R. A. M.
Embling, F. G.
English, F. J.
Evan, T. D.
Evans, N.
Eyels, E.
Eveleigh, C. J.
Eveleigh, W. C.
Everett, F. A.
Farmer, F. H.
Farraday, J.
Fell, T. C.
Few, R. D. J.
Ferris, F.
Fisher, E.
Fisher, H. E.
Fisher, J. C. H.
Florey, H.
Ford, D.
Ford, W. F.
Forest, W.
Forteath, W. V.
Fortune, J.
Fowler, H. J.
Fowler, T.
Fox, J. W.
Frost, F.
Frost, F. H.
Fry, W.
Fulker, J. N.
Fullaway, W. J. T.
Fuller, J. W.
Gale, H. W.
Gale, W. W.
Gardiner, A. D.
Gardiner, C. W.
Gee, A. G.
Gee, G. W.
Gee, W.
George, H. G.
George, W. E.
Gibbs, H.
Gibbs, J.
Gibbs, W.
Gill, G.
Gillard, S. T.
Glass, A.
Gleed, F.
Goodwin, J. W.
Gosling, H.
Gosling, W. H.
Goss, P. F.
Goddard, B.
Goddard, F.
Goddard, W. J.
Godwin, H.
Golby, H. L.
Golby, J. H.
Goodenough, A. J.
Goodenough, S. T.

Goodman, H. H.
Gough, F.
Govier, A.
Grace, W. J.
Graham, J.
Grant, J.
Gray, T. C.
Green, A. L.
Green, A R.
Green, E. R. B.
Green, J.
Green, J. C.
Greer, H. A.
Gregory, F. J.
Greenaway, J.
Gribble, F.
Griffin, G. M.
Griffin, P. C.
Groves, E. W.
Groves, W. A.
Gubbins, J.
Guley, E. G.
Gunning, A. E. T.
Guthrie, R.
Hacker, G. T.
Hacker, L. T.
Hackman, C.
Haggard, C. E.
Haines, J.
Hale, A.
Hall, A. W.
Hall, E. G.
Hall, W. J.
Hancock, E. W.
Harding, T. N.
Hardyman, H. E.
Harman, C.
Harris, J. H.
Harrison, A.
Hart, R. P.
Hartwell, W. W.
Hatcher, G. L.
Hatherell, A. P.
Haward, F.
Hawkins, A. E.
Hawkins, W. H.
Hawkins, W. H.
Haylock, F. C.
Haynes, O. M.
Hayward, N.
Hayward, W. A.
Hazel, E. J.
Head, W. H.
Heap, R. W.
Heath, G.
Heath, H. T.
Heath, J. W.
Heavens, S. H.
Hedges, W. E.
Hemmings, W. J.
Hemmins, R. A.
Hendon, E. E.
Henstridge, R. R.

Herman, J.
Hibberd, A. E.
Hibberd, E. G.
Hicks, F. H.
Higgs W. G.
Hill, J.
Hillard, H. C.
Hillier, C. S.
Hillier, R. R.
Hind, F. W.
Hinder, C.
Hinder, P.
Hinder, R. J.
Hinton, H.
Hiscock, F.
Hobbs, G. C.
Hodges, S. P.
Hole, C. H.
Holley, S. P.
Hollick, E.
Hollister, C.
Holmes, A.
Holt, H. H.
Howard, J.
Hughes, A. S.
Hughes, C. N.
Hughes, G. J.
Hughes, H. J.
Hughes, S. J. A.
Hughes, W.
Hughes, W. G.
Humphries, E. C.
Humphries, L. J.
Hunt, A. V.
Hunt, J. W.
Hunter, W. S.
Huntley, J. H.
Hursey, T.
Hurst, W. J.
Hutchinson, J. F. E.
Isaacs, F. H.
Jackson, R. J.
Jacobs, H.
Jago, R.
James, A. H.
James, F. A.
Jeffcutt, S.
Jefferies, A. H.
Jefferies, W. H.
Jefferies, J.
Jeffery, W.
Jefford, L. A.
Jeffries, W. E.
Jenkins, F.
Jenkins, J. K.
Jenner, A. J.
Jew, A. E.
Johnsey, L.
Johnson, A.
Johnson, H. E.
Johnson, T.
Johnstone, C. W. T.
Jones, A. W. E.

Jones, A. W.	Liddington, W. E.	Minett, J.	Pearse, W.
Jones, C. E.	Liddon, J. H.	Mobey, F.	Peart, H. G.
Jones, C. E.	Lindsey, E. A.	Moody, W. J.	Peart, J. J.
Jones, E.	Little, H. G.	Moore, L. F.	Pedder, A. L. K.
Jones, F.	Little, W. R. A.	Moreman, R. P. E.	Pegler, P. J.
Jones, F. G.	Loder, R. A.	Morgan, F. J.	People, O. C.
Jones, F. W.	Lockey, T.	Morris, C. V.	Perry, T. H.
Jones, P. W.	Lockey, W.	Morris, S.	Pettiford, E.
Jones, S. W. J.	Long, T.	Morris, S.	Phillips, S. R.
Jones, W.	Looker, S.	Morris, S. R.	Pickering, V. G. A.
Jones, W. A.	Lord, R. C.	Morris, W.	Pickernell, R. W.
Jordan, A. V.	Love, W. R.	Morris, W. G.	Pickett, W. E.
Joyce, W. H.	Loveday, A. W.	Morris, W. T.	Pictor, T.
Keegan, T. H.	Loveday, F.	Morse, A. J.	Pidgeon, S. H.
Keel, H. A.	Loveday, H. U.	Morse, G.	Pidgeon, G. H.
Keen, P. G.	Loveday, R. G.	Morse, J.	Pike, C.
Keene, A.	Lovegrove, B.	Morse, R. H. D.	Pike, J.
Kent, A. J.	Lovegrove, W. J.	Morse, T.	Pile, J.
Kent, C.	Lovelock, F. G.	Mugford, H. N.	Pill, P. H.
Kent, F.	Loveridge, E.	Mutton, E. G.	Pitman, E. H.
Kethero, C. E.	Loveridge, T.	Nash, C.	Pitt, W. J.
Kibblewhite, G. F.	Lucas, T. H.	Nash, G. W. F.	Ponting, A. J.
Kimber, T.	Lugg, W. J.	Neale, W. G.	Ponting, E. T.
King, F. R.	Lynes, N.	New, W. C.	Ponting, R. A.
Knapp, C. E.	Lynn, H. T.	Newman, B.	Poole, T.
Knee, A. E.	Mabberley H.	Newman, F. W.	Poole, W. J.
Knee, D. A.	Malin, C.	Newton, A. E.	Porter, T. E.
Knight, F.	Manners, B.	Nicholas, E. J.	Postlethwaite, E. M.
Knight, G. E.	Manners, W. F. G.	Nichols, W. E.	Potter, J.
Lambdin, R. G.	Mannings, J. T.	Nippress, F.	Powell, T.
Lambert, E. A.	Mant, F.	Noble, E. L. D.	Preater, A. B.
Lambert, F. C.	Marchant, A.	Norris, J.	Preater, C. L.
Lambourne, A. F.	Marks, C.	North, A. S.	Preater, H. F.
Lander, C. C.	Marsh, J. L.	Norton, E. G.	Press, W. H.
Lane, W. A. G.	Marsh, L. E.	Norgrove, E. J.	Price, H.
Lanfear, A. E.	Marshall, A.	Nurden, W. J.	Price, J. P.
Lang, C.	Marshall, T. W.	Oakes, L.	Price, J. W.
Lapworth, J.	Marston, E.	O'Brien, D.	Prior, G. H.
Launchbury, C. E.	Martin, B. T.	O'Brien, H. F.	Probets, T.
Law, H. G.	Martin, L. F.	Odey, J. H.	Provis, H. G.
Law, J. W. A.	Martin, W. E.	O'Keefe, T.	Rawlings, F. H.
Lawes, A. G.	Martin, W. J.	Oram, F.	Reed, A. E.
Lawrence, E.	Maslin, T. H. J. W.	Osborn, G. H.	Reed, J.
Lawrence, G. W.	Mason, A.	Packer, E. G.	Reeves, F. J.
Lawrence, J.	Matthews, J. E.	Packer, J.	Reeves, H. T.
Lawrence, H. C.	Matthews, J. E.	Packer, J.	Reeves, R. H.
Lawrence, W. J.	Matthews, S. W.	Packer, W. M.	Reynold, H. K.
Lea, T.	Mattock, F. E.	Padget, W. G.	Reynolds, W. A.
Lee, S. G.	McDougal, A.	Page, F. J.	Reveley, V. M.
Legg, G.	McGrath, W. A.	Page, W. J.	Rhymes, S. C.
Legg, S.	McIlvride, G.	Paginton, G. A.	Richman, A. D.
Leggett, E. G.	McKay, M. A.	Painter, A.	Richman, A. G.
Leggett, W. S.	McNally, G.	Painter, W. E.	Ricketts, P. T.
Leighfield, S. F.	Mears, G. N.	Paintin, J. E.	Rixon, W. J.
Leonard, E. J.	Menham, R. W.	Palmer, R. T.	Robbins, D.
Leonard, F. C.	Merrett, H. J.	Palmer, W. W.	Robbins, H.
Leonard, P. H.	Mildenhall, C.	Partridge, R.	Roberts, C. W. H.
Lewis, E.	Miles, R. E. H.	Payne, F. G.	Roberts, F. F.
Lewis, F. J.	Miller, H. E. B.	Payne, G. F.	Robins, H. R.
Lewis, H. A.	Miller, H. J. G.	Paynter A. E.	Robinson, A.
Lewis, H. S.	Millin, T. G.	Pearce, A. J.	Robinson, F. I.
Lewis, J. W.	Millin, W. R.	Pearce, F. S.	Robinson, F. S.
Lewis, T. A.	Mills, A. W.	Pearce, G.	Robinson, J.

Robinson, W. J.
Roe, L.
Roe, T. F.
Rowland, E. T.
Rowland, E. T.
Ruddle, H. G.
Russ, G. E.
Russell, W. G.
Sadler, W.
Salloway, W. L.
Sanders, D.
Sansum, A. J.
Saunders, E. A.
Sawyer, G. F.
Scammell, M. F.
Scammell, S. H.
Schofield, S. W.
Screvens, F.
Screvens, G. W.
Scull, J. T.
Scull, P. F.
Scull, R. W.
Seager, H. A.
Seager, J.
Seager, P.
Sealey, J.
Sedgwick, C. F.
Selby, A. H.
Sellars, A. W.
Selman, C. F.
Selman, H.
Selwood, J. R.
Selwood, R. G. C.
Selwood, W. J. H.
Shakespeare, W. F.
Sharland, H.
Sharland, J. H.
Sharps, C.
Sharps, J.
Sheldon, W. G.
Sheppard, A. F. G.
Sheppard, A. W.
Sheppard, P. J.
Shergold, R. D.
Sherman, A. W.
Sherman, H. B.
Simmonds, W. A.
Simms, D. W.
Simpkins, C. H.
Simpson, O. G.
Sims, J.
Sinclair, W. A.
Singer, W. H.
Sinnett, S. A.
Skinner, W. J.
Slade, F.
Smart, W.
Smith, A.
Smith, A. S. A.
Smith, C.
Smith, C. C. B.
Smith, D.
Smith, F. W.

Smith, G. A.
Smith, G. J.
Smith, G. J.
Smith, H.
Smith, J. E.
Smith, R. R.
Smith, S. R.
Smoker, H. J.
Snook, B. C.
Southwell, H. A.
Spackman, W. E.
Speake, H. V.
Speck, G. F.
Spreadbury, B. B.
Sprules, P.
Squire, F. R.
Stacey, E. T.
Stacey, S. C.
Stacey, T.
Stanley, O. J.
Staples, H.
Staples, H.
Stevens, A.
Stevens, E. J.
Stevens, H. A.
Stevens, J. E.
Stevens, N. G.
Stevens, R. N.
Stevens, W. H.
Stones, C.
Stone, J.
Stone, W. E.
Strange, A. J.
Stratford, G.
Stratford, W. F.
Stratton, E. J.
Strevens, G.
Stroud, A. J.
Stroud, C. E.
Stroud, W. B.
Sturgess, E. J.
Sturgess, T. G.
Sullivan, J.
Summers, M.
Sutton, E. G.
Sutton, W. E.
Swanborough, F. E.
Swatton, R. J.
Style, H. E.
Styles, A. E. H.
Styles, C. O.
Tavener, P.
Taylor, C. D. B.
Taylor, F. W. G.
Telling, B. C.
Telling, E. W.
Thatcher, W. J.
Thomas, F. A.
Thomas, W. H.
Thornbury, H. J.
Thorne, C.
Thorne, J.
Thrush, B.

Thrush, G.
Tiltman, C.
Timbrell, F. H.
Timms, P. L.
Titchener, F.
Titchener, H. B.
Titcombe, A. W.
Titcombe, J. G.
Titcombe, J. T.
Titcombe, O. H.
Titcombe, W.
Tombs, E. M.
Tompkins, F. J.
Tompkins, G. J.
Toomer, W. V.
Topp, H.
Tovey, A. A.
Townsend, C.
Townsend, W. H.
Townsend, R. G.
Trueman, W. C.
Trueman, F.
Tugwell, F.
Tugwell, J. M.
Turner, T. C.
Turton, H. T.
Twyfield, T. W.
Twyford, J. R.
Tyler, A. G.
Vance, W. P.
Vickery, F.
Vickery, J. F.
Viner, F. R.
Vines, C.
Vines, W.
Vokins, B.
Wade, F.
Waite, A. G.
Wakeling, J. V.
Waldron, A. H.
Walker, G.
Walker, G. E.
Walker, H. J.
Walston, W. H.
Walters, E. C.
Walton, F. J.
Walton, H.
Warburton, H. J.
Ward, G. W.
Warren, H. V.
Wasley, F. C.
Wasley, W. G.
Watling, H. W.
Watts, I. C.
Watts, W.
Weaver, W. R.
Weaving, C.
Webb, C. G.
Webb, T. D.
Webb, A. H.
Webber, A. H.
Weeks, F.
Wells, C. A.

Wells, H. G. L.
Weston, A.
Westlake, A. L.
Whale, A.
Whatley, F. C.
Wheatcroft, F. G.
Wheatley, F. G.
Wheeler, T.
Wheeler, W.
Whetham, C. E.
Whetham, G. J.
White, E. G.
White, W. H.
Whitefield, E.
Whitefield, H.
Whiteman, C.
Whiteman, E. R.
Wiggall, C. H.
Wilcox, J.
Wilkins, A. E.
Wilks, A. H.
Wilcocks, C. W.
Williams, A. E.
Williams, C. E.
Williams, E. A.
Williams, H.
Williams, H. H.
Williams, J.
Williams, J. W.
Williams, T.
Willis, A. H.
Wills, W. H.
Wilson, C. S.
Wilson, E. J.
Wilson, H. D.
Wilson, J.
Wilson, W. R.
Wiltshire, C. H.
Winchurst, B.
Winchurst, S. J.
Winchurst, W. E.
Windridge, S. E.
Winslow, J. F.
Winstone, C.
Witts, W. R.
Wood, F. J.
Wood, W.
Woodham, J. H.
Woodley, W. H.
Woodman, A. F. J.
Woodward, A. V.
Woodward, G. W. J.
Woolford, A. E.
Woolford, S. F.
Woolford, H. S.
Wordley, G.
Workman, A. B.
Wyatt, J. H.
Yabsley, A. E.
Yates, A. G.
Yeo, T. D.
Young, A.
Young, D. W.

CHAPTER IX.

Towards Re-settlement.

1919.
The
Peace year.
The year 1918 might justly be regarded as being the limit to which this survey should extend, but 1919 was well advanced before an approach to a normal state could be discerned in the local life, and the Peace celebrations could not be held until somewhat late in the year. It will be better, therefore, to give a slight sketch of local matters without going into as much detail as the previous years have demanded.

Apart from troubles in the labour world, into which it is no part of this work to enter, the outstanding features of the year from a local point of view were the persistence of high prices, the resuscitation of many branches of the social life after their long lapse during the war, and the emergence of two great problems—Housing and Water Supply.

Persistence
of High
Prices.
Those who anticipated a sudden drop in the cost of living upon the cessation of fighting were sadly disappointed ; they had not considered the facts, that there was a world shortage of goods and means of transport, that enemy countries now became competitors for those goods, that the wheels of industry could not be started again all at once, and that the real value of the currency had altered. Paper money was the rule and very few people indeed had seen a sovereign of a half-sovereign for years, and in the course of 1919 it was admitted in Parliament that, owing to the rise in silver, large quantities of five-shilling notes were being printed as a measure of precaution and in order that they might be issued if necessary. But by this time people had grasped the fact that a sovereign, as they had known it, was a very different thing from a pound-note in the new circumstances.

£30's worth
for £100.
About the middle of the year an answer given in Parliament showed that, taking the qualities of the goods usually bought by working-class families, the pre-war values of the quantities now purchasable for £100 would approximately be :

in the case of Boots .... £30 to £35
,, Men's Suits .... £35 to £40
,, Cotton piece-goods .... £25 to £35
,, Woollen underwear .... £25 to £30

But these were not exceptional figures ; they merely illustrate the state of affairs in most articles—furniture, hardware, glass, china, etc.,—and the price of food, high as it was, was only kept from soaring indefinitely by the rigid exercise of control.

Relaxation
of Food
Control.
Few, perhaps, were so optimistic as to think that Food Control would cease soon after the declaration of the Armistice ; indeed, it would have been disastrous to remove control before supplies were plentiful enough to allow free competition, and the first experiments in the direction of abolishing control only demonstrated the folly of haste, for they were accompanied by an immediate rise in the price of the articles

concerned. Still, there was a gradual amelioration of the situation in many
directions, and the Food Control Committee, at its last meeting before
More   Christmas, was able to announce that after December 29th, the value
Meat.   of the meat coupon would be raised to 5d., whilst pork, poultry, game,
rabbits, and other specified meat foods would be sold free of coupons.
This relaxation went along with the revocation of the Sale of Pigs Order, whereby
most of the restrictions on the sale and slaughter of pigs were removed ; but the
maximum prices of pigs—21 /- per score live weight and 28 /- per score dead weight—
were retained, and dealers and curers had still to buy only on permits.
Bacon.   It was intended that, although bacon was freed from coupon, customers should deal only where they were registered, but at this meeting
of the Food Control Committee it was agreed to cancel, if the Divisional Commissioner
would consent, the registration order ; the reason given is illuminating, for it was
found that although the control price was 2 /4 per lb., some shopkeepers were
selling bacon at 1 /8 ; at the same time some of the 2 /4 bacon was so bad that
people were getting friends who were registered elsewhere to buy bacon for them,
since they themselves were tied to a retailer whose bacon was inferior and
was 2 /4 per lb. ; it was further stated that there was plenty of bacon in the town.

In January the situation was so promising that the Food Controller
Ration-books could announce that when the ration-books were used up in May no
Going.   fresh ones would be issued, but he gave a warning against endeavours
to revoke food regulations too soon.

Dear   The Food Control Committee considered about this time ;the high
Meat.   prices of meat and the unfair advantages enjoyed by the American
Meat Trusts ; frozen meat was the same price as English meat, and
the Committee resolved that the Food Controller should be advised that in their
opinion meat prices generally should be reduced and there should be a differentiation
in the event of a reduction, between home-produced and imported
Eggs.   meat. Another resolution protested against the high price of eggs—
5d. each wholesale and 5½d. retail.

Inspection   It was reported to this meeting that complaints had been received
Still   that at the railway-station buffet in New Town, soldiers and sailors
Needed.   travelling by rail were being charged 4d. each for oranges ; the
Inspector had verified this by purchasing there three oranges, weighing
9½ozs. altogether, for 1 /-, and the Committee thereupon decided to send a strong
protest to the General Manager. In view of such cases as this, and following a
warning from the Ministry of Food that since the Armistice there was manifest
a tendency to ignore the regulations, the Committee determined to keep a careful
watch on prices and to keep the inspectorial side of its work well in the foreground.

From February 16th, Margarine was freed from coupons and the
Coupon-   amount purchasable was unlimited, but butter remained rationed.
Free.   Marmalade was freed about the same time, and it was hoped that
sugar would soon be obtainable in larger quantities and at a cheaper
rate ; a resolution pressing for this was passed by the Committee unanimously,
though some speakers put the situation very clearly, pointing out that the Sugar
Commission had bought the sugar at high prices and had sold it to the retailers
at high prices, hence a reduction could not be expected till the stocks were got
through.

**A Control
Time-Table.**
A brief time-table will show the rate at which " de-control " was going on in some other commodities, or at which prices were being reduced :—

March 15th : Certificates for oil-cake and meal cease to be issued.
   ,, 17th : retail price of shredded suet reduced.
   ,, 17th : retail price of vegetarian butter reduced.
   ,, 17th : maize prices reduced.
   ,, 17th : price of Irish oats reduced.
   ,, 19th : Government cheese fixed at 1/6 per lb. retail.
   ,, 22nd: restrictions on the making of ice-cream removed.
   ,, 24th : the order governing the price of tea suspended and that governing distribution partly suspended.
   ,, 31st : control removed from imported bacon, hams, and lard.
April 1st : prices of live stock (cattle and sheep) increased.
   ,, 1st: growers' prices of potatoes increased.

**Coupons
Ended.**
The coupons in the ration-books ran out on May 3rd, but people were warned to keep carefully their books, which would continue to be used for the purchase of butchers' meat, butter, and sugar ; the sugar-ration remained at 12 ozs. per head, but the butter ration was raised to 2 ozs ; butchers were not to exceed the meat-ration of 4 coupons per head weekly (1/8 worth), but any surplus could be sold fairly amongst their registered customers.

To continue the time-table :—

**More
Relaxations.**
May 4th : Restrictions on the sale of jam removed, except that the maximum prices remained.
   ,, 26th : control of Caerphilly cheese ceased.
   ,, 31st : orders as to the requisition and distribution of condensed milk revoked.
   ,, 31st : control removed from calves and veal.
June 1st : maximum retail prices of sweets and chocolates removed.
   ,, 1st : lowest level of summer prices of milk reached.

All restrictions upon the sale and distribution of live stock were to be abolished on September 30th.

**Resignation
of the Food
Control
Officer.**
On April 30th, Mr. W. H. Bagnall resigned his position as the Local Food Control Officer, being about to leave Swindon ; the Mayor, Ald. C. A. Plaister, paid a high tribute to Mr. Bagnall's ability and zeal, and his services were also warmly recognized by the Hon. Executive Officer, Mr. R. Hilton, and by Mr. E. Mackelden who spoke on behalf of the Traders' Associations. In the early stages of the work Mr. Bagnall had had an enormous amount of work to do, some of it very tiresome and difficult, and much of it unpleasant. One incident of the early days recurs to one's mind and it will illustrate the mixture of

**An
Awkward
Customer.**
irritation and humour that often permeated the atmosphere of Mr. Bagnall's little office in Regent's Circus. The tiny room was crowded with a tired and worried throng of men, women and children, and Mr. Bagnall and his small staff were trying to get through their business as quickly as possible, and were quite as tired and worried as their applicants, when a burly navvy—a Hercules for size and strength,—pushed through the little crowd, and, fixing Mr. Bagnall with a malevolent glare, bawled at the top of his voice, " I say, Boss, am I a babby ? " Mr. Bagnall, somewhat annoyed by the intrusion, snapped
K

out, " What do you mean ? " " Well look at me, do I look like a babby ? " Mr.
Bagnall scrutinised him with his sharp, quizzical eyes and then replied, " No, I
can't say you do." "Then," said the navvy thrusting a diminutive scrap of raw meat
across the desk, " what's the good of that to me ? " It was his meat allowance,
and looking at the great fellow one could not help sympathising with him. Mr.
Bagnall managed to explain to him what sources he could still resort to and gave
him a supplementary ration for heavy workers, but for a time it looked as though
the outraged son of Anak was going to add Mr. Bagnall to his ration.

By thousands Mr. Bagnall was spoken of as " The Food Controller," being
a much more important personage than Lord Rhondda himself, and they credited
him with unlimited powers of withholding or granting supplies. His services to the
Food Control Committee were invaluable, and the smoothness with which the
system worked in Swindon was due to the energy and tact which he brought to the
work. His resignation was an indication that the days of Food Control Committees
were numbered ; they were already being advised from head-quarters to reduce
their staffs in view of the lessened amount of work ; but although their active
functions would almost cease by the end of June, their formal existence under
the existing arrangements lasted till November 19th. There were, however, many
signs that a measure of control would be needed right through the winter ; unlimited
competition at a time when there was universal scarcity would certainly be
disastrous, and this was well illustrated when the control over veal was removed ;
the controlled wholesale price a week before was 10½d. a pound, but within the first
week of June prices had trebled, and a calf three weeks old, weighing 96 lbs., fetched
£15, or 3/3 a pound.

Sugar　　　　In April applications for extra sugar for making jam from home-grown
for Jam.　　　fruit were again invited, and shortly afterwards it was announced
　　　　　　　that these would be met in full this year,—an announcement that
nonplussed many, who, arguing that they would receive three-quarters or two-
thirds of what they applied for, as was the case last year, had ordered generously
and now found themselves credited with a large quantity at 7½d. per lb.

　　　　　　　Milk prices formed the subject of a discussion between the Food
The　　　　　Control Committee and a deputation from the Swindon Dairymen's
Committee　　Association early in May. A travelling commission had been making
controls　　　enquiries with the object of fixing prices in various areas ; the
Milk.　　　　Divisional Commissioner had suggested a scale for this area which
　　　　　　　gave—Producers' maximum price : May 1/4 a gallon, June 1/3,
July 1/6, August 1/8, and September 1/10 ; Retailers' maximum price : May
June and July 2/-, August and September 2/4. The deputation argued that Swindon
prices should be 1d. less than London prices which were 2/- to 3/- a gallon retail
through the period named, but the Committee decided to adhere to the suggested
scale, and milk was 6d. a quart in Swindon from May to August 1st. After that
date, however, the price rose to figures that were a national danger, imperilling
the welfare of the infant population and exciting keen indignation against the
central authority for fixing the producer's rate so high as to necessitate these retail
prices,—7d. a quart in August, 9d. in October, 10d. in November, and 11d. in
December.

　　　　　　　One of the most serious items in the family budget was coal. Ration-
Coal and Gas. ing was maintained, and except for very small comsumers the ration
　　　　　　　was reduced. But there was hardly need to ration people whilst

prices were so high—45/- a ton in March, 51/- in October, and 52/6 in November,—and this for any rubbish the collieries chose to dump on the coal consumers. Towards the end of November a reduction of 10/- a ton was announced for December, but as an increase of 6/- a ton had been made only a few weeks before, the mystery of coal-prices was only made greater. The price of gas in Swindon rose still higher in 1919, going up to 4/6 per 1000 cubic feet in April and to 5/3 in September, when meter-rents were also raised 50% (4d. to 6d.) and stove-rents 200% (2d. to 6d.).

Municipal Charges. In March the Council notified the public that the water-charges would be increased by 33⅓% and from April 1st the electricity charges were raised to 7d. a unit for lighting and 3½d. a unit for power. The workmen's fares on the trams were also raised 50% and no fare was to be less than 1d.; the fare for the general public was 1½d. from the Centre to the termini.

Removal of some Drink Restrictions. The restrictions upon the hours during which licensed houses could sell alcoholic liquor were relaxed somewhat in March; the week-day evening hours for the sale of such drink were made 6 to 9.30 p.m., and 6 to 8.30 for "off" sales, and certain restrictions affecting the sale of spirits and the supply of drink with meals at hotels were withdrawn. The evening opening hours of licensed houses were extended to 10 p.m. a couple of months later, and shortly afterwards the "no treating" order was cancelled; the price and quality of beer continued, however, to be a constant source of complaint, and the supply was not equal to the demand, houses frequently running quite out of beer or stout. In Swindon there had been next to no grumbling at the Drink restrictions, and many licensed victuallers, whilst looking for more freedom and extension of business hours, had no desire to go back to the pre-war condition of things. The complaints that were voiced in Parliament and in the daily press emanated from the great mining and industrial areas, and in no wise represent the public opinion of Swindon; circumstances in those areas are doubtless very different from those of the quiet Wiltshire town, where multitudes missed their accustomed glass on many an occasion, but it is pleasant to reflect that they did it with a good grace.

The survey of the question of food prices and control and kindred matters has already taken much more time and space than was anticipated, and there are a host of details, not without interest, that could be discussed; but this seems a convenient point for leaving the subject, although control may yet go on for a long time, and may even become in some form or other a permanent feature of government. Swindon, like other places, felt the pinch of scarcity at times, but it must be recorded that privation, in the usual sense of the term, was not experienced during the war. The policy of Control had turned out a success far greater than could have been hoped, and now it has passed away the remembrance of little vexations will be lost in gratitude for the regular supply of necessities secured to all classes alike. In Swindon, too, gratitude should be felt toward those men who worked unremittingly on the Food Control Committee to make the system work smoothly and fairly; criticism was of course often heard, but it was recognized that they strove for justice for consumers and tradesmen alike, and never was any hint made casting a reflection upon their probity and sense of justice. They realized that a grave responsibility lay upon them, and that sense never ceased to guide their deliberations and decisions, and it is but right that record should be made that Swindon was a happier and more contented town because of their labours.

Vegetables for the Navy; 5th year. Few supposed that the Committee for supplying vegetables and fruit to the Fleet could lay down its task immediately upon the cessation of hostilities, but at the same time no-one looked forward to another whole year of service from that date ; yet the Vegetable Products Committee was called upon to continue its efforts for another twelve-month and responded with the same zeal as it had displayed hitherto.

Thanks from the Navy. At the beginning of the year Admiral Beresford wrote, " I wish to congratulate you heartily, both in my own name and on behalf of my Committee, on the splendid way in which you have steadily and quietly contributed to winning the war. In this tribute to your devoted and patriotic labours I wish to include everyone who has so generously co-operated with you." The Admiral also went on to say that a large coloured portrait of Admiral Beatty, signed by the gallant head of the Fleet himself, was being sent as a token of the Navy's appreciation of the Committee's labours. Very soon afterwards two of these portraits arrived—one for Mr. Trowbridge, the chairman, and one for Mrs. Trineman, the secretary,—along with a beautiful engraving for each of the members of the Committee, inscribed, " With grateful thanks for all that you have done for the Grand Fleet," and signed personally by Admiral Beatty. At the same time a badge was presented to Ald. A. E. Harding in recognition of his valuable help during the last Summer, when 14 tons of vegetables were obtained from the Show at the Town Gardens.

Mr. E. Jerome Dyer wrote from London about the same time, saying that many branches were closing on account of the scarcity of vegetables and saying how cheered the Central Committee was by Swindon's steady support. The Swindon Committee, too, felt the shortage, but was only spurred on to greater efforts and in the February meeting the Chairman was able to announce that the past month was the best they had ever had in respect of cash contributions, excepting the month of the Show ; for the total for the month was £21 7 : 7, inclusive of collections of nearly £10 made at the various Cinemas by the permission of the proprietors.

The Mine-Sweepers. The General Secretary, Mr. E. J. Dyer, had hoped to bring the work to a close about the end of June, but later he appealed for a continuation of the Committee's work on behalf of the mine-sweepers, of whom 20,000 were engaged on the Northern Barrage. The Chairman, after reading Mr. Dyer's letter to the Committee, said that Swindon was one of the first in the field and they were determined to be in " at the death," and he had no doubt of the continued support of the public,—sentiments that were heartily endorsed by the Committee. And so, for another three or four months the Committee stood by the stout-hearted sailors who were daily risking their lives in clearing the seas of the deadly mines which menaced our navigation, opening the seas for the passenger, food, and troop ships.

A Big Consignment. In August a special consignment of cabbages—2,000 purchased by the Committee and 600 given by Mr. A. Currey,—was sent off for the mine-sweepers on the Norwegian coast ; they were fine specimens weighing 6 or 7 lbs. a piece. The Secretary said that they had been induced to buy the cabbages by a conversation they had had with a man of the fleet, who said that they of the fleet had to pay as much as 2 /6 or 3 /- for a cabbage. The figures seem too gross to believe, but they will not be doubted by those who know how soldiers and sailors were victimised at the ports by the cowardly knaves, without patriotism or generosity, who only sought to make a fortune out of their ignorance or necessities.

One of the strongest inducements to the Committee to be steadfast in its labours was the gratitude which its efforts called forth. The Navy, with the sailor-man's traditional frank and open-hearted spirit, repeated its thanks time and again ; letters of appreciation continued to flow in,—from the Cyclops, the King George, the Erin, the Agincourt, the Tara, the Victorious, the Irene, the Prince Royal, and many others, as well as from the naval base at Aberdeen.

The Naval Review. As a small mark of its appreciation the Admiralty invited representatives of the various branches to a naval review off Southend on July 21st, and Mr. Trowbridge and Mr. Trineman attended on behalf of the Swindon branch. There were about 500 representatives present, and the Admiralty did all in its power to give them every possible mark of courtesy and respect, and entertained them royally, whilst ship after ship voiced the thanks of the men in ringing cheers. A government department is usually regarded as a soulless thing, but the Admiralty did honour to itself by the grace with which it showed its thanks for the long services of the men who had helped to look after the health and comfort of the men of the Navy.

Despatches for the Year. During this fifth year of its activities the Committee despatched to the naval bases at Aberdeen and Rosyth 120 packages of fruit and vegetables amounting to 5¼ tons, and 10 truck-loads of vegetables amounting to 28½ tons, giving a total of 33¾ tons of which from five to six tons went to the mine-sweepers. Gifts in kind fell off considerably after the Armistice was declared ; but fortunately the Committee had a fair balance in hand, and with that and the fresh donations received vegetables and fruit to the value of £224 : 8 : 6 had been purchased.

The Last Meeting. The final meeting of the Committee was held on November 3rd, just about a year after the signing of the Armistice, and there were present the Chairman (Mr. W. H. Trowbridge), the Secretary (Mr. F. W. Trineman), the Mayor (Ald. C. A. Plaister), Ald. A. W. Haynes, the Town Clerk (Mr. R. Hilton), and Messrs. A. J. Gilbert, G. Davis, P. Crockford, A. J. Bennett, H. Haine (of Sevenhampton), and Geo. Gibbs (of Wanborough).

Death of the President. The Committee heard with much regret that the President of the General Committee in London had recently passed away ; Lord Beresford had been greatly devoted to the work, concerned as it was with the well-being of the thing he perhaps loved most on earth— the British Navy—and his death was a severe loss to the whole country. On behalf of the Committee in Swindon a letter of sympathy had already been sent to Mr. E. J. Dyer, the Honorary Director.

Swindon 3rd out of 800. The Secretary gave the results of the five years' labours of the Swindon Committee ; it was a magnificent record, placing Swindon third on the list of 845 branches. Fruit and vegetables to the extent of 324 tons had been contributed by the branch, of an estimated value of £9,072. Donations in cash had amounted to £344 : 4 : 5, of which £325 : 1 : 9 had been spent on fruit and vegetables, the rest going in printing and general expenses. Swindon had the honour of being the last branch of all to send off a consignment,—25 bushels of apples in November,—the gift of Miss M. E. Story-Maskelyne, of Purton.

The persistence and enthusiasm of this Committee were beyond all praise. When the work was inaugurated it was expected to last but a few months ; when, however, time passed by and the need of its efforts only grew greater, the Com-

The Chairman's Thanks.

mittee's determination grew with the need, and at the end of five weary years it was found as strong as at the beginning. The Chairman, in his farewell speech, expressed warm thanks to many of the chief supporters; he said, " The first gentleman to give the Committee a lift up was Mr. Haine, of Sevenhampton, who read in the local newspaper of the Committee's doings, and immediately gave them an acre of cabbages; he also induced his neighbours to give similar support, and they readily responded. As the result of one visit by the Committee to Highworth 25 tons of good food was obtained for the Fleet. Then, on Mr. Haine's suggestion, they went to Draycott and saw Mr. J. H. Hussey, who gave them an acre of cabbages." Mr. Trowbridge also alluded to the splendid assistance of Messrs. Compton's employees, who had subscribed £63 : 15 : 10, and to the Chamber of Commerce which had contributed £40 from its Waste Paper fund. He valued the results of the Show in the Town Gardens at £500, and said that Mr. Trineman's dog " Floss " had collected £26 : 9 : 2. Mr. Trowbridge also testified to the help the Committee had received from the Town Clerk, the Town Hall Staff, and the successive Mayors, from Mr. A. Currey, of Wroughton, and from Mr. R. Bathe, the Market Superintendent.

Finale.

The final act of the Committee was to present to the Mayor one of the engravings already alluded to, after which the Mayor made a formal presentation to the members of the Committee of the engravings that had been sent a short time before by Admiral Lord Beresford; besides those members already named as present at this last meeting, the recipients included Messrs. C. J. Averay, A. Currey, C. Hill, A. E. Harding, F. Austin, R. M. Forder, W. E. Morse, H. J. Scotton, T. S. Taylor (Idstone), R. Bathe, and Mrs. Trineman who had so ably filled her husband's place in his absence.

The Allotment Holders.

The Allotment Holders had undoubtedly done much to save the situation in 1917 and 1918, and when the Allotment Holders' Association of Swindon and District met in their second annual meeting in March, 1919, there was a justifiable note of triumph in the utterances of the speakers. The president, Ald. S. E. Walters, pointed with pride to the membership, now numbering a couple of thousands, and anticipated the time when there would be two such associations in Swindon. There was a good deal of protest when it was said that the allotments upon the Recreation Grounds would probably soon be resumed by the Town Council, and a deputation was chosen to interview the Council upon the matter. The Act of 1917 gave them security of tenure for two years from the close of the war and for a further three years if the Railway and Canal Commissioners consented, and it was urged that after the labour spent on getting into good condition land that had been devoted to sport for years, the holders should have at least five years' tenure.

An evidence of the Association's vitality was seen in an important conference held at the Mechanics' Institute a week or two later, when delegates from Gloucester, Somerset, and North Wilts met to discuss the subject of federation,—a suggestion favourably received by the Swindon representatives. The idea was supported by Mr. J. Randall, the Organising Secretary of the Agricultural Organisation Society, Western Branch, and he was asked to come down to a subsequent meeting to advise the plot-holders upon the subject that was disturbing many,—the possibility of having to give up their plots before long. The gathering resolved, " That the Corporation be asked to retain the recreation grounds as allotments, and to do their best

The Recreation Grounds.

to find some other play-ground for the children." This was precisely the situation feared by many when the project was first mooted, but no one who realizes the terrible anxiety and forebodings of 1917 will blame the project any more than he will find fault with the desire to retain what had cost so much toil and expenditure. Much as the Grounds were needed by the children,—for the schools were unable to continue their usual sports,—the Council abstained from disturbing the allotment-holders before they could offer them fresh land, taking steps at once to acquire suitable plots adjacent to the borough, such as the 65 acres at Mannington Farm for which the Council was negotiating in November, 1919.

The Trip It is a pleasant contrast to turn to the evidences of the revival of
Resuscitated. the social life of the Borough. First, perhaps, in general interest is
the fact that the annual "Trip" was resuscitated and was fixed for July 4th; this was a great boon to many families and especially to the children, though the G.W.R. Company had striven during the war to give their employees an opportunity for a change in the Summer ; but now families and groups of friends could take united holidays as of old. Those people, however, who
1½d. a mile. were not in "The Works" were not so fortunate, as fares were 50%
above pre-war rates, and no cheap fares were granted. The inconveniences of travel, however, owing to shortage of trains and the great numbers of people travelling, effectually repressed any inclination to go far afield, even if one could afford the exorbitant fares.

The Swindon Town Cricket Club was re-established at a meeting
The Town presided over by the Mayor, Mr. C. A. Plaister, on March 24th. The
Cricket Club war had put the club in a tight position, but Mr. F. P. Goddard
Re-estab- had generously remitted three years' rent—£90—that was due to
lished. him, and Mr. R. Reynolds, who proposed the re-establishment of
the club, said that although they would be faced with a liability of £30 for 1918, he felt sure Major Goddard and the Town Council would meet
them generously. Mr. Reynolds alluded with feeling to Mr. F. G.
Fallen Dean and Mr. P. O. Bown, who had fallen in the War, to Mr. Rawlings
Members. who would be unable to play again, and to Mr. B. T. Wilson, still
in hospital as a result of serious wounds. Mr. C. H. Agar, of Stanton Fitzwarren, was elected President, Mr. G. W. Mathews Secretary, Mr. C. Williams Captain of the First Eleven and Mr. E. W. Goodman Captain of the Second Eleven.

Another revival, welcome to the children of the Town, was that of
Revival of the Juvenile Fête, held in the G.W.R. Park on August 9th ; the
the Juvenile Council of the Mechanics' Institute, whilst trying to curtail expenses
Fête ; as much as possible and disallowing the not altogether desirable
"side shows" that used to attend the fête, were determined to make it a really good "Victory Fête," and it is a maxim in Swindon that when the Committee of the Mechanics' Institute takes up a thing they make it "go."

The Swindon Horticultural Society again held its August Flower
and of the Show in the Town Gardens. This, one of the most beautiful of
Flower Show. Swindon's annual events, had been sadly missed. There had been
during the War some very fine exhibitions of vegetables, but one missed the pure beauty and grace that characterised the Flower Show, and it must have been an unspeakable pleasure to the Secretary, Mr. A. E. Harding, to see the blooms come into their own again.

The Post-Office more active. A more prosaic revival was that of the postal activities. During the latter part of the War the public had really been hardly treated, for with a plentiful supply of female labour there was no need to close the offices during the dinner interval, just when working-men could use the offices, especially as they did not open till 9 a.m., and closed at 6 p.m. Recently the office hours had been from 9 a.m., to 7 p.m., but towards the end of May they were slightly increased and were from 8.45 a.m. to 9 p.m., and the delivery of letters was increased from two a day to three.

Local Elections resumed.

A Lady Councillor. The Municipal Elections, held on November 1st, signalised the resumption of normal municipal life after the long suspension of elections except incidental contests such as that held in the King's Ward in March, when Mrs. Noble won the distinction of being Swindon's first Lady Councillor by a majority of 4 votes over those polled for Mr. A. C. Booth. This by-election was caused by the death of Mr. W. H. Williams, who had been a member of the Council since the incorporation of the Borough in 1900. Mr. Williams had been one of the most active members of the Council and had passed through most of the offices on the various Committees, being elected Mayor of the Borough in 1905. Mr. Williams' successor, Mrs. Noble, was made an Alderman after the November elections, which were remarkable chiefly for the successes of the Labour Party at the polling-booths; the new Mayor, Ald.

The New Mayor. S. E. Walters, was Chairman of the Swindon Labour Party and had been an honoured member of the Council for many years; his election to the Mayoral office had no connection with the party's triumph at the poll, and he entered on his year of office with the unanimous support of the Council.

The Swindon Town F.C. re-invigorated. The term "resuscitation" can hardly be used in connection with the Town Football Club, for it had not lapsed during the War, although its existence had been precarious; professional football had been abandoned and the team's activities had been carried on by amateurs.

But early in the Summer of 1919 steps were taken to ensure a good season, and the 22nd Annual Meeting of the Town Football Company was held on June 4th, under the most promising auspices. The Chairman of the Directors, Mr. A. J. L. White, presided over a good company of shareholders and directors, to whom a satisfactory statement of the Club's financial position was made; the balance sheet showed:—

	£	s.	d.
Balance brought forward	59	4	6
Gates, and from other Clubs	732	9	5
Entertainment Tax collected	97	14	5
Gates (Prisoners of War Fund)	9	3	3
S. Taylor's benefit match	48	14	0
S. Taylor, grant from the F.A.	10	0	0
TOTAL	£ 957	5	7

After paying all expenses the Directors were left with a balance in the bank of £128 : 11 : 4. In view of the repairs needed at the County Ground, satisfaction was felt at the Directors' action in opening a depreciation account with the sum of £150.

In Memoriam. Mr. White paid a touching tribute to the memory of the four players whom the Club had lost during the war and also of one brilliant young amateur who had rendered good service to the Club. The four players were Messrs. Bathe, Brewer, Milton and Wheatcroft, and along with them Mr. Harold Warren had fallen in the great struggle; Mr. F. G. Wheatcroft was a lieutenant in the 5th East Surreys and was killed in action at Bourlton late in 1917 ; Mr. H. Warren had been awarded the Military Medal only two months before he was carried off by influenza in November, 1918, in France, where he was serving as a corporal in the Army Service Corps. Mr. White hoped that the Club would show the reverence and gratitude due to these gallant five by some tangible memorial, and it was generally felt that a brass tablet should be placed in the dressing-room at the County Ground.

Another name that claimed a tribute was that of Dr. S. Maclean ; the deceased gentleman had for a long time been very closely associated with football in Swindon and the County and had been Chairman of the Company. His death on July the 21st, 1918, had created a great deal of feeling in the Borough, as he had been called up to Trowbridge and passed as fit for Military Service only a few hours before he was taken seriously ill whilst visiting a patient ; he was 49 years of age.

The club bids fair to maintain the reputation it acquired before the War, and early in the 1919-20 season it won a place well up the Southern League Table, standing 7th on the list at the end of November.

A Swindon Tragedy. Every great war has its aftermath—deaths from ailments and injuries contracted during the war, deaths from accident during the "clearing-up," suicides, deaths of broken-hearted friends, and so on,—but one hardly foresaw such a tragic incident as that which stirred the heart of the town on Good Friday, 1919. A company of Swindon boys made an excursion on Good Friday morning to Liddington Hill, exploring the trenches opposite Chiseldon Camp—those long white lines that will remain for a long time as ugly scars below the ancient battlements of Liddington "Castle." Whilst the rest were having lunch, seven boys strolled behind the butts in search of bullet lead and one of them found " something like a rolling-pin " sticking out of the ground ; he pulled it up, and disregarding a comrade's warning to put it down " in case there might be something in it that would explode," he carried it off to some comrades who gathered round to examine it. Soon afterwards the boy rolled the object along a board into a trench, and a terrific explosion followed. Three boys—F. A. Cosway, F. J. Rawlinson and S. Holt—were killed and two others were injured by the explosion of the object, which was a live trench-mortar shell lost when the troops had been practising on the hill. All the boys were scholars of the Wesleyan Central Mission Sunday School in Clarence Street, and at the funeral, attended by one of the largest crowds ever seen on such an occasion in Swindon, the scholars of the Sunday School walked with the mourners behind the remains of their old comrades.

New Industries. Towards the middle of 1919 unemployment, though not so rife in Swindon as in some other industrial centres, was a source of a good deal of anxiety. Some hundreds of men, many of them ex-soldiers, were out of work, but a hopeful sign for the Borough lay in the preparations that were being made to re-establish three factories that had been diverted from their original purpose. One of these was the factory in Newcastle Street, formerly occupied by Messrs. Gundry as a rope and sail factory ; this was taken over by a firm of engineers from London (Messrs. Garrard & Co.) for the manufacture of small motors and tools, and it was hoped that before long they would employ as many as 500 hands. Then, again, Messrs. W. D. and H. O. Wills re-opened their factory during the Summer, giving employment to a large number of young people, chiefly girls, in the making of cigarettes ; those who saw the admirable steps taken by the firm to safeguard the health and comfort of their young employees were full of praise for the conditions of the factory, whilst the work was light, clean, and well paid. Finally, the Victoria Works in County Road, previously used by Messrs. Compton, passed into the hands of a private firm engaged in the production of clothing.

Flag-days. The first half of 1919 was punctuated by the " Flag-Days " that had become so familiar during the previous war-years, but they had become so frequent that large numbers of people had come to regard them with indifference.

On January 11th, Mr. A. Manners, Madame Dockray, and Mrs. H. T. Kirby arranged a flag-day to raise funds sufficient to wind up the Miss Manners Fund for Christmas Parcels to Soldiers and Sailors,—a fund that had won immense appreciation from large numbers of Swindon's sons serving abroad.

At the end of March Mrs. H. T. Kirby organized a flag-day to bring to a close the Swindon and District Branch's part in the National Egg-Collection for the Wounded Soldiers, raising the sum of £62 : 17 : 8½.

The Swindon Victoria Hospital Aid Committee held its annual " Rose Day " on May 31st, with the result that it was enabled to hand £200 to the hospital after defraying expenses to the amount of over £70. Later on the Secretary, Mr. W. Butt, published a list of collections and contributions amounting to £66 : 18 : 1½, obtained at a flag-day in aid of the hospital on August 23rd.

But, as has been suggested, the public was growing tired of these **The Mayor's** frequent street-collections, and in June the Mayor issued the following **Substitute.** notice, which reflects the general feeling and at the same time seeks to devise a means of abating the frequency of the calls made upon the public, without stopping up the channels of their generosity :—

TOWN HALL, SWINDON,
2nd June, 1919.

DEAR SIR OR MADAM,

WAR CHARITIES, ETC.

HOUSE TO HOUSE COLLECTION, IN LIEU OF FLAG DAYS.

I send you on the other side a list of War and other Charities, in aid of which I have been asked to make an appeal for support during the present year.

In former years large funds in aid of these Societies have been generously supported by means of Flag Days, but it has been felt for some time that too many Flag Days are not desired by the Public, and I have, therefore, decided with regard to the Funds set out on the other side, not to have any Flag Days, but to make one general appeal to the generosity of the inhabitants of Swindon for funds in aid of the Societies named.

The total sum realized will be equitably apportioned amongst them by the Ladies' Committee which has dealt with these matters during the period of the War.

Although the War is over, the above organizations are still carrying on their good work, for which there is great need, and I respectfully and earnestly appeal for your kind support.

I shall be glad if you will kindly place your contribution in the envelope sent herewith, and it will be called for in the course of two or three days.

I am, yours faithfully,

C. A. PLAISTER, *Mayor.*

List of War and other Charities referred to.
1.—The Hon. Evelina Haverfield's Comforts Funds, for the Serbian Soldiers and Prisoners.
2.—The Serbian Relief Fund.
3.—France's Day.
4.—The Lord Roberts' Memorial Fund.
5.—St. Dunstan's Day.
6.—Sailors' Orphan Homes.
7.—Armenian Refugees (Lord Mayor's) Fund.
8.—Vegetables for the Navy.

Prince of Wales' Fund, etc.   During 1919 a further £100 was received by Swindon from the central committee of the Prince of Wales' National Relief Fund, and was utilized in the assistance of cases averaging 8 per week.   This brought the total amount received from the fund up to £1491 : 5 : 0, a little more than quarter of the sum subscribed by Swindon (£6,384 : 9 : 8).

From the King's Fund—a fund that had never " caught on " in Swindon and to which local subscriptions had been small,—the Borough received more than its proportion ; for £550 : 0 : 0 was received in 1919 for the assistance of 11 discharged soldiers and 2 widows.

As regards the Mayor's Local War Fund, used for cases not covered by the other two funds, the local subscriptions up to Dec. 31st, 1919, amounted to £1,166 : 7 : 11, and by the end of the following year the total receipts reached the sum of £1,217 : 6 : 9. As has been indicated already, this fund was established primarily for assisting disabled men or the widows and children of those who fell in the war, particularly by giving them training in suitable occupations, and this was being done at the date of writing.

Housing.   It has been remarked that the questions of housing and water-supply were two great problems facing the Swindon Corporation in 1919. **The Dearth of Houses.**   It was about the end of 1918 that the general public of Swindon began to awaken to the fact that there were not sufficient houses in the Borough to meet the needs of the population.   In this Swindon was only in the same position as most other centres of population, and the general shortage of houses was at first a puzzle to many ;   " For four and a half years " they said, "hundreds of thousands of our young men have been killed; the houses we had before the war are still standing ;   there should be houses to spare instead of there being a shortage."   But they lost sight of important facts ;   firstly, where a husband was killed, the widow did not cease to need a house ;   secondly, for those four and a half years England's youth had been getting married ;   and thirdly, for, nearly all that time no fresh houses had been built.   Whilst the war was being waged the want had not been so very pronounced ;   a young soldier married a girl and whilst he was in the army she frequently lived at her home or with his parents. Then, again, many a young married couple, upon the calling-up of the husband, gave up their house and stored their furniture, the wife going to her home or finding work and going into lodgings.   Thus, early in the war there was a " slump " in the value of house-property and happy was the man who bought a house then !   But as time went on a change was experienced ;   numbers of young men who had remained at home in civil employment or in munitions work had married, and there was a big demand for houses.   Doubtless, now, rents would have gone up considerably, had it not been for the fact that by Act of Parliament landlords were prohibited from raising the rent of houses below a certain value, except by the amount of the increase in the rates ;   the tenants, too, were protected from arbitrary notice to quit, and so it was of no use for a person in need of a house to attempt to buy unless he was also guaranteed possession : if this could be guaranteed, surprisingly high prices could be obtained, but if not, it was of little use to attempt to sell, as no one would buy house-property as an investment under existing conditions.

But when the demobilized soldiers began to arrive home, the lack of houses began to be felt acutely. In Swindon it was practically impossible in 1919 to get a house, and extremely difficult for a married couple to get two rooms, for which the usual charge was 25 /- or 30 /- per week, furnished. Houses that would have fetched approximately £400 in 1914 were sold for something like £700—possession of course being guaranteed.

The Women Move. The Women's Section of the Swindon Labour League raised the question in November, 1918, by a resolution which they forwarded to the Town Council and the Local Government Board ; it was as follows :—" That this conference of representative residents of Swindon, ... believing the good housing of the people to be an urgent social reform, demands that the Government take immediate steps to compel local authorities to provide adequate housing schemes to be financed out of public funds, in order to provide the houses needed at the end of the war ; but that no private enterprise shall receive public money for such a purpose ; and that no building materials be released for the construction of such luxury-buildings as hotels and restaurants until the demand for adequate housing schemes has been met." The resolution then went on to demand that in any schemes proposed women should be consulted as to the planning of the houses, and to specify the minimum accommodation the houses should afford.

The Housing Committee. The Town Council appointed a Housing Sub-committee, of which Councillor H. J. Gregory was Chairman, on March 26th, 1919, and the Committee got to work at once ; they found that 1,000 houses were required in Swindon, of which 350 were needed immediately, and it was their intention to build a model suburb from which the ugly features and discomforts which have spoilt the greater part of the town should be absent. The Committee inspected 44 possible sites and sent deputations to visit the garden-cities at Bourneville and Harborne and also to inspect the concrete houses which were being built at Chepstow. Finally they selected a site abutting on Whitworth Road and Cricklade Road, known as the Hurst Farm Estate, which was partly occupied by allotment-holders who were the Council's tenants. The site met with the approval of the Local Government Board's Inspector and of the Housing Commissioner for the South Western District, and altogether about 100 acres were acquired, which, allowing 10 houses to the acre as was the Committee's intention, would provide the thousand houses which were needed. The site was the healthiest on that side of the town, being high and airy and having a south aspect. Mr. Chappell, the Board's Inspector, said the site was one of the best he had yet seen anywhere, and the District Commissioner, Lieut. Col. Mozley, agreed with him.

Hurst Farm.

The Scheme. At first all seemed promising, for the Local Government Board accepted both the site and the Committee's plan. Councillor Gregory described the plan at a special meeting of the Chamber of Commerce held at the Town Hall on May 20th, only two months after the appointment of the Housing Committee. He told his audience that the scheme would involve an expenditure of £500,000 and probably of £750,000 or even more ; the Government was going to subsidise the local authority by an amount which would be the equivalent of a penny rate, and the burden on the local rates could not exceed 1d., subject to the conditions that the Council satisfied the Government that they had been economical on the whole scheme and that they were receiving a rent proportional to the cost. The plan which Mr. Gregory described gave an area of 13 perches to each house inclusive of the house itself; thus the houses would have plenty of garden space. There were to be no monotonous straight roads or dingy "backs," but the houses were to be grouped in twos, fours and sixes. Two school sites were arranged for and there would be two open spaces of about 4 acres each in extent, whilst space would be left for churches or public buildings. The main road was to run from the Whitehouse Bridge along St. Mary's Grove to the new district, and was to be 50 feet wide and 90 feet from house to house; subsidiary roads were to be 40 feet wide and others not less than 24 feet, but whatever the width of the road the spaces between the houses, across the street, were not to be less than 70 feet. The architect had presented plans of various types of houses, and the cost of the cheapest of these, consisting of two bedrooms and living-room and scullery, was expected to be £463, and other types were expected to cost £539, £676 : 10 : 0, and £720. Asked about the rent, Mr. Gregory said that with rates and taxes it would vary from 14/- a week for the cheapest to 21/6 a week for the best types,—a remark that elicited the comment, "And people grumble at 5/9." These figures were somewhat startling, for the houses were intended for working-men, but, as it turned out, the Committee had been unduly optimistic in its estimates.

Plans Approved. In July the Housing Committee was able to report that the Local Government Board had approved the plans for the first 24 houses and that, having considered alternative schemes for the supply of electricity to the Hurst Farm Estate, they had decided to adopt the overhead system of distribution. The Council resolved at this meeting to purchase from Major F. P. Goddard an additional 8½ acres of land and buildings adjoining Southbrook Farm at £90 per acre,—the same rate as they had paid for the 80 acres already purchased there.

About this time the Mayor, Ald. C. A. Plaister, addressing a meeting of the Independent Labour Party upon the Council's Housing Scheme, said that the Council had authorized the erection of 24 houses as an experiment, and that the probable cost would be from £490 to £680 each, according to size, but he warned his hearers that these figures were to be taken with all reserve, for nobody could say what the price of labour and materials was going to be. This, of course, was the crux of the matter, and the Committee was soon to learn that the estimates upon which it was going were far too moderate.

The Cost. When tenders for the first ten houses were invited, five were sent in, and the Committee were astonished by the figures. Councillor Gregory, speaking at the Council on September 2nd, said that the Housing Committee had done everything possible to reduce the cost, and he quoted figures as to the price of the different types in the scheme,—type "A," £774 : 5 : 0; "B" £1,020 : 5 : 0; "C" £922 : 12 : 6; he said the surveyor had conferred with the Housing Commissioner's engineer, and they had found that by making modifications in 27 different particulars they could save £750 on the ten houses, but he was sure that the figures given would be accepted by the Government as the lowest possible in the circumstances.

A Check. The publication of the figures of the tenders had caused considerable sensation, and at this Council Meeting a deputation was received from the Swindon Labour Party, protesting against the Council's entering into a permanent contract upon these lines and urging them to adopt temporary measures to meet the difficulty, instancing the army huts at Chiseldon. But the Council had already approached the War Office and the Central Housing Authority on this matter, and had met with a refusal to sell the huts or to sanction their use if obtained.

Mr. Nethercot, the leader of the deputation, said that the figures presented to the Council worked out at £9,320 for the 10 houses, and that the cost of making roads and laying sewers, etc., would bring the cost up to £1,200 or £1,300 a house, and he asked how working people could afford to live in such houses. His estimate may have been too high, but it was pretty generally agreed that £1,100 was about the average cost per house.

The upshot was that although the Housing Committee had recommended the acceptance of the lowest tender the Council refused to accept the tender and sent the whole question back to the Committee.

Further Plans. By the end of October the Committee was again ready with plans prepared by the Borough Surveyor for 50 houses on the land adjoining the proposed main approach to the Hurst Farm Estate, immediately at the end of St. Mary's Grove. It was resolved that the Borough Surveyor should be authorized to arrange for the taking out, by a Quantity Surveyor, of the quantities of materials, and that the Town Clerk should advertise for tenders for the erection of the 50 houses with bricks or concrete blocks, and alternatively giving figures for contracts to supply all the materials.

The Mayor, upon his laying down office in November, referred with regret to the fact that in spite of the Housing Committee's hard work there were yet no tangible results to show. In leaving the matter at this point one knows, however, that the subject had to be pursued by subsequent Councils, and one may hope that the ideas of the Housing Committee of 1919 may bear fruit in the form of a true garden suburb to Swindon, and that builders shall never again be allowed to disfigure the town with long rows of brick hutches packed as closely together as they dare put them.

A Comparison. As showing how the prices quoted above compared with what was actually being paid, it may be mentioned that a row of nice houses of about twenty feet frontage was begun in another part of the town before the war; the houses had three rooms and a scullery downstairs, three bed-rooms and a bath-room, and a moderate garden behind the house. The price at which the houses were to be sold was £550, but the war caused the work to be held up and it was not resumed till 1919, when the first house completed—the nest-egg so to speak—sold for £900, and £1,100 was being asked for the others. In face of this the cost of the houses that were proposed for Hurst Park seems reasonable, and is explicable by the great advance in prices of labour and materials.

Water. The other great problem—that of giving the town an adequate supply of water—assumed a very serious aspect in the Autumn of 1919; the Summer and Autumn of that year were exceptionally dry, and from August the pressure was often so low that it was unable to raise the water to tanks upstairs, on the top of the hill. But when the Railway strike occurred at the end of September and the town was deprived of the large amount pumped daily from Kemble through the Great Western Railway Company's pipes, the strain on the municipal system proved too great and the reservoirs were practically emptied; although the end of the strike restored the Kemble supply the water-works could not, in consequence of the lowness of the springs, obtain the supply of water needed for the Borough, and for many weeks parts of the town had water in the pipes for only a very small part of the day.

In this connection it has to be borne in mind that the Ogbourne supply had had demands made upon it that had never been contemplated when it was inaugurated, for Swindon had now for some time been supplying both the Camp at Chiseldon and Stratton. It was obvious, therefore, that the Council must speedily find additional supplies of water, and it was with satisfaction that the public heard that a new supply was to be obtained at Poughcombe and that a provisional order had been obtained.

The Council and its Workmen. During the year the Council had taken steps to establish the relationships of the Corporation with its employees on a far better and more satisfactory basis than they had ever before held, for they had set up a Committee under the Whitley Council scheme and had adopted a 44 hour week of six days without reduction of pay for all classes of its workmen except those in the Electricity and Tramways Department, where the hours had already been fixed by the Committee on Production or by agreement with the men's Unions. All workmen were to have one day off in seven, overtime was to be paid for at the rate of time and a quarter up to 9 p.m., and time and a half after that hour, and double time was to be paid for Sunday labour. On April 1st the rates of pay had been fixed by an award of the Bath and South Western Conciliation Board at 1/2 per hour for painters, 1/1 for labourers, and 1/3 for other trades; but these were for a 46½ hour week, so in fixing a 44 hour week the Council augmented these rates so as to pay as much per week under the new arrangement as under the old one. Following on the constant unrest and dissatisfaction during the War, this was a notable effort by the Council to secure stability in its relations with the men, and the retiring Mayor spoke with justifiable pride in his farewell speech to the Council when he claimed that the steps taken to satisfy their employees were one of the soundest things this Council had done.

The Committees. The special committees that the war years had brought into existence had by this time ceased in some instances to exist; the Prisoners of War and Comforts for the Wilts Regiment Committee had finished its splendid work; the Belgian Relief Committee, the Camp Concerts Committee, the Committee for entertaining the Soldiers' Wives, and some others do not belong to 1919: the Committee for sending Vegetable Products to the Navy had taken on a new lease of life, but before the close of the year its work was done; the Local Employment Committee (the former Local Advisory Committee) and the Pensions Committee, however, were growing busier month by month, and the former had apparently "come to stay." But other committees arise as the old ones pass away, and although Englishmen have been rallied upon their love of Committees they are an evidence of the vitality of their local organization, keeping alive the sense of civic responsibility in a high degree; and so the latter part of the year saw the Housing Committee engrossed with the solution of a difficult problem, whilst the newly-formed Profiteering Committee held its first sitting on October 1st. It is no part of this work to trace the activities of this committee, but it was a direct result of war-conditions, and it is with a feeling akin to shame and indignation that one notes the necessity that led to the formation of Profiteering Committees all over the country. That any large number of people should find in their country's need the opportunity for amassing wealth and extorting undue profits from their brethren, is a monstrous picture, and is an ironical comment upon the pratings of those who at the beginning of the war spoke so glibly of the purifying influence of war. Happily the duties of the Swindon Committee were light, but that arose in some instances from the fact that the profiteers were far beyond its reach—dim financial and commercial personalities of whom the public have little knowledge, or soulless companies operating perhaps in distant lands.

Another new committee that sprang into being at the close of the year was an offshoot of the Local Advisory Committee,—the Juvenile Advisory Committee, upon which the Education Committee was strongly represented. It had a useful field before it, especially if a wide interpretation were given to its functions and if its work were frankly seconded by the employers of the Borough. [1]

---

[1] This Committee, after a couple of years' busy and useful activity, was "taken over" by the Education Committee in 1922, in accordance with the terms of a Government order making such action permissive on the part of the Local Education Authorities. It was felt in many quarters that the functions of J.A.C. approximated to the work of Education Authorities more than to that of Employment Exchanges, though in reality they shared the nature of both organizations. The J.A.C. dealt only with young persons up to eighteen years of age.

CHAPTER X.

Swindon Women's War-time Service.

(by H. G. B.)

No account of Swindon during the War would be complete without special reference to the splendid work done by the women of the town. This war has been spoken of as a " Women's War," because never before have the women of the country taken so active a part in the nation's struggle. When the war broke out and the women of England heard of the atrocities in Belgium, when they learned of the awful fate of many a poor wife and mother there, they were stirred to the depths and were anxious to help as far as possible in the complete overthrow of a power whose only right was might.

Variety of Women's Services. It has always been woman's duty to minister to the sick and wounded, and from the very outset of the war numbers of noble women offered their services to the Red Cross Societies. They left their homes, their leisure, and their sports, in order to become proficient in the art of nursing, and thus do something to alleviate the terrible sufferings of the brave men of the Army and Navy. But in this war women were not content with nursing only ; they found they way into many branches of trade and into many professions ; they were found in the office, behind the counter, on the land, at the bench, delivering the letters, in fact in a thousand and one places where years before people would have declared it was impossible for a woman to work ; but there they were, cheerful and efficient, enabling the country to " carry on " when it seemed that all her workers were wanted for fighters. How familiar the neat uniforms of the W.A.A.C., W.R.E.N., and W.R.A.F. have become ! The women of these corps were willing even to go to Flanders to work in aerodromes and other workshops, " doing their bit " by assisting in building aeroplanes, making and filling shells, and making munitions. Others felt drawn towards the land, and so one saw the "land girl," dressed in her smock and leather leggings, driving in her market-cart to town, or in charge of a drove of cattle. Perhaps her garb provoked a smile at first, and few would think of her as the heroine of the little song, " Where are you going, my pretty maid ? " which seems to conjure up the lass in her pink bonnet and lilac frock, with her pail and stool ; but folk soon ceased to smile, for the capable land girl proved her worth.

Swindon women were not lacking in their efforts to help their country. There were amongst them the truly patriotic who gave their time and talents ungrudgingly for over four long years in one way or another, to help to win the war or to ameliorate the sufferings it caused to England and her allies.

This chapter is not intended to give in detail the work of societies like the Prisoners of War Committee, the Local Red Cross Society, and similar organisations; the work of these bodies has been detailed elsewhere and a repetition here would be tedious; but it attempts to show in a collective way, though briefly, the amount and nature of the work done by the women of the town in the time of the Country's greatest need.

Red Cross Work. Almost immediately upon the outbreak of war the Red Cross Society in Swindon was organised, and a committee was speedily appointed with a view to forming Voluntary Aid Detachments in Swindon ; by the end of a week from their first meeting, two such detachments were formed and £322 collected, whilst another £303 was raised by September 24th. This work was under the presidency of Mrs. T. C. P. Calley, seconded by Mrs. Waugh. Then, when instruction was needed for the training of those willing to nurse, Miss E. B. Walker, of the Victoria Hospital, and Miss Dismorr, of Wroughton, gave them training in practical work. Soon a hospital was needed, and when the G.W.R. Swimming Baths were secured an enthusiastic staff of local ladies under Miss C. Deacon took charge. But all could not nurse and one must not forget those who gave a great amount of help by sewing and knitting ; the mothers' meetings and other societies made garments and bed-linen ; and here the girls in the schools should be mentioned, for there was scarcely a home where the little girl was not knitting a sock or scarf for " Tommy " or " Jack," and in many cases it was a giant task for the little fingers. The women of the town worked steadfastly, and the garments sent to Salisbury and to the Navy could be counted by hundreds, a detailed account being given in the sections dealing with the Red Cross Society.

But the work of the Red Cross Society did not end when the Baths were closed and the Hospital was moved to Stratton, and throughout all the long time that the war lasted and wounded men were needing nursing, the devoted band of workers stood to their posts. Some had suffered loss themselves, and this fact made them the more anxious to do what they could to lighten the sufferings of others. A sale at the Hospital was organised and brought in £91 : 9 : 5 ; concerts were arranged and the proceeds devoted to Red Cross work ; collections were made, and the women of the town were always found ready to assist in providing necessities and little luxuries for the men. It must be remembered that this work lasted not for a few weeks or months but for years, and the noble women who carried it on did so with unflagging energy. The arrival of fresh batches of wounded was sufficient to keep them devoted to their work, and there were many who gave up everything to this one task—caring for the wounded,—a task that was trying in the extreme, and a severe strain upon health and strength.

It would be impossible to name them all,—nurses, cooks, motor-drivers, collectors, and those engaged in other services which were indispensable. There were those who bought in the goods, those who made the garments, those who gave their time and talents to entertaining the men, those who took the wounded for drives or received them into their homes, and those who made gifts and loans. But mention must be made of Miss Rose, the Honorary Secretary, for her ceaseless work and furtherance of every scheme for the well-being of the Hospital, and of Mrs. Muir and Sister Whistler, who were awarded the Royal Red Cross. But it was of all the workers that the soldiers spoke when they praised the Hospital and referred to the happy times they had there, for, as more than one of them said when he was leaving, it had been a " home " to them.

This was the feeling that animated the gathering at the Bradford Hall at which the presentations were made to Mrs. Muir and Miss Rose. Mrs. Calley and Mrs. Waugh spoke in the highest terms of all. Wounded men who were fortunate enough to be sent to Swindon will always have in their hearts a warm corner for the town because of the devotion and loving service shown by so many of Swindon's women.

Work for the Belgians. The helpless plight of the Belgian refugees called [forth the pity of the women of Swindon with that of the women of every town. The sight of aged men and women and little children driven from their homes, and in many cases entirely destitute, stirred the sympathies of all, and efforts were made to provide for them and to ease their suffering as much as possible. Almost as soon as Belgians arrived in this country six large hampers of clothes were got together by the " Swindon Liberal Women " and forwarded to London. The local Belgian Relief Committee consisted entirely of women, with Mrs. Arnold-Forster as President and a succession of four most able secretaries in Miss Blake, Miss Arnold-Forster, Mrs. Tanner and Miss Withy. The ladies of this committee worked with great zeal and business-like energy and it was owing to them that houses were obtained and furnished, and maintenance was provided for refugees. Although the organization of the scheme was the work of the Committee their work would not have been successful if it had been not for the ready support of all who were approached for help. Some gave their time to collecting, and so successful were their efforts that up to September, 1917, no outside assistance had to be sought, and Swindon was one of the last towns in England to apply to Head-quarters for help. But thanks are also owing to those who readily subscribed money, food, furniture or clothing, and it was the response to their appeals that made the work of the Committee so successful, for Swindon has the proud distinction of being among the few towns in England that kept their committees to the end of the war,—a great tribute, surely, to the ladies who formed its committee.

Altogether, the women of the town cared for about 340 Belgians, who spoke in glowing terms when they were able to return to their native land Three ladies of the Committee were presented by the King of the Belgians with the " Queen Elizabeth Medal,"—Mrs. Arnold-Forster, Mrs. Tanner and Mrs. Tindle, and these distinctions, abundant y merited by the ladies thus honoured, but crystallize the honour due to a large company of women, whose steadfast labours were Swindon's recognition of Belgium's services in the cause of civilization, and the Allies' debt to her.

Work for the Forces. Although dealt with more fully in another part of the book, the work done by the Women of Swindon in providing comforts for the Wiltshire Regiment should be mentioned here, as, again, from its very nature it was essentially women's work. When, in August, 1914, the Mayor of Swindon received a letter asking for gifts for the Wiltshire Regiment, the ladies who were on the Prince of Wales' Fund Committee, with other ladies, formed a Committee, and under the leadership of Miss Slade organized a working-party whose energy was hard to beat. The names of this ladies' Com-mittee will be found in the section dealing with the work for the Prisoners of War, but tribute must here be paid to them and especially to Misses Slade and K. Handley. Through them the hundreds of pairs of socks, the hundreds of pairs of gloves and mittens, scarves, helmets, and other comforts were despatched to the men of the Wiltshires, who were experiencing their first winter in the trenches. They worked hard themselves and they begged hard, so that nearly every woman and girl was making some garment, either knitted or sewn ; and it speaks well for the women that the garments thus made numbered thousands. Then came the cry of need from the unfortunate fellows who were prisoners of war,—prisoners in the land of a foe who seemed to have lost all traces of humanity. Then the nature of the work changed and became more complex, for week by week parcels were packed and sent to the different camps where Wiltshiremen were known to be imprisoned. One cannot over-praise the workers who week by week for over four years were packing and despatching food and comforts to the men in the trenches in France, and the camps in Germany. Praise is due not only to the actual committee, but also to the 130 ladies who made the weekly house-to-house collection, and by whose unfailing energy £1,612 : 9 : 6 was collected towards this noble work. It is pleasing to note that their services were recognised by well-earned distinctions bestowed upon representative ladies. This, indeed, was not needed, for when each worker, who through love and pity readily gave her time and services for so long a time, remembers that some life was spared by her efforts, some father restored to his children, or some boy to his mother, it will be an ample reward, and no moment she gave to the work will be regretted.

Caring for Billetted Soldiers. Perhaps the women of Swindon collectively showed their kindheartedness to the greatest degree at the outbreak of the war, when thousands of troops were billetted in the town. It was not shown in the work of a special committee who gave up their time for some specific object, but it was a spontaneous outburst of kindliness extended by the bulk of the townsfolk to the soldiers; " I'll do my best for him, Sergeant, I've a boy of my own joined up and billetted somewhere," or " I've no one who could go in my own family, and so I'll do my best for those who are going to fight for us : " and so in hundreds of dwellings " Tommy " was made to feel at home. These men will never forget the kindness they received in Swindon, and when they reached France, letters from base and trench expressed their gratitude ; for next to writing home, many of them felt it their duty to write to " friends " in Swindon, who had made their first experiences of soldiering as pleasant as possible.

Providing for their Leisure. Besides the endeavour to make the men feel at home, efforts were made to enable them to spend their leisure time pleasantly and profitably, and the thousands of men in the town, and the thousands more stationed at Chiseldon Camp were given a welcome at the Town Hall, week by week, and enabled to spend a pleasant time,— to enjoy a comfortable tea, to hear good music and songs, and to have an opportunity for reading and writing. In connection with this good work one should mention Miss Deacon, who was responsible for the catering week by week, no easy task in the difficult days of " shortage," and also Mrs. Perry, who was the Treasurer and Secretary. Nor must one forget the ladies of the town who gave their talents as well as their time in visiting the adjacent camps and providing good concerts for the men stationed there ; Madame Dockray and her Ladies' Choir will live in the memories of many of the lads, and their fame has reached even to Australia and New Zealand.

Helping the Navy. As regards work done by women for the Troops, the Committee for providing vegetables for the Navy owed a great deal to Mrs. Trineman. When Mr. Trineman was called away she stepped in and admirably filled his place as Secretary for this committee; thus a splendid work was kept going. And surely among the ladies of the Town who should be mentioned and honoured for special war work, " Flossie," Mr. Trineman's collie, must be included, for she patiently did her little bit, and collected no less than £20 : 13 : 9½ for the Navy. Moreover, many of the woollen garments made in Swindon found their way to the Fleet, and lads who were keeping watch at Scapa Flow or serving on destroyers scouring the black waters of the North Sea or the Channel, were thankful for the warm muffler made by some unknown girl at home.

Cheering the Women. But there were others, whose lives had been made sad and lonely by this great war. There was "Tommy's" or "Jack's" wife and mother, whose part—patiently waiting at home,—was no easy one ; perhaps it was sometimes harder to live expecting the worst, going through each day's monotonous routine with a brave but bursting heart, than it was to do deeds of valour in the excitement of the fight ; it was certainly more monotonous, and there were kind hearts in Swindon who thought of these lonely ones, and who endeavoured to bring a bit of sunshine into their clouded lives. Chief among the women who carried on this thoughtful work were Mrs. Saddler, Mrs. H. C. King and the band of helpers associated with them. Every Wednesday the Club for soldiers' wives had tea at the Town Hall and enjoyed for an hour or two music and songs, varied by helpful and practical addresses ; and the appreciation of the women was shown by the way in which the attendance was maintained. It was indeed a labour of love to cheer for a short time the anxious hearts of wives and mothers, and in this case the women workers owe much to the support of Mr. Ald. J. Powell, who made their work his special care.

On the Pensions Committee. Another group of lady workers formed part of the Pensions Committee, and almost entirely did the work of distribution connected with it. Since 1916 a committee of ladies had met monthly at the Town Hall in order to overlook the provision made for orphans of soldiers and sailors. They visited the homes of the fallen or disabled men, and saw that some provision was made for their dependents. They also visited the Camp and Hospital at Chiseldon and interviewed men about to be discharged and gave them advice and help. This Committee consisted of Mrs. Arman, Mrs. Guthrie, Mrs. Gray, Mrs. Hemmings, Mrs. Tuck, Mrs. Warren, and Mrs. Whitworth, while Mrs. Haynes and Miss Crisford assisted on the Finance Committee.

Flag Days. The splendid work done by women in connection with the Flag Days is very evident from the figures showing the amount collected and detailed elsewhere. Many were the Saturdays on which the streets were patrolled by bands of ladies of all ages, who with a winning smile persuaded the passer-by to buy a flag, and if he escaped the wiles of one he was pretty sure to fall a victim to another a little further on. So persistent were the vendors of the little tokens that at last, in sheer desperation, and hoping for peace, even the hardest were overcome. But the sellers of the little badges were not tired out after one or two long Saturdays ; their efforts were unending, and one gentleman was heard to declare that if the war lasted another year he should have a "Season Ticket." Though they appeared so cheerful, inviting the passer-by to buy a flag for the Prisoners of War Fund, the Red Cross, France's Day, Wounded Horses, or Blinded Heroes, and many more worthy objects, their work was very tiring. They will be missed, but not forgotten, standing for hours, sometimes in the broiling sun, sometimes in the biting cold, and often even in the pouring rain. By their kindly action and labours the many and varied philanthropies benefited to the amount of about £5,000.

The Girls' Clubs. The enrolment of so large a number of men in the Army and Navy necessitated the employment of a great many women and girls. Some of these found employment in the locality of their own homes, but hundreds left their native towns and congregated in large centres of population which in many instances came to be known as "munition areas." Swindon became a "munition area," and soon numbers of girls were working in the munition depôt or the powder factory. Many of these were away from home and friends. They had nowhere to go for entertainment or amusement, and were often unhappy and lonely. It was thought that some kindly influence should be brought to bear on these, and some concern was felt as to how they spent their leisure time. It was with this object in view that, in the Autumn of 1914, the first Girl's Club was formed at Gorse Hill, through the energy of Miss J. R. Payne, Superintendent of the Evening Classes for Girls under the administration of the Swindon Education Committee. The need of such work among the girls of the town was felt by many and Miss Payne quickly gathered sympathetic workers, foremost amongst whom were Mrs. Arnold-Forster, Mrs. Currie, Mr. T. Butler, Chairman of the Education Committee, the Rev. J. Simons, and Mr. G. Burkhardt. A house was rented at Gorse Hill for social purposes, and there the girls spent many happy hours. The curriculum was suited to the tastes of girls of all types, with its varied subjects, including debates, art, needlework, home-nursing, first-aid, music, drill and country dancing.

Owing to the great success of this venture a more ambitious scheme was conceived including the whole town. Accordingly in April, 1915, the Girls' Club Union was established with Mrs. Arnold-Forster as its first President. The objects of this Union were to form a link between existing clubs, to stimulate and help the work of individual clubs, to start fresh clubs where needed, and to promote friendly competition between these organisations.

In July, 1917, owing to the pressure of war-work amongst the women and girls of the town it was felt that a hostel should be at once formed to provide suitable accommodation for these war-workers. Mrs. Currie, the newly elected President, was ably seconded by the Mayor, Mr. A. J. Gilbert, and Mr. Alderman Butler. A month later the premises of Messrs. Wills and Co., in Belle Vue Road, were advantageously obtained. For the support of this work a public subscription was raised, whilst the movement was in close touch with the Central Y.W.C.A. The first warden was Miss Robb, M.A., who also undertook charge of the Gorse Hill Club. This venture again justified itself, for owing to the energy of Miss Robb the clubs at the Hostel and Gorse Hill were a decided success. On every Saturday night the Club at the Hostel threw open its doors to the young soldiers of the Camp at Chiseldon, and the girls and men met in happy comradeship. Mirth and music helped to spread a homelike atmosphere over these happy gatherings, and the commanding officer at the Camp was warm in his appreciation of the good work done at the Hostel.

In January, 1918, the Central Y.W.C.A., which had previously borne a partial financial responsibility, felt that the time was come to assume full control over the Hostel, and this they retained until April, 1919. Their action thus set the Club Union free for other efforts. In February, 1918, the Comrades Club, under the auspices of the Girls' Friendly Society, was started in Fleet Street, Miss Mitchell being its first organiser.

Yet another Club was started for girls resident in the west end of the town by Miss Shallcroft, the Mistress of the Jennings Street Evening Continuation school, and it was very successful in spite of drawbacks in equipment due to scarcity of funds. Another club was opened at Sanford Street School to cater for the needs of the central part of the town, but this club was short-lived owing to the lack of workers. About this time the Committees of the Girls' Club Union and Ladies' Advisory Committee for evening classes were amalgamating, thus correlating the education given at the evening schools and the social atmosphere which the Club Union provided.

Girl Guides. Mention must be made to the link forged between the Girls' Club Union and the Girl Guides under the able leadership of Miss Ceris Williams, the Captain of the 1st Swindon Company of Girl Guides, which was formed in November, 1914, in connection with the Sanford Street Congregational Church. Starting with fifteen guides, the company reached the number of forty-two guides and five officers by the year 1920. From its inauguration the company engaged in various kinds of war-work, including work at the Red Cross Hospital and at Canteens. The girl-guides collected magazines for the troops, and helped considerably in collecting the waste paper. Several guides won the War Service Badge and the Commissioner for Wiltshire presented the Company with a shield for which the patrols compete annually; it goes to the patrol which gains the most points for punctuality, attendance, neatness, etc., and has won the most badges. In February, 1919, the first Swindon Company gave a concert which realised £18 : 11 : 10, and which enabled them to buy tents, ground sheets and other material, so that they were able to enjoy two week-end camps during the Summer.

An account of the Girls' Club Union would not be complete without mentioning the highly successful Club Contests organised by Miss Eveline Smith and Miss Summers, the Secretary, who had succeeded Miss Payne as Superintendent of the Girls' Evening Classes. These included contests in music, recitation, drill, and country dancing, and the competitors gave excellent public demonstrations of their skill and their delight in the work. There were also competitions in housewifery, dress-making, and plain needlework, and the work thus submitted showed a very high standard of efficiency. These contests gave evidence of the undoubted ability which many of these young women possessed, and which the Girls' Clubs are helping to foster. The Club Union was fortunate in having Mrs. James Currie as its President. Under her sympathetic guidance the work flourished. She was ably assisted by Mrs. Arnold-Forster, Mr. and Mrs. Gilbert, Mr. and Mrs. Haynes, and Mr. and Mrs. Plaister, during the terms of their mayoralty. Mr. T. Butler was its Treasurer from its inception and the Rev. J. Simon the financial Secretary. Under their leadership was a company of many ladies who rendered splendid services, Miss Bullock, Miss Chowles and Miss Mizen (who worked indefatigably for several arduous years at the Gorse Hill Club), Misses Goldsmith, Sacret, Shallcroft, Smith and Withy, with Mrs. Whitley and Mrs. Whitworth, and Miss Summers in whom the Club Union found a most able Secretary. The Union had satisfied an urgent need of the young women workers of the town, and its work has been fourfold—physical, technical, moral, and recreative. In these clubs girls have been able to meet their friends in a cosy and comfortable room, they have been kept in touch with the refinements of life, of music, art, dancing and poetry, whilst the moral and spiritual aspect cannot be over-rated.

The Girls' Shelter. Another example of the interest taken in the welfare of girls was the opening of a Shelter for Girls, in April, 1914. A house was taken in Prospect and suitably furnished. The objects were to provide shelter for any girl who might find herself stranded, whether through her own fault or not, to keep in touch with girls who had been rescued from bad surroundings, and to deal with cases unsuitable for the Workhouse. The Officers and Committee who were responsible for the work were :—the President, Mrs. Story-Maskelyne ; the Honorary Treasurer, Miss Beadon ; the Hon. Medical Officer, Dr. Moore ; the Hon. Secretary, Mrs. Hodsoll ; and the Executive Committee which consisted of Mrs. Arnold-Forster (Chairman), Miss M. Beadon, Miss Barr, Mrs. Brooks, Mrs. Gavin, Mrs. Harvey, Mrs. Hodsoll, Mrs. Muir, Mrs. Shawyer,

Miss Stephenson, Mrs. Swinhoe, Mrs. Waugh and Mrs. Whitworth, with Mrs. Cragg, the Superintendent. During the first year the Committee met with many difficulties, especially in regard to the increased cost of necessities. The Shelter had to be closed for two months, August and September, owing to the outbreak of war, but in spite of these obstacles good work was done, and thirty-six girls had already passed through the Shelter, having been assisted to a right course of life and preserved from a disastrous one; many of them were quite young. In July, 1915, the Shelter was moved to 89, Clifton Street,—" The Haven "—which proved to be much more convenient, and in November Miss Blake took over the duties of Secretary, as Mrs. Hodsoll had left the town. November 22nd was fixed by the Committee as " Pound Day," when the public was asked to make gifts in kind, a pound of some commodity to be the minimum amount; it proved a very successful venture.

The second year saw the work of the shelter carried on even more successfully than in the first year, 477 visits were made during the year; there had also been 52 admissions to the shelter, and out of these 21 were " rescue cases " and 22 "' preventive," the majority of these girls being between the ages of 14 and 20. The Balance Sheet for the year was as follows :—

INCOME		£	s.	d.	EXPENDITURE.		£	s.	d.
Balance from 1914	....	43	16	1	Rent and Expend.	....	26	8	6
Don. & Subscriptions	....	88	12	6	Salaries and help	....	47	10	3
Pound Day, etc.	....	56	17	4	Provisions	....	68	17	11
Other Sources	....	76	5	2	Furniture and Repairs	....	31	14	4
					Travelling and Homes	....	28	2	8
					Coal and Gas	....	20	9	5
					Other Expenditure	....	38	5	1
					Balance	....	4	2	11
		£265	11	1			£265	11	1

The following year the report of the year's work showed that 36 cases had been admitted during the year, and of these 27 had been " rescue cases," and about 30 others had been visited and helped in various ways. The balance sheet for the year showed the Committee to have a surplus of £36 : 17 : 7½ in hand.

The year 1917 revealed how real was the need of such work in Swindon, for during that year 45 girls had been admitted to the Shelter, of whom two had come back a second time; of these 28 were "rescue cases " and six " preventive." During the year the Committee had suffered a double loss in the retirement of Miss Blake and Miss Cragg, both ladies having worked with great energy and devotion for over two years ; they were replaced by Mrs. H. W. Reynolds and Miss Skinner, of whom the latter had been well acquainted with " rescue work " for many years. During Miss Skinner's absence for a month about Christmas-time, Miss Treneer carried out the duties of Superintendent with great satisfaction to the Committee, who were very grateful for her timely assistance. The balance sheet for 1917 showed a satisfactory state of the finances. The subscriptions for the year amounted to £81 : 12 : 6, and donations to £123 : 7 : 0, including £100 which was an anonymous gift and which saved the situation ; but the envelope collection was £10 less than in the previous year.

In 1918, 723 visits were paid, 34 girls were admitted of whom three came back for the third time and two for the second time. This alone proved the great need of continuing the work. The girl of the period had become used to independence at a very early age, and the result was not always good.   These girls needed a friendly hand and a shelter to which they could come when they saw their mistake, and many expressed their gratitude for the help and sympathy they found at the shelter.

Baby Welfare.   The appalling loss of life during the war emphasised the great need of caring for the infants of the race. Life is always sacred, but the fact that thousands of England's noblest and best were being sacrificed on the battle-fields of Europe made it a bounden duty to do all that was possible to preserve the young life at home.   England awoke to the fact that, as it has been put, it was as dangerous to be a baby in London as it was to fight in Flanders. Committees, therefore, were formed whose business it was to establish clinics, to assist and instruct mothers, and to see that the infant had a fair chance of living.   In this important work Swindon was ready to do its share, for in 1914 the Town Council established a Maternity Centre, which received much assistance from the Wilts Nursing Association and the Women's Co-operative Guild, and which is doing a good work in the battle against ignorance and prejudice.

In connection with the " Baby Welfare " movement in Swindon a " Baby Show " was held in the Town Gardens, and over five hundred babies were entered for competition.   The judges must have had a very difficult task, but it was a great triumph to get together such a crowd of jolly babies, all well cared for and brimful of health.   As an evidence of the real interest Swindon had in the welfare of the child, Nos. 36 and 37 Milton Road were purchased and converted into a Maternity Nursing Home, opened in June, 1917, and placed under the care of Nurse Langcaster.

Women in Industry.   Swindon women were not behind-hand in their efforts to carry on the work of the nation while the men were abroad, and it fell to the lot of many women to " carry on " in the Factory, at the desk, in the school, and in many other ways.

On Munitions.   In Swindon the Munitions Factory and the Powder Factory gave work to hundreds of girls and women ; when the large factory belonging to Messrs. Wills was taken over by the Government for munition-work, the girls employed there were given the first consideration, and thus many Swindon "lassies" were employed in "feeding the guns."

In Offices.   Then women were seen replacing men in shops and in offices, and in many instances proved their worth and won the commendation of their employers. Classes were held to train girls for business, and to fit them to become efficient clerks, and those who had received a good general education were taught typewriting, short-hand, and business methods ; many availed themselves of this opportunity and the result was that many offices were practically staffed by women and girls ; the Great Western Railway Company employed hundreds of girls in the offices during the war, and so competent did these become that many were retained after the war. The Post Office was one of the first to engage women workers, and in all the Swindon Post Offices responsible duties were carried out by women ; the work was heavy for the duties were more than usually onerous owing to the great amount of work entailed by pensions and war loans, and were still further increased by Swindon's proximity to the large military camp at Chiseldon. But not only were girls and women employed in the post-offices, they took the place of many of the postmen who had joined up, and it became the rule to find that

Post- Women.

the " postman was a lady." This must have been very hard and trying work, for the bags were sometimes very heavy, the weather often very inclement, and people wanted their letters early in the morning. Whatever the circumstances, however, the post-girl always seemed cheerful, and Swindon should be grateful to those who were not afraid to undertake this hard task. The number of women and girls engaged by the Post Office in Swindon was considerable for a town of Swindon's size ; between August 1914 and Christmas 1918 the total number engaged on indoor duties was 54, the maximum at any one time being 45 ; on the outdoor staff the total number engaged was 52, and the maximum number at any one time was 27 ; in addition to these, more than 50 others were employed during the Christmas Seasons 1916, 1917 and 1918, for periods of a fortnight.

Tram Conduct-resses. The Town Council, too, found itself under the necessity of utilizing women's help while the men were at the Front. In March, 1917, women were engaged as Tram Conductors, and although Swindon did not get so far as some towns and have women-drivers, all the conductors for a time were women ; this also was no light task, for the work was tiring, the hours long, and the management of the passengers, especially at the dinner hour, was often trying. In the following September girls were introduced into the Town Hall as clerks, with the happiest results.

Back to Teaching. The schools in Swindon would have suffered considerably if it had not been for the women who were ready to come back and take up once more the arduous task of teaching. In this case more than willingness was required, for long training and experience are necessary to fit anyone for teaching ; it therefore fell to those who had once been teachers to take it up again and to leave their homes and go back to school. Swindon was particularly fortunate in having such a band of capable " Reservists," and thanks to those who were fully qualified and willing, the schools were for the most part adequately staffed during the whole period of the war. The Education Committee was spared the awkward predicament experienced by towns which had only about half the requisite number of teachers, and where only half the scholars could go to school at once, the other half running the streets at a time when it was most injurious to them both morally and physically. During the War the Swindon Education Committee engaged many supply teachers, several of them going back to the very schools they had left only a few years before ; apart from supply teachers engaged for reasons that are always operative, the highest number working at any one time in the schools in the places of men in the Army, was forty-one.

Domestic Difficulties. Altogether Swindon has cause to be proud of its women during the great upheaval. The very queues which were seen in the street, day after day, when mothers and wives had to wait sometimes for hours for necessary articles of food, were composed mainly of patient women who hid their anxiety under a cloak of mirth. Grumble they did, and no wonder, for the hours thus spent in weary standing seemed wasted, and many mothers had to bring their little ones with them ; but they knew it was their part in the great struggle, and that it must be borne with good grace, when so many of their men were fighting in France, or guarding the High Seas, and thereby enabling them to get food at all.

But after the long and tiresome waiting the food was not what was necessary to build up the young ; it was lacking in nutriment. And so, to enable people to get the maximum amount of nourishment out of the food that was available, women came forward to instruct their sisters, and lectures in wartime cookery were gratuitously given by the Domestic Teachers on the Education Committee's staff. Visitors to the different centres were encouraged to inspect and discuss the various food-preparations, they were given lists of foods with their relative values, and printed sheets of recipes; four exhibitions in shops were opened in different parts of the Town, and later on, so that full advantage could be taken of the fruit crop, lessons were given in preserving fruit. None but the housewives themselves know what cares the food difficulties laid upon their shoulders. Apart from the worry of finding suitable food and of providing the necessary variety, there was the difficulty of handling unaccustomed articles of diet, the combating of the prejudices of their families, and, heaviest trial of all, the sight of their children ailing or disfigured by sores on account of the insufficiency of essential constituents in their diet. " Cranks " may say they were " never better in their lives " than when they were compulsorily rationed and fed on " substitutes "; the women know better, and nothing is gained by hiding the fact that the children suffered severely from the food conditions imposed by war.

Effects of the War on Woman's position. So varied and widespread were the activities of the women of the town throughout the long period of war, that justice cannot be adequately done to anything like all branches of their work. Many of them brought to it an idealism of which few men are capable, devoting themselves with almost religious fervour to the task they had taken up, and displaying to the full that patience and steady persistence that are so strong an element in the feminine nature. Untried and unsuspected powers revealed themselves, and their work during the war gave women a position in the social organisation far higher than they had taken before, constituting a permanent gain to the social weal. In industry they demonstrated superior fitness for certain forms of work, and the peculiar conditions of the time raised the standard of remuneration much above the disgracefully low rate that formerly prevailed, and taught woman to set a higher value upon her services,—by no means an unimportant gain in feminine education.

It would be as ungracious as it would be illogical and unjust to ignore the great services rendered by the sober majority of women and the substantial gains reaped by society from their efforts, just because a frivolous and small minority failed to rise to the high level of the rest. Undoubtedly the war had a demoralizing effect on some, and in Swindon, as elsewhere, the heartless pleasure-seeker, the vulgar imitator of men-workers, and the selfish spendthrift were not unknown; but these were far less obvious in Swindon than in many towns similarly placed, and the Borough has abundant cause to be proud of the order that reigned in the town, the sane and healthy atmosphere that prevailed, and the serious sense of duty and service displayed by the women and girls. No tribute can fully acknowledge the debt due to them.

The Right Hon. the Earl of Suffolk, Wilts Battery of the 3rd Wessex (R.F.A.).

PART II.

THE LOCAL MILITARY UNITS.

CHAPTER I.

The Swindon Company of
The Wilts (Fortress) Royal Engineers.

Just before war broke out the Wilts (Fortress) Royal Engineers (Terr.) were undergoing their annual training in camp at Fort Purbrook, Portsmouth, under their officers, Major F. G. Wright, Capt. Flitcroft (adjutant), Capt. C. S. Wilson, Lieut. J. Dawson, and Second Lieut. G. E. Knapp, and Coy. Sergt. Major H. C. Rodda. Upon the rumour of the imminent outbreak of war a Special Service Section was detached and sent to Weymouth to undertake fortress work. At the declaration of war they were rejoined by the rest at Weymouth, where they began work upon the Portland defences, comprising about six miles of trenches and wire entanglement. The formation of a second line unit was begun in September, and it was immediately recruited from Swindon, where, before going to Weymouth, it underwent six weeks' training; it held its parades in the Great Western Railway Park, took route-marches in the neighbourhood, and was exercised in general field-work on the Okus fields abutting on the canal. Then the unit was transferred to Weymouth under Lieuts. Tyrwhitt, D. Williams and Piggott, and Coy. Sergt. Maj. Fricker; there a few of them were chosen to fill up gaps in the first line unit due to the dropping of men who were medically unfit, and the first line was put through a course of intensive training under Capt. Wilson, its work embracing heavy bridge-building, trench-digging by night, route-marches with full kit, physical training, etc.

Foreign Service. On January 20th, 1915, this first line unit left Southampton for Havre on board the S.S. *Blackwell*, the passage taking sixteen hours; then followed a tedious and uncomfortable train-journey in horse-boxes to St. Omer, whence the men marched to their billets at the village of Heuringhem, near St. Omer. Here the men, working alongside regular soldiers of the Royal Engineers—a detachment of the 31st Company—and other Territorial units, were put through many tests and were inspected by various officers, giving every satisfaction to the General by their efficiency and soldier-like qualities. At this place the Wiltshiremen and another west-country company of engineers remained for six weeks, meeting with the kindest treatment at the hands of the inhabitants; eight Swindon men were lodged in one farm-house, and when the time came for them to leave, the entire household broke into tears, the little boy refusing to go to school and sobbing at the loss of the friends he had learned to love in spite of their foreign speech.

Ypres. By a roundabout route the men now marched to Ypres, taking three days to make the journey and lodging each night in some old barn or other building that had already been used by French or British troops. At that time the city of Ypres was still quite sound, and shops and restaurants were carrying on business as at ordinary times; the Wiltshiremen were billeted in an old convent or school in the rue de Lille, and were given twenty-four hours rest; but they had their first experience of bombardment that very night, and on the next began work by conveying material to their advanced dump on the road to St. Eloi, where they made their first acquaintance with the horrible stench that was not the least of the horrors of that devastated belt of country. It was on this night that the Company suffered its first casualties, L/Corp. J. Kent and Spr. Nash being wounded by rifle fire. The work for the next few weeks consisted of wiring, renovating old trenches, and general field work ; two sections would be out at a time, whilst two were preparing R.E. material ; two or three men were wounded whilst out on field-work. Work was now transferred to a point further out on the St. Eloi road, but the men retained their billets in Ypres, setting off to their destination at about 6 p.m., arriving there about 9 p.m., and starting back before daylight ; in their new position they were engaged in constructing a trench along the bank of the Comines canal, and at the same time another body of engineers was boring tunnels through the opposite bank—about twelve or fifteen feet in height—to serve as hidden approaches to the country beyond the canal. This was secret work and the men were not allowed to talk or smoke ; it lasted about three weeks, and none was wounded, though a few were knocked by spent bullets destined for other marks.

It was about this time that Coy. Sergt. Maj. Rodda was awarded the French distinction of the Medaille Militaire for his valuable work on a survey round Brigade Headquarters near Verbranden-Molen. Later in the year—in November—a French general pinned the medal on his breast in the big square of Steenevoorde, near Hazebrouck, speaking in warm terms of the exploits of him and his comrades.

An interesting letter from Lieut. G. E. Knapp speaks of the visit of the Bishop of London to Ypres at Easter ; the writer says, " This afternoon (Easter Eve) I heard the Bishop of London address the troops. Afterwards he came and shook hands with me. I told him I knew the Rev. Winnington Ingram (the Bishop's nephew), who was at St. Luke's, Swindon, and he was very interested . : . . . . We have had wretched nights the last two or three times. I was out all last night, and it was drizzling all the time. I go out again to-night, but hope soon to do some work by day. It will be a nice change after a month of digging and entanglement in the dark . . . . . It must be awful for the poor fellows in the trenches this weather, but they are cheerful all the time."

Brielen and the Yser. The Wilts R.E's. were now moved from Ypres to a farm behind the Yser canal and the village of Brielen, and were put on a job that was making but poor progress ; this was the erection of huts for troops about to go into the firing line. Capt. Wilson pushed on the work with energy, and it was very well executed ; the huts were first occupied by the 1st Cavalry Division, and then by a division brought straight from the North of England to help to stem the German advance ; but these were immediately shelled out, and the work of the engineers was reduced to match-wood.

The work was by no means without its dangers ; enemy aeroplanes were constantly reconnoitring, and the Engineers' Camp could not escape notice. In it, at Brielen, was a gigantic barrel standing on end, having a tap near the bottom ; it was for the water-supply of the men and was well protected by sand-bags. Just behind the camp was a hidden 9 inch gun which was causing the "Boche" considerable annoyance, and at length he determined to suppress it ; an aeroplane was sent to locate the nuisance, and the observer espied the barrel, mistaking it for the gun ; in a short time forty 5.9 shells were poured upon the camp, the men having to bolt for safety, and the gun, which the enemy thought he had destroyed, was unmolested.

Big Bridge over Canal du Nord (Havrincourt).   Swindonian and New Zealand Officers.

Bridge over Canal du Nord, nr. Havrincourt, erected by Swindon R.E.'s and New Zealanders.

Meanwhile, two sections had been taken off this work and had been put on bridge-building on the Yser Canal ; this was shortly before the second battle of Ypres, which began on April 22nd, 1915, made famous by the gallant defence of the Canadians and notorious by the German resort to the infamous method of attack by poison-gas.

First Distinctions. The work on the Yser Canal continued, consisting of the maintenance of bridges, and the swinging of two pontoons across the canal at sunrise and sunset ; it was necessary to hide these pontoons from the enemy, so they could only be thrown out during the night. So well was the work of the Wilts Engineers done, that Distinguished Conduct Medals were conferred on Sergt. O. Davis and Spr. F. Perry. These two members of the Company gained their decorations for a particularly smart and courageous piece of work. The hostile artillery opened a heavy fire on the Canal and one bay of the only available bridge was knocked out by a direct hit. Seeing that the French battalion on the opposite bank was suffering heavily, Sergt. Davis and Spr. Perry went at once, on their own initiative, and effected temporary repairs, so that the French could get their wounded back to a dressing-station without delay. About an hour later the remainder of the Company was brought up to make permanent repairs. Capt. Wilson, Lieuts. Dawson and Knapp, and Coy. Serg. Maj. Rodda were mentioned in despatches ; Lieut. Dawson was promoted to a captaincy and shortly afterwards left for England to take command of the second line company, and Lieut. Tyrwhitt replaced him in France ; 2nd. Lieut. Knapp was promoted to 1st Lieutenant.

The work was now very varied, and one job for which the detachment won high praise was the construction of the approaches to a heavy bridge. They were fortunate as regards casualties, though often exposed to shrapnel, and the same good fortune attended their neighbours, the Cornwalls, working alongside them.

A Chance Meeting. On this huge battle-front men would go for months at a time without meeting acquaintances from home, and when such encounters occurred the day was reckoned a red-letter day. Pte. Hollister, of the 1st Wilts, writing from Belgium, tells of the pleasure he and his mates experienced at suddenly falling in with a body of Swindon R.E.'s, who were changing their position. This was at Vlamertinghe, between Poperinghe and Ypres, just before June 15th and 16th, when the Wilts regiment was so badly knocked about at Hooge. The engineers were preparing for a well-earned rest and were leaving Ypres ; they were taken by motor-lorry to Dranoutre on the Locre road, just behind Mt. Kemmel, where they went into huts ; here they were very comfortable, and their eyes were gladdened once more by the sight of cultivated ground, green fields and trees, and good roads.

Bailleul. The unit was now split up ; fitters, turners, and other tradesmen were put into workshops at Bailleul, where for several months they led the humdrum life of mechanics, being engaged largely on mining materials for the Royal Engineers and other work for the defences of the army front, such as electrical lighting for the tunnels at Messines, hutting, etc. The rest were put to work on second line trenches with Belgian soldiers, repairing trenches and making reinforced concrete machine-gun emplacements in Kemmel Hill and the neighbourhood, and doing other field work of a like nature.

At Bailleul the War Council sent an inspector to examine the saw-mill set up and worked by the Wilts Engineers, and he was delighted with what he found ; he discovered that they were running the engine and saws by steam generated entirely

L

from the refuse of the mill, and the whole Company gained special mention by the War Council for the economical running of the establishment.

Various Jobs. Work continued on these lines to about the end of July, 1916; amongst other jobs executed by the Wiltshires during this period mention should be made of the dug-outs and machine-gun emplacements constructed in Ploegsteert Wood, the new R.E. dump at Steenwerk, and also the commencement of the first Australian casualty clearing-station in France at Trois Arbres. This was the earliest contact of the Wilts engineers with the Australians, whom they described as " top-hole chaps," speaking in high praise of their splendid physique and conduct.

Even to non-technical readers detailed accounts of many of these jobs— had it been feasible to give such accounts,—would have been of great interest. For an example one may glance at a comparatively small one,—the repair of a lift-bridge at Houplines in February, 1916. The bridge, roughly like a table with four legs, could be raised to allow barges to pass underneath, and was not unlike the old " Golden Lion " bridge at Swindon with an overhead structure. One leg had been smashed by a German shell, and the Wiltshire R.E.'s had to repair it, and as it was only seven hundred yards from the front line the work had to be done at night; no noise was to be made, and no lights were allowed. The damaged corner of the bridge was lifted by the aid of screw-jacks and a reinforced concrete splint was applied to the fractured part, some stones from the adjacent church being used for the purpose and the concrete being mixed on the floor of the front room of a neighbouring house. The task occupied several nights, and although bullets used to whistle overhead the company sustained no casualties, working in a hollow.

To Bronfay. A change came suddenly on August 2nd, when orders were received at 6 p.m. to pack up and be ready to entrain at 11 a.m. next morning for an unknown destination ; this meant the recall of detachments from Armentières, Nieppe, Steenwerk, and other places, and packing up in the dark. The train journey lasted twenty-four hours and finally ended at Bray, in the Somme district ; by the time the men had reached there and off-loaded it was dark, and they slept under trees until daylight, when, after breakfast, they marched to Bronfay Farm, a distance of twelve miles. The march was very tiring, for the men were out of condition after their comparatively quiet life about Bailleul, and on the way up they incurred the German counter battery-fire. After camping, dinner was prepared by the cooks, but in about an hour the company was shelled out by the enemy, suffering casualties amongst both men and horses, and so they had to seek another pitch, which they eventually found at an old French gun position known as " the Ledge." Here they stayed some weeks laying on a water-supply and putting down several miles of two-inch and four-inch pipe-lines. This marked the beginning of their second stage of actual fighting, and their establishment was temporarily increased by twenty-five men from home, whilst Lieut. Carroll replaced Lieut. Knapp, who went to England on sick leave.

The first job was to relieve a company of R.E.'s laying a 4 inch pipe-line in the Carnoy Valley ; the line was carried up to Montauban and finished in a horse-watering point and a water-cart filling-point. The state of the valley in wet weather in the winter is unimaginable by any but those who saw it ; the mud was so deep and extensive that it was impossible to leave the path constructed without risking one's life, and horses that had stepped aside were lost and had to be shot. It was here that the men got their first sight of the tanks.

Besides constructing the pipe-line just spoken of, the company undertook the maintenance of another from Suzanne to Bronfay Farm, and as their area of operations gradually extended small detachments were located in several dispersed places. This describes generally the work that occupied the winter of 1916—17, though in October the camp had been shifted to " the Citadel," near Fricourt. In November Coy. Serg. Major Rodda had been granted a commission in his own company,—a rare privilege, the rule being to move a man to another unit upon his **Fargny** being made an officer. The detachment under him effected the **Mill.** installation of a water-pumping plant at Fargny Mill, on the Somme river-side west of Peronne. The work was going on from November 1916 to March 1917, and the station was the largest then in the country, consisting of three sets of 70 horse-power petrol-engines driving Pearn's triple plunger pumps, which forced water through a 6 in. main over a hill 275 feet high; this line was about six miles long and ran through Maricourt to Trones Wood; it was to have gone further, but was brought to an end on account of the German retirement in 1917. Besides the engines just mentioned there were in the station four 40 h.p. sets driving turbine pumps for 4 in. mains over the same hill. The men had to endure trials both from the weather and the enemy; the cold was intense at times, and one night the thermometer fell to —15$\frac{1}{2}$° C., and the river, whose normal flow was two miles an hour, froze solid, at the same time rising 18in. owing to the freezing of the weirs. All the winter the station was only two thousand yards behind the front line; the German artillery was then shooting by time-table, firing from mid-day to 2 p.m., or at 4 p.m., or at both times, and never at any other period of the day; the station enjoyed astonishing immunity, for although shells pitched all around it, there was never a direct hit and only dirt was spattered over the huts, which were on the actual front line of the fighting of 1914-15.

Hardships and Fireworks. Right through this winter the men suffered real hardships. The detachment under Lieut. Knapp that was laying the line in the Carnoy Valley had at the same time to maintain the water supply through the whole of that system, and the working conditions were most severe; patrols had to be kept going throughout the twenty-four hours; break-down parties were turned out at all hours of the day and night to repair pipes burst by frost or smashed by shells, and as these were all buried at a depth of 2ft. 6in. the men were often up to their knees or hips in water and mud during long spells in keen frost or pouring rain. Their headquarters were near " Minden Post," in a ravine, and these and every part of their area were subject to hourly shelling, day and night, for many weeks. Lieut. Knapp lived in a bell-tent, and on two occasions it was riddled by shrapnel whilst he was in his valise. But the excellence of their work was not unrecognised; the Company was complimented, together with the 142nd A.T. Coy., R.E., upon the fact that the water supply system for which they were jointly responsible during the winter operations on the Somme was the only one in the neighbourhood that did not fail during the very severe frosts of January, 1917.

Just before Christmas 1916, Lt. Carrol had to leave for home, suffering from shell-shock, and his place was taken by Lieut. D. Williams.

In spite of hardships and fatigue the men could not help being struck by the wonder and beauty of the spectacle that lay before them every night. One tells how he used to sit admiring the vivid and intensely interesting fire-work display— the exploding shells, the various kinds of signals, such as those consisting of six lights on a line gently floating across the sky, the barrages, the creeping barrage which came into use about this time, and the phosphorus and thermite shells which burst into showers of golden rain. And in the daytime there were the observation balloons, of which sometimes forty could be counted at once, British and German.

Another change in the personnel took place about February, 1917, when Lieut. Williams was posted to a new R.E. formation,—an electrical-mechanics company, and Lieut. Dawson, voluntarily relinquishing his rank as captain, rejoined his old company in place of Lieut. Williams.

Various Tasks. Owing to the retirement of the Germans to the Hindenburg line, the Wilts Engineers were moved to Foucaucourt, south of Peronne, and set to construct a corps head-quarters camp, a task which they executed for the most part in pouring rain. The next move was to Villers—Carbonnel, where they had to build the Fourth Army head-quarters, including a large number of huts and offices and a water supply system, receiving high praise for the excellence of the work and the speed with which it was accomplished ; here they met Sir Henry Rawlinson, the Fourth Army commander, who made a point of riding through the Company's camp every morning and having a chat with one or other of the men. Other pieces of work done about this time were the erection of an Indian casualty clearing-station and the building of a railway station platform for loading wounded on ambulance trains.

On the completion of the army head-quarters the company was turned on to bridging at Peronne, with orders to complete four steel-girder bridges over the Somme in five days ; at the end of the third day the fourth bridge was ready for

Dunkirk.
Capt. Wilson
Leaves.
launching, when orders were suddenly given that the company was to go to Dunkirk. Dunkirk was almost as dangerous as the battle-field, for bombing by the enemy was a nightly occurrence, as many as 300 bombs being dropped in a night upon the town and neighbourhood; an undisturbed night was practically unknown for the four months the Company was at Dunkirk, and they had several narrow escapes. They were at Dunkirk from June to September, 1917, and in June Capt. Wilson was decorated with the Military Cross for his long record of devotion and ability. Whilst here the company formed another R.E. dump, and a detachment went to Bray Dunes to construct a casualty clearing-station with material brought down to them by barges on the canals. Another detachment was engaged in the docks, fitting up drinking-water tanks and petrol pumps on Thames lighters that had been brought over. In September, 1917, Capt. Wilson was promoted to be Major and given command of a work-shop company, and Lieut. Dawson replaced him as Captain in command of the Wilts R.E's.

A detachment was now sent to Pont Rémy, near Abbeville, to form a musketry school for the Fourth Army, a piece of work involving both speed and great effort ; but here again the excellence of the Wiltshiremen's work won great praise from high authorities. In November the rest of the men moved from Dunkirk to Amiens for work on billetting areas, and eventually joined their comrades at Pont Rémy, assisting in the completion of the musketry school.

On the Front again. The British offensive and victory at Cambrai on November 20th, 1917, caused the engineers to be suddenly called once more to the battle front, their orders being to go to a certain spot on the Bapaume-Cambrai road ; not knowing the locality and lacking sufficient information, they halted and detrained from their lorries in full view of the Germans ; they were immediately under hostile fire and several were wounded, and had to do the best they could to establish themselves in trenches and under hedges. The sergeants found a bell-tent and in the dark erected it on a hill; they slept there that night and awoke in the morning to find that they could see the Germans walking about in Moeuvres; naturally they lost no time in finding safer quarters, and the tent received a direct hit just after the sergeants had left it.

The first few days in the new situation were by no means comfortable, and the men's first duty was the filling of mine-craters in the road while exposed to machine-gun fire; they suffered considerably, too, from hunger, for they were without rations for five days. It was in these circumstances that Quartermaster Sergt. Duck won his Distinguished Conduct Medal for conspicuous bravery. Owing to continuous shell-fire and the fact that rations had not reached the unit, the men had had no hot food for several days. At last a stew was on the fires, when a shell-blast overturned the lot. Duck at once went and got another stew going, single-handed, as the area was being rapidly vacated, and with the help of volunteers got the food away to the half-starved men. The orchard in which this took place, on a bare hill-top at Boursies, was under heavy shell-fire all the time, being under direct observation from Bourlon Wood. After several strenuous days and nights orders were received that the company should go to Bihucourt to take over the construction and maintenance of the water-supply system, work which occupied about a fortnight.

The Yellow Line. A detachment sent to Vaulx-Vraucourt was engaged on work of vital importance, in constructing the line of defence which was afterwards famous under the name of " The Yellow Line," and the work comprised fresh trenches, entanglements, machine-gun battery positions, and dug-outs, stretching over about two miles ; the work was carried out under conditions of strict secrecy, and when the Company head-quarters moved to Ervillers in December, the same class of work was carried on from this fresh centre. So the work went on till the enemy began his great offensive on March 21st, 1918, advancing against Amiens. " The Yellow Line " proved its worth, for it held up successive attacks till the close of the day, with terrific slaughter of the Germans ; they had not previously observed the machine-gun emplacements that the engineers had constructed, and the machine-gunners wrought terrible execution amongst the advancing waves of infantry, wiping out attack after attack. The emplacements were mentioned by the German Commander in an account of the fighting, to the effect that " the advance was held up all day by a number of cunningly concealed machine-gun emplacements."

Hardships of Retreat. Now began a series of trials before which the hardships hitherto experienced by the Company paled. During the day they had been standing by, waiting for orders and being shelled out of their camp ; in the afternoon they were ordered to move to their company head-quarters, and they did so in open order in order to avoid the shell-fire ; as soon as they arrived they were despatched with a large labour-party to construct during the night a length of trench only about five hundred yards in front of the advancing foe. Meanwhile their head-quarters had moved back to Boiry St. Rictrude, and this meant that as soon as the men had done their trench-work they had to march to the old head-quarters and then to the fresh locale. They arrived at Boiry at 7 a.m., and immediately tried to get a little sleep, but at 9 o'clock they had to turn out, pack, and move to the village of Adinfer, where they arrived at 10 o'clock. At the same time an officer had been out and sited a new line of trenches, which, however, were never dug owing to the rapidity of the German advance. Next morning the company marched back to Boiry St. Martin and made a fresh line of

trenches, going back then to Adinfer for a night's rest.   In the morning orders came
to move again to Bienvillers-au-bois, where the officer in command was summoned
to a conference of R.E. officers at Monchy-au-bois for the consideration of further
trench-construction, at 6 p.m. receiving orders to site a trench-line from Adinfer
Wood to Essart and then to go back to Bienvillers and march his company to Essart
by 9 p.m., picking up a working party of nine hundred on the way in order to dig a
portion of the line.   The duty was successfully accomplished by 6 a.m., and the
party set out to return to Bienvillers for rest ; but the return was effected with the
greatest difficulty, for the men were so fatigued that numbers fell by the roadside
and it was almost impossible to arouse them from sleep.   Even now there was little
respite for the company, for they were awakened at mid-day by a report—which
afterwards turned out to be false—that the enemy was advancing on Hannescamps ;
as they were on the point of moving to La Bazeque, five aeroplanes flew across,
attacking them with bombs and machine-gun fire, inflicting several casualties upon
the company.   The aeroplanes flew low, at about 200 feet, and all appeared to
be British, having British markings ; about twelve men were hit.   Arriving at
La Bazeque, they were given a large barn as their quarters, but had to come to an
amicable understanding with a squad of pigs who were already in possession.

The Purple Line.   From now began a period of frantic trench-digging, and soon an
orderly system of defence was evolved ; chaos gave place to organization, and from Adinfer to Fonquevillers a definite line of trenches was
constructed.   The men had settled themselves in a ravine close
to Berles-au-bois, and in the construction of this new " Purple Line " did excellent
work, and had the gratification of seeing one trench named " Swindon Trench " ;
a bridge which had to be made to enable field-guns and ammunition to cross the
trench was suitably named " The Golden Lion Bridge."   This work was attended
by much risk, for the enemy's fire was very heavy, but although many of the labour-
party suffered, the Wiltshire R.E.'s were remarkably fortunate.

The Great Advance.   On the morning of August 21st, 1918, famous for the great attack
by the Canadian 17th, 6th and 4th corps, the Wilts company had
to construct a horse-watering point under severe shell-fire at Douchy,
where most of the R.F.A. horses of the corps on each side of the
Company's own—the 6th—had to water; they earned great commendation for their
energy and the long hours they worked, several men working continuously for
thirty-six hours to ensure success.   It was afterwards proved that if this point had
failed the line would have had to remain stationary, even if it had not been
necessary to move it back ; all the other watering-points broke down, and this
became the only one available for some miles around ; the traffic there was
tremendous ; several thousands of horses were watered there, and one of the
engineers says, " The country was black with them ; I didn't think there were so
many horses in the world !"

Then onwards during the triumphant British advance the company installed
watering-points at Courcelles, Ervillers, St. Leger, Mory, Behagnies, Vaulx-Vraucourt
and Lagnicourt,—work which necessitated successive transfers of head-quarters,
notably from Berles to Courcelles, and thence to Vaulx-Vraucourt.

The Ramp at Royaulcourt.   From the latter place a detachment was sent back to Boyelles R.E.
dump to form a bridging dump there, after which the company set
about making a " ramp," or sloping platform at Royaulcourt, to
enable traffic to pass into the dry course of the Canal du Nord at
Havrincourt Wood ;   this ramp was a fine piece of work, for it was

THE WILTS (FORTRESS) ROYAL ENGINEERS. 247

300 ft. long, 10 ft. wide and had a gradient of about 1 in 15. The spot was under the direct observation of many German balloons and subject to daily shelling, and was the scene of severe losses, for during a German attack on Havrincourt a working party of thirty-one men was caught by the German barrage, and eight were killed and twenty wounded ; it was here that Sergt. Marsh was severely wounded in the head, and won the Military Medal for conspicuous gallantry, and L/Corp. Beck and Spr. Henry were awarded their decorations for fetching in a wounded man.

The Big Bridge. These severe losses caused the company to be sent back to Boyelles for a rest, and there they were occupied in sorting material preparatory for the erection of a bridge ; but the change in the military situation caused this project to be dropped, and the company was joined with a New Zealand tunnelling company and set to erect over the Canal du Nord, near Havrincourt, a steel girder bridge, Hopkins' type, of 180 feet span. The camp was therefore moved to Hermies. This bridge, the largest military bridge erected in the country, proved of much interest to the authorities, and Sir Douglas Haig himself inspected it twice during the course of its construction ; 14 officers and 310 men of other ranks were engaged upon the work ; the weight of the bridge was 110 tons and its launching weight 120 tons, whilst its launching length was 240 feet. The task was completed in the astonishingly short time of 104 hours.

Now ensued the formation of water-filling points at several spots in the direction of the British advance, and the company head-quarters moved to Estourmel, the village being fitted up by the company for the accommodation of the Sixth Corps Headquarters. Then came more water-supply work at Boistrancourt, Boussières, etc., and having shifted camp three times in this area, the company made a further move to St. Hilaire, where they had half-a-day at road-cleaning. Solesmes having been captured by the British on October 20th, the Wilts R.E.'s were ordered to reconnoitre and build a bridge at Solesmes ; the reconnaissance was made on the morning of the 21st, the work was begun in the afternoon, interrupted twice by enemy shells and gas, and continued without a break until the bridge was completed at mid-day on the 23rd ; it was necessary that it should be ready by then so as not to delay the advance.

Having worked continuously for so long, the men hoped for a short period of rest and sleep, but they were dismayed to receive an order from Gen. Harvey to leave their friends of the Sixth Corps and to join the First Army for extensive heavy bridging.

Douai. The Armistice. After three days' wandering via Cambrai and Douai, they arrived at the village of Raches, and were set to repair the bridge over the Scarpe and also the one crossing the railway in Douai. The latter was an intensely interesting problem in engineering, one part of the structure weighing about sixty tons and needing to be lifted back into its original position ; there was great difficulty, too, in obtaining the necessary men and material. The work was marred by a sad occurrence only the day before the armistice was signed, for a delayed German mine exploded fifteen feet away from a party of six working on the bridge, and every one of them was injured.

The campaigning was over, although there was still work for the engineers to do and an immediate return to civil life was not possible. They remained at Raches till the 8th of January, 1919, when they were moved by train—a tedious three days' journey—to Andenne, a place eleven miles east of Namur, situated on the bank of the Meuse in a beautiful, hilly district. There was little to remind them of the enemy,—only a total absence of metal door-handles, a huge bridge across the Meuse replacing that which the Belgians destroyed to check the invader in 1914, and, a sadder reminder, a cemetery where some civilians were shot and buried alive by the brutal violators of Belgian independence.   From here the Company moved to Troisdorf, in Germany, at the end of January, and remained there until they were disbanded on November 19th, 1919.

One cannot but remark the frequency with which the Swindon Company of R.E.'s. had been praised for the excellence and expedition of their work.   Their duties had be·n very varied, almost unintermittent, and accompanied by much hardship ; their success was largely due to their indomitable pluck, combined with high mechanical intelligence developed by their education and training in Swindon and its factory, and also to the good health and physique fostered by the bracing air of their native Downs.   Their story is one of which Swindon may be proud ; the list of honours won by members of the Company and which is here subjoined speaks for itself, and these but reflect the spirit shown by the whole Company, and the honour it deserved.   It is sad to reflect that their gallant **Death of** leader, Major C. S. Wilson, M.C., did not live to see the return of the **Maj. Wilson.** men whom he led to France in 1914 ; just a fortnight before the Armistice was signed he fell a victim to the influenza scourge that was then carrying off many in most parts of the world ; he died on October 27th, 1918. His services had been officially recognized, but those who served under him best knew and appreciated his skill and his devotion to his work and his men ; by them his death was mourned as a personal loss.

HONOURS GAINED BY THE COMPANY.

Major C. S. Wilson : mentioned in despatches, 31-12-'15 ; Military Cross, Summer, 1917.
Capt. J. Dawson : mentioned in despatches, 31-12-'15 ; Military Cross, 9-10-'18.
Capt. G. E. Knapp : mentioned in despatches, 31-12-'15 ; Russian Order of St. Anne (with swords).
Lieut. H. C. Rodda : Medaille Militaire, 6-11-'15 ; Recommended for Gallant and Distinguished Conduct in the Field, London Gazette, 31-12-'15.   M.C., 2-6-'19.
Sergt. O. Davies : D.C.M. (London Gazette, 14-1-'16).
Sergt. F. G. Perry : D.C.M. (London Gazette 14-1-'16).
Sergt. A. W. Edwards : ⎫
S/Sgt. J. Oakford : ⎪
  ,,   H. Eaton : * ⎬ Recommended for Gallant and Distinguished Conduct in the
  ,,   J. S. R. Gale : ⎪ Field (London Gazette, 31-12-'15).
L/Cpl. S. Bellinger : ⎪
  ,,   H. Shorland : ⎭
Sergt. H. T. Gutridge : Mentioned in despatches (London Gazette 15-6-'16).
II. Cpl. H. A. Viner : Mentioned in despatches (London Gazette 15-6-'16).
Sergt. Ellen : Mentioned in despatches (December, 1917) ; M.S.M. (June, 1918).
Sergt. H. W. Ponting : Mentioned in despatches (London Gazette 18-5-'17).
A/Co. Sergt. Major J. E. Duck : D.C.M. (London Gazette 31-5-'18).
L/Cpl. V. Beck : M.M., 8-10-'18.
Spr. T. B. Henry : M.M., 8-10-'18.
Sergt. W. E. Marsh : M.M., 18-9-'18.
Spr. E. Culling : M.M., Nov. 1918.
Spr. G Caudle : Croix de Guerre (Belgian).
L/Cpl. S. Bellinger : Special Mention in despatches, Jan. 1919.

* NOTE—Staff Sergt. Eaton, serving under Major Wilson in No. 4 Workshop Company, was killed in action and awarded the M.M. during Gen. Carey's operations at the German attempt to break through in the Spring of 1918.

CHAPTER II.

The Wilts Battery of the 3rd Wessex R.F.A.

The 3rd   The 3rd Wessex Brigade of Royal Field Artillery consisted in 1914
Wessex Bde. of three Territorial batteries, viz., the 1st Battery, or Wilts Battery,
(Reserve) composed chiefly of Swindon men with some from the surrounding
R.F.A. neighbourhood, the 2nd or Hants Battery, and the 3rd or Dorset
Battery ; for the sake of brevity they were spoken of as the 1/3, 2/3,
and 3/3 Wessex R.F.A. respectively.

The 3rd Wessex Brigade was commanded by Col. E. H. Bedford-Pim, and
Captain De Gidley was Adjutant of the Brigade. The Wilts or 1/3 Battery, with
which alone this sketch is immediately concerned, was under the command of Major
the Earl of Suffolk ; his second in command was Capt. Goldsmith, who, when Lord
Suffolk at a later date went to Mesopotamia, took his place ; the other officers
were Lieutenants Godwin (of Swindon), Robinson, Nunn, and Glynne (of Stratton)
who became Captain of the Second First Battery (2/1 Bty.) of the Wilts R.F.A.
when it went out to India under Major Burdon. The strength of the Battery was
140 men and their officers.

As was told at the beginning of this work, the Battery only returned from its
annual training at Larkhill, proud of the honours it had won there, on Saturday,
August 1st, 1914, and on Wednesday, August 5th, the first contingent
The Wilts of eighty officers and men left Swindon, under Col. Bedford-Pim
Bty. Leave and Major the Earl of Suffolk, for active service, in ignorance of
for India. the field of service to which they were going. They were taken to
Farlington Racecourse, Portsmouth, where they remained for a few
weeks, and then the 3rd Wessex Brigade, R.F.A., with all three batteries, set sail
for India from Southampton on October 9th, arriving at Bombay on November
9th, 1914 : upon arrival the First-First Wilts Battery (1/1 Bty., 3rd Wessex)
entrained for Delhi, which was their station for about three years and where they
formed part of the vice-regal guard.

The 2/1   No sooner had this battery left Swindon than the formation of a
Wilts Second-First Battery (2/1 Bty., 3rd Wessex) was begun. This
Follow. battery was trained at Plymouth, Malmesbury, and Swindon, and
received a final inspection at Prospect Hall by Major W. C. Burdon
on December 10th, 1914. The 2/1 Battery left Swindon for Southampton on
December 12th, and Major Burdon telegraphed a Christmas greeting to the Mayor
of Swindon, Mr. W. E. Morse, from Port Said. On their arrival at Bombay on
January 7th, 1915, the battery went by train to Secunderabad and settled down in
their quarters at Trimulgherry—a military station three miles from Secunderabad—
where they found a hot supper awaiting them after their thirty-six hours' journey.

At Trimulgherry the 2/1's relieved the "Chestnut Battery," or "U" Battery,
R.F.A. (regular troops), who went to France. The Wilts Battery formed part
of a contingent of 2,068 officers and men, including the Oxford and Bucks infantry,
which formed the garrison of Trimulgherry for the next two years. The

" Hyderabad Bulletin," speaking of the new arrivals, commented upon the superior physique of the Wilts Reserve Battery, attributing it to the fact that the men were " mostly engaged in engine-building."

Life at Trimul- gherry. Trimulgherry is the chief military station of the Nizam's dominions, and the camp proved a comfortable spot ; the men had to undergo heavy training, but they were prepared to make themselves at home and soon wrote to the Town Clerk of Swindon asking for books and papers for their reading room. The Wilts Battery made a name for themselves by their prowess in sports—in hockey, horsemanship, football and cricket, and also in " hunting," the hare being replaced by two rough-riders who left a paper trail behind them. On July 22nd, 1915, the troops arranged a fine concert in the theatre at Trimulgherry at which Major Burdon presided ; he, too, wrote about this time to the Mayor of Swindon thanking him for gifts sent by the Committee for providing " Comforts " for the troops. Amongst the honours gained by the Wiltshiremen at Trimulgherry were both the " Terrier " Football Cup and the Wessex Brigade Billiard Shield,—the latter now resting in Swindon.

The 1/1's at Delhi and Meerut. Meanwhile, the 1/1 Battery had been undergoing most thorough training in the north of India. They remained at Kingsway Camp, outside Delhi, until the end of March, 1915, doing training such as was hitherto unknown in India,—eight hours a day as against the usual four hours done by regular troops,—practising gun-pit digging, all night firing, starlight firing, horsemanship, etc., and going through their gunners' laying-test and fuse-setting tests. This severe training rendered the men splendid horsemen and gunners in all respects, and before long they wrested the Brigade trophy from the experienced regular artillerymen.

On March 23rd, 1915, the Battery made the usual summer move to Meerut, establishing themselves in the barracks known as the " Rocket Lines," just outside the city. Training was continued here, and the men had their first experience of overhauling their own guns. The character of the battery, comprising as it did men of an extraordinary number of skilled trades,—fitters, turners, smiths, carpenters, wheelwrights, painters, etc.,—made it quite independent of any outside assistance, and they never had to call in any help from elsewhere to deal with any of the numerous needs of the battery throughout its career.

Recreation was found at Meerut in the Swimming Baths, where polo matches, diving competitions, and all manner of aquatic sports were frequently held, and in cricket and football matches. But both men and horses suffered severely from sickness, for the summer was the hottest known there for twenty years ; the battery had twenty to thirty regularly in the hospital, besides about five and twenty convalescents in the hills, and thus the ordinary duties fell very heavily upon the rest.

A Great Triumph. Returning to Delhi in October, 1915, the battery prepared to show its mettle in the forth-coming divisional training ; they formed part of the 16th Indian Division, and the place chosen for the divisional training was Ghaziabad, thirteen miles from Delhi on the Meerut road. Here the Battery won the Brigade Firing Cup and was described as " the most efficient battery of R.F.A's. at present in India," being highly complimented and entertained to dinner by the Earl of Suffolk.

Lord Chelmsford, the new Viceroy, being due at Delhi in April, the Battery— as part of the vice-regal guard—was detained in the plains a month longer than usual for the purpose of escorting him to the vice-regal lodge upon his arrival. It was about this time that the first draft of Swindon men arrived from England, and they went straight on to Meerut, where the Battery joined them late in April.

Losses. The second summer in Meerut was saddened by two deaths,—the first in the Battery,—both due to heat-stroke ; the victims were Dr. Vizor, of Malmesbury, and Corpl. Axford, of Folkestone Road, Swindon. A loss of a different kind, but one felt by the men, befell the Battery when Lord Suffolk left for Mesopotamia ; his place as Major was taken by Capt. Goldsmith, Col. Bedford-Pim being still in command.

Returning to Delhi in October, 1916, the Battery began to send its first drafts to Mesopotamia, for the men were now thoroughly seasoned artillery-men, fit for any service. The place chosen for brigade-training this season was Tuklakabad, two days' march from Delhi, and the troops had their coldest experiences on the plains, ice being seen for the first time for some years. The Battery held firmly to the Brigade Firing Cup which they had won the year before, justifying the high opinion that had been formed of their prowess.

Now and then the men were able to indulge their taste for sport whilst they were in the plains. They used to run a pack of hounds—greyhounds and whippets,— and chased jackals and silver foxes. At times they were able to have a little wild pig-sticking, a sport generally reserved for officers only, and on these occasions they had sometimes been favoured by the presence of the Countess as well as the Earl of Suffolk. But the men of the 1/1 Battery had probably less opportunity for sport and sight-seeing than the members of many other units in India ; they were never over their complement, and the duties of the Battery were always very exacting ; there were always men on the sick-list, and the hands of the rest were thus full of work.

This season was marked by two brigade-trainings, the second being a final training for the purpose of making selections for the drafts to Mesopotamia alluded to above. The second training took place at Roorkee, eleven days' march from Delhi, in the North-West Provinces. Here the Battery was despoiled of the Brigade Firing Cup by the Hants Battery, but although they lost the cup they still could reflect with pride that it was won by a territorial unit and that it remained in the Wessex Brigade.

The Afghan Frontier. The 1/1's stayed at Roorkee till after Christmas. Then came news that they were wanted on the Afghan frontier where there was a state of unrest, and about February they left by train for a border station between Rawalpindi and Nowshera. There the 16th Indian Division was for the first time assembled complete. Advanced troops—cavalry, motor-transport, and airmen—were sent forward to quell disturbances, and their engagements were noteworthy as being the first in India in which aeroplanes were used ; the guns remained in the rear with the infantry and the divisional motor-transport, and the Battery was engaged in severe open firing practice, remaining on the frontier till the end of March, 1917.

Lahore. The men now went down to Lahore on garrison duty for the summer. Lahore has been called the " White Man's grave " of India, and the Battery found the name was no empty title. Very soon an outbreak of cholera occurred, and people were dying in swarms in Lahore ; by the promptitude of the commanding officer the troops were saved, and for three months they were shut up in their camp, every place outside being " out of bounds ; " but two bad cases of enteric fever occurred in the Battery, and the heat claimed several victims.

Besides several who were not Swindon men, at least five Swindonians were mourned by their mates,—Bt. Serg. Maj. H. George (the eldest son of Mr. Reuben George), Dr. Leonard, Gnr. Mills, Dr. Pearce, and Bombr. Rand.

During these three tedious months the men found time hang heavily upon their hands, and they had to occupy themselves as best they could in the camp with draughts, billiards and football played amongst themselves. When, however, the R.F.A. brigade sports could be held the Swindon lads proved their mettle by carrying off all there was to be won.

After the cholera had passed away, about the end of June, 1917, the Battery was sent out on night-firing to prepare for brigade-training, and then in November went for its annual training to Hoshiarpur, in the Jalandar district, north of the River Sutlej. Here, for the first time since they parted from them on Farlington Racecourse in 1914, they met the 2/3 Wessex Brigade, also up for training.

Leaving Hoshiapur in January, 1918, the battery returned to Lahore for the summer season, and, but for a good deal of sickness, passed a quiet time there. In April the men had the first intimation that all 1914 men were recalled for service in France or England ; this meant the final dispersal of the Swindon men, as many had already gone on drafts to Mesopotamia and Egypt and the men received after the first draft from England had been men of all kinds, not Swindonians. The 1914 men who returned comprised thirty-six " A1 " men destined for France, and about fifteen " D.3 " men for England ; they were brought home by Col. Bedford-Pim and Major Goldsmith, and as they were dispersed to various units the 1/1 Swindon Battery passed out of existence.

Formation of the 3/1 Reserve Battery. To return to England ; on the departure of the 2/1 Battery for India under Major Burdon, the cadre of the Battery was left behind to form a Third First (3/1) reserve battery, which was stationed at Swindon for eight months under the command of Lieut. Adamthwaite, of Cirencester. The Ammunition Column lay at Malmesbury under Capt. A. L. Forrester. In February a draft of about forty joined the 51st Highland Division at Blackheath, proceeding with them to France within a month. This draft was not large enough to form a complete battery, but it kept together well in France and had a distinguished career ; it remained in France till the end of the war, and had a good share of distinctions to its credit. Driver Scull won the D.C.M. and M.S.M., for gallant services as a runner under fire. Bombardier A. A. Buttle won the M.M. for the courage and sang-froid with which he ran his canteen in the front line under heavy bombardment ; and Serg. W. Gosling was awarded the V.C. for his courage in unscrewing the fuse from a bomb that had fallen only ten yards away, thereby saving many lives.

Movements of the 3/1 Battery. In June, 1915, the 3/1 Battery went from Swindon into camp at Cheddar under Capt. A. L. Forrester, spending about three months under canvas. Whilst they were at Cheddar a draft of them formed a section of the 1/1 Wessex Divisional Ammunition Column, and went to Lyndhurst, passing two months there under canvas ; then, owing to bad weather, they marched the twenty miles to Bournemouth in the latter part of November, 1915, and went into billets there. They stayed in Bournemouth till the close of March, 1916, going then to Salisbury Plain. Here they found their old comrades of the 3/1 Battery established at Rollestone Camp, whither they had moved from Cheddar, and the 1/1 Wessex D.A.C. took up their quarters in a part of the same Camp.   At the end of April all D.A.C's were disbanded, and the draft rejoined its old battery.

Another draft of about fifty non-commissioned officers and men left the 3/1 Battery early in December, 1915, to join the No. 3. (T.F.) Artillery Training School under Lieut. Lester, and they were transferred with the School to Larkhill.   This school was approximately two thousand strong and was used in training the "Derby" men, and, later, the "Conscripts"; it was a "draft-finding brigade" under the command of Lieut. Col. E. H. Cheke and then Lieut. Col. S. G. Gouldschmidt.

From Cheddar the Battery had moved into billets at Exmouth about the beginning of September, staying there till February, 1916, when it joined the School of Instruction at Kettering under Col. Saunders, R.A. ; a month later the whole school moved to Rollestone Camp, Salisbury Plain.   At Rollestone the R.F.A's had probably more training and more arduous work to do than any other regiment there, and the work was made more trying by the untoward conditions of the weather and the surface of the country.

Drafts to India.   The first draft to India left Rollestone in terrible weather ; the draft numbered over two hundred, and they marched the seven miles to Amesbury in driving snow and sailed in a blizzard from Devonport on February 6th, 1916.   They reached India early in March, entrained to Delhi and then went straightway to Meerut leaving the 1/1 Battery in Delhi waiting for the new Viceroy, Lord Chelmsford,   After a fortnight's quarantine at Meerut some of the draft were sent to the Dorsets at Bareilly and some to the Hants at Umballa, as the number of the draft was in excess of the needs of the Wilts Battery.   Later on, when the 1/3 Brigade was divided into two batteries of six guns each instead of three batteries of four guns each, old comrades were brought together again.

Shortly afterwards a second Indian draft consisting of about fifty men left England, reaching India in May, 1916 : they joined the 2/1 Battery at Trimulgherry, which, with the Oxford and Bucks infantry, had now formed the garrison since 1914.   The draft was put into an isolation camp forthwith, and then, as there was no room in the barracks, remained for three months under canvas, occupied in light duties till they were acclimatized.

At this station there was not a Y.M.C.A. hut, but its place was taken by a " Sandy's Home,"—one of those institutions founded by Miss Sandy, and very highly valued by the troops in India.

2/1 Battery Leaves Trimul-gherry; Bangalore.   In September, 1916, the 2/1 Battery was sent from Trimulgherry to relieve the Devon Battery at Bangalore, and there underwent fairly arduous training.   Bangalore is one of the finest towns in India, with a climate not unlike the English climate at its best, and on account of its beauty and fertility it has been called the " Garden of India."   The men found there the 9th Hants Regiment and the Royal Sussex Regiment ; there was a Y.M.C.A. hut in the camp, and the city afforded plenty of amusement with its numerous English shops, the cinema theatres and dances, and the many places of interest in and about the town ; thus the men had a very pleasant time at Bangalore.

Early in November, 1916, the Battery went into camp at Rajankunti, thirty miles north of Bangalore, for their annual training, returning to Bangalore about the end of January.   Drafts were now being sent out frequently to Mesopotamia, and these, being placed on the strength of the various units to which they were attached, are lost to the Wilts R.F.A., and cannot be followed here in detail ; the sketch of the career of the 5th Wiltshires will, however, give some idea of the field of these men's labours and the great events in which they played a part.

During their sojourn at Bangalore, about half a dozen men were chosen to undergo a trade test for army mechanics, and the test was given them by a Swindonian, Mr. Barker, of the Railway Works at Bangalore.

The 2/1 Battery left Bangalore in the autumn of 1917 and moved north to Kamptee, nine miles north of Nagpur, where they found life very dull in comparison with the gaiety and brightness of Bangalore. They stayed here but a few months, and had but little training as the country was very rough and most of the season was the wet monsoon ; one day when the men were out firing, a gun began to founder in a bog, and twenty-two horses were needed to pull it out. On the whole the men were very thankful to get moved from this dreary camp. It was here that the Battery lost Major Burdon, who was made Colonel of the Jubbulpore Brigade, R.F.A., and was succeeded by Capt. Joblin as Major, he having come to the Battery from Mesopotamia.

The 2/1's at Meerut and Delhi. Early in 1918 the Battery was moved to Meerut, and after about a month or so they marched to Kingsway Camp, Delhi, forming part of the viceregal guard. The stay in Delhi was varied by a spell in camp at Roorkee, a hundred miles north of Delhi, and during their residence at Delhi the Wiltshiremen maintained their reputation as sportsmen by winning the " Williams " Football Cup. The men had a holiday every Thursday, and by permission of the officer they could go out in the country shooting buck or pea-fowl,—a privilege that many availed themselves of. The more aristocratic sport of " pig-sticking " was reserved for the officers.

When the Viceroy went to Simla for the summer, at the end of April, the 2/1's returned to Meerut, a few being lucky enough to be sent from there to the hills. Sergt. Maj. Weston left the Battery at Meerut, having been made a lieutenant in the Labour Corps and going back to Trimulgherry. Many in

Deaths at Meerut. Swindon were saddened to hear that Q.M. Sergt. Jago died at Meerut on May 16th, 1918 ; his services in Swindon as Bandmaster of the 3rd Wessex Military Band had won him deserved esteem, and the town as a whole heard the news with a real sense of loss : he had enjoyed excellent health in India and died of a ruptured heart the day he was taken ill. The Battery suffered another serious loss a few months later when, on October 29th, Sergt.-Fitter R. G. Loveday, of Swindon, died in the hospital of Meerut from pneumonia during a severe epidemic of influenza which caused much mortality amongst the troops.

The winter of 1918-19 was spent at Delhi like the previous winter and the 2/1 Battery was there when the armistice was signed. The news was shortly afterwards followed by serious nationalist riots at Delhi which were not unconnected with a lecturing visit of Mrs. Annie Besant to the city, during which she addressed meetings of the natives from public platforms and in the streets. The R.F.A's were mounted as cavalry armed with rifles, and for about three days kept guard over the civilian quarters. The usual visit to camp at Roorkee was made, and from there all men over forty years of age were sent home.

To Afghanistan. The cessation of hostilities naturally led the men to anticipate speedy demobilization and all the 1914 men had their kits packed ready for home, but they were held back by the trouble in Afghanistan ; so the Battery returned to Meerut in April 1919, under orders to stand ready for Afghanistan. Towards the beginning of June the men left Meerut for Afghanistan, being on board the train for nearly a week and finally detraining at Fort Chaman, about a hundred miles beyond Quetta on the way to Kandahar. The fort had been captured a few days before by the 102nd Battery (Devons), the Kents, and the Duke of Wellington's Regiment (regular troops) along with several native regiments. Here the Battery remained as part of the garrison till September, 1919. They found the life monotonous : the fort—a very fine specimen of fortification having a marvellously intricate system of internal connections,—is situated in a sandy desert surrounded by high hills, and sand-storms are frequent. The Battery saw no fighting, but the infantry had slight skirmishes further out and brought in Afghan prisoners daily,—men whose huge proportions astonished the British soldiers. The diet of the troops was sufficient but " deadly dull," and there was a good water supply from cisterns constructed under the orders of Lord Kitchener when he was Commander-in-Chief in India. In fact, the Battery found this experience at Fort Chaman—their only experience of active service—the dreariest of their Indian duties, and the chief incident was the wreck of a hospital train going from the Fort to Quetta, which was destroyed by the collapse of a bridge ; several were killed and wounded, but although some of the Wilts Battery were present they had the good fortune to escape.

Through the Kojuck Pass.   In accordance with the terms of the treaty with Afghanistan the troops evacuated the Fort in September, and returned to Gulistan, about halfway to Quetta. The artillery returned by a forced march of nearly fifty miles through the Kojuck Pass and a continuous series of mountain passes, this being the first time a brigade of artillery had ever been through. The march took them thousands of feet up the mountains amongst precipices of appalling depth ; the first night some reached the appointed camping-ground, but some of the horses were too exhausted to get there, and gunners, including lads from Swindon, passed the night under their guns on a narrow shelf of rock overhanging a sheer drop of many hundreds of feet.

Home.   The Battery stayed at Gulistan a few weeks, and the 1914 men left for Quetta and then for Karachi ; they sailed for England on board the " City of Marseilles," being brought home by Capt. Rose who had gone out with them as a second lieutenant in 1914 ; they arrived at Liverpool on November 22nd, 1919, having been absent from home exactly five years. The 1915 men and the cadre of the Battery returned a month later ; they came to Swindon, but there were very few Swindon men amongst them.

All original members of the Wilts Battery had the Territorial Long Service Medal, and doubtless those who served in Afghanistan will receive the Afghan medal. But it would seem but right that these men, who served from the commencement of the war and whose garrison service in India released the regular troops for service in France, should be allowed, if not the 1914 star, some special decoration that would be equivalent to it as a record of voluntary self-sacrifice and loyalty.

" B " Battery of the London Division.   In the early part of 1916 a new battery of the Wilts R.F.A. was formed at Rollestone Camp, with a complete equipment of horses and guns, and was sent to Codford Camp under Capt. Martell to complete the 303rd Brigade R.F.A., London Division ; it was composed of Swindon, Dorset and Hants men, forming " B " Battery, and had an eventful and varied career before it.

This battery went to France with the 60th (London) Division in June, under Major Cullern, with Lieutenants Whitehead, Roach, Philpott, and Alexander ;

Capt. Martell could not go, having had an accident that kept him at home. The non-commissioned officers were Sergt. Maj. Webb, Q.M. Sergt. W. Jones, and Sergts. W. Cuff (" A " sub-section), Sherwood (" B " sub-section), N. Tovey (" C " sub-section), and Chaldlecotte (" D " sub-section). The Division landed at Le Havre, went thence by train to St. Pol, and then trekked to Frevin-Capelle which was to be their wagon line ; there they relieved the 51st Division, and thus came into contact with the draft that had left Swindon in February, 1915, to join this division at Blackheath and which had been fighting with the 51st Division in France ever since.

At Vimy Ridge. Within four days of landing in France this new battery was in action. From the wagon-line " A " and " C " gun-detachments went into the line at Vimy Ridge, " B " and " D " detachments followed them the following night, and during the next two nights they had three " S.O.S." calls from the front line, firing about a hundred rounds per gun. From now the battery was continuously engaged till it left France in November, undergoing the various experiences of the artillery,—bombardments nearly every other day, gas attacks, and the shock of neighbouring mine-explosions. On August 13th, the whole Battery was for twelve hours shelled with eight-inch shells ; the bombardment was witnessed by His Majesty the King from Mont St. Eloy, and he sent two aides-de-camp the next day to ascertain how the Battery had fared, believing that they must have been annihilated ; they had, however, not experienced serious casualties or injury to the guns.

A week later the Battery was subjected to a gas-attack, but they were favoured by the shape of the front at that point ; for the front formed a horse shoe bend and a slight wind caused the gas to drift away to the right, just clear of the backward-bending line. Two days after this, at Neuville St. Vaast, two of the guns were detached from the 303rd Brigade and were temporarily attached to the 300th Brigade, manned, however, by their own men,—" B " Battery under Lieut. Philpott. These guns—eighteen pounders—were sent forward to cut wire, but after they had fired three rounds the Germans ranged upon them with " pip squeaks," following these up with eight-inch shells, and the men had to take cover ; they were for two days under such close observation that they could not get their guns out, and when they finally succeeded in doing so it was only done under heavy shell-fire.

Just before the Battery left Vimy Ridge the Germans shelled Acq and the wagon-lines at Frevint Capelle were in imminent danger. The Division left on November 6th, 1916, being relieved by the 1st Canadian Division, and, going first to Mont St. Eloy, was taken thence by motor transport and rail to Marseilles, where they were quartered in St. Valentin Camp till they left for Saloniki on December 6th.

In Macedonia. The 60th Division, with the 303rd Brigade R.F.A., arrived at Saloniki on December 10th, 1916, and they were in Macedonia for six months, about the same length of time as they had spent in France. They immediately trekked to Pataros on the Doiran front—the field of action in which the 7th Wiltshires were already engaged,—where they stayed for about six weeks, passing upon the whole an uneventful time. They had, however, one or two interesting experiences whilst at Pataros. One was on the anniversary of the destruction of the zeppelin at Saloniki ; on this occasion the enemy sent a fleet of twenty-three aeroplanes to bomb Saloniki, and " C " sub-section's gun was for the time being converted into an anti-aircraft gun, being mounted on six-foot French gun wheels. Another time " A " and " B " sub-sections went forward to a little village—Brest—and started firing at dawn with the object of releasing a body of

Ramp on the Canal du Nord (Royaulcourt) constructed by Swindon R.E.'s. A spot where Swindon men were killed

infantry that the Bulgars had surrounded in a neighbouring village,—an object that was successfully attained.

About the end of January, 1917, the 303rd Brigade was moved via Janus to the Vardar front. When they were in the neighbourhood of Janus they received orders to extend and clear away from the road and take cover ; immediately a heavy bombardment broke over them, both artillery and aeroplanes joining in the attack, and the Brigade suffered several casualties. The same night the Battery got into position with six guns at Karasuli.

Engaged at the Cedemli Ravine. An exciting piece of work fell to the lot of " B " Battery about a month after they reached Karasuli. For three nights parties of the Battery were engaged in laying wire to forward observation posts and in forming gun-pits of wire and camouflage ; then they received orders to throw two guns forward to the Cedemli Ravine in order to cut wire on the " Nose," a commanding point on the Bulgar lines. Between 4 and 5 p.m. they cut the wire, firing at about 750 yards (fuse 0), and then they were discovered by Bulgarian aeroplanes, which swept the ravine with machine-gun fire, flying so low that the men in the aeroplanes could easily be seen ; so hot was the fire that the gunners had to take close cover. When the aeroplanes had gone Lieut. Philpott and his men ran the guns along the Cedemli ravine under the observation of the Bulgars, placed them behind an over-hanging rock, and from that vantage-point fired a hundred rounds at the enemy. For this exploit Lieut. Philpott received the M.C., and Sergt. Lawrence, who was attached to " B " Battery, was awarded the Military Medal.

And now the whole battery kept up a continuous bombardment for thirty-six hours. The firing began at dawn and was intended to cover an infantry attack. The attack, however, was not successful, for just as the infantry were going through the gap cut by the guns in the wire the Bulgars played a searchlight upon the gap and of course concentrated their fire upon the spot. The infantry retired and the two forward guns rejoined the rest of the Battery.

Three days later the Battery was shelled at Karasuli with 4.5 centimetre shells ; ammunition pits were blown up, and " A " Battery was quite destroyed with some casualties amongst the men. Two guns, under the charge of Lieut. Roach and Sergt. Tovey, were sent to the rear, and they were shelled for four hours by gas-shells; when the bombardment was over seven feet of gas lay in the ravine where they were stationed. These two guns were to cover the other four in their withdrawal from Karasuli preparatory to their return to Saloniki. The Battery now trekked to Kilindir, where the left section (2 guns) was in action for four hours but came out without having fired a round. During the next three or four days they were trekking back via Sarigol to Saloniki, where they stayed at the Dudular dump, just outside, for about three weeks, re-equipping before leaving for Egypt in June, 1917.

To Palestine. The 60th Division was intended for the Palestinian campaign conducted by General Allenby, and only stayed in Egypt long enough to be re-equipped : the re-equipment was carried out at Ismailia, whither the troops were taken by rail from Alexandria, and then they trekked alongside the Suez canal to El Fardane and Bellah ; from Bellah they entrained to Kantara, staying there a couple of days before completing the rail-journey via El Arish to the rail-head, whence they trekked across to Tel el Farah towards the Beersheba front. Here they were in touch with the Turks, and Major Cooke took forward a party consisting of himself, Lieut. Philpott, Sergt. Tovey, and Sergt. Letch, to reconnoitre the enemy's position on " Hill 70." When the party was

seen by the Turks and came under rifle-fire, Major Cooke put his comrades behind
a hill and went forward alone under fire, completed his reconnaissance and returned
to them in safety.   On its return the party was shelled by " pip-squeaks," but got
back safely after spending twenty-four hours in the saddle, Major Cooke having
settled upon the position for his six guns.

Going forward to Beer el Asani, quite unsuspected by the Turks, the six
guns were there put into action guarding the wells or cisterns, and at night advanced
to Major Cooke's position with horses muzzled and guns muffled, going into it in
battery column at about 11 p.m., without alarming the enemy whose trenches
were only half a mile away ; there were no gun-pits, and the guns were protected by
only a stone empalement in front.   After Major Cooke, with a telephonist and a
small party, had gone forward and dug a hole in the rock for a forward observation
post the Battery waited for the dawn, when they began firing on the Turkish trenches ;
the firing lasted, on and off, for twelve hours, when the Turks gave way and the
British advanced to their objective, " Hill 70 " ; the advance was made under
shell-fire, for the Turkish artillery covered their retreating troops, and on its way
forward the Battery passed Turkish dead and British field ambulances bringing in
wounded Turks in their own captured carts.

Beersheba.   " B " Battery stayed a night and a day at " Hill 70 " and then
advanced towards Beersheba ; they were in action for four hours
just outside the town, and when the British cavalry entered Beersheba
on October 31st, 1917, Turkish aeroplanes bombed the place : the artillery entered
when the aeroplane attack was over, and settled down for three days awaiting
intelligence as to the enemy's position.

The next advance was to Wadi Sharah, and in addition to heavy fighting all
day with the Turkish rear-guard the men had to endure much privation on account
of the difficulty of getting water ; at this time one pint of water per day had to
satisfy a man for all purposes.   At Wadi Sharah the advancing British captured
machine guns, much ammunition, and a large quantity of general supplies, spending
the night there.

A Memorable Engagement.   The following day, November 7th, 1917,—the day of the capture
of Gaza,—was the most memorable that the Battery had yet exper-
ienced.   Their objective was the Tel el Sheriah wells where the Turks,
entrenched in trenches six feet deep, made one of their most obstinate
stands.   The Battery left Wadi Sharah at about 7 a.m., and as they were going on
in column of route about an hour later they received orders to halt and take position
for action.   " B " Battery was now in the open, with a wadi or ravine between two
and three hundred feet deep in front, and the Turkish guns commanded their
position.   One gun was sent forward under Lieut. Philpott to put down machine
guns which commanded the Battery's front ; this was accomplished, and for the
feat Lieut. Philpott was given a bar to his Military Cross.   Meanwhile the Battery's
horses and transport were put forward in the ravine for protection.   " B " Battery's
guns were the first to open fire, and as they did so the Turks retaliated heavily ;
they got a direct hit on the gun-limber of " A " sub-section, wounding Lieut. Hollis
and Gunner Francis (Signaller), but the ammunition was saved from explosion
by the fact that the gunners' kits were piled on it.

The position now was that " B " Battery was in a trap and had to be supported
at all costs ; fresh batteries were rushed forward, coming through the Turks'
barrage at a gallop and losing men all the way.   Altogether, the Battery was
exposed to machine-gun and shell fire for nine hours.

At 11 a.m., a lull in the firing allowed the men to get a little lunch, and the opportunity was taken to send Sergeants Tovey and Tiley down the wadi to see how the wagon-line had fared. They found that the transport had suffered terribly both in men and horses ; three times had the wagon-line been compelled to move under heavy shell-fire, and for his gallantry during these operations Gunner Durnford received the Military Medal on the field. Twenty-three were killed or wounded in the wagon-line and fifty per cent of the horses were knocked out. Amongst the killed were Gunners Loder, Macdonald, Marshall, and Neville, Drivers Hicks and Morton, and Corporal Lepler. The wounded included Sergt. Chaldlecotte, Q.M. Sergt. Jones, Signaller Hancock, Driver Gale and Driver Gibbons who died later. A serious loss also befell the Battery during the action, when Driver Simpkins, of Swindon, and two others were killed ; they had to lay a quarter of a mile of telephone wire, and at the end were just digging their pit when one shell killed all three.

Towards afternoon heavy shelling began again, wrecking the viaduct and the railway-line across the wadi, and several staff-officers were killed at the observation post on a hill adjacent to the Battery's position. Eventually, however, the position was captured and at the station a fine supply of stores was taken—bullocks, fowls, three big barns of grain, and other stuff as well as machine guns. The Battery was ordered to advance about 5 p.m., and proceeded along the wadi up a neighbouring hill where they camped for the night. A very welcome arrival—and a very timely one—was that of Bombardier Baker with a supply of cigarettes ; about a fortnight before he had been sent back to buy supplies of these as the men were very hard up for tobacco, and at the close of this trying day he arrived with the coveted luxury.

The advance continued the next day, November 8th, and after about five miles a small air-craft station was captured with two guns and a hangar but no aeroplanes ; the guns went into action there, and then the advance re-commenced. The British were now going over undulating country, and so the firing took place in spells, as the position afforded sight of the enemy ; thus the Battery moved on, firing section by section, to the village of Hoog,—a place made memorable by the splendid charge of the Middlesex Yeomanry, covered by " B " Battery's guns, when the cavalry captured several guns under point-blank fire ; this charge has been aptly described as " a second Balaclava Charge," and was the subject of much newspaper comment.

The Battery had to pause at Hoog on account of the serious loss of horses through the bad watering conditions ; the officers did all they could, and a party travelled all night to seek water and then had to haul it from a well seventy feet deep with a canvas bucket at the end of a length of telephone wire, giving a bucketful to each horse.

To Jerusalem. From Hoog the direction of movement was changed, for the British force now made a sweep to the westward to Gaza and then back to Tel el Sheriah where the Battery was re-equipped, preparatory to its taking part in the advance on Jerusalem. They trekked via " Junction Station " to a point at the foot of the hills commanding Jerusalem, taking up their position at Costel, where they came under fire, on December 6th. On the morning of the 7th fighting was going on at Nebi Samwel (Samuel's Tomb) and the Battery opened fire on the Turks retreating along the Nablous Road. The next day the position was advanced to Kolonich, and the Brigade Colonel (Col. Bailey, D.S.O.), Major Cooke and Lieut. Philpott, M.C., reconnoitred toward Jerusalem to pick up a position nearer the city. They went, however, right into Jerusalem and were told by the inhabitants that Jerusalem was surrendered ;

**First in
Jerusalem.**

Lieut Philpott, therefore, went back and on the morning of the 9th brought in the left section ; they entered the city and dropped into action, being the first British troops to enter the Holy City ; amongst them were some Swindon lads, and it is perhaps pardonable to emphasize the fact, not generally known, that a battery of the Wilts R.F.A., attached to the 303rd Brigade R.F.A., in the 60th Division, has the honour of being first in Jerusalem. So uncertain was the position at the time that whilst Major Cooke, with Sergt. Lawrence, was in the Post Office taking over all documents, etc., a company of Turkish troops passed the office not knowing of the surrender, and Major Cooke went out and took them prisoners. Three hours later the Infantry came in ; the rest of the Battery came in also, and as they entered the left section advanced further into the town and opened fire on the Turks retreating in disorder down the Nablous Road. Soldiers who were in Jerusalem say it was a piteous sight to see the inhabitants falling on their knees before the British troops, thanking God and their deliverers for release from the Turks, and possibly also full of apprehension as to their immediate future. The Turks had taken what they liked and paid for nothing, but the tradespeople did what they could to indemnify themselves when the excitement was over by making the newcomers pay pretty stiffly for any purchases, apparently regarding the shilling as the smallest British coin.

The left section position was now made the wagon-line and gun-position in one for the whole of " B " Battery, and they were in action all night. After staying in Jerusalem about a week, the Battery moved northwards to Shafat (*Nob* of the Old Testament), remaining there also about a week and then moving to a point near Beit Hanina (*Ananiah*) between Shafat and Nebi Samwel, where they spent Christmas in pouring rain and in the enjoyment of little more than a small ration of " bully beef."

**The Turkish
Counter-
Attack.**

It was clear that the Turks were about to make a strong attempt to re-take Jerusalem, and they brought up two army-corps, including new troops from the Caucasus, threatening Jerusalem from the north and east. The British line lay across the Nablous Road near Tel el Ful (*Gibeah*) and the London Division occupied the portion of the line near Beit Hanina, about a mile west of the road. The enemy began his attack soon after midnight of December 26th, by an assault upon Tel el Ful and at Beit Hanina. The Londoners met repeated attacks with magnificent firmness, not yielding a foot of ground ; two companies defending Beit Hanina itself were attacked four times with stronger forces each time, five hundred picked troops making the last assault, but they beat back every attack. All this time the Battery was heavily engaged in the support of the infantry, being in fact at the focus of the Turkish objective, and " C " Howitzer Battery " wiped out " the enemy machine-guns by direct fire. The Turks made a last big effort about noon, assailing the whole London line except Nebi Samwel ; they came on with desperate courage, but were met with equal bravery and repelled with the bayonet Then by a masterly counterstroke General Allenby drove in the Turkish right, and, having suffered tremendous losses, the Turks fell back along the Nablous Road, the British guns following up and driving in their rearguard.

On the 28th the Londoners attacked Er Ram hill (*Ramah*), capturing prisoners and machine-guns, and engaging the enemy rear-guard, and the next day they occupied Bireh (*Beeroth*), nine miles north of Jerusalem, the Battery entering on the 31st. Throughout these operations, so heavy and exhausting in themselves, the men's hardships had been intensified by the severe cold and by keen winds and heavy rain, and the movements of guns and supplies entailed enormous labour on tracks made slippery with deep mud.

Going to Jericho. From Bireh " B " Battery moved back to Jerusalem for a so-called " rest," and were billetted on the Mount of Olives, but they were in action all the fortnight they were there, firing on the Turks at Talat ed Dumm (" The Good Samaritan's Inn ") on the Jericho Road. Leaving Jerusalem, the Battery participated in the attack on Talat ed Dumm and the advance on Jericho,—captured on February 21st, 1918,—having much stiff work to do on the way ; they spent three weeks on a hill just outside the village, covering the road from Jericho across Jordan whilst the Australian cavalry were clearing the plain. Moving to " Mount 40 " (" the Mount of the Temptation ") the Battery was bombed by Turkish aeroplanes the first day ; thence a movement was made to the east of Jordan, across which, at that time in full flood, the R.E's. threw a pontoon bridge to replace the bridge blown up by the Turks. Pushing on through the ancient province of Perea, the force reached Es Salt (the modern name of *Ramoth Gilead*), but a strong Turkish force advanced against it, and a hasty but orderly retreat was made to the foothills on the east bank of Jordan ; the retreat was made under hard conditions, and the force lost some guns in the course of it. This expedition had lasted about a fortnight, and, re-crossing the Jordan next day, the Battery spent about three weeks more on " Mount 40."

Crossing Jordan.

Now the Battery was ordered back to Bireh, travelling by a forced march of a fortnight via Jerusalem to Bireh and on to Jufna, north of Bethel, where they were severely bombed, and then to Atara (*Ataroth*). They went into action there, C and D guns being mounted as air-guns ; there also they came into contact with some Swindon R.F.A's from India, and stayed at the place for several weeks. Again they are hurried back to the Plain of Jericho, and spend there a couple of months in the middle of the summer (1918) amidst dust up to the ankles and often very short of water.

The Final Blow. But the close of the war in Palestine was nearer than men realized, and General Allenby needed the guns for his mighty blow outside Jaffa which opened the way to the north. By night-marches the Battery hastened across to Sarona (*Sharon*), north of Jaffa, travelling by the main Jerusalem-Ludd road and hiding by day in the German orange-groves. The great advance began at dawn on September 19th, 1918, with a tremendous bombardment of the Turks on the coast-road,—eighteen pounders, four point fives, six-inch, eight-inch, and great naval guns firing almost axle to axle. " B " Battery helped to swell the terrific hurricane, continuing firing till they had discharged three hundred rounds per gun, creeping barrage ; then at about 9 a.m. the advance along the road began, the Indian cavalry passing through the Battery with flags to mark the route ; the Turkish first-line trenches were only three thousand yards in front of the Battery, but by the time the guns reached them the Ghurkhas had made them a road across the battered area ; then on the guns went at a trot as far as a swamp five miles or so ahead, where they captured four 5.9 c.m. guns and stores and stayed for two hours resting and watering the horses.

The direction of " B " Battery's advance was towards Nablous (*Shechem*). At Tel Karam, about fourteen miles from that town, the force of which the Battery formed a part captured ammunition dumps, motor lorries, and vast quantities of supplies, and the Australian Cavalry secured the gold that was on its way to the Turkish troops. Four days later or thereabouts the Battery went into position nine miles from Nablous ; the road as they advanced presented an appallingly ghastly spectacle, strewn thickly with dead horses and the corpses of Turkish soldiers, but those who went further said that the sight was far more horrible five miles further on.   However, the Battery got no further, for that night they heard the Turkish army was beaten.   The cavalry went right away to Damascus which they entered on September 30th, but the work of the Battery was done.

Finis.   Tracking gradually back through Sarona to Ludd, the men entrained to Kantara and then to Alexandria, which they reached about the end of November, waiting there for demobilization.   They were quartered at Sidi Bish camp and spent Christmas there, but their home-coming was deferred by the outbreak of troubles in Egypt.   An insurrection at Damanhour caused the authorities to refit the men as cavalry, and for a month they did patrols of twenty miles by three detachments, night and day, at Damanhour.   When the revolt was quelled they returned to Sidi Bish, and gradually—not as a body—they were demobilised and sent home.

The movements of " B " Battery of the 303rd Brigade, R.F.A.—A Wilts battery that preserved its identity to the end of the war,—have been traced in some detail because they illustrate the career of many drafts sent from the 1 /3 Wessex R.F.A. ; but these became attached to various units in many different areas, and to follow their different careers would be an impossible task unless one were prepared to trace the movements of individual men.   But there is no need to do this, since " B " Battery shows what Wilts gunners could and did accomplish.   The Wilts Battery has occasion to be proud of the efficiency of its gunnery and the spirit of its men.   They " played the game," whether engaged in the tedious years of garrison life in India or in the strenuous life of the battle-field, and they played it well.

End of 3 /1 Res. Batt.   To return to Rollestone Camp.—Soon after the departure of the battery whose work has just been described, the cadre left at Rollestone became known as the " No. 3 Reserve Brigade," and its Sergeant-Instructor of Signals was a Swindonian, Sergt. Hapgood.   The " School " left Rollestone for Bulford in the middle of 1916, and there recruits continued to come in from Swindon, but with a large proportion of men from all parts,—" Derby men."   Drafts were going off regularly to France and several left between June, 1916, and August, 1917, being posted to various units ; amongst the men who thus left Bulford was Reg. Sergt. Maj. Cunnington who brought honour to his battery by gaining the Military Medal in France.   In October, 1917, a draft also left for Mesopotamia.

Shortly afterwards the Reserve Brigade was broken up and the men were dispersed amongst various units overseas and at home.   One officer, Lieut. E. W. Pim, a nephew of Col. Bedford Pim, was wounded in France and came home to England only to die.   Sergt. Maj. G. Jones, who had formed part of the cadre of the 3 /1 Battery ever since its formation three years before, went to France, and after serving at Ypres and then in Italy, was sent as Sergeant Instructor to the 4th Army School of Gunnery at Amiens.

On the last day of 1919 members of the 3rd Wessex Brigade, R.F.A. met for a dinner and concert at the Drill Hall, Prospect Place, with a view towards re-kindling the enthusiasm for the old Battery.   The festival was held—so the notice ran—" under the Distinguished Patronage of the Commanding Officer, Col. Bedford Pim, and Officers " ; but Col. Bedford Pim's colleague who had accompanied him to India, Major the Earl of Suffolk, was no longer living to participate in his Battery's revival.

The Earl of Suffolk. Henry Molyneux Paget Howard, 19th Earl of Suffolk and 12th Earl of Berkshire, had been Aide-de-camp to Lord Curzon throughout his term of Viceroy of India, returning to England in 1904. He took up his residence at his stately seat at Charlton Park and took great interest in the work of the Wilts Battery of the R.F.A. in which he had the rank of Major. As has been seen, he accompanied the 1/1 Battery to India; but in the autumn of 1916 he took the opportunity of engaging in more active service in Mesopotamia. It was during a victorious advance in the third week of April in 1917 that he was killed; a shell burst near him as he was commanding his battery in action; he was struck by a piece of shell and died soon afterwards, being buried on the battlefield.

The Earl was a man of singular charm and had a high sense of public and private duty; in Malmesbury and the neighbourhood his loss was severely felt and sincerely mourned. At the time of his death the Countess and her three young sons were at Simla, waiting the end of the dreadful struggle. Before she left England to join her husband in India she had devoted herself to benevolent work at home, being one of the first in England to offer hospitality to the Belgian refugees, and allowing the beautiful mansion in Charlton Park to be converted into a military hospital.

The Wilts R.F.A. Battery was one of the first in the country to recruit again to its full strength, for by October, 1920, its complement was made up and it was anticipated that a fresh battery would have to be made to embrace the recruits still flowing in. Major J. S. Barkworth was the Commanding Officer of the Battery, and under him the Swindon R.F.A.'s resumed the training that made them one of the most efficient units of Territorial Royal Field Artillery in the world war of 1914-18.

CHAPTER III.

The Swindon Squadron of
The Royal Wiltshire Yeomanry.

The R.W.Y. The Royal Wiltshire Yeomanry is the oldest yeomanry regiment in the British Isles ; to give it its fuller title it is " The Prince of Wales' Own Royal Regiment of Yeomanry," and H.R.H. the Prince of Wales is its Colonel-in-Chief. The regiment was embodied in 1779, as is attested by a copy of an old charter which, hanging in their Headquarters, must have often attracted the gaze of old members of " D " Squadron. " D " Squadron, recruited in Swindon and the district around, was the junior squadron of the four squadrons into which the regiment was divided, and its strength before the war was about 120 men. It is the story of " D " Squadron—the Swindon squadron—that is here outlined, from the time when it was mobilized in August, 1914.

First call On August 6th orders were received that the Yeomanry were to be
to Service. sent to Cheltenham forthwith on special duty ; just before 9 p.m., ten blasts on the Great Western Company's "hooter" gave the men the signal to turn out, and very soon about a hundred yeomen were assembled at the Vale of the White Horse repository in High Street. The squadron was under the command of Major R. A. Poore, D.S.O., a distinguished officer who came of a gallant fighting stock, and who had served in the Royal Wilts Yeomanry for over twenty years and had fought throughout the South African War, in which he won his D.S.O. With Major Poore were Capt. Palmer, second in command of the Squadron, Lieutenants Buxton, Henderson and Ward, and at 11 p.m. the squadron left the Midland and South Western Station by special train amidst the cheers of an enthusiastic crowd that had gathered to see them off. The squadron returned to Swindon the next day, having been engaged in guarding the viaducts, bridges and signalboxes between Swindon and Cheltenham.

D Squadron For reasons of organization it was decided to split up " D " Squadron
Dispersed, amongst the other three squadrons of the regiment ; the 1st Troop therefore, joined " B " squadron at Devizes, the 2nd and 3rd Troops, with the Gun Section under Capt. R. Awdry, went to " A " squadron at Warminster, and the 4th troop joined " C " squadron at Chippenham ; Major Poore went to Headquarters at Chippenham to take charge of recruiting.

and The regiment met and formed at Winchester towards the end of
Re-united. August, being billetted in the College, and remained there about a fortnight, engaged in drill and in guard-duty at the station and the tunnel. From Winchester the Yeomanry trekked to Crawley, Sussex, staying there three days, and thence to Worth Park, Three Bridges, where they camped in the park. The men now underwent medical inspection and were inoculated, and volunteers for active service were called for ; " D " squadron volunteered almost solidly,—all, in fact, but eleven men, of whom seven were medically unfit for active service. And now, to the men's great delight, Major Poore re-joined them and was received with acclamation, and " D " squadron, who had been very sore on

account of their dispersal, was re-formed, " C " squadron being split up instead.

Training. The regiment remained at Worth Park till near the end of September, when a move was made to Tyes Cross, near East Grinstead. Drafts from Chippenham brought the regiment up to fighting strength, and the men went into strict training, being a regiment of the 1st South Western Mounted Brigade, consisting of the Royal Wilts Yeomanry, the North Somersets, the Hants Carbiniers, the Hants Royal Horse Artillery, with the Wilts Field Ambulance and Wilts Army Service Corps.

In December the men moved out of tents into huts at Forest Row—a spot that calls up memories of appalling mud and deadly monotony in the minds of many Swindonians, R.A.M.C. men and others. At Forest Row **Swimming Horses.** training went on until June, 1915, and the men were keenly interested in a new feature of their work,—training the horses in swimming the river. At first the horses were taken across on a continuous line of rope, and whilst some men were attending to the horses others made a raft out of a general service wagon to convey the equipment and men across. Afterwards the rope was dispensed with, swimmers rode the horses into the water and then slid off their backs and swam the animals across, the equipment and the rest of the men going over by the raft. In this work " D " squadron broke the record for the Brigade for they completed the crossing of the River Ouse in 42 minutes ; this included galloping up, off-saddling, crossing with machine-guns and full marching equipment, and remounting,—a remarkable achievement when it is considered that there were about 150 men, 170 horses and 2 machine-guns with ammunition-packs.

When the time came for the Yeomanry to leave Forest Row for Willingdon Camp, near Eastbourne, they left the happiest memories behind them, and a gratifying tribute to their conduct was paid them by the Vicar in a paragraph in the Parish Magazine.

Ordered out. From Willingdon Camp the men were moved to Lewes in September, 1915, where they met with a very hearty welcome, and there the order for active service, impatiently awaited by most, was received.

" D " Squadron was to have the honour of being " first out," and was immediately despatched to Winchester for equipment ; they were attached as Divisional Cavalry to the 38th Division, and when Queen Mary inspected the division " D " squadron had the post of honour and led the division round the parade-ground.

On December 3rd, " D " squadron, with the regimental Headquarters, embarked at Southampton, the squadron being under the command of Major A. Palmer, and the whole under Lieut. Col. Ulric Thynne, D.S.O. On the morning of the 5th the men disembarked at Havre, went by train to St. Omer, and then trekked all night through rain and snow to the Headquarter billets of the regiment at Enghuingatte, near Therouanne in the Hazebrouck district.

In the Trenches. Now began trench-instruction in real war conditions, and the troops went out one at a time ; number 4 troop—Mr. Locker-Lampson's— went out first, having a week's training in the front line at Laventie with the Coldstream Guards ; they were relieved by number 3 troop, Mr. Ward's, who went in with the Grenadier Guards. The division now changed its area and the squadron went to St. Venant, from where the 2nd troop, Mr. Davy's, went into the front line with the Welsh Guards at Laventie. The 3rd troop was now sent as the escort for the General of the First Army at Aire, relieving a troop of the 11th Hussars, the rest of the squadron being meanwhile at St. Venant, where many of the men were engaged on detail duty, such as despatch riding, road reconnaissance, and revising the road-map. or acting as traffic orderlies. Here Christmas was spent, the 4th troop now being in the line under Mr. Locker-Lampson.

And now a move was made to Paradis, and the remaining troop, the 1st, under Mr. Simmonds, had its turn at trench instruction with the Royal Welsh Fusiliers, of the 38th Division, at Lacoutre in the Armentières sector. The gun-section had a strenuous time, for it was in the line all the time, the two guns relieving each other alternately. Working parties were also drawn from each troop in turn and were instructed in patrol work, wiring, trenching, and general trench discipline, and the same work was continued when the squadron moved to Hinges, near Bethune,

First Casualty. about the end of February, 1916. It was at this time that the squadron suffered its first casualty, Trooper S. Perrett being wounded.

The British army was now preparing for the great Somme offensive in the summer of 1916, and in March the squadron moved to Boulogne for cavalry training with the Fourth Cavalry Brigade in anticipation of being needed in the coming offensive. The training only lasted a fortnight, and then the squadron

On the Somme. returned to the forward area and was sent almost immediately up to the Somme, to form there a corps cavalry regiment of the 4th Army Corps, the regiment comprising " D " squadron of the Royal Wilts Yeomanry, and two squadrons of the South Irish Horse, and being under the command of Lieut. Col. Ulric Thynne. This was about April, and the Headquarters of the regiment was fixed at Heilly, where a great deal of work was done, consisting of regular training for the offensive, duty with working-parties, and police duty in the forward area ; then on the eve of the great attack the Yeomanry moved up to the front and prepared for action, being stationed on the Morlancourt-Menalt road.

As is well known, the Somme offensive, launched on July 1st, failed to realize the hopes based upon it ; the cavalry stood by, ready to follow through and play its part, but had no chance to do the work it was intended to do. The Yeomanry was largely occupied in observation work in the front line—very risky work, in

Death of Lieut. Simmonds. which " D " squadron suffered a great loss in the death of Lieut. Simmonds, commanding the 1st Troop ; this gallant officer. keenly devoted to his duty and beloved by his men, received his mortal wound here and died in England about two months later ; another casualty occurred at the same time, and Trooper Griffin, who was with Mr. Simmonds, was awarded the Military Medal for conspicuous daring in the performance of observation work.

The R.W.Y. A Corps Cavalry Regiment. The squadron continued to be engaged thus until November, 1916, and was then sent to a rest area near Abbeville, where the Irish squadrons left the regiment and were replaced by squadrons " A " and " B," thus making the regiment a coherent unit—the corps cavalry regiment of Royal Wilts Yeomanry. After spending a week here the regiment went to Sailly-le-sec where the British had taken over part of the French line, being occupied there for a couple of months on police and traffic work.

Death of Major Palmer. It was about this time that " D " squadron suffered another heavy loss by the death of Major A. Palmer, who had been with them all along, and now was taken ill and died in Amiens hospital after an operation for appendicitis ; Capt. Henderson, recalling this loss at a re-union of the squadron after the war, said, "We all knew Major Palmer well and we all loved him.   To me, his death was the greatest blow I received while out in France,"—a tribute confirmed by Major Horace Mann in the words, "Major Palmer was one of the best fellows in the world, always cheery, always bright, and the regiment lost a tremendous asset by his death." Major Palmer's place was now taken by Capt. Horace Mann.

Mention might be made at this point of a member of the squadron who subsequently brought honour to his regiment and himself.   Corporal Wiseman was sent home as a casualty from the Somme, and was subsequently drafted out to the Gloucester Hussars in Egypt ; in the campaign in Palestine his gallantry secured official recognition and he was decorated with the D.C.M.

Peronne.   In February, 1917, the Germans had evacuated the Ancre sector, retiring beyond Peronne, and the Yeomanry was given the order to get into touch with the enemy and to reconnoitre,—that is, they were to fight an advance guard action.   They trekked to Moislains—which now became
Fighting   the regimental Headquarters—through the devastated area, early
at Nurlu.   in March, and sent out troops to patrol and get into touch with the Germans ; this was effected very speedily near Nurlu, a large force of Uhlans, motor machine-guns and cyclists being encountered.   For a fortnight this advance guard action continued, the Royal Wilts Yeomanry now definitely fighting independently ; in a cavalry encounter they forced the enemy to evacuate Nurlu in the most trying weather conditions ; in an exposed country, utterly devoid of cover or billets of any kind, the troops endured the utmost rigours of the winter, facing rain, snow, and a murderous blizzard ; the only sleeping shelter they had consisted of bivouacs made from waterproof sheets ; they had to be up at 3 a.m. to secure their horses, to set off in the dark, and were sometimes twenty miles ahead of the infantry, not turning in again till after dusk.   During this time the horses suffered terribly, for there was no shelter for them, and in spite of the devoted attention a cavalryman always gives to his horse numbers died of exhaustion and exposure.

Tincourt   After Nurlu, the Yeomanry captured Aizecourt-le-bas on the right
Wood.   of Nurlu, and then Tincourt Wood ; the Wood was held by machine-gunners, who allowed the Yeomanry to get into close range before firing, and it was here that Trooper McNally was killed.

A Cavalry   Acting in conjunction with the 8th Division, the Yeomanry now
Charge.   moved on Heudecourt, capturing the village and the wood.   This action afforded some thrilling moments, and was the occasion of the Yeomanry's first charge, made through a barrage of enemy artillery fire over flat country devoid of cover.   Three machine-guns were reported in the wood, and "D" squadron was given the honour of shifting them with the sword ; the Yeomanry held at the time a low hill facing about three-quarters of a mile of flat ground that would have to be covered ; the Germans trained their guns upon the brow of the hill behind which the squadron was forming, in anticipation of an infantry charge, so that when the squadron went over the horses met a hail of bullets about their legs.   Capt. Henderson led the charge, but so withering was the machine gun fire—and it was soon apparent that there were more than three guns at work,—that the squadron had to withdraw after covering about a quarter of a mile.   Eventually the place was taken under cover of British machine-guns, the men advancing on foot.

**Major H.
Mann
Wounded.**
During the course of this action Major Horace Mann was severely wounded in the back by shrapnel; he was carried back safely by some of his men and eventually sent to England, his place being taken by Capt. Henderson. The squadron lost four or five killed in the action and many more were wounded, whilst the horses suffered heavily.

Honours.
The regiment was awarded several decorations for its gallant part in this engagement, including, for "D" squadron, the Military Cross for Lieut. Gunning, who was in charge of the 1st Troop, and the Military Medal for Corp. Oscar Pakeman and Corp. Avenell.

Patrol Duty.
Heudecourt was the last action in which the Yeomanry was engaged in the German retreat of March, 1917. The regiment remained at Moislains, and "D" squadron went into the line a troop at a time to do dismounted patrol work. On one of these occasions two battle patrols went out to stir up the enemy in Honnecourt Wood; the patrol on the left of the wood was to draw the enemy's fire, whilst the other was to creep in under cover of darkness during the diversion. But the Germans turned out to be in very strong force, and the patrol on the left had a very hot reception and was forced to withdraw; the other patrol covered their withdrawal, driving the Germans back and bringing back the killed and wounded; in this affair Sergt. Joyce displayed great gallantry and was awarded the Military Medal.

**Not a
"Soft Job."**
This patrol work was dangerous and trying for the nerves; one gallant fellow was killed whilst doing his duty as point on an officers' patrol—a patrol that brought back most important information; he was seen to fall, but although diligent search was made for him afterwards, when the enemy had been driven back, they were never able to find any trace of him. It was probably about this time—the retreat of the Germans from Peronne,—that the Yeomanry did its most useful work, and no small part of its success was due to the splendid esprit de corps that permeated all ranks, and the invariable support which the officers received from the non-commissioned officers and men. As will be seen shortly, the Yeomanry were subsequently turned into infantry and so were in a position to compare the life of a cavalryman with that of a foot-soldier; no one will minimise the hardships of the infantryman's service, accompanied as it was during this war with unparalleled horrors; but there has been a disposition in some quarters to regard the cavalryman's duty as a "soft job." Few infantrymen had a worse job than the men of the Wiltshire Yeomanry who went out as patrols in order to draw the enemy's fire. Moreover, when some of their men were in trenches those who remained behind had the horses to look after, and one man with four or five horses on his hands is pretty fully occupied; even when the men were "resting," the horses were a continual source of work, and there was none of that entire leisure which the infantry enjoyed in their rest camps.

Dismounted.
When the Yeomanry left Moislains they trekked to Dunkirk, the corps of which they formed a part taking over a part of the Belgian and French front; there they were engaged on police patrol work until in July 1917, to their deep disgust, the order came that they should be dismounted. Forthwith they marched to Boulogne, delivered their horses at the depôt, and returned to Dunkirk for a week, when they were sent to the 3rd Infantry Brigade Depôt at Rouen; after ten days of infantry training the whole regiment was drafted to Kemmel, in September, 1917, and there embodied in the 6th Wilts, sufficient men of the 6th being sent to the 1st and 2nd Wilts to make room for the Yeomanry.

About this time the sad news was received that "D" squadron's
Death of   former chief, Major Roger Alvin Poore, D.S.O., was killed whilst
Major Poore. in command of his battalion of the Royal Welsh Fusiliers on Sept.
26th. He had not been associated with the Yeomanry in France,
but his twenty-four years' service with the regiment had endeared him to his men,
and they were looking forward to a renewal of the association after the war. The
Colonel of his regiment, writing to Mrs. Poore, said, " Your husband's command
behaved most gallantly in the action and has covered itself with glory . . . . He
helped and supported me most loyally ; indeed, I do not know how I shall get on
without his wise advice. He was one of the most gallant gentlemen I have ever met."

Properly speaking, the story of the Wilts Yeomanry during the war ends at this
point, but a brief sketch of their subseqent service is needed to round off the story.

The 6th Wilts formed part of the 19th Division and the men soon
With the   found themselves in the line in the Ypres sector, remaining there
6th Wilts. till November, when they moved out on divisional rest at Lynde,
near St. Omer ; they had suffered severe casualties and even their
rest was not allowed to pass unbroken ; news came that the Germans had broken
through at Gouzeaucourt in the Cambrai sector, and the regiment proceeded by a
forced march lasting three days to Ribecourt in the front line. They had twelve
days in the line, coming out on December 23rd to Havrincourt Wood, where they
spent Christmas Eve and had the pleasure of sharing in the parcels sent from
Devizes and the puddings provided by Miss Manners' Fund. The regiment went
into action on Christmas Day at Welsh Ridge, facing Cambrai, their transport lines
being in Havrincourt Wood, and this time they were in the line twenty-three days
without a break until they were moved to Haplincourt on rest.

It was pretty well known that March, 1918, would see a tremendous
Annihilated German offensive, and in anticipation of this the 6th Wilts Regiment
at Morchies. was engaged in rehearsing for the occasion. As expected, the Germans
began their attack about 4 a.m. on March 21st ; the regiment got
into battle order and went up to the attack about 4 p.m. at Morchies. They took
their objective, suffering very severely, and held on for two days ; but they were
surrounded and hopelessly situated : permission to break through was therefore
given to those who could get back, but only about thirty succeeded in reaching the
British lines, which had now fallen back some distance. The 6th
Deaths of   Wilts was practically annihilated, a large number being sent prisoners
Major S. C. to Germany. Major C. S. Awdry, the second in command, an old
Awdry   Yeomanry Officer, was missing, and no news has every been heard
and Col. A. of him since. Colonel Lord Alex. Thynne was wounded at Morchies,
Thynne.   and although he rejoined later he was soon afterwards killed.

The few survivors of the Yeomanry had not done with fighting,
The   and they were present as part of a composite battalion in an action
Survivors. on Wytschaete Ridge in April, helping to stem a fresh German
offensive. They were finally drafted into the 2nd Wilts, and when the
Armistice was signed only about half a dozen of the Yeomanry were still actively
serving. Fortunately the men captured at Morchies had not long to wait for release,
but in that time Sergt. H. Godwin died in hospital at Hamburg in September.

Capt. Henderson, speaking at the re-union already referred to, said
Losses.   he had the names of some 23 or 24 officers and men of the squadron
who fell in the service of their country, and there were others the
addresses of whose next-of-kin he had been unable to ascertain.

The Re-union. This re-union took the form of a dinner given by the officers to the men of " D " squadron at the King's Arms Hotel, Swindon, on June 25th, 1919.   The tables were laid for 87 guests and were adorned with beautiful flowers sent by Mrs. Palmer in memory of her gallant son, Major Palmer.   Major Horace Mann, M.C., presided, and was supported by Capt. the Hon. H. Henderson, Major G. Buxton, Capt. J. Duck, Capt. H. Davey, Capt. H. Ward, Capt. Fletcher, M.C., Lieutenants H. Gregson, Du Fosse, E. G. Flower, Gunning, M.C., A. Twine, and J. Anthony, and the Chaplain, the Rev. W. L. Waugh. It was a most delightful and enthusiastic company that shared the hospitality of the hosts, and amongst the guests were youths who were already crippled veterans, returned prisoners from Germany, and men who had been drafted home from the Yeomanry and had completed their service in other regiments.   Even then a number were still serving and the Chairman alluded with esteem to Squad. Sergt. Major Northover, who had accepted a commission and was with the Army on the Rhine ; the face of Swindon's Champion boxer, Lieut. H. Freeth, was also missed, he, too, being with the Army of Occupation.

Recon-stitution. One of the objects of the gathering was to take steps for re-constituting the regiment, of which Major H. Mann had been temporarily appointed Commanding Officer, though he hinted that the post would be taken by Capt. Henderson, a piece of information received by the men with hearty applause.

During the war the Yeomanry, and in particular " D " Squadron—the Swindon squadron,—received little notice in the journals, but enough has been said to show that they performed a great deal of absolutely necessary work, which entailed great risk to all concerned, and that they worthily upheld the traditions and honour of the premier Yeomanry regiment of the British Isles.

CHAPTER IV.

The Swindon R.A.M.C.

The 1/1 Coy   Prior to August, 1914, there was one unit of 114 men of the Royal
S.W.M.B.F.A.   Army Medical Corps (Territorial Forces) in Swindon. It was subse-
                 quently known as the " 1st line of the 1st unit of the Wilts R.A.M.C.
(Territorial)," or, more accurately as the " 1/1 South Western Mounted Brigade
Field Ambulance,"—in brief " the 1/1 S.W.M.B.F.A." As this was succeeded by
a 2nd line unit, and that in turn by a 3rd line unit of the same denomination, they
will in the following sketch be merely indicated by the abbreviations 1/1, 2/1, and
3/1 —technical terms that clearly show that the units are successive companies
of the same primary unit.

The local chief of the Swindon R.A.M.C. was Major R. Swinhoe, whose warm
interest in the Company and whose excellent tuition had rendered it an exceptionally
efficient unit of the Territorial Ambulance service. As is well understood, a good
chief who lacks a good Sergeant Major is like a man who has lost his right hand, and
Major Swinhoe and the Company were equally fortunate in having a fine officer
in Sergt. Maj. Banks, who, after supervising the formation of the 2/1's, was succeeded
at Swindon by an experienced first class Warrant Officer—Sergt. Maj. W. Whittington, who formed an admirable trainer of the young and raw recruits who were to
form the 2nd and 3rd companies.

At the time when war was declared the 1/1 unit was in camp on Salisbury
Plain at Fargo, engaged in the annual general summer manœuvres of the Territorials,
and about a half of their fortnight had been thus spent. They were immediately
marched to Pewsey and thence to their depôt at Swindon to await sealed orders
that should dissipate the swarm of rumours that kept the men in a state of continual
excitement. They were not allowed to remain long in their homes, but were
ordered off almost at once to Winchester, leaving Sergt. Maj. Whittington and a
small staff at the Drill Hall in charge of the Depôt. Major Swinhoe, too, was detained
in Swindon by his important local duties and the necessity of setting about the
formation of the 2/1 unit immediately.

After a short stay at Winchester the men were moved to Forest Row
Forest Row. in Sussex, where they settled down for the winter of 1914-15, being
            all the time under the command of Lieut. Col. Haydon, of Marlborough.
Here their time was spent in general field-ambulance work, comprising the working
of an actual field hospital attached to the brigade stationed there ; the daily routine
comprised physical exercises, lectures on field-ambulance work, general nursing,
disease, and sanitation, and practice in their ambulance duties. Still, as the weeks
wore on, the men were insufferably bored by the monotony of the camp, the unspeakable mud out of which the huts rose like islands, and the lack of sufficient
recreation. Twice did a party of these Swindon lads send home for a parcel of French
grammars and texts, anticipating that they would soon find themselves across the
Channel ; and after splashing through the mud to the marquee for a dose of sanitation from the " Green Book" they would flounder back to " stew " a bit of French
in a corner of their hut. Classes were formed for the study of French and were

conducted in the Ladies' Golf House by ladies of the neighbourhood, one of whom was Miss Eardley Wilmot, the composer of the charming song, "The little grey home in the west." It was only because of their high spirits and pluck that the lads were not quite "disgruntled" by the long and exceptionally wet winter of 1914-15.

The 2/1 and 3/1 Coys. Meanwhile, in Swindon, Major Swinhoe was forming the 2/1 unit, begun in September, 1914. It was filled up almost at once and spent a short time in training at Swindon, during which period it sent about four batches of about a score of men each to Forest Row, the 1/1 unit sending at the same time similar batches to the 2nd General Hospital at Brighton on short courses of instruction in which some of the 2/1 men participated. After its brief training in Swindon the 2/1 company was despatched to Bowood, which Lord Lansdowne had opened to the military. Major Swinhoe, Sgt. Maj. Whittington, Lieut. Mason, and Sgt. Tomkinson were left in Swindon for the purpose of forming another company—the 3/1 company,—which was formed in May and joined the 2/1's at Bowood early in June.

Bowood. At Bowood the 2/1 company spent the whole Summer of 1915, being as fortunate in their summer quarters as the 1/1's were unfortunate in their winter quarters. Some, of course, found the delightful spot monotonous since the only town accessible to them was the pleasant little borough of Calne, but most of the men will look back to that summer as the happiest episode in their military career. They had plenty of training and instruction to undergo, for they did not begin, as the 1/1 unit did, with a considerable store of experience ; and they served a Field Camp Hospital for a considerable body of troops in that area, Major Swinhoe being the senior surgeon and medical officer.

2/1's at Maresfield. At the close of the Summer the men returned to Swindon, and for a short time they were billetted in their homes, awaiting further orders. Then the 2nd company was moved to Tiptree and thence to Maresfield in Essex. Major Swinhoe, Sergt. Maj. Whittington, and one or two others remained in Swindon with the 3rd line unit, and Major (afterwards Lieut. Col.) C. W. Edwards was transferred to the command of the 2/1 unit ; with him were Capt. P. W. Mason, Capt. Keir, and Capt. Jollands as transport officer. In Sergt. Maj. W. Tomkinson the company had an ideal officer, who won the confidence and esteem of officers and men alike ; he proved himself a most capable soldier and his consideration and care for the men have left a deep impression upon their memories. Thus the 2/1's settled down at Maresfield for several months' training of the same character as the 1/1's underwent at Forest Row.

3/1's at Swindon. The 3/1 unit remained in Swindon, and as there were still a few vacancies the formation was completed early in November ; about three weeks later it was inspected at the Drill Hall by Brig. Gen. Lumley, who said that for newly-recruited men they were as smart a set as he had ever inspected,—an encomium that justly gave such gratification to their commanding officer that he forthwith gave them a holiday. Towards the end of November, when the unit was barely six months old, an order came for a draft of sixteen men to go to Egypt to join a R.A.M.C. (Terr.) field-ambulance ; the draft left at once, via Southampton, and thus it fell out that the first draft for foreign service came from the latest formation, and consisted of raw recruits, whilst highly-trained men

Royal Wilts Yeomanry (Swindon Squadron) in huts at Forest Row.

Royal Wilts Yeomanry (Swindon Squadron) in Camp.

were pining for change from the endless repetition of well-known duties at their camps. The places of these men were filled by fresh recruits, chiefly clerks from the Great Western Railway Works, and the unit remained in Swindon for five months, till the Spring of 1916, the men being billetted in their homes.

3/1's to Winchester. At the end of this period the 3/1 unit was ordered to Winchester. Major Swinhoe was, most unfortunately for the unit, prevented at the last moment from accompanying it by ill-health and the pressure of his many important duties. The situation was indeed disappointing in the extreme ; Major Swinhoe retired from the command and the men went off to Winchester without an officer, Sergt. Maj. Whittington alone being responsible for seeing them safely there. As the men marched to the Great Western Station the Major received the salute from his doorstep in Sheppard Street, and the men keenly realized their forlorn condition in thus parting from their chief at the moment when they most needed him. At the station the unit joined a Bath unit, the 3/2 S.W.M.B.F.A. (Terr.), under Major Norman Barnett, of Bath, and henceforth until their dispersal the two units were associated under his command. One can imagine that it was with no pleasant feelings that the Swindon men found themselves under strange officers, their identity being almost obliterated by their association with the Bath unit under its own officers.

At Flowerdown Camp, three miles outside Winchester, the 3/1 men remained from April to October, 1916. Some of them had a welcome change at harvest time, for the War Office, in response to the farmers' complaints of lack of labour, released for a few weeks men who had some knowledge of farm-work, and about thirty of the Swindon lads thus got several weeks' leave, going to farms at Gloucester, Tewkesbury, Cheltenham and elsewhere. During their farm service the men received 2/6 per day from the farmers, who also provided board and lodging ; their personal army pay ceased for the time being, though separation and other allowances for dependents of course went on as usual.

Movements of the 1/1 Unit. In July, 1915, the 1/1's left Forest Row to go under canvas at Willingdon Camp, Eastbourne, moving in October into empty houses at Ocklynge, Eastbourne. There was a reception hospital where the men were regularly engaged, and orderlies were also sent daily to assist at the " V.A.D." hospitals at Urmston and Kempston ; moreover, the evacuation of wounded demanded frequent service at Eastbourne station.

A fresh move was made in February, 1916, to Mistley, Essex, where the men went into billets until May when they went under canvas in Mistley Park. Whilst here, they were engaged at the reception hospital at Manningtree, and the designation of the unit was changed to " The 7th Cyclist (1/1 S.W.Mtd.) Bde. F. Amb."

The next movement was made in August, 1916, to Bromeswell Heath Camp, Woodbridge, and the unit's designation was again altered to " The 3rd Cyclist (1/1 S.W.Mtd.) Bde., F. Amb." The stay here was marked by a serious outbreak of cerebro-spinal meningitis (or "spotted fever ") in the Brigade, and numerous cases were admitted to the reception hospital, being subsequently evacuated to the Isolation Hospital at Ipswich, where about half-a-dozen of the Wilts Company were put on duty. Corp. Manderson, of Marlborough, one of these, contracted the disease through contact with cases and died at the Isolation Hospital.

The last change before its dispersal was to Grundisburgh, Suffolk, where the unit went into billets in October, 1916. About this time Col. Haydon was promoted
M

to Brevet Colonel and was honourably mentioned in home despatches for good service at home.

These changes of scene and experience had made the 1/1's a thoroughly competent R.A.M.C. company, and had not been devoid of interest. Whilst they were at Forest Row and Eastbourne they had fairly well covered the pleasant county of Sussex in the course of their frequent practices and manoeuvres. In Essex and Suffolk they found a different field ; they had their first sight of a zeppelin the very night they arrived at Mistley and soon had regular experience of raids by the German " taubes " ; whilst the terrible batches of wounded in the hospitals showed them some of the horrors of the war.

End of the 3/1's and 1/1s. By a General Army Order issued in October, 1916, all third line units of the R.A.M.C. were abolished ; the 3/1 unit was therefore split into two, half going to the 1/1 and half to the 2/1 unit. By this time the 1/1 company was at Woodbridge, in Suffolk, and the 2/1 company, having spent a short time at Wingham Wells in Kent, was now 'at Bossington Rectory, Adisham,—a spot about eight miles from Canterbury.

Whilst the 1/1 company was at Woodbridge and Grundisburgh it gave valuable assistance to the East Suffolk Hospital, at which convoys of wounded were received weekly or oftener from Flanders and France, and their aid was particularly needed at the time of the great Somme battle in July, 1916. During the time the 1/1's were at Woodbridge one of the chief R.A.M.C. centres—that at Ripon—was moved to Blackpool, which became the great centre for R.A.M.C. training prior to despatch overseas. Here, in January, 1917, the bulk of the 1/1 unit was transferred ; a few days after Christmas they had been inspected by Brig. Gen. the Earl of Shaftesbury at Grundisburgh, when he told the men that the time had come when every " A.1." man was urgently needed in the field, and he was only too sorry that on account of ill-health he was unable to accompany them. A draft just short of a hundred was immediately sent to Blackpool, leaving Colonel Haydon with Sergt. Maj. Bones (who had succeeded Sergt. Maj. Banks upon his transfer) to form the new 327th Home Service Field Ambulance. This, therefore, was the end of the 1/1 South Western Mounted Brigade Field Ambulance.

Blackpool. At Blackpool the men found thousands of R.A.M.C. men from all parts of the country, and drafts were sent overseas almost daily.

Thus the 1/1 unit now loses its identity ; they are not sent away as a unit, but old friendships are broken up as the men are gradually dispersed in small groups or as individuals, going to replenish field-ambulances in France, Mesopotamia, Russia, Macedonia, and India ; one Swindon man went to Sierra Leone, and another was with General Allenby at Jerusalem. It was a disappointing ending to a long course of training as a unit, but the men had by this time learned that army life was a continuous course of surprises and disappointments, and there was nothing for it but to take each day as it came.

Just before the half of the 3/1 unit joined the 2/1's at Adisham, a draft of about twenty had left the 2/1 unit ; quitting Adisham in October, 1916, they went to Tweezledown Camp, where they found a similar draft of twenty men who had just arrived from the 1/1 unit, and eventually the members of both drafts were despatched to Saloniki and Mesopotamia. The rest stayed at the Rectory till November, and then all—that is the 2/1's and the 3/1's who had joined them,—moved to Ipswich, being billetted in the town till about February, 1917. Whilst they were at Ipswich all the nursing orderlies were picked out and divided equally between the East Suffolk General Hospital at Ipswich and the Ranleigh Road Military Hospital at Ipswich. The former was a gigantic general hospital to which many annexes had been added to provide accommodation for wounded, and the latter was a brand-new Council School converted into a hospital to receive the overflow from Colchester Military Hospital.

End of the 2/1 unit. In February, 1917, the majority of the Swindon men were passed on from Ipswich to Blackpool, where the same fate befell them as befell their brethren of the 1/1 unit.

Thus, before the war was over, three Companies of R.A.M.C. men, each about 120 strong, had been raised in Swindon, had been trained, and for the most part had been sent overseas. Not all of these survived to return home, for when demobilization freed the men and allowed a review to be taken· it was found that several had lost their lives in their Country's service and in the performance of that beneficent work that the R.A.M.C. carries out on the battle field, often for friend and foe alike. These heroes of the Red Cross were:

Heroes of The Red Cross. Ptes. Beales, Bangs, Blackwell, Bown, Crocker, Lambert, Manning, Rixon, Vokins;

Ptes. Gleed and Greer who died in hospital in France;

Ptes. Morris and Schofield who died in hospital at Aberdeen.

Honours for Swindonians. The Swindon Royal Army Medical Unit has been honoured in certain of its members:—

Mr. E. Harris, a teacher under the Swindon Education Committee, gained the Military Medal at Courcelles, in August, 1918, and a bar to his M.M. at Cambrai, in September, 1918;

Mr. Fred G. Paul (106th F.A. Corps), was awarded the M.M. in December, 1917, for "gallantry and devotion to duty in action"; and

Mr. R. Green received the D.C.M. and Croix de Guerre for gallant and courageous work at Ypres, Messines, Bailleul, etc.

Although not a member of the Swindon Company, Mr. P. F. Arnold should be mentioned here. He was the first Swindon man to be mentioned in despatches; in June, 1915, he was mentioned by Sir John French for gallantry in rescuing wounded; he had been present at Mons, the Aisne, Hill 60, etc. Mr. Arnold was the son of the manager of Swindon Sewage Farm.

CHAPTER V.

The Wiltshires in India and Palestine.
The 4th Wilts.

The "Terriers." Of all the battalions of the Wiltshire Regiment, Swindon was most closely associated with the 4th, for it was the battalion that included the Swindon " Terriers." When the old volunteer system disappeared in 1908, being replaced by the Territorial system, amongst the territorial forces then formed was a new battalion designated the Duke of Edinburgh's Wiltshire Regiment of Territorials,—the 4th Wilts. It consisted of many units scattered over the County, and the " H " Company was the Swindon company. At the opening of the war 152 Swindonians were included in the Battalion.

First War Service. At the outbreak of hostilities the Battalion was in camp at Sling Plantation, Bulford Camp, undergoing its annual training. It at once received orders for Plymouth, and the Battalion marched from Bulford to Salisbury, where the men lay out on Cathedral Green and were most hospitably received by the citizens ; at 11 p.m. the men entrained for Plymouth, arriving early the next day, and relieved the Gordon Highlanders in the forts, being split up here and there amongst the forts. Here they remained until the evening of Sunday, August 9th, when they returned to Durrington Camp on Salisbury Plain and it was whilst stationed here that the Battalion volunteered for foreign service,—meaning, of course, service in France; they were, however, ordered to India on garrison duty, and were thus the means of relieving regular troops for active service.

In sketching the career of the Battalion it will be necessary to allude to two distinct units or battalions, the first being designated the First-Fourth (1/4) Wilts Regiment, consisting of the original Territorials, and the second being designated the Second-Fourth (2/4) Wilts, consisting of the second-line unit that was recruited as the reserve battalion directly the 1/4 battalion left. There was also, later on, a 3/4 Wilts Battalion that remained at home as the reserve battalion, but this will not need further notice.

The 1/4 Wilts set sail. The 1/4 Wiltshire Regiment embarked at Southampton on board the " Kenilworth Castle " on October 9th, 1914, and sailed the same evening. The Earl of Radnor was the Colonel in command, and with him were Major A. Armstrong, second in command, Major H. Willis, Capt. Bond (Adjutant), Lieut. A. A. Taylor (Quartermaster) ; the Company Commanders were :—

" A " Coy. Major Bennett.
" B " Coy. Capt. the Hon. Geo. Herbert.
" C " Coy. Capt. McKay.
" D " Coy. Capt. Phillips.

" E " Coy. Major Randell.
" F " Coy. Capt. Vicary.
" G " Coy. Capt. J. Phelps.
" H " Coy. Capt. D. C. A. Morrison.

The Medical Officer was Capt. Waylen, and other officers were the brothers Lieut. J. G. Arkell and Lieut. T. N. Arkell, Lieuts. Merewether, Pye Smith, Knight, Angus, Lockhart, Viscount Folkestone (Lord Radnor's son), Holman, Elliot, Brown, Redman, Hiles, Morris, Hodding, and Carson.

Along with the Wilts were details of the R.F.A. and the 7th Hampshires ; the convoy was a large one, and amongst the troops were Devons and Somersets, and the 3rd Wessex Brigade Reserve Battery, R.F.A., consisting of Wilts, Hants and Dorset batteries. The vessel called at Malta and coaled at Port Said, spending four days at Suez, and then crossed the Indian Ocean amidst a good deal of suppressed excitement, as it was known that the notorious German cruiser, the "Emden," was operating in those waters. The convoy arrived safely at Bombay,

Arrival in India. however, and the Wiltshiremen disembarked on November 12th, being the first Territorial forces that India had ever seen ; the first to set foot on shore were the Dorsets, who claimed the honour by right of their proud motto, "Primus in Indis"—"First in India,"—adopted on account of the fact that Dorsets were the first English Troops ever engaged in service in India.

Delhi. The 1/4 Wilts at once entrained for Delhi, where two companies, the "G" Company and the "H" or Swindon Company, were detailed to go direct to garrison duty in the Fort of Delhi. This was a most important commission, as the Fort is the refuge for the whole European population of Delhi in the case of a native rising, and the Swindon lads were very proud of the honour and responsibility laid upon them. Capt. D. C. A. Morrison was appointed Fort Commandant, and the Garrison consisted of one Master Gunner and one section of Garrison Artillery, one section of Machine Gunners, 200 Infantry, and 300 Transport mules and bullocks with their drivers. The Infantry were all trained in big gun drill so that they might assist the Artillery if occasion should arise. The life of the men in the Fort was somewhat restricted compared with that of men in camp, for not more than 25% of the Garrison was allowed out of the Fort at any time ; this was considered a great hardship, as the men were on guard twice and sometimes thrice a week, and they had therefore very little time for sight-seeing.

An interesting Commemoration. At Delhi the Wiltshiremen had the gratifying experience of participating in an annual festivity that had peculiar significance for them, although, speaking exactly, it is the 1st Wilts. whom the festival concerns. On December 21st and 22nd, 1845, the Wiltshire Regiment had played a gallant part in the battle of Ferozeshah. In that year the Sikhs of the Punjab made an attack upon the British territory east of the Sutlej, and upon the date mentioned Sir Hugh Gough attacked the Sikh fortified camp at Ferozeshah,—a position bristling with cannon, crowded with defenders, and protected in front with brushwood and water-courses. The Wiltshire Regiment attacked across the difficult ground in face of a terrible fire, losing no less than 7 officers and 281 n.c.o.s and men killed or wounded, but they were led to victory by the n.c.o.s. The Commander-in-Chief in his despatch said the Regiment had "done all which the most heroic gallantry and the most determined resolution could have achieved." This victory is celebrated every year by the 1st Wilts Regiment wherever they are stationed, and on this occasion the 1/4th, stationed in the historic land where their forefathers won the victory, celebrated it by a splendid ball in the skating-rink at Delhi. At the dance the band was conducted by Band Sergeant A. E. S. Fluck, of Swindon, and Sergeant T. P. Burns, also of Swindon, acted as Master of the Ceremonies. The men were provided with an excellent

Christmas dinner, the sergeants acting as waiters, and a jovial entertainment followed the dinner.

Life in Delhi. Until they left India, Delhi was the headquarters of the 1/4th, and their life was comparatively hum-drum; the battalion was comfortable in its fine camp at Kingsway, outside Delhi, and most of the men will regard their stay in India as a pleasant episode in their lives; on the whole they were left pretty much to themselves as regards the provision of entertainment, but some of the ladies of Delhi were most kind in offering hospitality, and many of the men brought away delightful memories of the reception accorded them in some homes; one youth, with happy simplicity, remarked, " You don't know what a lovely creature an English woman is till you see her in India." Nor were the men forgotten by friends at home; in May, 1915, the Mayor of Swindon received letters of thanks for tobacco and other small luxuries sent to the men, and giving a good account of their health; several received Christmas parcels provided by the funds raised by Miss Manners at the Empire Theatre, and Messrs. Ansties, of Devizes, kindly sent packets of tobacco.

In the heat of summer the troops were of course removed to some hill-station as far as possible. In 1915 the station was Kailana, about two miles from Chakrata, to which half the battalion, along with any sick, were despatched. The rest stayed behind at the Secretariat at Delhi, for it is worthy of note that for three seasons the 1/4 Wilts acted as the Vice-regal Guard, an honour usually enjoyed by Regulars for two seasons only. This Summer—in May, 1915,—the first draft **The First Draft.** to Mesopotamia was sent from the Battalion, being attached there to the 2nd Dorsets; it was followed by two or three later drafts and their story becomes merged in that of the units to which they went.

Sport. At Kailana the old Wiltshire enthusiasm for sport was well in evidence, and the men were delighted by the result of the Competition for the Kailana Association Football Cup. The regimental team was composed of about six Swindonians, and the other players hailed from Melksham, Marlborough and Bradford. The team went through the tournament without once meeting defeat, and carried off the Cup with a score of three wins and five drawn games out of the eight matches. The keen interest of the men and their exultation over their success are testified by many references to their triumph in their letters home.

The Battalion re-occupied its quarters at Kingsway about September and spent the winter there, and many Swindon homes bear witness to the intelligent interest of their lads in the marvels of the strange land to which they had been led, and photographs of the tower at Tuklakabad (the Kutab Mina), the Elephant **A Visitor from home.** Gate, or of the marvellous tracery of the mosques have become familiar household ornaments. Early in 1916 Professor G. H. Leonard, of Bristol University and an old friend of the Swindon Workers' Education Association, paid the Wiltshiremen a visit at Delhi; he wrote home in high terms of the Y.M.C.A. tent at the camp which he described as really " a home from home." Professor Leonard found the men delighted to chat about Wiltshire, and keenly interested in Mr. Reuben George's articles in the " Advertiser " and in Mr. Alfred Williams' " Life in a Railway Factory," of which one of the men showed him a copy.

January 1st was a day of mark, for that is " Proclamation Day," commemorating the realization of D'Israeli's design to have his Royal Mistress proclaimed " Empress of India." On that day in 1916 the troops were all paraded outside the fort for inspection by the Viceroy, Lord Hardinge; and later on, when his term of

An Honour. office expired, and he was succeeded as Viceroy by Lord Chelmsford in March, 1916, the Wiltshires lined the streets of Delhi as a guard of honour for Lord Hardinge upon his departure from the capital of the Moguls.

It was shortly after this that Capt. Morrison was invalided home, having been Station Staff Officer at Delhi Fort for about twelve months.

The summer of 1916 was spent by the whole Battalion at Chaubattia, near Raniket, within sight of the Himalayas and amidst glorious surroundings. They returned to Delhi when the cooler weather of Autumn set in, being sent to Tuk-lakabad where the old fortresses of Delhi stood, and famous for its remarkable tower as well as for its tall iron pillar of very ancient date ; there, along with the Somerset Light Infantry, Gurkhas, and Nepalese, they underwent brigade training.

On the 30th of January, 1917, a ceremony took place in the grounds of the Vice-regal Lodge, Delhi, described by the "Pioneer" as being both "picturesque and memorable." It was the presentation by the Viceroy of decorations and medals gained during the war by Indian officers, non-commissioned officers and men. Guards of Honour were furnished by the Wiltshires and Garhwal Rifles, a hundred men from each battalion, the combined guards being commanded by Capt. J. W. Phelps, of Swindon. His Excellency, attended by the Commander-in-Chief and Headquarters Staff, inspected the Guard of Honour, commenting on the smartness of the men and their fine physique, afterwards proceeding to present the decorations, whilst the recipients received hearty applause as they stepped forward during the recital of their gallant deeds.

Poona. The last few months of the 1/4 Wiltshires' service in India were spent at Poona. In March, 1917, they arrived at Poona just in time to see their comrades of the 2/4 Wilts depart for Allahabad ; after being encamped for a month on Poona race-course they spent five months at Kirkee, near Poona, then entrained to Bombay and put to sea on September 15th, 1917. They were no longer on garrison duty ; they were on " active service."

Prior to this, Lord Radnor, who had been made Brigadier General, had returned to England. Major Willis, Capt. Phelps, and Capt. Vicary were now transferred to the 2/4 Wilts.

On Active Service. Their destination was Egypt, and they were to form part of General Allenby's forces in Palestine. Their base was Kantara, on the Suez Canal by Lake Ballah, where they spent about a fortnight in order to complete their equipment ; thence they went by rail to Bela, on the coast some miles from Gaza, and marched into their reserve position before

Gaza. Gaza. The men now began to experience the real hardships of active service, and they found the march to Gaza very trying, especially on account of the difficulty of obtaining a sufficiency of water. The battalion was under the command of Col. A. Armstrong, who had succeeded the Earl of Radnor, and Major Bennett, transferred from the 2/4 Wilts at Poona, had replaced Col. Armstrong as major ; the Swindon company was under Capt. T. N. Arkell.

First Losses. The Wiltshires at once began to participate in the actual fighting, and one of the first to fall was a Swindon lad, Pte. J. H. Woodham, and the letter sent by Capt. T. N. Arkell to the stricken parents illustrates very sympathetically the way in which so many of our sons perished in distant lands ; the Captain says,—

" It is with the deepest regret that I sit down to write and tell you about the death of your son, Private J. H. Woodham, who was killed this morning. A raid on the Turks had just taken place (which was a great success), and they in return started to shell our trenches heavily at about 4 a.m. Your son was in a trench with three other men carrying out his duty by standing-to with his rifle-grenades, when an unlucky shell landed in the middle of the trench and exploded. All four were wounded, your son so severely that he died shortly afterwards. It seems an act of Providence that all four were not killed. One of the wounded was Private R. M. Wills, who also comes from Swindon. Please accept my sincerest sympathy in your loss, which is also the Company's, where he was very popular.

The letter of Col. Armstrong, who was himself shortly to lay down his life for his country, breathes the paternal spirit that marks the highest type of British Officers and exhibits a depth of feeling that could only be found in a truly noble nature :—

" I can't speak too highly of your son, or all the lads, for that matter. They are to me as my own children, so I can feel most deeply for you. Your son never regained consciousness after he was hit, and died a few minutes after. He was buried with his comrade, Pte. Goodall, who was killed at the same time, and a cross marks the spot. Like so many gallant sons of England he leaves his body in a foreign land. He died giving his life for his country ; he could not have done more."

These are only specimens of multitudes of letters that every post was bringing to English homes, and the little grave marked by a wooden cross in front of Gaza has myriads of counterparts in many lands.

It will be remembered that Gaza was taken by the British on Nov. **Advance on** 7th, 1917, and that ten days later they were in Jaffa. Then came **Jerusalem.** the advance on Jerusalem ; the 1/4 Wilts took part in this advance, fighting its way through the Judæan Hills, They spent the night of November 20th in a monastery and were heavily shelled by " Johnny Turk " the next morning at about 5.30, suffering nineteen casualties, amongst whom was Viscount Folkestone, wounded in the ankle. The same day, November 21st, the men sighted Jerusalem at about 9 a.m., and marched all day without further fighting. The next morning they went into action again ; Col. Armstrong was in command of the Brigade and the Battalion was taken into action by Capt. T. N. Arkell with only three other officers to command companies. It **A " D.C.M."** was here that Pte. Gosling, of Swindon, was awarded the " D.C.M." for gallantry whilst engaged as a runner ; the Battalion suffered a number of casualties that day but these included no Swindon men. The Wilts were now only about 5 miles from Jerusalem, but during the night **Nebi** they changed their position and next morning were in sight of Nebi **Samwel.** Samwel, i.e., Samuel's Tomb, which the Turks continued to shell heavily all day, damaging the monument to some extent. The Battalion suffered some losses that day, including Pte. Carpenter of Swindon.

Thus the Wiltshires did not actually enter the Holy City, their line of advance taking them to the left of it ; but they were accorded the honours of the capture of Jerusalem along with the troops privileged to make the actual entry. It was in the course of this forward movement that Capt. Merewether, of Salisbury, was killed, with several others amongst whom was Sergt. J. Cowley, of Swindon. Capt. T. N. Arkell, too, was wounded some ten days after the fighting at Nebi Samwel ; that was on December 1st, during desultory firing by the Turks upon a hill-position occupied by Capt. Arkell and a small outpost.

On the approach of the wet season the Battalion was relieved and **Winter** brought back to Ludd—the Lydda spoken of in Acts ix.—and spent **Duties ;** the rainy season at El Tireh, close by. Here they were by no means **Ludd.** idle, for they were busily occupied in collecting the enormous stores of ammunition abandoned by the Turks in their retreat. For instance, in January, 1918, they collected and sent down the line as salvage the following enormous quantity :—

Small arms ammunition	77,740 cartridges
Machine-gun ammunition (in belts)	96,600 ,,
	174,340
Bombs (various)	2,070

Other large quantities were collected at various times, but the foregoing statement will sufficiently illustrate the importance of the work.

Repulse at Rafat. The attack on the Turks was renewed in the Spring of 1918, and the Wiltshires lost many men in an abortive attempt to advance at Rafat, somewhere about thirty miles east by north of Jaffa and north-east of El Tireh; amongst the slain was Sergt. W. R. H. Wilson, of Swindon, killed on April 10th. After this stroke of ill-fortune the men were stationed in the Wadi Belat and moved about in the many wadis that intersect the old land of Ephraim from east to west, until they were brought into the line again at Berukin, in the vicinity of "Tin Hat Hill" and "Toogood Hill"; they stayed six weeks in the front line and had a very quiet time, returning to Ludd after a brief rest in order to practise for what was to be their last "stunt."

The Advance Renewed. The fresh British advance in Palestine began on September 19th, 1918; the Wilts left their station by night, reaching a secret position at Muelevis about midnight, where the troops were concealed in the orange-groves which abound in that part of the fertile Vale of Sharon; there they remained in hiding all the next day, and after dark they took up their positions ready to attack at dawn. Their position lay about ten miles or so north-east of Jaffa, between the two great historic roads,—the one the ancient coast-road from Egypt to Phoenicia and Syria, and the other, branching from the coast-road at Ashdod, being the old caravan-route from Egypt to Damascus. The way was barred by three lines of trenches, but these were commanded by British heavy artillery and the fire of the monitors off the shore; the bombardment was so effective that the infantry suffered less than they had expected, and in about three hours the Wilts had captured the trenches and had advanced five miles to Miskeh and to Et Tireh, a mile beyond; their victory was, however, clouded by the loss of many gallant comrades, including their leader, Col. A. Armstrong, D.S.O., and Lieut. Dodrell. One man writes,

Death of Colonel Armstrong.

"You will have heard long before now that we have lost our Colonel. He will be missed very much by the regiment, especially those who served in India with him. One of our men told me this morning all about the "stunt."

Our Colonel, as I expected, was in the very front line leading his men in the attack. They had just gained their first objective when he was struck by a bullet which passed through his left shoulder and body, and came out of his right side. He died three hours later. It is very sad, especially in view of the fact that with the taking of this objective and a small objective our work was finished.

The officer who carried on when the Colonel was hit (A/Capt. Knight) was also killed. Our men took the village headed by the Brigadier General. I am told our Colonel had a presentiment that he was not coming through this "stunt" alive. He told them before the action that the flag with our badge on it (which he held) was to fly from the top of the highest building in the village at a certain time, but he should not put it there, but the one who carried on in his place would see to it. The flag was flying before the time stated . . . . . .It was a great day, but the loss of our brave Colonel cast a gloom over the battalion."

Another   It was during these later operations that Sergt. Batchelor won the
" D.C.M."   D.C.M. He trained in the Swindon Company for two years before
the war, and his and Pte. Gosling's D.C.M's were a source of great
pride to " H " Company.

This was the last taste of actual fighting for the Wiltshires ; another regiment
had struck across from the coast, thus cutting off the Turks, and the way was open
for the cavalry who began their famous march to Damascus, reached on September
30th, and Aleppo, which was taken on October 26th. The Wilts were engaged in
raking-in prisoners, escorting them to the rear, and in road-making. They got
as far north as Haifa, at the foot of Mt. Carmel, stayed there a few
Back to   days, and then were taken back to Ludd, which they left towards the
the Base.   end of November; to return to their base at Kantara, Turkey having
been granted an armistice on October 30th,

This brief survey cannot give even a faint idea of what hardships the men
endured in this land that was once described as " flowing with milk and honey."
The extremes of heat, thirst, and verminous plagues on the one hand, and cold,
deluges and mud on the other, tried the men to the uttermost, and one wonders that
so many came back alive, even though it was with shattered nerves and damaged
constitutions. And yet these men retained at all times a kindly thought for " the
folks at home "; nothing brought home to the writer more vividly the great-hearted-
ness of these noble fellows than the sight of two large collections of plants of India
and Palestine collected and mounted in exercise books for his little daughter by a
gallant Swindon soldier. He, modestly content to praise alike his officers and his
men, will hardly pardon this trifling allusion, but the " H " company would never
pardon the omission of the name of their Sergeant Major, for Instructor Sergt.
Maj. Thorne, an experienced soldier, proved a father to many a Swindon lad as
well as a staunch support to his officers.

In the course of its service the 1/4 Battalion lost by death 201 men, besides
several officers ; the number may seem small beside the terrible figures for the 1st
and 2nd battalions, but in ordinary circumstances it would be deemed a serious
loss, and the actual deaths bear but a small proportion to the total number of
casualties.

The 2/4   On the departure of the 1/4 Wilts Battalion for India measures were
Wilts.   at once taken to form the 4th Reserve Battalion, known henceforth
as the " 2/4 Wiltshire Battalion." It was formed on September
26th, 1914, under the command of Lieut. Col. F. G. Parsons, D.S.O., late of the
Queen's West Surrey Regiment. It very soon went into training at Trowbridge,
its Headquarters, and speedily reached a strength of 1,200 men. The men always
spoke most cordially of the people of Trowbridge for the kind way in which they
entertained the men during their stay there.

The 2/4 Battalion, like the 1/4 Wilts, volunteered for foreign service, and
it should be emphasised that both the original 1/4 and 2/4 Wilts sent abroad were
wholly composed of men who volunteered, and both battalions contained a large
number of Swindon men. The destination of the battalion was India, but prior to
that it had been chosen for France with the rest of the Wessex Brigade ; billets
at Guildford had already been selected and some of the men had already communi-
cated with their appointed hosts there ; but India was being bled of her soldiery,
and it was necessary to send troops there to replace the regulars, who were doubtless

amongst the finest types of modern soldiers. For that reason, and because the 2/4 Battalion was but half trained, it was sent to India.

Besides Lieut-Col. F. G. Parsons (Commanding), there were with the Battalion Major H. Herries-Crosbie (2nd in Command), Major F. W. Giddings, Capt. G. R. Blake (Adjutant), Capt. F. J. Sparks, Capt. E. C. Pinckney, Capt. A. S. Hoare, Capt. C. W. Maggs, Capt. G. E. Anstie, Capt. J. Callaway, Lieuts. N. J. Awdry and A. V. H. Beaven, etc.

Embarked for India. On December 12th, 1914, the Battalion left Trowbridge for Southampton, and the same day went on board the hired transport "Saturnia"—a vessel of the Donaldson Line that had been engaged in the Canadian trade. The vessel departed in the evening—a dull, cloudy, and somewhat cold evening—on its three weeks' voyage, with something like 2,000 men packed aboard; everyone was in the highest spirits and the men crowded the sides as the vessel passed in semi-darkness down the Solent, to see the hospital ships with their glaring lights and brilliantly illuminated Red Cross, and to wish a silent good-bye to the shores of "Old Blighty" fading in the gloom. There was a strong "Channel swell" running, and by morning all but the best of sailors were sea-sick; it was not till the convoy of which the "Saturnia" was a member had got across the Bay of Biscay that the men found their "sea-legs."

A Collision at "Gib." Things went smoothly, with the ordinary troopship routine of rations, scrubbing decks, guards, physical exercises, etc., until Gibraltar Rock was sighted, and then, just as day was breaking, a small Spanish three-masted schooner ran into the "Saturnia" and almost completely wrecked herself; she was under full sail with apparently no one on watch, and she struck the troopship at an angle of about 45°, the shock shaking out her masts and splintering her bowsprit. The "Saturnia" put out a boat, and the men cut away the wreckage whilst the transport stood to windward to break the heavy seas; a cruiser was hailed from Gibraltar, and very soon a French boat was towing the wreck into port.

Xmas at Pt. Said. By this time the rest of the convoy was about an hour down over the horizon, and the "Saturnia" had to go on alone. She kept well to the North African Coast, having a fine view of Algiers by night, and arrived at Port Said soon after day-light on Christmas Day. The vessel coaled on Boxing Day, and the experience was one of which the men talked for long afterwards; the vessel was permeated with coal-dust, the men were as black as the natives, and they found traces of coal dust amongst their belongings months afterwards in India; the dust lay "inches thick" on decks and mess-tables and the men devoured a considerable quantity with their food, but they were full of the gaiety of youth and took a keen interest in the endless chant of the natives at their work, in the divers who fetched up coins from the sea-bottom, and in the hawkers of fruit who swarmed around.

Arrival. Dropping her pilot at Suez, the "Saturnia" had an uneventful voyage down the Red Sea and across the Indian Ocean to Bombay, arriving on January 8th, 1915, almost as soon as the rest of the convoy. On the same boat were some Wilts R.F.A's., Dorsets, Devons, and Somersets, and in spite of the discomforts of a troopship the whole party landed in good health and spirits after a really good voyage made in quite creditable time.

Poona. On disembarking, the Battalion boarded a train that was waiting at the dock, and travelled by night across the Western Ghats to Poona. Here they settled down to hard training—musketry, signalling, drill, route-marching, etc.,—and they supplied all the guards for the great arsenal at Kirkee, close by. On March 1st a party of twenty left for Peshawar where for three weeks they were attached to the 1st Royal Sussex Regiment, and underwent a course of " Interior Economy " (barrack life and duties) for three weeks ; on their way up they had the delightful experience of being put up for the night by their comrades of the 1/4 Wilts in Delhi Fort. Shortly after the return of this party

First draft the Battalion was temporarily split in two, the right half going to
for "Mespot." Mhow (13½mls. from Indore) and the left half remaining at Poona. About this time volunteers were invited for the first draft for active service ; nearly every man was anxious to go, but the number was limited to 40 n'c.o's. and men and three signallers, the sections of the Battalion at Mhow and Poona supplying half the number each. The draft was put under Lieut. G. L. Heawood, quite one of the most popular of the officers, and so young that when he first volunteered for the draft he was refused. The draft was destined for the Indian Expeditionary Force (D) in Mesopotamia, and sailed on board the transport " Varsova " for the Persian Gulf on August 16th, 1915 ; the signallers went to the 41st Wireless Signal Company (afterwards called the 2nd Wireless Signal Squadron) and the rest of the draft joined the 1st Oxford and Bucks Light Infantry, reaching the regiment early in September on the Tigris. This draft thus formed part of the 6th Division under General Nixon. Successive drafts followed as time went on, but as they were attached to various other regiments upon arrival, they ceased to claim attention as the 2/4 Wilts, although in time nearly all the original 2/4's found themselves in Mesopotamia. What the men went through in that terrible country can be gathered from the meagre summary given under the heading of the

Its Fate. Fifth Wiltshires, though it is to be remembered that many of the Fourth were there before the Fifth arrived. As regards this first draft, they had their first fight at Kut-el-Amara on September 28th, suffering two casualties,—slight wounds. The draft was very badly hit at Ctesiphon on November 22nd, 1915, where 10 were killed and 16 wounded, and later losses soon almost wiped it out ; there were Swindon men in the draft and some of these were amongst the last to get out of Kut before its investment by the Turks when the gallant General Townshend sought to hold out till reinforcements could reach him.

Shortly after the first draft left for the Persian Gulf the two halves of the Battalion were re-united at Poona. About this time Capt. E. C. Pinckney wrote

A letter from Kirkee to the Mayor of Swindon on behalf of the Swindon men
to Swindon. there, saying, " It was most awfully good of your Committee to send such a handsome present of tobacco and cigarettes. It was thoroughly appreciated, and it is a great joy to those out here to be remembered by those at home. Your kind present was divided as fairly as possible among the Swindon men, and a little remaining over went as an additional present to the men of the draft going out to the (Persian) Gulf. The men wish me to thank you and your Committee most heartily for your kindness, and I should like to add my gratitude as well. The men are very well, only one being in hospital at present, and he is not a Swindon man. This speaks well for the lads, as Swindon and Poona are decidedly different."

A Change After spending two years at Poona and Kirkee the Battalion had
of Station. a change of stations, moving to Allahabad in the April of 1917. Although the men knew they were going to a much hotter station, most were pleased with the prospect of a change, for the guard duty at Kirkee had become very monotonous ; at one period over a hundred men had to

be found daily to guard the ammunition factory, arsenal, and other important points ; this meant that the men were often able to have only two nights a week in bed—sometimes only one,—whereas each man was supposed to have three nights in bed between his guards. At Allahabad the Battalion relieved the Manchester Garrison Battalion, and one company, under the command of Capt. J. W. Phelps, went straight to Benares ; it is usual for the garrison at Allahabad to find a company for duty at Benares—about ninety miles from Allahabad and one of the most interesting cities in India,—the company being changed every three months.

Drafts. Thus the 2/4 Wilts Battalion was now definitely one of those charged with maintaining the interior security of India, and was located in the centre of a very seditious area ; this meant that all hope of being sent on active service as a battalion was gone. A great many of the original battalion, however, saw service, as drafts were being sent regularly to Mesopotamia and Afghanistan ; six drafts of about thirty men each were sent off rather quickly when the Machine Gun Corps was in process of formation ; it should be remembered that all these men were volunteers, not one having to be detailed for service, and the strength of the Battalion was kept up by new drafts from England.

Heat and Riots. Allahabad is one of the hottest stations in India during the summer, but 1917 was not an excessively bad season, the highest temperature being 115° in the shade ; but during May and June in 1918 the shade temperature went up to 124°, and the men were severely tried ; during those two months the Battalion lost five or six men as a result of heat,— nearly as many as the total lost during the previous three years. It is the usual practice during the hot season to give all, as far as possible, a change to a hill-station. This was effected in 1917 by sending the Wiltshires to Jalapahar, near Darjeeling ; they went in three parties of about two hundred each, the first going in April for two months and being relieved by the second party at the end of June ; the third party went up in August, but was unfortunate in having to return in October on account of what is known in the Battalion as the " Arrah riots." Arrah is about a hundred and fifty miles from Allahabad, and towards the end of the summer quarrels between the Hindus and Mahommedans led to serious rioting ; about the last week in September the Wilts Battalion was sent for, and every man that could be spared from Allahabad was sent to Arrah ; the contingent sent numbered about two hundred, under the command of Capt. Hoare, and reached the scene of the disturbances about midnight ; they patrolled the city with fixed bayonets, and the display of force had an immediate and salutary effect for all was now quiet for a couple of days ; then news came that the trouble had broken out afresh at Dehri and Sassaram, about sixty miles away, and the greater part of the Wilts contingent was despatched to those places. Dehri was found to be in a state of great disorder and looting was going on in the central bazaar. No shots were fired, but many arrests were made and it was not till after about ten days' hard work and the arrival of a party of the 7th Hussars that a normal state of affairs was re-established. The Wilts detachment remained in the district for about six weeks, under the command of Capt. Phelps during the last three weeks, Capt. Hoare having fallen sick; but as no further outbreaks occurred it returned to Allahabad in November. There also some trouble had been experienced and the troops remaining at head-quarters had been kept busy for several days, earning the praise of the Brigadier General for the tact they had displayed in handling the situation.

The Hills.
The usual routine life was carried on again till April, 1918, when half the Battalion was sent again to the hills at Jalapahar. The spot is situated in the Himalayas and is overlooked by the vast mass of Kinchinjunga,—the second highest peak in the world,—and the first journey up to Darjeeling on the mountain railway is an experience never to be forgotten. Darjeeling itself is the Queen of Indian holiday resorts and people who have travelled say that it is not only the most beautiful place in India but one of the loveliest in the world. It was only two miles from this delightful spot that the Wiltshiremen were encamped, and the change from the stifling barracks at Allahabad must have been unspeakably welcome.

In February, 1918, Capt. Phelps went to Burmah as Cable Censor, being stationed at the wireless station at Victoria Point on the Siamese frontier; Major Willis went to Secunderabad in charge of a Training depôt.

The Armistice.
Field training always takes place during the winter months, and on November 1st, 1918, half the Battalion started on a five days' march to Barkacha Camp, about fifty miles from Allahabad.

Hard field training was begun, but on the 12th of November news of the armistice was received. The camp was not much of a place for the celebration of the glad news, but the most was made of the occasion by lighting a huge bonfire and holding a concert. The field-training was completed, and naturally the men were eagerly looking for orders for England, overlooking the length of time required and the difficulties to be overcome before their places could be taken by troops from home. Moreover, frontier troubles broke out in north-west India, serious riots took place in Amritzar and the neighbourhood, and all movements of troops were suspended. Thus the 2/4 Wiltshire Battalion was practically " standing to " all the summer of 1919 at Allahabad ready to move at a moment's notice if needed. The end came, however, at last, and after spending a week in Deolali concentration camp the Battalion embarked for England on the 11th of October, one half coming straight to Plymouth and the other coming via Marseilles and Boulogne.

Home.

CHAPTER VI

The Wiltshires in France—The 1st, 2nd, and 6th Wilts.

The Wilts Regiment. The history of the Wilts Regt., were it fully written, would form a stirring record bristling with famous names—Quebec, Saratoga, Sicily, Ferozeshah, Sebastopol, Taku Forts, Etchowe,—and the Regiment has always, since its formation, been one to whose lot a large share of the hard grind of soldiery has fallen. Its history in the late war has been in accord with its tradition; few regiments have suffered heavier losses, have gone through severer strain, or have won greater glory. The story is far too long and complex to be told here, where nothing but the barest outline can be given, and that but very imperfectly; but many Swindon men were in the various battalions, and some record of where they went and what they endured ought to be given.

Battalions. Before the war was over there were in existence eight Battalions of the Wilts Regt., and, briefly summarised, their fields of operation were as follows:

(a) Battalions 1 and 2 were in Flanders and France right through the war;

(b) Battalion 3 was the reserve battalion for these, remaining at home and constantly sending forth a stream of drafts;

(c) Battalion 4 was the Territorial Battalion, consisting of the two battalions known as the 1/4 and the 2/4 Wilts, both engaged at first on garrison duty in India; the 1/4 Wilts eventually fought in Palestine, whilst nearly all the original 2/4 Wilts found its way in drafts to Mesopotamia;

(d) Battalion 5 fought through the Dardanelles campaign and then in Mesopotamia;

(e) Battalion 6 reached France early in the war and remained there till the end;

(f) Battalion 7 served in Macedonia and then was transferred to France;

(g) Battalion 8 remained at home as a reserve battalion eventually being merged in the 3rd.

Thus, nearly every important area of the fighting had some part of the Wilts Regiment engaged in it.

Position in Aug., 1914. At the declaration of war the 1st Batt. was lying near Portsmouth, the 2nd was engaged on garrison duty at Gibraltar, and the 3rd or Reserve Battalion was at Devizes, but was destined soon to be established at Weymouth. The 4th or Territorial Battalion, was in camp undergoing summer training; but it has received separate treatment as being more intimately connected with Swindon. [1]

Despatch of the 1st Wilts. The 1st Wilts Battalion, commanded by Lieut. Col. Hasted, was very early on the continental field of operations. Sailing from Southampton it landed at Le Havre on August 18th, as part of the First Expeditionary Force, which consisted of the 1st, 2nd, 3rd and 4th Divisions; the 1st Wilts was in the 3rd Division, forming part of the 7th Brigade. It was soon involved in the most critical operations then going on, for, after disembarking, the men entrained for the Belgian frontier and were soon

[1] **Pages 276—286.**

face to face with the Germans. The Germans were bent on annihilating Lord French's "contemptible little army," and the 1st Wilts was one **Mons.** of the regiments of the line that suffered most. On reaching their destination on Sunday morning, August 23rd, at Ciply within sight of Mons, they began trench-digging and after about an hour were surprised by German shell-fire; all Sunday night they "sat tight," but the fire was so hot that at 8.30 a.m. they had ,to retire, and thus began the terrible fortnight of fighting and marching that could have been endured only by the finest troops in the world. All the world held its breath during this fortnight when each day's newspaper showed the battle-line drawing nearer and nearer to Paris, and it was with heart-felt relief that men saw the foe pulled up sharply at the River Marne on September 5th; then began the Battle of the Marne and the recoil of the Allies **The Battles** which carried them to the River Aisne by the 15th. At Aizy, on **of the Rivers.** September 13th, advancing in the face of withering rifle and artillery fire, the Battalion captured an important position by assault in the most gallant manner. During these historic weeks the 1st Wilts, like the rest of the British line, was doggedly retiring and then advancing, suffering the greatest hardships of warfare, and gallantly fighting against tremendous odds. A soldier of the 2nd Dragoon Guards gives us a glimpse of them at the Aisne :

"On our left at the Battle of the Aisne were the Wiltshires, located in trenches just outside a wood. The Germans came through the wood in mass, and when at the edge charged the Wiltshires with bugles blowing and yelling like demons. We watched breathlessly, but the boys knew what was doing. At about seventy-five yards range an officer sprang from the trench and yelled 'Fire !' Then the Germans got a taste of Hell in the form of 15 rounds a minute. They wavered like drunken men. The Wiltshires then sprang from their trenches and charged with the bayonet. It was awful suspense while they rushed, and then came the impact. It was a horrible din, but at the finish what remained of the Germans fled back through the wood, and as dusk settled down all that could be heard were the groans of the wounded."

It is a ghastly glimpse of what was going on all through these weeks,—one of many incidents that it would be impossible to record, and that were taking a heavy toll of precious lives. Lieut. Col. Hasted was wounded early in the battle of the Aisne and was succeeded in the command by Major Roach.

It was about this time that an incident occurred which was repeated **"Ve are** in other forms more than once during the War. A German corps **de Vilts."** attempted to surprise an English battalion, and sent forward the front files dressed in uniforms taken from the killed and wounded of the Wilts Regiment. The English commander was suspicious and gave orders to fix bayonets, but the Germans called out, "Nein, nein ! Leedle mistake ! Ve are de Vilts." The dialect was hardly suggestive of the Downs, and the English officer gave the order to charge.

After the Battle of the Aisne the German pressure began to be **To Ypres.** very dangerous in Belgium, and it became necessary to extend the line the whole of the way to the coast ; to do this and join hands with the retreating Belgians and the inflowing stream of reinforcements, it was decided to transfer a part of the British army from the Aisne region to the Ypres district. There were many difficulties and dangers in this strategic operation, but it was carried out almost without a hitch, and amongst the troops moved was the 1st Wiltshire Battalion, soon to be joined by their brethren of the 2nd Battalion.

The 1/4 Wilts in India. Guard of Honour Inspection.

The 1/4 Wilts in India. Guard of Honour Marching off to Post.

Arrival of the 2nd Wilts. The 2nd Wiltshires, having been brought from Gibraltar, left Southampton in the first week of October about 1,300 strong, and landed at Zeebrugge. They formed part of the 21st Brigade in the 7th Division (consisting of the 20th, 21st, and 22nd Brigades) under General Capper. Two brigades were sent to Ghent and one to Bruges to hold the Ghent-Ostend line and cover the retirement of the Belgian army from Antwerp, which was captured by the Germans with their big guns on October 9th. The 2nd Wiltshires were with the Bruges section and then fell back on Ostend harassed by German aeroplanes. The retirement to Roulers now commenced, and the town was reached by the Wiltshires by train from Ostend; the two brigades from Ghent arrived in a terrible condition owing to their forced march. At Roulers they captured some German prisoners. The Division now retired to Ypres, one brigade doing the journey by train, and the remainder going on foot with the Wiltshires forming the rear-guard; on the march they had little fighting, although they were forced to deploy on several occasion..

Sanctuary Wood. The 2nd Wilts now took up an entrenched position in Sanctuary Wood about five miles from Ypres; this was on October 18th, and for six days the Division, numbering some 20,000 men, held the position against 80,000 of the enemy. The 21st Brigade occupied a position near Becelaire, and the 2nd Wilts was given the honour of holding what was the key of the position on the left. This they held for nearly a week against overwhelming odds: the Germans sought to turn the British position by sending an enormous column against the Wilts, and their commanding Officer, Lieut. Col.

Sacrifice of the Wilts. Forbes, gave the order to charge; the Battalion was practically enwrapped by the masses of the enemy and suffered heavy losses in killed, wounded, and prisoners. Lieut. Col. Forbes and about half the Battalion was captured, but the German object was not attained, and about an hour later the 1st Army Corps came to the relief of the British. Colonel Forbes might have saved himself and his men by a retirement, but he would not abandon his trust, and the action of the Wilts was a noble act of self-sacrifice in the interests of the whole British Army. During this battle the 2nd Battalion lost 28 officers and 650 other ranks, leaving only one officer and 254 men fit for service. The 7th Division suffered about 10,000 casualties in the terrific defence they had made and was temporarily withdrawn from the line.

After this disaster—practically annihilating the 2nd Battalion for the time being—the 1st Battalion came up and replaced them in the position they occupied, holding it till about the middle of November, when they were moved to the Kemmel position.

On November 17th the Germans delivered a desperate attack and the 7th Brigade was heavily engaged; the 1st Wiltshires distinguished themselves in the action by a gallant charge, led by Capt. Cary-Barnard. Unhappily, Major Roach was killed in this action, and the command devolved upon Major Blake.

After the 1st Battle of Ypres the front remained practically stationary until the Spring offensive of 1915, the 1st Wiltshires staying in the Ypres sector, and the 2nd Battalion in the Ploegsteert and Fleux Baix sectors; but it was by no means a quiet time, for the bombardment was incessant and raids frequent. An officer of the R.H.A., writing home early in December, says,—

"You will be delighted to hear that the Wiltshires did a most magnificent piece of work three days ago. A regiment had been turned out of its trenches by the German shell fire. The Wiltshires were ordered to re-take them, and not only turned out the Germans again, but also gained an extra 500 yards of ground. No troops could really advance against our fellows now, who are simply mad. One of our chief difficulties now is to make our fellows take sufficient cover and not lose life unnecessarily."

Both battalions spent Christmas in the trenches; the 1st Wilts occupied trenches on the Kemmel front, one of which—the notorious " J " trench—was only 30 yards from the German position; this trench had apparently no bottom and was only a big ditch full of water and mud, in which the men floated about in half-barrels, never daring to show a head above the edge of the parapet. The 2nd Battalion was in the neighbourhood of Neuve Chapelle in trenches which were only from 300 to 400 yards distant from the enemy. The wet weather made the life in the trenches most trying; a doctor who was with the Wiltshires at the time says, " There is a lot of water in the trenches, the clay is horribly sticky, and very often one gets stuck and you have to get someone to help you to move. If you get wet even up to your waist, as many men do, there is no chance of getting anything dried until you come out of the trenches. You simply have to stand in your wet clothes . . . . When I left we had been in the same trenches for about ten weeks, and the weather was playing sad havoc with them, so that in places they are falling down. There was water standing in the bottom, and platforms had to be erected so that the men could keep clear of it. It was not possible for the men to sit down, and often they would have to go for the three days without doing so." A kind of informal truce between the 2nd Wilts and their opponents was arranged both on Christmas Day and Boxing Day between the hours of 9 a.m. and 4 p.m., during which period the English were chiefly employed in recovering and burying their dead, and conversations were held between members of both armies; the doctor says, " One of the soldiers recognized a German who had been working with him in Yorkshire; they were apparently old friends, and had a long talk together."

Life in the Trenches.

By Christmas, 1914, both battalions had received large drafts of " Kitchener's men; " the first draft, consisting of about 500, left England on November 28th, and joined the 2nd Battalion, and two drafts joined the 1st Battalion in December.

The services of the Wiltshires hitherto had not passed unnoticed, and shortly after Christmas Lieut. Col. R. H. Steward, speaking at Devizes Barracks, announced that he had received a letter from Capt. Pollen, in which the officer said, " His Majesty the King lately expressed these words to me: ' The Wiltshire Regiment has done splendidly in this war. In fact, I can say that no regiment has done better.' " Their losses, however, had been severe; to repair those of the 1st Battalion, besides the reserves of that battalion previously sent, over 1000 men of the 3rd Battalion had had to be drafted into it, and of the 2nd Battalion 500 were prisoners in Germany, not to mention its appalling losses in killed and wounded.

Praise from The King.

1915. Neuve Chapelle.

Both the 1st and 2nd Battalions were engaged in the desperate battle of Neuve Chapelle on March 10th, 11th, and 12th, 1915,—a battle in which the British lost 572 officers and 12,239 men killed and wounded; the town had been subjected to continuous bombardment for months and when captured by the British was a mere rubbish-heap. After its capture the Germans delivered repeated counter-attacks in mass, suffering terrible losses but failing to re-take the hard-won position. The Wiltshires suffered heavily especially the 2nd Battalion, which lost in killed 7 officers and 58 men, and in wounded 11 officers and 210 men; amongst the wounded was Capt. Gillson who was in command of the Battalion.   A man of the 2nd Wilts writing home said, "It was a terrible fight, for all my poor mates fell, and how I came through is a miracle. We are proud to say we drove the Germans out of their trenches and captured about 1,000 prisoners. The Germans don't like cold steel . . . . It was a terrible sight to see so many dead with which the ground was littered." Amongst those who lost their lives here was Pte. Ralph Cotton, the eldest son of the Rev. J. W. Cotton, the Minister of Prospect Primitive Methodist Church; he died at the military hospital at Boulogne a few days after the battle, being only nineteen years of age.   On the 12th the 1st Wilts and the 3rd Worcesters had made an unsuccessful attack on the German position at Lindenhoek; they had reached their position for attack by 2.30 a.m., and the attack was timed for 9.15 a.m.; it was, however, postponed till 4.15 p.m. ; but the artillery bombardment had revealed the coming attack and the Germans had had plenty of time to prepare ; Lieut. Calley, a nephew of Gen. T. P. Calley, was killed by a shot from a sniper about an hour before the men went " over the top ; " " A " and " B " companies of the 1st Wilts attacked, and " C " and " D " were their supports ; owing to the German preparedness the two attacking companies were annihilated.

2nd Battle of Ypres. From now the Wiltshires were engaged in almost continuous fighting for a long time ; both battalions participated in the second battle of Ypres, which began on April 22nd ; in May they are found fighting at Ypres, Festubert, Hooge, and other places in Flanders, the 1st Battalion having moved from its position on the Kemmel front to trenches upon the Dickebusch front.   The 2nd Battalion, being laid in the Ypres salient, was especially exposed and suffered many casualties.   Both, again, took a memorable part in the fighting about Hooge and Festubert in June, especially on June 15th and 16th, winning many distinctions and honourable mention in Sir. John French's despatches.   The 2nd Wilts, between Festubert and Givenchy, attacked at 6 p.m. after a bombardment of the German positions that had lasted several days ; this bombardment was, for that stage of the war, a very terrible artillery assault, though it was soon eclipsed by later demonstrations of what artillery could do.   The attack proved a failure owing to the fact that the flank supports did not get up in time, and the 2nd Wiltshires suffered so heavily that they had to be drawn out the next morning, being replaced by the 2nd Bedfords in the original line held by the Wilts.

Sad news to Swindon. But the same post that brought home the General's despatches also brought sad news to many a Swindon family,—such messages as these :—

" I am taking the liberty of sending these photos by the request of your son, who, I am extremely sorry to say, was killed in action on June 16th. He was struck by a bullet from a machine-gun, and died almost immediately. He did not suffer much, and passed away very quietly.   I hope your dark hours will be brightened by knowing that your son died a hero and did his duty."

Again, " Your son was killed just behind me, the same shell covering me with earth. I am afraid he was a bit nervous that night.   He thought that he would not come through the day safely, and I tried to cheer him up all I could.   He was killed whilst sitting down in the communication trench, and must have died instantaneously."

On June 16th the 1st Wilts suffered severely, when they and the 9th Brigade were co-operating in an attack upon the German positions ; the 9th Brigade did not attain its full objective, and the Wilts advanced further than it did, thus having both its flanks exposed ; the result was that the Wilts, consisting of " C " and " D " companies, had to retire to what had been the German first line with heavy casualties and had forty to fifty of their men captured.

The Wiltshires were in this neighbourhood all the rest of the year, helping to hold the Ploegsteert—Armentières Line, and occupying one position after another; thus, the 1st Wiltshires were fightng in the Ypres salient from early June to July 11th, holding positions on the St. Eloi front for the latter half of July and on the St. Jean front from August 3rd to the 23rd, back on the Ypres salient from then to September 26th, holding a position on the left of Hill 60 from October 7th to the 17th, and in the Ploegsteert trenches from October 24th to January 23rd, 1916. They underwent a severe trial from September 1st to the 3rd, when about 90 of them were holding the famous Hooge crater, left of the Menin Road ; the Germans got their range exactly, and for four hours—3 o'clock p.m. to 7 p.m.—rained shells upon them ; it was surprising that even so many as thirty-six survived the ordeal. Lieut. Col. Brown had now assumed command of the 1st Wiltshires. The 2nd Battalion, after a short period of re-construction, had been put into the line at Richbourge l'Avoue in July, and subsequently moved to the Givenchy sector.

New Battalions. Meanwhile the 5th Battalion had finished training and was now in Gallipoli, the 6th had reached France, and the 7th Battalion, which had been formed at Codford Camp in 1914, left its billets in Marlborough in May and trained at Sutton Veny ; whilst the 8th Battalion was rapidly growing, its numbers having reached 500, and these had left Trowbridge for camp at Weymouth. The drain upon the 3rd Battalion was heavy and persistent, for the severity of the losses of the two battalions in France may be judged from the fact that in May Lady Lansdowne announced that 622 men of the Regiment were prisoners of war.

In spite of their hard fighting nothing could daunt the spirits of the men at the front ; some of the Swindon lads write home for a football, and during a rest they are found arranging concerts, a football tournament, and sports,—from which, however, they are suddenly recalled to the hardships of the trenches.

The services of the Wiltshire Regiment hitherto had been recognized by many decorations bestowed on officers and men, and in September the Commanding Officer of the 1st Battalion, Lieut. Col. A. W. Hasted, received at the hands of the King the insignia of a Companion of the Most Distinguished Order of St. Michael and St. George. But what had been done by the Wiltshire Regiment was but a small part of what lay before them, and the great Autumn offensive of 1915 made cruel demands upon them. When, on September 25th, Sir John French and General Joffre launched a combined attack in Flanders—in the neighbourhood of Loos and the Hulluch-Vermelles Road—and in Champagne, both battalions were deeply involved, the 2nd Wiltshires especially suffering severely. The

The 2nd Wilts at Loos. Battalion had been in reserve-billets behind the line for a week prior to the attack ; on Thursday, the 23rd, they marched in a drenching downpour to a village five miles back for final preparations, and then on Friday, towards mid-night, set out for the trenches, which they reached at 3.30 a.m. on Saturday, getting well into the firing-line by 9 o'clock. They played a very prominent part in the centre of a body of troops ordered to attack an important position near Loos, advancing under a terrible enfilading fire that only allowed them to run a few yards and then lie down ; early in the assault their Commanding Officer, Lieut. Col. B. H. Leatham, formerly of the 2nd York-shires, was killed, other officers fell, and many men were mown down by the terrible hail of bullets.   Colonel Leatham's loss was a sad blow to the Battalion, for he was an experienced and gallant officer, having served in the South African Campaign and having been mentioned in despatches and decorated with the D.S.O. in this war.   The position attacked was captured by the Wilts and their comrades, lost, re-taken, again lost, and finally captured and held.   Maj. Gen. H. E. Watts, C.B., C.M.G., paid the men of the Wilts a high tribute after the battle ; he said, " You were ordered to attack and you advanced in a very well organized formation, and in a straight line.   There was no hesitation, and there was no holding back to see whether others were coming or not.   Every man went straight on and was evidently determined to get there.   That was the result of very good discipline, combined with the sense of duty and the right spirit . . . The Wiltshires, I know, will go home with a reputation second to none."

The 6th Engaged.   The 6th Wiltshires received their baptism of fire at Laventie, losing 4 killed and 7 wounded ; then the Battalion took over some trenches at the "Canadian Orchard," near Festubert, on August 30th, occupying them till September 15th ; this spell was marked by a minor but severe action. It was a historic dash forward ; the 6th gained several lines of trenches, but then had to retire a little way ; many wounded men lay out amongst the dead in the open for two days, between the English and German trenches, and many gallant fellows lost their lives in trying to rescue the poor sufferers, until the officers had to forbid the further sacrifice of valuable lives.   Amongst the fallen was 2nd Lieut. W. Moore, son of Dr. S. J. Moore, of Swindon ; he lay for two days between the trenches, and eventually managed to crawl back only to die as he was being carried away.   With him also fell another Swindon officer, Lieut. C. Coleman.

On September 25th, the 6th Battalion was engaged, like the other two battalions in the great battle about Loos.   Meanwhile, the 1st Battalion had been doing their part in the Ypres salient, where, on September 25th their Division made the counter move for Loos by attacking at Hooge ; the Wilts were supporting the 2nd South Lancashires and were not called upon to attack, but suffered heavily under shell fire on the Menin Road.

General Watts' prophecy as to the reputation of the Wiltshires has been ful-filled, but their name was already famous in their native land.   A high tribute to them appeared in the " Nineteenth Century " for December, 1915, in which Professor J. H. Morgan, the Home Office Commissioner with the British Expeditionary Force, vividly reproduced a conversation with a wounded Wiltshire soldier, who relates in his native dialect his own experiences during an advance near " Wypers " (as the British soldier, like his predecessors in earlier Flemish wars, always called Ypres). Speaking of their capture of a house defended by Germans :—

A Wiltshire Peasant Knight.   " By the toime we got to thic house there were only 'bout fifteen of us left.   We had to scrouge our way in through the buttery winder, and we 'eerd a girt saddle inside, sort o' scuffling ; 'twere the Germans makin' for the cellar.   And our Capt'n posted some on us at top o' cellar steps and led the rest on us up the stairs to a kind o'tallet wheer thuck machine-gun was.   And what d'ye think we found, Sir ? . . . There was a poor girl there—half daft she wur—wi' nothing on but a man's overcoat.

And she rushed out avore us on the landing and began hammering with her hands against a bedroom door and it wur locked. We smashed 'en in wi' our rifle-butts, and God's mercy I we found a poor 'ooman there, her mother seemingly, with her breast all bloody an' her clothes torn. Oi couldn' mak' out what 'er was saying." After relating how they succoured the poor soul, who had been unspeakably mal-treated, the man related how they had to smoke the Germans out the cellar, bayon-etting them as they dashed forth. "An' when it wur done and we had claned our bay'nets in the straw, Capt'n 'e said, ' Men, you ha' done your work as you ought to ha' done.' . . Oh Christ ! they be rotten bad. Twoads they be I I never reckon no good 'ull come to men what abuses wimmen and childer. But Oi'm afeard they be nation strong—there be so many on 'em." Professor Morgan sat whilst the man chatted about his little boy and his sweet-williams in his cottage garden near Wootton Bassett, but he felt the poor fellow would never see them again, and when he called next day at the hospital the bed was empty ; the chivalrous Wiltshire labourer was dead.

The Germans began their inevitable counter-attack upon October 8th, north-east, south-east, and south-west of Loos, and the strenuous fighting in which the Wiltshires were engaged is shown by the casualty lists—frequently appalling in length—which continued to appear with monotonous regularity throughout the Autumn. The positions won were, however, maintained and the Wiltshire Battalions were engaged in holding the trenches about Ploegsteert all the Winter, and the first half of 1916.

Six Battalions Abroad. By the end of 1916 the Wiltshire Regiment had five Battalions out on active service, for, besides the three in Flanders the 5th Wilts were now at the Dardanelles, and the 7th had been sent to the Saloniki scene of operations, whilst the 4th Wiltshires were doing garrison duty in India ; the 8th Battalion, which had been training at Poole, was, however, disbanded before the close of 1915 and amalgamated with the 3rd, which now had the responsibility of feeding all the battalions on active service, instead of the 1st and 2nd only, as hitherto. The 7th Battalion had landed in Saloniki in October and there were between 150 and 200 Swindon men in its ranks ; their place was up on the Doiran front, and Sergt. C. A. Thorne, writing at the close of the year to Swindon for some sports-equipment for the men, said that hitherto their casualty-list was but small. This battalion also, before the end of the war, was to find itself upon the French battlefields and was to help in chasing the Germans back to their own land.

1916. In 1916 the 1st Wilts were not engaged in any serious action till April ; from January 24th to April 10th they were occupied in battalion and brigade training and in marching down country to the Vimy Ridge sector, and on April 11th they went into trenches on the Arras Road near **Vimy Ridge.** Vimy Ridge. From now till May 31st they were engaged in holding the sector, and it was one of the most arduous periods of their service; the German attack was so fierce that for twenty-nine days—May 2nd to the 31st —the Wilts were in the trenches without a break ; on Sunday, the 21st, when the Germans made a heavy onslaught on the 47th London Division who were on the immediate left of the Wilts, the Wilts had as much of the bombardment as the Londoners and lost heavily ; in fact, in the course of these twenty-nine days the Battalion had approximately five-hundred casualties, and the people at home were dismayed by the long lists appearing in the " *Advertiser* " and " *Herald* " on May 12th, 19th, and 26th. On the 31st the men were moved back to St. Eloi and immediately entered upon a course of intensive brigade-training for open-field work in preparation for the British Somme offensive.

The 1st Wilts were engaged in brigade training, as has been said, in the neighbourhood of Chelers from June 1st to the 14th; then they began marching southwards to take up positions on the Somme front where the " Big Push " of 1916 was to be made. On July 2nd they arrived by night in Aveluy Wood just north of Albert, sheltering in trenches for the night ; the next day they entered the firing line at Authuille behind the Thiepval front.

Thiepval. They entered at once upon a period of very arduous work, for the very next day was spent in hard duty under heavy shell fire till the men were nearly done up, and at 7 p.m. they had to attack over the fighting area of La Boiselle; they cleared the road between Contalmaison and La Boiselle, suffering heavy losses. Having by their vigorous assault gained their objective before night, they spent the night in consolidating the position, and again pushed forward in the morning. The Germans counter-attacked but were repulsed, and Contalmaison was securely held. On the 9th the Wilts were relieved, but their casualties amounted to 40% of their strength, and included Lieut-Col. W. S. Brown, who was killed. The last two days of this fighting were days of heavy rain and the men were up to the knees in soft mud ; but the Battalion had done splendidly ; twice in the week they had been called upon to take a piece of the enemy line and had succeeded in the effort ; their gallantry was recognised by the bestowal of many honours.

Right through July the 1st Wilts were continuously engaged in this neighbourhood. On the 26th they were fighting in Trones Wood, and a French journal speaks of them as " fighting stolidly round Pozières." But their **Beating the** most famous exploit in the Somme Battle belongs to the latter part **Prussian** of August, when the 1st Wilts and the Worcesters met the Prussian **Guard.** Guard face to face and came off victors. The affair began on July 24th, in the vicinity of Thiepval. After a hurricane bombardment lasting till the afternoon the Wilts and Worcesters left their trenches, swept over " No man's land "—the stretch of dirty brown earth furrowed and pitted by shells— and up a disused German trench, till they poured over the German parapet right on the top of the 28th Infantry ; the British found them crouching low and still cowed by the fearful bombardment they had undergone. Within ten minutes of the start the first batch of twelve German prisoners was in at battalion head-quarters. Then followed some very stiff fighting ; the Wilts and Worcesters advanced up the Hindenburg trench which was full of men armed with bombs and machine-guns, until they reached the Koenigstrasse trench—a straight cutting of 250 yards with a strong machine-gun post at the further end, full of Germans, and strengthened by bomb-stops ; but the Wiltshires blew up the barriers and bombed their way up, finally capturing the trench.

The next day was devoted chiefly to mutual shelling, but the following day opened with a heavy German bombardment which increased in intensity as the day wore on. A messenger to the rear on his return passed unknowingly right over a part of the captured trench which was now obliterated ; before he realised it he had reached the German trenches, passed over, and saw crowds of Prussians crouching down in readiness to attack when the signal should be given ; the man bolted and got back through the two zones of fire unscathed ; he informed the commanding officer of what he had seen, and a message was sent to the rear asking for a concentrated artillery fire upon the German front line.　About 7.30 p.m., the first wave of Prussian infantry emerged from their trenches, but under the terrific hail of shells they staggered and began to melt away ; none got more than fifty yards before their line broke and fled ; a second wave had the same fate, and the Wilts and Worcesters, who had been standing to with rifle-bombs and grenades, went " over the top " and in a hand to hand fight completed the failure of the 93rd regiment of the Prussian Guard Fusiliers ; but the price of this double victory was a dreadful list of casualties.

The 2nds at Trones Wood. The 2nd Battalion had spent the first half of 1916 in trenches at Carnoy and Maricourt, having been transferred, with the rest of the 21st Brigade, from the 7th to the 30th Division on the Somme.　On the 8th of July the Allies were attacking in the direction of Guillemont, and the village was covered by Trones Wood, an enormously strong position.　After several abortive attacks on the wood, the 2nd Wiltshires were ordered to attack it.　They charged magnificently through a storm of shot, bayoneted and shot the machine-gunners who did not surrender, and captured hundreds of prisoners.　Then they held the position against repeated counter-attacks and heavy shell-fire.　Lieut. Col. Gillson was wounded, and the Battalion lost altogether 11 officers and 200 men killed and wounded.　Their gallantry won and deserved the highest praise, and was recognized by the French by special mention in their Order of the day.　The 21st Brigade, after another unsuccessful attempt to capture Guillemont on July 23rd, was withdrawn from the area for re-construction.

The 6th at the Somme. The 6th Wiltshires, during the Somme Battle, were on the La Boiselle-Fricourt line.　On July the 2nd and 3rd they participated in an attack upon La Boiselle by means of which a large part of the place was captured.　Their losses, however, were heavy, 350 being killed, wounded, or missing, which number was raised to 380 by the time the Battalion was moved back on July 29th ; the killed included four officers and twelve others were wounded. The latter part of July was spent at Mametz Wood where the Battalion took over an advanced line in the neighbourhood of Bazentin le Petit, consolidating and strengthening the line until they were relieved on the 29th.　The Battalion was now exhausted and heavily reduced ; it was therefore withdrawn to Cocquerelles for re-construction.　Then, early in August, the division of which it formed part (the 19th) was sent to the Kemmel sector.　At this period Lieut. Col. Walter Long, D.S.O., had command, having been appointed to succeed Col. Jeffreys in December, 1915, the latter having been severely burned in a dug-out accident.

High Praise. Sir Douglas Haig honourably mentioned the Wiltshires, Worcesters, and Gloucesters for their distinguished work at Thiepval ; the charge on the 24th was a magnificent exploit, and the defence on the 26th was even finer ; the journals were full of tributes to the valour of the men who had repulsed the best of the Kaiser's troops, and a French journal said the English never showed themselves so brilliant as on this occasion.

During July the first drafts of " Derby men " began to be received at the front, and an officer of the Wilts speaks of those who joined them as " a splendid lot of fellows."

" Plug-Street " again. Thiepval and Combles were occupied by the British on September 26th, and in October the 1st Wilts were sent back to their old field— the Ploegsteert-Armentières line, where they spent the winter of 1916-17, sometimes in one sector and sometimes in another in this area. In the soldiers' phrase there was " nothing doing " through the winter, though this means merely that no great action was experienced, and that bombardments, raids, listening posts, etc., were the ordinary routine. Again did the 1st Wilts spend their Christmas Day in the trenches, having their Christmas festivities on Christmas Eve and moving in the next day. They were out again for New Year's Day.

The 2nd with the Tanks. The 2nd Battalion, after a short period of re-construction following the Somme battle, were soon in the line again, attacking in the neighbourhood of Flers in October,—an engagement for ever memorable as the first in which tanks were used. Many in Swindon will remember how for several days before the action it was whispered about the town that the Germans were about to have an unpleasant surprise ; little was said openly on account of the stringency of the military orders, but many had a fairly clear idea of what was afoot and were waiting eagerly for this attack. After Flers the 2nd Wiltshires moved to the Arras sector, remaining there through the winter of 1916-17.

1917. Amongst the first casualties announced in 1917 all Wiltshiremen heard with regret that Brig. Gen. Walter Long, C.M.G., D.S.O., had been killed in action on January 29th, falling at the head of his brigade at Hébuterne. He had been actively engaged from the beginning of hostilities, being with his regiment (the Scots Greys) during the retreat from Mons in 1914 ; he was afterwards appointed to the command of the 6th Wiltshires and attained the rank of Brigadier General in November, 1916. The gallant officer had won distinction in the South African war, and his reputation as a brilliant soldier had been greatly enhanced in the present war, during which he had been several times mentioned in despatches by Lord French and Sir Douglas Haig. Although his family was not closely connected with Swindon, the town always felt much interest in their neighbours in West Wilts, and there was much sympathy in Swindon for General Long's parents, Mr. Walter Long (the Colonial Secretary) and Lady Doreen Long, whose occasional visits to the Borough had won them many friends.

The 2nd Wilts at Arras. On Easter Monday, April 9th, 1917, the battle of Arras opened, and the 2nd Wiltshires were again involved in a sanguinary struggle that wrought great havoc in their ranks. If it were not for the glorious heroism displayed by the Battalion and the incalculable services it rendered the British army by its repeated sacrifices, one might be tempted to speak of it as " this ill-fated battalion." At Arras they fought with unsurpassable heroism ; they passed unflinchingly through open country right up to the German trenches, but there they were stopped by the barbed wire, which the artillery had failed to cut. It was a heart-breaking experience, but they dug in on the spot and held the ground they had covered ; the losses, however, were terrible, and, to add to their sufferings, a dreadful blizzard came on and many wounded died who might have been saved. The casualties amounted to 16 officers and 363 non-commissioned officers and men.

After the battle of Arras the 2nd Battalion was moved to the Ypres sector and participated in the third battle of Ypres,—part of the great advance designed to wrest the Belgian coast from the Germans. The Battalion secured the objectives allotted to it at the opening of the battle, but the great design was thwarted by the abominable weather then prevailing, which made the battle area a swamp.

The 1st at Meanwhile the 1st Battalion was sharing in the attack on the Messines **Messines** Ridge, delivered on June 7th, securing all its objectives at a com-**Ridge.** paratively small cost. On July 31st, they also took part in the assault made by the 25th Division from West Hoek Ridge upon Glencorse Wood and Inverness Copse, but the rain and mud rendered all the fighting unavailing. Lieut. Col. Ogilvie had by this time resumed the command of the Battalion.

The 1st Wiltshires were next in the line at Givenchy and towards the close of the year they moved to the Somme area. The 2nd Battalion also remained on the Flanders front till the close of 1917, being in the line on Messines Ridge in September ; early in 1918 they moved to St. Quentin, Lieut. Col. Martin having replaced Lieut. Col. Gillson in the command.

At the beginning of 1917 the 6th Battalion was still upon the Somme front in the neighbourhood of Hébuterne, and it remained there till early in March ; on the 4th of that month the Battalion set off from Euston Camp to march to Flanders, reaching the Dickebusch positions by the 31st of March. The following two months were spent in holding positions on the Wytschaete front, the work being varied by spells of training ; at the end of April, when the Battalion was holding the left of " Hill 60," about fifty of the men were attached to the 1st Australian Tunnelling Company, returning to the Battalion after a fortnight's work with them.

The 6th at The first week of June was devoted to preparations for the attack on **Messines** the Messines Ridge, and after digging assembly trenches at Vierstraat, **Ridge.** the 6th Wilts went into support trenches in readiness for the assault. They took part in the victorious attack on the Ridge on June 7th, advancing over the Y Wood and Wytschaete sectors whilst the 1st Wilts were advancing on the Neuve Eglise sector. Then followed several weeks of hard and dangerous trench work on the Messines-Ypres front, until the 6th Battalion turned out for a well deserved six weeks' rest at Seningham, near St. Omer, where they remained till September 10th. Back to the front line, the Battalion spent a week in holding positions on the Kemmel-Wytschaete front,

Passchendaele and then on the 19th moved up to assembly positions on the railway **Ridge.** bank on the right flank, ready for the attack on Passchendaele Ridge ; on the 20th of September the Battalion formed the right flank of the attack on the Ridge, and at that point the assault was a complete success, though the Wilts suffered heavily from machine-gun fire. Everyone knows what a long and costly struggle ensued before the Ridge was finally secured early in November ; from September 21st to November 4th the 6th Wilts were occupied in holding and fortifying the new positions on Passchendaele Ridge, but by the time the ridge was wholly taken it had swallowed up an appalling number of lives ; amongst those who died there was a brilliant young officer—Capt. H. H. Williams, commanding " C " company of the 6th Wilts,—who was a teacher under the Swindon Education Committee, and had made rapid strides in his profession ; he showed equal promise in the Army, and had been mentioned in a despatch from Field Marshal Sir Douglas Haig in April, 1917 ; he was again similarly mentioned for " gallant and distinguished service in the field " in this fight for the

Passchendaele Ridge in a despatch from the Field Marshal dated November 7th; the gallant youth was only 23 years of age and had served since the outbreak of war.

The 6th Wilts were resting at Lynde from November 11th until December 7th. By this time the chief area of activity was the Cambrai region, where, on November 20th, General Byng with his " Tanks " broke the " Hindenburg Line " in front of Cambrai. Great hopes were aroused by this victory, but the German reaction began ten days later and it was necessary to bring up fresh British troops. On December 7th the 6th Wilts were taken by train to Blairville, and for the next four months they were holding and fortifying positions along the " Hindenburg Line," chiefly in the neighbourhood of Marcoing and Ribecourt.

It should be remarked that in the fall of 1917 the Royal Wilts Yeomanry had been dismounted and incorporated in the 6th Wiltshires. They brought to the Battalion 25 officers and 350 men ; amongst the officers were Majors W. F. Fuller and C. Awdry, and Lieuts. D. H. Davy, H. G. Gregson and M. G. Sumner.

1918
The great
onslaught.
When the great German offensive opened, the 25th Division—including the 7th Brigade of which the 1st Wiltshires formed a battalion,—was in close support, the 1st Wiltshires lying in reserve at Achiet-le-Grand. They were at once sent into action in front of Frémicourt and the Bapaume—Cambrai road, and were attacked by the Germans on March the 23rd, in appalling numbers. They bore a gallant part in all the fighting about Liverval, Boursies, Morchies, and Vaulx-Vraucourt, but though constantly attacked they were not dislodged from any position by the enemy's assault. The ordeal was very severe, but when the Division was withdrawn the Commander-in-Chief was able to say, " when withdrawn from the Somme area the spirit of the Division was exceptionally high." The Battalion had held its ground magnificently, and honour was reflected upon the whole battalion when Capt. R. J. F. Hayward, M.C., was awarded the Victoria Cross for gallantry of the highest order.

From the Somme the 1st Wiltshires were transferred to the Ploegsteert Wood area, and were soon involved in the Lys battle ; thus, when the German onslaught began there, the 1st Battalion was holding the enemy on the now familiar ground of " Plug Street," and the blow fell on them there on April 10th. On that day the Germans succeeded in getting round on the right about dawn into Ploegsteert Wood, and also broke into Ploegsteert village and made a nest of machine guns there. The Cheshires,Wiltshires and Staffords held for two days on the left of the line with Germans actually behind them, and forced the Germans back again out of the greater part of the Wood. On the night of the 11th the men were ordered to abandon the Wood, where they were nearly surrounded, and to fall back on a line in front of Neuve Eglise and La Nieppe.

The 1st at
Neuve Eglise.
At Neuve Eglise the Wilts and Cheshires made a memorable stand, holding continuous attacks in vastly greater force than their own for some days. The Germans had definite orders to break through the line of the main road from Fletre to Bailleul at all costs, and every day that they could be held back was invaluable to the Allies. The Germans did their best, and the fighting was most desperate ; wave after wave came on and failed. " The enemy broke through into the ruined streets, and small parties of Wiltshires, Worcesters, and others sprang upon them and killed them or were killed, and fought desperately in back yards and over broken walls and in shell-pierced houses wherever they could find Germans or hear the tattoo of machine-guns. Several times the enemy was cleared out of most of the town and our men

held the hollow square containing most of the streets, and defended it as a kind of fortress, though with dwindling numbers, under a heavy fire of shells and trench-mortars and machine-guns." The defenders not only held their own till other troops came up and relieved the pressure on the flanks, but when that was done they broke into a counter-attack, captured and brought back five machine-guns, and drove back the enemy in confusion, killing great numbers of them,—an astounding feat of arms and of grim courage. Unable to take Neuve Eglise by assault, the Germans at length shelled it so fiercely that it became a death-trap, and, in silence and unknown to the Germans, the Wilts with their comrades withdrew behind the village to positions on the Bailleul Road. This was preliminary to further withdrawals, and on April 15th, the enemy gained possession of Bailleul.

It was about this time that Lieut. Col. S. S. Ogilvie fell into the hands of the enemy ; he, with another officer and some orderlies, had been captured in a dug-out, having been prevented from getting out by a very strong barrage. Col. Ogilvie's career had been one of great distinction ; enlisting as a private in 1914, he was a captain in the 1st Wiltshires at the desperate struggle at Thiepval in July, 1916, when Lieut. Col. Brown was killed, and for the time being Capt. Ogilvie succeeded to the command of the Battalion. As Lieut. Colonel he re-assumed the command in July, 1917, and in the magnificent stand made by the 1st Wiltshires in March, 1918, at Frémicourt, on the Bapaume road, Lieut. Col. Ogilvie earned the distinguished honour of a second bar to his D.S.O.

An Exhausting Defence. During the retirement of April the Battalion, fighting continuously, suffered enormously, and when it was withdrawn from the line on April 14th, its total strength had been reduced to about one hundred, and all its officers were amongst the casualties. By the 26th of the month, however, after a hasty re-organization it was again in the line under the command of Lieut. Col. Cade, assisting in a counter-attack upon the Germans at Kemmel ; there Lieut. Col. Cade was killed. In May the Battalion, along with the rest of the 7th Brigade, was moved southwards to Champagne—the Marne area,—having been relieved in its former position by the French ; here, on the 27th, the enemy attacked in great force and the 1st Wiltshires, at Bouffignereux, again suffered very severely, its Commanding Officer, Lieut. Col. Furze, being amongst the wounded.

The Battalion was now so reduced that it had to be made part of a composite battalion, continuing to play its part in retarding the apparently irresistible advance of the Germans ; but the whole 25th Division, of which the 1st Wiltshires formed a part, was so depleted by the exhausting struggle that it became necessary to disperse it, and the 1st Wiltshires were sent to the 21st Division, with whom they were **Turn of the Tide.** in the line at Mesnil and Beaumont Hamel in July, and at Miraumont and Le Sars in August. The tide had now begun to turn; and, instead of retiring, the allied forces were ready to advance ; by a night march on August 21st, the Wiltshires rendered valuable help to the British attack on August 22nd ; they participated in the capture of Beaulencourt on September 1st ; in the advance that followed they shared in the fighting at Epehy and Gonnelieu, reaching the Hindenburg Line by October 4th. Still advancing and fighting continuously—at Ovillers and Vendegies on October 23rd—the Battalion traversed the Mormal Forest, crossed the River Sambre at Berlaimont, and fought its last fight on November 8th at Aulnoye, within about ten miles from Mons, where, four years and eleven weeks before, they had begun the long and bitter struggle.

The Price of Victory. Few, however, of the heroes of 1914 could have been present at Aulnoye to see how completely Fortune's wheel had turned since the Wiltshires doggedly retired before the Teutonic hordes; for, besides its numerous losses in officers, the Battalion had lost 1,423 non-commissioned officers and men killed on the field or dead from wounds or disease,—a terrible price for one battalion to pay. The Battalion had been among the first to land in France, and for over four years had been on active service, mainly in French Flanders; it had taken part in innumerable engagements from the Belgian coast down to the River Marne, and in all it had displayed the tenacity and resolution that had caused the old " 62nd Foot Regiment " to be regarded as one of the most reliable regiments in the British army. To the long lists of battle-honours on its colours has now been added, " The Great War, 1914-1918," but only those who fought in its ranks can realize the suffering, endurance, sacrifice, and valour that these words comprehend.

Destruction of the 2nd Wilts at St. Quentin. The Great German offensive of March, 1918, destroyed two of the Wiltshire battalions—the 2nd and the 6th. The Germans were staking their all on this tremendous assault, and everyone remembers with what apprehension the world watched the early successes of the enemy and how nearly they attained their object. The full force of the blow fell on the 2nd Wiltshires on March 21st at St. Quentin, where they were holding the line by a system of forward redoubts. The first waves of German infantry, supported by indescribable bombardments, rolled up through the fog in the early morning; the Wiltshires held tenaciously to positions shattered and obliterated by shell-fire, inflicting frightful losses on the successive waves of Germans; but there was no end to these waves, and finally the Battalion was overwhelmed with a loss of 22 officers and over 600 men, Lieut. Col. Martin being amongst the captured.

Capture of the 6th at Morchies. The 6th Wilts were left in the Marcoing sector on the Cambrai front, and there they remained through the first ten or eleven weeks of 1918. On the night of March 21st–22nd, they were marched to fresh positions at Buegny, moving up in the morning to Morchies and digging new positions behind the village. On the 21st the great German attempt to smash the British army had begun, and as the 6th Wilts were digging at Morchies the British front was even then breaking; the Wilts were supposed to be two miles behind the front line, but they were under heavy artillery and rifle fire. All day long on the 22nd, the Germans were attacking at various points, driving in all posts in front of the Wilts, who returned the fire and realized that they were in reality part of the front line. As the day wore on the Germans were advancing everywhere, the British artillery retired, and an unsuccessful counter-attack by tanks left the Wilts practically surrounded. The night was fairly quiet, but the Wiltshires heard the Germans in Morchies about 500 yards in front of them, and their aeroplanes were enormously active.

On March 23rd, the Wilts could see the Germans concentrating about two miles away, but now the British artillery support was lacking, and when the German attack began between 10 and 11 a.m., it was plain that the Battalion's position was hopeless. Even at mid-day they still held their positions although their right flank was broken and the German infantry was getting behind them, but they could have got clear if ordered to do so, as they knew every inch of the ground behind them and had practised the retirement thoroughly. From 11 a.m. until 5.30 p.m. they were subjected to exceedingly heavy concentrated German artillery fire, and between 5.30 and 6 p.m. the British front was completely broken ; on both sides there were enormous casualties, but of the 6th Wiltshires, surrounded as they were, all but the merest handful were either killed or captured ; about thirty only escaped to the British lines, Lieut. Col. Lord Alex. Thynne being amongst the number, and, in the circumstances, it was on the part of any a piece of incredible good luck if he got through. It will be remembered that the dismounted Royal Wilts Yeomanry were part of the 6th Wilts at the time of its annihilation at Morchies, and amongst the captured were Swindonians who formed part of the Yeomanry. The 6th Wilts had not gone down in dishonour ; all day long on the 23rd they knew theirs was a forlorn hope ; from their elevated position they saw the German flood gradually sending its waves around their position, which became an island assailed by the enemy on all sides ; the shell and rifle fire made a continual storm about their heads, and comrades were falling all about them ; but still they held on, fighting to the end till human resistance could do no more. " Morchies " will remain in the annals of the Wiltshire Regiment a name that calls up conflicting feelings of grief and pride.

The gallant colonel of the 6th Wilts, though fortunate enough to escape capture, was wounded at Morchies; the second in command, Major C. S. Awdry, was missing after the battle and no news of him has ever been gained ; but in that terrific hurricane of shells many a man must have been killed and buried by the same shot, and doubtless the brave Yeomanry officer sleeps where he fell on the field of honour, with a crowd of the infantry whom the fortunes of war had sent him to lead.

Only a mere handful remained out of the Battalion ; that night they received a draft of eighty-five, and with a battalion strength of 120 they took up a new position with the rest of the Division. Then began a regular system of taking up new positions,—holding the enemy up for a few hours and then withdrawing,—until they had withdrawn through Bapaume after four days of continuous fighting, and on March 24th the Germans claimed Bapaume and Peronne.

Between March 21st and 28th the 6th Battalion, below strength to begin with, lost in killed, wounded, and missing, 12 officers and 477 other ranks. After the German offensive has exhausted itself, the sorely tried 19th Division, including the 6th Wiltshires, was taken by train from Doullens and Caudas to Strazelle on April 1st. They were marched thence to Locre, where the Battalion was re-con- structed under Lieut. Col. Monreal and Major Garthwaite, a draft of 550 men joining the remnant still in existence. Of the existing officers only Major Garthwaite and Capts. Kent and Harris had come out with the Battalion in July, 1915.

The 6th again Shattered. No sooner was the 6th Battalion reconstructed than a fresh trial shattered it again ; it was sent into the line near Oostaverne, and on April 10th was assailed by an overwhelming force of Germans ; it made a desperate and gallant stand, but the odds were too great and the Battalion, with a loss of more than four hundred men, was forced out of its positions, Lieut. Col. Monreal being amongst the slain. Continuous fighting during the ensuing weeks still further depleted its ranks, and in May the remnants of both the 2nd and 6th Battalions were merged in one, under the command of Major Rapson, and then of Major Shepherd, until Lieut. Col. Lord Alexander Thynne took command.

The 2nd and 6th remnants merged. The new Battalion was sent to Champagne, fighting in the neighbourhood of Epernay, and was warmly thanked by the French Commander-in-Chief for its gallant assistance to the 6th French Army in stemming the German advance in that quarter. Transferred to the north in August, along with the rest of the 19th Division, the Battalion was engaged in the neighbourhood of Hinges, successfully advancing the British line there. It was here that the gallant colonel of the Royal Wiltshire Yeomanry, made by the fortune of the war the commander of an infantry battalion, was killed ; Lord Alexander Thynne, having done valuable service with his Wiltshire Yeomen, proved an equally capable commander of infantry, and, having survived the terrible disaster of Morchies, it was a stroke of bitter irony that he should fall on the eve of a victorious peace. His position was taken by Lieut. Col. Beaver, who led the Battalion in the final advance ; it advanced to Cambrai in October, captured Eth on November 4th, and by Armistice Day had pushed on as far as the neighbourhood of Bavay, a few miles from the Belgian frontier.

Death of Lord A. Thynne.

The Cost. Both the 2nd and the 6th Battalions had a terribly heavy death-roll during the war ; apart from its heavy losses in officers, the 2nd Battalion lost 1,305 non-commissioned officers and men,—only 118 less than the deaths in the 1st Battalion,—and the 6th had the third biggest list in the Wiltshire Regiment, for it lost 624 non-commissioned officers and men, just 23 more than the 5th Battalion.

It should be noted that after the amalgamation of the remnants of the 2nd and 6th Battalions a new 6th Battalion was formed in England; it was conducted to France by Lieut. Col. Rapson in June, 1918, and took part in the closing scenes of the war. It was engaged in September in stiff fighting at St. Eloi, and also in October at the passing of the River Scheldt.

The 2nd Battalion is an old regiment of the line, formerly the " 99th Foot," with an honourable military record behind it ; but the 6th Battalion was called into existence by the exigencies of the present time, and it proved itself worthy to stand by the old regular battalions ; it passes out of existence with the establishment of peace, and only its colour remains, hanging in the Church at Devizes, a monument of its great sacrifices and valour.

The 7th in France. The 7th Battalion of the Wiltshires played a part in France in these closing months of the war, for in June, 1918, they left Saloniki for France under Lt. Col. Hodgson, travelling by train through Italy and France to Dieppe, where they were embodied in the 151st Brigade of the 50th Division. In October this division was actively engaged in the great advance that brought the war to a close, and made a victorious attack upon Bony, in the Hindenburg Line on October 3rd. The next day the 7th Wiltshires captured Prospect Hill, near Govy, but paid a heavy price for their success, having about three hundred casualties. Further losses were suffered two days later when the Battalion attacked Guisancourt and Villers Farm,—a fruitless operation in which " A " Company especially suffered. Their next important engagement took place on the railway embankments and in the orchards east of Le Cateau on the 17th and 18th of October, when the fighting was very severe.

A fortnight later the 7th Battalion had reached the Sambre ; they shared in the great attack on the Forêt de Mormal on November 4th,—an assault crowned with success but fraught with severe losses, especially amongst the officers,—and the next day they crossed the River Sambre by pontoons at Hachette Farm.

After the armistice the 7th Wiltshires remained in France whilst demobilization was being effected, they themselves being disbanded in June, 1919.

Thus four Wiltshire battalions saw service in France. The record of their deeds can never be fitly written, but were it recorded as it deserves to be it would form an epic unsurpassed by any in stories of heroism, endurance, and sacrifice. Here it has been possible to do no more than outline their story, but enough has been told to show the reader what valour and tragedy mark its various chapters. Few regiments suffered more than the Wiltshire Regiment, none has a more glorious record.

2/4 Wilts. Church Parade, Poona.

2/4 Wilts, Swindon Company. Return from Church Parade, Poona.

CHAPTER VII

The Wiltshires in Turkey and Mesopotamia.

The 5th Wilts.

The 5th Wilts at Cirencester. The 5th Battalion of the Wiltshire Regiment was formed at Tidworth in August, 1914, and underwent its training at Cirencester. On Monday, December 14th, 1914, 850 officers and men of the Battalion arrived at Cirencester from Salisbury Plain, and after inspection by Brig. Gen. Travers they were billetted in the town ; the remaining 250 men, who were home on furlough, came in on the Wednesday. The men were welcomed to the town by Mr. E. C. Sewell, the High Steward of Cirencester, who expressed the desire of the townsfolk to do all in their power to make the men comfortable and to provide them with recreation during their stay,—a promise amply fulfilled by the kind folk of Cirencester, who that same week were receiving with equal welcome the South Wales Borderers, thankful to exchange the wooden huts of Draycott for the hospitality of the ancient " Queen of the Cotswolds."

On February 23rd, 1915, the Battalion left Cirencester after more than two months of hard training in most trying weather. Before their departure the High Steward wrote to Lieut. Col. W. S. Brown a letter expressing high appreciation of the splendid behaviour of the men, a spontaneous tribute and one expressed with such genuine feeling that it left the Wiltshiremen with the kindest memories of their hosts.

To Gallipoli. It is not necessary to dwell further upon the training of the Battalion at Woking or their movements before they embarked at Avonmouth on the steamship " Franconia " on July 1st, 1915. Their destination was the Dardanelles, and they landed at Cape Helles (through the steamship " Clyde ") on the 16th of July, moving to " Anzac " on August 2nd.

There were of course some Swindonians in other regiments already at the Dardanelles, and one of the earliest of the brave fellows who fell in this awful campaign was the eldest son of Mr. J. P. Kirby, the clerk to the Swindon and Highworth Board of Guardians. Coy. Sergt. Major J. H. Kirby was living in New South Wales when war broke out, and he left for Europe with the first Australian contingent ; he was killed in action on May 2nd, 1915.

On Gallipoli the Battalion was commanded by (amongst others) Lieut. Col. Carden, Lieut. Col. A. C. Lewin, C.M.G., D.S.O., who afterwards commanded the Brigade, and Lieut. Col. Throckmorton, of the Royal Welsh Fusiliers.

Chunuk Bair. During the fierce fighting in August, the 13th Division won great glory, and two of its units especially—the 5th Wiltshires and the 6th Loyal North Lancashires—who were sent to hold Chunuk Bair, were almost annihilated whilst performing prodigies of valour. To quote the " Egyptian Gazette " for April 25th, 1916, " these men of this ' Iron Division '—after this terrible baptism of death so valiantly endured it has earned that glorious name—supported such losses as have rarely been endured in war."

N

The details of these momentous days are given succinctly in a letter from Lance-Corp. A. G. Scott, of Swindon, who was awarded the D.C.M. for gallantry at Chunuk Bair. After speaking of the fresh landing at " Anzac," he says the Wiltshires had to make fresh positions on the 6th of August, and "dug in" before dark, losing several men in the course of the work. On the 7th the Australians passed them, bringing in about 600 Turkish prisoners. The Wilts remained in those trenches till Sunday night, the 8th of August, and then were sent to reinforce troops who had
The Turkish onslaught. taken "Hill 71" on Monday, the 2nd of August, taking over the front trenches. On August 10th at dawn they were attacked in enormous force, great numbers of Turks coming up on every side ; the Wiltshires were exposed to a terrible enfilading fire, having no communication trench to the rear, but only a slight gully. They were ordered to charge with the bayonet through this gully, and did so through a furious hail of shot ; but of 900 men only 200 got through, and amongst the killed was the Colonel of the Battalion.

Trapped in the Gully. The men hoped to get through to the beach, but the Turks blocked up the lower end of the combe with machine-guns. So there the survivors were trapped, taking what cover they could and seeing first one and then another of their comrades falling victims to snipers during the day. When night fell about 150 of the survivors managed to escape out of the trap under cover of darkness, leaving about twenty men still in this valley of death, of whom only five were unwounded. It is to be remembered that this awful experience was taking place during the tropical heat of August, and that parching thirst and lack of food intensified the sufferings of the hapless men. Darkness enabled the little band left behind to search for water, and they
Fifteen days of Torture. found a little muddy water, which, with some biscuits, helped to sustain them ; they attended to the wounded, and found the dead bodies of the major and adjutant. For fifteen days these men endured unspeakable sufferings in the gully ; the Turks knew they were there, and searched for them at night, and the men saw them robbing the dead whilst they themselves hid in the bushes. During the day they were exposed to the scorching heat and dare not show a sign of their presence ; at night they were exposed to almost equally intense cold and knew that Turks were prowling about searching for them ; for ten days they were without food ; the wounded died, and gradually the number of the little band was reduced to seven. At length two of them—Lance-Corp. Scott and Pte. R. Humphries,—crawled out at night ; they were seen by the watchful foe, determined if possible to let none escape, and were fired at, but they got through and on Wednesday, August 25th, they met some New Zealand soldiers who brought them in. Capt. J. W. Greany, of the 5th Wilts, received the news from the two who had escaped, and at once determined
Rescue. to rescue the others if it could be done. That night some Wiltshires and New Zealanders went out to seek them, but their plans were spoilt by the moon ; they ran into a Turkish patrol and came under rifle fire. The next night the rescuers were more successful, for they found the men, now half dead, and managed to get them away though exposed to heavy fire. Capt. Greany himself carried back a wounded man on his back, and at the same time gained much information of military value, his gallantry and services being recognized by the bestowal of the D.S.O. upon him. One of the seven survivors,
Honours. Pte. W. J. Head, abundantly earned the D.C.M. which was afterwards conferred upon him ; he was wounded three times between the 10th and 26th of August ; he collected food for the entrapped

party from the dead bodies lying about the gully—the sole source of supply,—and by his splendid endurance, services and qualities of leadership did much to keep up the courage of his comrades. As has been mentioned, Lance-Corp. Scott, too, and his comrade Pte. R. Humphries were awarded the D.C.M.

There were no doubt thousands of thrilling examples of courage and endurance exhibited during the great struggle of 1914-18, most of which will pass unrecorded, but there can be few more thrilling than this terrible battle of the 5th Wiltshires and the Loyal North Lancashires at Chunuk Bair and the fearful experiences of the beleaguered band in the infernal gully,—experiences of which this meagre account can give barely a hint. The whole 13th Division, under Major Gen. Shaw, suffered enormously and lost 6,000 men out of 10,500, and the offensive of August, 1915, was the last great effort made to dislodge the Turks from Gallipoli.

Honoured by the Czar. About this time some twenty officers and men of the 5th Wiltshires, the Berkshire Regiment, the Gloucester Regiment, the Berkshire Yeomanry, and the Gloucester Yeomanry were decorated by the Czar with the cross or the medal of the Order of St. George for gallant conduct at the Dardanelles ; of the Wiltshires the number included three non-commissioned officers and four privates.

Towards the close of December, 1915, the Wiltshires along with the rest of the troops were withdrawn from Suvla, and went to Cape Helles for the evacuation in January, 1916. As is well known, the withdrawal from Suvla and "Anzac," announced in the House of Commons on December 20th, was a magnificent operation most successfully executed, and the Turks, though in closest contact with the British troops, were quite unaware of what was going on.

To Egypt. The 5th Wiltshires were transported to Egypt, in ignorance of what their future field of operations was to be, though from their position they must have suspected that there was every probability of their being sent to Mesopotamia, where General Townsend was even now closely invested in Kut-el-Amara. They remained in Egypt, resting and training, for about two months, at a time of the year when the temperature and weather conditions of the northern district make the climate both healthy and pleasant. There the Wiltshires gave proof of the wonderful marching qualities for which they have always been noted, when on February 12th, 1916, at Port Said the Battalion carried off the Brigade endurance championship with flying colours, winning all four prizes.

A Peaceful Victory. Teams of about a dozen men from each company of every regiment in the Brigade entered for the test, which consisted of a race in full marching order over a course of nearly three miles, mostly on loose, yielding sand, under a brilliant sun. The teams had to finish at the rifle-range, where biscuits had to be brought down by rifle-fire. "A" Company of the 5th Wilts won easily, under Sergt. A. F. Love ; they passed the finishing-post in exactly 28 minutes and knocked down their twelve biscuits in thirty seconds : they carried off the 1st prize with 51 points, whilst the other prizes went to "D" Coy. with 39 points, "B" Coy. with 36, and "C" Coy. with 33—a notable triumph for the Regiment, causing the Brigadier-General to say that he would not fear for the success of the winning team in any military competition in any command in England.

Leaving Egypt. Lieut. Col. Throckmorton was now in command of the Battalion, and when orders came for it to go to Mesopotamia along with the rest of the now famous 13th Division, he conducted it thither, arriving early in March, and destined to fall with hundreds of his men a month after arriving in that unsavoury land. From now until the close of the war—over two-and-a-half years—the 5th Wilts Regiment's story lies in Mesopotamia.

Mesopo-tamia.* In the annals of the 5th Wiltshires "Mesopotamia" will remain a name of glorious memory, though to those who fought in its parching heat and drenching rains, its suffocating dust and abominable mud, it may be like the recollection of a nightmare, In this distant field, where they seemed cut off from civilization and from the true scene of the great struggle, they and their fellows struck a deadly blow at the combination that threatened civilization, and restored the prestige of the British name when it had suffered eclipse by the capture of General Townsend and his meagre force at Kut-el-Amara, after a siege lasting from December 3rd, 1915, to April 28th, 1916.

Events prior to the arrival of the Wilts. The Mesopotamian Expeditionary Force had left India in October, 1914, arriving at Fao on November 6th ; after considerable fighting the campaign of 1914 was ended by the capture of Qurna, situated at the confluence of the Euphrates and Tigris, and it left the British in control of the whole delta and the course of the river up to Qurna, including the important city of Basra.

The campaign of 1915 opened with a victory over the Turks at Shaiba, part of the defences of Basra, and in June Townsend began his glorious but tragic advance towards Bagdad ; he defeated the Turks in the second battle of Qurna on June 1st, and captured Amara on the 3rd ; General Gorringe, operating on the Euphrates, captured Nasiriyeh on July 25th, and Townsend, steadily pushing north, captured Kut-el-Amara on September 28th; here, in view of his small force and his long line of communications, the British general should have stayed, but General Sir John Nixon, Commander-in-Chief of the Expeditionary force, considered that he was strong enough with the forces at his command to take Bagdad. Consequently

Ctesiphon. General Townsend pursued the enemy, reaching Aziziyeh by October 5th and Ctesiphon by November 21st. Here, after a four days' battle, the British force was so thinned that it had no alternative but retreat, reaching Kut on December 2nd, after a march that had tried its endurance

Townsend in Kut. and its general's skill to the utmost ; here, in a great loop of the Tigris, they "dug themselves in" to await reinforcements which were even then only just being shipped at Marseilles ; these consisted of the 3rd and 7th Indian divisions.

First efforts to relieve Kut. These reinforcements reached Ali Gharbi, about 60 or 70 miles below Kut, on January 5th, 1916, and within a fortnight two-thirds of the relieving column, pushing on under General Younghusband, were sick, wounded, or dead. On January 7th the first battle of Sheikh Saad

Battle of Sheikh Saad. began, lasting three days, and although the Turks were forced to retire, the relieving force lost 4,262 of General Aylmer's column,— losses that completely overwhelmed the scandalously inadequate medical organization. The next few weeks were spent in futile and

Failure at Es Sinn. costly attacks on the Turkish trenches, culminating in the disastrous attack on Es Sinn on March 8th. This attack should have been deferred until the arrival of General Maude with the 13th Division, of which the 5th Wiltshires under Lieut. Col. Throckmorton formed a part ; they were even then entering El Orah, 30 miles or thereabouts distant, but the attack on Es Sinn was precipitated by the fear—unfounded, as it turned out,—that

* Mr. Edmund Candler's excellent work "The Long Road to Bagdad" (Cassell ; 2 Vols.; 35/- net) is the source of the *outline* of the history.

Townsend could not hold out, and by the expectation of the river's rising by March 15th. The result was that the attackers were defeated in a terrible assault on the Dujaila Redoubt, and the relieving force had to settle down into trenches at El Orah, its base.

Arrival of the Fifth Wilts. It is at this point that the *5th Wiltshires* began to play a part in the struggle. As though their martyrdom in the inferno of Gallipoli had not been enough, they were thrust into this land of barren sand and pestilential swamp where the same stubborn foe that had successfully resisted them at Gallipoli barred their way to Kut and Bagdad.

In Camp at Sheikh Saad. The first two battalions of the *13th Division** arrived at El Orah on March 8th, the very day of the attack on Es Sinn, and the complete division was encamped at Sheikh Saad, a few miles below El Orah, by March 25th ; the *5th Wiltshires* formed part of the *40th Infantry Brigade.*

Mr. J. C. Gilbert, the son of Councillor A. J. Gilbert, was with *the Wilts,* holding a lieutenant's commission, and he graphically describes the march of *the Wiltshires* from Sheikh Saad to El Orah, the advanced base, He says,—

A Swindonian's Experience. "On the night of March 31st, we marched from Sheikh Saad to Orah, a distance of seven miles over open country. Unfortunately we got a very heavy thunderstorm, and, as the country floods very easily, the conditions were awful. The irrigated ditches were full of mud and water, and, being too large to jump, you slid down one bank and crawled up the other. The trip took from nine p.m. to five a.m. The pack mules had to be hauled up the sides of the dykes. None could stand and everyone was wet through and covered with mud up to the eyes. The next day was fine, but the night the absolute limit, and there were very few tents. I slept in a small bivouac tent with three others and a pool of water. We did the seven miles in mud like Draycott at its worst and the dykes extra. Having had a few hours of sunshine I have dug myself out. I am at present sitting in the corner of a trench in the sun, clad only in hat, shirt and shorts ; my boots, socks, tunic and putties are drying in the sun. When dry the clothing stands upright."

Until April 5th no further attempt to break through the Turkish lines was made, and the conditions of trench-warfare prevailed here as in Flanders except that the area covered by trenches was far deeper than anything on the same length of front in Flanders, though held far more lightly. There were no resources in camp as there were in France to vary the monotony of the spells of relief, and regiments were even known to grumble at being relieved, for there was always a little chance of excitement in the trenches where the Turks gave little trouble with artillery.

Engaged at El-Hannah, But on April 5th the turn of the *13th Division* came. The time fixed for the break through at Umm-el-Hannah was 4.45 a.m., and the *40th Brigade* (including *the Wiltshires*) had sapped to within 100 yards of the enemy's trenches and to within 70 yards of his wire, now broken down by the British gun-fire. Every man knew his exact time and place, for they had repeatedly rehearsed the attack on a plan to scale. The Turks evidently knew what was coming, for they had evacuated the front trench-line except for a few rifles and a machine gun. At 4.45 our bombing parties crept over the parapet and were in the first trenches in a few seconds ; they passed on and found the second and third lines empty, and then crept on under the artillery screen to the last line, a full mile in the rear. The Turks had fallen back on a

and Falahiyeh. position at Falahiyeh, 3 miles behind el-Hannah, and the *40th Brigade,* which was leading, came under heavy fire at 1,000 yards, and advanced to within 400 yards when they dug themselves in and waited for

* ‡In order to follow the movements of the 5th Wilts the reader should bear in mind the three terms here indicated,—13th Division, 40th Brigade, and the regiment. They will be italicised as they occur.

dark ; then they rushed the position, and the 38th and 39th brigades came in and cleared out the Turks at 7.45 p.m. The casualties during the day amounted to 1,912 ; the field was a naked stretch of mud and clay, without a particle of cover above ground, but the Division, although full of fresh men, had fought like veterans.

The Turks made their next stand at Sannaiyat, where they occupied **First attack** three lines of trenches, flanked by the river on their right and by the **at Sannaiyat.** Suwacha Marsh on their left. The 7th Division came up at night to relieve the *13th Division*, and in the dark lost the track ; consequently they were delayed and at 5.30 a.m. on April 6th, when it was quite light, found themselves 800 yards from the position ; they were met with a terrible fire at 700 yards, and after advancing 200 yards had to fall back and dig themselves in. They lost terribly both on this day and on the next, their casualties amounting to 2,650, and it was demonstrated that it was a fatal mistake to attempt anything in daylight.

On April 9th the *13th Division* delivered a second attack on the **Second attack** Turkish position at Sannaiyat at 4.30 a.m. ; some of *the Wiltshires*, **at Sannaiyat.** the Welsh Fusiliers, the King's Own and the North Lancashires got in, but very few got back. The Turks had behind the third line a marvellous labyrinth of bomb-chambers which it was impossible to locate, and the British first line was subjected to a shower of grenades from these hidden points ; the second line lost direction and the attack was paralysed. The Division lost from 1,600 to 1,700, making a total of about 3,600 casualties in the *13th Division* in the two attacks at Falahiyeh and Sannaiyat.

And now the Tigris rose in flood and the weather was appalling, with terrible thunderstorms, waterspouts, hailstorms, and hurricanes ; the water broke into the trenches and men even had to swim for their lives ; the narrow waterlogged front at Sannaiyat became, for both British and Turks, a " recognized impasse." Between April 5th and 9th, *the Wilts* lost about 30 officers and 700 men killed or wounded, many of the latter being drowned in the floods. The Regiment had the misfortune to lose in this terrible struggle at Sannaiyat its gallant Commander, Lieut. Col. Throckmorton, and the command passed to Capt. Bosanquet, M.C., of the Duke of Cornwall's Light Infantry and then to Capt. Robertson, of the Gordon Highlanders, until relieved at the end of April by Lieut. Col. R. H. Heseldine D.S.O., of the King's (Liverpool) Regiment.

The Wilts   Lieut. Gilbert wrote of these engagements as follows :— **engaged.**

" 7th April, 1916.
Was in a very hot show, day before yesterday. This division drove the Turks back about six miles. Should be in Kut in a day or so. Capt. Boot of the Cheshires was killed quite close to me. We are still advancing. We had the H.C. in the trenches at 6 o'clock this morning.

8th April, 1916.
Lice are the trouble.
As I told you, this Division went into the trenches on Sunday evening last, closed up into the front line trenches on Tuesday night to attack at dawn. After spending a very cold night, packed into trenches very tight, we got over the parapet at nine minutes to five and attacked at five to five, to find that the Turks had practically evacuated the position, leaving only about fifty men there.
We of course went right through, reformed at the rear of the position and pushed on, came up with the Turkish rearguard, entrenched, extended, and the *40th Brigade* advanced to about five hundred yards of them under very heavy rifle and machine gun fire. Our artillery is magnificent, and shuts theirs up every time. We dug in and hung on until dusk, when the 38th Brigade went through us and made a big advance. The 6th and 7th

divisions went through them and are now engaging them. The extent of the advance was about six miles. The division, particularly this brigade, made a great name for itself. We are now in support, holding some converted Turkish trenches.

We, of course, have no kit, and hardly find a waterproof sheet warm enough at night, but it is too hot during the day to carry more."

Victory at Belt Aieesa. In view of the hopelessness of an attack at Sannaiyat in the conditions now existing, the attempt to break through was transferred to the other side of the river, and the 7th and 9th brigades made a successful attack on Beit Aieesa on April 15th to the 17th ; this was followed by a tremendous counter-attack by the Turks, and the *13th Division* had to send reinforcements ; two battalions of the *40th Brigade*, of which the *Wiltshires* were one, reinforced the left flank, which the 8th Brigade had gallantly held against many heavy assaults. But it was the 7th Brigade, on the right flank, that by its coolness and steadiness saved the day and converted what might have been a severe reverse into a memorable victory ; the Turks lost in killed alone 3,000, and besides a proportionate number of wounded they lost 400 prisoners.

Capture of Kut by the Turks. On April 22nd a third attack on Sannaiyat was made by a composite Scotch battalion of Black Watch and Seaforth Highlanders ; they " got in." but their rifles were choked with mud and useless for firing, and a fearful struggle in the liquid mud of the water-logged trenches ended with no result. This was the destruction of any hopes of relieving General Townsend, and Kut fell into the hands of the Turks on April 28th.

Trench Life and Tropical Hardships. The summer was now at hand ; even if the pressing need for a forward movement had still existed the heat would have compelled the relieving force to relax its efforts. The Turks also were suffering from their heavy losses, and the threat of the Russian General Baratoff advancing from north-western Persia compelled them to reduce their Mesopotamian army : they therefore evacuated the Es Sinn position on May 19th and the British occupied it. No further operations could be undertaken till the winter, and a period of great hardship and suffering for our men ensued ; the heat was terrible, the thermometer recording 125° in the shade, which meant at least 130° in the tents, and for five months the men suffered tortures that none but those who have endured them can conceive ; fearful havoc was wrought by disease—cholera, dysentery, scurvy, boils, jaundice, and many other forms of sickness,—and every week 2,500 were evacuated at the clearing hospital at Sheikh Saad, and in addition to the crowds that filled every hospital in the country 15,000 sick left Basra for India in a month ; drafts of reinforcements arriving at Basra almost melted away before they reached the front, and, to crown all, the medical resources were entirely inadequate to cope with the situation. Such were the conditions in which the *5th Wiltshires* and their comrades in arms spent the summer and autumn of 1916, longing for the winter which should bring the lesser trials of the battlefield, even great as they were. The whole division had gone down from Es Sinn to Amara in July to re-form and receive reinforcements, and it returned in time to participate in General Maude's winter offensive.

General Maude's Offensive. General Maude's offensive opened on December 13th with a surprise march by the Cavalry Division and the 3rd Corps (including the *13th* and 14th Divisions) upon the Shatt-el-Hai—the old bed of the Tigris joining Kut, on the Tigris, with Nasiriyeh, on the Euphrates. The Turks at Sannaiyat who were opposed by the 7th Division were kept

Establishing a Position West of Kut. in their trenches, and Turkish reinforcements were drawn there by a heavy bombardment, and the night march on the Hai was entirely successful ; the *Wiltshires* were the first regiment to cross the Hai, and later the cavalry crossed and pushed on to the Shumran Bridge across the Tigris, six miles above Kut. On the night of the 14th our airmen bombed the gun-boat removing the pontoons, which were cast adrift, and the Turks left on the west bank could only cross by ferry. The following day the 38th and 39th Brigades pushed to within 600 yards of the Hai bridge-head guarding Kut on the south-west and then dug in ; in order to protect their left flank the 35th and *40th Brigades* spread out two miles to the westward.

The Wilts at Mahomed Abdul Hassan. January 9th to 19th was devoted to the capture of the Mahomed Abdul Hassan loop of the Tigris below Kut, an operation that fell to the 3rd Division and had to be achieved before any attack on the Hai salient could hope for success. This attack began on January 25th, and the *Wiltshires* were called upon to play a leading part in it. Their brigade—*the 40th*—were attacking on the east bank of the Hai ; Mr. E. Candler, the official " Eye-witness " of the Mesopotamian Expeditionary Force, says, " I was with *the Wiltshires* in the trench when they went over. They looked thoughtful and a little strung up, but there was no tiredness about them. When the yellow flags were hoisted to show that they had got in, I crossed over and found the enemy's firing trench broken up by our artillery and heaped with dead, the parapets fallen in on a debris of rifles and ammunition and litter of all kinds. We captured two officer prisoners, 136 rank and file, three trench mortars and a machine gun. During the day the Turks made repeated attempts to bomb us out of the ground gained, both on our flanks and in attacks directed down our communication trenches on to our centre. *The Wiltshires* and Royal Welsh Fusiliers stood their ground and out-bombed them every time." Thus the *40th Brigade* closed in on the Turks on the east bank day by day, being relieved on February 1st by the 8th Brigade, only to be called out on the night of February 2nd for a flanking movement. Between January 25th and the 31st the *40th Brigade* had dug 7½ miles of trenches, besides repairing and re-wiring 4 miles of captured trenches.

Clearing the West Bank. By February 10th the Turks were driven across the river to the bank of the Hai where the Turks had all the while been making a magnificent resistance, but had been gradually pushed back till the 62nd Punjabis entered Kut liquorice factory, in the angle formed by the Tigris and the Hai on the west, on February 10th.

In the Dahra Bend. The next stage was to clear the Dahra bend in the Tigris, above Kut, an operation that took from February 11th to the 15th. The *40th Brigade* lost 330 on the 15th when the final blow was struck, but they and the 35th Brigade captured prisoners to the extent of one-eighth of the Turkish general's whole army, for the enemy, driven back on the Tigris, surrendered en masse ; 2,200 prisoners were taken, vast quantities of material of all kinds, and two brigadier-generals. The rain, for which the Turks had been praying, came that night ; but it came too late, for the British now held the Tigris right bank for thirty miles, from Sannaiyat to Shumran. The river was now swollen to a width of 400 yards and flowed with a strong current ; in places it expanded to 800 yards, and the crossing of such a river with a determined enemy on the far bank seemed a hopeless project, but it was to be accomplished.

Crossing the Tigris. February 23rd, 1917, was the day chosen for the attempt to cross the Tigris, and the project was magnificently executed by men of the Norfolks, Hants, and Gurkhas at three different points in the Shumran bend ; the first boats pushed off at 5.15 a.m., and in spite of hot fire landings were effected, and by 4 p.m. a bridge had been built over which the transport was already crossing ; 600 prisoners were taken in the day, which concluded by seeing the infantry established on a ridge astride the bend. Meanwhile, on the Sannaiyat position an attack had been begun the day before with the object of drawing Turkish troops from Shumran, and it was continued on the 23rd ; it had been thoroughly rehearsed and was supported by splendid gunnery. The success

Capture of Kut. was complete, at the cost of 1,414 casualties ; the Turks had lost heavily and now beat a hasty retreat, leaving Kut empty. The river was now clear for the Navy, and on February 25th the *40th Brigade* saw with delight our gunboats coming up the river, ready to join in the pursuit. The *13th Division* had crossed to the eastern bank of the Tigris the day before to take up the chase and had a stiff encounter with the Turks, then making a stand to cover the withdrawal of their guns from Sannaiyat. This was the last serious fight till March 7th, by which time the Turks were making a stand on the River Diala.

At the River Diala. The *13th Division* led the attack at the Diala, and the 6th King's Own of the 38th or Lancashire Brigade were the first to cross the river ; crew after crew was destroyed, and every effort to establish a footing failed. The attempt was renewed on the night of the 8th by the Loyal North Lancashires ; this time a footing was secured, the attackers being protected by the dust raised by the barrage ; the little party held on till night and when they were relieved had come almost to their last cartridge.

The Wilts surprise the Enemy. That night the *Wiltshires* effected a crossing higher up the stream, and their action was such a surprise to the Turks that their footing was established before the enemy realised what had occurred, and by 9.30 a.m. all the 38th Brigade had got across. The way was now clear to Bagdad, which was entered on March 11th.

Bagdad.

But there was no rest for the *13th Division* in Bagdad ; they and the 14th Division continued to advance on the east bank of the Tigris whilst other forces followed the railway on the west side ; these latter had to fight a stiff action at Mushadie, whilst the eastern arm was concerned mainly in preventing a junction between the Tigris force opposed to them and the Turkish 13th Army Corps on the Persian frontier ; this was retiring before the Russians and now held a strong position on the British right in the Jebel Hamrin range. To prevent a junction, which would have enormously strengthened the opposition to the British advance, the 39th and *40th Brigades* attacked the Tigris force at Dogameh, whilst the 8th and 9th Brigades engaged the Jebel Hamrin force. The latter operation was unsuccessful and the Turkish 13th Army Corps got across the Diala, but were prevented from

The Wilts Charge at Dogameh. achieving their purpose by the success of the 39th and *40th Brigades* at Dogameh where they had to attack across a perfectly smooth cement floor—the " Marl Plain." Mr. Candler says, " The *5th Wilts* made a memorable advance over the last thousand yards of flat. They started a bare 500 strong, though they were the strongest battalion in the brigade ; 195 dropped going over, including seven officers, but they got in and drove the Turks from their line of rifle-pits in front of the position." At night the Turks fell back on the River Shatt-el-Adhaim, and entrenched themselves near its confluence with the Tigris.

The battle of Dogamch took place on March 29th, and it was intended to attack the Turks at their new position on April 11th, but on the 10th the Cavalry Division, which was containing the Jebel Hamrin Turks, reported that they were advancing in strength, and the attack had to be deferred whilst the **Fighting in** 30th and *40th Brigades* went to the support of the Cavalry ; they **the Desert.** made a night march of twenty miles from the Shatt-el-Adhaim across the desert, meeting the Cavalry near Shialah ; here began a battle in the open which developed into a running fight lasting four days, at the close of which —on April 15th—the Turks had taken shelter in the hills.

The course was now clear for the forcing of the Adhaim, and this **Forcing the** was splendidly executed by the 38th Brigade, 500 prisoners being **Shatt-el-** taken ; the cavalry then came in and captured 700 more, so that **Adhaim.** the entire force disputing the passage of the river was annihilated.

The Jebel Hamrin army, however, was by no means disposed of, and **Finishing** with the object of saving Samarrah—the next British objective—it **the Jebel-** advanced from the hills down the Shatt-el-Adhaim and took up a **Hamrin** strong position at Dahuba. The leading division only was at Dahuba **Force.** and the second was some miles in the rear, when a prompt attack on the first force drove it back on the second ; the whole Turkish force then **Battle of** fell back to a very strong position astride the Adhaim near the foot **Band-i-** of the Jebel Hamrin ; here, at Band-i-Adhaim, on April 30th, was **Adhaim.** fought the bloodiest battle of the Mesopotamian campaign in proportion to the numbers engaged. The *40th Brigade*, with the Cheshires and South Wales Borderers, was chosen for the decisive blow in the centre supported by the 38th and 35th Brigades on the right and left. They advanced at 5 a.m. across a bare plain, behind a heavy barrage, and drove the Turks out of their trenches. It was a splendid attack, and in their zeal the Cheshires and Borderers overshot the objectives assigned to them, captured eight guns and 800 prisoners, and had the Turks fairly beaten. Suddenly, however, a duststorm arose that hid the whole battlefield, and under cover of it the Turks counter-attacked with their main reserve ; they passed right in front of the 38th Brigade without being seen and delivered a tremendous blow on a very narrow front ; they recaptured seven of the guns and 450 of the prisoners, and the Cheshires and Borderers were enveloped. The situation was saved by the Machine-gun section and the *Wiltshires* and Royal Welsh Fusiliers, whom General Lewin hurried up to support the imperilled regiments ; they held up the counter-attack, and when the dust-storm subsided at 4 p.m. the artillery got to work. By 9 p.m. the Turks were routed and the Jebel Hamrin force was entirely broken. This was the end of the fighting in the campaign of 1916-17.

But already the 7th Division had entered Samarrah, moving along **In Samarrah.** the railway and fighting two desperate battles at Istabulat on April 21st and in front of Samarrah on the 22nd,—battles that should live in the annals of British gallantry. Samarrah was now the British summer quarters ; the last month of the campaign had been strenuous, but the result was seen in the capture of 3,000 prisoners and 16 guns. The summer of 1917 was quiet but for a few minor incidents, until operations were resumed towards the close of September, when movements began both on the Euphrates and the Tigris.

On the Euphrates the object aimed at was the capture of Ramadi ; it was
attained by fine soldiership, and the Lower Euphrates was closed to
Clearing the the Turks as a supply-base. Meanwhile the Jebel Hamrin force
Jebel had been threatening trouble to the Tigris army, and the *13th Division*
Hamrin. and the 14th were set the task of dislodging it from its position in
the hills. On October 18th the *40th Brigade* occupied Deli Abbas, west
of the Diala River, the 38th occupied Mansuriyeh on the east, the 35th was in the
centre, and the 36th and 37th worked along the ridge of the Jebel Hamrin. The
object was to envelop the Turks and when the cavalry got round to the rear the
end seemed accomplished ; but during the night the Turks slipped through the net.
The operations were, however, not fruitless, for the Jebel Hamrin force ceased to
be a menace to the British flank.

North of Samarrah Turkish threats compelled a further advance up the Tigris,
and the enemy was driven northwards until the British occupied Tekrit on Nov.
5th.

The Turks now evaded conflict as much as possible, and the British forces
were strengthened by the junction with the Cossack forces under General Bicharakoff
from the Persian front. The Russians co-operated with our army in clearing the
Turkish 13th Army Corps out of the Jebel Hamrin, a task in which the *40th Brigade*
played a leading part ; on December 3rd the *40th Brigade*, as part of a general
assault, surprised the Turks in a frontal attack after a night march in the hills west
of Deli Abbas, and two days later they cleared the Sakal Tutan Pass near Kara
Tapa, attacked the Turkish left and gained the hill crests ; in the course of these
operations the *40th Brigade* spent two nights without their first or second line
transports, and it was fortunate that the cold spell did not set in a few days earlier,
for the weather now turned bitterly cold. Had the men been exposed to the terrible
inclemency of the winter in these altitudes without proper provision the consequences would have been disastrous ; as it was, the expedition was a severe test
of endurance.

Apart from the interest of the story, the following diary of these
A Swindon operations of the *5th Wiltshires* in the Jebel Hamrin hills has a
Lad's Diary. special local interest, for it was drawn up by a Swindon lad—a private
in the *5th Wiltshires*,—and it is a striking illustration of the well
trained type of mind that Swindon sent into the Army. The young man was one
of the early volunteers, led to enlist by a lofty and single-minded patriotism.

Dec. 3rd. 5th Wilts proceed in motor lorries to the base to the Hills, pending
1 a.m. offensive operations in Jebel Hamrin Hills.
5 a.m. Moved towards hills ; entered and reconnoitred. Plan of approach
to hills :—

See page 316 (Plan No. 1.)

About Passed well into ridge ; saw two Turkish field guns complete with
8 a.m. teams, etc., under escort of S.W. Borderers. Later, passed old mud
fort held that morning by Turks but captured by S.W. Borderers.
Signs of hurried flight of Turks to be seen everywhere, viz : fresh
meat, clothing, saddlery, shells, etc. Later, was on outpost duty
until about 5 p.m., then proceeded to Bde. H. Qrs. near main pass.
Turks said to be holding pass. Remained at Bde. H.Q., all night,
except R.W. Fusiliers who occupied pass. Turks retreated.
4th Dec. 5th Wilts commenced march through pass and passed through Cheshires
7 a.m. and S.W. Borderers, then holding pass ; R.W. Fusiliers had gone on

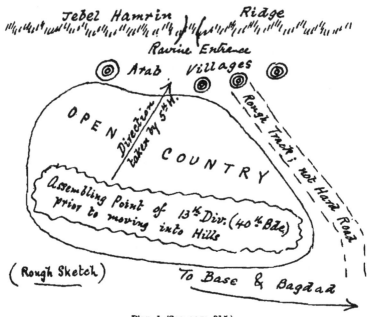

Plan 1 (See page 315.)

ahead. Marched about 14 miles to river and broken bridge about 10 miles from Kara Tapa. Turks said to be holding position 8 miles ahead. Rough plan of camp for this night :—

See page 317 (Plan No. 2.)

5th Dec. 7 a.m.	5th Wilts crossed river and after 10 minutes halt began march to left flank of Kara Tapa; forced march of 2¼ hrs. Turks retreated and held position at Kara Tapa village and surrounding hills.
10 a.m.	Reached flank position. Attack had opened on right flank and centre by 14th Division and S.W. Bdrs; 8th Cheshires supporting S.W. Bdrs. attacking main village; R.W. Fus. supporting 5th Wilts attacking left flank.
About 10.30 a.m.	5th Wilts "A" Coy. opened attack on flank, followed by "C" Coy. supporting. Battery to left of Wilts was severely shelled with shrapnel; guns out of action for a bit, but later did fine work, silencing Turkish battery on left flank.
About 11 a.m.	Turks commenced falling back; village in the hands of S.W. Bdrs; troops on right and left flanks steadily obtaining positions of the Turks.
About noon.	Turks abandoned position and were in full retreat, cavalry pursuing.
About 3 p.m.	5th Wilts took up outpost positions for the night, "C" Coy. facing Kifri. Coal mines at Kifri seen burning at night, destroyed by Turks.

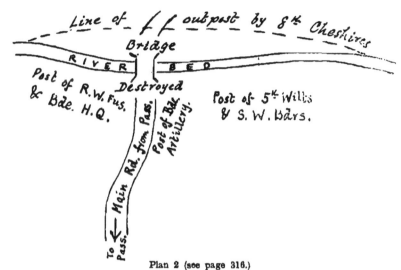

Line of f f outpost by 8th Cheshires
Bridge
RIVER BED
Post of R.W. Fus. & Bde. H.Q.
Destroyed
Post of 5th Wilts & S.W. Bers.
Post of Bde. Artillery.
Main Rd. from Pass.
To Pass.

Plan 2 (see page 316.)

40th Brigade too exhausted to press on further; in fact it was not intended.

6th Dec. Remained in position all day till 4 p.m., then drew in outposts, joined Battalion H.Q., and began retirement to river and broken bridge. Perfect silence the whole march back that night. Reason of retirement not known definitely: movements very strange.

7th Dec. Re-entered and marched through main pass. Terrible dust-storm all the way; no water available; condition of troops terrible but they stuck it. About 5 p.m., camped for the night. Dead beat; too exhausted to eat; the water was a sure " Gift of God."

8th Dec. Marched off for original camp, reaching it about 1 p.m.; settled
About down to usual routine of duties. Offensive stunt over; Turks
9 a.m. routed from Kara Tapa and broken up: positions safe for a while. Rough sketch of attack on Kara Tapa :—

See page 318 (Plan No. 3.)

Before the Spring was over the Division had captured Altun Kupry on the Lesser Zab.

It must be remembered that simultaneously with this successful conquest of the Tigris basin and the Persian border, equally good progress was being made by the forces entrusted with the conquest of the Euphrates basin, where Hit, Khan Baghdadi, Haditha, and Ana were successively occupied, carrying the Euphrates force about as far up the river as the other branch had advanced up the Tigris.

In the summer of 1918 the *13th Division* was again occupied in a big
Clearing drive beyond the Jebel Hamrin; it brilliantly defeated the Turks
Southern at Tuz Kharmatli, on the great road from Bagdad to Mosul via Kifri
Kurdistan. and Kerkuk at the base of the Jebel Hamrin, and entered Kerkuk on May 7th, thus clearing Southern Kurdistan. The Division retired

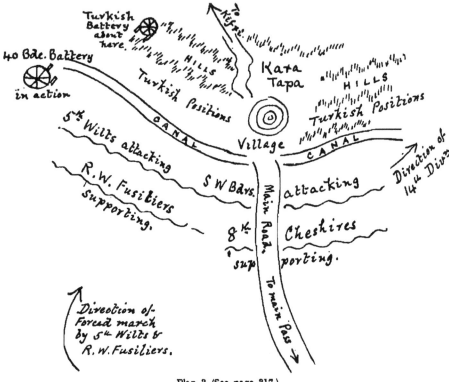

Plan 3 (See page 317.)

to Tuz Kharmatli for the summer of 1918, and in the autumn again advanced and occupied Kerkuk and Altun Kupry, which places the *Wiltshires* held at the time the Armistice was declared.

Changes in Command. Lieut. Col. R. H. Heseldine, D.S.O., after having commanded the *5th Wiltshires* in all their operations since April, 1916, left the Battalion after the victory at Tuz Kharmatli in the Spring of 1918 ; he had earned the regard of his men by his unremitting attention to their physical well-being and his determination that, for marching or fighting, they should always be as fully rationed as was possible in the circumstances. He was succeeded by the Adjutant, Temp. Capt. R. Scorer, M.C., with the rank of Temporary Major, who was relieved in November, 1918, by Capt. (Acting Lieut. Col.) L. Kettlewell, D.S.O., an original member of the Battalion.

Whilst speaking of these changes one may at this point conclude the details. The last mentioned officer left the Battalion to join the Political Service in February, 1919, and was succeeded by Capt. (Acting Lieut. Col.) H. E. Wood, of the East Lancashires, who commanded the Battalion and the cadre until its return to England. The distinction of being the only officer who served with the Battalion during the

whole of its existence belongs to the Quarter-master, Capt. G. R. Rumsey, M.C.
The Armistice forestalled a winter compaign, but on October 31st,
The the day before the Armistice was signed, General Marshall enveloped
Armistice. and captured the whole Turkish army on the Tigris at Kalaat Shergat,
about 50 miles south of Mosul. The great general whose genius had
made this possible, and who had restored the prestige of the British arms after
the disaster of Kut did not live to see the consummation of his work, for General
Maude had now been in his grave nearly a year ; he had died of cholera at Bagdad
on November 18th, 1917. But in no area of the Great War was victory so
complete as in Mesopotamia, nowhere had greater hardship been more bravely
overcome and nowhere had our men had to fight with more dogged determination.
The *5th Wiltshries* came down to Amara for demobilization in
Demobiliza- February, 1919, and the cadre left Basra in May ; they were detained
tion. in India during the trouble on the Afghan frontier and did not arrive
in England till August, 1919. The men who were not eligible for
demobilization proceeded to Kasvin, in Northern Persia, where they joined the
1/4 Hampshire Regiment.

The Wiltshire Regiment is proud of its history, and has a name in the British
army as one of the most indomitable regiments of infantry ; the 5th Battalion,
having undergone the most trying labours in perhaps the two worst areas of the
Great War,—Gallipoli and Mesopotamia,—not only worthily upheld the glory
of the Regiment, but added lustre to its noble record. The cost, however,
was terrible, and amongst a crowd of young and gallant Wiltshiremen some of
the best of Swindon's youth now sleep on the barren hills by the Dardanelles or on
the scorched plains of the Tigris. The total deaths, outside the officers, was 601.

The colours of the Battalion, along with those of the 6th and 7th Service
Battalions, hang in St. James' Church, Devizes, at which town the cadre was
disbanded in September, 1919.

CHAPTER VIII.

The Wiltshires in Macedonia.
The 7th Wilts.

The 7th Wilts. The 7th Wiltshire Battalion—the "Shiny Seventh," as it came to be called from its superior smartness,—was formed at Codford Camp, near Salisbury, in the autumn of 1914, remaining there under canvas till near the close of the year. It then went into billets at Marlborough until May, 1915, and then, after a short recruiting campaign at Devizes, finished its training at Sutton Veny, near Warminster. Lieut. Col. Rocke, its Commanding Officer, gave his men an exceptionally thorough training, the results of which were very evident when the Battalion went out on active service, proving once more that good discipline and perfect training are the key to efficient soldiership.

France. In September, 1915, the Battalion was ordered to France, and after reaching Amiens it remained in the neighbourhood of Amiens and Villers Bretonneaux marching, countermarching, and training until it was sent into the trenches at Fricourt in October. Suddenly, however, the Battalion was withdrawn to Villers Bocage and fitted out for Saloniki; after a night march it entrained at Amiens and for three days was travelling by rail to Marseilles,—a slow, tedious journey in uncomfortable and greatly overcrowded trucks. Thus the 7th Wilts, on its first visit to France, saw no real engagement though it had a taste of trench-warfare, which, however, by no means prepared it for the stiff trench-work it was destined to do in Macedonia.

To Saloniki. The sea-journey to Saloniki on board an old battleship—H.M.S. "Hannibal"—took ten days, for on account of the danger from submarines the vessel had to follow a circuitous route which took it almost into Alexandria ; but towards the end of November the Wiltshires landed at Saloniki and took up their quarters in camp at Lembet, quite near to the city.

At this time both the military and the political situations in Macedonia and Greece were very critical. The British 10th Division was retiring through Serbia on to the Doiran line, and the 22nd Division was encamped on the Monastir road. The whole Greek army was concentrated around Saloniki, bitterly hostile to the British and French, in a position to destroy the Allied force if a chance spark should start the flames of war ; at the same time the British naval guns commanded Saloniki and Athens and were in a position to destroy these cities if the Allied armies were attacked. The Greeks would only allow one train a day to communicate with the British troops in the interior, so one may imagine how difficult the situation was for the 10th Division. Saloniki itself was a nest of thieves and murderers and reeked with filth and disease ; at once the 7th Wiltshires took over the town-guard, and before long established order in the city, the Provost Marshal complimenting them highly for the way in which they had restored order and preserved property.

The Bird-cage Line. The Battalion was engaged in forming the line of fortifications that enclosed Saloniki about seven miles or thereabouts away ; the line was known as the " Bird-cage line," and on the British portion of it four divisions were established. The winter was a most trying time for the troops, providing them with their first experience of the terrible blizzards and Vardar winds whilst they had no shelter but canvas ; storms and floods taught the men how to bivouac with nothing but a waterproof sheet in the open country ; and they were short of fuel. All the time the work was exceedingly heavy, for it consisted of sheer hard digging with nothing but pick and shovel in the solid rock for eight to ten hours a day. Rations, too, were very short and very monotonous. Thus, although they had no fighting, the winter of 1915-16 was very trying, and the men were exposed to frequent air-raids by zeppelins and aeroplanes, one of the former being brought down in the Vardar marshes.

The work on the Saloniki fortifications lasted till June, 1916, varied by occasional treks into the hills as far as the Struma. In the early part of 1916 the strain was eased somewhat by the gradual removal of the Greek army to the south. Then came the Allied note to Greece in June and the concession of the Allies' demands, and the military authorities at Saloniki were free to develop their plans. General Sarrail very cleverly occupied the public buildings of Saloniki while the Greek soldiers were attending the King's name-day celebration, at the very time when the Wiltshires were holding an assault-at-arms at Lajna, on the Langaza Plain, just outside the city.

The Doiran Line. The Wiltshires were now (June, 1916) sent up country as far as Gnojna, south of Kukus, and then went on, trekking by night amidst occasional prairie fires ; by day they had to lie, motionless and " camouflaged," in the bare open country under a broiling sun, to escape the observation of the Bulgars and the attentions of the German travelling aeroplane squadron; thus they went on until they took over from the French part of the Doiran line at Kalinova. There they found the Bulgars established in positions practically impregnable, well designed and well constructed, where the great natural advantages of the country had been marvellously adapted for defence by the best military art. The Wiltshires lay about seven miles in front, and for the next month big fighting-patrols, operating for twenty-four hours or more, were sent out regularly and paved the way for a closer advance to the Bulgarian lines. During one of these Lieut. Goldie, of the 7th Wilts, and his servant were out sketching, and suddenly encountered a number of Bulgars whom they dispersed, capturing much material and successfully bringing it back in a retiring action. The hill upon which the affair took place was named " Goldie's Hill " upon the military maps and became a notorious place for raids. The work of the patrols sent out by the Wiltshires, organized chiefly by Lieuts. Goldie and H. Thomas, of Swindon, was characterized by the splendid discipline and coolness of the men, a result of Col. Rocke's fine training.

Severe Fighting. In August, 1916, the patrols had made a further advance possible. On the first night of this advance the Wiltshires began to " dig in," though in the hard rock this consisted of little more than making shallow depressions ; in these they lay out all the next day, camouflaged, and dug in again at night. This went on for three days, and each night patrols and listening posts were thrown forward. And now a general attack by the Bulgars was developed under a heavy artillery bombardment ; in the course of the engagement, Capt. Hughes, of Marlborough, went out with another officer and

o

a patrol of about a score of men ; as they advanced to a hill-crest the advance party of the patrol was suddenly met by rifle-fire, and the junior officer was killed whilst several other casualties were inflicted on the patrol ; Private Berry, with the utmost gallantry, went back up the hill and carried his officer back under fire,—a deed for which he afterwards was decorated with the Military Medal.

Owing to the fact that the Bulgarian artillery fire was not raised, the Bulgars could not develop their attack as was intended, except in a few places where they were repulsed by machine-gun and rifle fire. The British artillery could give no support to their own men, being without proper maps and having no register of the ranges ; thus the infantry had to rely upon its own efforts entirely. " A " Company of the Wilts sent out a fighting-patrol, consisting of a platoon and a Lewis-gun, which gave an excellent account of itself, and " C " Company was attacked on a hill called the " Bastion," repulsing the enemy with rifle fire. All that night the men sat still with fighting-patrols out, waiting for the Bulgars, each company holding at least two thousand yards of very broken country with only a little " concertina wire " in place ; any communication with other units was most difficult. The result of the advance was to bring the Wilts lines about four miles nearer, to positions at Cedemli, whilst the Oxford and Bucks regiment took the first point—the Horse Shoe Hill—of the famous " Pip Ridge,"—and the French advanced right up to the main positions at Doiran on the British right. In these positions the men settled down to digging-in, raids, patrol-work, etc., remaining there till October, 1916.

Summer Trials. The summer had proved as trying, though in a different way, as the winter had been. The heat was intense, mosquitoes were a plague and a source of danger, and sickness made alarming ravages amongst the troops ; malaria on the Struma front and malaria and dysentery on the Doiran front practically wiped out whole battalions. The Macedonian Expeditionary Force had a larger proportion of men laid low with sickness than any of the other expeditionary forces, and although the medical organization was good the effort to keep well was a moral struggle as well as a physical one ; men had to have " character " to keep well, and had to fight against the tendency to break down before an insidious enemy. The Wiltshires stood the trial better than any of the units in the Saloniki forces, thanks to Col. Rocke's excellent discipline and care for his men ; the good training of the "Shiny Seventh" in England now told, and the gallant commander's men had by this time learned the value of a discipline that at one time had perhaps seemed to them more irksome than useful ; certain it is that no commander stood higher in the affection and respect of his men than did the punctilious commander of the 7th Wiltshires.

As time went on the splendid sanitary organization that was evolved effected tremendous improvement as regards sickness ; the sanitary regulations were most strictly enforced, and personal cleanliness, the use of parafin, the protection of food and utensils from flies, the wearing of mosquito veils and the protection afforded by mosquito nets,—these and like matters were made important matters of discipline, irksome but highly beneficial.

At Doiran. About October, 1916, the Wiltshires were moved to Doiran itself, in front of perhaps the most wonderful natural position of defence in the world. They there sat in front of the Bulgars until April, 1917.

Owing to the necessity—military and political—of preserving the greatest secrecy as to conditions and operations in Macedonia, next to nothing was allowed to appear in the papers concerning affairs there, and in many quarters an impression was gained that the opposing forces simply sat and watched each other with very little fighting. As one of the Wilts Regiment remarked, "If you left Johnny Bulgar alone, he would let you alone ; but if you stirred him up he would make it pretty hot for you," and the impression alluded to was to an extent confirmed by the experiences of one famous regiment that had let him alone. But the Wiltshires and their comrades had a very different experience. In the period between October, 1916, and April, 1917, they were engaged in the usual trench-warfare, except that food was scarce on account of the activity of submarines on the sea line of communication, and digging in the solid rock was carried on under frightful pressure—ten hours a day—in anticipation of the Bulgar attack. In their positions the Wiltshires were under the constant supervision and artillery control of the Bulgars who, from their commanding position, overlooked the entire country down to Saloniki. The British, however, executed numberless raids, and one of the biggest was that of the Wiltshires on a Bulgarian work marked as " O.2." on Christmas Eve, 1916.

A disastrous Attack. In April, 1917, the British troops had orders to attack these formidable positions ; they did so, and the first British general attack was over in a marvellously short time with the men's having a chance to do the Bulgars scarcely any damage at all. "C" and "D" companies of the Wiltshires rallied three or four times after being nearly shattered by terrible machine-gun fire, but were soon quite "wiped out ; " the very few that got through were caught on the wire, which the artillery had failed to cut, and were bombed there whilst trying to get through ; only Lieut. Dixon, of Pewsey, and a party got through, doing considerable damage to the enemy in front of them,—a feat for which he was awarded the Military Cross. "A" company advanced across a very big and steep ravine right against the lake side, and were likewise wiped out by trench-mortar fire and bombed on the wire ; a few did break through and died fighting ; whilst "B" company did wonderful work all night in fetching in the wounded. The Wiltshires lost in this brief but terrible fight nearly all their officers killed or wounded, and three hundred other ranks.

On the left of the Wilts Battalion was a huge ravine, five hundred feet deep at least, which was the scene of awful losses. The Devons had to advance over this and about half the Cornwalls followed them. Nearly all who went into the ravine were killed by concussion—an unparalleled occurrence in warfare—and died without a mark upon them : the few who did get across had no support, and at dawn a little band consisting of about ten men with Capt. Passmore (M.C. with bar), of the Devons, came back after fighting through the night with stones. The horrible ravine itself was choked with dead.

The Scots of the 77th Brigade came up to the attack, but their advance did not develop and they were sent away before dawn. The Wiltshires—or rather the handful that remained—held to their trenches for another two days under severe artillery fire, waiting for the counter-attack which, however, failed to come, and then they were relieved by the Scots.

A Sequence of Hardships. Upon the top of this awful and tragic experience came further hardships. When the Scots took over the line the Wiltshires had to make a forced night-march, and had then to spend all day making ready to move with their complete equipment to another front. Considering that they had been in their last position about six months, and remembering how even in a small establishment things get lost and mislaid in the course of a few weeks, one will realize what a gigantic task it was for the remnant of the Battalion to get together and pack within twelve hours, after a night spent in marching, the whole Battalion equipment ; besides this, all the transport was very weak and short owing to the damage done by the bombs of the German Travelling Air Squadron.   Then followed another frightful night-march over hilly country, lasting from dusk till nearly 10 a.m., to Snevce.   The Wiltshires are famous in the British Army for their marching powers and few regiments could have endured this exhausting sequence of events.

On the Snevce front and the Vardar.   The next night the Battalion took over part of the Snevce front, fifteen miles of front being held by a single brigade.   Here the Bulgars were four miles away, the positions were to some extent already dug, and reinforcements arrived at the Battalion.   After about a fortnight at Snevce, the Wiltshires marched to the Vardar where the old routine of trench life went on with the Bulgars a mile away.   About that time the enemy was very busy making raids, and every effort had to be made to season the recruits to the dangerous and nerve-shaking work of the fighting patrols.

The Battalion remained on the Vardar till August, 1917, when it was sent back to the Snevce front.   Here they found that conditions had changed since they left that front, for the Bulgars had been allowed to get complete control of the four-mile-wide strip of " No-man's land " that separated the combatants.   This was not allowed to continue, and again the Wiltshires were engaged in what was practically open battalion warfare, sending the Bulgars back on their main line again. This involved some " very pretty fighting," and in a battle at Akindzali Wood, when the Bulgars fled at the sight of a bayonet charge, Lieut. Col. Soames was wounded ; he had succeeded Lieut. Col. Rocke, invalided home, and came to the Wiltshires from the King's Royal Rifles.

Cut off as they were from home and from the great bases in France, the Saloniki forces had been almost without anything in the way of amusement and recreation. Things improved in this respect in 1918, and one of the first serious efforts to enter-tain the men at the front was the production of a pantomime,—" Robinson Crusoe," —excellently stage-managed by Capt. Tucker, of the 7th Wilts.

Leaving Macedonia.   The Battalion stayed in the line till the summer of 1918, when it was summoned to France.   Enough has been written to prove that the 7th Wiltshires were no whit behind their fellows of the other battalions in courage and endurance.   Their long exile in Macedonia was a period of great hardship and the Battalion suffered severely both from fighting and sickness ; but they left with a noble record to which fresh pages were yet to be added on the fields of France.

France.   The 7th Wiltshires left Saloniki with parts of the 22nd and 26th Divisions for France in July, 1918, and in France they were embodied as the 50th Division, which had been annihilated in the great German offensive in March.   They were now under the command of Lieut. Col. Hodgson, with Major Bayliss as second in command, having as company-commanders Captains Longland, Hulbert, Sawtell and Fairchild.   They "vegetated" at Forges-les-Eaux for three weeks, and were then sent to Dieppe for five weeks, and one can imagine how delightful was the change to these pleasant spots in France after the scorching heat and rocks of Macedonia.   The next move was to Coisey, near Amiens, and then to Combles.

When the Allies' final advance began the 7th Battalion was engaged in its first " big affair " at Le Catelet, and from then it was fighting incessantly, making a notable stroke on October 4th, when it captured " Prospect Hill."   The Wiltshires joined in the pursuit of the Germans to Le Cateau, being held up there for a fortnight. Continuing the pursuit of the retreating Germans they were engaged in the Forêt de Mormal on November 4th, crossing the Sambre next day.

The pursuit of the Germans involved continuous fighting and was a severe strain on the men; many who had come safely through the Macedonian campaigns went down in these last days of the war, and amongst them was Coy. Sergt. Major C. A. Thorne, who left his work at the Employment Exchange in Swindon at the outbreak of war to volunteer for service in the Wiltshire Regiment; during his three years in Macedonia he gained the D.C.M., and was mentioned in despatches, and already in France he had been again recommended for distinction for gallantry; but on October 13th he was killed in the transport lines by the bursting of a shell, after having come back safely from the front line.

The Armistice, signed on November 11th, found the 7th Wiltshires at Solre le Chateau, and they remained in France during the demobilization, being themselves finally disbanded in June, 1919. The colours of the Battalion now hang alongside those of the 5th and 6th Service Battalions, in Southbroom Church, Devizes.

The town of Marlborough, where the 7th Wiltshires were billetted for several months during their training and which by its kindly hospitality established a kind of proprietory interest in the Battalion, has been fitly chosen for the site of the memorial to those of the Battalion who lost their lives in the struggle. The memorial was unveiled by Field Marshal Lord Methuen on October 2nd, 1920, and the inscription tersely summarises the history of the Seventh : it reads thus—

" To the glory of God, and in memory of the officers, non-commissioned officers, and men of the 7th Battalion Wiltshire Regiment, who fell in the Great War, this monument is erected by their comrades. The Battalion trained in Marlborough during the winter of 1914-15 ; served in France, September to November, 1915 : Macedonia, November, 1915, to June, 1918 : France, June, 1918, to November, 1918. The record of those who fell and a roll call of the Battalion is deposited at the Town Hall." *

About a hundred of the officers and men of the Battalion were present at the ceremony, and amongst them were Lt. Col. W. J. Rocke, C.M.G., the first commanding officer of the Battalion, Major C. W. Hughes, M.C., Major C. K. Hulbert, M.C., Major H. Waylen, M.C., Capt. H. W. Lloyd, M.C., D.S.O., Captains Longland, Sawtell and Mackie, and Lieutenants Vacher, Pavey, Meyrick, Pounds and Wort.

The Mayor of Marlborough testified to the admiration felt by the borough for the Battalion and its pride in their achievements, and Lord Methuen recalled how, when he reviewed them before they left England, he was so impressed by their high state of efficiency that he told Lord Kitchener that if the 7th Wilts was typical of the new battalions he was to be congratulated on the character of the armies he had created.

So there, in the delightful little Wiltshire town, on a lovely autumn day when everything around spoke of beauty and peace, the buglers sounded the " Last Post " to the memory of brave comrades sleeping in France and Macedonia, whilst many of those standing by reflected that they owed the peacefulness and security they were now enjoying to the sacrifices and labours of the lads whom they entertained five years before.

* The 7th Battalion lost by death, besides several officers, 249 N.C.O's. and men.

THE ROLL

OF

SWINDON MEN WHO SERVED

In addition to those who fell in the GREAT WAR, enrolled in the ROLL OF HONOUR
(on Page 203).

It is impossible to frame a perfectly complete list of the Swindon men who enlisted, but the following is probably as complete as one could hope to draw up in view of the many removals of families from the town and the failure of many to reply to the numerous appeals for names. The list comprises the names of those for whom certificates were issued ; they were obtained partly from the replies sent to the Town Hall in response to appeals for names, and partly from the lists of discharged men drawn up by the War Pensions Committee, and these have (at the cost of enormous labour on the part of Miss Slade and helpers whom she enlisted) been embodied in a rough register which gives the name, address, number, rank, and regiment or ship of each one enrolled. It will be a thousand pities if these sheets remain unused, and it would be a public service on the part of anyone with sufficient leisure and patience who would transcribe them, properly arranged and checked, into a well-bound volume to be placed amongst the Town Records or in the Museum.

A few names of others known to have enlisted have been added from personal knowledge, but an attempt to use supplementary lists from the schools failed because they contain the names of a great many old pupils who had long left the town and were domiciled elsewhere. Had it been realized at the beginning of the war how important this matter was, a card-index might have been kept from the outset, and a register of unique value and interest could have been formed therefrom. As it is, the following list is a wonderful array of names for a town like Swindon, and to these must be added the thousand names of those who fell, recorded on pages 203 to 206.

Abbott, R.	Addison, Walt. B.	Allen, Geo.	Aplin, Ern. H.
Abbott, Jas. T.	Adkins, Ern. G.	Alley, Edgar	Archer, Thos.
Abrams, Alf. G.	Adlam, Reg.	Alley, Jesse	Archer, Wm. Hy.
Absalom, Thos. S.	Akers, Thos.	Allsopp, Roy	Archer, Wm.
Absalom. Alb.	Alder, Fredk. E. E.	Amor, Bertie	Archer, Wm. Jas.
Ackling, Wm.	Alder, Walt. J.	Amor, Edgar	Archer, John
Ackrill, Ern. F.	Aldridge, Arth.	Anderson, Alex.	Archer, J. V.
Ackrill, Geo. A.	Aldridge, Wm.	Anderson, H.	Archer, Ern. G.
Ackrill, Leon. F.	Alford, Louis	Andrews, Wm. G.	Archer, Jno. Owen
Acott, Arth.	Alexander, Alf. G.	Andrews, Alf. C.	Archer, Fred. Jos.
Acott, David	Alexander, Arth. D.	Andrews, Wm. Hy.	Archer, Leon J. D.
Adams, Frank	Alexander, Geo.	Andrews, Walt. G. H.	Archer, Robert
Adams, Lionel, N.	Alexander, Chas. E.	Andrews, Frank G.	Archer, A.
Adams, Graylon, B.	Alexander, Stan. J.	Andrews, John	Arkell, Thos.
Adams, Alf. J.	Alexander, Chas. R.	Angell, Tom	Arkell, Alb.
Adams, Geo. V.	Allard, Fredk.	Angold, S. E.	Arman, B. J.
Adams, Bertram	Allen, Wm. C.	Angold, Frank L.	Arman, Chas. E.
Adams, Isaac	Allen, Wm.	Annett, Vernon G.	Arman, Alf. R.
Adams, Thos.	Allen, Dennis	Ansty, E. J.	Arman, Reg. A.
Adams, C. L.	Allen, Ed. Wm.	Ansty, H.	Arnold, Percy F.
Adams, Wm. J.	Allen, Chas.	Applegate, W. H.	Arshur, Wm. Jas.

Ashby, Mark
Ashfield, B. G. J.
Ashfield, Cyril T.
Ashman, Jas. W.
Ashman, Ern. S.
Ashton, Jno. Gordon
Ashton, Arth. R.
Atkinson, Bern. H.
Atkins, L.
Attrill, H. M.
Aubertin, Hy.
Ausden, Chas.
Ausden, R. S.
Ausden, Jno. C.
Ausden, Geo. E.
Austin, F. H.
Austin, Geo.
Austin, Thos.
Avenell, H. Wm.
Avenell, Alec.
Avenell, Wm. Jas.
Avenell, Ed. Thos.
Averay, H. E.
Averay, H.
Averies, Stan. J.
Avern, Wm. Ivor
Avern, J. W.
Avern, H. I.
Avery, A. E.
Avery, S. G.
Axford, A. E.
Axford, Fred
Ayliffe, R. C.
Ayres, Thos. W.
Ayres, Hy. J.
Ayres, Ern. J.
Ayers, Ern. A.

Badmington, Jno.
Baggs, H.
Bailey, Ern. G.
Bailey, S.
Bailey Hy.
Baker, Alf.
Baker, Arth. M.
Baker, Ch. A.
Baker, Edw. J.
Baker, Edw. R.
Baker, Fredk. N.
Baker, Reg. A. F.
Baker, Thomas
Baker, Thomas
Baker, Vic. C.
Baker, Wm. J.
Baker, Fred. H.
Baker, Alb. J.
Baker, Reg. A.
Balch, A. J.
Balcombe, F. C.
Baldwin, A. E.
Baldwin, C. E.
Baldwin, G.
Ball, Sid. A.

Ball, W. H.
Ball, M. W.
Ball, Chas.
Ball, G. W. A.
Ball, Alb.
Ball, A. E.
Ball, F. A. T.
Balsdon, Thos.
Bambridge, Ch. H.
Banbury, A. E.
Banner, Nich.
Bannister, A. V.
Bannister, H.
Banyard, Alf. J.
Banyard, Arth E.
Barber, Ed. H.
Barber, Wm. Jos.
Barber, H.
Barefoot, Ern.
Barford, Alf. Jno.
Barke, Edwin
Barkham, Rob.
Barnard, Hy.
Barnard, Jno.
Barnes, Chas. P.
Barnes, E. A. T.
Barnes, H. H. J.
Barnes, W.
Barnes, W. A.
Barnes, A. J.
Barnes, Tom
Barnes, E. G.
Barnes, F. T.
Barnes, W. H. F.
Barnett, A. E.
Barnett, A. H.
Barnett, H.
Barnett, W. J.
Barrat, H. S. L.
Barrett, Geo.
Barrett, Fred
Barrett, Hy. G.
Barrett, Jas. H.
Barrett, W. J.
Barrett, Geo. H.
Barrett, Norm.
Barrett, F. W.
Barrett, Jesse
Barron, W. J.
Barter, Percy
Bartlett, Hy.
Bartlett, Alb. R.
Bartlett, Frank
Bartlett, Chas.
Bartlett, Wm. Alf.
Bartlett, Jno.
Bartlett, George
Basden, Chas. A.
Basing, J.
Basing, W.
Batchelor, P. J.
Batchelor, Jno.
Bateman, Ern. J.

Bates, A. W.
Bates, H. A.
Bath, St. John A. C.
Bathe, Wm. H.
Bathe, Geo.
Bathe, Sydney
Batt, Stanley
Batt, Henry
Batt, Vincent
Baycroft, Chas.
Bayley, Chas.
Baylis, Alb. P.
Baylis, F. J.
Baylis, W. E.
Bayliss, Alb. J.
Bayliss, Art. J.
Bayliss, Horace
Bayliss, Alf.
Baxter, F. C.
Baxter, E. C.
Baxter, Jas.
Baxter, Ed. Ch.
Beames, Alb. E.
Beames, W. H.
Beale, Albert
Beales, G. F.
Beasant, Alb.
Beasant, Ern.
Beasant, Edw. A.
Beasant, F. T.
Beasant, H. E.
Beasant, Jack
Beasant, John
Beasant, R. F.
Beasant, W. F.
Beasant, Fred G.
Beasley, T. M.
Beaven, C. P.
Beaven, H. W.
Beaver, S.
Beazley, A.
Beazley, V.
Beazley, F.
Beazley, J. J.
Beck, V.
Beckinsale, Chris C.
Beddon, L. P.
Bedford, O. R.
Bedwell, Rob.
Bee, W. G.
Beechey, W.
Beechey, P.
Bees, A. E.
Beint, E. J.
Beint, W. E.
Belcher, C. M.
Bell, Harold, J.
Bell, Robert L.
Bell, A. C.
Bell, Wm. E.
Bell, Arth.
Bell, Chas.
Belsham, Arth.

Bellinger, Stan. C.
Bendall, Jas.
Bendell, Wm. Hy.
Bendell, Wm. F.
Bennell, Jas. A.
Bennell, Walt.
Bennett, Alf. C.
Bennett, Alb. H.
Bennett, Hy. E.
Bennett, Wm. H.
Berry, Rob.
Berry, N. A.
Berry, Walt. C.
Berry, Wm. H.
Berry, Walt. W.
Besant, Trev. St. Jno.
Besant, Geo. A.
Besant, Benj.
Bevan, Alf. E.
Bevington, Alb. W.
Bevington, Thos. H.
Bevington, Ern. A.
Bezer, A. G.
Bezzant, Jno. W.
Bezzant, Jas.
Bick Chas. A.
Biggs, Sid.
Billett, Tom
Billingham, Wm.
Billingham, Fred W.
Billinghurst, Fk.
Binding, Wm.
Bingle, Sam. G.
Bingham, G. Hy.
Bingham, Jas. E.
Bingham, Royston L.
Bingham, Wm. C.
Bint, Walt.
Birkett, F.
Birks, Geo. A.
Birt, Jesse C. J.
Birt, Syd. C. V.
Birt, Wm. G.
Bishop, Arth.
Bishop, Fk. E.
Bishop, Hy. B.
Bishop, Herb. G.
Bishop, Tom H.
Bishop, A. E.
Bishop F. E.
Bishop, R. F.
Bishop, Ed. G.
Bizley, Alb. Hy.
Bizley, Wm. A. H.
Bizley, Wm.
Blackall, Harold
Blackman, Arth. E.
Blackman, A. H.
Blackman, Jos. Jno.
Blackwell, Alf. E.
Blackwell, Thos. H.
Blake, F. A.
Blake, D. C.

Cann, R.
Cann, Vict. W.
Cannings, A.
Cannings, E.
Caple, O. J.
Capper, A. H.
Carey, Jas.
Carey, Jas.
Carew, Leon E.
Carnell, Walt. J.
Carner, F. J.
Carpenter, G. E.
Carpenter, Hy. Jos.
Carpenter, Wm.
Carpenter, A.
Carpenter, Har. F.
Carpenter, Thos.
Carpenter, Hy. Jas.
Carpenter, F. Geo.
Carter, Frank
Carter, Leon J.
Carter, Jno.
Carter, Wm. C.
Carter, Wm.
Carter Isaac
Carter Isaac
Carter, B. L. L.
Carter, Herb. G.
Carter, B. H.
Carter, W. J.
Carter, C. H.
Carter, Allen
Carter, F. G.
Carter, Chas.
Carmody, Jno.
Carr, Percy R.
Carrivick, W. J.
Carver, V. C.
Carvey, A. E.
Carvey, Wm.
Carvey, C. F.
Carvey, Chas.
Case, E. J.
Castleman, L. C.
Castle, Jno.
Castle, Edg.
Castle, Chas. H.
Caswell, Walt.
Cathcart, E. H.
Candle, L.
Cavalot, C.
Cave, Geo. Fr.
Cave, Geo. F. J.
Cavey, Ern. E.
Cavey, Hy.
Cavey, Eth. J.
Cavelot, C. A.
Ceutler, A. J.
Challis, Geo.
Chamberlain, G. J.
Chambers, J. W.
Chambers, A. J.
Chambers, E. J. H.

Chambers, E. J.
Chambers, P. H.
Chambers, E. O.
Chambers, S. W. T.
Chandler, W.
Chandler, H. G.
Chandler, F. G.
Chandler, Thos.
Chandler, W. C.
Chandler, E. R.
Chandler, E. W.
Chapman, C. W.
Chapman, Ed.
Chapman, Fk.
Chapman, W. J.
Chapman, W. P. E.
Chapman, Fredk.
Chapman, Jas.
Chapman, Rob
Chappell, G. S.
Chappell, A. C.
Chappell, H. J.
Chard, Stan.
Chard, Hy.
Chegwidden, E. A. H.
Chequer, Clar. N.
Chequer, F.
Chequer, Wm. A.
Cherry, G. N.
Chesterman, A. F.
Chesterman, H.
Chew, A. Geo.
Chew, A. Jas.
Chew, Fk.
Child, Alb. J.
Child, Wm. A.
Child, Jno.
Child, Alf. R.
Chilton, Sid. R.
Chilton, Saml.
Chilton, Ern. G.
Chirgwin, F. J. H.
Chirgwin, A.
Chirgwin, J. G.
Chitty, Alf.
Chivers, Jno. A.
Chivers, Jos.
Chivers, W. L.
Chivers, E. T.
Christian, A. W. H.
Chubb, Ed.
Chun, Wilf. R.
Chun, Edgar
Chun, Geo.
Church, Hy.
Church, G.
Churchill, Alf. A.
Clack, Ron. R. P.
Clack, Stan.
Clack, Wm. G.
Clack, Sid A.
Clack, A. J.
Clack, Rob.

Clack, Hub. G.
Clack, Herb. G.
Clapham, G. F.
Clapham, Jno. F.
Clapham, F. W.
Clargo, Francis
Claridge, F. E.
Claridge, F.
Claridge, A.
Clark, Reg.
Clark, Wm. M.
Clark, Jno.
Clarke, P. B. F.
Clarke, Wm. T.
Clarke, Wm. E.
Clarke, Walt. S.
Clarke, Wm.
Clarke, Ern.
Clarke, Wm. G.
Clarke, Fred. H.
Clarke, Jonas
Clarke, Fred S.
Clarke, Hub. J.
Clarke, Walt.
Claughan, T. O.
Cleave, G. H.
Clements, Wm.
Clements, F. C.
Clements, G. T.
Cleverley, H. G.
Cleverley, O. W.
Cleverley, Walt.
Clifford, Alf.
Clifford, Wm. J.
Clifford, G. H.
Clifford, Wm. N.
Clifford, E. K.
Clifford, H. J.
Clifford, G. H.
Clifford, W. S.
Clifford, Wm.
Clinkscales, H. C.
Clissold, H. A.
Cockbill, C. J.
Cockell, J. M.
Cockey, J. E. L.
Cockhead, Wm.
Cockhead, Jim
Coker, Ern.
Colbourne, F. P.
Colbourne, Arth. R.
Colbourne, Leon D.
Cole, Walt. H.
Cole, Ed. G.
Cole, Ern.
Cole, Arth.
Cole, C. E. S.
Cole, Alb. E.
Cole, R. J.
Cole, F. W.
Cole, Hy.
Cole, R. J.
Cole, W. F.

Coleman, J. C.
Coleman, F.
Coleman, C. J.
Coleman, A. H.
Coleridge, A. K.
Collard, L. F.
Collard, C. H.
Collard, J. W.
Collett, Fred
Collett, H. R.
Collett, A. J.
Collett, F. L.
Collett, Sid.
Collett, Thos. G.
Collett, Nelson
Collier, Chas.
Collier, W. E. K.
Collins, Ern.
Collins, A. E.
Collins, Frank
Collins, F.
Collins, A. T.
Collins, W. H.
Collins, W. S.
Comely, F. C.
Comer, W. J.
Comer, A. J.
Comley, C. A.
Comley, Alb.
Comley, Alb. Clar.
Comley, F. W.
Comley, R.
Comley, T. W.
Comley, F.
Comley, T. J.
Comley, W. Hy.
Compton, Stan.
Compton, Geo.
Connett, Geo.
Conway, J. C.
Cook, Wm. A.
Cook, Percy
Cook, Wm. H.
Cook, Walt. F. C.
Cook, Wm. G.
Cook, Ed. Jos.
Cook, Reg. A.
Cook, Percy A.
Cook, Chas.
Cook, Fred
Cook, Fk. I. A.
Cook, Vincent
Cook, Jos. T.
Cook, Wm.
Cook, Alb. J.
Cook, Fk.
Cook, A. E.
Cook, Jesse.
Cook, A. J.
Cook, C. H.
Cook, Walt. J.
Cooksey, A. E.

Cooksey, P. A.
Coombs, A. J.
Coombs, A. T.
Coombs, Fred
Cooper, A.
Cooper, A.
Cooper, Chas. Geo.
Cooper, G. E. E.
Cooper, K.
Cooper, Fred. Jno.
Cooper, Hy. G.
Cooper, Fred
Cooper, Geo.
Cooper, Wm. A.
Cooper, Arth.
Coote, H. J.
Copp, Sam
Coram, E. H.
Corbett, Wm.
Corbyn, P. A.
Corbyn, P. D.
Cording, G. H.
Cording, G. H. (Jun).
Corgrove, W. H.
Cork, F. P.
Cornish, W. J.
Cornley, Chas.
Corpe, Chas.
Corser, H.
Corser, R.
Cotton, Fred
Cottrell, F. W.
Cottrell, Jacob
Cottrell, E. G.
Cottrell, C. F.
Cottrell, Walt.
Cottrell, Jno.
Coughlin, P.
Couling, J. H.
Court, T. F.
Cousens, D.
Cousin, A. J.
Cousin, D. P.
Cousin, F. J.
Cousins, E. J.
Cousins, S. C.
Cousins, A. H.
Cove, Thos.
Cove, E. A.
Cove, Hy.
Cove, E.
Covey, H.
Covey, T.
Covey, F.
Cowan, David
Cowan, W.
Cowley, H. R.
Cowley, G. E.
Cowley, A. W.
Cowley, H. W.
Cowley, Wm. H.
Cowley, A. J.
Cowley, Walt. H.

Cowley, H. J.
Cowley, E. W. C.
Cowley, Vict.
Cox, Alb. H.
Cox, Geo.
Cox, Wm. Jno.
Cox, E. Jas.
Cox, Alf. T.
Cox, A. E. J.
Cox, W. C.
Cox, A. E.
Cox, L. J.
Cox, W. W.
Cox, A. W.
Cox, J. E. G.
Cox, A. Jas.
Cox, Alf.
Cox, Wm. Chas.
Cox, Alb.
Cox, Alf. Jno.
Cox, Ern. Geo.
Cozens, A. W.
Cozens, E. H.
Craddock, E. H.
Craddock, L. J.
Craven, G. H.
Crawford, J. S.
Crayford, W.
Crayford, G. D.
Creswell, A.
Crew, A. S.
Crewe, D. R.
Crewe, V. C.
Crippen, Geof.
Crippen, P. J.
Cripps, L. G.
Cripps, A. G.
Cripps, G. O.
Cripps, C. H.
Cripps, A. E.
Cripps, H.
Crisford, Rev. K. N.
Critchley, H. M.
Crocker, A.
Crocker, G. F.
Crockett, S.
Croft, J. F.
Crompton, W. J.
Crook, A. J.
Crook, A. G.
Crook, H. J.
Cross, C. E.
Cross, Wm.
Crossley, Geo.
Crumbie, C.
Cruse, J.
Cruse, Sid
Cryer, F. E.
Cudmore, R. W.
Cuff, Wm.
Cull, W. G.
Culley, Jacob
Cullingford, T. W.

Cullingford, R. P. M.
Cullingford, J. A. G.
Cullingford, R. C. H.
Cummins, W. H.
Cumner, Wm.
Cumner, O. G.
Curle, Chas.
Curtis, H. F.
Curtis, W. T.
Curtis, E. G.
Curtis, S. E.
Curtis, F. W.
Curtis, B. W.
Curtis, P. G.
Cusworth, H. W.
Cusner, T. A.
Cuss, F. G.
Cuss, E. J.
Cuss, Fk. Geo.
Cuss, A. E.
Cuss, W. H.
Cuss, W. H.
Cussons, Chas.
Cussons, E. C.
Cutler, A. J.

Dabbs, A.
Dadge, Gilb. Geo.
Dadge, Geo. J.
Dadge, Frank
Dafter, Hy. Edw.
Dafter, Harry R.
Dainton, Geo.
Dance, Wall.
Dance, Herb. C.
Dance, Arth.
Dance, Frank
Dance, Francis J.
Dance, Hy.
Dangerfield, Geo. P.
Dangerfield, Fred
Daniell Frank W.
Daniels, Geo.
Daniels, Jno. Ed. Ch.
Daniels, Cyril H.
Dark, Tho.
Darling, F. W.
Darlington, Chas.
Dash, Herb. Geo.
Dash, Everett
Dash, Hy. R.
Dashfield, Chas. A.
Dattin, Fredk.
Davey, Walt.
Davidson, Archi. H.
Davies, Clem. L.
Davies, Jno.
Davies, Jno.
Davies, J. Edw.
Davies, Edwin D.
Davies, Wm. J.
Davies, Frank
Davies, Geo. R.

Davies, Herbert
Davis, Alf. O.
Davis, Arth. E.
Davis, Ernest J.
Davis, Thos. Hy.
Davis, Albert
Davis, Harold C.
Davis, Arth. Herb.
Davis, Geo.
Davis, Walter
Davis, Samuel
Davis, Edgar F.
Davis Herb. Hy.
Davis, Cyril Geo.
Davis, Albt. Edwd.
Davis, James H.
Davis, Alfred
Davis, Alb. E.
Davis, John J.
Davis, Oswald
Davis, Fredk. Geo.
Davis, Chas. J.
Davis, Chas. E.
Davis, Wm. Jno.
Davis, Joseph Geo.
Davis, Arth. Thos.
Davis, Ernest
Davis, J. F.
Davis, Archie Frank
Dawe, Wm. P.
Dawes, Chas.
Dawes, Arthur R.
Dawkins, C. P.
Day, Jack F. Ed.
Day, Leslie
Day, Lawr.
Day, Wm. Hy.
Day, Wm.
Day, Wm. Edw. Levi
Day, Ernest A.
Day, Herbert Tom
Day, J. H.
Day, Edwd. Walter
Day, Alf. Jno.
Deacon, Fredk. S.
Deacon, Tom
Deacon, E. S.
Deacon, Wm. Hy.
Deacon, Wm. Hy'
Dean, Clarence L.
Dean, J.
Dear, Thos.
Deeth, J. W.
Deller, Chas. Wm. D.
Dent, A. E. C.
Dent, Richard Jno.
Dent, Chas. Fredk.
Dennet, Harold
Denton, Walter Wm.
Derrick, W. F.
Dew, Alb.
Dew, Alb. V.
Dewe, Reg.

Dewe, Stanley
Diamond, Hy. G.
Dibben, W. H.
Dibben, R. J.
Dibbs, W. H. R.
Difford, F. A.
Dickenson, Geo. Fdk.
Dixon, Wm. J.
Dixon, Robert
Dixon, Raymond
Dixon, Wm.
Dixon, Wm. Th. N.
Dixon, Aubrey J.
Dixon, Chas. Wm.
Dixon, Jno. R.
Dixon, P. Eric
Dixon, Ern. F.
Dixon, Geo.
Dixon, Hy.
Dobson, E. Geo. Herb.
Dobson, Wm. Chas.
Dodd, Fredk. Wm.
Dodgson Lawrence O.
Dodgson, Herb. W.
Dodson, Leon V.
Dodson, Francis Wm.
Dodson, Fredk. J.
Dodson, Percival
Doell, Samuel
Dolan, Hy.
Dolman, Wm. Chas.
Dolman, James
Done, Herb. Chas.
Done, Ernest
Done, Chas.
Dore, Joseph Jesse
Doughty, Fredk. Edwin
Douglas, Algernon Wm.
Dowd, Joseph
Dowdell, Jas.
Dowding, Geo. Hy.
Dowding, Fredk. R.
Dowding, Wm. Ed.
Dowell, Chris Geo.
Dowers, Rob. H.
Dowling, Edwin
Draper, Jno. Wm.
Draper, Percy W. J.
Draper, F. H.
Draper, G.
Draper, T. J.
Drew, H.
Drew, E. S.
Drewett, W.
Drewett, Stan G.
Drewett, Frank
Drury, W. J.
Drury, Fred. L.
Drury, Leon.
Drury, Phil. Chas.
Dry, F. J.
Dry, A. E.
Duck, John Wm.

Duck, James Edwin
Duck, Wm. Arthur
Duck, Walter E.
Duffill, Harry
Duffill, Ern. A.
Dunford, Arthur J.
Dunford, John Hy.
Dunmore, Fredk.
Dunmore, Wm. Joseph
Dunmore, Arthur
Dunn, Hy. Chas.
Dunn, Hy.
Dunn, Wm. Jas.
Dunn, Herb. Hillier
Dunn, Frank
Dunn, John
Dunn, Fred
Dunscombe Will
Dunsford, Hy.
Dunstan, Rich.
Durbridge, Alb. Edw.
Durbridge, Alb. Edw.
Durbridge, John
Durham, Thos. J.
Durham, Edw. Hy.
Durham, Frank
Durnford, Hugh
Durrant, Harry
Dutton, Thos.
Dutton, J.
Dyball, Arthur
Dyer, Percy W.
Dyer, Syd. A.
Dyer, Lewis Edwin
Dyer, Wm. Upfold
Dyke, Har.

Eagleton, F. W. G.
Eagleton, E. A.
Eagles, Chas.
Ealey, Arch. C.
Ealey, Herb. D.
Ealey, Wm. Hy.
Eames, B.
Eamer, Wm.
Earnshaw, Cyril
East, Rich. Jas.
Easter, W. C.
Eastbury, C.
Eatwell, Alb. E.
Eatwell, Chas.
Eatwell, Jno.
Eatwell, Hy.
Eatwell, Alb.
Eatwell, B. J.
Eaton, Walt.
Eaton, Geo. Hy.
Eborn, Ern.
Ebrey, R.
Eburne, Geo.
Edens, W. H.
Edge, G. F.
Edge, V. J.

Edge, Chas.
Edgington, Thos.
Edmonds, F.
Edmonds, Wm. I.
Edmonds, Wm. Rob.
Edmonds, Hy. S.
Edmonds, A. J.
Edmonds, Walt.
Edmonds, Wm. Francis
Edmonds, F. Jas.
Edmunds, Fred
Edwards, Hy. Jas.
Edwards, Jno.
Edwards, Chas. F.
Edwards, Alb. W.
Edwards, Hy.
Edwards, Wm. G, M.
Edwards, Wm.
Edwards, Thos. Hy.
Edwards, Fredk.
Edwards, Sam.
Edwards, Jas. Hy.
Edwards, Arth. Fk.
Eggleton, Jos.
Eldridge, Fred. Hy.
Eldridge, Jas.
Eldridge, Jesse E.
Elford, W.
Elines, Har. Jos.
Ellen, Alf. Har.
Ellen, B.
Ellen, Thos. Fk.
Ellery, Geo. T.
Ellicott, Hy.
Ellicott, Wm.
Elliot, Percy
Elliott, H. R.
Elliott, L. D.
Elliott, Percival
Elliott, Hub. Jos.
Ellis, Arth.
Ellis, Sidney
Ellis, F. E.
Ellison, Sid. Geo.
Ellison, A.
Ellison, Tom
Ellison, Gerald
Elston, Hy. Jas.
Elton, Oliver
Elton, Mark
Elton, James
Embling, E. T.
Embling, E. L.
Embling, F. H.
Embling, Sid. Geo.
Embling, Hy.
Embling, Alb. E. G.
Embling, Geo.
Emery, Chas. F. W.
English, I. H.
Etherington, Stuart F.
Evans, F. E.;
Evans, F. H.

Evans, Dan. J.
Evans, Har. F.
Evans, Arth. A.
Evans, Wm. H.
Evans, Hy.
Evans, Jas.
Evans, Walt.
Evans, Jno. M.
Evans, Thos.
Evans, Hy. Jno.
Evans, Bert W.
Evans, Frank
Evans, Jas.
Evans, Wm.
Eveleigh, Leon G.
Evemy, M. F.
Everett, Geo.
Everett, Arth.
Everett, Jno. A.
Everett, Ed. Geo.
Exton, Wallace B.
Exton, Wm. Alb.
Exton, Hy. Jos.
Eyres, L. L.
Eyres, Reg. Jno.
Eyres, D. G.

Faith, C. F.
Faning, Hy. E.
Farmer, Jno. H. J.
Farmer, Fred R.
Farmer, Jas.
Farncombe, Fred W.
Farrell, Jas.
Farrow, I. B.
Fell, Stan. L.
Fell, Chas. A.
Fell, Alb. Chas.
Fell, Thos. C.
Fenemore, Wm. J.
Ferris, Wm.
Ferris, Wm. Jno.
Ferris, Chas. G.
Ferris, S. A.
Ferris, Herb. G.
Ferris, R.
Ferris, Maur. V.
Ferris, Geo.
Ferris, Geo. B.
Ferris, Edw. M.
Ferris, Wm.
Ferris, H. G.
Fessey, Jos. B.
Fiddes, L. H.
Fiddes, F.
Fido, Arth. A.
Field, Jacob
Field, Percy R.
Field, Walt.
Field, F. J. M.
Field, Grantley
Finch, Hy. G.
Fincham, Doug. G.

Fincham, Alb.	Fox, Fredk. F.	Gardner, Dan	Gill, Giles,
Findlay, Rob. A.	Foyle, Hy. Ed.	Gardner, Alb. E.	Gillett, F. C.
Findlay, Geo.	Frampton, F. C.	Gardner, Chas. E.	Gillman, Walt. Jno.
Finn, Reg. F. M.	Francome, C. R.	Gardner, Maur.	Gillman, A.
Finn, Thos. F.	Francome, A. H.	Gardner, H. E.	Gillman, Fk. Alex.
Finn, Chas. J.	Frankis, H. R.	Garner, Ern.	Gilmore, Alb. Rich. B.
Finn, Chris. A.	Frankis, A. H.	Garratt, J.	Gilmore, Har. Edgar
Finney, Wm. H.	Frankis, W. E.	Garrett, W.	Gilmore, Lancelot Chas.
Finney, Rob. J.	Franklin, Alb.	Garrett, Fred Rich.	Gingell, Ed. Jno.
Fisher, Fred A.	Franklin, Ar. V.	Garrett, Ern. Geo.	Gingell, Fred
Fisher, Arth. E.	Franklin, Hy.	Garrett, Walt. Jno.	Gingell, Fred
Fisher, Thos.	Franklin, Wm.	Garrett, Dick I.	Gingell, Wm.
Fisher, Thos.	Franklin, Dav. H.	Garroway, Geo. Ed.	Gladwin, W. H. M.
Fisher, T.	Franklin, V. G.	Gavin, Rev. J. H.	Glass, Ern.
Fisher, Thos. F.	Freebury, Wm.	Gay, Thos, Geo.	Gleed, Fk.
Fisher, Hy.	Freebury, Jno. Hy.	Gealer, Syd. Jno.	Gleed, H.
Fisher, G. W. H.	Freebury, John	Gealer, R.	Gleed, Alf.
Fisher, Fred	Freebury, Reg. Ed.	Gee, Franc. Sidney	Gleed, Alf. F.
Fisher, F. J.	Freegard, Har. W.	Gee, Fred Jas.	Glover, Wm.
Fishlock, W.	Freeman, Thos. A.	Gee, Wm. Hy.	Glover, Ern.
Fitchett, Fred J.	Freeth, Donald, M.	Gee, Oct. Fred	Glover, Wm. Jas.
Flay, Geo.	Freeth, Hubert	Gee, Chas. H. J.	Goatley, Geo.
Fleming, Rob.	Freewin, Wm. T.	Gee, Alb. Geo.	Gobey, Geo. E.
Fleming, H. J.	Frost, Frank	George, Hy. Sam.	Goddard, Franc. Ern.
Fletcher, Wilf.	Frost, Fred	George, Wm. Ed.	Goddard, Arth. W.
Fletcher, Fk.	Frost, Chas. J.	George, Ed.	Goddard, E. G.
Fletcher, Jno. Reg.	Frost, Rob. Wm.	George, W. E.	Goddard, Stuart G. W.
Flint, Ed.	Frost, Alb.	Gerring, Wm. Jno.	Goddard, Wm. Fred A.
Flower, Arth. Reg.	Frost, A. G.	Gerring, Alf. Chas.	Goddard, Chas. W. R.
Fluck, Alb. E. S.	Froud, A.	Gerrish, Isaac Jno.	Goddard, Jas. Nelson
Fluck, Rob.	Froud, Alb.	Gerrish, Leslie G.	Goddard, Fred Chas.
Follit, Arth. H.	Froud, Sid.	Gerrish, Reg. J.	Goddard, Alb. Geo.
Ford, Ern. G.	Froud, Ern.	Gibbs, Hy. Chas. M.	Godden, Jno.
Ford, Wm. E.	Froud, Ed. Geo.	Gibbs, Geo.	Godding, Wm.
Ford, Alb. E.	Froud, Chas. E.	Gibbs, Geo.	Godsell, Ed. Fk.
Ford, Ern J.	Fulcher, C. H.	Gibbs, Fred Jno.	Godsell, Geo. Fred
Ford, Kenn. E. T.	Fulker, Jas. N.	Gibbs, Ed. Alf.	Godsell, Percy
Ford, Rich. L. G.	Fuller, L. T.	Gibbs, Fk.	Godsell, Wm. Chas.
Ford, Wm. Fk.	Fuller, E.	Gibbs, Sidney R.	Godwin, Arth.
Foot, I. W.	Fuller, F.	Gibbs, Rob. Har.	Godwin, Ed. Jas.
Forrest, Fred	Fuller, Geo. C.	Gibbs, F.	Godwin, Ern. Walt.
Forrest, Jos.	Fulton, F. W.	Gibbs, W.	Godwin, Wm. Hy.
Forsey, F. Hor.	Fulton, G.	Gibbons, Thos.	Godwin, Jas.
Forsey, Alb. E.		Gibson, Geo.	Godwin, Tom D.
Forsey, Bertr.	Gabb, Franc. Th. S.	Giddings, Jno.	Godwin, Alf. H.
Forster, Rob.	Gale, Jno.	Giddings, Alb. Wm.	Golby, Ern. A.
Forster, Geo. Hy.	Gale, Jno.	Giddings, Wm. Hy.	Golby, Jas. Jno.
Fortune, J.	Gale, Percy Hb.	Giddings, Wm. Hy.	Golding, Wm.
Fortune, A. E.	Gale, Wilf. Syd.	Gilbert, Jno. Cliff.	Goldsmith, Ern. Walt.
Foster, Har.	Gale, Wm. J.	Gilbert, Archie	Goldsmith, Sid. Wm.
Fowler, Hub. W.	Gale, Jno. S. R.	Gilbert, C. M.	Goldsmith, Chas. Jno.
Fowler, Harry	Gale, Rob. C. B.	Gilbrey, Geo.	Goodall, Tud. Jno.
Fowler, Herb. Hy.	Gale, G. E. V.	Gilby, Alb. Ed. V.	Goodenough, Fred
Fowler, Stan. G.	Game, Hy.	Gilder, Herb. W.	Goodman, Phil.
Fox, Jno. A.	Gammage, Hy. Ed.	Giles, Fred W.	Goodman, C.
Fox, Leop. C.	Gane, Jas. Wm.	Giles, Geo. Wm.	Goodman, Alb. Geo.
Fox, Wm. A.	Gardiner, Herb.	Giles, Wm. Andrew	Goodman, Ern. Wm.
Fox, Jno. W.	Gardiner, Geo. Hy.	Giles, J. T.	Gore, Arth. Jas.
Fox, Alb. Hy.	Garlick, Arch.	Giles, L. G. W.	Gore, Fred. Elijah
Fox, Stan. T.	Garlick, Maur.	Gilfoyle, Rich.	Gore, Chas. H.
Fox, Percy	Gardner, Ashley Fred	Gilfoyle, Wm.	Gosling, Reg. Chas.
Fox, Jno. C.	Gardner, Eric Chas.	Gilfoyle, Ed.	Gosling, Wm. Fred.
Fox, Chas. E.	Gardner, Harold	Gill, Franc. W.	Gosling, Cec. Wal.

Gosling, Cec. Hy.
Gosling, Arth. Evett.
Goss, Fk.
Goss, Percy Fk.
Gough, F. E.
Gough, Franc. Hy.
Gough, Hy. Maur.
Gough, F. J.
Gough, H. H.
Gough, C. W. G.
Gough, Cyr. W.
Gough, Jno. Leon.
Gough, Wm. Scott
Gough, F. W.
Gough, Wm. Jno.
Goulding, H.
Govier, W.
Govier, Edgar Alb.
Grace, Wm. Geo. G.
Grace, Geo. Hy.
Grace, Thos.
Grace, W. H. W.
Grace, Ed.
Grant, Wm. H.
Grant, J.
Grant, Alex. Victor
Graves, Alf. Ern.
Graves, Fred G.
Gray, Geo.
Gray, A.
Gray, Percy Fk.
Gray, Ern. Chas.
Gray, Bert. Huish
Gray, Chas. Alb.
Gray, Sid. Jas.
Gray, Wm.
Gray, Jno.
Grayhurst, Alf.
Green, Horace Jas.
Green, Wm. E. R.
Green, Stan. H.
Green, Jos.
Green, Hub. S.
Green, Ar. Ed.
Green, Wm. Jas.
Green, Hy. Wilf.
Green, Jno. Hy.
Green, Reg. Fk.
Greenaway, H. C. H.
Greening, Fred S.
Greening, Ashley J.
Greenwood, Ern. W.
Gregory, Wm. Hy.
Gregory, Thos. Alb.
Griffin, Wm.
Griffin, F. C.
Griffin, J. H.
Griffin, Stan. V.
Griffin, Hugh
Griffiths, Alf. Ed.
Griffiths, Hy. C.
Griffiths, Alb. E.

Griffiths, L. A.
Griffiths, Fred
Griffiths, Fred A.
Griffiths, Gordon
Griffiths, A. G.
Griffiths, Ch. Fred
Griffiths, Hy.
Grist, Alb. Har.
Grist, Wm. Geo.
Grover, Arth. Jno.
Groves, Wm. Alf.
Grubb, Ed. W.
Grubb, Chas.
Guley, H. C.
Gullis, A. H.
Gunner, Franc. Th.
Gunston, Franc. H.
Guy, Wm. V.
Gwillim, Percy Wm.
Gwyther, Jas. H.
Gylby, Leon. W. B.

Habgood, Percy
Habgood, Robert
Habgood, J. R.
Habgood, Wm.
Hacker, Harry
Hacker, Harold
Hacker, Herb.
Hacker, Oscar C.
Hacker, Wm. N.
Hacker, Reg. A.
Hacker, Albert
Haddrell, George
Haggard, Sam J.
Haggard, Fred V.
Haines, Sid E. J.
Haines, Geo.
Haines, Fred. W.
Haines, Wm.
Haines, James
Haines, Albert
Haire, Lionel E.
Hale, Alf.
Hale, A. W.
Hale, Chas.
Hale, Richard
Hale, W. Jos.
Hale, Hy. J.
Hale, Wm.
Hale, Fred Wm.
Hales, George
Halestrap, H. J.
Halestrap, S. J. W. T.
Hall, Thos.
Hall, H.
Hall, Arthur
Hall, Chas.
Hall, Alb. W.
Hall, H. W.
Hall, Edwin
Hall, S.
Hall, E. G.

Hall, Walter
Hall, Wm. Jasper
Hallett, Wm.
Hallett, H.
Hallewell, E. T.
Hallewell, W. J.
Halliday, F.
Hamber, R. H.
Hamblin, F. A.
Hamblin, Rich G.
Hamblin, H. W.
Hambidge, W. F.
Hambidge, A. S.
Hambidge, G.
Hamley, Albert
Hammond, James
Hammond, Arthur
Hammond, George
Hancock, Har. F.
Hancock, Fred J.
Hancock, F. C.
Hancock, E. G.
Hancock, Chas. J.
Hancock, Frank
Hancock, Har. J.
Hancock, Wm. A.
Hancock, Ern. Wm.
Hancock, Alb. F.
Hancock, Ed. F.
Hancock, A. P.
Handel, Ar. Wm.
Handel, F. V.
Handy, Jos.
Hanks, Walt. Chas.
Hanks, C. V.
Hanks, Percy
Hanley, Alb. R.
Hanson, Thos.
Harfield, W. E.
Harding, H.
Harman, Chas.
Harman, G. H.
Harper, G. A.
Harper, Wm.
Harper, Wm. Edg.
Harper, Frank
Harrington, A.
Harris, Ben. S.
Harris, Clarence
Harris, Chas. W.
Harris, Colin
Harris, Chas.
Harris, Ern.
Harris, Geo. D.
Harris, Hy.
Harris, Fk.
Harris, Jas. E.
Harris, Jas. E.
Harris, Jos. H.
Harris, Sam.
Harris, Sam. J.
Harris, Walt. R.
Harris, Walt.

Harris, W. E.
Harris, Wm. J.
Harris, W. C.
Harris, W. Ingram
Harris, Leon.
Harris, Geoff.
Harrison, W. F. P.
Harrison, F. G. Hy.
Harrison, E. J.
Harrison, Geo. Hy.
Harrison, W.
Harrison, Chas.
Harrison, W. Geo.
Harrod, Frd. Jno.
Harrod, Edward
Harrod, Harry
Hart, Jno. Hy. P.
Hart, A. V.
Hart, Walt. Hy.
Hart, W. G. S.
Hartless, R.
Haskins, Thos.
Hastings, Tracy V.
Haslam, Jno.
Hartley, Fredk. A.
Hartley, Chas. W.
Hartley, Wm.
Harvey, Wm.
Harvey, A. Chas.
Harvey, Jas. L.
Harwood, S. Chas.
Hatcher, Chas.
Hatcher, W.
Hathaway, Hy. Wilf.
Hatherall, A.
Hatherall, Sid. E.
Hatherall, G. W.
Hathrell, John
Hatten, Arthur H.
Hatton, C. J.
Hatton, Fredk. A.
Hawkes, F J.
Hawketts, Frd. Ed.
Hawkins, A. E.
Hawkins, Alf.
Hawkins, Chas.
Hawkins, Frdk.
Hawkins, G. Edw.
Hawkins, Jas. H.
Hawkins, John
Hawkins, Walt. F.
Hawkins, Wm. Chas.
Hawkins, Wm. H.
Hawksbee, E. F. E.
Hay Stan. F.
Haydon, Thos.
Haydon, Walt. H.
Hayes, Herb. E.
Hayes, E. H. Jas.
Hayes, F. W.
Hayes, Ed.
Haylock, Frd. C.
Haynes, Bert.

Haynes, Ar. Hy.
Haynes, Fred. A.
Haynes, Wm.
Haysom, Ern. Jno.
Haysom, Ern. C.
Haysom, Reg. A.
Hayward, Rob. W.
Hayward, H. G.
Hayward, S.
Hayward, Wm.
Hayward, J. J. G.
Hayward, Francis H.
Hayward, Tom
Hayward, Alb. Tom
Hayward, Alb. R.
Hayward, Geo. Sam.
Hayward, Jos.
Hayward, Jas. E.
Hayward, Nelson
Hazel, H. Chas.
Hazel, W. J.
Hazel, Alf. Thos.
Hazzard, Chas.
Hazzard, Harry
Hazzard, H.
Head, Cornelius
Head, Edg. E.
Head, Franc. W. J.
Head, S. A.
Head, Rob. J.
Head, G.
Heath, Chas.
Heath, W. Clar.
Heath, E. Chas.
Heath, Frd. Chas.
Heath, Frederick
Heath, Fred
Heath, P. J.
Heath, Reg. Jack
Heath, Wilf. P.
Heavens, Ern.
Heavens, R. Ray.
Heavens, Art.
Heaver, F. C.
Hedges, Hy. Jas.
Hedges, Geo.
Hedges, Wm. Jas.
Hemmins, Reg. T. C.
Hemming, Geo. Wm.
Hemmings, Rob.
Hendy, Fred C.
Hendy, Jos.
Henley, P. G.
Henley, W. F.
Henly, Edg. B.
Henstridge, Albert
Henty, Hy. G.
Herbert, Edw.
Herbert, Edwin
Herbert, Hy. V.
Herbert, Frd. H.
Herbert, W. F.
Herbert, Walt.

Hermon, James
Hern. Thos. Hy.
Herring, Ern. Edw.
Hester, Hy.
Hewer, Alf. Jas.
Hewer, Jno. Wm.
Hewer, Wilfd.
Hewer, John Hy.
Hewer, Cyril Red.
Hewer, Thomas
Hewer, George
Hewitt, I.
Hewlett, A. M. H.
Hewlett, Fred Thos.
Hibbard, P. F.
Hibberd, G.
Hibberd, Wm.
Hibberd, Wm. G.
Hibberd, J. T.
Hibbert, John.
Hickmott, Wm. G.
Hicks, Wm. J.
Hicks, Edward
Hicks, John
Hicks, Thomas
Hicks, Fred
Hiett, Hy. Chas.
Higgins, Reg.
Higgins, Herb. Fk.
Higgins, Geo. J.
Higgins, Wm. G.
Higgs, Jas. W.
Higgs, Wm. E.
Higgs, Geo. Hy.
Hilborne, Wm. Geo.
Hill, Harry
Hill, G. Rich.
Hill, Chas. J.
Hill, P. A. C.
Hill, Thos. A.
Hill, Stephen
Hill, Edward
Hill, Frd. Chas.
Hill, Jno. Thos.
Hill, Sam.
Hill, Arthur
Hill, C. H.
Hill, F.
Hill, R. J.
Hillier, Wm. Jas.
Hillier, Har.
Hillier, Sid. David
Hillier, Alb. Bert
Hillier, Arch. G.
Hillier, George
Hillier, Wm.
Hillier, Thomas
Hillier, Hy. Geo.
Hillman, Ed.
Hills, Row. Hy.
Hilton, S.
Hinder, Art. R.
Hinder, Chris. G.

Hinder, Har. J. E.
Hinder, Har.
Hinder, E. J.
Hinder, Thos. Wm.
Hinton, I. H.
Hinton, Chas. Geo.
Hinton, A.
Hiscock, Alf. Norm.
Hiscock, Valentine
Hiscock, Art. Wm.
Hiscocks, Geo.
Hiscocks, F. J.
Hitchcock, Hy. S.
Hitchman, Ron. Frk.
Hobbs, Reg. Chas.
Hobbs, Wilf.
Hobbs, Ern. R.
Hobbs, Alf. Hy.
Hobbs, Fred Geo.
Hobbs, Alb. Edw.
Hobbs, Wm. P.
Hobbs, Ern.
Hobbs, Thos.
Hobbs, Chas. Hy.
Hobbs, Hy. Jas.
Hobbs, Alb. Wm.
Hobbs, Wm.
Hobbs, Ern. E.
Hodges, Art. Hy.
Hodges, Her. Stan.
Hodges, Reg. Vic.
Hodges, Ern. H.
Holder, Hy. Wm.
Hole, C. H.
Hole, E. W.
Hole, Jno. Ed.
Holley, Wilf.
Holley, H. C.
Hollick, F. G.
Hollick, Eric C.
Hollick, Art. E.
Holliday L./Corp.
Holliday, James
Hollier, F.
Hollister, W. Edw.
Hollister, Chas.
Holloway, Wm. Thos.
Holloway, Geo.
Holloway, A. P.
Holman, Wm.
Holmes, Wm. Jos.
Holt, C.
Homer, Alb.
Honey, S.
Hookings, Fk. E.
Hookings, Hy. Thos.
Hooper, Art.
Hooper, Geo.
Hooper, Sid. Rich.
Hopgood, John
Hopkins, Percy Wm.
Hopkins, Jno. Hy.
Hopkins, Jas. Hy.

Hopkins, Ern. G.
Hopkins, F.
Horan, Frank
Hornblow, Fred H.
Hornblow, Walt. G.
Hornblow, And. Jas.
Horne, David
Horne, Francis H.
Horrell, Chas. Hy.
Howard, I. T.
Howe, Jno. Hy
Howe, Ern. Alb.
Howell, Geo. Tom
Howell, W. J.
Howell, W. H.
Howell, Alf. Jas.
Howlett, Ern.
Howlett, Cecil
Howse, Hy. Jas.
Howse, Jas.
Huband, Ern.
Huck, N.
Huckson, Harold Jas.
Hughes, Walt. G. D.
Hughes, Alb.
Hughes, Walt. Jno.
Hughes, Geo. A.
Hughes, Chas. N.
Hughes, Arth.
Hughes, Chas. E.
Hughes, Jno. E.
Hughes. Ern. Reg.
Hughes, Geo. Hy. M.
Hughes, Wm.
Hughes, H. F. A.
Hughes, T.
Hughes, W. H.
Huggins, Chas. N. E.
Hulbert, Geo. R.
Hulbert, Sid. G.
Hulbert, Fred
Hulbert, Hy.
Hulbert, Wm. Jas.
Hull, Per. Jas.
Hulme, Frank
Humphries, Wilf. J.
Humphries, Wm. H.
Humphries, Alb. Wm.
Humphries, Tom Jas.
Humphries, Wm. Stan.
Humphries, Hy. J.
Humphries, Sid. Jno.
Humphries, Alb. Wm.
Humphries, Chas.
Humphries, Percy E.
Humphries, Geo.
Humphries, Alb. S.
Humphries, Jesse
Humphrey, Fred
Hunt, Hy. C. Jno.
Hunt, Jno. Wm.
Hunt, Jno. Wm.
Hunt, Hry.

Hunt, Walt.
Hunt, Chas. Percy
Hunt, Sam.
Hunt, Herb. Wm.
Hunt, K. R.
Hunt, Geo. E.
Hunt, Alf. W. C.
Hunt, Alb.
Hunt, Thos. Dav.
Hunt, Ewart
Hunt, E. F.
Hunt, Edwin J.
Hunt, Wm. Fk.
Hunter, Ralph
Huntley, Herb. Chas.
Huntley, Vic.
Huntley, A. J.
Huntley, Rich. W.
Hunter, Jno.
Hurcom, F. S.
Hurcome, Geo.
Hurn, Reg. E. J.
Hurrell, Geo.
Hurst, Jno. Geo.
Hutchings, G.
Hutt, C. J.
Hyde, Jack E.
Hyde, Rob. E.
Hyde, Oliver, E.
Hyde, Henry

Iles, Ewart S.
Iles, R.
Iles, Walt. J.
Iles, Wm. Jas.
Iles, Percy E.
Iles, Sid.
Iles, Ern. A.
Iles, Edw.
Iles, Hub. C.
Iles, Chas. E.
Ilett, Alb. W. T.
Imms, Wm.
Imms, D. N.
Inge, Fk. C.
Ingram, Geo. H.
Ingram, Jas. H.
Ingram, Fk. A.
Innes, R. K.
Instone, Hy. G.
Irish, A. H.
Ireland, C.
Ireland, W. E. G.
Ireland, H. W. T.
Ireson, Jas. W.
Isaacs, Fred
Isgar, F. C. J.

Jackson, Fred Hy.
Jackson, Geo. F.
Jackson, Jno.
Jackson, Joshua
Jackson, J. T. B.
Jackson, T. G. J.

Jackson, Wm. J.
Jacobs, Chas.
Jacobs, F. E.
Jacobs, Wm.
James, Walt. C.
James, Alf. W.
James, Geo. W.
James, Har. F.
James, Jonah, C.
James, Rich. G.
James, Wm. H.
James, Wm. E.
James, Wilf.
Jannaway, A.
Jansen, J. W.
Jarvis, Alb. G.
Jarvis, Geo.
Jarvis, Hy. R.
Jarman, Har.
Jarman, J. S.
Jefferies, Alb. E. E.
Jefferies, Ch. A.
Jefferies, Ed.
Jefferies, Jas. S.
Jefferies, Jno.
Jefferies, Jno.
Jefferies, Wm. E.
Jeffery, Alf.
Jeffery, Wm.
Jefford, Fk.
Jelly, Sid. F.
Jenkins, J. K.
Jennings, Syd. R.
Jennings, W. E. J.
Jennings, J. W.
Jermy, Jno.
Jerome, Wm.
Joachim, E. F. W.
Jobson, Wm.
Johnsey, W. L.
Johnsey, T. I.
Johnson, Alf. J.
Johnson, A. N.
Johnson, Ern. H.
Johnson, Ed.
Johnson, Fk.
Johnson, Fred
Johnson, Har. G.
Johnson, Geo. E.
Johnson, Hy. J.
Johnson, Jno.
Johnson, Norm.
Johnson, Wm.
Jones, Alb. A.
Jones, Alg. B.
Jones, Alf. S.
Jones, Arth. W.
Jones, Bert. W.
Jones, Chas.
Jones, Chas.
Jones, Chas.
Jones, Ed. R.
Jones, Ed. G.

Jones, Edwin P.
Jones, Frank
Jones, Fred W.
Jones, Geo.
Jones, Geo. E.
Jones, Gord.
Jones, Horace, C.
Jones, Jno. D.
Jones, J. C.
Jones, Norm. W.
Jones, Owen H.
Jones, Osw. F.
Jones, Lambert
Jones, Rich. E.
Jones, Rich. M.
Jones, Rob. E.
Jones, Rob. G.
Jones, Wm.
Jones, Wm.
Jones, Wm.
Jones, Wm. G.
Jones, Wm. H.
Jones, Wm. R.
Jones, Wilf. R.
Jones, Wilf.
Jones, Thos. C.
Jordan, F.
Jordan, H. H.
Jordan, A. V.
Jordan, Edg. J.
Journet, Fk. H.
Joyce, J. J.
Joyce, A.
Joynes, Alb.

Kane, Arch. O.
Kane, Frodk. C.
Kane, Wm.
Kane, Geo. W.
Keating, A. M.
Keefe, Frank
Keefe, Thos.
Keefe, Alb.
Keel, Hub. J.
Keel, Lawr. H.
Keel, Norm. R.
Keen, Andr. U.
Keen, Hub. S.
Keen, Geo.
Keen, Arth. C.
Keen, Wm. G.
Keen, Walt. J.
Keen, Wilf. H.
Keene, Chas. F.
Keene, Jesse
Keene, Bert
Keene, Percy G.
Keene, H. J.
Kelly, Percy
Kemble, Ald.
Kemble, Arth. A.
Kemble, W. H.
Kempster, C.

Kendall, Percy J.
Kennett, Arth. H.
Kennett, Geo. R.
Kennett, Wm.
Kennett, Har. Jas.
Kennea, Alf. T.
Kennyfec, Ed.
Kent, Ch. F. G.
Kent, Ch. Hy.
Kent, Hy. F. E.
Kent, Herb. Hy.
Kent, Hy. Jas.
Kent, Herb.
Kent, Ern Hy.
Keogh, Jno. Jas.
Kerridge, Ch. Ed.
Kerslake, C. G.
Kethero, Ern Hy.
Kethero, Wm. Jno.
Kewell, Wm. C.
Key, Alb. J.
Key, Geo.
Key, Thos. S.
Keylock, Wm. H.
Kibblewhite, E. H.
Kilby, Wm.
Kilford, Wm. Jas.
King, Alb. S.
King, E. H. V.
King, Fred
King, Fred, Jas.
King, Geo. Hy.
King, Geo. Thos.
King, Jno.
King, Peter
King, Wilf. E.
King, A.
King, A. J.
King, Basil
King, C. J.
King, Francis
King, H. J.
King, Jos. Hy.
King, Rob.
King, Walt.
King, Wm. Jas.
King, W. Ern.
King, Dennis H.
King, W. J. A.
King, Walt. J. A.
King, Alb.
King, Ed. E.
King, Jno.
King, Hy. Jas.
King, Fred W.
King, Alf. J.
King, Wm. A.
King, Wm. C.
Kingston, Chas. J.
Kinneir, Har. P.
Kirby, Doug. Wm.
Kirby, Fred
Kirby, Jno. Ed.

Kirby, Chris.
Kirby, Wilf. Hy.
Kirk, Rich. Wm.
Kirk, R.
Kirk, Jno. Wm.
Kirk, Wm.
Kitching, Chas.
Kitson, Ed. A.
Knight, Chas. J.
Knight, Arth. H.
Knight, G. R.

Lacey, Leslie
Lainchbury, Chas. R.
Lake, Wm. T.
Lamb, Chas.
Lamb, Vic. E. O.
Lambourne, Doug. R.
Lambourne, Fred
Lambourne, Wm.
Lambourne, Alf. Hy.
Lambert, Ernest
Lambdin, R. G.
Lambdin, W. E.
Lampard, Wilf Ew.
Lamport, Frd. Percy
Lamport, Wm. Alb.
Lamprey, Wm.
Lancaster, J. L.
Lancaster, A.
Lang, Jno. F.
Langcaster, Alb. V.
Langdale, A. Hy.
Langdale, L. J.
Langley, G.
Langley, R. C.
Lander, Art. Ern.
Lander, Art. Ed.
Lander, Chas. C.
Landon, Bucklee
Lane, Chas.
Lane, Frd. Thos
Lane, Dav. A.
Lane, Walt. F.
Lane, Har. S.
Lane, Wm. Jas.
Lane, W. J.
Lang, Jack
Lanham, Thos Perc.
Langley, R.
Lapworth, Frdk. Jno.
Lapworth, John
Largent, S. H.
Last, A. S.
Last, W. J.
Latter, Vict.
La Touche, G. H.
Lavington, W. O.
Lavington, C. Jas.
Lavis, W. E.
Law, Wm. M.
Law, Jno. W.
Law, Ben

Law, Ern. Godf.
Law, Frd. J. C.
Law, Mark M.
Lawes, Alf. G.
Lawrence, Saml.
Lawrence, Alb. Ed.
Lawrence, Chas.
Lawrence, E. C.
Lawrence, Franc. Jno.
Lawrence, Frd. Wm.
Lawrence, Geo. Thos.
Lawrence, Henry
Lawrence, Joseph
Lawrence, Thos Val.
Lawrence, Wm. Jos. F.
Lawrence, William
Lay, Chas.
Lay, Ed. Wm.
Lay, Frank
Lay, Jno. H. V.
Lea, Art. Wm.
Lea, David
Leach, W. E.
Leach, Reg. Bert.
Le Cappelai n, Geo. Hy
Ledwidge, Michael J.
Lee, Wallace
Lee, Graham
Lee, Stan.
Lee, Reg.
Legg, Alb. Ed.
Legg, Art. Rich.
Legg, Jno. Hy. J.
Legg, Hy. Jno.
Legg, Wm.
Legg, Arthur
Legg, A.
Legg, S.
Leighfield, Mark Jas.
Leighfield, A.
Leighfield, Reg. Alb.
Leighfield, Wm. Chas.
Lenham, R.
Lennie, Jno. Flem.
Leonard, Arnold Jas.
Leonard, F. C.
Leonard, Geo. Herb.
Leonard, Reg.
Leonard, Percy H.
Leonard, Sid. Alf.
Lester, Alb. Hy
Lester, A. H.
Lester, W.
Lester, Jo.
Lester, Herb. A.
Lester, Reg. W. Jno.
Lester, Tom Frd.
Lester, Wallace F.
Lester, Wm. Jas.
Leveson, John
L'Evine, Ken. M. L.
Lewington, Stan. J.
Lewis, Thom. A.

Lewis, W. E.
Lewis, F. J.
Lewis, Reg. Walt.
Lewis, Edg.
Lewis, Rob. Jno.
Lewis, Hard. Geo.
Lewis, Alan J.
Lewis, Alb. Sid.
Lewis, Chas. Alb.
Lewis, Frd. Wm.
Lewis, Geo. J. V.
Lewis, Hy. Geo.
Lewis, Robert
Lewis, Rob. Thom.
Lewis, Wm. Chris.
Lewis, Wm. Oliver
Liddamore, Art. C.
Lidbury, F. S.
Lidbury, Alb.
Liddiard, Edward
Liddington, Alb. Ed.
Liddington, Jno. H.
Liddington, Percy Har.
Lindsey, T. H. L.
Lindsey, Wm. John
Lindsey, Art. Ern.
Lindsoy, Frd. Chas.
Lindsey, Walt. T.
Lintern, P. R.
Lintern, Guy
Linnegar, Harry
Lilly Geo. Ed.
Litten, Herb. W.
Little, Alf. W.
Little, W. R. A.
Little, Melton
Little, S.
Little, P.
Llewellyn, Harold
Llewellyn, H.
Llewellyn, Herb. Edg.
Llewellyn, Thos. Alf.
Llewellyn, Thos. J.
Lloyd, Frdk.
Lloyd, Edw. Hy.
Lloyd, Reg. P. J.
Loader, B.
Lock, Frd. H.
Locke, Fk. C. H.
Lockey, Alb. Geo.
Lockyer, Joseph E.
Logan, John
Loker, Wm. A.
Long, C. F. W.
Long, Jas. Chas.
Long, Arthur
Long, Alf. Fk.
Long, John
Long, Walter
Long, Hy. A.
Longstaff, O. W.
Looms, George
Lord, Geo. Hy.

Lord, Rob. C.
Lott, Herb. L. G.
Love, Alg. Ed.
Love, Fred.
Love, S.
Lovell, Har. Ed.
Loveday, Alb. Jer.
Loveday, Fred
Loveday, Geo. Alb.
Loveday, Jno. Woold.
Loveday, Jas. B.
Loveday, Head U.
Loveday, Fred W.
Loveday, W. Fred
Loveday, John
Loveday, Thos. G.
Lovelock, Ern. Wm.
Lovelock, Herb. Sid.
Lovelock, Frd. Grah.
Loveridge, S.
Lovesey, Ern. Ed. Geo.
Lovibond, F. I.
Low, W. J.
Lowe, Arthur
Lowe, Herb.
Lowe, Ern.
Luff, Wilf. J.
Luckman, Fredk.
Lucas, Ern.
Lucas, J.
Luce, Joseph J.
Lumkin, Regd.
Lusty, Art. Geo.
Lusty, Chas.
Lusty, Edw. Jno.
Lusty, Geo. Thos.
Lydiard, Herbt.
Lye, Alf.
Lye, Chas. E.
Lyne, Hy. Geo.
Lyne, Ernest
Lynes, Norman

Mabley, Thos. Wm.
Mabberley, Alf, Chas.
Mabberley, Frank
Mabberley, Arth. Reg.
Mackman, Jas. Ed
Macpherson, Ch. Stua.
Macpherson, Geo. T.
Macpherson, Jno.
Madden, Thos. Hy.
Maisey, —.
Major, Alf. Ed.
Major, Eden Jas.
Major, Harold
Major, Wm. Geo.
Malin, Chas.
Malken, Frank
Manfield, Wm. Jno.
Manly, Frdk.
Manners, Ed. C.
Manners, Herb. F.

Manning, Art. Thos.
Manning, Ed. Wm.
Mant, Hy. Geo.
Mantell, J.
Mantell, Ch. Hy.
Manton, Ern. Ed.
Mansbridge, Chas.
Mansfield, Thos. Wm.
Mapstone, Edg.
March, Jas. Alb.
Margetts, Frdk. G.
Marks, Thos. J.
Marks, Wm. Thos.
Marks, Frdk. C.
Marks, Rob. Geo.
Marley, Frdk. T.
Marsh, Chas. J.
Marsh, Wm. Thos.
Marsh, Eric
Marsh, Harry
Marsh, Arth. J.
Marsh, Fred
Marsh, Fred
Marsh, Hy. Wm.
Marsh, John
Marsh, Wm. Jno.
Marshall, Frk. E.
Marshall, Arth.
Marshall, Wilf. Hy.
Marshman, Tom O.
Martin, Wm. Hy.
Martin, E.
Martin, Ralph R.
Martin, Frank
Martin, W. H.
Martin, Alf. R.
Martin, Arthur
Martin, Arth. A.
Martin, Herb. A.
Martin, Reg. J.
Martin, Wm.
Martin, Wm. D.
Masetto, Gaetano
Maskell, Franc. H.
Maskelyne, Jas. A.
Maskelyne, Wm.
Maslen, H.
Maslin, A.
Mason, Hy. J.
Mason, Har. F.
Mason, Bert. A.
Mason, Alb. Ed.
Mason, Arthur
Mason, Bert. Eg.
Mason, Jno. Wm.
Mason, Dr. P.
Massey, Wilf. R.
Massey, A. E.
Matthews, Ger. Wm.
Matthews, John
Matthews, Ch. Jas.
Matthews, Edm. J.
Matthews, Ern. R.

Matthews, Geo. L. E.
Matthews, Art. Reu.
Matthews, Jas.
Matthews, Jno. Edg.
Matthews, Geo. Oct.
Matthews, Har. Reg.
Matthews, Hy. Ob.
Matthews, Les. Hy.
Matthews, Trev. C. J.
Matthews Walt. Hy.
Matthews, Wm.
Matthews, Wm.
Matthews, Wm. J.
Matthews, Har. W.
Matthews, Jas. Ed.
Matthews, Geo. Sid.
Mattews, Alb. Vi.
Matthews, Frank
Matthews, John F.
Matthews, Vic. Row.
Matthews, Wm. E.
Matthews, Jacob E.
Matthews, Stan.
Matthews, A. T.
Mattingly, Geo.
Mattingly, Geo. E. J.
Maunder, Art. Hy.
Maunders, Geo. C.
Mawer, W. L.
May, Ern.
May, Percy
May, Harold
May, Doug. G.
May, Art. E.
May, Art. G.
May, Jno. S.
May, Percy H.
May, Wm. R.
Maybury, Vern. J.
Mayell, Sid. E.
Mayell, Wm. Jno.
Maynard, Geo. Hy.
Maynard, Thos. Alec.
Mayo, Tom C. E.
Mayo, Walt. C.
Mayo, Wm. Alb.
Mazzoleni, Cecil F.
Mazey, Jas, H.
McCarthy, Jno. F.
McCarthy, Jos.
McCarthy, John
McCue, Matthew
McGovern, Daniel
McGrath, Rich. T.
McLean, Matthew
McLellan, Jno. Hy.
McNally, Sid. B.
McNally, Wm. Thos.
Mead, Leon F.
Mead, Wm. Geo.
Meader, A. E.
Meader, Wm. Hy.
Mears, Geo. N.

Mears, Alb. Ed.
Medhurst, Harold
Mees, G. E.
Melhuish, John
Merchant, Sid.
Messenger, Alf. J.
Messenger, Geo. Frd.
Messenger, Jos. Wm.
Metcalfe, Chas Hy.
Middleton, Alb.
Midwinter, Hubert
Mildenhall, Arth. M.
Mildenhall, Walt.
Miles, Alf.
Miles, Wm.
Miles, Ern.
Miles, Fred. Edm.
Miles, Harold
Miles, Alb. Jno.
Miles, Chris.
Miles, Ed. Alb.
Miles, Humph. J.
Miles, Jos.
Miles, Chas. D.
Millard, Reg. H.
Millard, Ern. W.
Miller, R.
Miller, Alb.
Miller, E.
Millet, Sid. Jas.
Millin, Thos. G.
Millin, Wm. R.
Mills, Arth.
Mills, Arth. S.
Mills, V.
Mills, Fred
Mills, Alb.
Milsom, Alb.
Milsom, Ern.
Milsom, Fredk. G.
Milton, Sam. J.
Minchin, Thos. H.
Minchin, Chas.
Minto, Alex. B.
Minto, Archie, J.
Minto, Wm. H. L.
Minty, Fk. Ed.
Mitchell, Thos. Edg.
Mitchell, H. C.
Mitchell, Jas. Fred
Mitchell, S. W.
Mitchell, Geo.
Mittens, Edwin L.
Mobey, Ern. Chas.
Mockridge, Lewis Rich.
Modley, Wm. Hy.
Money, Ern. Jno.
Monks, H.
Monks, K.
Moody, Wm. Geo.
Moore, Hy.
Moore, Alfred
Moore, Lot

Moore, H.
Moore, Joseph
Moore, Hy. Geo.
Moore, Thos.
Moore, T. H.
Moon, Sam. Frd. Jno
Moorman, Frd. Chas.
Moran, Patrick
Moreman, L. R.
Moreman, Wilf. B.
Morgan, Frank
Morgan, Alf. Jno.
Morgan, Clar. W.
Morgan, Vic. Jno. F.
Morkett, Ralph
Morris, Chas. W.
Morris, L.
Morris, Frdk.
Morris, Harry
Morris, Jno. Chas.
Morris, Jas. Ed.
Morrison, And. W. J.
Morse, Ewart
Morse, Jno.
Morse, A.
Morse, Sidney
Morse, Alb. Arth.
Morse, Cecil
Morse, Chas. Wm.
Morse, Edwin
Morse, Ern. Wm. Geo.
Morse, Frd. Mark.
Morse, Hy.
Morse, Jesse
Morse, Ralph Ray
Morse, Sidney
Morse, Sid. Fk.
Morse, Wm. Chas.
Mosely, A. H.
Moses, A. E. W.
Moses, Bert. T.
Moss, Wm.
Moss, Alb. Sid.
Moss, Thos. Alf.
Mortimer, Wm.
Mortimer, R. H.
Morton, Edw. Jno.
Moulding, Sam.
Moulder, Percy
Mountjoy, B.
Mountjoy, G.
Mountjoy, Jas.
Moxey, Percy J.
Mudge, Edw. Jno.
Mulcock, Geo. Jas.
Mulcock, Alb. Ed.
Mullins, Thos.
Mullis, Alf. Jas.
Mullis, Wm. Jno.
Mulraney, Christop.
Mulraney, Jno.
Mulraney, G. G.
Munro, Lloyd Alex.

Munday, Hy. F. G.
Mundy, Frdk. C.
Mundy, A. M.
Mundy, Geo. B.
Mundy, Alb. H.
Mundy, Alf. Jas.
Murrel, Jas. W. T.
Murphy, Wilf. Hy.
Musetano, Don. Wm.
Musty, S. H. J.
Mutton, Ch. A. L.
Myers, C.

Nash, Chas. E.
Nash, Fran. Hy.
Nash, Perc. Wm.
Nash, Perc. G.
Nash, Walt. Wm.
Nash, S. G.
Nash, Edg. T.
Nash, Har. G.
Nash, Wm.
Neabard, D. J.
Neal, Jos. C.
Neal, Arth. T.
Neale, Wm. F.
Neale, W. G.
Neil, G. C.
Nethercot, Reg.
Nethercot, Rich.
Neeves, Wm. J.
Neville, Ch. E.
Neville, Wm. C.
Neville, Reg.
New, Fred W.
New, Thos. Hy.
New, Raym.
New, Fred G.
New, Tom.
Newman, Alb.
Newman, Ern. E.
Newman, Jas.
Newman, Rob.
Newman, Wilf.
Newman, D.
Newman, Norm. T.
Newman, W. J.
Newman, L. J.
Newman, J. H.
Newman, Ivor G.
Newman, Har. V.
Newman, F. W.
Newman, Alb.
Newman, Jas. W.
Newman, Walt.
Newman, Sid A.
Newman, Walt. J.
Newman, Bennett
Newport, Percy J.
Newton, Alb. E.
Niblett, C. W.
Niblett, A. H.
Nicholls, Ben.

Nicholls, Dav.
Nicholls, Rowl.
Nichols, Ern.
Nichols, Wm. E.
Nippress, Em.
Nippress, Geo.
Nixon, Mich. J.
Noad, Philip H.
Noble, I. H.
Noble, C. J.
Nock, S.
Norgrove, Edg. J.
Norman, Hy. A.
Norris, Hy. V.
Norris, Law J.
Norris, Lewis
Norris, Walt. J.
Norris, Wm. A.
Norris, Hy.
North, Percy G.
North, Alb. E.
Northover, Rob. W.
Northway, Sam. J.
Norton, W. O.
Notley, Jas. H.
Nunn, Bern. W.
Nunney, Wm. Ch.
Nurden, W. J.
Nurden, Fred J.
Nutbeam, Claud
Nutbeem, Fred C.
Nutman, E.

Oakford, C.
O'Brien, Aeneas
O'Brien, Felix
O'Callaghan, Dennis G.
Ockwell, Jno.
Ockwell, Ch. M.
Ockwell, E.
Ockwell, Sid.
Ockwell, Ern. J.
Ockwell, L. F. F.
Ockwell, Wm. Geo.
O'Connor, Chas.
Odey, J. H.
Odey, E. C.
Odey, W. R.
Ody, Wm.
O'Keefe, Reg.
Oldrewe, E. T.
O'Neil, L. H.
O'Neil, J. R. T.
O'Neil, T. J.
Onions, Enoch
Oram, P. T.
Oram, Chas.
Orpwood, E. F. R.
Orum, A. E.
Orum, Chas.
Orum, Chris.
Osborn, H. L.
Osborn, J. W.

Osborn, H. V.
Osborne, W. J.
O'Shea, T.
Osman, R. H.
Ostler, H. G.
Ovens, E.
Ovens, H. J.
Ovens, S. H.
Ovens, F. S.
Owens, H. J.
Oxborrow, F.
Oxley, A.
Oxley, H. P.

Packer, Clem. J.
Packer, Frd. W.
Packer, Herb.
Packer, Jos.
Packer, Jos. Geo.
Packer, J.
Packer, M. J.
Packer, Thos.
Packer, Wm. Med.
Packford, Frd. Chas.
Packford, Nor. Per.
Padgett, Alf.
Padgett, Jno. Jos.
Padgett, Rob. Thos.
Page, Alb. Ed.
Page, Frank
Page, Fred
Page, Hry.
Page, Hy. Steph.
Page, Sid. Chas.
Page, Sid. Art.
Page, Thos. Wm.
Page, V. L.
Pagett, Jos.
Paginton, W. J.
Painter, Alb. Jno.
Painter, Alb. Wm.
Painter, Art. Wm.
Painter, Edw. Geo.
Painter, Ern. Wm.
Painter, Edwin C.
Painter, Frd. C.
Painter, Hy. Ed.
Painter, Merv.
Painter, Thos.
Painter, H.
Paisey, Art. Wm.
Pakeman, O.
Palfrey, Percy
Palmer, Alb. Edw.
Palmer, Arth.
Palmer, A. W.
Palmer, Fd. Hazel
Palmer, Jas. Edw.
Palmer, Rich. Thos.
Palmer, Rob. J. A.
Palmer, Wm.
Palmer, Walt. Wm.
Pane, Arth.

Panting, Fred
Parbutt, Jas.
Parfitt, Frd. Geo.
Parfitt, H. M.
Parker, Rev. G. W.
Parker, Frd. Art.
Parker, John
Parkinson, Geo. Clem.
Parratt, Har. Thos.
Parrish, Geo. Wm.
Parry, A. E.
Parry, J.
Paisley, Alb. Ed.
Parsonage, Geo. Thos.
Parsons, Rob. E. V.
Parsons, Step. Chas.
Parsons, Wm.
Partridge, Ernt.
Partridge, Percy
Partington, Joe. Doug.
Patterson, Hy. Jas.
Paterson, Cyr. J.
Paterson, Gordon
Paterson, Francis
Patton, Geo. L.
Patton, Ralph N.
Paulding, Frd. J.
Paul, Chas. T.
Paul, Frd. Geo.
Payne, Arth.
Payne, Art. Rob.
Payne, Edwin P.
Payne, Frank
Payne, G. F.
Payne, Geo. Fk.
Payne, Jno. Hy.
Payne, Wm.
Peake, Alfred
Peaple, Andrew H.
Peaple, H.
Pearson, Jos. E
Pearson, Thos
Pearce, Alb.
Pearce, Alb. Ed.
Pearce, Alex. S.
Pearce, B.
Pearce, Cyr A.
Pearce, Edward
Pearce, Ed. Frck.
Pearce, Fk. Hy.
Pearce, Frd. Jas.
Pearce, Geo.
Pearce, Jno. Arn.
Pearce, Jos. Edw.
Pearce, Lionel, H.
Pearce, Perc. Jno.
Pearce, Reg.
Pearce, Thos. I.
Pearce, Victor
Pearce, Wm. Jas.
Pearce, Wm. Jas.
Pearce, Wm. S.
Pearse, Wm.

Peart, Chas. G.
Peart, Wm. G.
Peart, Hy. Jno.
Peck, Geo.
Pegler, Leo. Thos.
Pelling, A. J.
Pelly, Wm. J.
Pengilly, Thos. Fk.
Pennycook, A. V.
Pepler, Alb. W.
Perham, John K.
Perham, H.
Perkins, Alb. H.
Perrett, Jos. Jno.
Perrett, Wm.
Perrett, Wm.
Perry, Franc. H. R.
Perry, Fk. S.
Perry, Fk. Chas.
Perry, Jno. Lew.
Peters, Alf.
Petters, Wal. Wm.
Pettiford, Edw. H.
Pewsey, Harry
Peyton, Geo. Jas.
Phelps, Thos. C.
Phelps, Jno. W.
Phillips, Alf. Chas.
Phillips, Elton J.
Phillips, Ern. Cec.
Phillips, John
Phillips, Ern. Jno.
Phillips, Geo. P.
Phillips, Hy. Jas.
Phillips, Jno. Gor.
Phillips, Rich.
Phillips, Wm. Ed.
Philp, Jno. H.
Philpott, Wm. S.
Pickering, Ar. Chas.
Pickering, Fk. F. W.
Pickering, N. S. J.
Pickett, Ar. Ern.
Pickett, Alf. Reg.
Pickett, Hub. Wm.
Pickett, John
Pickford, L.
Picton, Edw J.
Pictor, W. E.
Pidgeon, Herb. F.
Pierce, Aub. W.
Piff, Wm. Har.
Piggott, Ed.
Piggott, Geo.
Pike, Cec. Her.
Pike, Edg. Fk.
Pike, E. J.
Pike, Wm. J. C.
Pile, Rich. Jno.
Pill, Percy
Pillinger, Ern. H.
Pilot, Ern. E.
Pilot, A. G.

Pilot, W. E.
Pincott, Ar. Jas.
Pincott, Ralph
Pinnegar, Ar. Hy.
Pinnegar, Arth.
Pithouse, Wm. E.
Pitt, Wm. J.
Pitt, Lancelot
Plaister, Hor. Ray.
Plaister, A.
Platt, Art. Les.
Platt, Gordon R.
Platt, Per. Har.
Platt, Stan. C.
Platt, Stan· H.
Platt, Wm. Jno.
Plenty, Geo. W. B.
Plimley, E.
Plomer, Ar. Reg.
Plowman, Alb. T.
Plumb, Jas. J.
Plumley, E.
Plyer, F.
Poake, Geo. E.
Poletti, A. E.
Pontin, A. T.
Ponting, Arth. A.
Ponting, A. H.
Ponting, Alf. Jos.
Ponting, James
Ponting, Chas. R.
Ponting, Edw. J. C.
Ponting, Edwin C.
Ponting, Hy. Jno.
Ponting, Hy. Wm.
Ponting, Leo. Geo.
Ponting, Robert
Ponting, Sid. Hy.
Ponting, Walter
Ponting, Wm. Jno.
Pooke, Frank
Poole, Alb. Ed.
Poole, F. R.
Poole. Alb. Theo.
Poole, Har. T.
Poole, Hy. Jas.
Poole, Jas. Frdk.
Poole, Wm.
Pope, Chas.
Porter, Alb. Ed.
Porter, Alick
Porter, Ern. Hy.
Porter, Ern. Geo.
Porter, Geo. Hy.
Porter, Hub. G.
Porter, Oliver, W.
Porter, Reg. H.
Porter, Stan. E.
Portlock, Rich.
Potbury, Mau. A.
Potter, John
Poulton, Rob. Jno.
Pounds, Edg. W.

Powell, Ern. W.
Powers, Chas. W.
Poynter, Chas. W.
Poynter, Rob.
Poynter, Wal. Frd.
Poynter, Wm. Geo.
Pratt, Jos. Step.
Pratt, Fdk. Thos.
Preston, Wm. Alf.
Price, Wm. Jno.
Price, Harry
Price, Rich. Jno.
Price, Alb. Wm. C.
Price, Rich. Geo.
Price, Alb. Edw.
Price, Reynallt
Price, Wm. S.
Price, Fred Wm.
Prictor, Chris. J.
Prince, Chris Geo.
Prince, Isaac Jno.
Probets, Alfred
Probets, Herbert
Proffitt, F.
Prosser, W. B.
Proudler, Hedly A. K.
Provis, N. J.
Prowton, Wm.
Pryce, Hy.
Pryor. Hy. E. V.
Puffett, Wm.
Puffett, Arth.
Puffett, Sid.
Puffett, Walt. G.
Puffett, Wm.
Pugh, Perc. G.
Pullen, Thos.
Purnell, Ar. Wm.
Purnell, Frdk. G.
Purnell, Wm. C.
Puzey, Jno. Hy.
Pymm, Ed. C.

Quarrell, A.
Quest, H.
Quick, Edwin R.

Racey, Chas. Hy.
Radbourne, Ed. Jas.
Radmore, P.
Radway, Alb. Hy.
Ralph, Sid.
Rand, Alf. J. H.
Randall, Alf.
Randall, Ed. J.
Randell, Walt. E.
Rashley, W.
Ratcliffe, Jas. Wm.
Rawlings, W. C.
Rawlinson, Fred
Rayer, Harold
Razey, Wm. Chas.
Razey, Alf. S.

Read, Thos.
Read, Ar. Ern.
Read, Henry
Read, Geo. Wm.
Read, Harry
Read, Walt. Geo.
Read, Wm. Ed.
Read, Wm. Jno.
Reason, Geo. Chas.
Reason, Wm. F.
Rebbeck, J. A.
Rebbeck, W. T.
Redman, Geo. Wm.
Redman, Hy. Jn.
Reed, Dav. C.
Rees, Harold, N.
Rees, Wm. Jas.
Reeson, H.
Reeson, V.
Reeves, Ern. Thos.
Reeves, Hy.
Reeves, Jas.
Reeves, Reg. G.
Reeves, Wm. Chas.
Reeves, Geo.
Reeves, Wm.
Reeves, Ern. Walt.
Reeves, Jno.
Reeves, Fred
Reeves, C. E.
Reeves, W. H.
Rendel, Ray. G.
Rendell, Stan. E.
Retter, Rob. R.
Retter, Alb.
Reynolds, G. W.
Reynolds, W. A.
Reynolds, Alb.
Reynolds, Ern. Har.
Reynolds, Wm.
Rennison, Hy.
Rice, Eric T.
Rice, W. J.
Rice, Alb. Har.
Rice, Hy.
Rice, Stan.
Rich, Jno. Ben.
Richards, Ben. J.
Richards, Clif. Jno.
Richards, Hy. Jas.
Richards, Perc. Stan.
Richards, Thos. E.
Richards, Wm. Hy
Richards, Geo. V.
Richardson, Ed.
Richardson, Hy.
Richens, Hy.
Richens, Fred Alb.
Richens, Sid. Jos.
Richens, Thos.
Richens, Wm. E.
Richens, Wm. Thos.
Richmond, Har. Geo.

Ricketts, Rich. R.
Ricketts, Percy Thos.
Ricks, Jno. Wm.
Ricks, Jack
Ricks, F. J.
Riddall, Percy
Rigden, Ed. Hy.
Riley, Ed. J.
Rivers, Ern. Abr.
Rivers, Alb. Ed.
Rivers, Ar. Reg.
Rivers, Chas.
Roach, Ch. Ern.
Robbins, A. H.
Robbins, Wm. J.
Robbins, Sam. Ern.
Roberts, Frid. F.
Roberts, Ar.
Roberts, Alb. Er.
Roberts, C. W. H.
Roberts, Jno. F. C.
Roberts, Clif. J. S.
Roberts, Alf. L.
Roberts, Walt. R.
Roberts, Evan L.
Roberts, G. Reece
Roberts, Geo. Reece
Roberts, Geo.
Roberts, Ar. Jas.
Roberts, Har. Dav.
Roberts, Albin J.
Robertson, Alb.
Robertson, Frank
Robins, Wlt. Hy.
Robins, Ed. R.
Robins, Wm. E.
Robins, Wm. Hy.
Robins, Jno.
Robinson, Wm. Hy.
Robinson, Ar. M. C.
Robinson, Wm. Chas.
Robinson, F.
Robinson, J.
Robinson, T.
Robinson, T. H. J.
Robinson, W. J.
Robinson, Hy. Geo.
Robinson, Alb. Jos.
Robinson, Stephen
Robinson, Norm .F.
Robinson, Wm.
Robson, R.
Rodda, H.
Rogers, Lewis
Rogers, W.
Rogers, Thos. S.
Rogers, Chas. Har.
Rogers, Ed.
Rogers, Laur. E.
Rogers, Herb.
Rolfe, Sid.
Rolfe, Thos.
Rolls, Alb. Ern.

Romans, A. G.
Rootes, F. R.
Roper, Leon. W. H.
Rosby, Ralph W.
Rose, Nath.
Rose, Franc. Geo.
Rose, Hy. Jno.
Rose, Alb. Chas.
Rose, P. A.
Rose, Geo. T.
Rose, F. G.
Rose, Fred Wm.
Rouse, Ed. Ger.
Rouse, G. S.
Rouse, Jno. Thos.
Row, Thos. D.
Rowse, Jno.
Rowland, Thos. J.
Rowland, S. H.
Rowland, Arth.
Robie, E. W.
Ruddle, J.
Rudman, Hy. C.
Rudman, Wm. F.
Rudman, Walt. J.
Rumble, Leon
Rumble, Fk. Ed.
Rumble, Wm. Ed.
Rummery, Alb.
Rumming, Hy.
Rushan, Phil. S.
Russell, W.
Russell, Wm. Jas.
Russell, Fred
Russell, Howard
Russell, Jas. Th.
Russell, Wm. Ed.
Russell, Jas.
Rymills, Wm. Alb.

Sadler, W. G. N.
Sadler, Geo.
Sadler, Wm. Geo.
Saddler, Thos.
Sage, T. W.
Sainsbury, Jas.
Sainsbury, Tom
Sainsbury, Wm. Thos.
Salter, H. F.
Salvage, Cyril M.
Sanderman, L. H.
Sanders, Clif. W.
Sanders, Geo.
Sansom, Wallace
Sarahs, Geo. H.
Sarahs, Fred C.
Sarahs, Jno. Ed.
Samworth, Geo.
Samworth, Perc.
Saunders, A. W.
Saunders, E. F.
Saunders, J. G.
Saunders, Chas. Wm.

Saunders, Sid. Geo.
Saunders, Wm. Jas.
Saunders, Rich.
Saunders, Anthony
Saw, Ben.
Sawford, Geo.
Sawtell, Hugh
Sawyer, A. J.
Sawyer, A. E.
Sawyer, G. F.
Sawyer, Wm. Thos.
Sawyer, Charlie
Scadding, Sid. Jas.
Scarlett, S.
Schmitz, B. F.
Schoerthal, Hy.
Schulze, Geo. W.
Scott, Fred Jas.
Scott, Jno. And.
Scott, Geo. Wm.
Scott, A. G.
Scott, Wm. J. L.
Scott, Wm.
Scrivens, Ed. J.
Scrivens, W.
Scutts, Chas.
Scutts, Wm.
Scutts, Hy. Geo.
Scutts, Richd.
Scutts, Bert.
Scutts, Hy.
Scutts, E. W.
Seager, Thos. R.
Seager, Jas.
Sealey, Steph.
Seaman, Hd. D.
Seddon, Jno.
Sedgwick, Jos. Thos.
Selby, Geo. A.
Selby, Fred B.
Selby, Wm. J.
Sellwood, Arth.
Sellwood Arth Jas.
Selman, G.
Selman, Chas.
Selwood, Wm. Hy.
Selwood, Fd. R. G.
Selwood, Hbt. Wm.
Selwood, Frk. C.
Selwood, Alb. Wm.
Selwood, Hy.
Selwood, Ed. T.
Serridge, Wm.
Sexton, D. W. H.
Seymour, Jno.
Shackell, Pcy. S.
Shackell, P. S.
Shadwell, A.
Shakespeare, Alb. E.
Shallcroft, Hy. Hd.
Shalwell, N.
Sharland, Hy.
Sharland, A. E.

Sharland, Wm. J.
Sharland, Frd. Geo.
Sharman, F. R.
Sharman, Wm.
Sharman, Syd.
Sharman, Alb. Wm.
Sharp, C. Hy.
Sharp, Alf.
Sharpe, Geo. A.
Sharpe, Wm. Hy.
Sharpe, Wm. C.
Shail, Edg. Wm.
Shail, Rob. G.
Shaw, Alf. Chas.
Shaw, Jack E.
Sheldon, Ern. Jno.
Sheldon, Frd. Geo.
Sheldon, Hy. J.
Sheldon, Frd. Gran.
Sheffield, Stan. H.
Shergold, Herb. Stan.
Shergold, Herb. Jas.
Shergold, Frd. D. W.
Shergold, Thos. A.
Shergold, Ern. Wm.
Sheppard, Reg. Chas.
Sheppard, Philip
Sheppard, Wm.
Sheppard, Hy.
Sheppard, Tom. Alb.
Sheppard, L. A. F.
Sheppard, Sam. Chas.
Sheppard, Wm. Chas.
Sheppard, Rob. Head.
Sheppard, Walt. W. N
Sheppard, Bert
Sheppard, Fred
Sheppard, Harold
Sherman, Wm. H.
Sherman, Wm. E.
Sherwood, Walt.
Sherwood, T.
Sherwood, Ar. Jas.
Sheward, D. H.
Shewry, Hy.
Shewry, Wm.
Shinner, Ern.
Shipton, Franc. Wm.
Shipton, Ed.
Shipway, Jno. Chas.
Shipway, Walt. Tom
Shirney, Arth.
Shittrall, Chas.
Shorrock, E. W.
Shorten, Wm.
Shurgold, Ern. W.
Shurgold, Herb. J.
Shurmer, Hy. Alb.
Shurmer, Arth.
Shuttlewood, Wm.
Silk, R. E.
Sillett, Herbert
Silto, Wm.

Simmons, Wm.
Simmonds, Wm. A.
Simons, Philip
Simons, Thos. H.
Simons, F. H.
Simpkins, George
Simpkins, Enos. Wm.
Simpkins, Ern. H.
Simpkins, G. W.
Simpkins, Sid. T.
Simpkins, Geo. Hry.
Simpkins, Harry C.
Simpkins, G. J.
Simpkins, M.
Simpkins, W. A.
Sims, Charles
Sims, David E.
Sims, W. G.
Sims, D. W.
Sims, L.
Sims, E. J. V.
Sinclair, A.
Singer, L. C.
Single, Jas. E.
Sinnett, Sid. A.
Sinnister, J. Edwin
Skane, Art. Jas.
Skeates, Ed. Geo.
Skeates, Sam. A.
Skeates, Tom
Skinner, Arthur
Skinner, Stuart, Ed.
Skinner, G. E.
Skull, Stan.
Skull, Ar. Geo.
Skull, Hy. Ed.
Slade, Wm. A.
Slade, C. E.
Slade, Martin J.
Slade, Jas. Wm.
Slater, A. J.
Slater, Geo.
Slatter, A. Percy
Sleeman, Charles
Slempson, E. S.
Smart, A. T. A.
Smart, Hy. Jms.
Smart, Wm. Jas.
Smart, Chas.
Smart, Ern. Geo.
Smart, Hrb. Chas.
Smart, Jno. E.
Smart, Hy. J.
Smart, Hub. Sid.
Smart, Alb. Edwin
Smith, Ar. Wm.
Smith, E. A.
Smith, Ern. A. M. L.
Smith, E. H.
Smith, Frank
Smith, G. T. D.
Smith, H.
Smith, Thos. M.

Smith, W. A.
Smith, W.
Smith, J.
Smith, Walt. G.
Smith, Wm. Thos.
Smith, Alb. E.
Smith, Hy. Jno.
Smith, Reg. Alb.
Smith, Ed. J.
Smith, Ar. Laur.
Smith, Jesse
Smith, Alec Wm.
Smith, Sam. N.
Smith, Walt. Shel.
Smith, Percy Sid.
Smith, Wm. Hy.
Smith, Herb. Is.
Smith, Chas. C.
Smith, Herb. A. T.
Smith, Wm. Pole
Smith, Rob. Jno.
Smith, Herb. Walt.
Smith, Ralph
Smith, Geo. Franc.
Smith, Wm. Rob. Ed.
Smith, Albert
Smith, Geo. Chas.
Smith, Chas. Hy.
Smith, Geo. Corn.
Smith, Alf. Ed.
Smith, Herb. Fk.
Smith, Wm. Jno.
Smith Alb. Chas.
Smith, Gilb. Chas.
Smith, Arth.
Smith, Stan. G.
Smith, Alfred
Smith, Aus. Geo.
Smith, Fred W. W.
Smith, Wm. Chas.
Smith, Syd. H.
Smith, Jno.
Smith, Horace
Smith, Hy. Jas.
Smith, Bertie
Smith, Arth. Wm.
Smith, Frank
Smith, Wm. Jas.
Smith, Walt, Geo. J.
Smith, Tom
Smith, Wm. Geo.
Smith, Ed. Fk.
Smith, Wm.
Smith, Tom
Smith, Alb. Ed. W.
Smith, Alb. Hy.
Smith, Geo.
Smithson, Jno. Wm.
Smithson, A. G. Head
Smythe, Rob.
Snelgrove, Wm. Rich.
Snell, H.
Snook, Geo. Frdk.

Snook, Sidney
Snook, Chas. Alb.
Snook, Jas. Henry
Snook, Ben. Chas.
Sobey, P. W.
Sollis, Wm. Ed.
Soloman, B. J.
Solven, B. Stanley
Somers, Austin
Souerbutts, Frank
Soul, Arthur
Soul, Wm. Frdk.
Southall, James
Southam, Arthur
Southby, Alb. Jas.
Southern, F. G.
Spackman, Sid. Frdk.
Spackman, T.
Spackman, Ern. C.
Spackman, Wm. Peter
Spackman, Wm. Peter
Spackman, C. W.
Spackman, George
Spackman, Wm.
Spackman Walt. Jno.
Spackman, George
Spackman, Jno. Walt.
Sparkes, F. Chas.
Sparrow, Frdk. Wm.
Speake, Edwin Geo.
Speake, Harold V.
Speck, Alb. Vic.
Speck, Herbert
Speed, H.
Speller, A. T.
Spicer, A.
Spicer, Herb. Thos.
Spong, Charles H.
Spong, W.
Spreadbury, R. R.
Spreadbury, F. F.
Spreadbury, B. B.
Springford, Thos Wm.
Spruce, Cecil H.
Spurlock, Ern. P.
Spurlock, Herb. J.
Spry, W.
Stacey, Ern. Frk.
Stacey, Frank
Stacey Mark
Stacey, Stephen C.
Stafford, A.
Stafford, Edw. E.
Stafford, Ed. Ern.
Stagg, V. H.
Stagg, Frd. J.
Stagg, W. F.
Stallard, Rob. Geo.
Stanaway, Wm. Geo.
Stanier, V.
Standish, Alex.
Standish, Irv.
Stanley, F. E.

Stanley, W. C.
Stanley, H. W.
Stanley, H. G.
Stapleford, Sid.
Steer, Fr. R.
Stephens, Thos. Alf.
Stephens, Fred
Stephens, W. H. F.
Stevens, Frank
Stevens, V.
Stevens, A. Geo.
Stevens, Norm.
Stevens, F. Hy.
Stevens, Alf.
Stevens, Ed. Jas.
Stevens, A. Wm.
Stevens, John
Stevens, Franc. Ed.
Stevens, Hy.
Stevenson, Frdk.
Stevenson, Robert
Stokes, Per. Ch.
Stone, Wm.
Stone, Av. H.
Stone, E.
Stone, Rupert J.
Stone, Herb. Hy.
Stone, Herb.
Stone, Mark.
Stone, J. R.
Stone, Geo.
Stow, S. L.
Strange, Walt. Geo.
Strange, H. P.
Strange, Rupert E.
Strange, Stan. Vic.
Strange, Alf. Geo.
Strange, Ern. Wilf.
Strange, A. W. E.
Strange, A. Jno.
Strange, Reg. Ch. J.
Stratford, W. F.
Stratford, G. Wm. Jno.
Stratford, Charles
Stratford, Alf. V.
Stratford, Frd. G.
Stratford, Wm.
Stratton, Ern.
Stratton, F. G.
Stratlow, E. J.
Street, W.
Streetly, H. W. T.
Streetly, Ch. W. J.
Strong, Herb. Geo.
Stroud, Wm.
Stroud, Ch. Ed.
Stroud, H. Geo.
Stroud, Edw. C.
Sturgess, Edw. A.
Sturmy, H. R.
Sturmy, Ar.
Sturmy, Jno. Ed.
Styles, Pat.

Vaughan F. A.
Venn, Arthur
Venn, Fredk. Albert
Venning, Wilfred
Verrinder, Percy
Vickery, Wm. Victor
Vickes, Hugh Cecil
Vines, Charles Wm.
Vines, Edwin
Vines, Walt. John
Vines, A. W.
Viner, A.
Viner, C.
Vincent, Cecil Wm. H.
Viveash, Cecil Chas.
Viveash, Fred. John
Viveash, Leonard
Viveash, Thomas Jas.
Viveash, Wm. Percy
Vowles, Fredk. Allan
Vowles R. V. J.

Wait, Chas.
Wait, Sam.
Waite, Wm.
Waite, Wm.
Waite, Cyril Henry
Wakefield, Wm. Vince
Wakefield, Walter
Wakefield, Jos. Thos.
Wakeling, Les. Jas.
Wakeling, G.
Wakeling, Wilf.
Wakely, Arth. E.
Waldron, E. J.
Waldron, Wm. Chas.
Waldron, Wm. Chas.
Waldron, Fr. Jno.
Walker, Geo.
Walker, Fred Jas.
Walker, Herb. S.
Walker, Wm. Hy. G.
Walker, Nath. Wm.
Walker, Walt. Jas.
Walker, F. Wm.
Walker, F.
Walker, E. J.
Walker, Jas. H.
Walklate, E.
Walklate, Robert
Walklett, Fred Harry
Wall, Llewellyn
Wall, W.
Wall, Ar. H.
Wall, G. W.
Wallace, Wm. E.
Wallace, Bern.
Wallbridge, Wm.
Walling, Edgar
Wallington, R.
Wallis, F. C.
Wallis, Ern.
Wallis, S.

Wallis, Fred
Wallis, Frank
Walman, Wm. Hy.
Walsh, R. A.
Walsham How,
        Rev. W. H.
Walter, R. J.
Walter, W. F.
Walter, J. E.
Walters, Har.
Walters, Fr. Fk.
Walters, A. W.
Walters, E. C.
Warburton, Hy. A.
Ward, Jno. Wm.
Ward, Albert
Warman, Wm.
Warren, R. F. Jas.
Warren, Frank
Warren, E. Jno.
Warren, John
Warren, Alb.
Warren, Ar.
Warren, F. E.
Warren, R.
Warren, Ed.
Warwick, Hy.
Warwick, Walter
Warwick, Sam.
Warrick, A. F.
Waterhouse, A.!E.
Watkins, Hy.
Watkins, Chas. Jno.
Watson, Alb. E.
Watson, James
Watson, Jesse W.
Watt, E. G.
Watts, Chas.
Watts, Alfred C.
Watts, Wm. Walt. Vic
Watts, Benj. Thos.
Watts, Tom
Watts, Alb. Ed.
Weaver, Jas. Chris.
Weaver, Alb. Ed.
Webb. H. W.
Webb, Alb. H.
Webb, Alb. Geo.
Webb, Percy Wm.
Webb, Wm. Thos.
Webb, Harry
Webb, Geo. Hy.
Webb, Fred
Webb, Chas. Hy.
Webb, Harry
Webb, F. G. D.
Webb, S. F.
Webb, R. M.
Webb, Wm. Jno.
Webb, Ar. Chas.
Webb, Norman P.
Webb, Geo.
Webb, C. S.

Webb, Chas. S.
Webber, A. F.
Webber, F. A.
Webber, F. J.
Webber, H. J.
Webster, Alf. Percy
Weeden, A. R.
Weeks, Edgar
Weeks, Alb. Hy.
Weight, B W.
Weight, Ar.
Wells, Fr. Jas.
Wells, F. J.
Wells, Chas. C.
Wells, T.
Wells, Chas.
Wells, H. E. L.
Welson, G. A.
Welsh, F. H.
Westall, F. G.
Westall, S. W.
Westall, W
Westbury, E.
Westcott, A. S.
Westlake, G. H.
Westlake, H. R.
Westlake, E. D.
Weston, Fred
Weston, J. R.
Westwood, Fred
Whale, H.
Whale, M.
Whale, W. W. C.
Whale, H. J.
Whatly, W. E.
Whatley, W. L.
Wheatly, J. H.
Wheeler, H.
Wheeler, W. R.
Wheeler, W. J.
Wheeler, W.
Wheeler, Harry
Wheeler, R. S. E.
Whettam, F. G.
White, H. T.
White, W. W.
White, Chas. Ed.
White, G. F.
White, T. H.
White, C. E.
White, Sid
White, T. E.
White, Jack
White, L. H.
White, Fred Chas.
White, W. G.
White, H. J.
White, W. Mc A.
White, Dennis
White, Wm. Geo.
White, Lionel A.
White, Hy. Chas.
White, Clement

Whitefoot, W. G.
Whitehouse, W. D.
Whiting, Hubert
Whiteman, J. E. F.
Whiteman, E. R.
Whiteman, W. F. J.
Whiteman, R. R.
Whiteman, L. C.
Whittaker, C.
Whittaker, Ed. G.
Whittington, Wm.
Whitworth, A. Har.
Whipp, T. L.
Whipp, Leslie
Wiblin, Chas.
Wickenden, W. E. B.
Wiggin, F.
Wiggins, F. T.
Wilcox, Edg. Frank
Wilcox, Fred
Wild, S. E.
Wilder, Percy
Wilkins, Rev. B.
Wilkins, A. G.
Wilkins, F.
Wilkins, Wm. Hy.
Wilkins, Fred
Wilkins, Nelson W.
Wilkins, Sid.
Wilkins, Walt. I.
Wilkinson, Geo. H.
Wilks, A. O. G.
Wilks, E. E.
Wilks, O. J.
Willawoys, Edward
Willcock, Francis
Willcock, E. Holman
Willcocks, A. J. T.
Williams, R. W.
Williams, Fred Thos.
Williams, Fred. Chas.
Williams, Leon. Hy.
Williams, Frank
Williams, David
Williams, George
Williams, Alb. Hy.
Williams, Wm. Hy.
Williams, Fred Jas.
Williams, E. M. F.
Williams, R. I.
Williams, Raymond A.
Williams, John
Williams, Fred Hy.
Williams, Fred Alb.
Williams, Wm. Geo.
Williams, W. E.
Williams, Reub. J.
Williams, Herb.
Willmore, Ern.
Willis, Syd. Geo.
Willis, Geo. Val.
Willis, Cecil
Willis, Fred

Willoughby, Fred
Willoughby, Thos. W.
Willoughby, Stan.
Willoughby, Alb. V.
Willows, Eli John
Wilson, Thos. Wm.
Wilson, Percy T.
Wilson, Jesse
Wilson, Thos. J.
Wilson, Geo. Chas.
Wilson, Bert S.
Wilson, Frank
Wilson, Fred W.
Wiltshire, Chas.
Wiltshire, Perc. R.
Wiltshire, P. T.
Wiltshire, Fred E.
Wiltshire, Wm.
Wiltshire, H.
Wiltshire, A. E.
Wiltshire, E. G.
Wiltshire, Ar. Ern.
Winchurst, Bert
Winchurst, Sam. J.
Winchurst, Wm. E.
Winchcombe, Wm. G.
Winchcombe, Wa. Hy.
Winchcombe, A. E.
Winchcombe, Fk.
Windman, Fred G.

Windslow, Alb. E.
Winslow, Oliver, F.
Winslow, S. M.
Winslow, Jos.
Winter, Wa. Geo.
Wise, Ern. Geo.
Wise, Frank
Withers, Alb. Ed.
Withers, A. G.
Withers, Hy.
Witt, Alf. Jas.
Witt, Dennis
Witts, F. P
Witts, F. T.
Witts, Hy.
Witts, Fred
Witts, Ern. E.
Wombey, Edwin
Wood, Ed. Cl. Ger.
Wood, Les. S. P.
Wood, G. C.
Woodall, Har. E.
Woodcock, Sidney H.
Woodcock, Leslie J.
Woodfield, A. W. G.
Woodham, Vincent
Woodhouse, Jesse V.
Woodley, H. T.
Woodley, F.
Woodley, S.

Woodley, H. Thos.
Woodman, E.
Woodman, H.
Woodroffe, Wm.
Woodward, Wm. E.
Woodward, P. R. H.
Woodward, Ern, Maur
Woodward, Franc. J.
Woodward, Wm. Jno.
Woodward, Alb.
Woodward, Geo.
Woodward, Walt. J.
Woodward, W. H. J.
Woodward, Aug. Geo.
Woodward, Wm. Hy.
Woof, Frank
Woolford, Ern.
Woolford, Jas. Ed.
Woolford, Hy.
Woolford, Wm. Thos.
Woolford, Wm. Jas.
Woolford, Ern. Ed.
Woolford, H.
Woolford, Ar. Chas.
Woolford, Fred Jesse
Wooster, Chas.
Wootten, Perc. Jas.
Workman, Sid.
Worthy, G.
Wright, Fred

Wright, Fred Jno.
Wright, Hy.
Wright, Walter
Wright, Thos. Jas.
Wright, Robert
Wright, Wm.
Wyatt, Stephen
Wyatt, Ar.
Wyatt, Jas.

Yarnton, W.
Yates, Chas. Wm.
Yates, Han. Rob.
Yates, Hy. Chas.
Yates, H.
Yeo, Har. Hy.
Yeo, Jno. Herb.
Yeo, F. C.
York, Perc. Hy.
Young, Dr. Gord.
Young, Chas. Jas.
Young, Daniel
Young, Jno. Hy.
Young, Rob. Jas.
Young, Wm. Alf.
Young, A. E.
Young, G. H.

Zebedee, Edward T.

JOHN DREW (Printers) Ltd., 51, Bridge Street, Swindon.

Index.

Lightning Source UK Ltd.
Milton Keynes UK
UKHW02f0839070618
323878UK00007B/576/P